TELECOMMUNICATIONS MANAGEMENT PLANNING ISDN NETWORKS PRODUCTS AND SERVICES

ROBERT K. HELDMAN

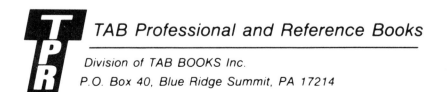

TAB Professional and Reference Books

Division of TAB BOOKS Inc.
P.O. Box 40, Blue Ridge Summit, PA 17214

To Valerie

This analysis has only been achieved due to the love, assistance and understanding of Valerie, as her husband searched over many years to conceptualize the networks, products, and services of the information era and to determine a better innovative planning process to achieve them. Hopefully, they will help provide a better world for ourselves, our children and our children's children.

FIRST EDITION

FIRST PRINTING

Library of Congress Cataloging in Publication Data

Heldman, Robert K.
Telecommunications management planning.

Includes index.
1. Management—Communication systems—Planning.
2. Business enterprises—Communication systems—
Planning. 3. Management information systems—Planning.
4. Telecommunication systems. 5. Telemarketing.
I.Title.
HD30.335.H45 1987   658.4'038   86-30002
ISBN 0-8306-2864-9

Questions regarding the content of this book
should be addressed to:

Reader Inquiry Branch
Editorial Department
TAB BOOKS Inc.
P.O. Box 40
Blue Ridge Summit. PA 17214

Contents

Why Plan?—Now Is a New Era for Management, But What Kind?—Managing Change Produces Opportunity, but for Whom?—The New Marketplace: Its Direction or Lack of Direction?—The New Technology: The Driving Force or Is It?—Changing Strategic Direction—Change Planning: Planning in Change for Change—The New Manager Planner: Playing in a New Game—Further Analysis—Observations: A Time to Change!

Strategic Planning—The Mission, The Vision—Strategy of the Strategies—The Strategic Game: Playing to Win—Business of the Business—Planning Buys Success—Planning . . . Needs . . . Processes—The Planning Phases—The Management Planning Process—Reviews and Decisions—Competitive Processes—Managing Change—Further Analysis—Observations: Strategic Processes

10 Information Networks, Products, and Services 264

The Info Ring: The Ring Switch—The Information Communication Complex—The Operations Support Center—The Metro Switch—The Intelligent Network Complex—The Access Switch—The Business Information World—What's a Switch?—The Private/Public Network—The Quality Information Network—The U.S. ISDN Network Architecture—The ISDN Marketplace—The Game—Further Analyses—Observations: A Complex Game

11 The Information Era 316

Strategies—The Formation Phase—Strategic Strategies—Further Analysis—Observations: The World of Planning in the World of the Future

Part 3: Case Studies and Workshops:
Information Networks, Products, and Services 333

12 Case Studies: Where Technological Possibilities Meet Marketplace Opportunities 335

1 Two Changing Worlds Collide 335

Impact of Telecommunications and Computer Technology on Our Future Society—High Tech West Inc.—Mid. Tech Tele. Inc.—Multi-National Inc.—Standard Tel Tech. Inc.—I-Change Inc.

2 New Missions—New Strategies 347

Apollo II—NewTel Inc.—Infolab Inc.—Central Research Inc.—International Technology Trade Center

3 Integrating Marketing and Technology 365

Top Down Planning for the New Users—Top Down Planning for the Network of the Future—Why Do Conceptual Planning—Conceptual Information Rings—What Will Be Realistic Needs of Society for Telecommunications at the Turn of the Century?

4 The Features World 393

Information Cubics—The Government's Playing Field—Feature Features—ISDN Requirements and Questions—Requirements Definition Phase Methodology—The Trillion Billion Dollar Decision

5 The Network Game 434

ISDN—What Constitutes a Network, System, or Product?—Product Definition Methodology—Who's on First, What's on Second

Acknowledgments

This document contains the results of many years of discussions and analyses with numerous knowledgeable associates as we, all together, attempted to play the game with new technological breakthroughs that change it every two years. Many of the basic theories were developed at North American Rockwell and then applied over the years to GTE, ITT, and Northwestern Bell, with each application enhancing and refining the theories. I wish to thank these firms for the opportunity, encouragement, and assistance to test them in "living corporate laboratories" in the competitive marketplace.

I have greatly appreciated the advice and counsel of my parents and family, as well as my many colleagues and friends, who will see their ideas, thoughts, views, and definitions expressed within this book. I hope they will be pleased to see them as integral pieces of the complete picture. Though they are too many to mention individually and some sources of my notes are unknown, I wish to acknowledge their contributions and individually thank L.L. Smith, a true lateral thinker, H. Wirsing, the pathsearcher, Henry Malec, the quality expert on quality prisms, Rich Margo and Claude Walston on program planning, Dave Lawson on system reviews, Fr. J. Burke, a great teacher, Hank Crowell and Henry Briggs on understanding people, CCITT planners on ISDN standards, Sr. Rosemary, a visionary administrator, Bellcore friends on new technology, Jerry Hanley on marketing to users needs, and Tom Madison, Dick McCormick and John Willemssen on playing the game, as well as Irwin Dorros, Desmond Hudson, Volker Jung, Koji Kobayashi, John Mayo, and Bill Norris for their views of the future information society.

In conclusion, I wish to thank all the previous members of my continuing education courses at George Washington University, for identifying the issues and questions a book such as this should address.

Hopefully, it does . . .

Preface

Today, as never before, management, planners and designers are faced with increasingly critical, complex, and costly decisions. As telecommunications integrates with data processing to extend the movement and processing of information to new areas of application, suppliers and providers must take more time to plan their new products, networks, and services to meet new users' needs. Through the turn of the century, their users will require more and more new features. The combination of integrated circuit technology, fiberoptics, sophisticated compilers, and new programming techniques can now economically achieve network systems that are truly physically distributed, causing a blur between traditional functional areas and interface boundaries.

This analysis is intended as a reference for those who are deeply involved in providing and supplying new networks, products and services for new users of *telecommunication information*. It provides an in-depth look at the building blocks of the future ISDN network architecture, in terms of technology possibilities, market opportunities, and governmental restraints. It indicates the type of *information marketplace* that could flourish in terms of its *users*, their *needs* and their resistance to *change* during the transition period to the functioning phases of the *information era*. In doing so, it provides detailed "looks" at *the marketplace, the players, technology, governmental decisions, and evolving ISDN architectures, structures, interfaces, standards, issues and questions.*

In so doing, we will take a moment to consider "visions of the future" in terms of information networks, products and services, as foreseen by several prominent leaders and decision makers of the *computer* and *communication* industries, as their worlds collide in the *formation phase of the infor-*

mation era. The "visions" presented are:

- The Changing Telecommunications Networks
  Dr. Irwin Dorros, Exec. V.P., Bell Communications Research

- User Needs and Network Strategies for the Nineties
  Desmond Hudson, Pres., Northern Telecom Inc.

- The Network of the Future
  Volker Jung, Pres. and CEO, Siemens Public Switching Systems Inc.

- A View of a Future Society Based on C & C Technologies
  Dr. Koji Kobayashi, Chairman and CEO, NEC Corporation Inc.

- Technology and Network Architecture
  Dr. John Mayo, Exec V.P., AT&T Bell Laboratories

- The Future of the Information Era
  William Norris, Former Chairman and CEO, Control Data Corp.

Hence, this analysis brings together top management, marketing, technical planners, and designers. It is intended as a working guide which defines a realistic process to understand each other's needs, interfaces and dependencies. For management, it will help eliminate expensive go no-go high risk decisions, as well as minimize the amount of risk per investment. On the technical side, it will return competitiveness and quality to products, and productivity to the designers. It will define the planning role of marketing and their interfaces to the technical analysis. This will enable firms to compete more effectively in the marketplace, with the right products at the right times.

This analysis identifies the new users in the communications and computer industries in terms of features, requirements and user types. It then translates *what* their needs are into specific services, which identify the next generation of ISDN (Integrated Services Digital Networks) information products. Analyzing the *what* may be broken down into several parts:

- Identifies the information marketplace by Industry and by User Type.
- Provides an analysis of the two worlds of ISDN:

  — ISDN Overlay Network of the 1988-1998 timeframe.
  — ISDN Wideband Network of the 1990-2010 timeframe.
  — CCITT/IEEE/TI standards.

- Reviews the governmental arena:
  — Inquiry III versus Inquiry II, MFJ, NCTE
  — Comparably efficient interconnection
  — Open architecture
  — Open standards
  — Open systems
  — Open protocols

- Defines future information services:
  - Features
  - Services
  - ISDN marketplace

- Provides a competitive analysis of the information marketplace strategies
- Analyzes "the human element"—the missing factor of the information corporation and the information marketplace.
- Considers "price for growth," tariffs, and the regulated, non-regulated marketplace.
- Packages specific applications for the new users of the information marketplace...
- Identifies the "collision and integration" of the two worlds of "C&C"— Computers and Communication within ISDNs, LANs, and WANs.

Processes and organizational structures are then described, as *how* to enable users, suppliers, and providers to achieve the right product, at the right time, for the right market:

- Analyzes change to survive in a world of change.
- Describes the relationship of mission, vision, goals, and objectives to strategic direction.
- Ties strategic direction to conceptual planning of new networks, products, and services.
- Identifies and defines the phases of the planning process.

  - Conceptual planning
  - Requirements definition
  - Product definition

- Overlays the planning process on the product life cycle.
- Describes the role of management, marketing and technical in terms of the planning phases.
- Defines the methodology for pursuing quality to the desired level of degree and extent.
- Provides the technical development process for successfully developing the desired product.
- Describes technology transfer processes between users, suppliers and providers.
- Considers the impact of the planning process on:
  - Market planning and user needs research
  - High technology products' architecture and structure
  - Product selection
  - Management commitment
  - Benefit analysis

- Identifies and discusses product development and a quality planning and implementation process to successfully achieve the "right" product and service.

- Defines the architecture and organizational structure for achieving preproject, preprogram, preproduct, and people planning processes that enable people to participate successfully.
- Defines checkpoints for management review and commitment as a progression of looks that reduce risk.
- Provides the framework for planning programs that provide a continuous array of network, products and services in a cost effective manner, enabling a transfer of technology from product to product in a changing market.
- Translates future products to business plans to strategic plans.

Therefore the objectives of this analysis are to interactively consider the *what* with the *how*, by first achieving a clear understanding of the purpose, activities, risks, organizational structures, dependencies, interactions, reviews, decisions, and expected results of several new innovative and useful planning and technology transfer processes for the future; and then secondly by specifically applying these theories, strategies and processes to help identify and define the right future networks, products and services for the telecommunications/information marketplace of the forthcoming information era.

La Petite Histoire

It has been said that "*we do not plan to fail—we just fail to plan*."

This brings to mind a little anecdote, about two adventurous young men, who had decided to take the day off from their studies and set off on a trip, far from the super highways to a destination approximately two hundred miles away. Having awakened bright and early, hearing the birds singing and seeing the bright blue skies, they were filled with such a sense of expectation, excitement and adventure that they refused to take the time necessary to find their missing maps. When faced with the unknown, they would simply use their instincts.

Once underway, at each crossroad, they made various masterful decisions, from checking the position of the sun to tossing a coin. However, as the terrain became quite complex, having twisted and turned through the densely wooded trails, they soon lost their sense of direction. Finally, several hours later, on turning a corner, much to their surprise, they found themselves not more than one mile from their starting point. With the day now nearing high noon, it was too late and they were too tired to begin a new journey. The opportunity for an exciting day was gone, as well as their enthusiasm, energy and resources. They had not planned to fail—they had just failed to plan!

This book is intended to be a road map, hopefully not left behind, but read and studied. As we move into a period of intense change, filled with future unknowns and opportunity, it is essential to use the right aids, especially those designed to manage change, to help achieve our destination. This analysis is intended to show the holes in the roads, opportunities to bypass, the slow moving traffic, dangerous conditions, and dead ends, as well as to indicate safe places to rest and relax.

Once a man was asked why he had taken time to build a bridge over a treacherous creek that he had already successfully crossed. He answered: "Why—to help those who come after me to safely cross, not tire, and reach greater destinations!" Hence, this book is for those who care to take the time to pause, to think, to learn perhaps a better way, an easier way, to achieve their destiny. I wish you a safe voyage!

Robert K. Heldman

Introduction

Over the seventies and eighties, planning has grown to maturity. Today 85% of the Fortune 500 corporations reported in surveys that they now emphasize planning. The initial stages of planning have been called various names, such as: Strategic Planning, Corporate Planning, Operational Planning, Long Range Planning, Short Range Planning, Prestudy, Advanced Planning, Market Research, Applied Research Planning, and Product Planning. There has been much confusion as to who should be doing what type of planning.

The process of producing a product through the various phases of its "life cycle" is the subject of much discussion by today's program management, whether the product is a network, a system, a program, a device or a service. High technology's complex, highly competitive arena has greatly reduced the margin for error. Regulatory changes, the economic environment, technological advances, and expanding user needs have caused major business shifts in many industries. This is especially true in the telecommunications industry, which is presently undergoing drastic changes to provide new integrated services for the *new information era users*. During these changing times, top management are more intensely reviewing their basic mission, strategy, organizational structures, personnel capabilities and procedures with questions such as:

- How do we identify the marketplace and become market driven?
- How do we currently perform?
- How do we tie our business plans, marketing plans, program plans and project plans to our strategic plans?
- What is our mission? Our vision?
- Where are we going today?

- What should our business be?
- Where are our costs?
- Is there a better way to operate?
- How much R&D do we need? How do we control it?
- How do we cut software development costs?
- How do we improve our support costs?
- What should be our strategic direction in this period of intense change and opportunity?
- What is the business of the business?

In turn, their marketing and technical managers, along with their systems analysts, are concerned with the following questions:

- What is ISDN? What is our market? Where is our market?
- Who are the new ISDN users? What are their needs?
- What should we provide? What are our products?
- What is the market for this particular product?
- How do the requirements for the "right" product become defined in the shortest time possible?
- How do we structure a network, product or service to meet the requirements with the most optimum design?
- How do we increase design quality and productivity economically?
- How do we provide products, networks and services that easily handle change?
- Is there a better way to plan, design, test and operate?
- What are our next families of ISDN products?

With these what and how questions in mind, this analysis takes a hard look at the basic market/technology planning and transfer processes to achieve specific ISDN networks, products and services for the telecommunications information world application. It shows logical and realistic planning and implementation phases and identifies the type of work performed during each phase by identifying the different factors, conditions, interrelationships and outputs of each phase. In one sense it is a book within a book, where the planning theory is one and the telecommunication-information application another.

The proposed process indicates decision points for management to review the technical progress. It emphasizes the conceptual planning, requirement definition, and the product definition phases as the key points for early management involvement in establishing strategy, products, and programs consistent with the corporation's mission. In addition, the process is presented in its skewed form, since in the real world, each phase does not abruptly begin where the preceding phase ends. However, its structure and management checkpoints remain consistent. Further analysis shows how multiple products can be time phased to enable maximum utilization of personnel and material resources. This will provide more realistic workloads, as well as a reasonable means for transferring technology.

The planning process is overlaid on a product life cycle to further clarify and refine its initial phases. Emphasis is placed on fully visualizing all aspects (purpose, function, organization, methodology, and personnel utilization) of "Product Planning." If the planning phases are realistically understood and implemented, this process can become an effective method for minimizing subsequent programming, hardware development, manufacturing, and support costs. This will help enable the firm to achieve very successful products in the marketplace. However, as will be shown, this type of planning must be performed with the right mix of management and specialists from the various disciplines of finance, legal, market research, systems engineering, programming, product engineering, quality, training, and support.

ISDN

For the sake of clarity and understanding, extensive analysis using case examples best exemplify the recommended strategies and techniques demonstrating their application to the information world. They will show the interrelationships between strategic and product planning in actual practice. For example: a detailed workshop methodology will be presented for understanding and identifying future ISDN networks, products and services.

Part I: Strategies and Plans

Chapters 1, 2, and 3 identify the reasons, strategies and programs for planning in a period of complex change, in terms of management, marketing and technical relationships, by addressing the most prevalent questions and problems that pertain to their various activities. The final section, *Conceptual Planning*, provides a realistic approach to innovative and creative thinking.

Chapter 4 describes the "Requirements Definition" phase in terms of degree and extent of emphasis. Various aspects are covered, such as features, performance, operation, support, limits, environments, future features, feasibility, risk, priority, and reviews. The specific interrelationships between marketing, technical, government, and management are carefully investigated in terms of the telecommunications information world of future features cubics.

Chapter 5 analyzes the "Product Definition" phase. Here the design and project planning processes are described that ensure that the product's architecture and structure meet the requirements to the desired level, required by management, before commitment to development.

Chapter 6 identifies the processes that integrate research and development efforts of the suppliers with the requirements of the providers and needs of the users. They are analyzed to show how the objectives, requirements and structures are defined and pursued in a manner that ensures the desired level of quality is achieved.

Chapter 7 defines the multi-facets of the processes in terms of their impact on people organizations and identifies the techniques for orchestrating the planning process in a multi-unit, multi-national environment to integrate marketing and technical together. It describes the interrelationships between universities and industry, as well as national and international standard committees and planning forums.

It applies the planning process to the world of telecommunications today, to its working level environment of lines of business, business plans, strategic planning, market planning, network planning, project planning and system planning and identifies its problems and opportunities for success in various organizational structures (the formal and informal). Operations will be considered in different culture conditions of various degrees of distribution of power, risk taking, formal planning, and willingness to change and meet new opportunities.

Chapter 8 will integrate all of the above thinking of the planning processes into the environment of today's firms that are currently involved with information networks, products and services.

Part II: The Information Era

Chapter 9 is an analysis indicating the type of world society that could flourish in the information era. It is overlaid on the conflicts and resistance that will occur during the transition period to the functioning phases of the information era in the twenty first century.

Chapter 10 is an in-depth look at the building blocks of the future ISDN network architecture in terms of technological possibilities, market opportunities, and governmental restraints.

Chapter 11 provides an analysis of the Formation Phase of the information era showing the views, plans, products, programs and concerns of its suppliers and providers in terms of financial strategies, business strategies, positioning strategies, players strategies, market strategies, architectural strategies, network strategies, product strategies, information service strategies, ISDN strategies, governmental strategies, and the overall strategy of these strategies.

Part III Studies: Networks, Products and Services for the Information Marketplace

Chapters 12 and 13 provides detailed "looks" at the marketplace, players, technology, governmental decisions, and evolving ISDN architectures, structures, interfaces, standards, issues and questions. This analysis consists of specific case studies and workshops for those who are deeply involved in "playing the game" of providing and supplying new ISDN networks, products and services for the telecommunication-information new users.

The case studies present a past experience, a technical/marketplace vision, or a specific technique that identifies the need for something different. Alternatively, they may address the future and its need for a new form of thinking.

Each workshop will have one or more detailed discussion topics that are designed for individual reflection or group discussion to bring out the participants' views and draw upon their different experiences. The topics will center on points made throughout the immediate section. Each workshop may also contain specific questions that emphasize the major points of the case studies. They are designed to force one to think and then make a decision or show indecision. The sequence of questions should cause a rethinking of answers to previous section's questions, as their ramifications are better understood.

Each chapter's observations will summarize its key points. A final conclusion will contain the major points, made throughout the book, for easy reference after reading the book.

Part 1

Strategies and Plans

Chapter 1

Planning For Change
and Opportunity
in The Information Era

Now is the time to bring together many of the major facets of the complex picture of change that today's management, planners, project leaders, and system designers are attempting to address, to show the scope and influence of change on technology, government decisions, competition, marketplace needs, top down planning, and management. These factors can then be applied to future information networks, products and services to demonstrate real problems requiring difficult decisions. In doing so, hopefully, we are drawn into the world of planning to see that to survive in the 90s and beyond will require considerable preproject analysis that enables innovation and management of change, using some form of top down planning process.

WHY PLAN?

Of course you plan! You would not be reading this book on planning if you didn't. In getting to the position you have today, you have probably developed a mental process that is quite effective. Perhaps you have not formulated it into a formal process. However, when things don't go exactly as envisioned, or others are not quite in sync with your thinking, it is nice to be able to identify where the differences or problems may be, in order to be more effective in the future. This is one of the purposes of this analysis—to provide a base upon which to cross reference your own particular planning processes with these ideas, processes, and techniques, which may make your work a little easier.

With this objective in mind, you might wish to take a moment, before reading this book, to write down your current processes for planning and making decisions, both formal and informal. Then compare them with those expressed throughout this book. Where they are similar, you will find reinforcement, where different you may wish to consider new ideas, or at least determine reasons why these differences occur. Future situations may find their application helpful. In any event, you should find this analysis on planning interesting, stimulating, and full of possibilities that may warrant your further investigation, especially as we all participate in this period of change.

The traditional industries of communications and data processing have entered the "corridor of crises" that established companies reach, when their standard base "bread and butter" product lines are threatened. Only this time it is the industries themselves that are threatened. Each has the opportunity to expand and take over a considerable portion of the domain of the other. The FCC and courts have attempted to control the situation by creating artificial boundaries. However, the uncontrollable changing technology, together with the new marketplace demand, has caused a continuous stream of new rulings to soften and modify these limits, so that in time, there are no limits at all. It has been jokingly said that "the situation grew and grew until it was gruesome," with lawyers, marketing, technical, and management locked in an endless sea of change.

These considerations could have been written for almost any business, as many facets of today's society are undergoing intense change. The principles, observations and recommendations are timely and universal. They have been developed over the last twenty five years, the hard way, by trial and error, under fire, in the intense business arena of the aerospace, defense, and telecommunications industries. There, they directly or indirectly affected the work styles of some half a million people. What was learned through this real world laboratory experiment was constantly reapplied, causing the strategies and techniques to be redefined and further developed to enhance their effectiveness. It is now time for them to enter the world arena, as they have been honed to a fine cutting edge. However, to be fully understood, a tool must be directly applied to every aspect of an especially challenging job. It is only then that its potential power can be appreciated.

As we move into the information era, there is great resistance as we give up the old ways and establish the new. Telecommunications—information firms are those first affected by the tremendous changes of the information age. Hence, it is appropriate to apply a process for handling change initially to these industries, and to demonstrate how those in it can not only survive, but become greatly successful. Therefore, this analysis concentrates on those involved in moving society into the information era. It contains a wealth of knowledge, gained from hundreds of conversations, and from experiences of people directly participating in this period of change.

Over the past five years, participants in workshops on these views have observed that though many ideas individually appear logical and straightforward, it is in their integration and application that the processes' unlimited expansion occurs. This is the key to their power, and unfortunately to their complexity. Problems today are not simple, requiring independent solutions for management, marketing, or research, using such aids as business plans, marketing plans, or project plans. The true solution is in bringing them all together and understanding those interrelationships, that make the whole greater than the sum of its parts. Here lies the hidden path to achieving successful solutions. In order not to fail, we must spend more time planning, especially in today's unforgiving intense period of international competition.

A thoughtful mother once said to her small boy, who was in a great hurry to play in the exciting world outside, but was constantly going back upstairs for something he had forgotten: "If you do not have a good head, you had better have good feet!" As we enter the new world of managing change through innovative planning, it is now time to take the time to think on how to be more innovative and effective. It is a new ball game, with new rules, new objectives, new players, requiring new tools. It is time to think out the game, before playing it, in order to save our energies for the game . . .

NOW IS A NEW ERA FOR MANAGEMENT, BUT WHAT KIND . . ?

Today, we are no longer faced with the unknown. During the 70s and throughout the 80s, technology was transforming the world by reducing all known electronic devices to the size of a microdot. Costs plummeted as U.S. firms moved VLSI facilities around the world, searching for the cheapest, yet still technically sophisticated labor force; but something happened along the way. The rest of the world learned the technology only too well and began to sell their own products back to the U.S. with better quality. Suddenly faced with this new intense competition, traditional firms found their entire product lines under attack. Some had taken so much quality from their product's design, that support costs had reached a full 30% of the initial R&D costs. The quality-costs-schedule design trade off priorities, in many instances were: schedule first, costs next, then quality. The slogan being: "Get it to the marketplace as soon as possible, then cost reduce the next version of it!" Quality was left for marketing advertisements to convince the prospective buyer with their single requirement being: "Make it attractive, the customer really doesn't care how it works!" or "Caveat Emptor—Let the buyer beware!" Subsequent problems were made the responsibility of the maintenance and support organizations, not design or sales. Raises and commissions depended on getting it into the customers hands, they were not tied to the total revenue to the firm, which, of course, is based on the formula:

Profit is equal to Sale Price *minus* Total R&D Costs and *Support*.

With this attitude, many firms today are spending $.30 on support for every $1 spent on getting the product out the door. With competition, less sales, shorter product life cycles, this adds up to disaster in today's business environment.

There also prevailed a do nothing, "leap frog," mentality of waiting a little longer for the next change in technology, in order to skip over the costs of one change to catch the next one. Unfortunately many firms that did not track the changes, also did not develop the technical, marketing and planning skills to realistically compete in the next wave. A case study will show how one firm, that was used to buying its way into technology, has lost billions in the 80s, due to having difficulty recruiting people with the right leading-edge knowledge. In the past, many of the nonleaders tried to solicit key personnel from those who had done it before, to come up with a similar version of the product for them. However, due to the amount of change, by the time they come up with another version, three to four years hence, it will have become obsolete. Still, when these general managers are asked to "spend for the future," their response usually is: "If I do so, I will simply be ensuring the success of my successor." Their personal success is tied to today's products. Of course, they will subsequently fail, and their successors will also fail. This is a no win situation for all involved!

Unfortunately, the competition is so intense, and the game is being played at such sophisticated levels, that the opportunity for "learning while playing" is gone. Many firms attempted, too quickly, to provide "office of the future" or "home of the future" products, and have bowed out, after losing several hundred millions with no sign of success. There have been numerous panic buy outs, where large firms tried to obtain needed products, developed by smaller more innovative firms. This was finance management's answer to the technical gap problem. However, they soon found that the costs were excessive, with small firms exchanging owners for the third time, at costs of up to 30 or 50 million. Also, by then, most of the good people had left the original firms. Hence, a more intense search for 1st and 2nd phase opportunities was their alternative solution. So they have feverishly reviewed "over the counter" companies for opportunities, causing much speculation in the stock market, with few real results in acquiring new successful products.

As seen in Fig. 1-1, the view today is no longer that of a submerged iceberg, which had a mammoth unknown size underwater, hiding the impact of future unknown changes. In the past, there has been much discussion, that we were only viewing "the tip of the iceberg." Over recent years, the dams holding back the sea have been broken by great advances in technology, lowering the water level and showing the iceberg with all its facets. The FCC and the justice department antitrust decisions have been made, opening the dams, letting out the remaining water, washing the iceberg ashore, to enable the impact of new competition to forever change the world of telecommunications and data processing.

Now the unknown is known, but the problem of today's management is how to obtain "life saving resources" for their industries, from this highly complex iceberg, sitting on their front beach. They could wait for the late summer to develop enough heat to melt it down, but, by then most of the resources would simply have returned to the ocean, and they would have missed a great opportunity. To take advantage of the situation, they must reassess and perhaps modify or change their management styles and take

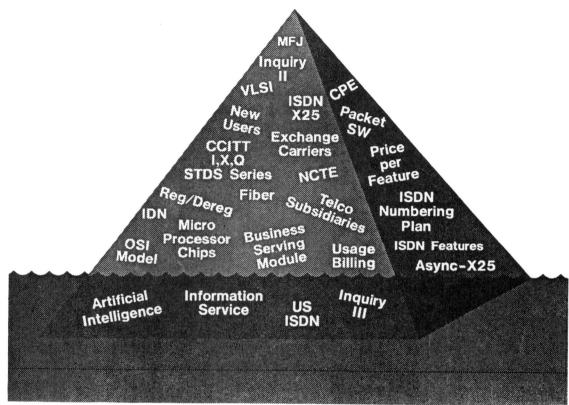

Fig. 1-1. The Facets of the Information Iceberg.

time to understand the new marketplace from the view of the future users of information. They must take time to understand the phases and shifts in technology and more carefully match the right technology with the right market to achieve the right product, in such a manner that they are neither market driven or technology driven but market-technology (Mark-Tech) driven. They must challenge and change the finer points of the government decisions to expand and wedge their products into greater markets.

Management must be willing to share power within the organization, enabling others to assist them in determining direction, by soliciting aid from the marketing and technology planners. Finally this new management must be able to take risk, recognizing that they are no longer in the world of evolution, but in the world of distinct abrupt change, with marked discontinuity points. We are back to the days when all that management had were such things as basic ideas and technical techniques; for example, a mathematical model of a possible future device called a motor. There is an interesting story, that the inventor of the motor was having difficulty obtaining entrance into the United States. His listed occupation was playing with mathematical num-

7

bers. Then, the leader of one of today's major firms, recognizing his potential, obtained his entrance and applied his models to make labor saving devices, such as washing machines, etc., for new unknown markets. Hence, we will see how management must establish an environment for new ideas, which we will call "Innovation Planning." They must take a more active role in planning, be willing to invest large sums of money on products of shorter shelf life and have a constant flow of new products to meet the changing needs of the "new users." This applies not only to top decision makers, but to all involved in "the new game." The technical, marketing and support divisions of the new lines of business must together manage change, or it will manage them, bypass them, and leave them—all of them—far behind. Now is the time to manage change . . .

MANAGING CHANGE PROVIDES OPPORTUNITY, BUT FOR WHOM . . ?

How often have we seen seminars advertising various management aids such as: "What you need are Business Plans that . . .," "You should use Marketing Plans that . . .," "Project Control Pert Systems will . . .," "Decision tables can . . .," "Financial models will . . .," etc. During the course of our investigation, we will consider these management support tools. However, we must first have a solid framework, upon which to structure them. What good are business plans based on old business opportunities, that are being drastically changed by deregulatory FCC rulings; marketing plans based on providing data communications for unidentified users; financial models based upon nebulous projections, so that the margin for error is near 40%-60% (a toss of the coin?); or design pert systems, having over 1000 nodes, which do not identify cross dependencies tied to new features? For these and other reasons, many bottom line driven general managers take a dim view of support aids. Since they have never achieved their true potential, many have been dropped after considerable time and effort had been expended. Some directors did tie their careers to pert systems, only to find that once their project began having many new requirements, the "perted design schedule" did not reflect "the design." In one case, it was found that technical management were spending so much of their time feeding the pert systems data, that they were not monitoring the design of the system at all. To their dismay, these more adventurous directors found themselves and their pert systems eventually removed. This was unfortunate, since these events caused a regression from using many of the new tools with any degree of confidence.

A part of the solution is for today's management to first employ a planning process which fosters innovation, to enable them to manage change. Nothing is stable any longer. Without a truly functioning planning process, many of these past management aids have simply become exercisers; where the real driving forces are two day (all day and night, off site) meeting, or late evening or Saturday morning strategy sessions. They result in strategies that have a few problems "yet to be worked out," and are therefore subject to change. Subsequent similar strategy sessions, as events change, may cause a redirection with a 90 degree shift.

Single person visionaries may still exist, but few are functioning as they did in the past. Most of today's firms have experienced corporate wars, power plays or hostile takeovers, leaving: confusion, dispersed power, and lines of business groups pulling in different directions. Unfortunately, in this environment, resulting from this form of reaction to change, direction becomes more and more illusive. Usually, loss of marketplace position, together with loss of profits, will be the catalyst to return to cooperation. By then, the need for a planning process to refocus energies in the right direction has become critical. In this more complex world, the era of dictatorial management is passing. It is true that a few must eventually set the direction, but the most successful direction occurs when many knowledgeable internal and external inputs have assisted in formulating the decision.

This requires a new participating role for management called *the manager planner* who interchanges ideas with appropriate groups within the organization. Today's firms are living in a changing world, where change must be embraced. It must become an integral part of the thought process of all involved. This requires understanding the economical shifts and the changes in society, along with the technical factors and user needs. Anyone can build a product, but knowing how to achieve the right product and projecting how long it will remain the right product is another story, isn't it? How to continue to have the right product throughout this era of change, and when to know the right product is no longer right requires a new level of sophistication in planning. The answer lies in having management from all disciplines—marketing, technical, financial and strategic—assume the role of manager planners, who must take calculated risks. We can no longer wait until the line of people, requesting a new version of our widget, is so long that its end cannot be seen.

Opportunities for tomorrow are achieved through difficult decisions today! Six to eight months will become a long lead time over the competition. Products will be built, purchased and provided with no guaranteed market. The manager planner must take the time to truly identify new opportunities and accept change, as a way of life. One vice-president once noted that he should begin spending at least 50% of his time planning, not as a prolonged "study it to death" planning exercise, but as a way of life, by adapting a planning process that naturally evaluates the forces on the marketplace, anticipates future user needs and enables decision maker leaders to easily shift and position their firm to appropriately meet the market. This brings an end to chaos, it launches new projects with enough lead time to be positioned, when "the window of opportunity" occurs. This is truly managing change to avail of every opportunity it offers.

THE NEW MARKETPLACE:
ITS DIRECTION OR LACK OF DIRECTION . . ?

Over the past twenty years, we have seen many changing forecasts and economic shifts in society. Several major industry collapses occurred when factories based upon bending iron into various metal parts closed down, as the first wave of the microdot technology's tremendous impact was felt. Major changes have taken place for the survivors. For example, an electronic manufacturing plant, that won an award in the 60s for efficiently bringing raw materials into one end of its mile perimeter building, and transforming it into step by step switching systems going out the other end, employed 14,000 people in the 1960s. Today the plant employs only 3,000 people. It has a white clean room environment and uses robotic devices and automated test systems to assemble highly sophisticated switching systems, whose software programs constitute 85% of the R&D costs. This is typical of the transformation of many of the older firms still remaining in the electronics industry.

There has been a shift to the Southwest sunbelt states and to the Northeast, from the Northwest, Midwest and even California, as firms attempted to relocate in new areas to attract high technology designers and programmers. (Especially after California housing costs became prohibitive.) However, as family ties reentered the scene, there has been some return, but to different industrial locations that catered to light industry. In the Midwest, farming, iron ranges, steel factories, and auto industries suffered greatly, causing a shift to telemarketing, credit card industries, and database centers etc. On the international scenes, trade deficits and labor employment restrictions required factories to assemble products in the "marketed" countries. The incoming industries' response was more automated factories. This further complicated the picture, as similar shifts took place in every European country, away from the heavy equipment industrial society, to the smaller highly automated high technology era. This now causes high unemployment throughout the world for the unskilled labor forces, introducing a two tiered society of those with education, skills, employment and opportunity, and those without.

As the computer moves to all aspects of the business and residential community, more areas become automated and under control of data driven systems. This forms the "usage basis" for the complex data networks to overlay on the voice networks. They will enable more and more information to be available to the manager-planners to better understand this changing world. The manager-planners will themselves become a major catalyst to cause the changes in the world that they are trying to understand. This will be a self fulfilling prophesy, as they seek more information and require more complex programming, to analyze the data, to become more sophisticated in meeting change in the marketplace. This in turn will cause more and more change, as new products, networks, and services are created to meet their needs for more data. In other words, they become their own best customer!! This will result in continuous growth of office computer usage, as computers begin to analyze, plot interrelationships, provide possible alternatives and consider impact of new directions, resulting from decisions made by those using earlier computer analyses.

As yesterday's youth, who grew up using the computer in school, enter higher management positions, the marketplace's resistance to various computer applications diminishes. More and more firms will shift to using the computer in every facet of its operation to cut costs, improve efficiency and productivity. This then creates and sustains the "information society," as those using it in the office extend its acceptance into their homes and their shopping, transportation, and recreation endeavors.

Information networks will enable satellite work locations of major firms to locate anywhere in the world. Initially, large metro cities, such as New York, are ringed by multi tenant work environments, where firms take floors of office buildings for their workers and tie the locations together by information networks. However, this is applicable for any location, and moving the work force to more rural areas with high quality of life factors will become more common.

The information era is requiring a much more sophisticated business and engineering education. The gap will widen between the technical and non-technical countries. Factories will return to the high technology countries, employing more technically proficient labor forces to control the highly automated operations. This will create vastly different markets than we have had in the 20th century. Machines and systems will have shorter shelf life as users demand more and more sophisticated information manipulation features. This will require a deeper understanding and new emphasis on the product life cycle phases, especially the initial planning phases and, of course, the termination phase. The days of numerous evolutionary hardware changes to products are over. If it cannot be accomplished easily with software, perhaps a new product offering should be considered, earlier than traditional product life cycles had once indicated.

Future user needs will have to be determined before projects are initiated. This requires a new way of thinking, a new way of operating. In periods of intense change, there are great rewards, but higher risk. No one ever made money on gold when it stayed at $32 per ounce. After gold was deregulated, the smart players knew when to get in, when to get out, and when the risks became too great to play the game. Fortunately the marketplace for which we are planning is not quite so volatile, but it does require well calculated risk decisions. In looking at the past growth of telecommunications and at its projected growth, there are ample opportunities for success. However, timing and identification of key shifts are essential, where too soon or too late can be very expensive. It is necessary through extensive market research to analyze industries such as retail stores, banks, insurance firms, state and federal agencies, and determine where and when they will be (or are) willing to spend their capital to make their goods better available to the customer, to have tighter control of their inventories, to improve the effectiveness of their office workers, to obtain data to facilitate more timely decisions, etc. It is a situation where attitude is more important than fact! The fact *that they need it* is not important. The fact *that they have decided they need it* is important!

This is no longer a *connect and collect* market. To insert a data packet switch, video conference center, or office image unit, requires fostering the origination and subsequent growth of entirely new markets. Losses must be tolerated, as customer appreciation and demand develops. The Bell system came out with a picturephone trial network in the 60s. When they did not have customer acceptance, they did not proceed with picturephone III or picturephone IIII until a successful offering was achieved. The same situation occurred with their data transaction network offering of the late 70s. Viewtext, a menu-driven data retrieval system for the home or shopping center market, had similar experience in its initial trial in Europe, as France and England began to learn the complexities of their customer's need for various "friendly" machine interfaces. The designers of the Macintosh personal computer of the mid 80s anticipated that meeting this particular need with their "friendly mouse" would be the key to their initial, but not necessarily continuing, success. The concept of "user friendly" then changed to become "friendly system to system interfaces" and "friendly operational facilities for new programs."

To truly understand what is needed in the marketplace, the market research survey questions must provide more effective answers. Some data surveys in the 70s went so far as to ask anyone on the street what they thought about such and such an offering. Others in the 80s were given to randomly selected employees of various businesses. Unfortunately, this form of research killed many product possibilities, due to uninformed responses. As we enter the totally new markets of the information era, there is a need to more carefully select the person to be questioned and to have knowledgeable researchers spend educational time to identify the possibilities in considerable detail before questioning. Also, in interacting with the potential customer, other new opportunities will surface than the ones initially considered. Hence, the analysis of what took place during the survey is sometimes much more meaningful than the mathematical results of the questions. Firms who leave this to research houses, just to provide a finalized summary report, will usually miss a great opportunity. To counter this, many suppliers and providers account teams have been established to work directly with the major and medium size customers to determine their requirements. A detailed process for working with the customer will be described in subsequent sections.

Marketing cannot assure the role of order taking. Gone are the days of regulated monopolies or controlled product offerings where, as noted earlier, enough customers must demand a new product or service that the risk is obviously zero, at which time, the firm may (mind you, just may) offer it. Yes, it is a new marketplace, an ever changing one, with numerous firms ready and able to meet its desires, especially when a telecommunication switching system now occupies a space no bigger than the size of a desk. There is no longer any need for a small army of people to develop it, and certainly less to support it. As more and more products enter the marketplace, the questions quickly change from "Do we need this product?" to "What are its features?"

Hence, we enter "The Feature Game." Unfortunately, as we consider various product's features, we are forced to resolve who can provide these products offerings. The Justice Department and FCC have made many changing boundaries rulings in separating telecommunications from data processes to encourage competition. It is extremely important to understand who can provide what, especially with the government's big footprints all over the flower bed. "What flowers can be grown? What varieties will survive a lot of trampling around? What flowers will be crushed, long before they bloom?"

These aspects must be carefully analyzed during the planning phases. The heavy handed attempt to separate and control the separation between traditional communication firms and data processing in the mid 80s, after divestiture, caused extensive questioning of artificial boundary limits between Customer Provided Equipment (CPE) and Network Central Office Equipment (NCE). These considerations must be understood in terms of "What opportunities exist where and for whom?" Unfortunately, in many cases the boundaries were left to the courts to resolve and have become a complex legal-political game, rather than one based upon more logical technical and market considerations. The changing limits on information features, regulated and unregulated products, tariffed or detariffed offerings, as well as conditions on products provided by CPE, the Telco marketing subsidiaries, or the basic Telco, must be carefully understood, as we move from Computer Inquiry II to III to IV to . . . rediscover regulation? . . . to . . . ?

Today, the opportunity for the *providers* to provide anything to the *users* exists, since the *suppliers* can more and more economically design and manufacture anything! However, each offering requires extensive funding. This points out the need for all three to be drawn together early in the planning phases of new products, instead of after the design is complete and the product is in the field. Usually, it is then too late to find that it is missing a critical requirement variation, to make it more useful and successful.

As always, the marketplace will be the deciding factor, not just the back design rooms. To truly understand it is a skill in itself. This analysis will discuss a successful proven technique for interacting with the marketplace early in determining future product opportunities. No longer can a casual idea easily become a successful product in the telecommunications world. On the other hand, with appropriate attention, a casual idea may be expanded into a successful family of product offerings. To keep up with the marketplace is now a necessity for survival, as noted on the last page of the last issue of an earlier electronics magazine of the 70s, which had decided not to remain in the marketplace (see Fig. 1-2). It indicated that its death was due to economic conditions in a changing marketplace. (Today, there are at least twenty new magazines in the electronics-information field.) It is indeed necessary to recognize shifts and opportunities, such as shifts from discrete electronics to integrated circuits, to logic computers, to programming, to personal computers, to database information systems, to... In order to survive, we must understand today the direction of tomorrow's marketplace, as well as have the desire to "play the game."

Editorial

death and birth

THIS IS THE LAST ISSUE

After more than 40 years of publishing history, the magazine has become a victim of the current economic problems facing the electronics industry.

To survive we must prepare for tomorrow!

Fig. 1-2. Birth and Death.

THE NEW TECHNOLOGY: THE DRIVING FORCE . . . OR IS IT . . ?

"As a result of technological change, today, we have, as AT&T's John Mayo has noted, four uncontrollable "killer" technologies (computers, fiber optics, memories and programming). Within each, new technology advances are literally destroying an earlier fundamental technological and in the process are propelling us to new worlds of possibilities" (Refer to Chapter 9). In the early 60s, a device called an Integrated Circuit (IC), was developed by Texas Instruments for Rockwell International's Autonetics Division to replace Minuteman 1 with Minuteman 2. It was to substantially reduce bays of equipment to a few multi-layer printed circuit boards, filled on both sides with these IC's. At that time, in lot sizes of 1 million, a dual register IC chip cost approximately $55. It was only able to store two bits of an 8 bit character. It would take 4 of these devices to represent an alpha-numeric 8 bit code, to store, for example: the letter A. Through 1985, we had progressed to Large Scale Integration (LSI) and Very Large Scale Integration (VLSI) devices, which can store from 8,000 bits (8K where K = 1000) to 16K, 64K, and 256K. Subsequent developments, at an ever increasing rate, enable storage of 1 million (1985), 4 million (1986), and 40 million (1996?) bits of information.

Today 1 megabit memory chips have about 2 million components. No one talks about theoretical limits anymore, although the space between molecules and between shells of the atom might be one such threshold. We are seeing 100 million components on a one millimeter chip for devices that have less than one micron spacing, that have switching times of 10 Pico seconds—that's 10 trillionths (10×10^{-12}) of a second. We also have circuits performing 90 billion operations a second, using Gallium Arsenide technology. The standard Apple computer of 1985 would be 10 million times faster using that power. Moving to instructions per second—the speed a computer functions, we can express this in productivity terms used today such as: horse power or crunch power or MIPS (Million Instructions Per Second). Single chip computers or micros have been doubling their power each year. That's like increasing an automobile's miles per gallon by 100% with each fall line. By this projection, the power of a micro in 1990 reaches 4 MIPS. If a 1970 car got 30 miles per gallon, it would get 30,000 M.P.G. at this rate in 1990. Supercomputers today such as a Cray computer, costing several million dollars, have the power of 200 MIPS. We begin to see why the slide rules of the 1960s are as obsolete as buggy whips. With similar storage changes, this means an Apple or IBM PC would have had the power to control an Explorer IV mission to another galaxy. The graphs in Fig. 1-3 show the trends of computer technology.

The second killer technology is "lightwave," which for our purposes is both fiber optics and laser device technology. The horsepower yard stick is bits/second/distance. Here, we are also seeing a doubling every year. Four Hundred Megabit (Million Bits/Second) facilities, that pass information 20-30 miles without regeneration, are now ringing our metro cities. *Lightwave photonics switches*, which have the ability to switch information at the speed of light, have estimated limits of ten billion megabits or ten million gigabits.

15

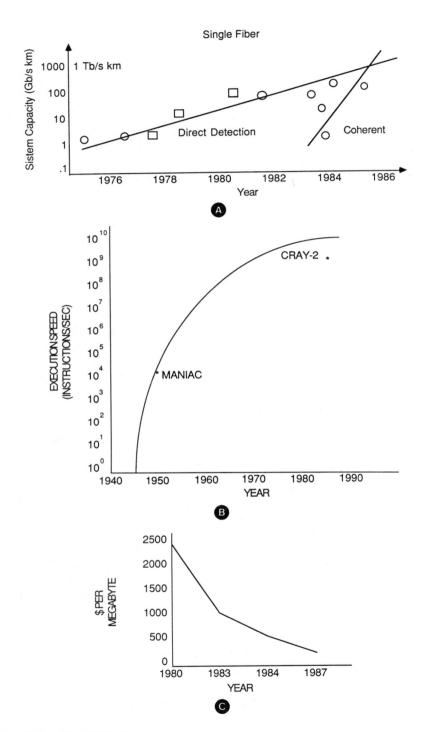

Fig. 1-3. Technological Forces.

Two billion bits per second would transmit the Encyclopedia Britannica, all thirty volumes, in less than two seconds, with an error rate of about one misspelled word. With these types of capabilities, we now have a situation where technology can easily move large amounts of information processing capabilities close to the user. Their terminals can work with the distant super computers that process megabits of information in a reasonable period of time. Networks can be designed to interface a large number of different users to systems that provide an array of features for solving a multitude of sophisticated problems.

There are today nearly 400 billion documents in storage in places such as libraries, offices, government files, etc. Some seventy billion or so are being added each year. For that information to be accessed, handled, and exchanged, it is probably realistic to say that most of it would never be retrieved or shared productively across a very wide spectrum of users. However, distributed computer systems, using the type of networks described, will be able to access and search large masses of this literature, once mass storage (the third killer technology) moves to such devices as the laser disk, which can store 250,000 pages of information. A naval architect could build a super tanker using one such disk.

Programming (the fourth killer technology) has developed from machine language (binary numbers) programs to high level languages (symbols) to a few that even respond to simple voice commands. They are structured into sets and subsets of functional modules that can be physically distributed throughout a computer's processors network. The total system decomposes into an array of processors working together, each resolving a piece of the problem, sharing resources and interfacing to special purpose adjunct systems. Micro memory technology, where storage costs only a few cents/bit, has reached fantastic breakthroughs. They are enabling the new exploding advances in the memory hungry sophisticated programming technology. Database management programs, that specially structure and access data, utilize advanced virtual memory techniques so that the amount of storage and its physical location are transparent to the user. These expanding computer, memory and programming technologies, when integrated together, have enabled terminals to change almost overnight from dumb to smart. As more and more artificial intelligence capabilities are added, they have even become somewhat intelligent.

Therefore, intelligent terminals, distributed networks, and super-mini processors are all complementing each other and competing to meet the needs of the new users. It has traditionally been left to the system designers to locate the work in the most efficient device. However, the picture is further complicated by the fact that each of these devices will be provided by many different manufacturers; each of whom desires to gain a major share of the marketplace. To ensure open competition, the Federal Communications Commission and Justice Department entered the scene to cause the break up of AT&T and to try and establish a level playing field (initially with limited success in this period of rapid technical change) via their enquiries, judgments, and waivers.

So technology can now locate or enable access to just about anything close to the user, by using physically distributed intelligent products connected by high capacity networks, provided by multiple vendors and carriers, offering a variety of features. However, in retrospect *who really* determines: What the users want? What the users are willing to pay for which features? Features offered in what products? At what point in time? Acceptable to which rulings made by the government? Who then, is really driving the use of the technology? Marketing? Technical? Justice? The users themselves? or strategic planners? It is time to take a closer look . . .

CHANGING STRATEGIC DIRECTION

Top management in every firm, participating in the transition into the information era, are greatly involved in establishing the strategic direction of their companies. Working with many levels of their management, they are attempting to direct their firms, without having constantly changing strategic direction. To change strategic direction is to have *opportunity;* to have changing strategic direction is to have *chaos.* In some firms, management is totally occupied with trying to manage chaos, not change. This not only is a nightmare for the management, but brings total frustration and finally indifference to the work force. In the mid 80s, a small midwestern college in South Dakota had a riot. The frustration level exploded as the school oscillated from being first directed to stop its liberal arts programs and change to a business school, and then stop and change back to a liberal arts school. Finally, a new president was brought in to restore order. He painfully set the direction, as a business school, but one specializing in utilizing the latest advances in information technology, emulating a Sloan or Wharton undergraduate program. Some students and teachers left, some came back, some new arrivals came. They finally had changed direction and had stopped the changing direction. Many believe that they can change a firm's direction from lower levels within the organization. In reality they can only usually influence a change in thinking. The direction of the firm will not change until its mission, strategic direction, and operating structure change.

For many years, over the 60s, 70s and early 80s, many visionary people described the opportunities of the information age. However, for the major common carriers around the world, data handling was only one to three percent of their business. They were quite comfortable in being voice carriers in a regulated environment. As will be seen in the case histories, it wasn't until the anti-trust cases were in full swing that a second look was taken of the situation. By then, it was too late. For many years, planners had presented the opportunities, but found that the information world was not in the mission of the firms. To change direction, to encompass new non-voice business opportunities, would require risk. Questions were asked such as "Why take risk when everything was running smoothly, when personal situations were satisfactory, when the majority of the people employed were happy and content? Why change a good thing?" Opportunity lost for doubling and tripling income with new markets was of little consequence in a regulated world. Unfortunately, it was exactly at this moment that the marketplace was changing. But holding companies, accountable to stockholders far distant from the marketplace, were unwilling to let individual unit communication companies do their own planning. This is the history of a past environment that required limited high risk planning. It is important to remember and understand, because the situation today is quite different. It is one of tremendous change. It is indeed one in which a great amount of stored change, that was never allowed to take place orderly, is being unleashed, unchecked, with limited government control, over a shorter period of time.

Unfortunately, at the same time, the four massive technology changes are occurring along with tremendous buildup demand for new products and services from the more sophisticated buyers. The demand is especially prevalent in this social era of change, as we have moved into a period of choice, when everyone wishes to choose for themselves, this or that. With this background, the challenge to today's management is to effectively direct these powerful forces. To do this the driving force should be *the strategy of the strategies,* which twists here and turns there, to establish, *the business of the business.*

Once a clear direction and strategy on how the game is to be played is developed, then the lines of business can be formed to establish their particular strategies, goals, objectives, and plans to move the firm in the desired direction. Without this overall direction, the dilemma becomes one of managing various lines of business, which are in a contest with each other, overlaying their conflicting alternatives to the customer. Also internally, there is extreme competition between business units for funding to support their projects, that meet particular business sales objectives, usually with no real trade off accountability of actual revenue to the firm. This can only begin to be resolved by first clarifying the *strategy of the strategy*, in order to achieve the *mission.* Unfortunately, in a period of intense change, that is a nice objective, but may be quite impossible. As the mechanic said to the anxious driver of the disabled car, "When I know what the problem is, I will fix the car." Unfortunately strategic direction issues are never simple. If the direction could be easily determined and set, it would be!

New Business Strategies

Firms, today, are usually a family of companies under a holding firm. Its multiple units are located throughout the country with a few foreign locations. (A company is not a firm unless it has an international division or office.) True multi-national firms, controlling separate autonomous major companies throughout the world, have yet another dimension of complexity, quite different from having an extended branch in a foreign country. Here, national pride, old world wounds and politics play a major role, especially where the work force have government protected guaranteed jobs. Over recent years, a slogan has developed that "small is beautiful." It had become time to return control back to the unit. The units argued that, since they were profit centers responsible for their own profits, they should have the responsibility to establish their own direction in the marketplace. Hence, massive upheaval has occurred, as case holders in the parent holding companies were reduced along with legions of financial and legal experts. Other firms are pursuing commonality across operating units, with various degrees of central planning and control.

A couple of Harvard business professors made the strategic "revelation" in 1984 to the academic and business world, that business had rendered such a short term view, due to financial concerns and constraints, that this was seriously damaging the long term viability of the firms. This of course had been known throughout the industry for years. Over the late 70s and early 80s, numerous blood baths had occurred, when general managers could not meet the marketplace's needs, as foreign competition entered with the right products (such as small cars), at the right time. Hence, their observation was not new, but it did cause management to stop and ask, if there really was a better way to operate, and that was new.

Post war industries had been run on military style strategic thinking such as "We wish to win the war. . .; to do so, we must take these three bodies of land surrounded by water. . .; the first, we will blockade. . .; the second, we will bomb. . .; the third we will take by assault. . .; the navy will use the 5th fleet, with X number and type of ships. . .; the marines will hit the beaches at 0600. . ." This was strategic planning at its best, with levels of strategies down to the final tactical deployment of resources. All in sync with the strategic direction and mission.

However, somewhere along the way, business direction planning became cloudy and one of profit for profit sake. Those who could cost reduce the product, sell a fantastic number in the marketplace, manipulate inventories, or cheaply purchase or milk "cash cow" firms became the strategists for setting direction. In fact, there was no direction except the mission statement, which became "Make a profit today and everyday!" The more immediate and larger the profit, the better for the individual. This was successful, as long as the firm had a solid base line of good products, relatively limited competition in the marketplace, and customers who were tolerant and willing to wait for new offerings.

In the 80s period of change, that philosophy, approach, and reward system were no longer effective. Firms, with all their units' products under competitive attack, then attempted to decentralize. Unfortunately, the business units in the information world, had thought that they could set their own destiny. They soon found that they were very much dependent on sister company offerings and the strategies of their competitors. Especially as the terminal devices interfaced more closely with distributed computer systems that were tied together with the transmission media to form networks. Today, their individual products are now only a small piece of that network, with its many interfaces and standards to be achieved before they can become a true offering. They soon found that their firms required a more specific mission, that truly established the overall direction.

Hence came the new wave of visions of firms in the mid 80s. Unfortunately, there may be a long dry spell as one travels along the way to reach the vision of an oasis. Sometimes it is accomplished with much difficulty, such as in a sandstorm. Also, care must be taken to be sure that it is not a mirage. *Not all visions are found to be realistic!*

Today, the game is further complicated by competing factors such as: "How much should the firm be market driven or technology driven? Should strategic planning and top management just set direction and then assume the role of referee or scorekeeper? How does a firm achieve balance? How do the customers' needs become identified with enough lead time to turn around and impact future product offerings? Must every big firm wait until a small competitor does it and then scramble to emulate or eliminate them? Do we need some form of planning, if so what kind..? We have strategic plans, business plans, marketing plans, financial plans, and project plans, but we never seem to have the right products. We don't seem to be really in tune with the market. Yes, it is indeed a complex game!"

The interrelationships between the suppliers, providers and users have become so gridlocked that few real advances are being made by very many firms. The intense arena becomes a game of chess to determine competitors' strategies, watching their actions, emulating their successes, merging with them, or buying them out. The more adventurous leaders have become more market competitive, keeping their strategies hidden until their offerings are available. No longer is it a game, where the leader announces a new product long before it is available, in an attempt to have the market wait for them. On the other hand, the followers are having difficulty introducing the new technology into their operations, since their people have not participated in its many previous versions. They are not able to leap frog technologies, as originally anticipated. This causes a widening gap between the leaders and the followers.

The government/industry/education situation is becoming equally complex, as governors promote high technology centers and high technology councils to identify new jobs and revenue sources in technological fields. A research and development consortium was established among many of the midwestern states in 1985 for their universities to share research, jointly work on common problems, and market technology to the world via an international trading firm. It was established with an advisory board of leaders from industry, state governments, and universities, with the hope that closer relationships with industry could establish working partnerships between industry and the universities on specific areas of mutual interest. Similarly, today, cross industry sponsored research and development partnerships are helping to cut R&D costs. A group of firms will share in the benefits, as well as the costs. However, the process of managing, directing, interfacing, and receiving the benefits require an acceptable multiple owner research laboratory technology transfer process. Such a process, that has had considerable success, will be presented later in this book. We will see how it ties R&D to the specific strategic direction of the owner firms, making it most effective.

A few books written on the social economic changes of America indicate that we have reached the last frontier. After explorers reached the boundaries of the Pacific Ocean and megatropolises replaced the small western cities, no more did we hear "Go west young man for fame and fortune." (Also the high technology slogan of the 50s and early 60s). Some advised in the 70s going off to outer space, the last frontier of the Star Trek series, or to explore the ocean for growing food and providing new habitats, based on the "20,000 Leagues Under the Sea" approach, using the Jules Verne and Jacques Cousteau's view that the oceans have great opportunities for mankind. Unfortunately, these new worlds were initially able to employ only a few astronauts and marine biologists. The frontier of the 80s became the computer design and programming arena. At the same time, others did venture to the other side of the ocean for international opportunities, only to find that "over there" the customs, education, and philosophies of life were an equal challenge to "over here." Similarly, many across the sea were venturing to their "over there," also looking for opportunity for their products.

International trade centers, constructed in the late 80s to foster new trade routes for the turn of the century, will use global networks to tie the world marketplace together. Hence, the search for the last frontier has begun to move us into the international game. It is another dimension, another game. As expected, governments attempted to step into this arena with quotas, tariffs and limits on technology information exchange. However, in reality today is now the time for the next complex movement of the marketplace. As the marketplace appears to change strategic direction to a new facet of emphasis, in actuality, it is simply taking its next step, *a giant step for mankind—into the information era . . .*

CHANGE PLANNING: PLANNING IN CHANGE FOR CHANGE

In the midst of a storm, many a captain has gained new respect for the changing violent seas and made plans for new designs to enhance the sea worthiness of his ship, to achieve the peace of mind presented in Fig. 1-4. During these times, many seek any port in the storm for safe harbor. Few return to the sea without implementing their plans, changing this or that to enhance their chances for survival. Only the foolish expect a different treatment from the harsh sea when they return. Similarly, racing skippers are constantly searching for better boat designs to win the race—to win the game. So it is, as we live in the transition period from the post industrial era to the information era. It is like the challenges of sailing in rough seas or trying to win highly competitive races. It is time to think and implement new approaches to the game of business, for indeed it is a continuously new and changing rough game.

We can no longer quickly and easily introduce new products from new ideas. It has become more and more expensive to design products and establish them firmly in the marketplace. The risks are great, since many of the product's features are totally new, in order to meet new needs, which have only been perceived and usually do not have enough users to justify their

Fig. 1-4. The Storm.

initial existence. Unfortunately, if the product does become successful, there will soon be many new (some better) products from the intense international arena, competing for the market. No longer is there a sacred cow or turf, where sovereign control by one entity can be maintained. Also, playing the game is more complex, due to the players lack of new game knowledge. Firms cannot easily draw upon past experiences, because the new technology and markets are substantially different, though in some respects, they are an extension of past offerings. It is this unassuming difference that lulls one into thinking the game is the same, when in fact it is an order of magnitude more complex. For example, providing a data packet switch is quite different from providing a voice switch, though both are switches.

Therefore, we are like the blindfolded men in Fig. 1-5, who were up too close trying to identify the elephant. They thought the tail was a rope . . . the leg, a tree . . . It is time to step back and consider the complete picture to obtain a complete solution.

To meet this challenge, the need for some form of planning process has been identified; one that is able to deal with new change and allow all levels of management to manage change. Ideas must be challenged and reviewed to determine if they have substance before going to the development stages of a product. We must have a process that encourages innovation. There is much discussion today on the need to have more innovation. Various government divisions are paying for extensive research in the business graduate schools to investigate this need. It is indeed a major concern, especially when we have so much technology available and so few good products.

Innovation is the process of understanding needs, creating new ideas, translating them into new concepts, that are further analyzed, challenged, understood, extended, modified and adapted to become appropriate solutions to the more fully identified and defined needs. See Fig. 1-6. This is indeed the challenge of today's society. We have lived for many years on the innovated solutions of our fathers and father's fathers, but their solutions were for different needs than we have today. We must have a process, that encourages a better understanding of today's needs and provides creative solutions. This we will call the *Innovative Management Planning Process*. Its purpose and life is to exist in a period of change, enabling those using it to manage change to create opportunity, using innovative concepts. Upon this process we will overlay several other parallel new processes to assist the manager planners such as:

- A process to identify new user needs
- A process to bring marketing together with technical
- A process to enable timely management decisions
- A process to control the product through its product life cycle phases
- A process to better utilize research and development
- A process to manage the pursuit of quality
- A process to transfer technology to the users
- A process to restore enthusiasm to the work force

24

Fig. 1-5. Up Too Close.

This innovative process will be the basis upon which to orchestrate these multiple processes for multiple projects effectively, using the appropriate personnel to achieve the goals and objectives of the various lines of business. It will be further identified, defined, and exemplified, as these versatile processes are overlaid on it. Together, they will make a formidable set of tools for the *new manager planner* of the 90s to plan, *during change, for change, to achieve effective change. . .*

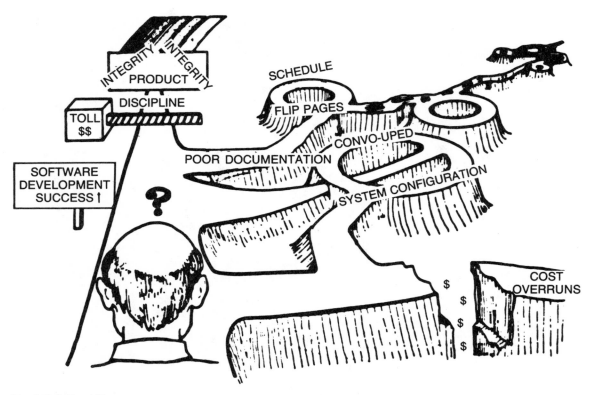

Fig. 1-6. A Road Map.

THE NEW MANAGER PLANNER: PLAYING IN A NEW GAME

The manager planner is the orchestrator of these innovative processes. However, an instrument, no matter how perfectly constructed, with whatever potential it may have, is actually only as good as its player. In the past some managers have not utilized opportunities to stop and think, such as performing a sufficiently detailed system design before beginning to develop the system. One firm in the mid 70s offered the Ossie award shown in Fig. 1-7 to anyone with the courage to give it to those in their organization who acted in this manner. Since there were a number of unemployed engineers and program managers throughout the 70s, and few project successes, perhaps more than just a few were presented the Ossie award.

The need for the Ossie has not changed with time. Note the multi-billions spent on the disastrous "Sergeant York Tank" in the mid 80s. Today, the problem is not only in building the system, but in determining what to build, when to build it, where to provide it, and for whom! The problems have reached such a level of complexity, that we must be careful to realize that they are

Fig. 1-7. The Ossie Award.

still solvable given the right tools. Ready to play the new game are today's new managers, system analysts, and planners from all disciplines. Those who are willing to face change without hiding from it have one of the essential characteristics required of the new manager planner. With an innovative planning process and its family of processes, they will have the tools to play the game successfully, but what about the competition?

No analysis on planning should be written that does not consider what others, such as the Japanese have done and are currently doing successfully. Americans and Europeans have come to believe that the Japanese must have hidden skills and processes that have enabled them to be more successful. So let's take a deeper look in order to later compare processes for strengths and weaknesses. The Japanese have made great strides in industry by transferring their citizens' sense of duty for their country and honor of family to the world of business. When the corporation assumed the role of a benevolent leader, whose managers were father figures for the workers families, it immediately obtained a benefit of having a dedicated work force, who did not wish to discredit their family by letting down their benevolent firm. These close parallel relationships with past traditions cultivated the efficiencies, productivity, and dedication that had once been achieved by firms in the U.S., after the great depression and war. People were thankful for their jobs then. They worked very industriously for a new opportunity for themselves and their children. They were proud and dedicated to their company.

Over the years, in Japan, firms continued to foster pride in work by setting difficult objectives and rewarding the workers with personal recognition, as percentages of the goal were achieved. They did not put a great financial distance between their presidents and managers, but used personal pride and responsibility as the motivation. For example, Japanese programmers have a five times greater reuse of past program modules in new programs than their American counterparts. One of the encouragement techniques was to put the programmer's name with his module and give recognition the more it was used to effectively help other programs to be successful. This required careful documentation of programs and time to structure the modules so they could be used by others. Hence, a quality emphasis in the initial programming requirements and a management emphasis to pursue quality where prevalent.

These techniques are extended to the assembly line. There, each worker reviews the work of the previous task and can stop the line, if the work is not up to standard. To prevent boredom, to establish pride and challenge, teams of workers are established on the assembly lines. For example, a team of workers will assemble the complete car, competing against other teams on the line. Management by consensus, not management by conflict (one U.S. firm's technique) is promoted, where all have a say and push for homogeneity and agreement. Another technique is the contract, where there is much negotiation until a person signs his or her agreement. Then it is up to that party to deliver in order not to lose face, so one and one's family aren't shamed in the company and community. These techniques employ a great deal of energy to manage, manipulate, encourage and work with the labor force. It is interesting to note that not only is the product achieved, but it is a quality product. This is because of their emphasis on quality as a strategic direction goal of the firm. It is part of their mission and the strategy of their strategies. Once the achievement is reached, the workers receive personal recognition, father image approval, and their families are well accepted in the community. (See *The Human Element* case study.)

In the marketplace, one single marketing firm may market the products from three research/manufacturing plants. All will build the product to the same requirements, established by a common marketing technical planning group. However, they may all build a different product that meets the requirements. The number of sales of the successful product will determine which firm's product architecture is successful. The winning firm is given a bigger percentage of the marketing effort for next year's products. Again success in the marketplace is transferred back to the successful manufacturer's employees and their families.

Unfortunately, our last 30-40 years have been spent in removing pride from work efforts, as those who were clever in reducing costs beyond reasonable quality limits were rewarded. As this quest to achieve greater profits for the firm was transferred to personal goals, the firms entered the age of the "bonus babies." It began with ball players and movie stars receiving mega dollar contracts. Later, this form of reward became perks and bonuses for management, as an incentive to reach sometimes unrealistic goals. This transformed some firms into having very short term profit views. We must be careful not to relate amounts of salaries to the loss of long term vision, but to the type of goals and objectives. Large salaries can definitely be useful incentives, if the goals are correct. (For example, the original profit sharing bonuses at a major retail store had created one excellent dedicated work force before it was removed.)

In the past, the auto industry has been a prime example of wrong goals and rewards. Japanese import restrictions throughout the early 80s were self imposed to protect a total loss of U.S. market to foreign industry. This was done to try to keep the large U.S. unskilled labor force employed and the U.S. Congress from imposing protectionism quotas. During this self imposed protection period, the net result was that the price of cars rose 60%, factories were automated to emulate the Japanese robotics, requiring 20% or so less unskilled workers, U.S. top management in the three auto firms reached 4.5 million dollar annual salaries, and car dealers continued to have long waiting lists for the new Japanese cars, the equivalent of which still were not available from the U.S. auto firms. Four years later, enormous trade deficits again caused Congress to turn to protectionism.

However, for many companies the Japanese situation indicated that something else was needed. Something did happen during this period. There was a definite change in some top management, who have worked extremely hard in an attempt to turn their companies around. Considerable effort has been spent over recent years to reestablish lost product lines with better quality products. This attitude is now becoming prevalent from the heads of many major companies throughout all their employees. Unfortunately, frustration has also occurred, where success in many cases is still elusive. Hence, the search for something to be more effective is the prevailing attitude in many firms. The time is right for change, for something new, to be more competitive, but what? Americans do not have the same motivational background as the Japanese. Therefore, how can this Japanese process, based upon different historical motivations, be successfully challenged by an American process, based upon meeting independent personal goals, financial rewards, and stockholder profit objectives?

Today is still a time of self interest, but understanding has occurred, after many major disasters, that survival is also a major self interest, along with respect, work enjoyment, and good relationships with others. People still need each other to help address highly complex issues. "No one is an island unto themselves." More and more people are realizing that working relationships are important not only for enjoyment, but harmony on the job translates into bigger profits for the firm and subsequently more personal wealth for everyone. Also, pride in work, personal satisfaction of achievement, and recognition for a job well done are still important to each new generation entering the work place.

The new members to the work forces have greater expectations than their parents, for more involved participation in the firm's efforts to achieve successful products. This underlines the need for having a planning activity in which many levels of people can participate. This also translates into the need for a process to enable management to define a specific mission and strategy. Internal bickering, fighting, and power clashes will be less prevalent by achieving better understanding and agreement to a less volatile, clearly defined strategic direction. This then enables the new players, the manager planners, to play the game. Successful performance will achieve shared profits for all the players of the team. There is a new world of opportunity. In this world, the team members, together, can achieve both recognition and profits. More profit sharing, stakeholder, and shareholder ownership will enhance cooperation, as one's ideas are used in one's company. Individual achievements that enable the group to win should be recognized and rewarded.

The new culture will enable the firm's management to play the game with their people. They must set direction, participate in the decision review processes, monitor current direction, remove obstacles, ensure that committees are not just forming other committees, and then allow the players to play the new game. With this delegation of responsibility further down the organization, the right level will be reached where the appropriate market and technology knowledge exist to meet the opportunity, especially as these opportunities demand more and more specific knowledge. This will foster a "buy in" by the key players. They become stakeholders in the endeavor, similar to the contract approach of the Japanese. Additional duties of the manager planners are to provide the training, processes, and organizational working relationships, which enable their players to be successful. During the play, fine adjustments are required, as they assume the coach roles, as well as that of the umpire. Hence, all play the game—together.

There is the need to know what is happening, to position and reposition the team to be at its best strength to meet the competition. This requires a deep understanding and constant monitoring of the game by management. "Participating management" do not just set general direction (especially that which may not even get the team onto the playing field) and walk away. They must become active in the game, but not always to the point of being the star hitter or pitcher. It requires maturity to win the game with strategic strategies, while participating as player coaches. It brings to mind the story of a terrible fire in the oil fields of an oil refinery. A team of company fire fighters arrived to bravely attempt to put the fire out. Anyone who has seen a raging oil refinery fire, understands their courage. As they engaged in the battle, a courageous manager went into a fire ridden operating house and re-routed the oil away from the fire area. He had used his head and quietly had supported the fire fighters to help them achieve their success.

Hence, the need for the manager planner, who can orchestrate many projects, using the appropriate people with highly skilled unique disciplines is evident. They will do this by knowing that with education comes an intense desire to participate, by recognizing that the secret to success in the new business arena is to enable the players to become the interested shareholder and stakeholders, by making sure that they have the right processes which will enable them to be innovative and effective, and by participating in the game with them. This then will require enlightened management, who will take the time to establish a specific mission and strategic direction, foster a return to seeking quality by managing the pursuit of quality, and establish processes, that ensure a logical flow from ideas to project completion. They will facilitate the "Ps," from Possibilities to Plans, Programs, Projects by Processes, using their People. See Fig. 1-8. This is the arena for the manager planner of the years to come to achieve new products, networks and services for the information age. It is our new frontier, it does not matter what level of management, or whether we are technical, marketing, or financial. We all must become manager planners to succeed in this intensely competitive game and play (and win!) the game together.

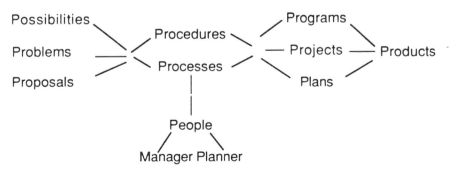

Fig. 1-8. The "P"s.

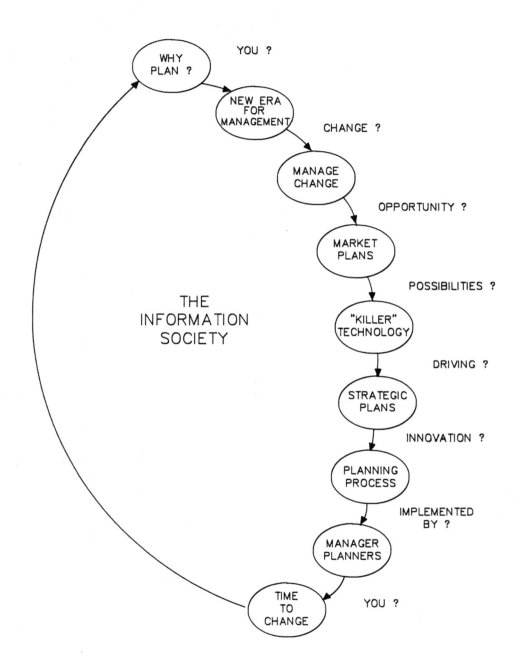

Fig. 1-9. The New Frontier.

A Time To Change, To Achieve New Opportunities

In step with these changes in the international telecommunication-information marketplace, now is the time to change, to achieve new modes of operation by management, such as the manager planner, to change to achieve the right mission, to change to achieve the right strategic direction with the right strategy of strategies, to change to achieve the right lines of business supported by the right organizations, to change to achieve the right processes enabling the right people, to change to achieve the right technology, to provide the right product at the right time, to meet the changing opportunities in the marketplace.

FURTHER ANALYSES

In Chapter 12, the case studies entitled *Two Changing Worlds Collide* and the workshop *What is the Strategy of the Strategy* directly apply these views to the information era, where we see in the case studies our resistance to change and in the workshop the need to understand the many aspects of the information era in terms of Phases of Change.

It is also interesting to note that though many of the strategies and processes are applied to the telecommunication-information industries, in reality, they are universal and can be adapted to many personal and business endeavors.

OBSERVATIONS: A TIME TO CHANGE

1. We all plan, but in a period of intense change, the mission, strategy of the strategies, strategic direction, and business of the business planning become the key driving factors to achieve success.

2. Independent solutions for management, technical and marketing are not the answer. We need an integrated solution, which ties business plans to marketing plans and project plans by using an innovative planning process, which brings them all together and makes the whole greater than the sum of the parts.

3. Management has a new role to play in sharing power within the organization and must take more risk, recognizing that the world of evolution of products is over. Products must be developed for totally new markets, taking time to be identified and developed by the right people. No longer is it a make and sale or connect and collect world. All levels of management, marketing, technical and finance must become to various degrees "The New Manager Planners."

4. Opportunities for tomorrow are achieved through difficult decisions today. Change must be embraced and become an integral part of our thought process.

5. Technology and the marketplace are in a new arena of intense competition. This is causing some to manage chaos instead of managing change. Some are losing great opportunities in not offering the right product.

6. There is a need for the manager planner to identify direction, using the right mix of disciplines at the right level in the organization, where the market meets the technology. There is a need for the player, coach, and umpire role of participating management, as they, with various levels of management and specialists of many disciplines, all play the new game together.

7. Now is the time to have a top down planning process that enables the new manager planners to provide the "right product," for the "right market," at the "right location," at the "right time" and to recognize when the "right product" is no longer "right," based upon understanding future user needs in terms of technological opportunities.

8. Now is the time to change, to achieve new opportunities.

The time is now!

Fig. 1-10. The Time Is Now. Now Never Waits.

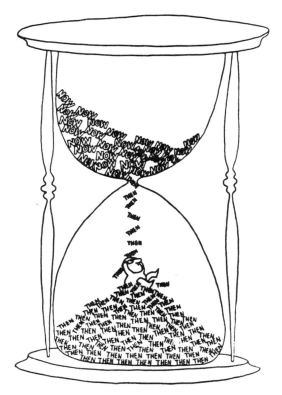

Chapter 2

Strategies and Processes

Let's take a moment to review the way we do business in the information telecommunications industry, to fully understand today's relationship between the user, the provider, and the manufacturer; the role of research and development; the mode of operation of strategic planning; the planning interface between strategic planning, and product planning and the relationship between system planning and the user needs. Let's see what's right and what's wrong with today's strategies and processes to determine what is needed, and what is not needed to enhance the role and decisions of top management. This analysis will consider how their mission and goals for the company can be more successfully translated to future products in the marketplace. In so doing, the hand off between preproject planning and project management will be clearly identified in terms of "product life cycle" phases, planning reviews, and management decisions. Today, technology can do most anything, the major problem is to determine what it should do.

As noted in "La Petite Histoire," we don't plan to fail, we fail to plan. Products, networks, and services' architectures and structures are based upon technology and requirements. Requirements are not only based upon user needs, but on both the short and long term objectives and strategies of management. Alternatively, too often, the subsequent decisions of what else the product should do are left to the programmer or logic designer to decide deep in the detailed design or testing phases. We have come to call them the "Else Conditions." There is a need for a living process which ties management to marketing and technical during the early phases of the product development and transfer of technology. This section will deal with these realistic problems and provide realistic solutions, some of which are currently being introduced and implemented throughout the world.

Major aspects of planning processes and their key interrelationships to the development phases of the product life cycle, as well as the technology transfer processes, will be identified and discussed. The role of participating manager planners will be defined, as well as their interface points to strategic and system planning. Finally, the impact of the processes on strategy and system architecture and structure, as well as maintenance and support will be reviewed in terms of the ultimate user and the marketplace, to show the need for a structured planning process and its impact on program and product development. This analysis provides a brief lead in to the topics of subsequent chapters to show their overlay on the planning life cycle.

STRATEGIC PLANNING

What's our strategy? We need a strategic plan! What's our strategic direction? We look like an organization searching for a mission! Can we change our strategy? Should we change emphasis?

In today's rapidly changing environment, especially for telecommunication information firms, we must have strategic strategies. Without them the corporate game quickly becomes a no win situation. Some firms have a strategic planning group. Those that do not have strategy sessions. No firm can successfully exist today, using one or two strategies that were established several years ago. As we look at various laboratories, industrial firms, telecommunication companies, or data processing firms, we see more and more of them recognizing this fact and formulating a strategic planning group. Establishing strategic direction requires a position of leadership and power, which will in all cases be challenged by the "informal" organization power seats. Hence, it is usually one job to determine direction and another to get it accepted. To only discuss one without the other would reduce the problem to a theoretical simplistic exercise. Both must be understood and integrated to form a true solution.

Strategic planning is closely tied to the mission of the firm and its goals and objectives. Today these are clarified with a vision description of the future of the company in various new marketplaces. Now one may ask; what does this have to do with building products or providing new telecommunication information services? We will see how providing future information network features and services is greatly dependent on a firm's mission and strategies. Traditionally, the governing board of officers set the general direction of the firm with a mission statement. Then, it was left to the various internal organizations to translate it into actions. Lets take a deeper look at how the mission of a firm can be used quite effectively to establish it in the "right" marketplace.

THE MISSION . . . THE VISION . . .

The mission statement should not be a generalized "wishy washy" collection of generic, vague concepts defining the charter of a company. From the mission statement should spring the life of the firm, the reason for its existence, the essential characteristics that differentiate it from others in the marketplace. Its character and attributes should be identified in terms of directional goals. Important specific objectives should be incorporated into the mission statement. Accompany the mission statement is the detailed vision description of the future world of the company in terms of the marketplace, technology and opportunity. It is not surprising to see how the mission and vision will set the framework and guide lines for subsequent financial decisions, that may not be fully statistically justified, other than by the statement "this is the reason we are in business." The statement usually is not very long; possibly only a single paragraph, or a single line or two; but it must capture all of the above considerations. The vision may be four or five pages to fully describe the new world of opportunity.

To establish the mission is not a trivial undertaking since a generalized mission statement can greatly undermine opportunities and limit the scope of the vision and its breath of future endeavors. It is therefore very important to carefully determine the reasons for the existence of a firm, the scope of its endeavors, its mode of operation, the pulse of its people, and its essential qualities and attributes.

Remember the story of the firm in the "gas light" business, that went out of business when electricity became available, because they had not realized that they were in the "light" business; or the railroads who lost a great amount of business, because airplanes began moving freight and people faster and easier. They did not expand their operations to include any form of transportation, but limited their scope to using two rails. Even in the 70's, we saw the telephone manufacturers and communication providers limit their vision to voice communications and not information, where information could be considered voice, data, video, image, text, graphics, whatever.

Many stories are told such as the one about a visionary planning group in one of the large telecommunication companies in the United States, that had spent years in the late 60's and early 70's going throughout the firm evangelizing about the possibilities and opportunities of the forthcoming information age. Many of its directors, vice-presidents, and presidents were in concurrence, but no one knew how to make it happen, because the firm's leaders saw themselves, as a voice communication company. It was not in their mission to seriously consider data. Data was only a small percentage of their business, so they left it to market groups to try and determine exact figures on how many data customers would be lined up for the new services in the 80s and 90s. Of course, future numbers, such as these, could not be proven. As more and more proof was requested, planners realized it was simply a delay tactic to not make a decision, and terminated their research. It was simply foolish to pursue, until top management was willing to change the mission and refocus the firm on these new opportunities in the marketplace.

After many years, and a reshuffle of management, the planners views were reconsidered. The mission and vision changed and the firm purchased for many millions the capabilities to provide data. Unfortunately, in attempting to do a quick buy in, because they were so late, these delayed expenditures drove the cost to the billion dollar level. Had they pursued it when the situation was not so obvious, using their research and development laboratories in the early 70s, they would have obtained the products and expertise with a minimal investment.

To change a mission usually causes substantial change to the direction of the firm. In periods of intense technological change, the longer it takes,the more difficult and expensive it can become. Hence, it is best to do it as early as possible, when the technological shifts and the marketplace demands are first understood.

Mission Statement—Vision Description

The mission and vision therefore should be periodically reviewed in terms of technological change, economic factors and shifts, and new demands from the marketplace. They should be streamlined, where necessary, emphasizing specific objectives. For effective results they should set the tone of the company, as much as the direction. A reasonable format would look like the following:

Mission

1. Purpose for the firm's existence (right to life).
2. Basic direction and scope of operation (charter).
3. Characteristics, attributes and qualities for which it stands (character).
4. Tone and mode of operation, such as aggressively handling change (pulse).
5. Image of the firm presented to the outside world, impact it wishes to leave on society, position in the marketplace, and responsibility to its owners (stature).

Vision

1. The future marketplace, its shifts in time.
2. Phases of technology to meet this marketplace.
3. Opportunity and problems presented in future scenarios, in terms of economic changes, user resistance, technology options, market opportunities.
4. Role the firm plays in the new game.

Though the mission is initially established by the officer group, working with its directors and advisory groups, it should be reviewed, changed, extended or modified, when it is challenged in the marketplace or as new opportunities arise, as noted by strategic planning groups.

Strategies

In the past, a separate group in the firm, different from the lines of business, not responsible for functional research or development areas, manufacturing or operation , marketing, or support, is traditionally charged with the responsibility to translate the mission into a specific direction. However, there is a substantial difference between specific direction and strategic direction. Strategic direction should be strategic, but also specific. This is key to success in today's market. Some have attempted to reduce strategic planning to the role of financial watchdog, where the group simply coordinates efforts to establish a general direction, allowing each research laboratory or line of business to determine their own particular goals and objectives. In this mode, the informal organization rather than the formal runs the firm by default. On the other hand, a too strong or too heavy handed strategic planning group, may, with limited knowledge, establish the wrong strategic direction for the firm, only to have it challenged and changed by the units, usually after various failures and disasters in the marketplace have occurred. Thus, balanced participation is necessary. See Fig. 2-1.

One successful technique is using marketing and technical advisors to participate in planning boards that cross the various research and development laboratories or lines of businesses of the operating companies, manufacturing firms, or research labs. There has been much written recently about stakeholders, shareholders, and stockholders planning strategies, which enables those who must define and implement programs to achieve a strategic direction, goal or objective, and be able to "buy in early," by having them participate in establishing the initial strategies. In this manner, some may say that these planning boards need only be facilitated by strategic planning. Of course, their achievements are greatly dependent upon the skills of the strategic planners in obtaining true strategic direction and not negotiated meaningless statements, that leave resistive participants to return to doing whatever they want with no accountability. A more reasonable alternative would be to have a strong strategic planning group, whose participants come from the effected units. The key attributes of the players should be their big picture view, their technical insights, their marketing understanding, their financial depth and their ability to logically determine direction and the possible effects of proposed directions on all aspects of the business, from R&D to operations and support. The planning group or committee require some form of planning process, which would assist these planners in understanding, defining and establishing:

- Strategic Direction
  - Specific Assumptions
  - Specific Risks
  - Specific Goals
  - Specific Objectives
  - Specific Priorities

- Strategic Plans
  - Business Plans
  - Financial Plans
  - Program Plans
  - Project Plans
  - System Plans
  - Marketing Plans

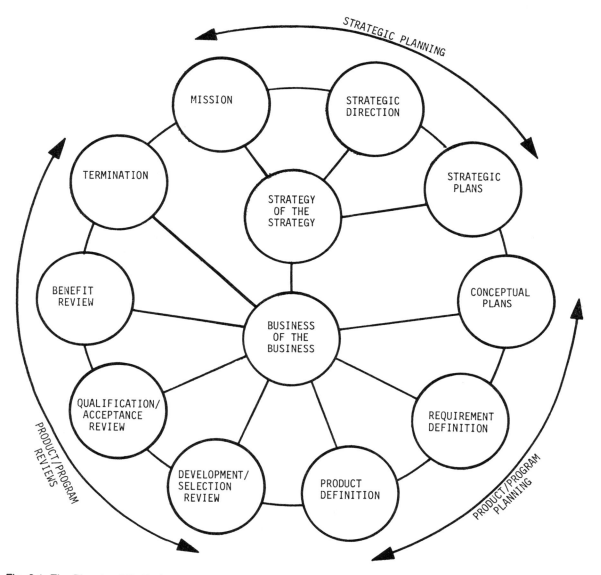

Fig. 2-1. The Planning Life Cycle.

Note the word specific. Strategic direction must be *specific*. It must track and map back into the mission statement and the vision. Some firms have attempted to substitute the vision for direction, but the vision is not nor should it be as specific as the strategic direction. For example, a telecommunications operating firm once set up a subsidiary to handle enhanced data communications, while the basic distribution firm was to give access to the world from any vendor or private network. The strategies for each firm were different and quite specific. The subsidiary was to be a collector of data customers. (It could provide access to the world, but should use the most economical means to achieve it, such as using the base company). On the other hand, the basic distribution network company was only allowed to provide access to the world and not compete against the subsidiary to collect customers. This strategy initially stopped the larger wholesale company from competing in the same market as the smaller sub. It achieved the objectives of the government, to provide access to information networks, as a common carrier. Later, as Inquiry III considered a bigger role for the distribution company to play using a non regulated separate accounting division, these changes had to be reconsidered in strategic planning to provide new direction and plans, as the marketplace opportunities changed, as governmental boundaries broaden. Those who anticipated and responded quickly to change would be better positioned to play the new game.

It is also important to separate goals from objectives. Many firms may miss several objectives and still achieve their goal. Hence, there is the need to separate and maintain emphasis and focus on goals, which may in actuality be only dependent on achieving two or three objectives successfully. Normally, objectives will come and go, but the goals remain.

STRATEGY OF THE STRATEGIES

It is important that strategic planning is not reduced to just financial planning though this is a major integral part. Many decisions can usually be reduced to financial trade offs, in favor of the more lucrative ventures. However, this is where the short term focus challenges the long term vision and financial viability of the firm, in the years to come. Normally, this cannot be made strictly on a financial basis due to future unknowns and it must go back to the basic mission of the firm, the reason for its existence, its image in the marketplace and its needs for future products.

The driving forces behind the mission, strategic direction, and strategic plans is the vision of where the firm is going and the strategy of the strategies on how it will get there. They are a reference structure base that are carefully analyzed from all directions and put in place, as an anchor point to which all strategies must connect. In times of change, the more successful management teams are able to reassess this strategy and when necessary move it to a more favorable position, being careful to move all attached strategies. It is usually the task of management of each line of business or research laboratory and strategic planning to work with the chief operating officers and the president to constantly assess all situations in terms of the visionary strategy and establish the underlying strategy of the strategies.

In considering the influence of the strategy of the strategies, it is not to be underestimated, as it drives not only the strategic planning functions, but twists here and turns there, to position the businesses of the business. We will see later how the business of the business strategy is the driving force for establishing the program plans, project plans, product plans, marketing plans, and financial plans that formulate the business plans. However, there will be a silent planning clash, similar to two locomotives hitting each other on a distant horizon, when a particular business strategy is out of line with the strategy of all the strategies.

Figure 2-2 notes the situation where any number of lines of businesses, units, manufacturing firms, or research laboratories are being governed by the strategy of the strategies. When one area is out of step or requires repositioning of the main anchor, it is then that this clash occurs and nothing will happen with that line of business until the conflict is resolved. Hence, there is a need for close interactions between strategic planning and business planning, using some form of management planning process, to resolve conflicts, define direction, establish interfaces, and obtain hand offs.

As noted, the strategy of the strategies should be based upon a market vision of where the firm is going and what it takes to get there. Today, there is considerable emphasis on establishing a business vision based upon a mar-

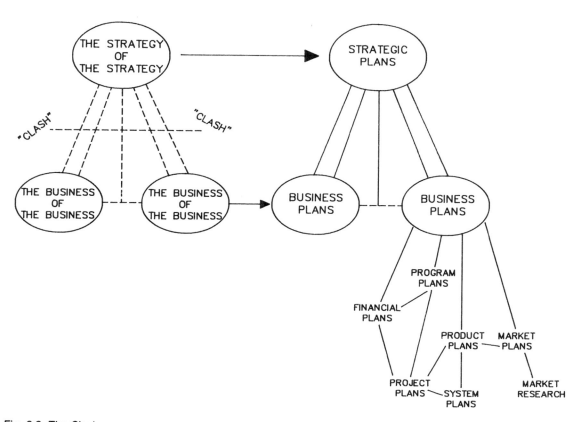

Fig. 2-2. The Clash.

ket and technical view for the firms that are specifically involved in providing networks, products, or services for the information age, since technology is capable for the first time of providing anything that the marketplace may need or desire. AT&T has announced their Universal Services vision (Section Nine); most firms have embraced some form of the Information Services Digital Network vision of the United Nations International Telecommunication Union-CCITT organization. Others in the past have called their visions such catholic names as Century 21, Global Communications, Digital World, etc. All were indicating a universal type of integrated service offering. Careful analysis must be made to understand their phases of implementation, and the features that will be offered at each phase to appreciate their differences. A vision is, in effect, a big picture look at future social phases, shifts in technology, needs of the marketplace, and an assessment of the resulting world, in which the firm will exist, in terms of opportunities and possibilities.

To achieve a truly complex objective direction requires making many timely strategic decisions, based upon the best technical, marketing, governmental, and financial considerations. It requires the skills of the master decision makers, who can put their finger on the heart of the problem and separate the possibilities into the possible. A good technique to obtain the right information for these decisions, is to use the right people within the organization, where the market meets the technology. In an era of choice, where people want to contribute, participate, and make their own decisions, their input and involvement becomes critical for subsequent success. This brings us to two main issues: risk and power.

Risk

First we will address risk. As issues become more and more complex, only the unwise pretend they have all the answers. To diminish the risk, strategic planning must work with many disciplines, such as marketing, technical, regulatory, legal, economics, manufacturing, support, costing, pricing, and financial. There is a need to take more than one look before a firm commitment is made. Commitments must be tied to decisions. In reality, without commitments, there are no decisions. With the decision must come accountability. The risk of making the wrong decision is lessened, in an environment of "participating management," who exchange critical information essential for the right decision. Risk is lessened, if a process for obtaining the decision exists, in which the decision makers not only have this chance to exchange ideas with the many disciplines, but are able to obtain several levels of exploratory analysis, before making large financial commitments. We will call this total participation process "top down planning."

Power

Power is a difficult, complex ingredient in the planning world. Many situations have occurred where power plays have deliberately destroyed major divisions of firms, as various general managers and vice-presidents clashed to control the destiny of a firm. The "craft of power" should be understood by all who engage in the planning world, to appreciate the meaning of the words "base motives." A colleague once described a particular situation by saying "think of the most base, self-serving, revolting reason for such and such to happen and you are probably nearer the real truth of the story." Leaders come and go on a daily basis, as some firms utilize "management by conflict" rather than the Japanese "management by consensus" techniques. In this "conflict" environment, there are usually several opportunities to see the impact of those who are unwilling to work with others, carving their own particular empire over many "dead bodies." In the more enlightened circles, these individuals are called "road blocks." Attempts are made to go around them and circumvent them, but failing this, the unpleasant task of removing them is usually left to top management. The wise have learned that by sharing power, they gain more power, as they become more and more effective and successful!

THE STRATEGIC GAME . . . PLAYING TO WIN!

The strategic direction should identify assumptions, risks, goals, objectives and priorities. These are then rigorously challenged in recursive analysis with strategic implementation plans in terms of organizational and resource allocation strategies, as subsequent business plans containing program plans, project plans, marketing plans, system plans, and product plans are overlaid and integrated around the strategic direction. In most situations today, this has become a "trial by fire" process against a direction, which is no more then a general, vague target. Correspondingly, new vague organizations are established to pursue vague objectives and goals. As the new organization stumbles along and gets closer to the target, the direction becomes more visible. Those who get close enough to see the marketplace, can then redefine the direction and reestablish a new organization to better address it.

Unfortunately, as we question past history and look for alternatives, we are usually faced with the dilemma that the game must be played to be understood and that the game itself is changing over time, so it is a constantly new game. With this dilemma, many are left to their own devices, to plan their own efforts, fight for their own turf, and get their own funding approved at program trade-off meetings ("silver bullet" wars), with the hope that they will somehow be successful or get promoted before the day of reckoning. It becomes a valiant difficult exercise, which should and could have been avoided, had there been a better, clearer strategic direction, with an acceptable plan of action.

The Game

To understand the tremendous change and amount of complexity of the game, let us look at what a large, multi-unit information firm must untangle in order to provide the right networks, products, and services for the information era. In so doing we will note only a few of the strategic goals and objectives that must be met to enable a telecommunication provider to be successful in the new governmental regulated/non regulated competitive marketplace.

Strategic Goals:

1. To provide total information communications for the new users in the information era.
2. To establish an aggressive marketing firm to provide specific information products or services to the user.
3. To automate internal operations to increase productivity and become a showcase of new product offerings for the world.
4. To promote and maintain the image of quality, integrity, and excellence in the marketplace in providing "leading edge" universal information networks, products, and services.
5. To become an integrator of selected types of "C & C" products in the marketplace and provide users access to the world.
6. To provide a good, long range return on investment to the stockholders.

Strategic Objectives:

1. To identify areas and boundaries, where telecommunications providers can expand their operation and scope via the Department of Justice waiver process.
2. To establish an architecture for the information network in terms of these applications and restraints, that enable the company to compete in the regulated, non-regulated areas using integrated, overlaid, and autonomous product offerings.
3. To establish divisions, subsidiaries, and holding company organizational structures to enable providers to satisfy regulated and non-regulated requirements more effectively.
4. To establish boundaries and relationships with the holding company between its subsidiaries, and information Distribution Companies (IDCs) divisions on new ventures and support areas.
5. To restructure groups and people to meet the above in terms of programs within expanded lines of business.
6. To define the detailed program/product/project plans, that establish specific technical and marketing objectives for all companies involved.
7. To define and establish a planning decision process to enable effective and timely utilization of management.
8. To establish a technology concept, requirements, and product definition planning program for future networks, products, and services.
9. To restructure and redefine tariffs and revenue objectives on a competitive basis, as well as overlay financial measurement and trade off programs.
10. To establish a 4 year/8 year planning strategy in terms of these new networks, products, and services using specific business plans.

BUSINESS OF THE BUSINESS

It may take several businesses to meet all of the objectives. The scope of a particular line of business can be quite complex, as noted by the following specific objectives, of an information distribution firm, acting as a wholesale communication middle man:

- Providing access to the outside networks from internal "enhanced services" networks per Inquiry III.
- Providing distributed switching at the closest point to the customer, using the most economical means possible.
- Moving functional areas into the deregulated area, having first determined the detariffed advantages, or after loss (real or potential) in the marketplace.
- Providing an "open architecture" interface to other enhanced carriers.
- Identifying costs, detariffing, and deregulating functions, such as new user network management and class feature packages.
- Migrating to distributed variable channel selectors for customer utilization of N number of channels or bits at a given instant of time and billed accordingly by using integrated ISDN switches;
- Providing in the non-regulated environment a new info business servicing unit, as an extended Centrex-type offering for the general public.
- Automating its internal operations to be the most efficient voice, data, video, transport middleman in the business.
- Offering public data and wideband switched networks with access to the world.

Note how these strategies tie directly back to the mission and strategic direction decisions. Hence, the business of the business is a complicated game, even to be just a middleman!

PLANNING BUYS SUCCESS

There must be an understanding that "top down planning" is not free. We have to "spend money to make money." In essence it is leverage, "a nickel today gets a dollar's worth of opportunity tomorrow." There is, as Mr. Milton Friedman once said, "No such thing as a free lunch." However, some lunches can be more expensive than others. Some can be more pleasant than others. Some can be more nourishing than others, at half the price. Planning can provide the right lunch at the right price, but it does require "paying for the meal before it's served."

In a period of intense change, to be successful, strategic planning must establish a reasonable and acceptable strategic direction, supported by appropriate business plans. This requires sharing the power, distributing the risk, and providing management with the right data, by using an "innovative" planning approach. Upon this planning vehicle, a series of implementation processes should be overlaid to aid in the day to day operation of the lines of business. If the strategic planning effort is not tied to the business effort, it will become a stale, unused, ineffective vehicle, which can do more harm than good. However, if used as the basis for all coordinating operations, in a manner that it becomes a living, breathing organism in the corporate environment, then it has a right to life and can be most effective in establishing and maintaining strategic direction. It should integrate the lines of businesses' business plans, program plans, project plans, and marketing plans, together with organizational and resource plans. These then form the total living strategic plans of the firm.

To achieve this, a management planning process (Fig. 2-3) based upon a planning life cycle (Fig. 2-1) is recommended, as the fine precision instrument, which the new participating management, the manager planners, can use to set direction, organize and coach the players, and referee the game. It has been demonstrated in the military and aerospace industries (see the High Tech case study), where the right amount of front end planning will enable products to be achieved using smaller development teams, with less manufacturing cost, with less support costs, and to be provided much earlier to the marketplace. They usually last longer than products that are hastily defined and redefined during their detailed design phases, as indicated in Fig. 2-4.

PLANNING . . . NEEDS . . . PROCESSES

Hopefully, by now we have accepted the need for more detailed planning, using some form of top down planning process to assist us in our

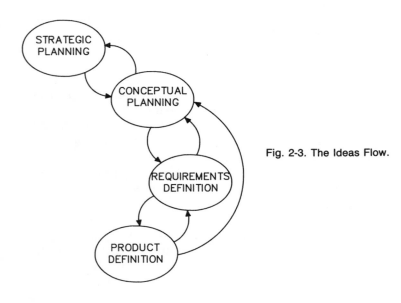

Fig. 2-3. The Ideas Flow.

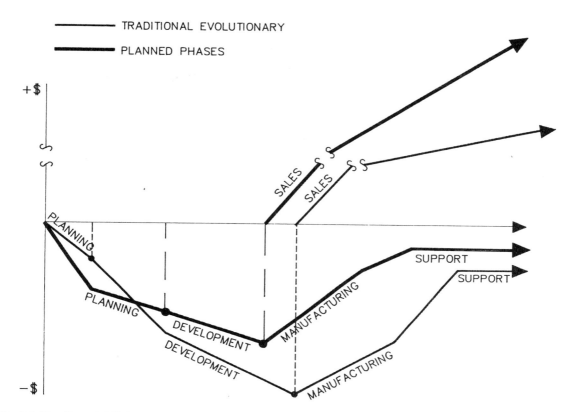

Fig. 2-4. The Financial Picture.

role as manager planner. To enable us to truly manage change, this process must:

- Foster innovation, enabling new ideas to be conceptualized into realistic applications.
- Help minimize risk and limit large spending, until financial commitment.
- Provide a forum for management decision makers, technical planners, and marketing planners to communicate and exchange ideas.
- Identify the technical and marketing studies, as well as the management decisions required during each planning phase.
- Translate mission and goals into networks and products or challenge and change strategic direction.
- Enable technology planning and technology transfer across users, providers, and suppliers.
- Identify the role of the various organizations and personnel involved in establishing the new product line strategies.

- Provide a review process that enables effective and timely management decisions.
- Provide a planning basis for management planners and marketing and systems specialists to easily monitor and foster the progress of an idea to a product.

Upon this process we will overlay the following processes:

1. An "innovation" process to foster new ideas, concepts, visions, and strategies, and bring all the forces and disciplines of the firm to enhance their scope.
2. A process to bring marketing together with technical realizing that:
   a) The future telecommunications network architecture and structure is going to involve several complex phases to achieve an "integrated services" voice data video network.
   b) The products that support this network will require intense marketplace user analysis over the next years to determine their requirements in terms of architecture and structure, that provides various features, protocols, signalling, and access to other ISDN networks, etc.
   c) These architectural layers of future features and services must be overlaid on existing and future networks in terms of governmental boundaries and restrictions in order to be provided in the most effective regulated, non regulated, tariffed, detariffed, cost and price basis.
3. A process to identify new user needs in terms of the major shifts of society.
4. A process to utilize research and development to achieve new products, networks and services.
5. A planning life cycle process that realistically overlays on product life cycle phases and is in sync with the normal product development.
6. A process that manages the pursuit of quality attributes to achieve the desired degree and extent of product quality.
7. A process to enable "participating management" to participate in order to obtain their commitment.
8. A process to establish working relationships between *multiple* lines of businesses across *multiple* units of *multi*national firms.
9. A process to enable active "interfaces to government" regulators, justice departments, and various communications agencies to promote a competitive marketplace.
10. A process to achieve interaction between educational institutions and industry, to obtain from the universities and colleges the right level of knowledgeable students as well as the kind of research activities that are needed by industry.
11. A process upon which to structure the firm and leverage resources.
12. A process upon which personal career growth and technology transfer

can occur to achieve a growing level of expertise within the firm.

13. A process to establish, modify, and extend a firm's mission, strategic direction, and strategic plans in a period of intense technical and marketing change.

14. A process to foster technology planning and transfer between units, educational facilities, government agencies, and industry suppliers.

15. A process upon which to overlay business plans of the lines of business, consisting of project plans, system plans, program plans, and marketing plans.

16. A process to achieve for the users the products, networks and services, that meet their needs.

An innovative process called the *Management Planning Process* will be the basis upon which to orchestrate these multiple processes for multiple projects effectively, using the appropriate people to identify and achieve the goals and objectives of the various R&D laboratories, manufacturing units, and telecommunication—information firm's lines of business.

THE PLANNING PHASES

The management planning process basically consists of four phases, as shown in Fig. 2-3. In this chapter's analysis, we have concentrated on the activities and impact of the first phase, strategical planning. Its activities; mission, vision, strategic direction, and strategic plans, are determined and driven by new business opportunities and strategies in a period of change. Each business unit will then translate these strategies into their particular networks, products, and services in the telecommunication world, using a basic understanding of the business of the business. The next three chapters will take an in depth look at the activities performed in the three major product planning phases. There, ideas are generated in an atmosphere of creative thinking in the conceptual planning phase; enhanced, modified and refined in the requirements definition phase; and clarified and structured into practical solutions in the product definition phase. One may ask how these phases relate to a product's life cycle, and whether we are performing overkill or redundant analyses.

If we have learned anything from past history of product developments, we have learned that it is very expensive to change a product once it has entered the field. A review of program bugs, performance, and throughput problems, etc., have noted a direct relationship of design faults and limitations to requirement changes. We will see how more top down planning will improve performance, shorten development time frames and reduce resource needs. However, to achieve results from more up front effort, there is a need to use a logical process to enable us to effectively play with ideas, understand needs, and translate them into solutions.

In reference to a typical sixteen phase product life cycle, Fig. 2-5, we can see how the planning process tucks very nicely into it's front end. The prod-

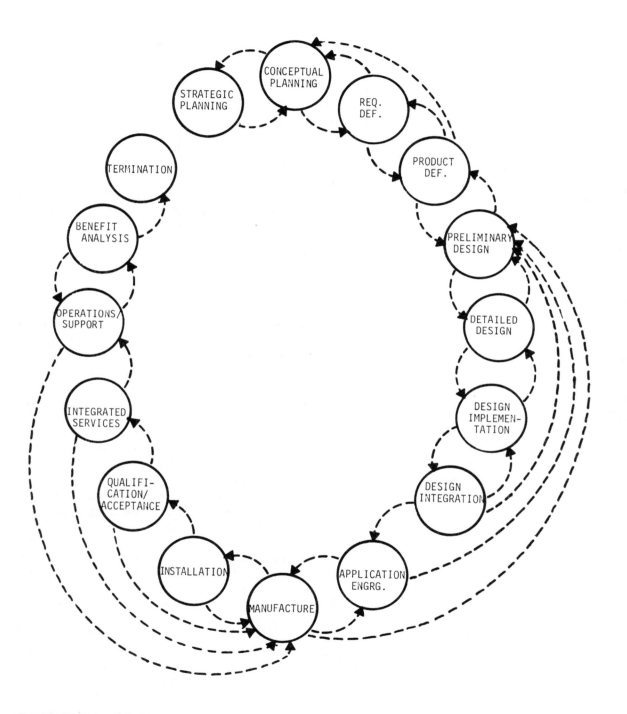

Fig. 2-5. Phases and Paths.

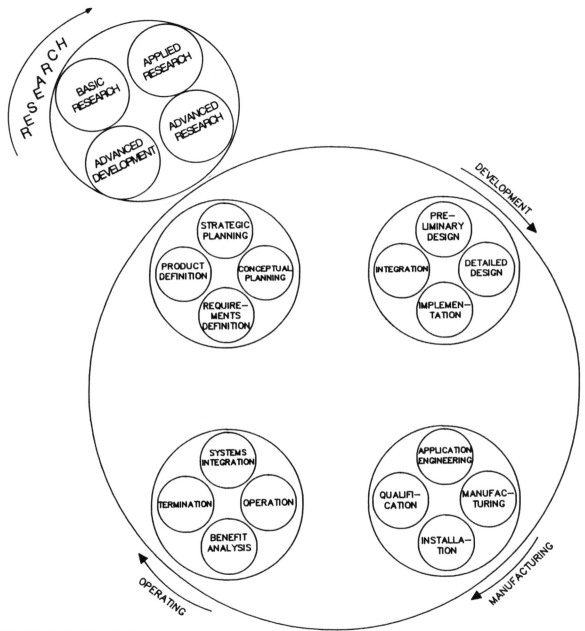

Fig. 2-6. Product Life Cycle.

uct life cycle overlays onto the planning cycle, as shown in Fig. 2-6. In Fig. 2-7, we see a more extensive view of the overlaying of several of the major processes, noted earlier; the marketing processes for recognizing user needs and providing them appropriate solutions; the flowing of ideas from research

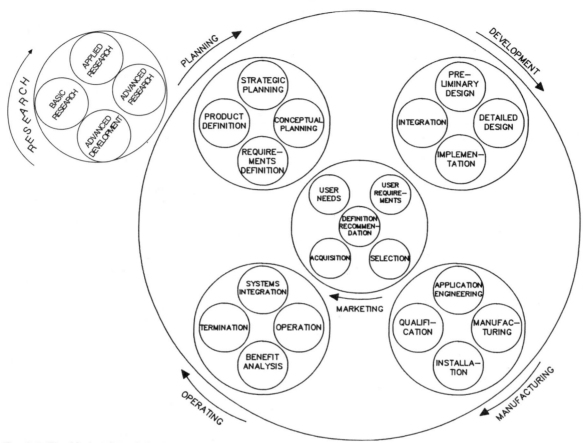

Fig. 2-7. The Marketplace Axle, The Technology Push.

to development of new products or services by the suppliers; and the efforts of the providers to integrate the user needs in the marketplace with the technology possibilities from the research and development labs, in order to obtain the right products at the right time for their customers.

The cycles on cycles within cycles in Fig. 2-7 show the flow of these three processes, as they integrate together into one major user/supplier/provider planning technology transfer process. Here strategic planning and the program/product planning phases become the crank to turn the Product Life Cycle, which is based upon the marketplace, in sync with the possibilities from technologies. These Figs. 2-6 and 2-7 are presented here in their final form. They will be carefully broken down and analyzed in the next chapters. They are noted here simply to show their interrelationship with strategic planning and their overlay on the four phase management planning process.

Experience has found that any worthwhile endeavor requires considerable thinking to be successful. Albert Einstein once said that he enjoyed a

"Danka Experiment"—a "Thought Experiment," as much as the actual experiment. He would think out a possibility and its resulting possibilities to a solution, before going to the lab to verify them. Such is the top down planning process. It employs this technique in identifying user needs and then defining and structuring new products to meet these needs. This thought process is essential for all our processes, as they attempt to enable us to:

- Obtain information
- Share information
- Coordinate activities
- Provide guidance
- Understand needs
- Identify tasks
- Design products
- Prioritize activities
- Insure quality
- Make effective decisions
- Motivate people
- Manage people
- Obtain commitment
- Establish interfaces
- Improve working relationships
- Solve problems
- Terminate obsolete products
- Have career growth
- Achieve the right solutions
- **Manage change**

Hence these processes, as shown in Fig. 2-7, will use the planning cycle as their basis for the interrelationships of Fig. 2-8.

THE MANAGEMENT PLANNING PROCESS

Now that we have a general idea on how various processes can utilize a four phase top down planning cycle. Figure 2-9 shows the phase one strategic planning interrelationships between top management, vice-presidents of the various lines of businesses, director level product planning boards and specialty advisory councils. Together, they establish the firm's mission, vision, strategic direction, and strategic plans. In this structural arrangement top management has its product line vice-presidents as their consultants, who have the responsible directors across the various lines of business as their planning board, which has various lines of business specialists and key managers as their advisory council. In actuality, top management has access to the planning board and advisory councils via strategy and recommendation sessions and reports. In turn, lines of business vice-presidents have access to recommendations by the various directors and specialists from other lines of business. Conversely, responsible directors and managers, as well

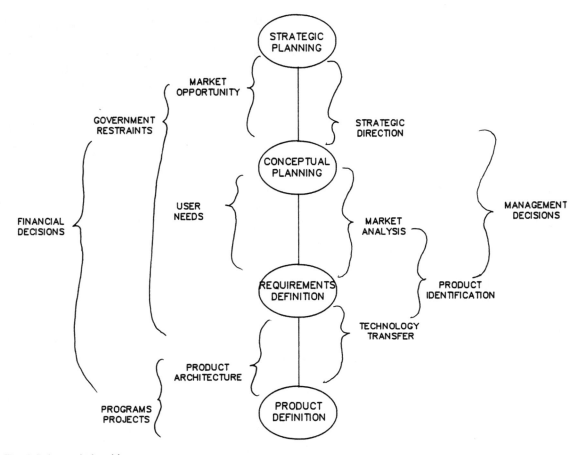

Fig. 2-8. Interrelationships.

as involved specialists have an opportunity to communicate the real issues, problems, and opportunities directly to senior decision makers. All in all, in actual usage over the past years, it has been proven to be quite effective in obtaining commitment by top management and early "buy in" by those responsible for implementing their direction, as they all participate and assume the role of manager planners together.

The process uses the review, as the decision point (or node) in the thought process for go, no-go, or rework decisions, as well as assessments of implementation resources and quality of output. Key decision makers switch from the planner to the role of judge, as plans are presented, modified, accepted, or rejected.

A series of strategies are developed, each refining the other, as the levels of mission, strategic direction, and plans are generated and then, as the corporation, in adapting to changing conditions, revisits to extend, modify, enhance, or change them. Hence, as the flow of ideas within the process takes place, the management game of monitoring and controlling the direction of the firm proceeds in an orderly fashion, enabling top management to make more effective decisions on timely information provided, by those responsible for ensuring its success.

At this time, the strategic planning group plays several roles. The vice-president of strategic planning, being part of top management, participates separately by working within the senior management team to establish understanding and agreements to various strategies, as well as by having a decision vote as a member of the strategy review board. The strategic planning group members assume the role of leading, coordinating and facilitating the product planning board and advisory council meetings across the lines of businesses, laboratory projects or manufacturing units. Within a unit, its vice-president and directors have responsibility for their own planning. The recommendations and strategies of the reviews must be reflected back into the strategic direction and plans of the firm, implemented in the business plans of the units and coordinated into the yearly and long range capital expenditure program.

In the event cross-laboratory or cross-lines-of-business planning activi-

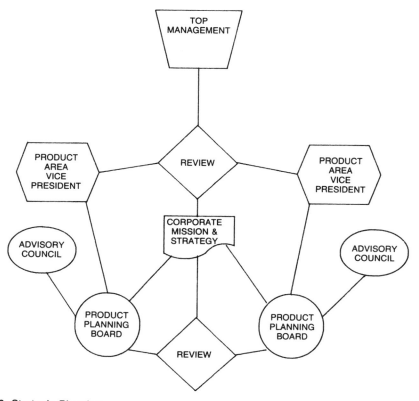

Fig. 2-9. Strategic Planning.

ties are needed, it may be reasonable for the firm to have a separate network/product planning group, consisting of members from marketing and technical, as well as strategic planning to formulate program/product teams to perform the initial planning activities, reporting to the product planning board. Alternatively, within the major lines of businesses the product planning teams may be formed with members from all involved and affected areas, with the team reporting to the lead line of business vice-president, but with their reports also going to the product planning board. If only one line of business is affected, the team consists of members who subsequently report to their own vice-president or internal directors. Depending on the situation, one or all modes of operation can be in place, but the main thrust of strategic planning is to ensure that the strategic direction is indeed reflected in the work activities, in order to be in the final business plans.

Business plans should reflect the planning activities of the lines of business in three phases of planning. As various ideas reach the product definition phase, their implementation should be defined in specific program plans, consisting of system plans and project plans, which indicate all aspects of the development schedule and resources needed to achieve the system architecture. Accompanying these plans should be the manufacturing, marketing, support, financial or operations plans for the product, be the product a device, program, system, network or service.

Each line of businesses' business plans may have plans for more than one product in different phases of its product life cycle. Once defined in the business plan, it is the task of the strategic planning group to assist in the coordination of the various business plans, and map them onto the strategic direction and strategic plans of the firm. Where they are out of sync, or have insufficient resources, conflicts occur that cannot be easily resolved. This is left to the officers to work out the appropriate funding. In this arena, the officers play the resource game, sometimes called "the silver bullet game," where silver bullets per the legendary T.V. western hero "The Lone Ranger" do not miss. Unfortunately in retrospect, each officer usually only has one silver bullet...

But what makes this process different is the fact that the game is being played around three planning phases, conceptual planning, product definition and requirement definition. This gives more substance to the game and less risk. See Fig. 2-10. More knowledge is obtained as each phase is implemented. This diminishes the risk of the unknown. As more effort is applied, more expenditures are required. This occurs over the three planning phases, as questions are addressed and answered, providing more and more information, before the commitment of large financial funds. This technique gives management three looks, each requiring increasing amounts of resource allocation to obtain more information. As more and more questions are resolved, more and more management "buy in" to the new venture. This greatly diminishes the need for substantial "silver bullet wars" in which the bleeding heroes return home with limited successes. By using cross lines of business planning boards in the strategy sessions and cross lines of business

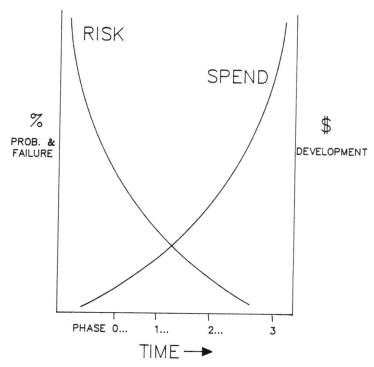

Fig. 2-10. Diminishing Risk.

participants in the product planning activities, early acceptance is obtained using this stakeholder/shareholder approach, where the implementers want to achieve their own recommendations.

In Fig. 2-11 we see lines of business planning being carried out under the guidance of the director's advisory group, and of course, responsible VP's. In this role of participating management, manager planners become coaches as well as planners. Selected specialist players, from within the units, plan in one of four planning groups: as conceptual planners, or as a member of the advance planning team, requirement definition team, and/or product definition team. Here, various disciplines, such as marketing, research, system analysts, program analysts, circuit designers, support system designers, financial, and legal experts are gathered to help move an idea from a concept to a product description. In this manner the product is pretty well defined before committing large numbers of people to actually perform the detailed design, test, manufacture, support, operation, and maintenance of it.

These teams can be established within a laboratory, across laboratories within a line of business, across lines of businesses, within one unit, across units, within one country, or across countries. It is the task of the product planning board and the director's advisory council, with individual VP's or a separate planning group to use their staff to coordinate these planning ef-

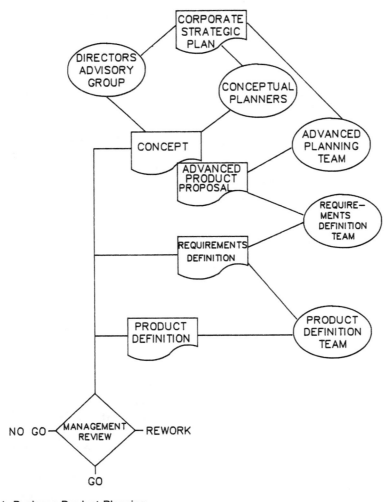

Fig. 2-11. Business Product Planning.

forts. As each phase is completed, a review is made of the outcome. At this time various interested affected parties may wish to participate. It is however essential to bring in senior management, depending upon the magnitude and extent of the possible outcome, to ensure that they become early shareholders to obtain their commitment. The make up of the review board members will be later described for each phase in subsequent sections.

REVIEWS AND DECISIONS

As we leave each phase for another, there must be appropriate documentation to support commitment decisions. These exits are checkpoints on the progress of the analysis. In actual practice, it is necessary during one phase

60

to initiate some activities of subsequent phases for long lead time items. This does not preclude an orderly conclusion of each phase with a recognizable check point.

The decisions made at these checkpoints can be implemented in a management decision support system. This may consist of information systems which store all key points made in a decision, so a historygram can be made on phase check points reviews to trace how many times a phase was revisited, for what reason, and with what decisions, for use by future projects. It should also be noted that the amount of documentation should be minimal. The purpose for each phase is to do the necessary analysis and move onto the next phase and not to provide phase activity just for the sake of phase activity. Planning does not need to be long and tedious with excessive documentation for documentation sake. When the effort is finished, the phase should be exited as soon as possible.

These phases are difficult to schedule, since they are searching for ideas or solutions. We must realize that time frames for them may not be easily defined. Blocks of times may be set aside with periodic reviews by management, until an answer is achieved. In most cases, the analysis periods of each phase should be relatively short. Depending on the pressure or innovative atmosphere of the firm and the creative capabilities of the participants, planning can be short but extremely creative. This will be discussed in Chapter Three at great lengths.

Once the planning phases are understood and used throughout the firm, several projects can proceed in an orderly flow from conceptual planning to product definition. With a smooth transition of people from project A, to project B, to project C. In this manner, knowledge can be moved across projects, as well as minimizing resources of equipment and people. In Chapter Seven, we will see how personnel can be shifted in time, and how resources can be better managed.

COMPETITIVE PROCESSES

Other processes exist today, from the five step (pre study, proposal, design, manufacture, market), to an eight step (data collection, problem definition, alternate solution, match objectives, requirements plan, documentation, approval, implementation), to other multiple task processes (some with up to fifty or more tasks). Over the past, we have had a tendency to define processes which were uncomfortable, restrictive, did not fit our mode of operation, were unrealistic, or did not generate innovative thinking. Alternatively, some believed the answer was to define a simple process and then have their people go use it and obtain success. They ignored the need for the participating manager planner, with the result that many firm's modes of operation were to answer requests for quotes with proposals which were usually the result of one month investigations. This then was their process for planning. Some worked several proposals at the same time. Some did one each week. This form of thinking led to quick decisions that the firm needed such and such a product, feature, or service. Then crash design troops were brought in to crank them out.

We need not agonize over the long term results of this type of planning, except to note that less quality, errors, wrong products, expensive products, no products, expensive support, no understanding of the marketplace, or no strategic direction resulted. No wonder U.S. businesses were no longer competitive with the Japanese and other nations in utilizing their own high technology in their own marketplace!

MANAGING CHANGE

We now have reduced our reaction to change to a manageable mode of operation. As we consider how some in the rest of the world have reacted to intense change, we see that there is large unemployment, as many wait for their government to control their industries and foster reemployment. They are frightened of change, afraid to move, and they have become dependent on their government to take care of them. In turn, the Americans continue to demonstrate that they are still determined to take care of themselves, have a great willingness to learn new ways and to relocate for job opportunity, are very creative with new gadgets, but are unable to build large time consuming projects that require extensive front end planning. We are great at evolving design, putting in refinements as time goes on, but slow to take the time to do it right the first time. We have a great "lets get on with it" motivation, while not really knowing where we're going.

Having reached insurmountable costs and over runs, many times we are forced to abandon good ideas. Over recent years, we've been unwilling or reluctant in the large corporate world to take new idea jumps, once a current product is successful. This has brought a rapid slow down of real research planning and prototype experiments, especially those that do not have immediate short term impact. With the result that various foreign countries have specialists who spend a great deal of time in our patent offices, or who participate on various large projects, and then return to their own country to redo the design better, after a more extensive planning period. It was noted in a prominent Japanese author's book on the information age, that the Japanese look for the Americans to come up with the ideas, but not to achieve them, because Americans do not know how to take the time to play with ideas until they can become successful products. This process will form the basis for meeting this challenge and help return our role of excellence in the marketplace, *enabling us to not only anticipate change but manage it.*

Results

We can now begin thinking about how we could utilize this process to obtain ideas, enhance them into feature requirements, and structure effective products that provide competitive solutions. By overlaying the product life cycle onto a planning life cycle, we can be very successful, as it enables timely management (commitment) decisions to pursue the desired level of quality, to truly identify user needs, to transfer technology from effective research to the appropriate product developments, and to use motivational career growth techniques. Planning for the new ISDN marketplace will be especially effective, as this form of innovative thinking is performed by the new manager planners, sharing risk and power, assuming planner, coach, and umpire roles to successfully provide the right product at the right time, to move society into the information era—by using this management planning process beginning now. See Fig. 2-12.

FURTHER ANALYSIS

In Chapter 12, we can see the application of strategic thinking in the case studies on Apollo, NewTel Inc., Infolab Inc., and Central Research Inc., as well as in the study on the International Technology Trade Center.

OBSERVATIONS: STRATEGIC PROCESSES

1. Strategic Planning should define the firm's mission, direction, goals, and objectives realistically in terms of specific usable strategies that apply directly to business plans.

2. The basic underlying strategy upon which all other strategies are developed, called the strategy of the strategies, is *the rock* that may have to be occasionally repositioned, as conflicts arise between strategic direction and business opportunities.

3. Processes for integrating market analysis and technology product planning should provide early market technology interfaces, and identification of interests for both to pursue.

4. Strategic planning, conceptual planning, requirement definition, and product definition activities work together in involving top management in decision making product planning, to ensure their strategic mission, goals, and objectives are realistically considered, and are consistent with possible product opportunities.

5. Business plans should contain system plans, market plans, and financial plans based on new networks, products, and services whose concepts, requirements, and architectures have been defined using formal planning phases, with reviews to ensure they're in sync with strategic direction. Then they can more easily be integrated across lines of business into the firm's strategic plans and capital expenditure programs.

6. Planning for hardware and programming products will require more sophisticated analysis before development to ensure the product's requirements, architecture, and structure will be consistent with the volatile, changing, complex world of the new integrated information networks of the future.

7. The three phases of product planning are extremely important in helping to establish a product strategy, consistent with corporate strategic plans, especially the conceptual planning phase, which closely interfaces with the strategic planning process.

8. A separate requirements phase helps ensure that a complete list of feasible requirements are considered at the initial period of product definition.

9. An extensive product definition period ensures that all features are initially considered in the design architecture. This is reflected in a feature matrix that is cross-referenced to a design's functional areas.

10. Pre-program planning performed in these more formal and detailed steps will enable a more efficient development/implementation program to produce/provide the product for the marketplace.

11. Expenditures on planning to minimize risk to the level required by management should be measured against expected product costs. Hence, for example, for a $40 million dollar development, 10% expended in planning could enable a detailed top down planning activity of perhaps thirty or so people for one year.

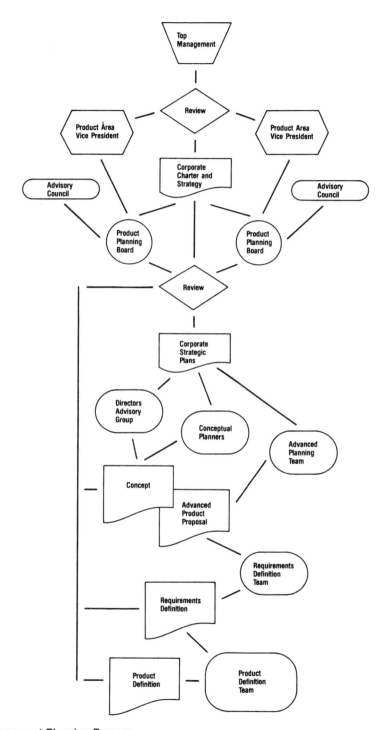

Fig. 2-12. The Management Planning Process.

Chapter 3

Top Down Planning: Conceptual Planning

Planning is difficult, painful, and essential.

In today's competitive telecommunications marketplace, it is mandatory to minimize risk, as much as possible, during the early stages of a program's or product's life cycle. To do this effectively, we must understand the forces and direction of the users' needs, technology, and various economic factors. The ultimate users will play a major role in the 90s, be they the information provider or the provider's customers. Over the 80s, an efficient process was developed that enabled users to better relate their needs to the suppliers and providers of future networks, products and services. This we have called the "top down planning process."

The product planning process consists of three separate phases: *conceptual planning, requirements definition,* and *product definition.* They provide a feasible integration of market research and technology research with the right level of involvement of top management, product planning teams, and prospective users. Each has a role to play and it is important to know one's point of impact, its extent and degree. The phases are defined in the next consecutive chapters followed by an overall summary. The major problems and obstacles, that must be overcome are noted, as well as areas of interfaces between suppliers, providers and users.

Before we begin, let us pause and ask ourselves "What is really needed to help make business projects more successful?" We have often heard statements, such as "If I had only known fifteen years ago what I know today, I would have done a lot of things differently." Yes, we do learn as we go along, that is the adventure of life. We all have a lot of accomplishments, but to achieve some of them has cost more pain than enjoyment. There is a need at times to do some things a little better, a little easier. Recently a lead programmer and veteran of many successful large complex systems, said; "Building systems today is like playing pinball. If you win, are successful, you get to play the game again, and again, and again... There is not much enthusiasm in building one's sixth complex computer project on a crash basis, with these tremendous pressures to get it out the door!"

Crisis management can be a continuous mode of operation. For example, the people of a respected laboratory worked night and day to design their new voice switching product, because their management had delayed decisions until their competition had done it first. After several years of this intense effort, this same laboratory was then asked to provide a new family of data switches, and to integrate them with the digital voice systems. It became another crash design effort back to back with the last one, with market direction still remaining unresolved in terms of two approaches; partially or totally integrated. This mode is very exhausting for the people, especially as the firm structures and restructures to meet changing strategies. Though it may settle down eventually, one must ask "Is there not an easier way, a better way?"

THE MISSING LINK

As we look at the difficult questions, "What should our business be?", and "What should our products be?", we need to link strategic planning to program/product planning, project planning, and system development. In the past, we have allowed management to do their planning separate from system/network technology planners. Then at some distant crossroad they meet. I remember the comments of the president of a major telecommunications company, when suddenly faced with having to purchase an extremely expensive data packet switching system to move information for a new untested market. "I want to position my firm in the information world, but why this way. I need to understand what is going on." "Why" is an excellent question!

Management today are more inquisitive, more involved, as they become more "participating" in leading their firms into the information world. They are being challenged with expensive, high risk decisions. Whether they are the supplier or the provider, as they assume the roles of manager planners, they will need to establish and share their vision of the future with their marketing and technical groups. In this manner, all effected players can feel more comfortable as to where they are going and the reasons why they are doing what they are doing to get there. Similarly, program/project planning must be more carefully tied to research, marketplace analysis, and project development. Many past projects have been stopped in the middle of design, when difficult new features could not be easily added, or as more and more features were added, especially when (as noted earlier) a project "grew and grew until grewsome."

Hence, there is a need to pause at the very beginning to think it out, in order to not only have *a* product, but the *right* product. We have entered a game where real success is determined by slight shifts. For example, a data communications packet switch can be achieved by different architectures, such as a stand alone system, one that is integrated with a voice system, or one that is physically distributed throughout the network. All will have a different impact on the marketplace with varying degrees of success.

We must be able to understand the new users, who they are, what they will really want, what they will buy. The days of a monopoly organization determining what will be provided are over. Those who respond to RFQs, RFIs, or RFPs know that requirements are very vague these days and that throwing quick system designs together to meet these vague requirements is not the way to go. There has been a mass exodus of tired system design team members, who no longer wish to play another game of "pinball." It is a difficult design world today, where the requirements for the next family of telecommunication systems is somewhat dependent upon users who don't really understand, what they want.

Thus, there is a missing link between what technology can do and what the marketplace wants. There is a missing link between developing a proposal, identifying the features, and designing a product. There is a missing link in initially determining the shifts and variations of a future product offering. There is a missing link between early integration of project management plans and product plans. There is a missing link between strategic planning and product program planning. This chain of missing links is a new phase in the planning of programs and projects.

It is the time, where thinking can be done. It is the place for playing with ideas, without the pressure of running to design or development. It is the time to get to understand the users and listen to what they want, determine what makes them tick and decide what they really need. It is the time to collect data, time to look it over, time to understand it, time to propose possibilities, time to share visions, time to construct blue sky considerations, and time to translate possibilities to realistic ideas. It is the time to find the right ideas, for the right product, for the right market . . .

As described earlier in the familiar fable of three blind-folded men attempting to understand and identify an elephant, one must look at the whole and not just separate parts. Similarly, the role of the conceptual planning phase in the product life cycle is analyzed here from several aspects in order to fully appreciate its possibilities. This section will address basic questions concerning conceptual planning such as "What is it?", "Where should it be done?", "How should it be performed?", "When and by whom?" Viewing it from these concerns will help clarify the conceptual planning phase and its areas of application.

The artists' concept in Fig. 3-1 shows that the multi-faceted structure, comprised of separate triangles, produces a perfect solid when they are integrated together. Similarly, the conceptual planning phase, consisting of separate functions (market analysis, technology analysis, creative synthesis,

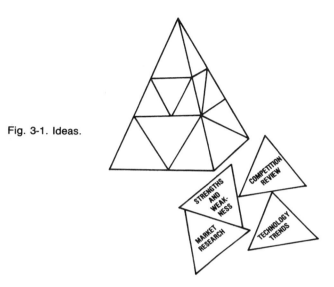

Fig. 3-1. Ideas.

feasibility analysis, management reviews and decisions) which, when integrated together, become a formidable solid management tool.

CONCEPTUAL PLANNING

What exactly is conceptual planning? What does it provide in relationship to strategic planning? What type of analysis is performed during this phase? To what degree? To what extent?

During the Conceptual Planning Phase, diagrammed in Figs. 3-2 and 3-3:

- New Products are conceived, specific customer requests are translated into prospective products, competitive versions of competitor's products are identified, and existing products' new applications and features are defined.
- Strategic goals and objectives are translated into potential programs, networks, systems, sub-systems, terminals, and devices.
- Trends are reviewed and considered in terms of future user needs, regulatory impact decisions, technology advances, economic environment, social advances of society and general direction of international and local political attitudes.
- Competitive analyses are performed, that indicate not only what the competitors have in the marketplace, but their possible future products.
- Internal capabilities are assessed in terms of strengths and weaknesses.
- Multi-unit trade off analyses are performed to indicate future products, that can be supported by the different corporation units.
- Financial projected costs versus sales trade off analyses of future product considerations are performed to insure their returns and risks are consistent with alternative investments.

69

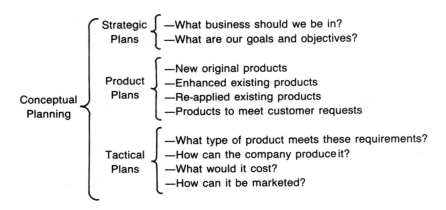

Fig. 3-2. Conceptual Planning.

- Market research—needs analysis and future society scenarios are performed to identify the most applicable products in future market time frames.
- Conceptual planning is performed using "think tank" analysis by "thinker" planners and managers, who are knowledgeable specialists in the field with perspective views that are realistic and timely.

Effective decisions can then be made using a formal review process by representative specialists from the marketing, programming, engineering (system), manufacturing, quality and financial areas. The output of this phase is an advanced product or products proposal, which indicates the market, the technology, the user requirements, the manufacturing impact, and the support requirements. It will provide a "limited" financial cost/market picture, as well as a plan of action for proceeding through the next phase (requirements). The strategic plans, goals, and objectives will be reviewed in terms of the advanced program/product proposal to ensure it is consistent with company direction. If not, this difference is resolved by either reworking the proposal or modifying the strategic plans. This inter-exchange is an on going recursive activity between strategic and advanced product planning. The conceptual planning phase includes a portion of the tactical planning activity to ensure the details of the product's features and technical structure are understood sufficiently to minimize some of the risks and make the review a more effective decision.

Hence, lateral thinking, creative exploratory analyses, user needs research, and technology applications analyses should be performed and achieved during conceptual planning, based upon strategic goals and objectives that provide the general direction for identifying new product lines. "Needs research" should be performed on a continuing basis to provide identification of "user types' attributes." Technological analysis and technique analysis should be explored in an "applied research" environment, to ensure concepts are based upon realistically feasible technology. Also, competitive products are technically analyzed to determine their cost, feature, performance, and technical attributes. Technical seminars and futuristic papers are reviewed and analyzed to assist in determining the future direction of technological advances that will impact future products considerations. Analysis and synthesis are recursively performed until the concept is finalized for review.

Multi-unit involvement is achieved by participation in the requirements phase. However, conceptual planning may require a joint working team to complete the conceptualization phase. A conceptual planning team may be formed to investigate an interesting concept or a particular product enhancement or application. This team can be coordinated by a conceptual planner or responsible manager. The conceptual planning team should analyze the concept to the tactical level considerations, in order to ensure it will be feasible in the product definition phase. The level and depth of the analysis is determined by the amount of change and risk to the corporation. User planning sessions are conducted to invite actual and potential users to share ideas,

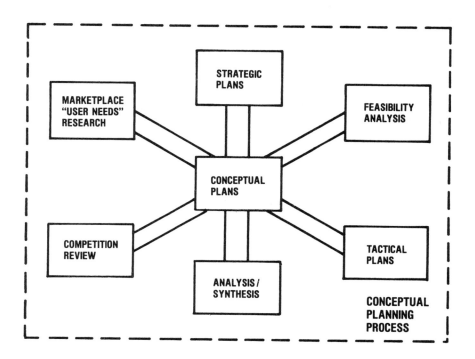

Fig. 3-3. Who?

wishes, and problems, as well as to inform, consider, and accept new proposals. Review is performed by specialists and top management to obtain an effective "go, no-go, rework" decision and corporate commitment.

Conceptual Planners

"Who does Conceptual Planning?"

The following thoughts and quotes, along with Fig. 3-4, identify planner types and their roles:

- "Perceptiveness is the key ingredient of the planner. It goes beyond originality, imagination, and creativity. It is the capacity to see ten things when ordinary people see two plus the ability to register that multiple perception into a novel work that is accepted as tenable or useful or satisfying by a group at some point in time."
- "The most creative act of all is the initial one. Conceptual planning requires the ability to ask a new question, see a new need, devise a new goal. Perception is a prime requirement to perform creative conceptual planning."
- "Planners must be cognizant of the real world and preferably flow between the planning and implementing phases to ensure that their views are applicable, realistic, and translatable into programs and products."
- New product conceptions, however, are usually made by conceptual planners, managers or specialists, who have apperceptive views based upon formal marketplace needs research, technical analysis, competitor reviews, etc. The attributes and goals that motivate planners are not usually consistent with other disciplines, such as managers (who enjoy managing people to accomplish specific tasks), marketing (who prefer to sell to a perspective buyer), engineering (who relish designing or building a unique interesting device), programming (who concentrate on conceiving a functional process algorithm), finance (who like to analyze all aspects of the monetary picture), manufacturing (who have satisfaction producing a particular widgit more economically in the most efficient manner). These are very different from conceptual planners (who prefer to review society, analyze trend data, propose future marketplace direction scenarios and identify products, that can best fit these analyses).
- Coordination in the 90s will be a major role of planners to bring together managers and specialists from the Marketing, Programming, Engineering, Manufacturing and Support disciplines, as the product world becomes more competitive, specialized and complex.

Planning should be a major activity of Management. Directors should have an advisory team consisting of selected managers and specialists within their organization, who meet periodically to plan new products, react to customer requests, consider product enhancements or new product applications. Subsequently, conceptual planning teams could be formed of knowledgeable managers and specialists to further analyze plausible recommendations.

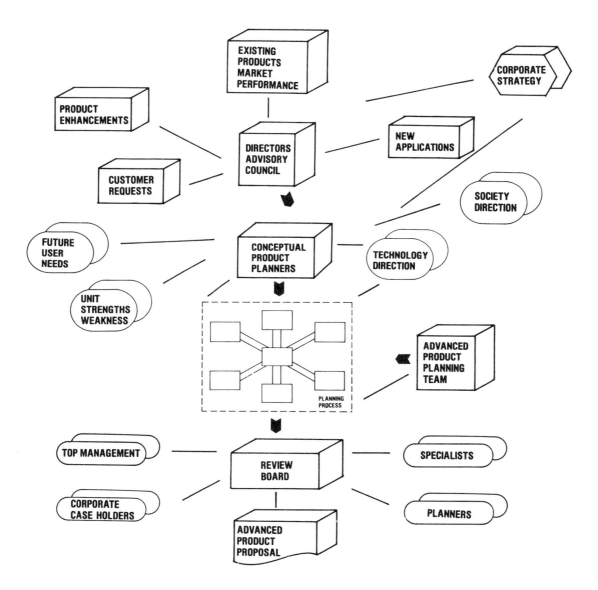

Fig. 3-4. Conceptual Planning Process.

Alternatively, a director of planning could have a small planning organization, that besides responding to the recommendations proposed by the advising teams, also performs the on-going planning activity. They will utilize many different types of personnel, to perform the various types of product planning. These types include original, customer requested, product enhanced, and product application. Their task is to coordinate advanced product planning teams that utilize specialists from the various disciplines in order to produce the detailed proposal. See Fig. 3-5.

Multi-unit product planning is usually reviewed by unit directors, the planning council, and the corporate R&D case holder. The corporate planning staff will be coordinating and monitoring planned programs relationship to corporate strategic plans. To broaden the spectrum of ideas and benefit from the academic/research environment, working relationships can be established with universities or university associated units. Finally, it is important to note that top management participation in the planning reviews is necessary to ensure that the conceptual plans are consistent with their thinking and to obtain their commitment decisions. This is mandatory for further phase analyses to be effective.

Effective Planning

As noted in these observations, continuous conceptual planning search for new products is not only desirable, but is necessary for survival. Planning for modified, enhanced, applied, customer requested products should be performed by advanced planning teams on a periodic or demand basis in a continuous search for product opportunities. Three or more plans should be in active consideration at any point in time. Once a project leaves the Concep-

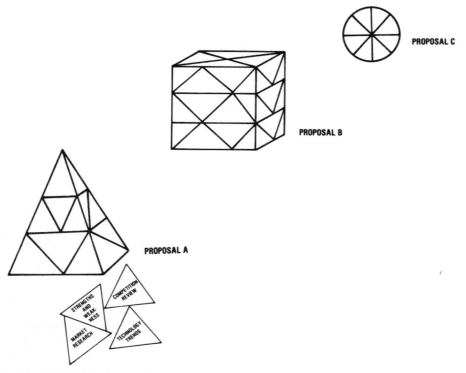

Fig. 3-5. Proposals.

tual Planning phase, another one enters. Strategic plans should be checked continuously against conceptual planning activity to ensure their goals and objectives are consistent with new ideas, new product enhancements, new applications, new opportunities.

THINKING

There are many techniques to aid the mind to think, but all depend on having data. If we were to go through a library in a successful consulting firm, we would see a large number of volumes on statistics of this or that, lists and lists of providers and suppliers' new products, as well as numbers and types of new customers who use or could use various potential devices or services. The first technique of a good consultant firm is to obtain a statistical view of their customer in terms of its current operation. This is one of the first steps to understanding their problems.

Though data collection is necessarily important, the key to conceptual planning lies in knowing what to do with the data. Conceptual planning takes a big picture view, by stepping back and looking for the forest instead of the trees. In doing so, all sorts of interesting observations will come to mind. We must use the data to feed our minds, but not too much, lest it become lost in just looking at the data. Some conceptual planners come to conclusions by simply projecting data or extending a current mode of operation. A few come in with a different view from another direction they are true "lateral thinkers." Most conceptual planners are looking for the interesting twist that puts everything in place. The one line statement that puts the finger on the heart of the problem, as in the Dr. Gillispie/Kildare movies of the forties, where Gillispie was always telling Kildare not to jump to conclusions, but to analyze the facts and then to pause and think until the real problem was identified. Usually, the initial data does not pinpoint the real problem, but by stepping back and doing some hard thinking and good analysis, we can achieve the right answer.

Systems teams attempt to break large complex problems down to separate smaller problems for more reasonable work areas. Conceptual planners do the reverse by taking numerous small separate statistics and observations and integrate them in their minds into a simple universal solution. See Fig. 3-6. Many examples of conceptual thinking can be found in the world of communications. For example, when the providers were having difficulty in finding enough large data customers to justify building new data networks, a conceptual planner observed that they could not expect their customers to do something that they would not do themselves.

"If it was so good for them, it must be so good for us as well. So why not automate our own operation via data networks and use it to train our people in the new technology by being our own best customer. Then use our new operation to be a showcase to introduce our customers to the way they could become better

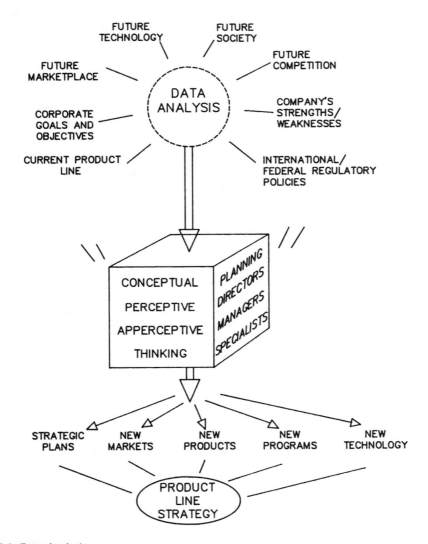

Fig. 3-6. Data Analysis.

by using our networks and products. Then if they don't use it, we will still be ahead by our new efficiency. If and when they do use it, we can keep our costs low, since a good portion of it will be handling our own increasing usage."

A Can't Lose Situation—the Right Solution

Another example of new thinking is for the voice network providers to build a small parallel data network and give it away at cost to customers who remain on their voice network. In this way their customers learn to use it without worrying about whether they really want to spend a great deal of capital. Hence, no resistance. They also do not consider leaving the voice network to build their own separate voice and data networks. Later, when their usage is up, they can decide if they really want it and are willing to pay for it. Which by then of course they do!

INNOVATION

There are several techniques to analyze and foster creative, innovative thinking such as:

1. *Information Thinking Rings* — This is a technique to foster understanding by big picture "doodling" sessions. This may be done individually or with one or more colleagues. Sometimes it is effective to bring together a small group of thinkers and build up a vision, in either a brainstorming session or a model building session. A model building session can develop concepts, by using rings of information. The first level of issues are noted in a ring. Then each variable has another ring of impact of further considerations. The impact of the impact is then determined for various levels, usually two or three. Then interrelationships and dependencies are noted, especially in relationship to time events of various aspects of the topic under question. Finally, the conclusions of the topic can then be determined and identified in terms of these cross dependencies. The

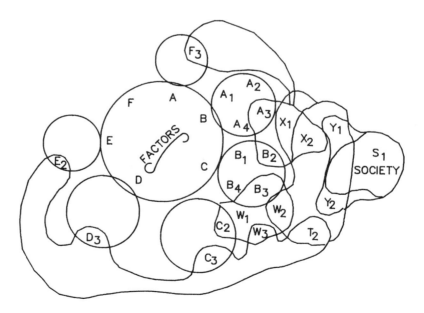

Fig. 3-7. Thinking Rings.

basic topic is not contained in the initial ring but is the underlying concern, as the rings are developed. Example: "What is society going to be like 20 years from now in terms of telecommunications?" See Fig. 3-7. Note that telecommunications itself is not in the initial ring. It will be what is concluded from the rings of information—The S ring. The model information rings are developed until one can then ask questions such as: What will society be like in the future? What will technology be in 20 years? What role does telecommunications play in meeting the needs of society in 20 years? After the rings are developed, there is a lot of data from which to draw upon and think. From this form of analysis a set of observations can be made. Their interrelationships and dependencies can be noted, from which a basic set of conclusions can be developed. These will probably identify various supporting analyses or further data collections that are necessary to substantiate the conclusion or at least to develop a better understanding. It should also be noted that the impact ring sessions are an excellent input of ideas and thoughts to the mind to enable a subsequent back burner analysis to determine a satisfactory answer to unresolved questions.

2. *Back Burner*—In order to analyze information, understand it, twist it, and turn it to some unique observation, we can develop the ability to feed the "back burner" of our mind. Later, usually at a unique moment, far distant from where/when one would expect, the answer will come to mind. It is like cooking a meal slowly on the smaller back burner of the stove. Until resolved, we exist in a mode of feeding and analyzing information on a periodic basis. Usually, during the initial analysis, an idea will come forth, which is not quite the answer, then later the right solution will occur.

3. *Brainstorming*—Conceptual thinking can also be a "brainstorming session." This chapter's work shop reference material was developed in a brainstorming session. It took a backward look at society 20 years ago. This was then used to trigger a look forward 20 years, from which a set of observations were made on the impact and type of telecommunications needed in the future. With the right players, these sessions can be a lot of fun and provide very unique and interesting insights.

4. *Discussion Sessions*—In this method two people complement each other and work closely to challenge and expand each other's thoughts, as they build up a universal view of the situation or problem together and make their observations and recommendations. Usually in explaining one's view to another, this will trigger a new level of thinking, especially as comments and enhancements are received from the other person.

5. *Then What*—In these sessions two or three thinkers gather together having first developed a strategy. They then extend the analysis by accepting the earlier conclusions, but ask the question: "Then what happens?" From this, the impact of the conclusion is examined from every direction—marketing, technical, political, legal, etc. From this may come a modified game plan, a more aggressive game plan, a different more

versatile product, more features based upon the original features, etc.

6. *Impact Thinking*—A well known Los Angeles employment industrial psychiatrist used a very novel approach to determine how creative a prospective employee would be on the job by asking new candidates to describe what the world would be like if we had suddenly developed a pill to replace food. Especially if it contained all the nourishment one needed and was so easy to produce that it could be mass produced and sold for two cents. Rather than say more, the reader may wish to think this one out in terms of levels of impact.

7. *Difference Thinking*—Starting from a basic asset, market shift, or technological change, one might "suppose" or "propose" that something different could take place under various conditions, circumstances, groupings, locations, and/or timeframes. This could be the removal or addition of a feature to a traditional business product or service. Alternately, it might be the extension or limit of a products' attributes. Some creativity seminars have proposed selecting a random word (person, place or thing) from the dictionary to cross associate visualized characteristics as an aid for conceptualizing new attributes or features by extending or creating new products and services. These conceptions are then viewed through a desired framework to limit and bound the possibilities into purposeful applications. Subsequently, proposed tasks are then resolved by a set of conceivable solutions which are usually based upon a singular group of changes, that will achieve new "different" networks, products, and services, meeting realistic user needs by providing desirable benefits.

8. *What If Thinking*—Jules Verne had a great mind that was indeed both imaginative and practical. It is important to play with ideas, to initially hold no boundaries, to allow the mind to float and speculate, to ask why (such as "Why do we go down roads that twist and turn, based upon earlier cow paths?") In asking why do we do things this way or that, and asking "what if" we could do it another way, we begin to see new possibilities. By then challenging these possibilities for practicalities, we can develop short and long term visions, such as those upon which Jules Verne based his exciting novels. Only a few have the rare gift of being able to sit and let the mind wander out the window to the blue sky above and then day dream in a fantasy world of possibilities, until an acceptable concept emerges, but many of us can push our minds to expand their self-imposed restrictions by using one of the thinking techniques to collect our data, analyze it for possibilities, and then reconsider the possibilities with practicalities. We should continually develop, as we go about our everyday business, a family of ideas that can be stored away for a quiet session in a quiet place, where we allow the mind to wander, where they can then be revisited and enhanced, to form innovative concepts.

9. *A Second Look*—Ideas generated using the above techniques can be extended, finalized, and become a more completed concept. An idea can usually be greatly developed, if it is allowed to have a second pass, as

it is being contemplated. Usually it should be left alone for a period of time, while other ideas are considered, some for completely different situations. Then when we are ready to readdress it, this is done in a fresh light. Usually, new concerns, limits, and conditions are imposed to see how the original idea flourishes. At this point ideas become solidified into a structure more able to withstand the rigors of future challenges.

10. *However Analysis*—We must never forget the story of tulip mania, that supposedly developed in the past century in the Netherlands. At that time everyone within the Netherlands had formed the consensus that a particular tulip bulb was very desirable and worth a great deal of money. They bid the price so high that everyone decided to grow their own and sell them. So the following year, everyone had their own bulbs. Since there was no market within the Netherlands, they went forth to sell them to the world. However, the world noted that although it was a very pretty tulip, it was not worth the ridiculously higher price than the other tulips that were readily available. So the market collapsed overnight. They had created in their own minds an unrealistic need. In conclusion, we may laugh at this, but we have seen American agriculture go through a tremendous shakeup, as farmers in the late 70s believed that land should be acquired at any price, using high interest bank loans to acquire it, at two to three times the initial price. Unfortunately, the artificial price collapsed during different economic conditions. Similarly, we have seen gold rise to $800 per ounce only to tumble back down to $295 per ounce. Hence the need for the second look, the relook, and the "however" analysis, where ideas are further developed and challenged in order to become solid concepts. At this point, they can then be eloquently defended and considered, as candidates for further investigation in the next planning phases.

UNDERSTANDING PEOPLE, THE MARKETPLACE, AND USERS

To truly obtain the right concept, we must come to understanding. We must understand people in the marketplace, what they are really like, what they really want or do not want, what they are really willing to pay for. Similarly, we must understand society, where it may be going, where it could go depending upon various conditions. We must understand economic shifts and opportunities in the international arena. We must understand our companies, their politics, their strengths, their weaknesses. The consultant must understand the client's present status, before proposing future solutions. With understanding comes identification of needs, as we move from data, to knowledge, to understanding, to a vision which we can share with others.

In this state we are able to begin to seek a solution. Now we know what is and is not important, as we look for those fine tuning twists and shifts, which provide the real market opportunities. For example, a firm established by three highly sophisticated companies to move wideband information in the 70s found that their customers were actually low speed data users of less than 9600 bit rate. In the 80s they had to restructure their networks to meet these different needs, with one of the owners dropping out due to disillusionment. Yes, there was the need for a new data network, but low speed instead of high speed. The shift to high speed will probably occur at the turn of the century, as many more wideband services are available. However, they should have structured their network based upon changing user needs, not just a preconceived need, which in actuality was a future need, not a present need.

People

As we develop concepts, several techniques have been recently developed for segmenting the marketplace. Since the marketplace consists of people, methods are used to identify people in terms of classifying them in various stereotypes and then marketing products and services to that particular type of person, for example: conservative or liberal. One such method is called psychicgraphics.

People Types. We all have the tendency, when we meet someone, to classify them. We have seen a list of opinions that run from the "Archie Bunker" type to "High Society" types. Market research has gone one or two steps further in developing more categories to distinguish the various characteristics based upon demographics, behavior and attitudes. Such as:

1. *Trend Setter*—Innovative, educated or self-educated, likes cutting edge.
2. *New Professional (Yuppie)*—Likes expensive new toys, works hard, physical sports, serious, career dedicated.
3. *Older Professional*—High income, education, successful, optimist, value government, live in cities, likes new concepts that solve interesting problems.
4. *People Person*—Enjoys social games, human interest, interactions, direction of society, new concepts.
5. *Homebody*—Family oriented, large households, high community interests, less national interest.
6. *Working Provider*—Worried, pessimistic, low risk taker, likes some but not all new concepts, must meet a real need.
7. *Traditionalist*—Afraid of change, limited education, loyal to family, likes things as they are, high resistance and slow to change.

We can then consider these "people types" in terms of new telecommunication services to determine those that may be more or less successful for particular types of persons. See Fig. 3-8. Using this methodology, market researchers can identify future markets using a matrix in which various features or possibilities are overlaid on the people types to project degrees of acceptance or resistance.

This is one of the many methods today for attempting to understand resistance and acceptance to change; however people come in many shapes and sizes as they enter the world of choice. They usually reflect more than one of the above stereo types over a period of time. Some will be influenced

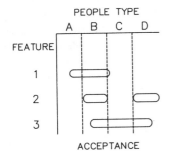

PEOPLE TYPE

Fig. 3-8. Acceptance Chart.

by another marketing philosophy, which is the use of television or the mass media to motivate them to want a particular product. This is where those in the back room decide what is best for the people, and determine how they will convince them that they need it.

It is interesting to spend time discussing future possibilities with all types of people and to listen to what they like and do not like about the ideas. Then consider what they are saying against their "people type" background to see areas of agreement or disagreement across people types. From this form of analysis come excellent enhancements to back-room planning. There is a trend today to say that back-room planning is wrong. "Just go to the street and talk directly to the people." This is a misconception. The good conceptual planners in the "back room" are never really in the "back room" but are always trying their ideas out on the clerk at the bank, the barber, the milkman, teacher, lawyer, and the town politician, and listening for new ideas and things they might want.

Hence, when the concept is initially considered, it is natural to discuss it with the affected people to see their reaction. This requires explaining it sufficiently so that it will be well understood in terms of its benefits to that particular person. If in actuality there is no real immediate use for it by such and such a particular type of person, this should be understood and considered in the conclusions. Hence, the interaction with people, as individuals, is a key ingredient to conceptual planning, as better and more focused understanding is developed. It is a two way street—ideas for new products can come from the people, or be originated in the back room then discussed with the various types of people to determine their reaction. From this interaction, ideas grow, are modified, challenged, and enhanced to become mature concepts, sometimes totally different from the original conception.

Example: By noting the number of misdialed digits, someone came to the realization that there is no feedback for persons using a touchtone phone, to indicate that the digits have indeed been sent. So a simple device was considered in the "back room," that would display the digits on any phone and sell for $9.95. After discussing this with a potential manufacturer, the device was given a clock as well. After discussing it with a mass marketing firm, the device was given a duration of a call timer. After discussing it with the network providers, it was given the ability to receive incoming digits and display the incoming number to show who was calling. After discussing it with various people using communications, it was given the ability to display the various names of persons calling rather than numbers. After discussing it with technology planners, it was given the ability to talk and tell who is calling, as well as receive verbal instructions on who to call. After talking to senior citizens, it was given a large display readout, so that they could easily see the numbers. Of course, it should still sell for $9.95, or perhaps there should be several sophisticated versions, at different prices?

The Marketplace

In reality, conceptual planning is done both on the street, and in the back room. It is and always must be in tune with the marketplace in terms of people. As more and more features are considered, we must determine who and how people will use them. See Fig. 3-9. Consider the viewtext trials in Europe—there we found that the mass market required a very simple interface for the TV set. Even the touching of the screen or pointing was not acceptable, if the instructions were at all complicated. The preferred interface was a talking TV, that asked a series of menu driven questions to the customers.

Formal Planning Process

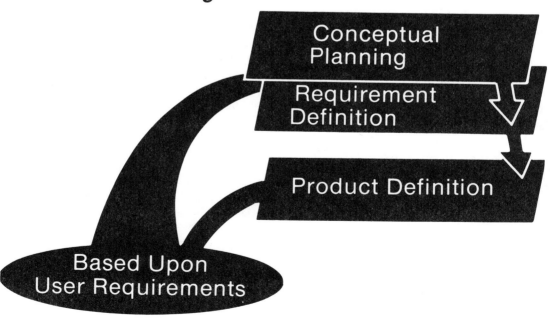

Fig. 3-9. User Planning.

Some have identified the marketplace in terms of class, mass, and trash. The MacIntosh computer designers wanted a series of programs that provided many new forms of sophisticated operations, using a friendly interface for the masses at home. As the programs were developed, they became such a challenge to the major software houses to have their programs accepted for the "Mac," that soon it became a symbol of class to have one's software working on it.

User Types

The market can also be defined in terms of user types. The "New Users" Case Study in Chapter 12 demonstrates how to identify the business market, in terms of user types and not people types; where user types are identified in terms of a specific mode of operation in performing business communication tasks. These are further defined by attributes and a range of specific values to further clarify the type of user.

The user type = function (mode of operation(attributes(range of values))).

In the case study, users from many businesses and industries are identified in terms of the tasks that they must accomplish in their specific work environments. The users modes of operation are identified in terms of specific communications to be accomplished per task. In this manner, we gain a view of future information users, such as inquiry/response users, data collection users, data distribution users, graphics users, etc. We can identify these users by describing what their technical telecommunication characteristics and attributes are in terms of connect time, holding time, transmission rates, error rate tolerances, etc. These can then be further defined in terms of ranges of values, such as low speed, medium speed, and high speed transmission rates. Other needs and indicators can be used to further divide them, such as requiring security, encryption, etc. This will produce, as the case example shows, an understanding of the marketplace in terms of various user's technical needs, as they perform their communication tasks.

The market's technical needs can then be further identified in terms of technology that is readily available in the near future, or that must wait for future technology! Hence, market needs can be technology phased. This then identifies new objectives for technology to meet these needs. On the other hand, technology that is looking for an application can be applied to existing user tasks or entire new operations. Here, we enter the recursive world of:

... Market - Technology - Market ....(Mark-Tech)

or:

...Technology - Market - Technology ....(Tech-Mark).

It simply depends on where we pick up the cycle:

The secret is to provide a planning phase, which can be entered either by a technical possibility looking for a market, or a market possibility looking for a technology. During the conceptual planning phase both meet, and enter recursive analysis to establish specific user needs, met by specific technology.

Organization

Conceptual planning can be used for any endeavor, from understanding user needs to reconsidering the mission of the firm. It is important to realize that it is just the beginning of a three phase sequence of looks and investigations. It should be considered a place for thinkers to meet, discuss, analyze, and think. It is a natural phase for planners from multiple international divisions to meet and look at opportunities in which each unit could work together to provide a piece of a future network or system or product. For example a multinational firm consisting of autonomous units that provide modems, terminals, switches, transmission devices, and fiber optics facilities requires a cross-unit planning activity. All need each other to help develop concepts of new networks in which their future new terminals interface to new modems, which interface to new switches, which interface to new databases via new satellites and facilities.

By using conceptual planners and advanced planning teams across units such as these, firms are able to identify realistic concepts acceptable for all. This applies across lines of businesses within individual companies, or across design groups on a preproject investigation, or . . .

USERS—PROVIDERS—SUPPLIERS

Figure 3-10 shows the interrelationships between the users, suppliers, and providers by using the conceptual planning phase. Here, providers analyze their users to understand the marketplace in terms of people types' and user types' needs and requirements. They also work with various suppliers to understand what technology can provide. This will identify areas in which they may use new technology. Of course, the suppliers are performing their own strategic planning and conceptual planning by working directly with the providers and the provider's customers, in order to direct their research efforts. In this manner, we achieve, via either the supplier or provider, better directed research and identification of more technical possibilities for the marketplace. This will enable the supplier to meet the needs of both the provider and its customer, the end user. Once the concept is complete with acceptable market and technology considerations, it is ready for a management review in order to exit to the requirements definition phase.

Review

What are the results of this phase? Who performs the review? What docu-

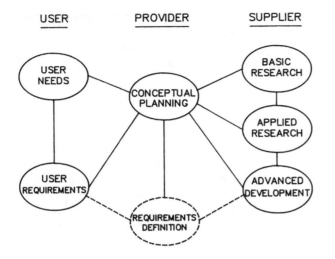

USER   PROVIDER   SUPPLIER

Fig. 3-10. The Pivotal Point.

ments are provided? How detailed are the reports? What form of commitments are made?

The review team consists of the "go, no-go" decision makers and their advisors. The type of product being proposed determines the level of top management involvement. Specialists should participate from all affected disciplines, programming, systems engineering, finance, marketing, manufacturing, and quality. To be effective, the decision to go, no-go, rework must be seen as a corporate commitment, realizing that each phase of the product life cycle has risk, with the risk being reduced as each phase is completed. However, the decision to proceed should be a serious corporate commitment and not simply a holding action for later phases' further analyses. See Fig. 3-11.

The following supporting analyses are provided for review:

- Marketplace Review and Product Strategy. This identifies the role of the product in the marketplace in terms of its possibility for success. The projected users are indicated with tentative quantitative estimates.
- Technology Review and Product Strategy. The type of technology that will make the product competitive in the marketplace is identified. It notes the technical capability of the company to design and produce the product, as well as dependencies between units, "buy rather than make" considerations, and new skills to be acquired.
- A feasibility analysis is provided on basic technical concepts that are essential for the product success. Areas of further study are noted.
- A review of the competition and their future products' strategies are provided to identify all competitive aspects needed for the product's success.

86

The general concept and specific advanced product proposal are provided in terms of user needs, technology, cost-sales projections, P/L statements, general development costs (projects), manufacturing impact, support studies, quality requirements, marketplace profile, financial considerations, corporate future impact, and risk. In addition, a plan is provided for implementing the next phase (requirements planning). This plan is modified after the review

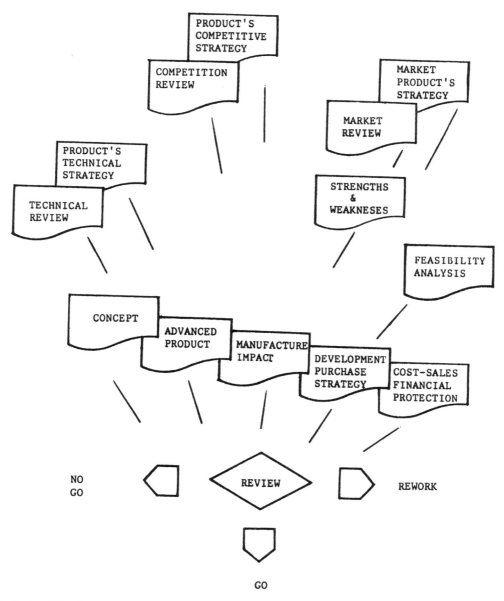

Fig. 3-11. Review What?

to be consistent with the decisions made during the review. A short review report by the review board documents conclusions and decisions made during the review. See Fig. 3-12.

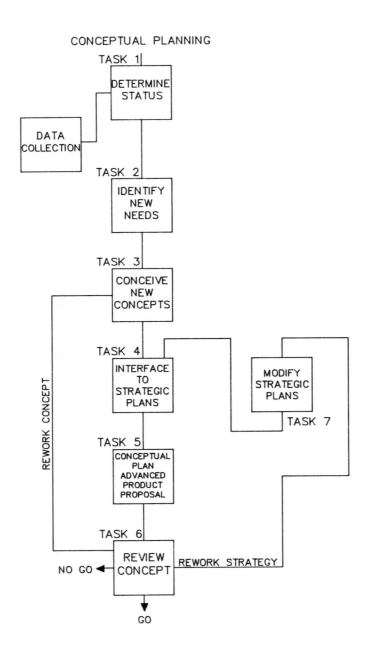

Fig. 3-12. Conceptual Planning Flow Chart.

Fig. 3-13. Conceptual Planning?!?

FLOW CHART: CONCEPTUAL PLANNING

During this first phase, planners define a future product's basic application, requirements, and feasibility. Its technical aspects, target product costs, and features are determined using both applied research and marketing research assistance. This will indicate the product's key market and why it is particular and applicable. These studies are performed for top management to the extent necessary to ensure that this is indeed the best product for the company in terms of market, technical capability, financial concerns, and overall success risks.

The net result will be a high level document called the "Advanced Product Proposal" that defines the product and its application. Once all major issues are resolved, the product proposal is presented to management for their formal concurrence. At this review management can retain the product in conceptual planning, terminate it, or allow it to proceed to the requirement definition phase, having only spent a small portion of their R&D budget on this phase:

- Enter phase from: strategic planning, statement of need, product requirements definition phase, product definition phase, preliminary design phase.
- Basic objectives: To perform short and long range planning, that reviews the marketplace and technology in perspective of company involvement.
- Dependencies: top level direction, market trends, technology trends, competition, regulation, financial, standards.
- Personnel skills: conceptual planners, market researchers, systems designers.
- % Calendar time of life cycle: 5% to 15%.
- % Cost of life cycle: 1% to 5%.
- Analysis considerations: utilization, marketability, commonality, technology, cost, feasibility, resource availability, timing, complexity, past products, components availability.
- Phase results: strategy direction plans, network, system, device, service proposals—advanced product proposals, general market/user requirements, financial consideration, technical feasibility studies, identified risks, approval for the requirements definition phase.

FURTHER ANALYSIS

The case study in Chapter Twelve, *Integrating Marketing and Technology* demonstrate how conceptual planning studies have identified the future new users of the information era, as specific "user types." They also show the evolution of the ISDN Network, using "overlays" that will encourage user information usage and growth, until replaced by the integrated wideband ISDN Network of the 90s, which is described later in Chapter Ten.

OBSERVATIONS: A TIME TO THINK

1. Conceptual planning is the missing link between program planning and strategic planning. It is the innovation phase, where ideas flourish, where marketing meets technology, and where technology meets the marketplace.

2. Data is essential for good analysis. In conceptual planning, it is used to obtain the big picture view to separate the forest from the trees.

3. During this phase little pieces or facets are put together to form the big picture. It is not a taking apart, but a building up.

4. Here the mind is stretched until it hurts. Tons of data are mentally searched for all encompassing simplistic solutions or opportunities.

5. As more firms structure around autonomous multi-unit profit centers and the application requires more integrated solutions, it is mandatory for cross-unit planning to occur around a think phase, before new endeavors are launched.

6. Participating management, the manager planners, must have something with which to participate. Concepts are presented to them at the review step of the conceptual planning phase. It is at this point that the strategic direction and future program planning have early interaction with the participating management.

7. Conceptual planning integrates basic research, applied research and advanced development activities in the laboratory with the market user needs and requirements research activities of the providers. It facilitates the "market—technical—market—technical" cycle, entered either from the marketplace or from a technical analysis.

8. The conceptual planning phase positions management thinking on timely market opportunities and technical possibilities.

Chapter 4

Top Down Planning: Requirements Definition Phase

In this third phase of the planning process, we must consider the interdependencies between users, providers and suppliers of telecommunications products. The product and service requirements definition phase follows the conceptual planning phase, during which preliminary ideas and concepts were solidified into conceptual plans and advanced product proposals that designate feasible technology to meet projected future marketplace users' needs.

The next phase, the requirements phase, is the most misunderstood phase of a product's life cycle. Traditionally, once the concept or basic ideas have been identified, only a brief period is spent on further clarifying the requirements. This is then followed by an intense effort to produce the design proposal, design schedule, human resource estimates, and projected costs. After the project is launched, the managers and designers spend considerable time and effort attempting to redefine what exactly they are to build. Normally, halfway through the design, many features have not yet been clarified and designed, so they are delayed until after the first production article, as a later release, in order to meet schedule.

The purpose of emphasizing this phase is to show the types of analyses that should be performed before the project is launched or the product purchased. The intent is to allow the program manager, design teams, and support teams to better understand the type of product required. This will later enable them to provide upper management and themselves with a realistic schedule to achieve their full support and commitment. Care should be taken to ensure that precious time is not wasted in aimless studies that are not

Fig. 4-1. Identifying New User Needs.

directly effective. If the requirements phase of a design project is brushed over too lightly, designers must constantly reassess what it is they are building.

Today's products must meet a particular niche in the marketplace. For example, a telecommunication product (be it a program, a device, a subsystem, or a system) is rapidly becoming part of a network. Hence, its interfaces, its features, its maintenance objectives, its size, its limits, and its quality of performance are dictated by its network application. No longer can a future communication device for the home or office be independently defined. It is now part of a rapidly changing system, which may require it to display the calling party, provide feature oriented electronic ringing, interface with a digital ISDN loop, or indicate that a voice message is waiting. Similarly, the future local central office switching exchange will have a completely different set of requirements than traditional plain old telephone service. The Integrated Services Digital Network (ISDN), for instance, will not be composed of systems physically situated in a central office. They will be dispersed throughout the local vicinity and into neighboring towns and villages in order to concentrate clusters of customers on a base switch.

FACETS

The features, maintenance, reliability, sizing, growth, interfaces, physical size, and environment requirements become extremely important to clarify, before attempting to structure the product's hardware and programming architecture. In order to ensure that these requirements are realistic, this may require supporting feasibility analyses to be performed concurrent with the requirements' definition to select techniques and resolve trade-off considerations. For example, a remote mountainous third world application's physi-

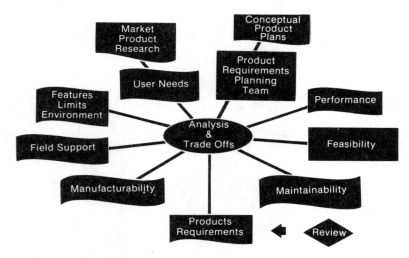

Fig. 4-2. The Requirements Planning Process.

cal distribution plant will affect the type of maintenance personnel and programming support requirements, which may require the selection of a particularly advantageous maintenance programming language, and operational support system.

Due to this complex changing application environment for future products, an extensive requirement definition phase should consider the following aspects:

Marketability. What features are absolutely required in the first, second, and third releases of the product? What other applications or versions will be marketed? How can the product be structured to be versatile, but still cost effective?

Manufacturability. What limits are imposed on the product to ensure that its production costs are minimized? What features and requirements will have major manufacturing cost impact or schedule impact? How do the company's strengths and weaknesses in its manufacturing capabilities affect the requirements? How will it be tested in the factory?

Reliability. To what degree of reliability should each portion of the product perform and still meet a system level reliability requirement? Do functional processors need to be duplicated? Triplicated? Do databases need to be duplicated? Alternatively, should they be provided in a different system with emergency access?

Maintainability. What level of maintenance person will support the system in the field? Will there be remote diagnostic analysis? What type of spares will be required to support the product? How can the product be designed to minimize spare costs? What type of physical and logical structure can best achieve the maintainability objectives? What performance impact and cost penalties exist? Will the system be located in a site requiring RFI shielding?

Quality. How do usability, integrity, efficiency, correctness, completeness, and adaptability objectives compete with cost and schedule? What is the "good will" name of the company worth in terms of expense and schedule? To what extent should it be a quality product? Define quality for a particular product. To what extent and degree will it be pursued? How?

Testability, Flexibility, Adaptability, Changeability. To what degree should they be determined, defined, and emphasized to ensure that there are no surprises after release of design, such as growth changes that cannot be added to data switches without shutting them down for two days or two hours or two minutes?

Security, Privacy, Confidentiality. In today's changing marketplace, these requirements can, if future marketplace emphasis exists, extend the life of the product and greatly increase sales, but architecture and structure may have to be drastically changed. Hence, if required or to be required, they must be considered in the initial design.

Human Factors. The most important objective consideration, as the others are achieved, is to ensure a reasonable market life. Human-machine communication for operating and maintaining operation is extremely crucial to the architecture of the product. How much must this interface be user friendly to be successful?

EXTENT AND DEGREE

The depth, amount, or level, in defining the requirements has always been a major problem. A recent survey of a hundred product managers indicated that 98% of their projects suffered substantially because the requirements were inadequately defined before launching the development. Regarding extent of definition, a prime example is the "else condition" for a program's conditional requirements. Here, a "coder level" programmer may make the most crucial decisions on how a product performs. During design, most inputs and their desired actions are adequately specified for their encoding, but the actions required for the other permutations of the input conditions are not. An example is the space shuttle postponement at 31 seconds before launch, when project control could not override an inadvertent system stop condition initiated by the control program. The reason for the stop was a suspected trouble, but the inability to override the suspected trouble was a programmer's "else condition."

In the 70s, one project in a major drive to identify all considerations and actions required decision tables to be written to the lowest level. Unfortunately, the law of diminishing returns took its toll and it was found more desirable to only implement the decision tables to a realistically manageable level. Thus balance is necessary.

Today there are several tools being developed to enable signaling protocols, input requirements, features, performance objectives, and limits to be described along with the alternative actions required, if they are not completely achieved.

FEASIBILITY

Anyone can conceive of a feature that may be desirable in the marketplace, but to make it a realistic requirement for a new product may require some form of feasibility analysis. Many requirements can be determined by a brief paper analysis. However, some are considered critical to the technical base of the project. They may require a separate feasibility support study. Effort spent in these studies will greatly reduce the risk for extensive additions to be added to a product's project cost and schedule commitments. Hence, an applied technology group should initially perform these studies to determine key hardware and programming techniques, during the preproject planning activities.

PRIORITY

Translating a wish list to a must list is always difficult. However, if it is not formally performed by system management, it will be informally achieved during the course of the development. More than one project has had numerous

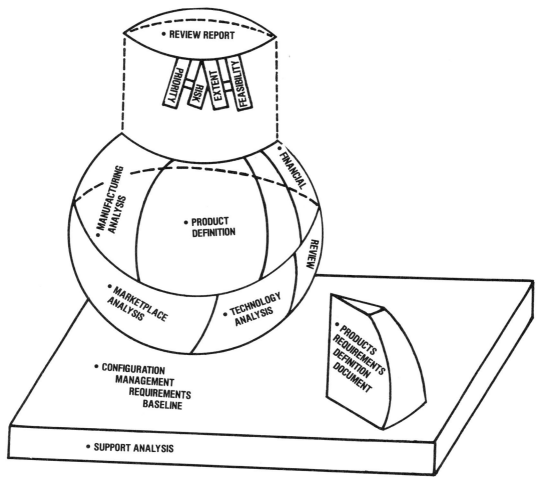

Fig. 4-3. Requirements Definition Document.

new releases or versions within six months after its release to manufacture, in order to obtain a product that provides the features and requirements it must have to sell in the marketplace. If these requirements are adequately prioritized in the beginning, this clarifies the design objectives and the project has greatly increased its chances for obtaining its goals. However, with too many requirements and goals which cannot all be initially achieved in the time allowed, then chance is the deciding factor, not management.

RISK

The purpose of an initial, extensive effort to fully understand the marketplace needs, and have the technology analysis, competitive analysis, requirements specification, and feasibility supportive studies is to greatly minimize risk. As each analysis is completed, the risk should be reduced. Many program directors have noted that these initial phases are by far the most critical. If they are not performed or are performed incorrectly, the missing analyses cannot be easily recovered during the life of a project.

METHODOLOGY AND TOOLS

Requirements are under intense review, analysis, clarification, and selection during the three product planning phases, the first three development phases, and when return paths are executed from subsequent phases for further modification and clarification of new features for new applications. Hence, there must be a method for controlling the status of the requirements and ensuring the integrity of feature reviews and product commitments. A typical example might be requirements for a North American digital switch. The requirements can be divided into three categories, such as required (must), desirable (wish), or negotiable (could). The extent of definition of the requirements may be in different stages: completely defined, partially defined, and undefined. As each feature is analyzed, its category is determined as being acceptable to the first release, 2nd release, 3rd release, pending further analysis, or not applicable. In addition, it usually will be necessary to expand definitions of each requirement and keep track of letters of clarification and agreement with the potential customer.

The requirements documents for most projects are changing documents, as more and more information and understanding is developed, during the product life cycle. An excellent management tool is a video access, time-shared word processing system, which enables a requirements document's sections to be maintained in a requirements database, but also enables all managers and designers to review and update the requirement's status and definitions. In this manner, the requirements document is indeed a "living document" throughout the project, in which revisions are kept in memory record files after each phase's review, to provide immediate reference to changes in requirements. This enables the requirements to be clarified, modified and expanded throughout the product life cycle and tracked to key product reviews and decisions. Later, each feature or requirement can be tied to the design by a cross reference number. This can be used to determine the cost of each requirement.

USER REQUIREMENTS

During conceptual planning activities, we identified people in terms of

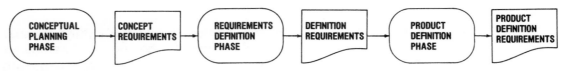

Fig. 4-4. The Planning Phase's Product Requirements.

types or categories in order to understand their motivations, individual needs, resistance to change and willingness for new endeavors. The case study *The New Users* presented a detailed analysis for identifying future telecommunication users in terms of user types performing various types of operations. There, a task for a given industry may have a series of telecommunication operations. However, a sort by operation indicated that a set of 20 or so operations are commonly used for a large variety of tasks of the different industries. This then became the set of basic user types, whose needs should be met by the new telecommunication networks, systems, and products. By overlaying these back on specific people types who will actually be performing the tasks, we can develop a better market segmentation and timeframe priority perspective for providing new products to meet their needs. For example, if most tasks requiring a particular operation occur in industries controlled by people types who resist any form of change, then this is not an area for initial emphasis. They will follow change, not make change. On the other hand data collection is a very competitive industry, where more aggressive people types are searching for more innovative methods. It may possibly become a leading industry. Iacocca, who turned Chrysler around, once said, "Satisfied people do not create change." This has been one of the problems with T.V. viewtext, which had attempted to provide the masses with information, when the masses only wanted to simply watch T.V.

Originally, telecommunication systems met only the providers' needs and not the providers' customers' needs. They had a set of transport features, but not features for the customers. It is only when we aggressively enter the world of the providers' customers, that we must seriously begin to differentiate between "wish," "must," and "could" features. As we analyze the various new feature considerations, it is useful to establish these three categories. As feasibility and impact studies are performed, interesting shifts of emphases will occur, as customer's requirements change from "musts" to "coulds" to "wishes." Specialized requirements should be carefully considered in terms of their impact on the whole. Some requirements fulfill a universal need and will be the basis for determining a new set of common features. Others are more specific and apply to a limited group of customers at a particular point in time. For example:

User Type A: One who wishes to perform inquiry/response data communications at a 9600 baud rate, using instantaneous network connections and having an error rate of one in ten million bits per second.

User Type B: One who is the same as user type A, but also wishes the message to be encrypted.

User Type A may initially be more universal than User type B. However, as more and more requirements are established across the various potential users, we will identify a new family of user types by expanding and modifying the previous set, but timing is important to first capture the customers and then provide them with more features as they need them. In other words, features that grow as the user's usage grows.

RESEARCH

Research activities, such as basic research, applied research, advanced research, and advanced development provide exciting new information for marketplace opportunities. Usually, basic research and applied research are particularly applicable to conceptual planning, as they look at new materials or consider new network possibilities for transmission, switching, and data processing applications. Then, as the concept is understood in terms of these possibilities, the analysis is moved into the advanced development and applied development arena, (which are sometimes called advanced research and advanced development respectively.) Here, advanced product development teams will establish specific detailed technical requirements for the new network, product, or service offering, based upon various feasibility analyses and tests. From these forms of research investigations, we will develop a clearer understanding of what is possible, as we further identify more specific user needs and user requirements.

USERS, PROVIDERS AND SUPPLIERS

As noted, the planning process establishes the linkage among these three players. We now have a logical location for users to discuss, with their providers and suppliers, what they need and what they require. During the more detailed requirements phase, concepts are further defined and clarified. Here, a general product concept may become two or three unique products with definite boundaries in terms of features and costs. As we will see in a later section, this is also where those who manage the pursuit of quality play a major role in determining the quality of a product. Quality is really achieved during the requirement phase and not later, after the product has already been built. Now is the time for the users and providers to clearly indicate to the suppliers what level of quality should be pursued for a particular attribute.

Interchange

Many techniques are being established to get the users together with their product planners and designers, such as one to two day conferences or forums. Over the years, user groups have proven to be a valuable asset to computer language compiler developers. An exciting new vehicle is the "round table" for discussion groups of knowledgeable planners and decision makers. Here, they are brought together to look at the future of society, technology and the marketplace. Each comes with extensive and indepth experience in a particular aspect of the field. These discussions usually have a reasonable mix of the providers and suppliers with a few knowledgeable users. The purpose of the "round table" is not only to analyze specific technical considerations, but to discuss the direction of society and telecommunications in terms of potential total information requirements for future networks, products, and services. Considerable effort may be spent in identifying interfaces and standards, that must be resolved before offerings can be made. In this manner technological and marketing possibilities are brought together to further develop and expand acceptable concepts from conceptual planning activities and to translate these concepts into more specific and realistic networks, products and services. Possible new features are identified, as ideas and views are exchanged among the key players. All benefit from these exchanges, since few future products can be developed autonomously without the network interfaces. Each participant will have a part to play, all will be successful, if the information society networks grow and expand.

CYCLES ON CYCLES WITHIN CYCLES

Many times we have heard the statements; "We must be market driven!" or "We can no longer allow technology to drive new products!" We have also heard technical people say "If we waited for marketing to tell us what they want, we'd have a long wait!" or, "We know what's best!" In actuality, both are right and both are wrong. Sometimes technological possibilities are so broad and complex that few people on the street really know what it means to them. At other times, people indicate needs, but technology may not be available to economically meet the need. Some needs are only considered in the light of the most recent newly identified technology. For example, digital networks are based upon pulse code modulation transmission techniques that were established in the early 30s by researchers in ITT laboratories, but it was not until the 60s that technology had advanced to the point of economically and reliably achieving it, as well as having user traffic of a volume that required it. Conversely, specific user needs may be identified and must wait for technology to catch up. For example, the Dick Tracy watch, having a portable T.V. and phone, or Jules Verne's rocket to the moon and submarine under the sea.

Hence, it is not a question of being market driven or technology driven. It does not matter which drives which. However, it is at this phase that they meet, and it is important that they meet *early* in the product life cycle. Here, realistic requirements in the planning life cycle of future endeavors are identified and established between marketing and technical groups. Here, we separate the could from the can, and the wish from the must, in order to have a well defined, prioritized list of requirements. During this phase, the requirements must be extensively ranked in terms of what the user really wants. Look at the lists of PBX features today! There are many conditions and variables that must be understood in implementing requirements. It is at this time that these detailed requirements must be defined in terms of what the market is willing to pay.

DECISIONS

Many times, large lists of requirements are given to designers to implement. These can usually be accomplished over a reasonable period of time.

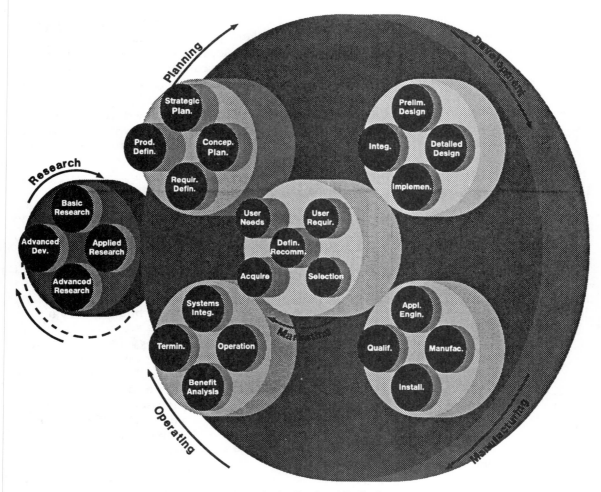

Fig. 4-5. Technology transfer to the Marketplace via the Product Life Cycle.

However, many designs begin to expand and grow, as numerous internal loops and exits are added, as the result of "else conditions." These are the actions that must take place, if the expected does not happen. For example, if you are to meet someone during the Christmas shopping rush, at some appointed place and time, you should also spend a few minutes discussing what to do, if you or the other person are late or fail to arrive due to difficult traffic or parking conditions. Hence, you have entered the "else" world, what else to do if conditions different than expected occur.

As we look deeper at defining requirements, we see that considerable effort is spent describing the expected conditions of a requirement and then identifying a sequence of desired operations, in terms of these possibilities. For example, an action F is dependent upon the conditions of variables A, B, and C being true. $F = A + B + C$. However, we must also define what happens, if A goes away before conditions B and C arrive or become true. $J =$

102

$A^- + B + C$ where A^- means A is not there or false. However, there are many other possibilities that can happen, which should also be identified such as $G = A^- + B^- + C$, $H = A^- + B + C^-$, $I = A + B^- + C^-$, $K = A + B + C^-$, $M = A + B^- + C$, and $N = A^- + B^- + C^-$. We can mathematically determine the number of possibilities. If we have one variable, which has two conditions, we can have two states A or A^-. Two to the 1 power equals 2. If we have two variables, we will have four states such as: $A + B$, $A^- + B$, $A + B^-$, $A^- + B^-$. Two to the power 2 equals 4. Three variables will have 2 to the power 3, or 8 possibilities, and N variables will have 2 to the power N possibilities.

A matrix such as the one shown in Fig. 4-6 may be used to identify primary and secondary actions, based upon various input conditions.

Alternatively, we may have a combination state map to indicate all possible actions. (Example: for three variables with two conditions (T or F), there are 8 possible actions, as shown in Fig. 4-7.) For various conditions of variables A, B or C, different states of existence are possible, during which various actions can be performed at each state. Now this can be extended for new conditions of new variables, such as D. This can provide new states and new actions performed within these states, as shown in Fig. 4-8.

As long as D is true, the other actions could take place, but whenever D is not true, then we should ignore all the other possible actions and only do the specific action or new set of actions identified for D. In some software programs, this becomes an IF, THEN, ELSE statement, meaning IF a condition is true (example D is true), then do all sorts of actions, depending upon the states of other conditions, ELSE when D is not true or false, THEN do a specific action or new set of actions and ignore the previous set of action possibilities.

Since a decision table can drive another decision table by an action state-

Primary Condition	Primary Actions
Secondary Conditions	Secondary Actions

If A is true and B is true	Then F is true
If A is true and B is true but C is false	Then F is false

Fig. 4-6. Conditions Map.

Variable — Condition

A	T	T	T	T	F	F	F	F
B	T	T	F	F	T	T	F	F
C	T	F	T	F	T	F	T	F

Action 1 Action 2 Action 3. . .   Action 8

Fig. 4-7. States/Actions.

ment indicating if certain conditions occur, then go on to decision table 2 or 4 or 100, we can then build up a matrix of decisions and actions based upon predetermined changes in conditions. Some system designers have attempted to design compilers that will directly translate these tables based upon user requirements to operational programs, that directly cause computers to perform the designed actions. Over the years there have been higher level languages developed to try to achieve this. There has been considerable effort in artificial intelligence, using "fussy" logic, where the robot can draw upon immediate dynamic results of present and past experiences. For our analysis we will use decision tables as a simple tool to collect our thoughts and indicate all the possible outcomes that we may wish from various situations or conditions as we further identify requirements. The better we define our requirements, the less we will leave for the programmers or designers

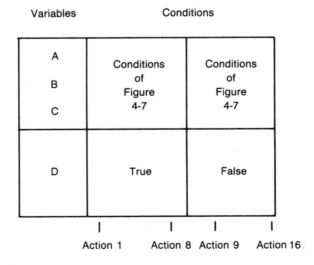

Variables — Conditions

A		
B	Conditions of Figure 4-7	Conditions of Figure 4-7
C		
D	True	False

Action 1   Action 8 Action 9   Action 16

Fig. 4-8. Variables/Conditions/Actions.

104

to determine later by themselves, what we would have wanted, as "else conditions."

LIFE CYCLES OVERLAY

As will be seen in Chapter 6, the requirement definition phase is one of the three key locations, where major life cycles and processes can interface and interact. Here, as the planning life cycle and product life cycle (Fig. 2-6) overlay on each other, requirements become a key driving force for the activities within each of these life cycles. This overlay also facilitates the following ramifications:

- Research becomes more directed, as concepts move from possibilities to more specific areas of impact. For example, general data network models leave the applied research activities to become the more specific advanced research and advanced development analysis models. Structures, interfaces and protocol standards are identified and established there, so that specific networks, products and services may be developed.
- Strategic planning becomes more intensified, as more specific strategic direction issues are being identified and challenged in the lines of business, as their plans containing detailed requirements are established, causing a reevaluation of strategic direction in terms of where the company is actually going.
- More research is required in more specific areas, as we no longer talk in vague generalities of possible customer needs.
- Technology transfer occurs, as more and more market needs are identified with new requirements for new types of technology.
- Product life cycles are initiated, as ideas leave the conceptual phase and enter the sequence of planning/development phases that end in an established product.

Understanding this phase in this light can enable one to use it to drive many other processes than the one from which the phase was entered. For example, as user's needs are translated to requirements; as market research considers a possible market, this is an opportunity to drive a research laboratory to reassess their own and other's applied research findings to determine which technique may be applicable for a particular definite application. (As noted earlier, the famous example is ITT's PCM theory of the 30s, being applied by AT&T to solve a problem of the 60s.) Hence the requirement definition phase of one Life Cycle can also drive other Life Cycles, as seen in this figure.

REVIEWS AND BENEFITS

The requirement definition phase output should be carefully reviewed by both marketing and technical management. Generally, it does not require se-

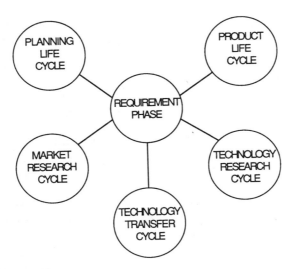

Fig. 4-9. Requirements Control Point.

nior management. In some corporate culture conditions, if it is performed for an internal project, it is usually best not to solicit their involvement, until the next phase. They may want a solution as to how to meet the requirements too early. This usually occurs immediately after having reached an agreement on what exactly the requirements should be. A feasibility model that demonstrates the key techniques required for success will usually accompany the analysis, so that management is reasonably assured, that the proposal can achieve its goals. Previous to the review, the strategy that is driving the company should be reviewed to determine if the new product is consistent with previous direction. If not, the review should have representation of senior management. The requirements definition review should provide the following major analyses to the extent necessary to minimize risk:

1. A program/product requirements analysis, approved by the requirement definition team, that clearly and concisely identifies and defines the family of requirements. These are defined to a reasonable level to limit "else conditions" in order to identify the product, network, or service. This extends the initial conceptual requirements to become the "living" requirements definition document. It is a base line document containing features/requirements, condition action statements, performance objectives, limits, maintenance requirements, growth and sizing objectives, dependencies, support objectives, interface requirements, device or technique dependencies, human-machine interaction requirements, cost objectives, environment requirements, packaging requirements, and priority recommendations.
2. Marketing and technology key feasibility studies are performed to ensure that both are adequately understood and resolved. These consist of mar-

ketplace analysis of user needs, future user needs, competitive products, competitive future products, environment shifts, social, financial, economic, and sales projections, as well as technology analysis of techniques, trends, tools and methods, technical architectures, structures, devices, and feasibility studies.

3. Financial analysis (general and very limited) of proposed development, manufacturing, operations, and support impact considerations are identified for subsequent product definition phase investigation, such as manufacturing support requirements, product engineering requirements, manufacture tools requirements, testing requirements, cost versus sales analysis, profit and loss analysis, buy versus make analysis, manufacturing and development overall cost objectives, support cost objectives, training cost objectives (user, manufacture, and field support), spares cost objectives, potential user documents and support tools costs, and pricing strategies.

4. A Product Definition Phase Plan for completing the next phase of analysis, such as: Methodology; Resources; Schedule; Supporting Studies; and Projected Phase Results.

5. Future studies and investigations authorized by management to be performed in parallel with the next phase or before entering the next phase are identified and committed.

6. Review report containing a Go- No Go decision with reasons for go, delay or termination, for later historical reference or reconsideration.

In looking at the Product Planning Life Cycle phases, Fig. 2-1, after products are developed, it is important to realize that the two subsequent phases are really an extension of the planning requirements definition phase. For in these phases we determine if we did achieve the envisioned products, networks or services, that meet our initial requirements. These phases are:

QUALIFICATION PHASE

The first article off the production line is put on what is sometimes called a "beta" test site, which is a friendly real environment feasibility test. At this point, the product should be tested to ensure that it does indeed meet the requirement specification. It is not a destructive test, but an operational test. Here, the environment is somewhat controlled to exercise the product in a manner that will verify its key operational objectives. Even though it is a friendly environment, it is sometimes called by many designers a hostile environment. It is the first non-laboratory, real world test. Considerable time should be left in the design schedule to reconsider portions of the design, as further details or new requirements may be redefined, as a result of these tests.

BENEFIT ANALYSIS

After the product has become operational, a periodical benefit verification phase should be entered to ensure that the product is still meeting the initial requirements and objectives. Too often, the reliability and performance objectives are never fully verified or officially revisited, until the product is deteriorating. Then, there is usually only the option of considering the termination of the product because its job is completed. Alternatively, a benefit analysis could be periodically performed during the operation. From this analysis, the preliminary design phase is logically (not physically) revisited in which new requirements are added to the still "living" requirements document and subsequently implemented in the design. Later, when it is determined that the requirements cannot be economically achieved to meet a changed environment, the need for a new product is clearly established.

The following is a list of observations and activities performed during the benefit verification phase, which, as noted, is "a periodic look" as an extension of the Requirement Definition Phase:

- Benefit data is collected from operational logs
- Earlier benefit models are utilized to analyze the data
- New benefit models may need to be developed
- Benefits are carefully reviewed and verified against original projections
- Recommendations can be made for changes or new requirements
- Marketplace and internal programs' are monitored against performance of existing program's operational results to identify obsolescence.
- If results indicate, a return to major strategy or new conceptual planning can be performed or the program may be terminated.
- Periodic operational review for benefits will readily indicate problems and inconsistencies that must be resolved
- New research and development can draw upon this analysis to provide more effective products
- Operational analysis should be continuously performed "On Line" with direct operational data
- Log performance record should be carefully monitored and reviewed for problems, changes, features required, as well as the operational results of new features
- Periodic exit to and from the benefit verification phase during peak and stable operational periods is required to ensure desired benefits are being achieved

This results in an orderly program from requirements to an operating Network, Product or Service with the right analysis and limited surprises.

FLOW CHART: REQUIREMENTS PLANNING

Once the conceptual plans are acceptable to management, before the project begins, there should be a complete analysis and definition of the product requirements, with some form of technical feasibility analysis performed to support the requirements to understand better the technical restraints, dependencies, performance, cost, and maintenance objectives. These anal-

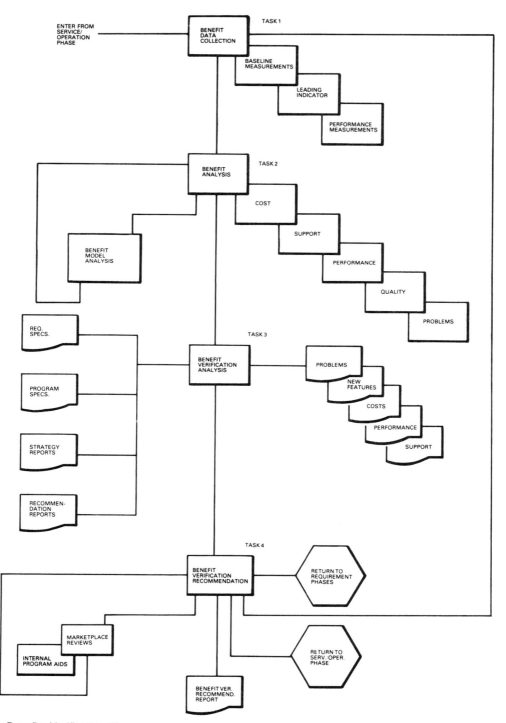

Fig. 4-10. Benefits Verification Phase.

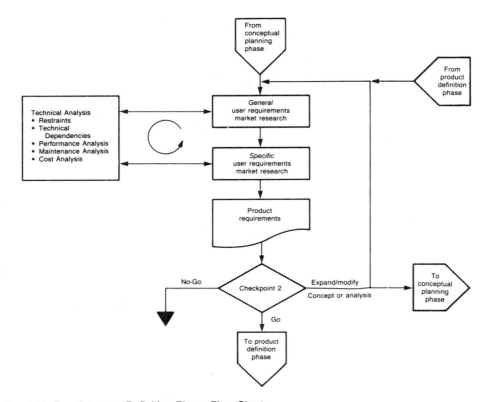

Fig. 4-11. Requirements Definition Phase Flow Chart.

yses should establish the requirements for the general overall operation, such as performance, maintenance, and packaging, as well as the user features that must be provided to be successful in the marketplace.

- Enter Phase From: Conceptual planning or product definition;
- Basic Objectives: To define operational and performance requirements, that the product must meet as well as user/customer features it must provide;
- Dependencies: Top level directives, market trends, technology trends, competition, regulation, financial, standards, available technology to be used at time of manufacture or service;
- Personnel Skills: Conceptual planners, market researchers, system planners, hardware/software requirement specialists, specific technology specialists, manufacturing specialists, human factor specialists;
- % Calendar time of Life Cycle: 5% to 15%;
- % Cost of Life Cycle: 5% to 10%;
- Analysis Considerations: Usability, integrity, efficiency, correctness, reliability, maintainability, flexibility, changeability, adaptability, testability,

modifiability, completeness, marketability, cost, security, privacy, confidentiality, risk, practicality, and human factors;

- Tools and Methods: flowgraphs, decision systems, P. and E., structured analysis, data analysis, interactive information retrieval systems, formal specification languages, configuration management tools;
- Exit Criteria: Requirements reflecting target user req., practical set of performance objectives, future feature objectives, reliability/maintainability objectives, cost/feature objectives, concurrence by management product review board;
- Phase Outputs: Product requirements definition (commercial specifications), interface control documents, requirements matrix, product definition phase implementation plan, approved analyses and plans, for decision report.

FURTHER ANALYSIS

In Chapter 12, case studies contain an excellent application of the requirements phase to the information era by demonstrating the Features World of Information Cubics, Feature Features and ISDN Network Requirements. This is then supported by a detailed ''How'' requirements phase methodology and concluded with a Workshop on *The Trillion Billion Dollar Decision.*

OBSERVATIONS: PENNY WISE AND POUND FOOLISH

1. The requirement definition phase is many times brushed over too lightly, causing design, schedule, cost, sales life, and quality problems.
2. The requirement definition team should consist of many disciplines and be able to delicately balance all their concerns.
3. Requirements will change from ''musts'' to ''coulds'' to ''wishes,'' as technology and cost impacts are considered.
4. Concerns will greatly diminish as technical feasibility studies are performed to validate the possibilities of successfully achieving key requirements.
5. Every hour spent in identifying, understanding, and defining requirements will save five to ten hours during the development phases.
6. The more ''else conditions'' that are defined, the better the product.
7. Big picture analyses, such as the *Information Cubics* are excellent vehicles to more clearly see the forest from the trees.
8. The requirements will challenge the concept, which will challenge the strategic direction. This will result in better identification and definition of products of the lines of businesses. These become the basis for strategic plans, which are more consistent with the strategic direction and the mission of the firm.
9. The requirements definition phase is one of the three natural locations for interfacing and interlacing the other planning, product, technology, market and research life cycle processes.
10. Entering the requirement phase from one particular process will enable it to drive other interlinking processes.

Chapter 5

Top Down Planning:
Product Definition Phase

This phase achieves the top level and functional level definition of the product, and the program to develop and support it. In today's highly complex technical arena, it is virtually impossible to economically build proper products in the traditional manner of jumping in with a couple of technologists and watching helplessly, as the product "grew and grew until it is gruesome." In the mid 80s, numbers peaked at one billion dollars for the product development of a particular firm's network switching product. Late to the market with limited sales, it did not achieve a reasonable return on this R&D investment, causing a write off, lowering a dividend to the stockholders, resulting in the eventual sell off of the manufacturing unit. Obviously, this practice will be less and less acceptable in the future.

One of the reasons for the high cost of high technology was noted by a professor of a database management course, as he exclaimed to his class, "Lists will rule the world." (Fig. 5-1) He may indeed be correct. The software that structures, accesses, controls, and processes these lists is becoming more and more complex and expensive, as we move deeper into our dependency on programming to control all aspects of our daily life. It has been said that three out of four programmers support past projects. It has also been noted that the reuse of previous modules (stored and used by other designers) has enabled Japanese programmers to generate five times more than the amount of software code of American programmers.

All aspects of these issues must now be considered in terms of the planning process, as the process establishes the requirement's architecture, struc-

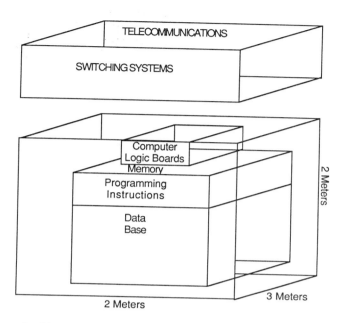

Fig. 5-1. Programming Lists Will Rule The World.

ture, functional, and sub-functional design of the product. Appropriate reviews, team approaches, participating management, logical product life cycle and formal planning phases can help bridge the reusable code gap, reduce the number of support programmers, and make the product more adaptable for change.

There is a need for a new approach to structure the product, be it a network, system, subsystem device, or service, as well as to define the program and resources to achieve it *before* the product is committed to development. Too often, 30 to 600 people are prematurely put on a project, where too much time is wasted and work overlapped, as they attempt to determine what they should build and how.

This phase is the final planning effort before launching the product into its development. It gives management a clear understanding of what they will get for their investment. It will enable a technical evaluation of the requirement's architecture to meet the full range of objectives and strategies, before commitment to development.

WHAT MEETS WHAT REQUIREMENTS?

Traditionally, the product definition phase consists of a small team, performing a two week to two month product proposal that is a reasonable attempt to meet basic features of the future product. This, together with projected costs, development resources and schedule, complete the product's "system level" analysis. Once the project is initiated and staffed, this analysis becomes the basis for beginning the preliminary design.

Usually, the product's design schedule does not leave time to reassess a premature launching. Project management is committed to meeting schedule milestones and staffing the project. If, midway into the detailed design, the architecture and structure are seriously challenged to meet a major requirement, performance, or cost objective, a great number of work hours will be lost, while a smaller group attempts to get the design back on track. The only chance of success, in the past, has been due to the tremendous effort by design teams and their expertise in having done something like it before for a previous company or project. In today's new environment of intense change in both requirements and technology, the product definition phase enables a deeper and longer analysis. In the earlier phases, considerable time is spent determining the requirements and their feasibility. In this phase, considerable effort will be spent in identifying the best architecture and structure upon which to base the design. This may require further clarifying and prioritizing of the requirements, as well as interactively modifying the design to meet a specific requirement feature or limit for performance, cost, and manufacturing.

To take one example: In 1963 a product team of an aerospace company spent over a year assessing the requirements for a new missile and structuring the design around a new device yet to be made, called an "Integrated Circuit," before committing the company to an extremely tight design schedule. It missed some of its interim milestones, but very successfully met the last one—the test launch. The overall project, including the nine month product definition phase, was performed in less time than earlier projects of the same magnitude with less complexity. At all points during the project's development, program management were more cognizant of the progress of the design. There were no surprises, the company made a great deal of money on the cost-incentive milestone-driven contract. It was so successful, that the program director received a new home as a bonus for his effective management.

Since that time other major companies have gone to the more extensive product definition phase, using the product team approach for planning and developing their more complex and volatile products.

This form of more extensive analysis should be performed to the extent necessary to reasonably reduce the risk to an acceptable level for management. On well-defined non-complex programs, the need for a long tedious study is considerably less than for complex new systems using new specialized VLSI technology, with very sophisticated software programs, or even systems that integrate complex existing systems, such as the "Sergeant York" multi billion dollar tank, which was cancelled after billions had been spent on R&D, where they ran research in parallel with development.

As noted earlier, we may have entered the planning process from either the marketing side, where an identified need is looking for a technical solution, or from the technical side, where a technology is looking for a market application. At this point, the need and solution must be truly understood in terms of each other. Too often we have seen a slight variance in the solution, as the need was not fully understood, causing the resulting situation to become worse than the original one. Many times the supposed *tool* has become the uncompromising *master,* where people become slaves to the computer. Instead of the computer being a help, it becomes a hindrance.

Further investigation may be necessary to clarify, change, delete and add to the requirements, as we consider various solutions in the form of architectures and structures. This is the period to analyze the trade off of potential designs and solutions for various requirements in terms of performance, cost, manufacturing feasibility, and support considerations. It is the time to determine, what is the "right product" for the "right market." If this is seriously addressed now, then the design will not be allowed, as noted earlier, to "grow until gruesome."

It is in a way analogous to building a house. During the strategic planning phase, you make the decision to build a home, perhaps, for a "ball park" amount of dollars. During the conceptual planning phase, the house takes on a general shape, as market analyses offer a range of ideas and costs. During the requirement definition phase, the details of the home, such as the type of kitchen, bathroom etc., are defined in terms of possible products. The concept becomes more and more specific, as the house begins to take on a definite shape. Finally in the product definition phase, the architect, having worked off a few feasibility sketches, does the first pass in designing a specific house for a specific lot, taking advantage of the slope of the lot to drop the garage to the basement level, in order for the room over it to become the family room, or, if on a level lot, to provide the garage at the main level and make the room above the garage a bedroom, etc.

Here, its potential appliances and materials costs can be estimated to determine the bottom line figure. In this manner various "musts" from the requirements phase are changed to negotiable "coulds," while some "coulds" are left to the world of "wishes," as the builder gives his cost estimates for the possible architectures and structures. In this process, the house concept, requirements, architecture and structure are now developed to the point where you and your builder can concentrate on how he plans to build the house. Now you must make the "go, no-go" decision to commit or not commit to building the house. Over subsequent design phases you can further determine what features from the "could" and "wish" lists you may decide to have at what new costs . . .

Here we see the methodology for taking the time to understand the impact of the various requirements, and if necessary, acquiring supporting market research. Many times, a particularly complex requirement may have a drastic impact on the architecture of a product. In past developments, some more complex requirements may have been omitted or only been roughly addressed to be solved later. Instead, each major requirement should be challenged in this type of preproject definition phase. If it turns out to be important, then the structure must provide for it. Later, we do not have the time to redesign for it, with the result that it would be left out for later versions.

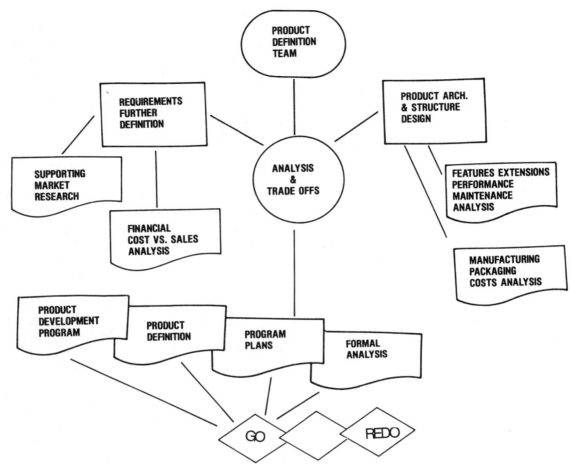

Fig. 5-2. Product Definition Phase.

For example, the digital communication channel synchronization technique, for moving voice in the new pulse coded mode, did not fully resolve the movement of information that contained random all zeros patterns of data, even though it was known that these data patterns could destroy the synchronization of the movement. As a result, a new network, in the late 80s, had to be overlaid to handle data in the "clear channel" 64 kilobit digital mode.

Similarly, manufacturing, maintenance, and operational support must be considered early in the design of the architecture and detailed structuring of the product. How many of us have thrown away an electronic "widget" because it drained the portable batteries too quickly—causing expensive replacement costs? Or a car whose engine was so crammed that it could not be repaired without removing everything? Over the years, both camps (manufacturing and field) have challenged previous designs, crying to the wilderness, that had they only been asked at the beginning, they would have ensured that it would have been designed this way or that.

Historically, how many times have suppliers seen a system evolve during the preliminary design phase to a design, in which one portion has an inordinate amount of work to perform over another, or where one subsystem is controlling the entire system from too low a level? On the other hand, we have seen systems divided into functional units, but subsequently found that distributing the work was impractical, causing the functional units to be reconfigured again and again, as the design developed throughout the detailed design and implementation phases. Similarly, the question of commonality between two different system designs has many times been a difficult goal, with each trying to use this or that of each other, as the systems are designed and redesigned. Also, the problem of changing interfaces of multiple new devices and systems over the life of a product has many times caused a premature shortening of a product's life cycle. Today, both the providers and suppliers have found the added problem of positioning a system in a network and continuously overlaying numerous new features from the integrated voice, data, and video worlds, as new possibilities are required.

Many of the above problems occur or are further complicated by not having the right architecture or the appropriate structure to achieve the goals and objectives, or by having the wrong goals and objectives. Furthermore, as systems became more of a blur between functions performed in hardware or software, we must have more uniformity across both these fronts. We have all seen systems with a good hardware architecture, but sloppy and inconsistent software, which causes great inefficiencies. This becomes more and more serious, as the capability of "physically distributing" portions of telecommunication and data processing systems becomes a major requirement. This adds another complexity to the problem as data processing systems have more front end, remote processing, and local—remote database manipulations, while telecommunications decomposes into networks of central and remote units of totally distributed nodal point systems. As we further consider the functions performed in the telecommunication systems and data processing systems, we see that they now have only a few differences, such as multi path control, multi user processing control, and complex mathematical operations. As time develops, we will see each take on the functions of the other, causing an eventual total integration of the two.

The two worlds of communication and processing have collided, integrating functions, using common technology to perform similar tasks and subtasks. See Fig. 5-3.

Both systems use logic elements from CMOS, I²L, Gallium Arsenide devices, motherboards of 8 to 16 multilayers, cables and connectors. All systems use computer chips, such as 8085, 8086, 8080, 8600 processors, memory devices such as; 64K, 256K, 1-4 meg memory chips, floppy disks, hard disks, digital disks, tape drives, CRT's, keyboards and printers, etc.

Information for both worlds will be either digital voice, digital data, or digital video, in the form of numbers moving down pulse code modulated

Network Switching/Transmission Systems

1. Terminals (phones, or data sets), to interface to system units . . .
2. Processors to receive incoming instructions . . .
3. Processors to search internal memories for routing instructions . . .
4. Processors to translate data to determine routing of call . . .
5. Processors to control a connection across a matrix of possible paths . . .
6. Matrix of possible paths (originally analog, presently digital, future packet and channel wideband) . . .
7. Software to monitor system for error conditions, software to diagnose error locations and recover by inserting standby processors, memories or new programs . . .
8. Data Packet Systems to move information to a central computer to receive, analyze and search for illegal conditions or update databases with new instructions and interface to various protocols . . .
9. Databases which define customer or office dependent information . . .
10. Modems to combine information so more than one customer can share facilities . . .
11. Facilities to move more and more information, gigabits instead of kilobits, as information needs expand and expand, as technology capabilities expand and expand—obsoleting older devices . . .
12. Keyboards, printers and CRTs to input and output from the system to give and receive various instructions . . .
13. Cross connect systems to enable different users to connect to different systems, providing different features . . .
14. Billing systems to monitor usage and bill customer . . .

Data Processing Systems

1. Data terminals, CRTs, keyboards and printers to interface to the computer to provide and receive information . . .
2. Processors to search for incoming instructions or poll terminals for packets of data . . .
3. Processors to compile code to direct a system of computers to use instructions and act on data . . .
4. Processors to execute instructions, reference database information and store new data . . .
5. Processors to control the sending and receiving of information to local and remote printers or databases, using greater wideband facilities . . .
6. Processors to monitor the operation for error, software to locate the faulty module and recover the system by switching processors, back up memories or remote systems to make data processing systems operational . . .
7. Data Packet Switches to move information to a centrally located computer maintenance center to access, analyze and search for illegal conditions, update databases, or provide new versions of operational/maintenance software . . .
8. Multiplexors, modems, concentrators to send and receive information to internal front end processors within an office complex or remote complex of single or multiple customers . . .
9. Protocols and code interfaces, that translate to internal protocols and codes . . .
10. Local area network interfaces to move information within a complex of building(s) at higher and higher megabit rates for high usage groups utilizing systems providing specific features
11. Clusters of memory devices to file information . . .
12. Billing equipment to monitor usage and bill customer . . .

Fig. 5-3. Tel Systems Versus DP Systems Chart.

(PCM) fiber optics or T type facilities, being manipulated by software in distributed central processing systems using data from database systems.

Both will provide numerous features, as customers demand more versatility in the future to have the systems provide many things to make life a little bit easier.

Today, systems are becoming more and more parts of a network, networks are becoming parts of layered networks, and devices are becoming parts of a system. Each becomes interrelated with the others. On top of all this, the suppliers have the new demands of the new users and their providers. They must ask them what they will really need or will buy. No longer can we rush the proposal of a general system to meet a vague requirement. Technology is too much of a micro-micro dot design, costing mega bucks to redesign. Software is now too complex, in some cases causing small armies of programmers to write and rewrite code, having various nebulous degrees of quality, requiring subsequent rework and extensive documentation with little reusability. Software costs are now 85%(some say 90%) of new development costs and 75% of support costs. Telecommunication systems that were achieved for 40 million dollars in the early 70s are costing 400 million dollars or more in the 80s. However, from all this change and pain has come some extremely interesting and exciting proven techniques, that if performed "early" in a product's life cycle, will greatly improve the quality, schedule, and costs of the development and operating phases. Hence, the need to perform a top down analysis, before the network, system, product, device, or service is committed to development or purchase, in order to truly understand what best meets initial and future requirements, justifies a more extensive effort! So let's take that deeper look.

WHAT ARCHITECTURE?

The architecture of a particular network or product line becomes an integral part of the firm's business-of-the-business plans, which in time become the strategic plans of the company, affecting the strategy of the strategy. We have seen where GM bought out EDS and later Hughes for approximately 5 billion dollars in a strategic effort to bring high technology to both the architecture of new automobile designs, as well as to its manufacturing plants. Their intent was to use robotics together with extensive information networks, enabling GM to become a "showplace" U.S. manufacturing firm. ITT bet its future (and fortune) in the telecommunication world on the design of its System 12 architecture, AT&T is moving to their universal network. Even the firms which have not established their particular "architectural trade mark" upon which they base their products, networks, and services, tell the world what they are by its conspicuous absence. No longer are reviews of products on an individual, stand-alone basis favorably received, if they do not tie into a higher order of evolution and offerings, such as Century 21, Network 2000, Universal Service, Network of the Intelligent Universe, the Information World, or the Dynamic Network Architecture.

A network, system, or product architecture should set the tone, direc-

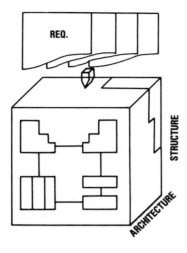

Fig. 5-4. Product Architecture/Structure
Per Requirements.

tion, boundaries, time frames, extensions, interrelationships, growth, over-lays, and bases upon which to structure particularly attractive facets of future offerings. Since all devices, subsystems, systems, and even services have be-come part of a network architecture, let us take a look at what a network architecture establishes:

- Basic boundary conditions
- Features and capabilities
- Guiding principles
- Framework for network structure
- Identifies standards
- Layers of structural levels
- Functions performed at each layer
- Performance characteristics and interface requirements
- Relationships of other network layers
- Definition of network components
- Movement and positioning of control information
- Ability to adapt to the various subsystems
- Plans for evolution to merge with other networks
- Specifics of the network   .
- Uniqueness and advantages
- Image it conveys and needs it meets
- Ability to determine status and reconfigure
- Types of subsystems and products
- Dependencies on designs, components and programs

Some have said that a network architecture should be a living entity able to take on a life of its own. In actuality, few reach this position, but would be content to achieve the distinction of being building blocks for future net-works. The resulting network should be identified in terms of a few big pic-

120

ture views, goals, and objectives, with a list of attributes and characteristics defining its right for life. To be effective, a network architecture should be designed to enable particularly favorable arrangements of unique features that offer timely flexibility and growth, and that can be economically and easily achieved.

As we look at various telecommunication architectures and structures to better understand this description, we see in the case studies an ISDN architecture model of an integrated voice data video network of distributed systems, using common wideband fiber optic, and digital interconnecting facilities. Its key goal is to provide in the future a universal plug, from which the user can generate and receive voice, data, text, image, still video and motion video information. Specific objectives for accessing various information channels are defined in the ISDN Case Study, using different levels of interfaces, standards, and protocols. Similarly, levels or layers of work partitions and boundaries have been identified, as well as maintenance and support objectives for billing and network control for various types of feature packages. It is then left to the individual suppliers and providers to selectively define their specific network and product line's architecture and structure to support this model.

Working within the network architecture are the various specific architectures, such as; that of a local area network, a telecommunication switching system or a data processing system. These more specific architectures will meet the high level network goals and objectives best, by first identifying a particular "open architecture" framework on which to interface their unique hardware and software structure.

First identifying a telecommunication switching system architecture's basic objectives is essential to segmenting the work in terms of functional areas and interfaces, for example an architecture that can:

1. Accommodate a wide range of users to 50,000, where in actuality over 1,000,000 users may be achievable.
2. Be cost effective at the lower end of 1000 users and grow in modular cost units, as size advances.
3. Ease customer design engineering to simplify packaging of features and options.
4. Enable new technology to easily be integrated into the design, as processors and memory power advances.
5. Distributed control, in terms of functional system distribution of each process's particular functions, where each processor performs a portion of the exchanges' overall operation, or in which each processor has a specific role in the hierarchy relationship with other processors.
6. Enable a variable bandwidth network, under customer control, in which the network is virtually non blocking.
7. Provide for several levels of maintenance from replacing cards to reconfigurating systems from remote or centrally located maintenance centers.
8. Exchange administration, traffic, and maintenance data with automated

operational support systems.

9. Standardize hardware and software interfaces in functional areas, using such concepts as "virtual" hardware and software.
10. Enable the overlay and subsequent integration of data and video information.

To meet a few of these objectives, a digital voice network configuration was established in the late 70s, where facilities were integrated with switches, becoming a multi-nodal point mapping of switches and facilities on topographical clusters of central offices, within a serving area. However, it was recognized at the time as being one of several needed architectures and would initially only apply to the rural or suburban environment with subsequent architectures for the metro environment of the future information world.

This architecture formed the basis for upgrading the telecommunication plants in the 1980 to 1995 time frame to digital, where voice analog frequencies were changed to number patterns and sent in binary form over this more error-free facility. Since the facilities are moving voice in the form of numbers, they are available, as a basis, to add data (kilobits of numbers) and video (megabits of numbers) to become a more integrated offering. This then was the architecture to meet the needs of the rural and suburban users, as a basis for a new family of digital voice switching systems. Later overlaid on them would be data and video functions, as indicated in the ISDN system architecture model, noted in the ISDN case study of Chapter 12. It was next used in

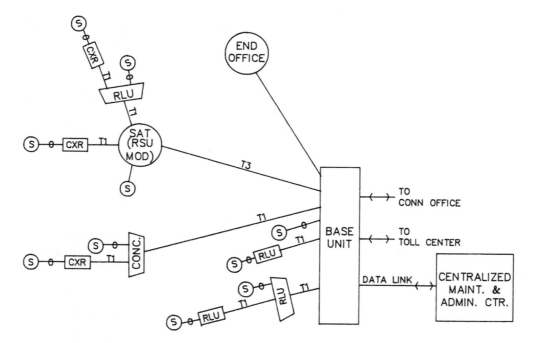

Fig. 5-5. Rural/Suburban Switching Systems.

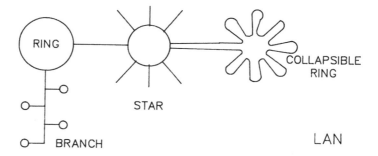

Fig. 5-6. LAN.

the metro arena to handle growth and enable digital fibers to be introduced into the local plant.

Similarly, local area network (LAN) architectures have been formed, based upon the ring, star, and branch configurations, where rather than being switched, users can exchange information and access databases via 2-20 megabit wide band facilities using different forms of modems (modulators/demodulators of data), concentrators, and contention systems for accessing available channels. Each terminal on the network has a unique identification to automatically receive and retrieve its information.

As time passes, local area networks within a multi-tenant building or on a college campus will tie to larger area networks (50 + Megabits) called Metro Area Networks (MANs), or Wideband Area Networks (WANs) and will integrate with private branch exchanges, business serving modules, or central switching systems to provide the best of both worlds, forming the type of configuration shown in Fig. 5-7.

WHAT STRUCTURE?

Indeed, many such models have been developed for local area networks

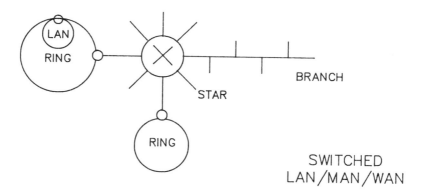

Fig. 5-7. Switched LAN.

123

or internally physically distributed designs, where facilities are integrated with switches, distributing portions of the switch, throughout a particular serving area. The high level architecture of the network of subsystems and devices is resolved by further partitioning the work and defining the sub programs. This leads us to the most optimum structure, upon which to segment both hardware and software designs.

Over the years, various hardware and software structures have merged, suggesting a new family of possibilities, as technology provides more and more processor power and inexpensive large memory devices. This enables programs to be written in higher level languages with more processor capacity available for message exchange, as work is further partitioned and functionalized. We have at our disposal such techniques as finite state machines, finite message modules, virtual hardware, virtual software, virtual processors, virtual databases, extensive communication buses, operating systems, and control languages for specific areas, such as list processing, database management, as well as menu and procedure oriented human-machine interactions. All of these become the building blocks for new system designs.

These vehicles establish a specific configuration basis, upon which the hardware and software interrelate, and in which various entities are hidden from each other, so that modular growth can provide extensions, changes and additions transparent to the user or higher levels of the software. Here change does not affect the levels above it. It also enables, from a designer point of view, interface boundaries to be established, enabling levels of work to be designed and tested in parallel and then integrated at these boundaries. Hence, hierarchical hardware structures (Fig. 5-8) are complemented with layered software structures (Fig. 5-9) using top down structured analysis.

Here for example, as noted in a past trade article on fully distributed system structures, the main system functions are derived from generic specifications and arranged in a hierarchy:

System functions are decomposed into subfunctions, then these subfunctions, in turn, are decomposed into further subfunctions and so on, until we finally arrive at basic entities, where all entities to these functions are clearly and explicitly defined and documented. The optimum decomposition should minimize the complexity of the resulting subfunctions and provide the simplest interfaces between them. Communication between functions can be achieved directly or through standard procedures depending upon the priority, amount, and complexity of the problem being solved at that particular level, using the following criteria:

- Each subfunction must have a well defined purpose.
- All interfaces should be simple.
- Software must reflect hardware modulability at lower levels.
- Execution speed and memory capacity are of major concern for the total operation of the system.
- The structured, top-down design results in well documented and comprehensible hardware and software. Programming and detailed design are carried out only after the function is defined, designed and its working interfaces have

Fig. 5-8. Top Down Structured Levels — Hardware.

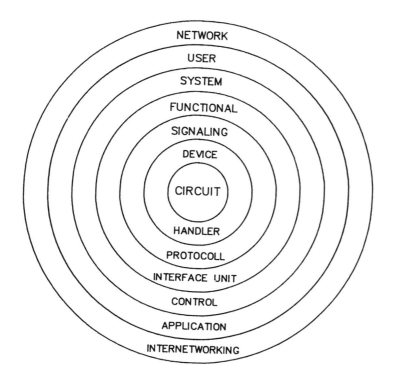

Fig. 5-9. Top Down Structured Layers — Software.

been completely determined.

- High level language coding such as CHILL, PL1 and specialized problem oriented languages (LISP), C and A1 can be tailored to the functional and subfunctional models to insure efficiency and accuracy in coding.
- Models can be separately structured to specific user requirements and tested to ensure performance and capacity objectives are met for the specialized features.
- Future features can be considered to ensure that the architectural structure is consistent with long range objectives, or at least to indicate where inconsistencies will exist.

In this manner a hardware module is surrounded by one or more layers of software. Together, the hardware and software become a virtual machine to the programmer. The more complex the task, the more layers, the more intelligent the virtual machine appears. Those working in higher hierarchical levels (the outer layers) do not need to know in detail the implementation of the lower level functions. Thus, an application programmer coding a device handler, where the device handler is the software module associated with a particular hardware device such as a terminal, need not know how the message handler, network handler or operating system function is implemented. Hence, localized changes will only affect one or two functional areas.

Another type of architecture forms a feature driven structure, where primitives are written as a basic set of software modules, which can be collected together using a set of commands to form a software program, tailored to meet a particular customer's needs. These commands form an input language to a compiler, that builds user dependent software, and can be easily written by service providers and not the product suppliers. This architecture has long been a design objective.

A different type of virtual machine is obtained, when the structure accommodates high level languages. Here the programmer sees a machine which understands high level statements, but the microprocessors execute only machine level code. In this case the programs can be written in a language independent of the microprocessor, on which they will run and can be tested "Off Line" at a different location with coding and error trace aids. Finally, the program can be written at a generic level, not machine or application level, by changing its database or adding particular submodules.

These architectures and structures are usually for state driven applications, where various activities are performed to arrive at a given state and depending upon conditions at the time of arrival, the system operation will go to the various other states. Hence, a state flow chart or map can be developed to support the hardware and software structure with a series of decision charts to identify all known user requirements and else conditions, to further define the architecture and structure of the product.

MORE PRECISELY . . .

The above techniques are used to erect various software structures with identified hardware structures, using communication buses that interface data and instructions between subsystems, functional areas and subfunctional areas. They constitute the top level design for the system in terms of the services it may perform. When this is achieved to a satisfactory level to ensure that there will be no surprises during the project development (or system purchase), we have completed the product definition architecture and structural analysis.

The product's architecture must be defined to closely conform with all the requirements to the functional area level, with all major interfaces and protocols identified. Its basic structure should be initially formulated to meet performance, new features, growth, and reliability objectives. The extent and degree of design is subjective. There is a point when the risk is minimized and the feasibility is assured. Then the product's initial architecture is complete. The functional area and sub-functional area design can then be completed later, in the preliminary and detailed design phases.

To advance the design to the detailed level for each functional area, their interfaces and database structures must be fully defined. Areas that do not have this detailed design definition are identified to indicate risk or the need for additional time in the preliminary design phase, later in the development. As the sub-functional areas are extensively further defined, the functional areas are firmed up and completed with minimum restructuring of new boundaries. Chapter 12 case studies give a view of the complexities of the level of definition required for the network architecture, hardware architecture, and hardware and software structures. It demonstrates the need to formalize these architectures and structures to a sufficient level before launching the project, by using a more detailed requirements and product definition phase. In actual practice, in order to achieve these architectural functional and subfunctional objectives, the product definition phase can begin at a reasonable point midway into the requirement phase and be performed together in parallel.

As Fig. 5-10 indicates, the requirement phase must be sufficiently established before the product definition phase. In this manner, the requirement document, completed in the requirement phase, becomes the solid basis for the product definition phase architecture and structure. During the product definition phase, the requirements in this document are further addressed clarified, revised, added, and extended. The requirement documents are then changed accordingly. Thus, it remains a living document throughout the design. However, requirement changes should be less and less, as the design subsequently develops due to cost and schedule impact. After the Preliminary Design Review (PDR) at the end of the preliminary design phase, few if any requirement changes are tolerated. Usually no changes after the Critical Design Review (CDR) near the end of detailed design phase.

Thus there is a need for this predevelopment phase to set down the requirements and provide a logical, top-down design solution, before the project is launched. In this manner, difficult decisions of launching massive projects becomes lessened, as more and more is understood from these planning phases. Of course, as a note to the cynical, balance is needed on the

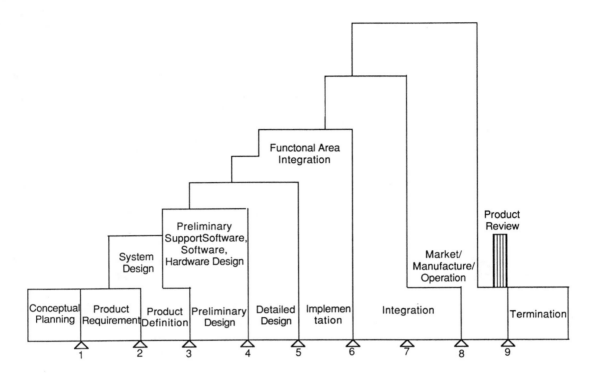

Fig. 5-10. Skewed Phases.

degree and extent of analysis that can be provided at this point, but experience has proven that initially thirty people of a possible 300 person project, can save up to two years of schedule, and achieve a quality project if allowed to perform a 6 to 12 month product definition phase. Of course for small projects this translates to four to six month endeavors by ten to fifteen people. The net result will be to have a top level architecture supported by a top-down structured design to the functional level with major structures pursued to the subfunctional level. Though the functional and subfunctional levels may change in the actual project development, the high level structure will remain solid. In the worse case, if only an acceptable architecture and high level structure are all that are achieved, it would have been enough, because then we appreciate the complexity of the problems left for design to resolve, and we can initially apply the right resources to resolve them.

SCHEDULE, COSTS, QUALITY

During the product definition stage, the quality of design, the cost of the product, and the development schedule are constantly in intense conflict. It is important to identify areas of conflict early in order to enable management to make the appropriate trade-offs, before launching the development, after which these objectives usually attain a "schedule-costs-quality" priority relationship. If the "good will" name of the firm is important, then quality must be built into the design initially rather than added (if possible) on recalls or "field modifications." However, if "anything to meet schedule" is the real priority, this "anything" must be realistically understood in terms of future market, manufacturing, and field support impact. At that point the only planning activity should be to repeat the words "schedule," "cost," and "quality" over and over, until it is understood and accepted that this type of emphasis on design will indeed cause schedule to reduce the quality of the offering.

The case study analysis on the "Pursuit of Quality," provides an alternative approach. As noted in Fig. 5-12, the delicate balance can be achieved between schedule and productivity by using the planning and development processes to obtain a quality product at reasonable costs. These processes enable both management and technical designers to determine how much they will pursue quality objectives in each of the planning and development phases, in terms of allocating the resources and allowing schedule impact. The analysis is quite extensive in showing how the different "quality prisms" representing all the "ilities" (maintainability, reliability, reusability), can be pursued throughout each stage to achieve a supporting array of solid pyramidal structures, upon which to provide the product.

In addition, a ranking algorithm is described for financially relating efforts to achieve different levels of quality objectives across families of products to various degrees. This enables one to say we will pursue quality in this product, or products of this type, with a 70% effort versus a 20% effort for a different type of product. It does not define the quality achieved, but the amount of effort expended to pursue it. This usually becomes a one for one mapping with actual quality achieved. In this manner, quality is truly considered in the design-requirement trade-offs equation and not just given lip ser-

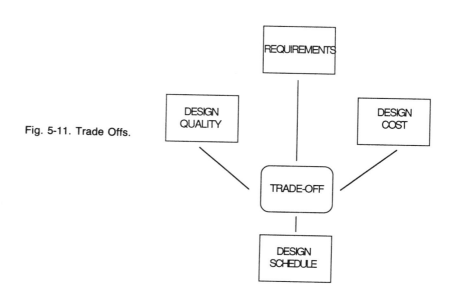

Fig. 5-11. Trade Offs.

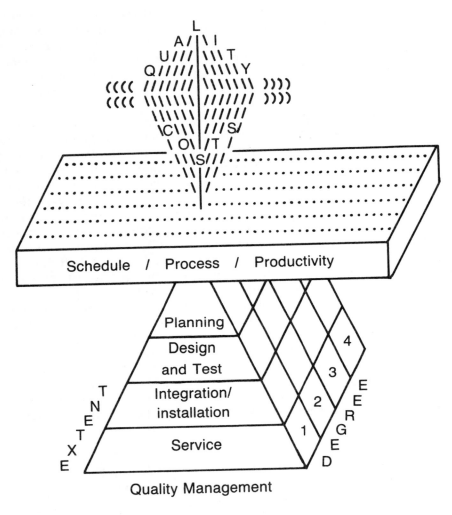

Fig. 5-12. The Delicate Balance.

vice. In the past, quality had simply been a general goal, whose requirements, other than reliability, had never been vigorously pursued in the cost, schedule, and quality trade offs.

In the future, quality will become a network problem, as numerous manufacturers supply products for an "open architecture." Hence, the need to pursue quality across suppliers, providers, and users in forums and working committees in which a series of ISDN U.S. "quality" network objectives and standards are established.

THE PRODUCT TEAM

The success of any project resides in its people. The product definition team should consist of future designers and managers from marketing and systems, who will be affiliated with the project over its life cycle. Thus, the decisions they make during this phase will be their commitments affecting their own future. Their efforts will not be later thrown out or ignored by subsequent new technical development, manufacturing, or marketing teams. In this manner the knowledge gained from this analysis is retained, as much as possible, with the project. Later members will move to other projects in technical or management positions to further apply this knowledge. For example, for the suppliers who will be developing the product, one or more new product team members should represent the various disciplines of programming, system engineering, marketing, conceptual planning, and requirements planning, with support specialists from finance, manufacturing, quality, reliability, field support, etc. As required, support studies in the market and finance areas will be performed, as well as technical feasibility studies by the advanced development labs in programming, computer design, packaging etc.

These product definition teams should be established by both the supplier and provider for determining new networks, products, or services. The providers will work with their future customers, their users, for additional requirements and with their suppliers, for future product designs. In this method they can effectively represent both themselves and their users in establishing new architectures for future endeavors with their suppliers. As providers, they should design their new network and service offering using marketing, network, technical, operations, maintenance, and database support personnel. They must carefully design their offering to the detailed architecture level, with the functional level structures to identify required subsystems. In working with suppliers during either the development or selection phases, they should consider the impact of various supplier's architecture, structure, and subfunctional-level designs on their present and future service requirements. In packet switching, for example, some suppliers are integrating various packet capabilities into their system's present architecture, some have adjunct systems, some are going to different types of future architectures. Thus each type affects performance throughout, for different patterns of customer user input. This effects crucial network architecture throughput, depending on the provider application and the type of users.

The product teams of the suppliers may be seen in Fig. 5-13 where they perform the quality-cost-schedule considerations against the requirements. These product teams of the suppliers and providers will be further discussed in Chapter 7, but are noted here to indicate the need to establish these types of teams, as a normal ongoing activity, prior to the program or project initialization. They will usually cross lines of business, having representatives from each respective planning organization, as well as obtaining a few specialists from a shared central brain trust. These are what were called "system teams" in the aerospace industry.

THE PLAN

Now that the solution has been identified in terms of not only a high level

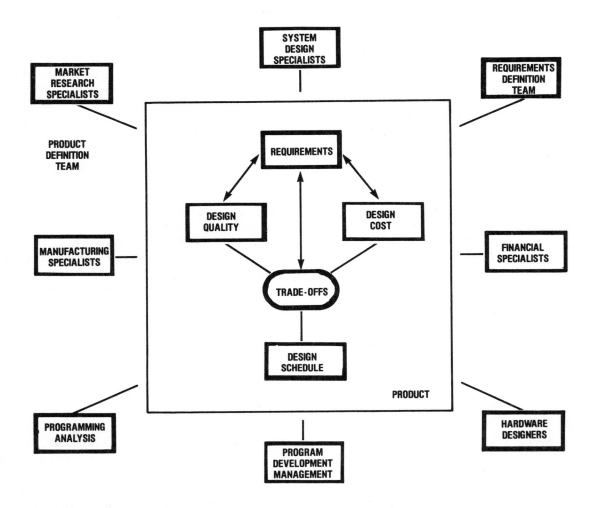

Fig. 5-13. The Product Team.

architecture, but a detailed level functional and subfunctional level structure for the particular network, product, or service, we have the opportunity to appropriately address the next phases of analysis. If it is the selection phase for purchasing an existing product, then we should accompany our recommendation with an implementation plan for using the proposed solution. On the other hand, if we are a supplier about to launch the product, as a new development program, it is time to define the plan of action for achieving this product.

This plan of action has come to be known as the project or development plan, which accompanies the system plan of technical analysis defining the product's architecture and structure. The project plan will define the design/test schedule, people, resources, cross dependencies and work flow for each functional area identified in the system plan. The program plan will define the overall program in terms of the project plan and the system plan. It will also contain the financial plan for the total program expense and revenue picture, together with the marketing plan and manufacturing plan. The market will be identified, as much as possible, per product type, feature, version or family, as well as in terms of entrance, segment, location, position, distribution, time frame, advertising, and schedule.

In the past, this program plan has become quite vague in the pre-development stage, causing difficult trade off decisions by top management, between one program and another. This has been one of the keys to success in Japanese ventures. They have always used extensive front end planning to provide their management with a great deal of information before launching a program. Also, it has been observed that the Japanese are extremely good at perfecting American ideas and packaging them into solid, high-quality products. If we enter our project developments with the type of careful analyses provided by the product definition phase, we will also be able to achieve a good design analysis follow up during the design phases. This has always been missing from U.S. commercial designs. Most designers only have, at most, a short window after integration to redesign aspects which may really only work together as a "cluge" (a design term indicating thrown together). This is a key point of the product definition phase. A double impact is achieved. The designers get a second look at the right point in the design phases, and later, the testing and integration is smoother, because the design is better, causing less rework. Thus we achieve a higher quality product.

We also have the opportunity to obtain a realistic schedule from project management now that the subfunctional building blocks have been identified in terms of interfaces and dependencies. In the past we have been very good at "perting," but not so good at "perting" a realistic program with the right cross dependencies. Once, a telecommunications switch was "perted" with 10,000 nodes, but with only a few cross dependencies, because at the beginning very little was known about the actual architecture. The project group and system management were just "perting" for "perting" sake. Also, the right amounts of resources, the types and disciplines of people and tools is quite questionable, if the architecture and structure is not firm. This many times becomes a crash activity at the commencement of each new project, as management tries to hire new people, while not knowing for sure just how many or what type are needed. On one project the number of maintenance software designers grew from 10 to 60, as the design became more and more identified and complex to meet the reliability objectives.

Three groups, which greatly benefit from all this, aside from the project and technical groups, are marketing, manufacturing, and finance. For the first time, they have had an early input and can watch a product, which they have had a chance to understand from its very beginning, develop under their own eyes, instead of being called in near the end, to build this thing, sell this thing, or provide more money to finish this thing!

ANALYSES

Though this is a planning activity, it is important to establish the planning analyses, as the front end of a program or project development, selection, or purchase. Figure 5-14 demonstrates how the reports from the planning phase, particularly the product definition phase, neatly fit into the supplier's project documentation tree.

The product definition analyses should map back and reference the requirements to ensure that all the features are considered in the design. They should contain the generic architecture document, which identifies the family tree of all subsequent sub-functional area design documents, interfaces, and database documents. These documents are maintained throughout the project by system level designers and are the basis not only for design, but for the PERT schedules, type of resources (people and equipment), and cost projections.

For example, the pricing of telecommunication products may be on a cost per feature basis. This type of requirement-architecture-structure cross-reference will greatly facilitate cost accounting per feature and enable the marketing and grouping of common features. Since the original high level design was initially broken down to the functional and sub-functional level, the high level architecture and structure should survive the second look even when portions of functional and sub-functional structures analysis are redeveloped during the preliminary design. Hence, these documents provide the initial documents for the preliminary and detailed design phases, where the top level, functional, and sub-functional designs are once again aggressively challenged. The results will be much more effective than just having had a general high level brush, as a generalized, simplistic design proposal.

We are now ready for real commitment by those involved in the decision. A great amount of effort has been expended in providing the right information. Management have had three looks at the progress of the analysis, as seen in Fig. 5.15, where ideas have moved from concepts to requirements to design for new products or specifications for purchasing existing products, depending upon a buy versus make decision at this review. For the supplier, part of the output of the system plan is to indicate which portions should be purchased or developed. Hence, the exit review of this phase is a major decision point.

THE DECISION

Eight separate documents (product requirements, product top level architecture, product functional/subfunctional area structure, product development plan, product support feasibility studies, product financial review, product marketing plans, and product manufacturing plans) are provided for review. The review board or decision team consists of top management, representatives of buyer or customer, program management, system management, marketing, finance, strategic planning, and manufacturing, as well as other affected areas such as training, field support, and applied research. This

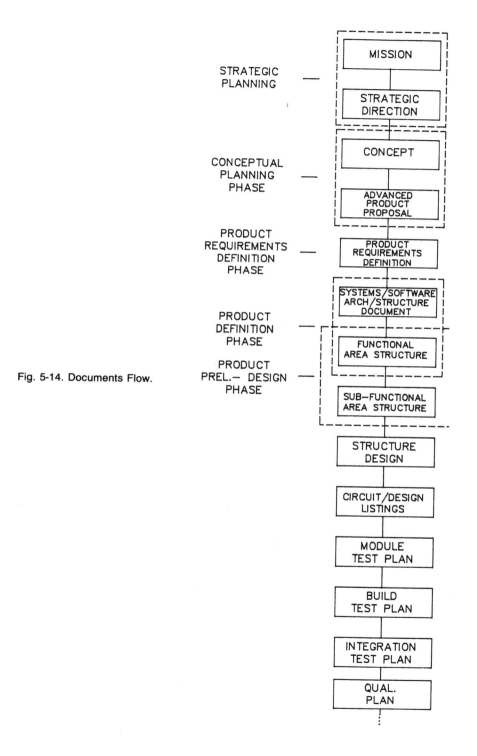

Fig. 5-14. Documents Flow.

STRATEGIC
PLANNING

CONCEPTUAL
PLANNING
PHASE

PRODUCT
REQUIREMENTS
DEFINITION
PHASE

PRODUCT
DEFINITION
PHASE

PRODUCT
PREL.— DESIGN
PHASE

MISSION

STRATEGIC
DIRECTION

CONCEPT

ADVANCED
PRODUCT
PROPOSAL

PRODUCT
REQUIREMENTS
DEFINITION

SYSTEMS/SOFTWARE
ARCH/STRUCTURE
DOCUMENT

FUNCTIONAL
AREA STRUCTURE

SUB—FUNCTIONAL
AREA STRUCTURE

STRUCTURE
DESIGN

CIRCUIT/DESIGN
LISTINGS

MODULE
TEST PLAN

BUILD
TEST PLAN

INTEGRATION
TEST PLAN

QUAL.
PLAN

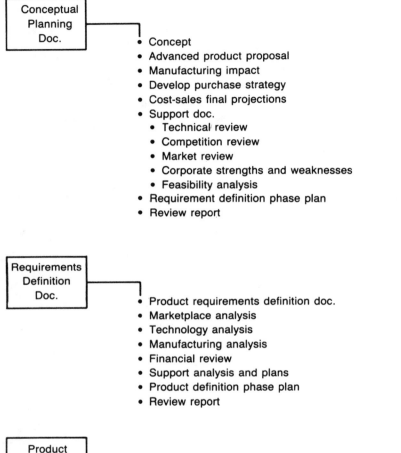

Conceptual Planning Doc.

- Concept
- Advanced product proposal
- Manufacturing impact
- Develop purchase strategy
- Cost-sales final projections
- Support doc.
  - Technical review
  - Competition review
  - Market review
  - Corporate strengths and weaknesses
  - Feasibility analysis
- Requirement definition phase plan
- Review report

Requirements Definition Doc.

- Product requirements definition doc.
- Marketplace analysis
- Technology analysis
- Manufacturing analysis
- Financial review
- Support analysis and plans
- Product definition phase plan
- Review report

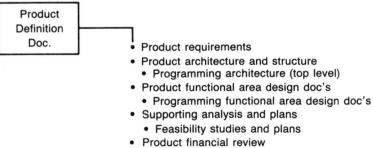

Product Definition Doc.

- Product requirements
- Product architecture and structure
  - Programming architecture (top level)
- Product functional area design doc's
  - Programming functional area design doc's
- Supporting analysis and plans
  - Feasibility studies and plans
- Product financial review
- Product marketing plans
- Product manufacturing plans
- Product development plans
- Review report

Fig. 5-15. Planning Analyses

product definition design review is the first of four major design reviews of the product's design. Each of the subsequent design reviews, the preliminary design review (PDR), the critical design review (CDR), and the qualification review (QR) covers the design to a deeper extent with different emphasis. It is a key top management decision point. The first being the strategic direction, then the approval of the conceptual plan. Next, depending on complexity, they may or may not have participated in the requirements strategy decisions, but they must now review those decisions in terms of the proposed solution, against their strategic direction. Now is the time for their "go, no-go" decision.

FINANCE

Financially, we now are at a point of commitment. Up to now it has only been an exercise for the marketing and technical people. Finance has only had to commit to funding market research, product definition design, feasibility tests and analyses to minimize the risk of the venture. They may have developed various mathematical models of projected results, but now is the time to seriously address their concerns of revenue loss and profits in terms of trade offs of the various requirements with specific architectures. It is time for the traditional financial bottom line reviewers to begin playing the new game differently in the early innings. It is a new world for finance, as they become players instead of judges, but it will be a world in which all will benefit from their involvement. The game will take on an added dimension, as more realistic financial impact considerations are tied to technical and marketing possibilities. However, it is an addition which can make the game more interesting, effective, and fun, or it can make it difficult, impossible, ineffective, and miserable.

For this reason, marketing and technical planners have been reluctant to bring in and involve financial planners in the past. Many financial types have attempted to divorce themselves from the realities of the marketplace, requiring unrealistic market revenue projections, justified to impossible levels, before commitment. This has the result that they were left to remain in a world of vague cost estimates and fantastic market revenue projections for the first year of production or offering. In the Telco environment this is called the "Connect and Collect" mentality. Connect a telephone to the network and collect monthly revenues. For each phone connected, X amount of average revenues can be projected. However, the marketplace is no longer a connect and collect (monopolistic) provider environment or make and sell (captive buyer) supplier domain. We now have the third dimension—the competitive marketplace and its fickle users, the unknown variables. What do they really want? What will they really buy? When will they really buy it?

It is time to bring knowledgeable, reasonable, financial considerations into the product decision. Risk must be addressed. Risk must be faced, accepted, discounted or discredited in the decision. Later, all involved should review the benefits of their decisions in terms of what has happened due to "no-go" considerations, as well as "go" considerations. For example, up to the mid 80s, telecommunications switching offices were replaced as new technology offered new advantages to more economically handle growth, maintenance, and operational features. For these reasons, suppliers and providers built and replaced electro-mechanical systems in an orderly manner, as the life of a switching system changed from a forty year life to a twelve year life.

It was left to the financial people to address depreciation rates and replacement costs, as well as capital programs to manufacture, operate and support these systems. However, with the breakup of Bell companies, both the suppliers and providers have emerged into the competitive arena of the multinational-multiunit world, where Siemens, Ericsson, IBM, and other such companies have survived for many years. It is one where financial decisions have been concerned with:

1. Units meeting the desires of their holding firms in which their expenditures are challenged in terms of what industry can provide the greatest return on investment.
2. Where to place the offering—Which unit can be most effective in the marketplace given present and future political, regulatory, and nonregulatory constraints.
3. The dilemma of obtaining new product lines to make them the bread and butter money machines for the company, replacing those that are under serious attack from the competition.
4. The need to achieve, maintain, or meet the company's mission in terms of its image. For example, how can one maintain the image of having a quality hotel chain, if the customer never knows what type of hotel he will enter? (If the company operates them without quality in remote locations, and with quality in the better locations of some of the major cities?) Sometimes funds have to be spent in order to have a full and consistent product line, where the designated return is not achievable on each product or each remote office. Hence, decisions are tied to the mission for justification, not revenue.
5. Managing lines of business situations, where the dominant, and sometimes ruthless, have gotten what they want and have no product accountability. In a controlled marketplace, there are always those who have controllable expenditures, where return on investment was not really a consideration. In the monopoly or captured customer marketplace they have survived, but in an open marketplace they cannot and must be challenged by financial and strategic planners.

Hence, there is a need for the financial people to aggressively enter the game at the point of the product definition phase, where their suggestions and concerns are seriously addressed. This will also provide them with the opportunity to listen to the real reasons, problems, limits, and boundaries under which the product can be achieved and offered. Using this type of process or methodology, final outcomes, benefits or lack of benefits can be considered for various requirements, architectures and structures.

Better architectures, that last longer, may cost more to last longer!

Hence, this will require financial analysts, planners and management to become manager planners to play the new telecommunication-information game of the 90s by making decisions to position the suppliers and providers in the new information world with a new base, to offer products, networks, and services that meet mission objectives, such as quality without justified return on investment in some instances, in order to maintain the overall image of the firm, to challenge new features to have some revenue considerations but to temper this with the amount of risk and the amount of unknown, to enable the lines of businesses to be accountable, to use a planning process in which all participate in the product definition phase, so they all will appreciate and understand the requirement-architecture trade offs, to be willing to deviate from the process, where necessary, to prematurely launch various products and ventures without the formal activities, but with the ability to monitor and augment with further planning, as situations may develop, to participate on a benefit analysis for determining impact of earlier "go, no-go" decisions, in terms of benefits from provided networks, products, and services, or the lack of them.

Hence, the product definition phase does become the "right" point for bringing together the many "right" disciplines, to come up with the "right" network, service, or product, with the "right" degree and extent of quality. These plans for developing or purchasing the product at this time are much more reasonable and unfortunately more accurate. This will cause management to have to face realistic estimates and not just "funny numbers," that grow and grow over the project. Management must adjust their thinking to realize that these numbers are what they would be getting near the end of the project and that they will not be growing, as those have grown on previous projects. Hence, a project may indicate 500 people of various disciplines peaking to 600 possibly 700, instead of 150 peaking to 225 or possibly 300. Many times, difficult decisions up front make easy decisions later. Sometimes, easy decisions up front make painful decisions later.

Thus we have provided a logical process for addressing the strategic direction, with the right programs for purchasing or building the necessary products, to achieve new networks or services. At this point we have an excellent understanding of the technical design and project resources and schedule considerations, needed to achieve the product in time to obtain a management commitment. These plans should be consistent with the strategic direction or challenge it. They will eventually become part of the business plan, which then becomes part of the strategic plans.

It is the end of the pleasant country road and the beginning of a major highway. It is time for the manager planners to assume the role of umpires and make a call at the plate. Is the player out, or safe? It is time to play the game—real dollars will have to be committed at this point. Due to a more extensive understanding, the decisions will no doubt be for big dollars with little change left over. Later, the projected project costs should decrease, as players, delightfully, find themselves ahead of schedule due to their more thorough top down planning.

> *All the planning is worth it,*
> *if the decision is a good decision...*
> *the right decision..!*

FLOW CHART: PRODUCT DEFINITION PHASE

Once management has given the go ahead for the product definition phase, the talents of many persons are utilized at various times in a group called the product team. They produce two separate documents, that further clarify all aspects of the project, before the firm's major resources are employed. It is a critical stage, because it is at this point that a product is flexible to change, to be molded into something that is marketable, manufacturable, and maintainable. Here the initial cost trade offs of various versions and configurations can be applied to make it truly economical. Similarly, its features and requirements can be fully analyzed and supported technically. This is especially important since the design can be successful, but if the original guidelines are wrong, the final product will not be a financial success.

Hence the "what" and future "whats" from the product requirement definition phase will be defined in accordance with the "how" and future "hows," by the technical analyses performed during this phase. There will be an iterative loop between the "whats" and the "hows" until both issues are mutually resolved in a manner acceptable to management. If the project passes this checkpoint successfully, it is now ready to enter the development process, with its approved project management plan (provided by the project team). See Fig. 5-16.

- Enter phase from: product requirements definition phase.
- Basic objectives: To define the network, system, device, or service, as a feasible response to proposed user needs, which considers all major issues, such as features, cost, etc.
- Dependencies: Available technology to be used at time of manufacture or service, manufacturing capability for both hardware and software, competitiveness of design in the marketplace.
- Personnel skills: Conceptual planners, market researchers, system planners, requirement specialists, technology specialists, hardware/software designers, manufacturing specialists.
- % Calendar time of life cycle: 5% to 15%;
- % Cost of life cycle: 5% to 10%;
- Analysis considerations: Features, performance, usability, integrity, efficiency, correctness, reliability, maintainability, flexibility, changeability, adaptability, testability, modifiability, completeness, marketability, cost, security, privacy, confidentiality, risks, safety, capital, and quality.
- Tools and methods: Simulation models, performance, reliability, cost, flow-

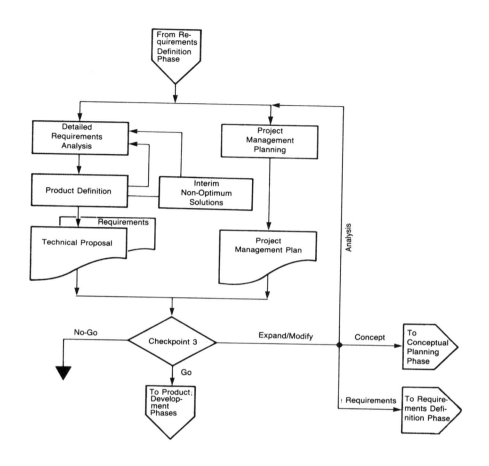

Fig. 5-16. Product Definition Phase Flow Chart.

graphs, decision systems, P. and E., structured analysis, data analysis, interactive information retrieval systems, formal specification languages,
configuration management tools.
- Phase review: Checkpoint 3, management decision point to allow the project to enter development, based upon analyses performed in this phase.
- Exit criteria: Requirements reflecting target user requirements, performance
  objectives, future feature objectives, reliability, maintainability objectives.
  Technical proposal of design architecture, performance analysis, maintenance analysis, cost/feature analysis. Project development plans reflecting costs, people, and support.
- Phase outputs: Product requirements specifications, program plan, technical proposal, development plan, marketing plan, manufacturing plan, test
  specifications, financial plan, and approved projects for further development.

Fig. 5-17. We Should Have Had
A Product Definition Phase!!!

FURTHER ANALYSIS

The Chapter 12 case studies for this material presents a complete view of ISDN, as well as a review of what constitutes a product, together with a detailed methodology on product definition. These analyses are then followed by a workshop on governmental restraints, using an analysis entitled *Who's on First—What's on Second.*

OBSERVATIONS: A NETWORK SOLUTION

1. Devices are becoming sub-systems, sub-systems are becoming systems, systems are becoming networks, networks are becoming functional nodes of a multilayered-nodal-network.
2. Physically distributed multiprocessor structures integrate transmission, switching, terminals, and data processing into a blur of configurations and boundaries.
3. The network architecture has become the critical key element in a firm's strategic strategies, upon which is based its families of products and services from its lines of businesses. Network architecture is now an integral part of a firm's strategic direction.
4. Hardware and software structures and support structures must interface and integrate to facilitate the firm's products, services, and network architectures.
5. Programming costs are now 85% of development and 75% of support. The major reason for this being a poorly addressed product definition phase, with too vague requirement definitions.
6. Preproject analyses in the product definition phase should not only clarify the desired architecture and structure, but identify a realistic supplier project development plan and provider implementation plan, based on achieving the "right" product.
7. The ISDN (Integrated Services Digital Network) international telecommunications model is the basis for "International Top Down Planning" of both technology and the marketplace in terms of user needs.
8. No longer, due to the complexity of the world marketplace, can one firm dominate over others in establishing standard interfaces. System or product interfaces are now dependent upon international network standards.
9. Hardware structures should be partitioned in terms of software layers to make work segments transparent across interfaces to enable ease of design, growth, change, and additions, to create virtual systems.
10. As memory becomes cheaper, processors more powerful, transmission facilities more wideband, features more complex, systems more physically distributed, interfaces more user-friendly, the product definition phase is needed more and more!

Chapter 6

Planning Processes

The preceding chapters have identified several processes and indicated the need for various interrelationships between functional organizations and groups. The marketplace was considered in terms of "User Needs" of various "User Types," across a wide range of "People Types." Over the period of our human existence, various organizations and structures have been erected to encourage and facilitate people's efforts to work together, to achieve great endeavors. This required motivating numerous marketing, technical and management people to exchange ideas and assistance.

Many times we have seen companies reorganize, only to reorganize again and again, hoping to find some structure in which people function better. However, these organizations in many experiences have become a series of disasters, because of the lack of processes to bring everyone together to work efficiently and effectively.

Before we reorganize (in the next section) let us first consider the needs that we are attempting to meet, in terms of processes that will enable the different disciplines to interchange ideas, develop programs, design networks, operate systems, support products, and provide services. Once we have a firm understanding of these processes, then we can structure organizations around them to facilitate their successful utilization.

Figure 6-1 denotes the family of processes that have been referenced in the preceding sections. When used together, they become a formidable set of tools for the manager planner of the 90s. Hopefully, we have now developed an appreciation for their need, having seen the complexity of a wide

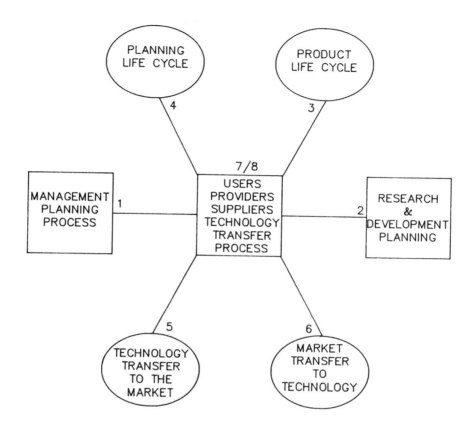

Fig. 6-1. Planning Processes.

spectrum of issues that need to be solved by people working together from many locations, throughout the world with different and unique skills. The following processes, shown in Fig. 6-2, must be coalesced, reduced, and simplified for easy utilization, in order to be functional management tools.

Considering the earlier statement that programming lists will drive the world, we may observe that processes enable people to not only write these programs, but write the "right" programs, that resolve the "right" problem. These processes are key to returning productivity to the large corporation, enabling people with different capabilities to work together in solving complex problems. In a society with different incentives than those of the Japanese, these processes are an important part of the solution, enabling better creativity to flourish and in so doing achieve better products.

These processes are based upon the four phase management planning process, of which each phase has been individually covered in the proceeding sections. Let us now take a deeper more perspective view of the phases, as they work together to allow creative ideas to become conceived and better defined with both management understanding and commitment.

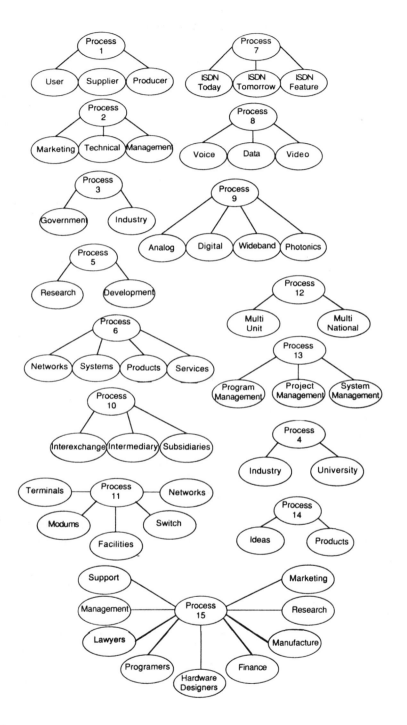

Fig. 6-2. Processes.

MANAGEMENT PLANNING PROCESS

The purpose of the management planning process is to involve management. Too often in the past, management has waited for either the marketing or technical group to work out a proposal and bring it to them for their approval, with the net result of attaining from them a "limited" concurrence. In the course of attaining this concurrence, the proposers usually "slit their own throats" by agreeing to provide the product, network, or service in one half the time, at one half the cost, as management push for better schedules and lower costs. Traditionally this has been the game, with management feeling more comfortable and in control, believing that they should probably get it accomplished at a significantly lower cost than what had originally been estimated and within 75% of the original schedule. Though they realize that this pressure may cause some problems throughout the period of design or implementation, they believed that the original estimates had been padded, or not carefully thought out and all will be reassessed later, once the design is underway.

This practice used to be a little game between management and the proposers. The proposers soon realized, that they would not get all their requests, and not wishing to slit their own throats did, in fact, pad a little here and there to cover their losses. However, as the marketplace became more selective and more manufacturers and providers competed for the same market, pressure mounted to have "something new," "something better." This soon became "something now." Hence, less and less time was spent at preproject planning. It became more a game of "promise them anything" to obtain management approval, get something started, then wait to see if "anything" would come of it.

For example, look at the funding game in Washington for new weapon systems from the Military—Industrial complex. Over time, congress became less decision oriented, and more resistive to large commitments, as the products became less successful. This developed a new dimension to the game. It was more important to obtain funds than to spend time on a good design. Also, if there were serious concerns after funding was obtained, no one could or would admit that the original design concept might have had problems, and that it should go back to preprogram planning. The attitude become one of "just put a few people on it, until we get the funding." Once funded, it became a major scramble to get "it", whatever "it" turns out to be, out the door. No one even looked back to see if "it" worked, since promotions were tied to getting "it" to the field.

Since organizations and people's mode of operation will be further discussed in the next section, for now we should only note the need for changing this approach in order to become more successful. To do so, we have indicated the need for management to become participating management planners and the need for active cross discipline planning, before the proposal is finalized and before embarking on some major project. The need for approval will become less and less of a problem, once understanding and participation is achieved. Then, honest estimates can be presented to manage-

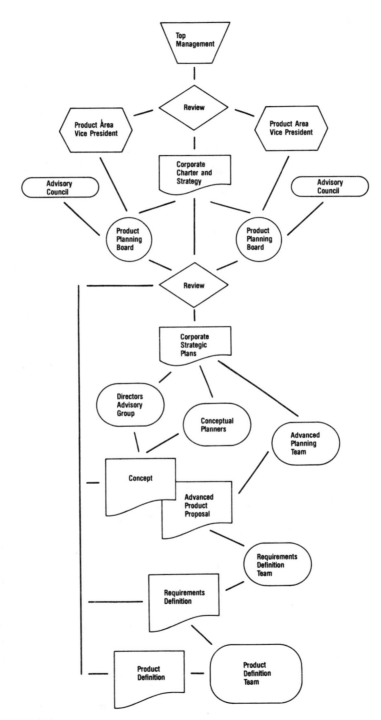

Fig. 6-3. Management Decision Process.

ment partners, enabling better evaluations, modifications and commitments to be achieved by all involved. The vehicle to foster and obtain this participation is the management planning process.

One of its key aspects is each of its phases' exit reviews. In this manner, management obtains three looks before commitment. It is reasonable to assume that if the work has been performed properly, meeting their concerns, then, at the time for commitment, they will be ready to commit. With these thoughts in mind, in reviewing planning techniques throughout the world, we make the following observations and note these key points, concerning the four phase management planning process, described in the previous sections:

- "We don't plan to fail, we fail to plan." In 1970, only 25% of New York corporations had a formal mission statement dealing with the underlying design, aims, and thrust of their companies. This lack of direction was reflected in a lack of strategic planning, product planning, and operation planning.
- Top management involvement in the decision making product planning reviews is necessary, to insure that their strategic plans are realistic and consistent with their products.
- Strategic planning is continuously refined and enhanced by the product planning and product definition analyses.
- Due to the demise of our auto industry, our attention has been focussed on Japanese management styles. As early as 1974, teams of product planning and development vice presidents and directors were sent to review the Nippon and Hitachi research and development labs. Their major finding was that Japanese companies perform a tremendous amount of planning to be able to compete for Japan Inc.'s share of the telecommunications market. After the war, the Americans financed Japan Productivity teams, and sent advisors. At a recent meeting some of the same teachers went back to learn from the students.

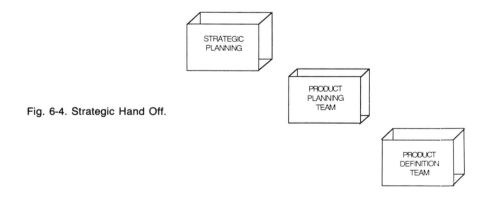

Fig. 6-4. Strategic Hand Off.

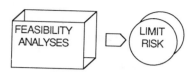

Fig. 6-5. Feasibility Analysis.

- Programming now reflects approximately 85% of a switching product's design effort. Today's "software problems" indicate whether a product has been ill-conceived, ill-defined, or hastily structured. Products which do not have a reasonable planning phase tend to be extremely error-prone, expensive, and difficult to use, and have no basis for new features.
- This is a planning process in which mission, objectives, product plans, product requirements, and product design flow together in a homogeneous manner to insure success in the development and support phases. Each planning phase covers new areas, as well as extends the preceding area's analysis.
- Technical feasibility analyses performed by systems planning, together with extensive market research by marketing, support the plans and minimize risk.
- The degree and depth of each phase analysis is determined by the product's complexity, and the amount of risk and change required by the company.
- To be successful, product planning requires top management involvement, with participating planners, managers, and specialists from various disciplines. A separate planning group activity is needed in which conceptual planners visualize products that meet both the technical advances and future marketplace needs.
- Product planning and product definition teams are formed from marketing, engineering, programming, finance, and manufacturing personnel to do the complex analyses for the conceptual planning, requirement definition, and product definition phases.
- Requirements can no longer be only vaguely understood before a product is committed to its development phases.
- In the product definition phase, the products' architecture and structures are extensively designed against all its major requirements (such as performance) before commitment to development. Unresolved areas that require later analyses are indicated to show risk. For example, the York Tank couldn't carry enough armor to protect its people and still get to the battle in time to meet its speed requirement. Unfortunately, speed was originally emphasized; where it would have rushed the people into the battle unprotected, to get them killed.
- The product definition team utilizes the specialists and managers who will be responsible for the development of the product.
- Programs developed for products, where both purpose and requirements are clearly identified and considered in their architecture, will normally take

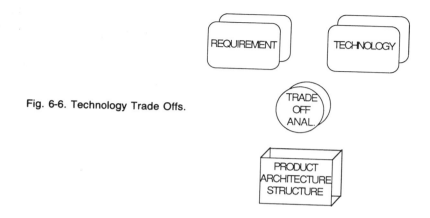

Fig. 6-6. Technology Trade Offs.

less time to develop and are relatively error free. The program development plan will be based upon a completely defined product proposal with supportive studies. This will minimize changes and enable its costs and resource projections to be more realistic.

- Planning for hardware and programming products, as well as services, for the 90s will require more sophisticated analysis before development, to insure that the products' requirements and their architecture and structure will be consistent with the changing, complex world of the new integrated information networks of the future.

- The three phases of "product planning" after strategic planning are extremely important in helping to establish a "product strategy" consistent with corporate strategic plans.

- The separate requirements phase insures that a complete list of feasible requirements are considered at the initial period of product definition.

- An extensive product definition period enables all key features to be initially considered in the design architecture. This is reflected in a cross-reference of feature matrixes to functional areas of the design.

- Planning performed in more formal and detailed steps will enable a more efficient development program to produce the product for the market on time with minimum errors. It will be a better base for new additions and will require less field support than previously attained.

- As noted earlier, expenditures on planning "to minimize risk to the level required by management" should be measured against expected product costs. Hence, for example, in a $40 million dollar development with 10% expended in planning, this would enable a $4 million dollar planning activity of 40 people or so for one year at $100,000 per "loaded" professional person cost; 30 people at $150,000 cost; or 20 at $200,000.

- In summary this planning process will definitely minimize risk and enable more effective and timely decisions to obtain products with a higher profit. This is achieved by increasing planning costs and cutting overall development costs, manufacturing costs, and support costs. More products will be sold by getting them to the marketplace on schedule, by having them meet their requirements and perform in such a manner that they are accepted by the users. They then can become the basis for future extensions and applications.

RESEARCH AND DEVELOPMENT PLANNING PROCESSES

One of the most difficult needs to be resolved in today's high tech arena, is to provide for an orderly pursuit of technology. Some firms have resigned themselves to giving their research laboratories a fixed budget in order to have ten or so research investigations pursued. Then they just wait for one out of the ten or so to be a success. Within the laboratories, there has always been a great mystery, between the basic research portion of the laboratory and the advanced development laboratory. If one were to ask what specific research studies will be used for new developments, blank looks might be observed, since an advanced development, in many cases today, uses only one or two aspects (if any), that may have come from one's own research. Usually, the system requires many devices and products developed from other manufactures, with the result that as research becomes more and more expensive, and a firm's current products are under intense competition, the first thing to be challenged is the basic research budget. The second is the applied research budget.

A current technique is to pool resources into a common research facility or consortium and share in the patents, ideas, and techniques generated. In this multi-owner arrangement, the problem of direction and control becomes an on-going game, as the various owners attempt to get their money's worth. On the other hand, some become a silent partner to a research institute and wait to be told of any breakthroughs. In the mid 80s the initial government guidelines for the RBOCs (Regional Bell Operating Companies) did not allow them to operate their own manufacturing plant. They did allow them to perform research to the level of feasibility models to determine what future networks, products, and services they might need to provide. This then became one of the bases for having a large shared network/product research and support program facility, called Bellcore, for the RBOCs. Next, the RBOCs requested overseas manufacturing capabilities to sell in the overseas markets. Later, domestic manufacturing was proposed when "open architecture" was implemented in 1988. Note: This, with the inter-LATA and inter-state Telco network requests, together with AT&T intra-LATA network operations, will eventually result in eight separate competing information firms, resulting from the former Bell System. See the case studies in Chapter 12.

Many multi-national firms would like to transfer technology from country to country to build special versions of a successful product for each particular country in order to market it to the world community. To accomplish this they used to attract expatriots to go to the selected country with the desired technology that was needed. As revolutions and economic conditions made this unattractive, the next technique was to establish a high technology center or telecommunications technology center as a technology transfer center to perform shared research, using a brain trust of American and international researchers. In this manner, their international work force were cycled through a central laboratory to upgrade their technical skills. Their charge was to utilize the results of their shared research by next jointly developing a common practical prototype in an advanced development laboratory. From this model, they would return to their own particular development laboratories throughout the world, to develop a version applicable to their individual country.

In the past, we have seen the universities, fearing a drain of the best brains to industry, and having a need to obtain more funding to finance their research and salaries, form unique alliances with state governments and industry. They have been willing to locate research laboratories on their campuses, funded by multiple-industry owners, in which their professors are able to carry on their research, share ideas and learn from their industrial partners. They have also provided technology transfer by continuing education programs, where recognized specialists from industry would be invited to teach and share ideas with other specialists from industry and their university or college associates. Recently, these endeavors have lead to another type of alliance (such as the Midwest Technology Development Institute) where state governors, presidents of many universities, and corporate leaders would jointly finance a research institute (not a building). Here, (logically, not necessarily physically) the various universities would share research for common profit oriented new technology business opportunities, sponsored by the participating states, in an effort to attract new businesses to their states in the high technology arena or to get a source of income from technology investors (both foreign and domestic).

Finally, there is the problem of maintaining funding for research endeavors. Unfortunately, this is a major problem when research becomes research for research sake, or when one success in ten projects becomes one in twenty or thirty without any immediate benefit or application. At this point the owners balk and either totally retreat, or resort to "cherry picking" those projects that have the best chance for success, and drop the others. Here, the research institutes usually have difficulty between their directors and owners in agreeing to the need to have on-going stability in order to attract and keep the best minds.

Hence arises the dilemma. How can owners monitor and direct a research facility to obtain what they want; and how can the research facility keep its owners satisfied, by pursuing the areas the owners really want, when in many cases it is difficult to communicate with the owners, until something actually is discovered? How can they work together and obtain agreement to pursue areas of higher risk, or areas that are not necessarily directly related to immediate needs, but part of the long range picture?

To accomplish these objectives, enable various arrangements and structures to foster the desired research, and transfer the successful endeavors into actual products meeting the needs of the marketplace, we need to use

Fig. 6-7. Basic Research.

- MATERIALS
- LIGHT SWITCHES
- TRANSMISSION MODELS

Fig. 6-8. Applied Research.

- DISTRIBUTED NETWORKS
- TRANSMISSION ARCHITECTURE
- AUTOMATED TESTING
- SWITCHING ARCHITECTURES/STRUCTURES
- MAN—MACHINE INTERFACE COMPILERS
- CALL PROCESS AND SUPPORT COMPILERS
- DATABASE MANAGEMENT COMPILERS.

Fig. 6-9. Advanced Development.

- NETWORK/TRANSMISSION
  ARCHITECTURES/STRUCTURES

- PROGRAMMING LANGUAGES

    ✔ CALL PROCESSING
    ✔ MAINTENANCE
    ✔ DATABASE MANAGEMENT
    ✔ MAN—MACHINE INTERFACE

a free flowing planning process, that ties the various groups within the research community together with each other and their owners.

The Research and Development Planning and Technology Transfer Process ties the Management Planning Process (in which the providers and suppliers identify and determine their own particular lines of business projects and programs) to the various laboratories' research and development efforts for new products, networks and services. Research and development are subdivided into four separate laboratories: basic research, applied research, advanced

Fig. 6-10. Applied Development.

- NETWORK/SYSTEM/SUB—SYSTEM/ DEVICE

  ✔ REQUIREMENT DEFINITION
  ✔ PRODUCT DEFINITION
  ✔ MARKET RESEARCH
  ✔ FINANCIAL MODELS

development (sometimes called advanced research), and applied development. Figures 6-7 thru 6-10 give a brief description of the types of analyses performed in each laboratory for the telecommunication world. The figures' notes demonstrate how analyses of basic materials or models can be further enhanced and be more specifically applied, as general ideas move to more and more specific applications. The figures indicate the hand-off points, as a particular laboratory transfers the technology on to the other laboratories who will further apply it. These laboratories may be under one roof in one firm or located throughout the world within many firms.

Figure 6-11 indicates that the research laboratory efforts become more and more influenced by both the provider and user, as requirements for the marketplace are imposed upon them. Their concepts then move to the supplier (producer), where preproject design, manufacturing requirements, and product structuring are performed.

Figure 6-12 notes where in the flow the product is reviewed to insure that it meets the original objectives and requirements of the supplier and provider. It is also reviewed to see how well it operates and functions, as well as how easily it can be supported by the provider of new services in meeting the needs of the actual users, and supported by the supplier in meeting the needs of the providers.

Figure 6-13 shows how a particular provider obtains technical possibilities from conceptual planning activities of the research laboratories. Later, these technical possibilities assist various suppliers (producers) in establishing requirements for new product possibilities with subsequent reviews of the proposed architecture and structure to see if it will indeed meet the concept and requirements. Similarly, Fig. 6-13 notes that the development laboratories must interface with the research laboratories on an on-going basis to work with new concepts and consider more detailed requirements, as they subsequently translate them to products.

This overall process is then seen in its entirety in Fig. 6-14. It should be recognized that this example is for the research laboratories, providers, and

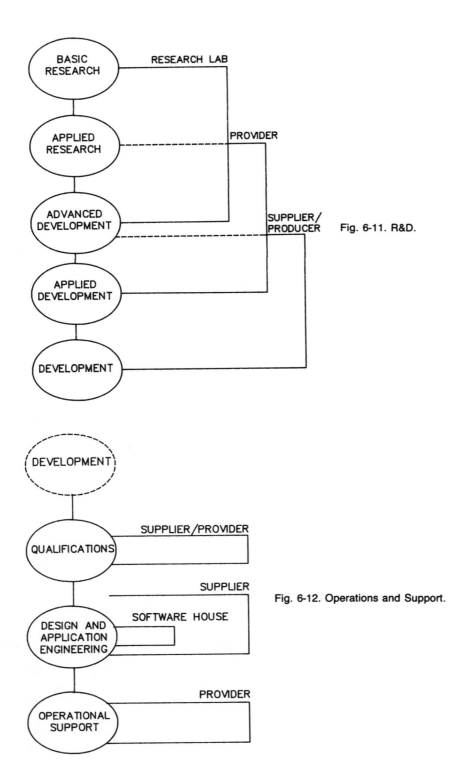

Fig. 6-11. R&D.

Fig. 6-12. Operations and Support.

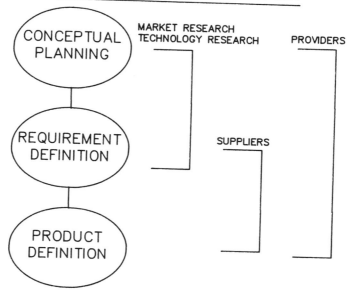

Fig. 6-13. Technology Planning.

suppliers, where the research laboratories may be both in the university and in industry, working together. We also can consider the provider as one of several owners who are using the management planning process to determine where they are going. In the case of sharing university and industry research, these four separate areas are where sharing can occur, based upon the three planning phases, as ideas move through the various phase relationships.

Based upon this model, if all involved parties are using their own separate but similar management planning process, they will be better able to reach agreement on the direction of the research and the types of benefits that each laboratory should produce. In this manner they will achieve a more directed research, but with the flexibility required by the researchers.

PRODUCT LIFE CYCLE

The phases and paths indicated in Fig. 6-15 clearly demonstrate both the ease and complexity of maneuvering an idea from conception to termination. This model has been proven over many years to accurately define all the major facets of a product's life.

The various phases are interconnected by specific paths. These should be studied carefully. Note that changes should not be made indiscriminately once the design is completed, but should be returned to design to reconsider

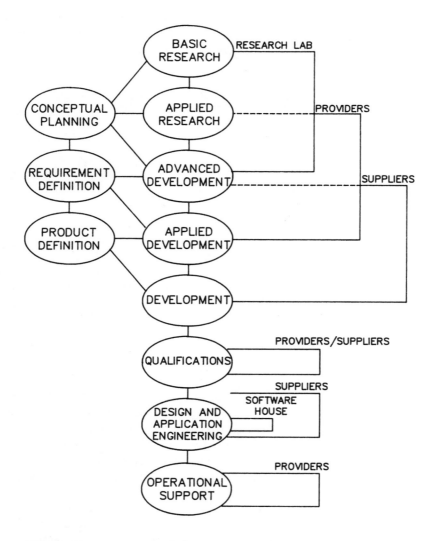

Fig. 6-14. R&D Planning and Transfer Process.

the basic design architecture that was achieved during the planning phases. If they cannot be reasonably accommodated within the technical and financial considerations, the new requirements should be evaluated in terms of the basic structure previously defined, during a revisit to the product definition phase. (Performed logically in time, but out of phase sequence.) If the architecture and structure is seriously challenged, then perhaps a new product is required, thus driving the analysis back to the conceptual planning phase, where again it must be judged against the overall strategic direction of the firm. An example of this is adding data packet switching to an existing voice switching product line, when the firm already produces separate data packet switches and where the packet traffic may seriously affect the voice traffic capabilities of the original system. This type of consideration requires a reassessment of the original concept of the voice switch and separate data packet switch requirements and architectures in terms of the strategic direction of the firm.

Each development and operating phase activity can be described in detail in terms of petition and the work flow of what tasks are performed by whom with what outputs. In the light of top down planning, we need to consider the relationships of both the planning and the operational phases to the development phases, so as to fully appreciate the need for integrating planning activities of the users, providers and suppliers in order to accomplish what has been planned.

THE PLANNING LIFE CYCLE

The many aspects of the planning activities that have been discussed throughout this book, are indicated in Fig. 6-17, as three manageable areas: strategic planning, product/program planning, and product/program review.

The previous sections have already described the activities of how the "strategy of the strategy" thinking moves missions to strategic plans and how the "business of the business" thinking moves conceptual plans to product definition. Hence, let us take a few minutes to consider how the "strategy of the strategies" establishes the "business of the business", and then is reconsidered in the reviews.

The "strategy of the strategies" is a term to describe the need to carefully consider the strategic positioning of the firm's products, networks and services with particular architectures, structures, and features in the appropriate lines of business. When one unit of a multi-unit firm is in trouble, or wishes to provide a new offering in the heavily integrated telecommunication marketplace, that particular unit cannot be separated from the whole. Its condition and future offerings must be considered in terms of the strategic direction of the firm. This is the job of strategic planning at the corporate level. There is only one location which has the power to control offerings of multiple units. This is a neutral area—the group responsible for the strategic direction of the firm.

Over the past, many business units, or lines of business that are considered autonomous profit centers have been in a constant tug of war, with corporate planning to obtain the freedom to control their own destiny. Over the late 80s, there has been a shift by major firms to return this responsibility back to the units in the form of planning activities. One firm went so far as to eliminate it's complete corporate division of case holders and system planners in a single sweep, only to find after several frustrating years, that due to the "integrated network", interface requirements for each of the individual products (terminals, modems, switches, fiber optics) of the various units were interrelated. The units needed each other, as well as a central division to work out boundaries, overlaps, shared research and marketing. Hence, a firm must be careful to keep its strategy decision makers capable of insuring the lines of business are firmly on the right turf. However, by the interesting hand-off to the lines of business, each has the charter to perform its own conceptual planning activities. Hence, the lines of business remain the planners of their own destiny. However, a central strategic planning group must lead, facilitate, coordinate, and advise the unit to ensure that its concepts are consis-

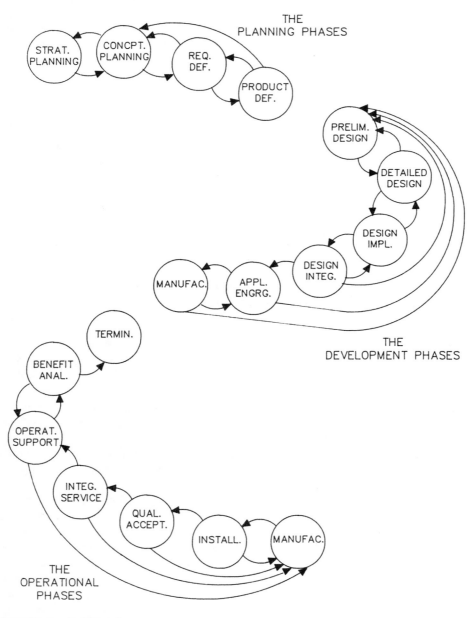

Fig. 6-15. Product Planning.

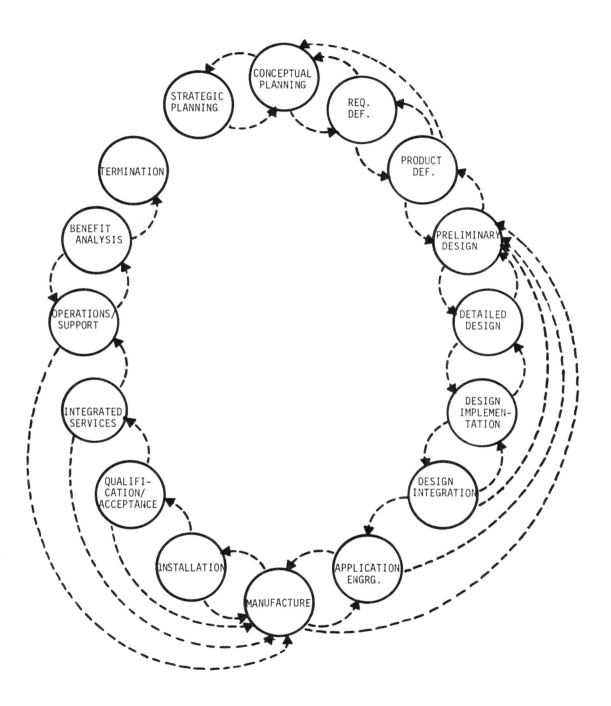

Fig. 6-16. The Product Life Cycle.

tent with the strategic direction of the firm and can be integrated together with other units to successfully become part of the corporate strategic plans.

Now let us take a deeper look at the Product/Program Review cycle (Figs. 6-15 and 6-17), in terms of the Product Life Cycle (Fig. 6-16). Here we see a buy/make decision, performed as part of the product definition phase review or during a subsequent phase, where a more detailed selection/recommendation analysis is performed. The planning requirements are then reviewed in terms of a recommended solution of what is available versus

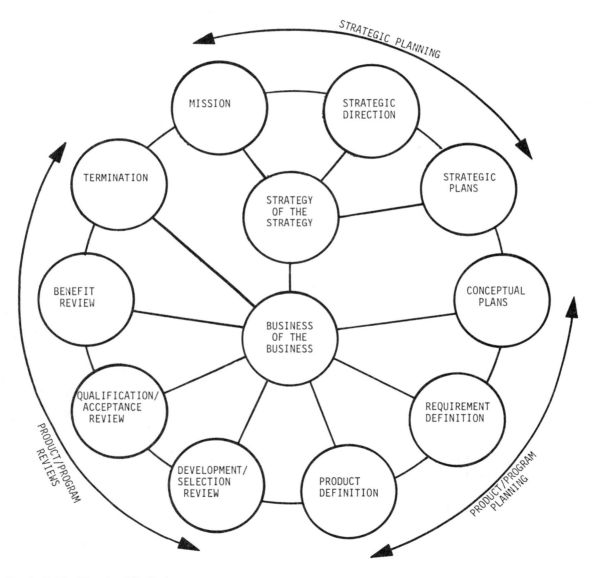

Fig. 6-17. The Planning Life Cycle.

162

designing a new product. Later, once the first product is installed, if it is the first article off the production line, it must pass extensive qualification testing to determine that it truly meets the planning objectives and requirements. Alternatively, if it is not the first unit, then it has acceptance testing to insure it meets the operational requirements.

During operation, there are periodic reviews to determine if the product is meeting expectations in terms of over-all performance and reliability as well as to see if the conditions under which it is operating are as projected, or if new requirements have occurred. Finally, termination may be necessary to provide for new products with new features to offer new services. Here, the termination review and subsequent post-mortem analysis are performed in terms of providing input for new product line strategies. The actual product termination is usually executed upon arrival of the new offering, but the decision to terminate the product line is made as a result of new opportunities, new techniques, and the performance of current product lines, as determined by benefit analysis reviews. Hence, the planning process has a complete life cycle from mission to termination.

TECHNOLOGY TRANSFER TO THE MARKET AND VICE VERSA

There has been much discussion on being technology driven or being market driven. In reality it really does not matter whether the cycle begins with a technology looking for an application, or a market need looking for a technical solution. What does matter is that they meet and work together. Recently, an experiment was performed by a major provider, where a two week, off-site meeting was held between technical and marketing people to provide a conceptual plan for the firm's entrance into the information world, based upon ISDN networks, products and services. There was considerable conflict the first week, a few walked out to return later, and one sought the assistance of a doctor for chest pains, perhaps due to tension. By the end of the second week, the two groups had broken into joint working parties whose final reports became the basis for the firm's ISDN offerings. All involved later said that it had been an outstanding experience. Each had learned a great deal from the other, but only after they had begun listening to what the others had to say.

The marketing people learned the possibilities and jargon of the new voice/data/video world and the technical people learned the reality of what the users may want or not want and what they may be willing to pay. It also showed the need for risk to proceed without a clear, well established marketplace. It was difficult to find users who really knew what they wanted. All in all it was a memorable experience, with the result that joint planning teams were established to proceed with the requirement definition and the product definition phases to form an in-house laboratory of planning activities to work with the outside research and development laboratories. Similarly, several major laboratories reviewed their planning process and constructed their new product planning activities, as well as their internal applied research and advanced development planning, around the planning phases of the product life cycle to achieve joint planning activities.

Now let us take a moment to fully consider the research life cycle, planning cycle, and market research cycle views and see how the revolving "product life cycle" has within it, the separate planning, development, manufacturing and support life cycles. In observing how it brings everything together, we will see that there are "life cycles" within "life cycles".

The market analysis can be overlaid on the product life cycle to feed the planning activities by identifying new opportunities, new features, new problems looking for a solution. This is seen as the driving shaft (the PULL) upon which the product life cycle turns, in Fig. 6-18. Note that all major life cycles, within the Product Life Cycle, are constantly touched by the marketing cycle.

As we attempt to understand new technologies under consideration in the suppliers (producers) laboratory environment, we must tie the planning

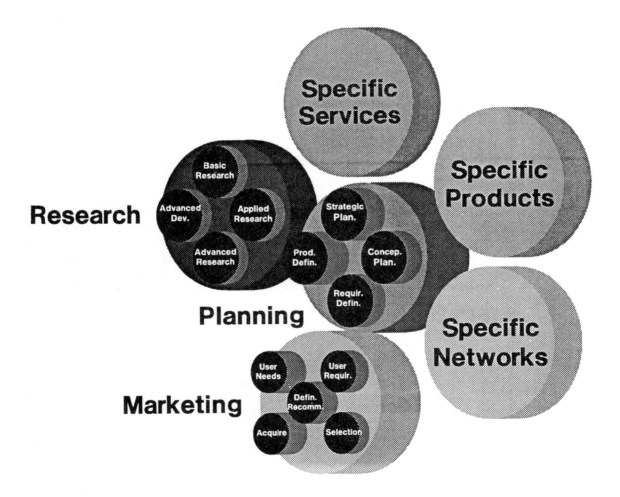

Fig. 6-18. Market Driven (Pull) / Technology Driven (Push).

cycle of the life cycle to the four research and development stages of investigation.

Hence, the product planning cycle touches both the marketing and the technology research cycles, and forms conduits joining them together at the right point and time, throughout a product's life cycle. These conduits connect and disconnect as the various cycles turn at different rates, overlaying, at some point in time, all aspects of the marketplace for each research laboratory to investigate and understand in terms of new technologies. The marketing wheel spins faster than the research wheel. As the product moves through its phases, moving from concept to requirements, the research wheel advances through its different laboratory stages, as noted in the research and development planning and transfer process (Fig. 6-14). All these wheels will turn in sync, as marketing application ideas are understood in terms of solutions, or as technical ideas are tied to market possibilities, through the planning phases of the product life cycle.

Thus, the resulting view, if one were to study Fig. 6-18 would be of the market place spinning quite quickly and slowly turning the product life cycle wheel, which is also being pushed by the technology research and development cycle to click it through the product planning cycle (the extended crank handle of the product life cycle) to achieve preproject plans. As the planning handle moves, so does the product's life cycle. If we viewed it from the other direction, the research and development cycle turns the planning handle, which turns the market cycle at a slower rate than the shaft upon which the product life cycle turns. Only the rate is different. Therefore, who really drives whom?

It is simply a matter of speed. If the marketplace is ready, it will move very quickly if it has the technology to obtain the products it needs. On the other hand, technology can push the marketplace to accept products. It will only take a little longer to overcome resistance and fine tune the product to fit in the emerging marketplace, unless the planners totally misjudged the market. In either case, when the market cycle interfaces with technology, beginning at the conceptual planning phase, the wheel will stop if there is not an acceptable market. This can occur at the concept, requirements, or product definition phases. The figures in Chapter 11 show the net result of all the forces working together to produce a continuous array of products, networks and services. This will then require a versatile process to integrate the users, providers, and suppliers and enable the various manager planners to orchestrate their planning, using the integrated market technology transfer process, as shown in Fig. 6-19.

The title of the figure indicates the process as the base, supporting the many players on top. Indeed, this is the way it should be. A process to be used by all needs to be stable, easily understood, easy to use, and accepted. The process in the picture is simply a composite of all the previous processes, with the addition of the select/acquire phase referred to earlier, to integrate the user and provider with the product life cycle of the supplier. By studying the figure, you can see how each of the paths integrate and interlace with

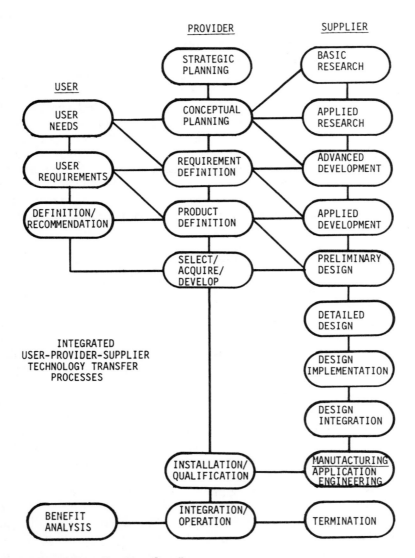

Fig. 6-19. Integrated Users/Providers/Suppliers.

the various planning activities of users, providers and suppliers. It should be noted that the supplier will also follow the same planning paths as the provider to drive its own research and development activities to determine its project and system plans. For the sake of clarity, the view is shown from the provider's perspective. (Hopefully, the laboratories will tolerate this perspective, since they are quite used to twisting designs and looking at them from another axis).

The figure demonstrates how all can work together by showing work portions with checkpoints and reviews that enable the Providers to provide the right solution for the right user needs, using the right products developed by the suppliers (producers).

TOP DOWN QUALITY PLANNING

As we pursue quality, the missing ingredient from our American product lines, we may wish to carefully consider this section's workshop. It defines an exciting quality management process called "Quality Prisms" for managing the pursuit of quality. This becomes an integral part of the answer to the Japanese productivity and quality challenge to our industries. It provides a top down emphasis on the pursuit of quality. It does not determine how much quality will be pursued, as that is dependent upon what the managers and designers determine for each particular product based on user needs. It will, however eliminate the nebulous quality endeavors that have been tied to the vague pursuit of quality for previous products. For example, today there are many fine techniques, as noted in the workshop in Chapter 13, for obtaining better software. The problem has been the lack of management support to provide schedule relief to achieve them, or to pay for the additional costs to perform additional tasks, sometimes with additional people. Hence, the process addresses the real problem, which is the need for a process to pursue the desired level of quality and indicate the extent and degree to which it will be pursued through the product's life cycle phases.

It has been said that quality, in the produced product, can be free. In the sense that one does not have to pay for it later by costly changes or loss in the marketplace, it is. However, as Fig. 2-3 from Chapter 2 on the cost of planning indicates, you pay for what you get. To pursue quality will cost, but to pursue it at the very beginning throughout the planning and development phases, before production, will reduce over all design, as well as manufacturing and support costs. This analysis provides a process to manage our pursuit of quality. It does not provide the tools to achieve quality, but does provide the missing platform upon which these tools must be supported to be effective.

FURTHER ANALYSIS

The case studies in Chapter 12, *Product Development/Technology Transfer Process, Methodology to meet User Needs and Process for Achieving the Delicate Balance*, provide proven processes for developing a successful quality product for identified needs of the user.

OBSERVATIONS: PROCESSES FACILITATE SUCCESS

1. Networks, Products, and Services in the 90s require planning and transfer processes to bring together users, suppliers, and providers.
2. Manager planners can utilize a family of planning processes, each expanding on the other to achieve a new dimension of effectiveness, where the whole is greater than the parts.
3. Each process for bringing together marketing, technical, government, research, and management overlays onto the four phase management planning process.
4. Do not put an organization together without a process to hold it together.
5. Desired levels of quality can be achieved, if we manage our pursuit of quality.
6. Processes must not be restrained by methodologies and procedures.
7. Marketing and technical need processes to integrate their thinking into a channeled powerful force.
8. Orchestrating multiple units with multiple disciplines to plan and achieve new networks, products, and services can be successfully accomplished and can indeed be exciting, by using the right processes to bring them all together.

Chapter 7

The 'P' Organization

Processes don't make plans, people do. Firms that wish to survive and compete successfully in these turbulent times of intense change, need to establish an organization that meets the challenge of the processes and the needs of the people who will use them. Processes need to be surrounded with an organizational structure that supports their successful usage. In reviewing the "Ps," noted in section two, and the planning cycle (the crank) of the product life cycle, what was missing was the structure to support the people, enabling them to turn the planning wheel.

A vehicle is required that will not only support, but also go a long way toward diminishing resistance to its operation and provide a mechanical advantage, so that any effort spent has a multiplier value, making it more effective. We all know that the best tool is one which is easy to use and takes minimum effort, so that anyone can use it. It is usually a well worn, lubricated device which requires very little work to get it going and runs a long way, even when the terrain is rough and up hill. It may, for example, figuratively take the form of a racing bicycle. We then need capable people to ride the bike, turn the pedals, participate in the race, and play the game. In reviewing the Japanese model, we see the dedication and job satisfaction that is now missing from U.S. industry. American industries had taken thirty years to demotivate their work force, while the Japanese were building a very dedicated working society.

WHY CHANGE?—WHAT'S DIFFERENT?

In the mid eighties, a prominent U.S. Congressman and Japanese Ambas-

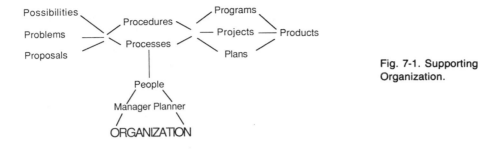

Fig. 7-1. Supporting Organization.

sador participated in a televised roundtable discussion on the seriousness of the Japanese foreign trade deficit of 30 billion dollars. The Ambassador indicated that Japan would begin opening up their markets to buy U.S. goods with extensive promotions, but the goods had to be worth buying. They would not force their people to buy inferior merchandise. In response, the Congressman, searching for something with quality, finally settled on our raw materials such as trees from Washington and then on the "Louisville Slugger" baseball bat, indicating that at least the bat was still made with quality. He admitted that our industry was in a sad state of affairs, noting that we must change to a new way of doing business. Today, many firms have also recognized this and are now finally ready to change, to be more competitive, and that's different!

The new work force for the forthcoming information era need a "different," planning-oriented organization, to enable them to competitively supply, provide, and use new complex information networks, products, and services. We are retiring the generation of people who grew up in the industrial revolution era. They made their living by devising devices which could be "cranked off" the assembly line. Firms were structured around the assembly line. Fear of losing one's job or piece part bonuses were used to turn the "assembly line crank." Rewards and promotions were awarded to those who could get the most "widgets" out the door at the lowest cost. A ready market was waiting on the other side of the factory door, who were willing to buy anything because of more sophisticated advertising. Those on the assembly line were the best customers of someone else's assembly line. It was a self-fulfilling picture. However, a barrier was crossed, when workers wages reached the point that they could own a house, and a car, and send their children to college. They had fulfilled the American dream.

As this happened, demands for more goods, the second car, private college, or a bigger house, caused a movement for the housewife to take a job in order to bring additional capital into the home, so they could live up to the Jones next door. This additional demand for goods was met with increasing prices, as factories could not meet the demand. Soon, it became an economic necessity for the wife to work along side the husband, in order to bring in enough income to meet the mortgage payment.

The American dream began to fade for the children of the working force of the 40s and 50s, as prices continued to rise in the 60s and 70s. By 1985 goods were up by a factor of five over the 1960 prices, but labor wages had only risen by a factor of 3 to 4, and in some of the unskilled jobs only by a factor of two. What was keeping these salaries down, were five major conditions. First was the basic shift from large electronic assembly lines to microdot clean room technology. Second was the doubling of candidates in the work force, now that both husband and wife were competing for the same jobs. Third was the slackening of demand for the various items since everyone already had two of them. (Two T.V. sets, two cars, two washing machines, two houses, etc.) Forth was the inability to assume any more debt—many were already "mortgaged to the hilt." Fifth was the shift to foreign locations to build the goods cheaper, so that the already debt ridden families could still have a lot of everything instead of a few well made quality items.

As this dilemma ensued, two attitudes prevailed. The first, preferred by some industries, was to simply milk the name of existing products, as long as possible. This allowed the near retiring management to retire along with their factories, which could no longer compete. The second was more acceptable to congress. It was various forms of protectionism to protect the labor force and provide taxable revenue on imports to supposedly keep jobs and give American industry a chance to compete. This simply translated into foreign manufacturing plants in America to manufacture the goods under the control of the foreign manufacturer. The net result would be jobs available to rural Americans at cheaper wages, with the new young families working on more automated assembly lines, under control of the foreign manufacturers. This then was the result of the effort to keep the cycle going as it had been in the 50s, except now with foreign owners.

What is different now is the introduction of the computer. As noted, even with a desire to do the job better, there is still a great disparity between buying power and the price of goods. There also are fewer children for the working families. Hence, there is still a lower demand for goods. Firms found it economical to maintain the price of goods and sell fewer goods by having less manufacturing costs. There was also a shift in the type of goods in demand. The new demand of a growing number of those with money became the more expensive $19,000 sports car instead of the four door family car. However, for those on the assembly lines, the price of the four door family car at $12,000 was too, high. They were losing the American Dream. At the same time, businesses experienced intense competition in their changing and shrinking market. They had great difficulty trying to motivate a disinterested work force to keep the costs down to compete with the foreign countries, whose labor forces worked harder for a great deal less money. Hence, the work force was and still is the weak link in the chain.

The technology for the information age met the challenge and provided the power of the microprocessor, the megabit memory, and the gigabit communication networks to support robotics and automated manufacturing plants, requiring less people. Note G.M's drop in the Mid 80s, from 780,000 to 600,000 in three years. Now less people are employed, but of a higher skill range. This will enable many to be paid more. This example shows the separation of the labor force into two camps; those *with* the higher skills and higher paying jobs and those *without* higher skills and perhaps without jobs. This long term trend may drive the economy back to the early 50s, where considerably fewer people had any major buying power. Hence we have less demand, causing less inflation, as fewer people compete for the goods. Subsequently, as the situation becomes severe, those without skills will be willing to work harder to keep themselves employed. (Some advertising firms today are running, not walking, back to the old philosophy that "20% of the people purchased 80% of the merchandise.")

Hence, there would be even greater pressure to get an education in order to have the skills required in the more automated world. The result being, through the turn of the century, a world dilemma, and not just a localized American or European problem, with business competition being tougher and rougher. The purpose of this analysis is to identify major shifts in direction to help understand what is happening in the marketplace, in order to determine how corporations, attempting to provide competitive products, will have to function to survive. As time passes, there will be many such shifts, but as we move deeper into the information world, the buyers, the work force and the users will be more sophisticated and knowledgeable. This shift was also noted by the advertising industry, as generalities are now being changed to specifics.

This means a better educated work force, and with education comes the desire to participate in all facets of the game and a desire to own better products. Quality is now important. This new workforce will have a desire to be with the best company, that is providing good quality products, a desire to obtain financial reward (substantial) in recognition for having helped the company achieve its quality products, a desire to be with a growth firm, so that jobs can be challenging, and a desire to be where the opportunity for better jobs and promotions exist. There will be more competition from both men and women with more education for the better jobs. There will be fewer jobs for running furnaces and steel plants, and more clean room environments with enjoyable working conditions. An unwillingness to work under dictatorial management will become prevalent, and the right atmosphere of the work environment will become essential. There will be willingness to move, (no longer a 40 year dedication to one firm) and a desire for a choice in the marketplace and on the job. With these new needs will also be the need for more multidiscipline participation to solve problems, which have become more complex. The world of stand alone, simple, singular products and services will become increasingly smaller and smaller, as the universal network grows to maturity, requiring many people to work together to resolve interface standards, structures, and architectures.

Therefore, we must spend more effort on organizations which motivate, support, and develop people who will use the processes to help them participate and work together to build these new complex products. With the "right" culture, we can obtain a growing, functioning and successful firm, with satisfied people, achieving their greatest expectations. The time and motion studies that simplified predetermined tasks and movements of the assembly line workers, are now a thing of the past. This type of work can be accomplished in the future by automated machines. So let us take a deeper look. What do we need? A structure based upon detailed procedures to regiment peoples' modes of operation, or "something else?"

ORGANIZATIONAL NEEDS

Telecommunications and data processing have become integrated in the new "network" game. They are no longer single autonomous industries. Their new products require considerable pre-study and technical expertise in many disciplines, working to answer specific questions to solve particular well identified problems. No longer are people who have done it before available from other firms. In addition, no single project can economically support all the studies needed to develop the required knowledge during the development's design cycle.

Thus, the new complex integrated networks of the 90s will require considerable new skills, that need to be developed, maintained, and applied over several projects to maximize the return on research investment. The full ramifications of these new networks should be understood in order to utilize a product's versions in more than one network.

Hence, planning groups are necessary to provide the "big picture" view, instead of determining products by technical or short view market studies. A family of products needs to be identified with a realizable mix of features and market priorities established by a logical market driven five-year plan of products for specific networks. This is the basis for product driven organizational structures to provide them.

The current situation, as noted by the chief executive of a major telecommunications firm, is as follows:

1. We have issues that pile up awaiting management decision, not because the managers are unwilling to make the decision, but because they are over-burdened, or do not have, on a timely basis, the information necessary to make those decisions.
2. We find changing and unpredictable demands placed on the organization by changing technology and changing competition. These demands over-burden elements of the structure from time to time.
3. We are faced with an increased diversity of products and services falling within our business missions, and simultaneously we see an increased interdependence between our various business units. This creates a need for more effective interchange between those units.
4. We see the increase in technological content of our business and find problems in making the maximum use of the most effective technical talent that we have in the organization. Organizational boundaries, including job titles, sometimes impede us from deploying our best talent across

our organization to make most effective use of it.

5. We find overly-long development cycles for new products or services and at the same time shorter product lives.

6. We have to be realistic, we have to be tough-minded in our recognition of our own problems, so that we can solve them. We need a willingness to accept change, these are the greatest strengths, we will need within the organization.

7. We need a new image. The most effective way to change the new image is to change the reality. This means that we have to look at changing our management approaches, our organization, our planning, and our implementation. We cannot get where we want to go by just doing what we have been doing, but doing it harder, faster, longer.

8. We need to become more marketing oriented. Many firms have insufficient strength in the marketing area. We see that Marketing is the most important, if not the only important thing, that we have to do. If we're going to be a successful company, we still have to do a much better job of identifying what the public wants and when they will want to have it available and be prepared to deliver it to them at a reasonable price and at a profit.

9. A second crucial area is one of management development. Despite the fact that most of us are overworked, we still haven't really begun to challenge our management to the degree necessary to produce the best results. This doesn't mean working harder. It means working more effectively and focusing on the important issues.

10. This leads to another area of concern—improved profitability objectives. We will continue to have very substantial demands for capital, and our earnings growth must be sustained on a reasonably consistent basis in order to make that capital available to us at a reasonable price. We must recognize that all of our businesses cannot be equally profitable. We must have within our organization a sufficiently balanced portfolio so that if we do identify those businesses which should invest and grow, those which we should conserve and protect, and those that should be phased out, we can achieve what we want to achieve. But it is clear that we cannot live in an environment where everyone's objective is "invest and grow." That just doesn't make sense. Our businesses have different risk characteristics, and as a result we must assign different return responsibilities to those businesses, rather than having an arbitrary percentage that applies to all businesses.

11. Another area that requires further study is that of servicing our products. If we are going to be successful in many of the business areas to which we intend to direct our attention, we must have a profitable service capability.

12. At the heart of some of our past and present problems has been a lack of adequate strategic planning.

These and other similar concerns have been recently expressed by today's concerned business leaders. As noted above there are many major needs, that must be resolved in order to develop new products, such as the:

- Need for marketing research and product planning to select a specific range of products over several competitive markets.
- Need for a wide range of specialists covering programming, transmission, traffic models, VLSI, and ISDN standards.
- Need to coordinate multiple units that provide interfacing products.
- Need for lead time to perform studies, before finalized definition of the product.
- Need to utilize highly complex, but effective, hardware and programming architecture design.
- Need for automated methods and tools to aid design, testing, and manufacture to improve quality and productivity.
- Need to utilize personnel in an orderly progression of products to transfer knowledge from product to product.
- Need to utilize most complex highly specialized skills over several projects.
- Need to provide development schedule relief by having many specific problems resolved on predevelopment models (similar to Japan's techniques to verify many technical concepts before commitment to development).
- Need to separate and integrate planning functions and identify their relationship to R&D and the Marketplace.
- Need to enable the work force to participate in all facets and work together.
- Need to motivate the work force.
- Need to train the work force. Skills need to be upgraded and obtained.
- Need to recognize and reward, to keep highly skilled employees satisfied and content with their jobs.
- Need to establish this type of new environment and culture.
- Need to establish an organizational structure that supports these needs and processes to bring people together.

If we were to look at our analogy of the bicycle, the style, seat, handlebars, headlight, pedals, wheels, and framework structure make up the organization. The process becomes the gear mechanism enabling one or more riders to more easily move the bicycle up and down hills through many marketplaces. The people are the racers, who are motivated to drive and pedal this beautiful, easy to use, quick to respond, light to the touch, comfortable vehicle, which is designed for going places that they would like to go, in a style which encourages them to be a part of the race. "To play the game . . ."

THE MANAGER PLANNER

To play the game means to participate, to become participating management. This requires having some way to participate. We have seen the earlier sections describe several processes, based upon a four phase management planning process, that enables management to meet with technical, marketing, and finance at the very beginning of ideas and help them advance net-

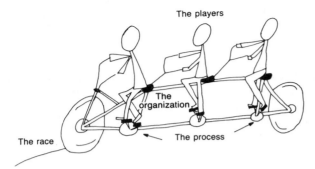

The players

The organization

The race

The process

Fig. 7-2. Playing The Game To Win.

works, products, and services. We have seen how the complexity of this game has grown to require a great deal of effort to understand outside factors, such as government decisions, ISDN standards, marketplace research of user needs and advances in technology research which render earlier ideas and techniques obsolete. We have seen this complexity extend itself into the heart of the firm's strategic direction and business plans. Thus, we have the need for large companies to be able to solve large problems, using the right groups of their people, from many disciplines, across business lines, across units, across countries.

The manager planners can orchestrate these processes, but they need a structure to support them. All levels of people within the organization need a structure, that enables them to participate with the manager planner. The specialists from the various disciplines need a structure that allows their views to be considered, before major decisions and commitments are made. Recent detailed discussions on organizations and structures with Japanese management indicated two points. The first was that everyone in their organization can participate, the second was that they carefully interviewed their people, before they were selected for the job, to insure that they were the type of people who could work together in their organization, and wanted to participate. Not only the managers, but also their people must participate together. Similarly, there is the need for the manager planner, who is supported by an organization, which encourages people to work together.

ORGANIZATIONAL STRUCTURE

The preceding chapters have identified twelve key ingredients required by the planning process. These are based on two premises. The first being that planning is now a must, due to the tremendous amount of change, the impact of technology, and the network architecture solution. Thirty percent of the task of supplying or providing new networks, systems, or products will be the planning of the products and programs to achieve them, (to the level described in this analysis) The second is that people should participate in the organization in councils, teams, and groups to resolve cross lines of business dependencies. In looking at structures, we see that a self contained line of business is usually too heavy to support itself, if it does not draw from various support groups. Usually, if its right to life is a single product, the collapse of that product in the marketplace will destroy the line of business and cause havoc with its people. Since it will have to carry all costs to support the single venture, even in bad times, its product or service prices may be too high, causing a further loss in the marketplace, which results in further price increases to support it, translating to disaster. Hence, the self sustaining project usually self destructs soon after it is launched, unless there is a sequence of new offerings to keep it going. The alternative structure, the matrix, is a structure by disciplines, from which talent is drawn for various projects, to which one returns after completion. This does not usually work at all from the human motivation aspect. One may find upon returning, that if there are no new projects, there is no new work, or if there are new projects, one is just a resource from a pool of "warm bodies," to be put on this or that endeavor at the whim of the resource manager, depending on how well one's previous work was performed. Also, the further away one is, the more forgotten.

The new project may demand new skills which the last project did not provide. Here, you can be cut off from new opportunities which would require new knowledge, unless you were lucky enough to have just been on a leading edge project. Thus, the motivation is to always only be on a leading edge project, or you will be left behind and subsequently be surplus and out the door. Similarly, matrix organization financing is always subject to 10 to 30% cuts, as it only obtains funding from projects, who only need it when they need it.

An alternative structure in the past has been one big technical project which does everything for everybody, with smaller dependent projects, customizing this or that, and with separate marketing groups to market its specialized versions. In this structure, costs are difficult to track and we must take the good and the bad with little opportunity to obtain competitive advantages here or there, as there is little incentive to change.

PREPROGRAM STRUCTURES

Over the years, aerospace, military, and telecommunication product research development firms used both the project and the matrix structures. Both have been efficient at various times, but neither have been totally effective.

The "network problem" began to emerge in the late 70s, along with the "complexity problem." Terminal lines of business need modems, which need switch interfaces, to be resolved before the products can be developed. All have become dependent on new technology, all are searching for early market indicators and few have taken the time in the past to do much interdependent product planning, before launching projects.

In considering the matrix and project structures, in Fig. 7-3, most firms have selected the project structure. However, most of the developments have had problems in coordinating the separate hardware, software, test, and quality groups within the project. Some groups seem to do little for long periods of time, simply waiting to be told the eventual design, in order to do their particular piece of support work. Correct and timely hardware/software discussions and trade-offs have become a major development problem. Issues and interfaces across function groups are difficult to track and coordinate. Only the hottest areas obtain attention, resulting in a constant series of hot issues.

We need to take the project structure and extend it into a program structure and make it more effective in bringing together the right mix of people with the right motivation to work as a group to achieve the total program (planning, development, and support). Within the preprogram, preproject, preproduct planning committees and teams, people can move from project to project to advance and foster their careers, and become, in effect, a knowledgeable matrix resource. In reviewing the program structure, we must consider the people and their mode of operation. The new program structure must now include the preproject analysis in which strategic planning, conceptual planning, requirement definitions, and product definition analysis are performed. This will precede a particular project and usually consist of possible multiple project analyses.

It may utilize a group of specialists from each laboratory, division, or line of business to perform this preproject planning, similar to the matrix specialists pool, but in this case they will be part of a preproject planning activity that is always working on leading edge ideas. They usually will move on to the project with their ideas, when it is well defined. One or two may remain in advanced systems teams for new products. We will call this new structure the people planning programs "P" structure or just "P" structure to differentiate it from the traditional project or matrix structures shown in Fig. 7-3. To enhance it, we must organize it and overlay people needs on it to make it an effective structure that supports and organizes many disciplines of people, planning and providing new products in an overall program, in an organization for people, a "people organization."

SUPPORT STRUCTURES

A reasonable objective may be to structure the firm in terms of establishing a program to provide integrated total network multiple product solutions for segments of the marketplace by the firm's lines of business. Many times two lines of business may market different versions of the same prod-

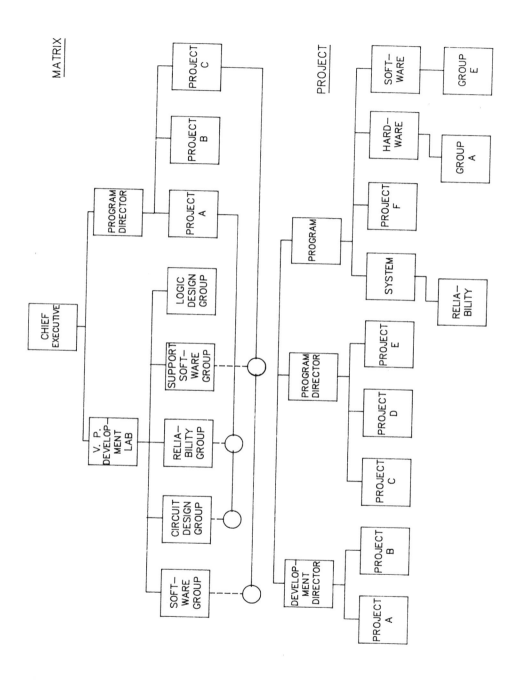

Fig. 7-3. Project Matrix.

179

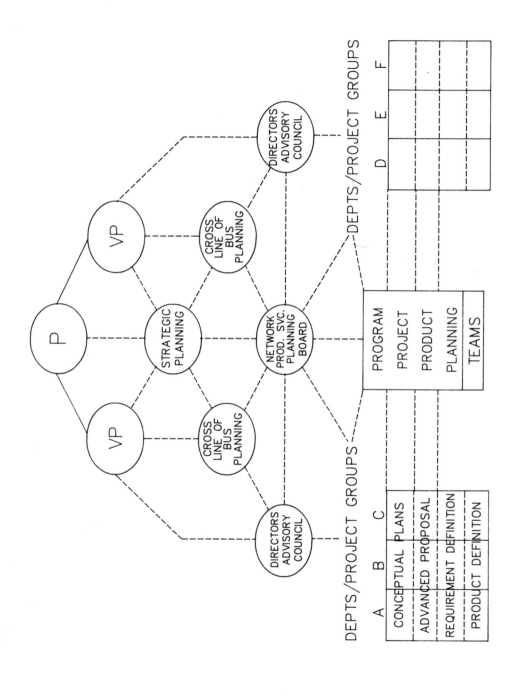

Fig. 7-4. The Planning Organization.

ucts to different market segments. Each line of business is given a wide enough program of several products or projects to support its existence. There will be some redundant disciplines with other lines of businesses similar to the project structure situation. However, for many disciplines that it may need, it can simply purchase assistance from a support organization within the firm. Support organizations can be subcontracted on a product line basis to support the lines of businesses. If these are obtained at substantially higher costs than in the marketplace, these additional costs will have to be covered as overhead and not applied directly to the lines of businesses. If the supporting organization is not efficient or is reluctant to provide the desired level of service required by the line of business, then of course the line of business should be allowed to go to other resources. The support organization of the product must support each line of business as separate customers, as would any other small business.

Hence, the support organization in a sense becomes a line of business, but not necessarily a profit center. It can have some of its costs as a reasonable overhead. The support organization may wish to farm various work projects to outside firms, so that it maintains a reasonable size, and acquire specialists to assist in meeting excessive schedules and demands only on a contractual basis.

In this manner we have a segmented firm competing in the marketplace, petitioned in a cost effective manner, with value added support centers, where each segment is handling several major integrated products, providing the total solution to their customer, supported in the most effective manner. However, to be a profit center there must be direct access to the real customer, control of support costs, and responsibility to perform or at least to approve planning.

THE "P" ORGANIZATION

The "preprogram, preproject, preproduct" organization, as shown in Fig. 7-5, moves the game from the program world to the preprogram world, recognizing that this is the new arena for the 90s and well into the twenty first century. Here "people planning programs" organizations utilize the processes that we have discussed throughout the book to create ideas and move them to products, as seen in Fig. 7-6. Figure 7-6 together with Fig. 7-5 indicate the need for the architecture of the new "P" organization, as shown in Fig. 7-7. This is sometimes referred to, as the new "people organization."

THE PEOPLE

Where does who participate how? How do they fit into the "P" architecture? How does planning interface with project management and system design? How do we achieve the best design? As we revisit figures of the

Fig. 7-5. The Focal Point.

processes from preceding sections, we can observe the need for various groups or types of people to perform unique functions within the preprogram oriented lines of business, to enhance their operational architectures to make them effective, as well as efficient organization structures.

Many of these needs apply to the providers, as well as the suppliers. They are:

1. The Manager Planner
2. The Strategic Planner
3. The Conceptual Planner
4. Advisory Councils
5. Planning Boards
6. Advanced Planning Teams
7. Requirement Definition Team
8. Product (System) Definition Team
9. Program Project Groups
10. Design Committees
11. Review Boards
12. Benefit Teams

Each appropriate individual or group of people have the following functions to perform:

- *The Manager Planner*—The participating management.

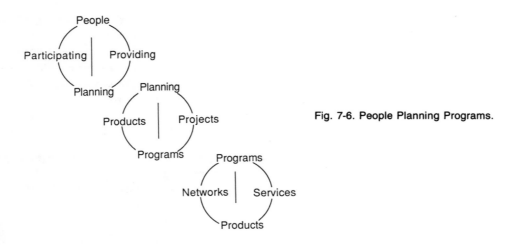

Fig. 7-6. People Planning Programs.

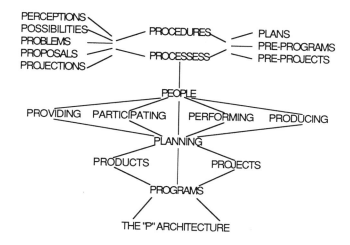

Fig. 7-7. The "P" Architecture.

Fig. 7-8. The "P" Organization.

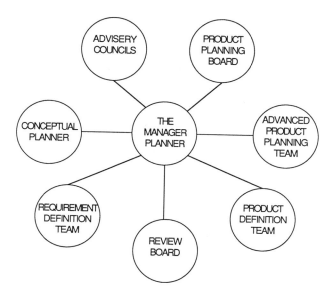

Fig. 7-9. People Planning.

- *The Strategic Planners*—A market, technical, finance oriented group, that work with involved top management and lines of business leaders to formulate strategic plans and help establish strategic direction, as well as facilitate and coordinate planning activities between lines of business, and across multiple units, and/or divisions.
- *Conceptual Planners*—Across lines of businesses, per unit or multi division. Big picture thinkers, who are technical, marketing, financial, society, and social oriented to identify market opportunities using technical possibilities. They work with advanced planning teams to further define new network, product, and service offerings.
- *Advisory Councils*—Market and technical business leaders, who participate in councils to provide strategic level advice to top management, in terms of business plans' impact on strategic direction.
- *Planning Boards*—A network, product, or service planning board that drives the planning process to pursue a strategic market/network architecture for the firm. It's participants cross lines of businesses, of units, and of divisions and report to top management of the firm, and the advisory council.
- *Advanced Planning Teams*—Conceptual planners from the various lines of business with the specialists from system and marketing planning within the lines of business, that define the advance product proposal.
- *Requirement Definition Team*—Participating players from the marketing and technical divisions, who work with various laboratories around the world, using market research, applied research, advanced development feasibility models to identify and define the product requirement specification.
- *Product Definition Team*—Consists of four groups: the system planning team, the marketing planning team, the project planning team and the program planning team. They produce the top level architecture and structure with functional and, possibly, sub functional partitions, the market plan, the project plan, the financial plan, and the manufacturing support plan. These are contained in the overall document, the program plan for a specific project or projects. The program plan becomes part of the line of businesses plans, which become the strategic plans of the firm.
- *The Program Teams*—These teams will be responsible for the program once the product definition phase is completed successfully. Hence, the exit review of the product definition phase will be facilitated by the program group. It must present not only the system, product, or service analysis, but also the project and support plans, as well as the financial and marketing plans. During the development phase, the program team will work with the customer (or lines of businesses), the project team and the various systems and support teams to provide top management with a detailed view of the progress of the program. In this manner, the schedule-quality-cost trade offs are brought to the highest level for consideration, during each phase of the development.
- *Design Groups*—The development program and the design should be well thought out before commitment. Hence, there is an opportunity to identify the type of people needed on each particular aspect of the project, in-

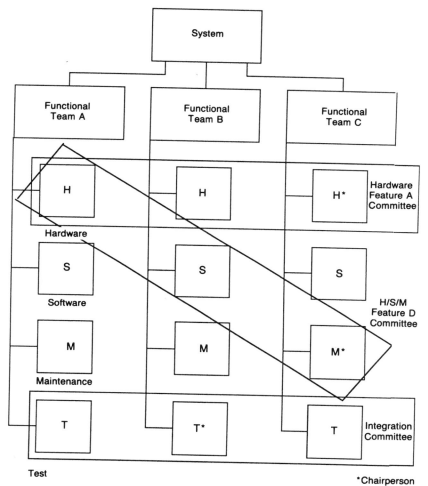

Fig. 7-10. The Function Committees.

stead of just general estimates of quantity of people. It also is an opportunity to identify work responsibilities, in terms of design groups composed of multiple disciplines that are developed by separate design teams, consisting of one or more system, hardware, software, manufacturing, test engineering, quality, and layout persons.

In this manner the hardware people develop the design, together with the software, and the test people. Here, the test person will understand the design early and correctly define the required test vehicle and integration plans. The quality person will have an early say on the quality and establish the acceptance and qualification tests to verify it. These have been major problems in the past. The system person is responsible for meeting the requirements and resolve the impact of new requirements on the design architecture.

- *Design Committees*—These committees will resolve cross design group design interfaces problems. For example, an array of working committees should be established, one for requirements, one for system design, one for interfaces using interface control documents (ICD), one for database design (global and local definitions), one for integration plans and testing, one for maintenance, one for human interface, one for quality plans and procedures, etc. There should be a representative member from each functional design area in each committee. In this manner there are not separate auxiliary groups looking over the shoulders of the few, who are doing all the design work. All work together to understand what it is they are developing, and assist in that development with their own area of expertise, early in the design and not after it has been completed.

  Each committee has a chairperson, who is responsible for seeing that their area of interest meets the system and requirement objectives. This chairperson is a member of a design team and may also be a member of the system team. Each chairperson of each committee is also a member of the systems steering committee, controlling the design of the system, product or service. The chairperson (usually the leader of the systems group) of the systems steering committee works directly with the project management group and the program director.

- *Review Committees*—These review committees are different for the various phases under review. As noted, the conceptual planning and product definition phase reviews, as well as the critical design review (CDR) (the end of detailed design) are key checkpoints for top management involvement, information, exchange and commitment decisions. The other phase reviews are more for the experts to track the progress of the project, with the exception of the requirements definition phase review, as noted in Chapter 3, which, depending on the impact on strategic direction may or may not require top management decisions.

- *Benefit Reviews*—Here, experts review the operational results of the ex-

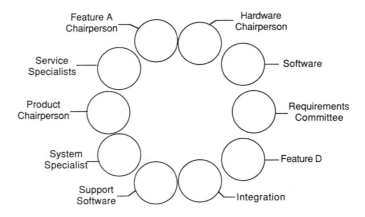

Fig. 7-11. The System Steering Committee.

186

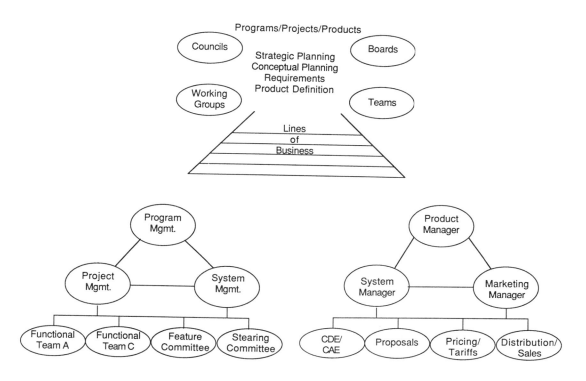

Fig. 7-12. The "P" Structure.

isting products in the marketplace to determine enhancements, termination, or new product needs, from the benefit analysis data. They report their findings to top management and project management.

When these teams, players, and committees are overlaid on the processes and the planning structures are in place, then the program and lines of business will be able to function successfully in the new "P" organization and respond to the increasing demands for new features and new products for the marketplace.

THE "P" STRUCTURE

A key to success is the one to one mapping of the design teams to functional areas identified in the product definition phase. This is the major reason for doing an extensive preproject architectural structure decomposition down to the functional and subfunctional level.

The cross committee involvement to identify subfunctional area components such as databases, interfaces, procedural software overlays, message structures, requirements partitioning, throughput, and performance models using chairpersons of each cross committee, as part of a system steering committee, is *key* to a system development program success.

Hence, we have obtained a living organization, not dependent on a particular project, having people transferring knowledge across projects and within projects, across lines of business and within lines of business, as they identify, design and provide programs for a succession of "right" projects, at the "right" time, using the "P" structure.

CAREER DEVELOPMENT

To play the game we must be able to play the game and want to play it. Over the years, much lip service has been given to the desire to provide a career path for the "fast trackers" or to provide training for "key" people, but in actuality, some fast trackers out ran their knowledge base, or key people leave the firm to work on projects with newer technology, so that they did not become technically obsolete. Others never had the opportunity to obtain the desired skills, which would enable them to become one of those "key" persons. As this became more and more recognized, no one wanted to be "left behind" on the old system. Salaries and promotions were tied to the new projects, with the result that fewer and fewer people stayed with the system long enough to see the results of their management decisions or designs.

The game degenerated in the 80s into a "promise anything" game, especially the "anything" that has an exotic architecture, that has some pizzazz. Some systems became extremely complex, just to be totally different. No one would remain on the projects to have to live with their commitments. Hence, one excessively cunning individual once said "Truth is only what it will obtain for me at that moment." He was eventually replaced, when, on a subsequent system, he was caught lying to a more sophisticated customer.

We can have a good organizational structure with good processes, but we must have knowledgeable people with integrity to utilize it. Figure 7-13 shows a reasonable technical/management career development program, overlaid on the product development phases. Here, an individual can progress on different projects over his and her career life, by moving from the implementation to systems planner and, depending on capabilities, becoming a conceptual planner, systems manager, or program manager.

A good firm will have their people participate on a series of projects to develop their skills, at least to the systems analyst position level, before offering an alternative management route. One enterprising person who saw Fig. 7-13, noted that the smart people get off the technical path after the first project and enter the management game. Unfortunately, this has been the case for too many potentially good management people, who desired to become fast trackers to reach high management positions. On the way, they made a few bad decisions, causing their downfall due to their lack of depth of technical knowledge, because, as Peter Drucker would have said, "they reached their level of (technical) incompetence."

Today's products have become integrated hardware and software systems, with intricate database structures. In order to attain the optimum trade

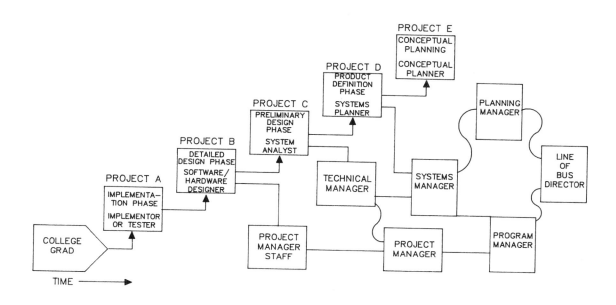

PROJECT E
CONCEPTUAL PLANNING
CONCEPTUAL PLANNER

PROJECT D
PRODUCT DEFINITION PHASE
SYSTEMS PLANNER

PROJECT C
PRELIMINARY DESIGN PHASE
SYSTEM ANALYST

PROJECT B
DETAILED DESIGN PHASE
SOFTWARE/ HARDWARE DESIGNER

PROJECT A
IMPLEMENTA-TION PHASE
IMPLEMENTOR OR TESTER

COLLEGE GRAD

TIME ⟶

PLANNING MANAGER

LINE OF BUS DIRECTOR

TECHNICAL MANAGER

SYSTEMS MANAGER

PROJECT MANAGER STAFF

PROJECT MANAGER

PROGRAM MANAGER

Fig. 7-13. Career Development.

offs in schedule, cost and quality, this requires a good understanding of these complex areas by all involved. This need for a much deeper understanding by management of the technical consequences of these trade off decisions, was also noted by the first female admiral of the navy, as she retired, when she commented on the lack of technical understanding and the long term impact of the financial decisions of the MBA graduates. It would, therefore, be advantageous for the individuals, as well as the firm to have the management path begin for the technical management inclined, at a minimum after project C and for project management after level B, as shown in Fig. 7-13, assuming 2-3 years on each project.

As technology changes every two years with many large projects lasting 4 to 5 years, there is the need for retraining all levels of personnel, either by internal courses or continuing education courses, with at least one specialized or refresher course every other year. In this way each person is up to date, so that they would be able to participate on every other (or third) project without the firm having to go outside to bring in new people and close out divisions of existing people.

To rekindle the dedication and motivation flame, the firm must first be dedicated to its people, enough to invest in them. (One of IBM's three key policies.) As we enter the new era of total information flow and we consider providing its new networks, products and services, there is the need for all involved to feel knowledgeable and comfortable in it. Those that win the intense competitive games in the marketplace will be those who not only know the game, but know the few winning ways to play it successfully.

Learning how to play it successfully, is for each of us to personally experience, but understanding the game in terms of its details and variations will give all of us a good edge. As the coach of a winning football team knows, the team's strength is also on the "bench" with ready, willing, and able players waiting to play the game. He develops that bench, spending at least a third of the energies and resources that he spends on his first team. He knows he will need them over the long season to have a winning season.

Figure 7-14 gives a quick guide on how a series of courses on planning, data, video, databases, and technology would apply to interested parties such as top management, directors, marketing, network planning, design, engineering, and operations. The extent of their interest can be defined as overview, 2nd level, and 3rd Level courses. The degree of interest within each level can be expressed as low, medium and high, representing type, intensity, and complexity of the courses at that particular level.

As we develop our management, various players will require different levels of knowledge, having different degrees of interest, depending upon involvement. However, the figures show that everyone requires some knowledge, from just an overview to an indepth course in design or operation, with various amounts of intensity at each level of the subject matters. In recent years, as the complexity and intensity of the game increased, senior management required a more detailed technical picture, in terms of high level overview, medium 2nd level, and some detailed third level analyses, instead of the traditional overview. The NCTE boundary issue ramifications have forced them to the second level considerations and the "open architecture" issue has required further analysis to the third level.

THE MANAGERS

As we consider new teams to achieve the product definition and product development activities, we will need new types of participating players and management. Too often in the past, planning was considered the "graveyard" for the out of favor, would be, or has been project leaders. With the result that the current product's systems management liked to re-do any advanced planning work the way they wanted it. However, as we have seen, the network game has now brought the company focus to the preprogram, preproject, preproduct planning phases. Attitudes must be changed about planning. Phases must be managed by respected and competent individuals, who have grown up in the development arena and understand the complexities of the various technical disciplines. They must also have a desire to work with the customer to better identify what the system should do. They need to participate early in the advanced product proposal, which defines the product architecture. It is not a holding tank, but a major arena requiring interested, knowledgeable, and respected players.

Conceptual, requirement and product definition activities are under the management of a planning organization in each line of business. Depending on the complexity of cross-line-of-business planning, it may require a separate planning organization reporting to the V.P. of strategic planning, respon-

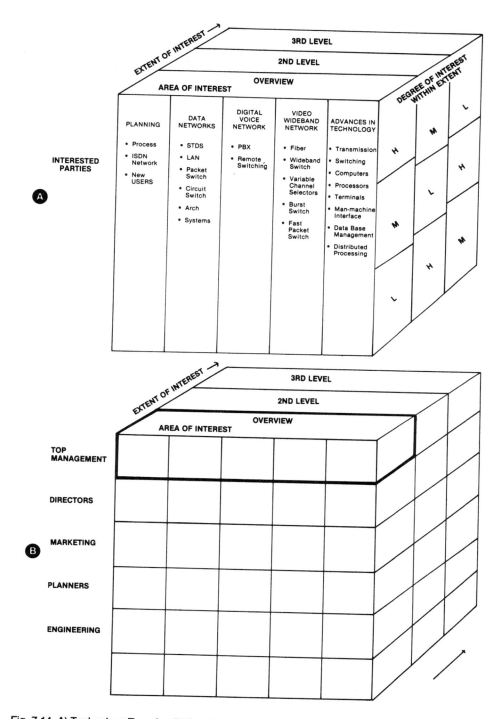

Fig. 7-14. A) Technology Transfer. B) Continuing Education.

sible to the product planning board and the senior executive responsible for the several lines of business.

The planning activities should be under the direction of planning managers, supported by program management of current or proposed programs or products. These development/implementation managers are sometimes called lines-of-business project/product managers. Once the product definition review decision is made in favor of a program, then program management will assume the responsibility, supported by the planning management. They must work together, as the program development manager provides people with the various disciplines to assist in each of the three planning phases (conceptual, requirement, and product definition). Future project programming management and systems people will participate in the planning reviews during the planning phases. Once the product enters the development cycle, the project manager will provide the reviews for the program management, who will usually only chair the critical design review phase, where the customer participates. The program manager will provide separate reviews to upper management.

The Planning Manager
- Working with multi-units to coordinate planning activities.
- Providing management briefing to top management.
- Scheduling/coordinating analyses with the various disciplines.
- Establishing feasibility studies with research and development.
- Obtaining market research for particular areas of concern.
- Establishing governmental considerations, positions and policies with legal departments.
- Identifying various lines of businesses planning opportunities and reviewing the status of current plans.
- Integrating conceptual plans with strategic planning to overlay mission and direction on future development plans.
- Working with lines of business strategic planning to overlay business plans into strategic plans.
- Providing management of technical and market resources in the three planning activities.
- Provide guidance to conceptual planners.
- Chairing planning phase review meetings.
- Working with the program manager.

The Program Manager
- Works with the planning manager.
- Providing guidance to conceptual planners.
- Becomes the customer interface.
- Organizes work activities with other disciplines involved in the project design and the development plan.
- Responsible for both the technical content, the delivery schedule and the costs of the product.

- Directs the systems and project control management activities.
- Identifies problems and manages solutions effectively, affecting schedule-quality-costs decisions.
- Tracks costs, deliveries and schedules.
- Coordinates integration and field support activities.
- Coordinates manufacturing and implementation activities.
- Negotiates contracts.
- Insures qualification of products to requirements.
- Assumes responsibility for requirement definition document's changes, additions, and deletions and their impact on the system by working with systems management and project management.
- Prepares proposals, explores areas with perspective customers, obtains agreements, makes contractual commitments, identifies additions, new versions, etc.
- Performs benefit reviews.
- Provides base line management reports.
- Monitors progress of program.
- Coordinates program reviews with top management.
- Identifies when new requirements should be addressed with a different product.
- Obtains phase review approvals from participating management.
- Determines product development cost picture.
- Resolves conflicting priorities across multiple units.
- Obtains necessary support systems needed to achieve the product.
- Coordinates sub-system's development/test integration programs.
- Provides the product deliverables to the customer.
- Insures timely delivery.
- Coordinates product releases and new version strategy.
- Provides customer training and support.

Product Manager

It is the product manager of the more service-oriented providers who controls, coordinates, prices, applies, modifies, tariffs, and delivers a particular product's service offerings where the product, such as a data packet switch, may be the vehicle to offer data input/output, transport, processing and manipulation features called "services." In this case, the product manager performs internal coordination and control, having decision making responsibilities. However, if decision and control responsibilities do not have authority or if authority is greatly limited to one area, such as marketing with no technical support, then as Fulmer's works have suggested, "they should not be called managers, but product specialists."

In fact, as there are levels of management in today's organizational salary structures, the title might be called product director, rather than product manager to indicate authority over major product area decisions, as well as to identify accountability. This observation, of course, applies to the product manager's counter part in the suppliers' design world, where the "program manager" could be called "program director." If the product's development and marketing are under one responsible person, who would be at the V.P. or executive director level, then the product manager will report to a program director. Here the product manager may be at the manager level, with more limited authority.

Systems Manager

Figure 7-15 denotes the two major market functions CDE/CAE that occur during the marketing of a product. System management provides customer design and application engineering to change and support the product. In the product management arena, the design changes of CDE are quite limited. If they are as extensive as the adaptation of a product from a generic design to a specific sophisticated design for a specific country, this would be performed under the direction of the program manager previously figuratively noted in the "P" structure. The product manager's systems management provide the technical support to the marketing managements' proposals and later customize the customer's Network, Product, or Service, help provide a qualification plan procedure or acceptance test with the suppliers quality assurance group and the customer, perform "beta" test trials or field tests with the supplier for new versions or applications, and may write new features in vendors' software to provide faster response to customers needs. If the products' suppliers provide primitive instructions, that can be easily used to develop new features. (These will have limited complexity until systems with user-friendly, feature-oriented, artificial-intelligence software are error free).

The systems group participate in the preprogram, preproject, preproduct/service planning activities of the conceptual, requirement definition, product definition phases of the "management planning process" with the representatives of the marketing manager.

Marketing Manager

The marketing manager provides the pricing, sales forecasting, advertis-

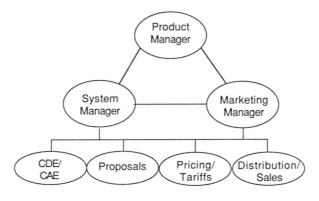

Fig. 7-15. Product Management.

194

ing, market analysis, market research, service policies/methods, direction to sales force toward target accounts, distribution policy, methods and departmental budgets, product improvement requirements, new product "feature" requirements, and product termination recommendations with postmortem reviews. Here a "marketing product life cycle" is established with a "market plan" for the six market life phases of the product: start up, growth, new features/versions, stable sales, decrease, and termination with support for remaining products in the field. (Some prefer to include new features in growth for five phases; others do not recognize anything other than growth or non growth for a four phase market life cycle).

The marketing group will work directly with the customer or may be part of a "single contact team" in order to provide a total solution to eliminate conflicting proposals and integrate offerings across product lines. The customer may be accessed through an intermediary or agent, as will be discussed later.

In this manner, the product manager obtains technical guidance and support from an internal system's group, who themselves may contract assistance from a supporting matrix group of hardware and software specialists. This provides capabilities to achieve fast technical response to the marketing manager's customers needs. By this system-market integration, the product manager obtains the "right" product support for the "right" market, in a timely manner. Again as noted, new product planning activities are supported by the product manager, using both the marketing and systems management to provide planning resources.

In the past, Telco's pricing was tied to tariffs and cost averaging to provide universal ubiquitous services. In the future, as the services are provided in the unregulated world using, separate accounting from regulated services, the pricing must be more in tune with the competitive techniques, in that basic costs are first determined and then various pricing philosophies and approaches, such as PRICE for GROWTH are used to obtain the bid, purchase or subscription. No longer should firms attempt to "milk a few customers" or "cream skim." They should provide for extensive movement and processing of volumes of information at small costs per unit handled, in order to have a growing market and not a growing amount of providers and suppliers for a "fixed" or "contracting" market which only results in fall-out of the number of suppliers and providers. Of course the game of "buy in" by a constant new group of providers and suppliers will artificially remove any profit for a long period of time and perhaps introduce extensive losses, depending on the new competitors' costs, labor market, automation of factories, type of new technology, and import tariffs.

Product Managers — Program Managers

These complexities have lead to the need for program managers, who have tasks quite different from product managers, and are more involved with developing new products than product markets, using project and systems managers. They are usually responding to governmental requests for bids or performing internal preprogram planning in the conceptual/requirements phases, It is there that they interface with product managers. Hence, in this preplanning arena, both the program and product managers' people meet to identify and define new products, networks, and services. Here the application "systems group" of the product group obtains the necessary avenue and power to indicate to the "systems teams" of the development group, what was wrong with past projects and what is needed in new products to better enable new feature packaging, maintenance, factory design and field support. It should be noted in the case of the suppliers, that the systems team of the product manager may in limited cases provide the actual product redesign for the factory. In this manner, they are totally cognizant of the design of the product, especially after development is finished with its first two years of factory support.

However, it is usually a full time job to support the factory. In most cases this is not advisable because the complexity of the product requires a separate factory product engineering "systems product group" to repackage the product for factory automation for manual or robotic assembly, as well as to work with the "factory automation systems group," which is responsible for the flow of design to the factory, automation of information flow in the factory, and "networking" of internal factory inventory flow and assembly operations.

This structure of distributed systems groups would look something like Fig. 17-16.

It is interesting to note, by observing the product life cycle phases, design committees and development teams, how systems designers from the nondevelopment areas can rotate through the development design groups, supporting development teams, as well as learning all aspects of the product in order to later perform their system design support function with the correct knowledge in their respective areas.

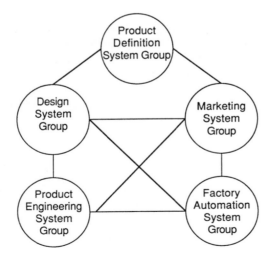

Fig. 7-16. Systems Groups.

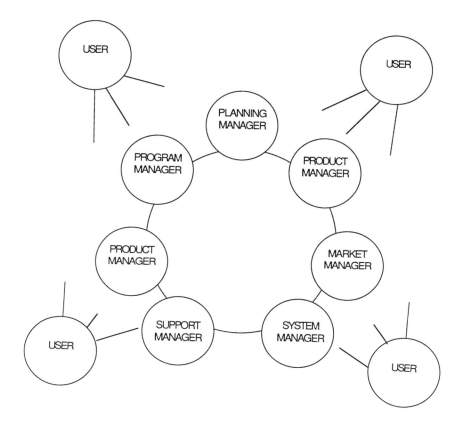

Fig. 7-17. Continuous User Interfaces.

User Agents

Interfaces to the potential and actual users must be carefully orchestrated. Some firms have gone to customer reps to coordinate activities of their various groups with the user and to respond to the user's "needs and requests." This can be seen in Fig. 7-17 as the users are addressed by the different groups within the firm over the product life cycle. It also becomes more complex, as several products may be required, each in a different phase of its market life cycle, overlaid on the product life cycle phases, especially as firms' units attempt to provide an "integrated" solution requiring features across products, simultaneous voice, data and video offerings for example.

This becomes extremely difficult, as the life of products shorten due to advances in technology, so the interval for various phases of customer interfaces are begging to overlap—for example new versions of current products that overlap with potential new features for new products. The impact on the customer, as the information era progresses, can not be underestimated. The net result will be a shield of planning and implementation advisors and consultants either on the user side or the suppliers and providers side.

User

- User Agents
- User Advisers
- User Providers
- User Consolidators
- User Groups

Firm

- Customer Account Specialists
- Client Specialists
- User Representatives

Intermediaries

- Local Service Providers
- Functional Area Providers
- Resellers
- Packagers
- Value added networks
- Consortiums

These areas represent and/or interface to the user, who may elect to select an intermediary, that will simply provide the user with various features and services from a cluster of multiple vendors that formulate a consistent total network solution.

Finally, the users become segmented into various information camps which provided a common family or array of tailored offerings, such as hospital-doctor networks, lawyers, factories, or schools. In any event we can see in Fig. 7-18 how the various groups will be working with the user, where preprogram product planning will play an ever increasing role:

PLANNING-DEVELOPMENT

There are many activities between planning and development, which complement and support each other's efforts. In this manner, those who participate in the early planning, bring their analysis to fruition during the development phases. The reviews conducted during planning become part of the full review program for the particular network, product, and service as it proceeds through design and development and then into operation. The cross-group, working-committee approach has been recommended for tracking, monitoring, designing, and reviewing technical progress of functional and subfunctional partitioned areas of the architecture, during the supplier's planning and development efforts. The provider should work with the suppliers as participants in their requirements committee and should have a similar effort to design their particular network or service offering, using working committees across lines of businesses with participating suppliers for similar

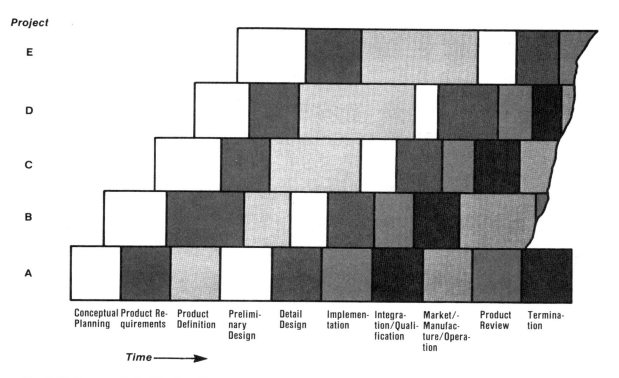

Project

E

D

C

B

A

| Conceptual Planning | Product Re-quirements | Product Definition | Prelimi-nary Design | Detail Design | Implemen-tation | Integra-tion/Quali-fication | Market/-Manufac-ture/Opera-tion | Product Review | Termina-tion |

Time ⟶

Fig. 7-18. Program-Project-Product Skew.

major mutual areas of impact. A study case takes a brief look at using design working committees to achieve a telecommunication switching product design. It demonstrates how the program manager uses the systems group to control and achieve the desired product and ensure that it meets its requirements. The system groups in turn uses design teams and working committees to structure the design.

Thus, all the preproject planning efforts to establish the right architecture and structure to meet the right requirements were effectively extended into the product's design by responsible systems, project, and program management, with their system analysts and designers.

MANAGING RESOURCES

The planning phases, development phases, manufacturing and operating phases can be used to balance resources as shown in Fig. 7-19. Many times a firm has begun three projects at the same time, because it had finally recognized the need for each endeavor, only to find that the required people and support systems were reaching unattainable peaks, with substantial drop offs, once the projects completed their implementation phase and the products successfully function their first year in the field. Since the planning processes give an early warning indicator by identifying what is needed and when,

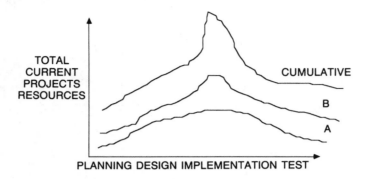

Fig. 7-19. Balancing Resources.

projects can be more carefully defined. and scheduled. Their architecture and structure can be designed in detail in the product definition phase by small groups of people. Then if the product is to be a development product by the supplier, the subsequent development phases can be skewed, so that an orderly human resource staffing, by type, can occur. See Fig. 7-20.

After we determine what type of people (not just generalized quantities) are needed and when, we can distribute resources. For example, project A's conceptual planners can move to the next project B, when the requirements and product definition teams take over project A. Later in development, some of the design teams can move to project B, when test and integration teams take over project A. However, in actuality, there would probably be alternating design teams working on every second or third project, with various people moving to positions of more expertise and responsibility.

The resource balancing can be obtained by viewing the company in the arena of providing multiple products sequenced after each other, but in a phase skewed manner. Not one after the other in series, but space sequenced in time, with people moving from project to project, as life cycles open up their respective phases. It is interesting to note that as they move to the next project, they leap frog technology and bring with them the best proven techniques from their past projects. This fosters training and career development activities, as they bring old skills to new tasks on projects of new technology.

The checkpoints of each phase were shown earlier. In practice, to balance resources, on multiple projects it may be necessary to begin phases before other phases end. However, as long as they do not prematurely begin, causing premature structures to be developed, before the requirements are known, this practice does not hurt and provides more time for a better detailed analysis to occur before final decisions are made. However, each phase must have an ending with a review checkpoint, before the subsequent phase can end.

Hence, balance can be achieved, enabling top down planning to drive the company at all times and prevent statements such as the following made many years too late by a chief executive officer who had the courage to admit past mistakes:

"There is no question that we have suffered from time to time from short-term goals. Let me cite just one example. We failed to undertake development of an electronic PABX on a timely basis. That was a conscious decision made on the grounds, that we could not simultaneously develop our electronic central offices and a line of electronic PABXs. I really wonder; if we would have reached a different decision had the issue been raised to an appropriate level, and had it been sufficiently examined on the basis of a long-term trade off analysis."

DECISIONS—DECISIONS

Who makes what kind of decision when? There are formal decision support processes, structures and models, which are based upon the following type of statement: "Decision flow analysis will identify decisions which should be made by modeling each management managerial decision, where possible, no matter how crude. It will determine information required by each decision and the design of the information system that will provide the data to enable the decision. Jobs may also be designed by determining job decision descriptions, identifying responsibility for them by indicating those decisions that are to be made by groups, and specifying the organization or decision making group. It also consists in the developing of measures of performance, procedures for making measurements, disassembling and using

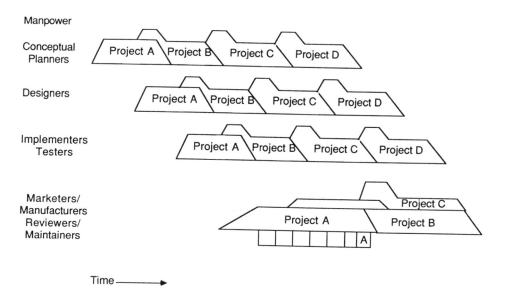

Fig. 7-20. Resource Distribution.

results, and incentive systems for motivating personnel to perform as well as they can."

The planning process reviews, within the "P" organizational structure using the teams, committees and review boards, meet the objectives of this decision model, without seeming to detail out a hard set of rules and procedures. It establishes a comfortable environment for making decisions, by the "right" people, at the "right" point and time. It brings the "right" information to the "right" level in the organization, both up and down, wherever the knowledge, power and influence exist. In this manner, those with the power share their power, but do so in a manner to minimize risk. The processes, supported by the organization, help manage risk. They bring the right information to the right people. If necessary, they, also, could be supported by a decision support system, which records all the decisions made at the phase reviews and documents the reason for the decision. It then could provide a more automated history log to enable subsequent review of the decision in the context of what happened, as the result of it. This will enable tracking of reviews, to determine if a particular strategy is revisited several times for different reasons. It also provides the basis for accountability of decisions, in order to provide appropriate rewards.

However, as can easily be recognized, with accountability (if heavy handed) comes fear and caution, so that no one may elect to make decisions, even though everyone should recognize that management may only be right an average 65-75% of the time (and that this is a desirable goal). Management may resist making decisions. Unfortunately . . .

"no decision is a decision no."

Hence, a lack of decisions usually indicates an overly cautious firm or one with too much negative accountability. This then brings us to the area of the culture of the firm and the environment, in which people are motivated, rewarded and encouraged to perform with even greater potential, than they could have imagined. Not on a one shot basis, as history had shown, where people really do not believe that they could have performed that well, but on a continuing basis. This was demonstrated in the Hawthorn Western Electric experiments in the early 50s, where people were taken from the production line to a pleasant controlled environment to see how well they could perform. They seemed to have unlimited amounts of increased productivity, simply by treating them with respect and allowing them to participate. It was not the better lighting, but the attention given to them. Unfortunately after the test, they were returned to the production lines with few changes, until the Californian Silicon Valley, having learned from these tests, established more worker motivation oriented production facilities.

CULTURE

"Culture consists of the norms, values and unwritten rules of conduct of an organization, as well as the management style, priorities, beliefs and interpersonal behaviors that prevail. Together they create, within an organization, a climate that influences how well people communicate, plan, strive, and share."

This is often an overlooked factor of a firm, as noted by the cartoon in Fig. 7-21 indicating a negative environment. For anyone who has lived aboard a ship, either sailing on a competitive racing ship or aboard a naval submarine or destroyer, knows the impact that the captain has on the crew. In earlier years it was called leadership or even management style. Some movies, such as *Captain Roberts* or, *Mutiny on the Bounty,* portrayed the impact that the person in charge can have on the operation.

Fig. 7-21. Whose Turf?

In some cases there is an "informal organization" individual, who by his or her personal aggressiveness or ruthlessness may endeavor to have an organization under his or her heel. In these instances, there is usually a constant clash between those attempting to run the firm with one management style and the other simply attempting to have power. Most of today's enlightened management are willing to assume some risk, but sharing power is usually another story. In some firms the negative use of power is destroying creativity, homogeneity, trust, working relationships, compromise, and willingness to enhance and expand others ideas. In these situations the best structure, process, and team or committee of well trained capable people will not augment individuals who are in powerful positions and misuse this power. These people must be removed, as they are "roadblocks" to any real successful ventures that are not directly sanctioned and sponsored by that particular individual.

On the positive side, many firms have leaders who treat others as they would like to be treated themselves. They are there to block for their people, not roadblock! They understand that everyone is successful, if all the forces of the company are functioning to make it a success. As noted earlier, in a recent discussion with a Japanese advisor to the chairman of the board of one of the largest banks in the world, he was asked "How the Japanese worked together so successfully?" He responded that candidates for top jobs are interviewed, before they are given positions, to determine exactly what type of people they are in terms of their management style, motivations, and capabilities, to ensure that others can work together with them and under them. He also reemphasized how everyone in the firm attempts to make "the firm" successful, and not just themselves. If the firm is successful, then they are successful, and they share in that successful environment with satisfaction.

An aerospace program director who turned around a major project, which was headed for disaster, was asked what his key to success was. He simply stated that he was there to help his people, and spent 40%-60% of his time with them, until they finally accepted him and told him their real problems. Then, he was able to move the company to back their efforts. It was no longer a situation of building the product in spite of the company, but building it together. His willingness to listen and be available was his key to success. Others have created vehicles for their employees to air problems and differences and ask the firm to change this or that, or to provide various things, such as day care centers, health facilities, flexible working hours, or to just encourage people with "can do" and "pride" type campaigns. However, the latter forms usually has little effect without the others.

We have all seen what happens when things are "not so good;" when financial objectives are not being met; when the project does not work; the market objectives are not being met; when the product is late. It's in these situations, where a culture, established by real leadership, provides an environment to continue to foster motivating relationships and reasonable objectives, like the store owner who rented a stadium to sell all the furniture in the warehouse, in order not to have to lay off any employees during tough economic times. Motivation of employees, overcoming resistance to change, willingness to take risk in the marketplace, spending money on planning for the long term view and providing a new offering of high technology networks, products, and services, many times conflicts with the "meeting the bottom line" emphasis to slice expenditures. All these things formulate the environment, in which people perform in a negative or positive manner depending on the direction and emphasis of the chief executive officers. Note how quickly the atmosphere of the same sailing ship can change with a different skipper.

A tried and true technique is to establish a culture in which rewards and recognition are tied to how hard people tried, rather than the results. As long as people are encouraged to work together and to become a working team, in which all levels of management and various disciplines respect each other, listen to each other, support each other, and try to meet the high expectations which each has for the other, how can they go wrong? Especially if there is a supportive organizational structure, that has the ability to encourage people to trust and communicate with each other and share ideas and information, remove negative competition between internal groups and establish accountability with understanding, by using processes to make their work more effective and enjoyable!

Hence, participating management will work with their people, provide leadership, coach, review and make commitment decisions to help them to achieve their endeavors successfully. A Japanese businessman was asked, "What happens if the 15% growth bottom line was not met this year; would the stockholders sell the stock?" He indicated that people in Japan today are looking for a solid long term view firm, but he admitted that some would sell. However, many would buy, since the large participating Japanese financial world is really looking for a firm that will be successful, over the full long term period. He, also indicated that "if the firm did have the long term look, it usually does not get into very many short term problems." Hence, the Japanese firm's leaders will do a great deal to ensure that the long term prosperity of their company is protected.

In America we now have a new breed of money managers making multi-million dollar commissions, as they constantly move billion dollar pension fund resources from stock to stock depending upon momentary Wall Street concerns for a particular day. There is a new mood in the financial world, having seen the net negative result of what has happened over the years with these investments constantly reversing the market. The pension fund controllers are considering managing their own funds with a longer, steadier look. In time, this type of influence will enable firms to better operate with long term concerns. However, as interest rates change and the market responds with speculative emotional advances, as much as 100 points a week followed by panic sell offs, logic does not prevail and big investors play the market shifts with little concern for individual firms making great profits, using leveraged money accounts. It may be time for the mature firm to separate itself from trying to constantly please wall street and concentrate on achieving its own success and survival in its product's marketplace.

Fig. 7-22. A Japanese Saying, Meaning "Together As One".

CONCLUSION

Figure 7-22 notes a Japanese firm's visionary objective for "the office of the future," A literal translation of the saying being; "No man on the saddle, no horse under the saddle." This means that the horse and the man are one unit in complete harmony. The horse does not feel that he is carrying a man and the man does not feel that he is riding a horse.

We have not attempted to copy the Japanese process for achieving quality products. What has been presented are effective methods for our culture in the western world today. It fosters new working relationships, using new processes under new organizational structures and cultures, enabling everyone to participate to their maximum, working together, as one, to meet the challenge of the new frontier—the information era—in the firm of the future—The Information Corporation.

FURTHER ANALYSIS

The case studies *Participating Manager Planners, Design Committees, Multi-Unit Planning and a Universal Planning Process* demonstrate the ideas and concepts presented in this chapter.

OBSERVATIONS: PEOPLE NEED ORGANIZATIONS THAT SUPPORT PROCESSES

1. Provide a process that enables people to function successfully. Provide an organization that enables the process to function successfully.
2. People need organizations which foster a climate that enables them to embrace change, take risk, share power, motivate and reward efforts (not only successes), and encourage participation.
3. Today's and tomorrow's organizations must support people with higher skills, who have the desire to keep learning and advance their careers in technical, marketing, or management in an orderly progression over multiple projects.
4. Multiple projects and programs can be time-phased to minimize cumulative resource requirements and enable the transfer of knowledge obtained from preceding endeavors.
5. Participating management needs an organizational structure that enables them to participate not only efficiently but effectively.
6. A planning organization is needed, in each line of business, which works across lines of business to provide many integrated offerings.
7. The project and product type organizations are enhanced by the "P" organization, where people participate in a "people planning programs" oriented organization, in which preproject, preprogram planning is performed, using shared resources across divisions and lines of business.
8. The planning teams and design committees should both establish interfaces with R&D laboratories and market research firms for the type of technology transfer and market feature/shift information required at the various phases of the management planning process.
9. The review process becomes a decision process, as major endeavors are reviewed at the "right" time and place, by the "right" people, to obtain the "right" management commitment.
10. Playing the game with the "right" organization, with the "right" process, with the "right" people is less exhausting, more efficient, more effective and considerably more fun, as the firm becomes a formidable opponent in the internationally competitive telecommunications information world marketplace.

Chapter 8

The Information Corporation

The previous chapters considered several techniques, processes, and organizational structures, as well as various modes of operation to achieve "the transfer of technology to meet identified 'market driven' needs." Due to the number of changing variables of the future telecommunication information market and challenging technological possibilities, a management planning process was presented that facilitates the exchange of ideas between marketing, technical, government, and users. These innovative management tools enable a "series of thinking/action looks" to take place, in order to bring out the various hidden facets, conditions and aspects that more fully identify the issues, to better define the problem, in order to provide the right solution.

This maps well into today's management operating style, where thinking is tied to action in thinking/action cycles. Managers often instigate a course of action simply to learn more about an issue. One implication of action/thinking cycles is that action is often part of defining the problem, and not just implementing the solution. The act of collecting more data often changes the nature of the problem, as part of the cognition process.

As discussed, the future information society will be based upon several complex steps in which technology and marketing will become the push-pull forces. This will require a new type of organizational structure, the "P" structure, that enables management to participate in a world of change and make commitments with less personal risk. As seen in Fig. 8-1, the interconnecting location is sometimes difficult to pinpoint, where the new game will be played for future voice, data, video networks, services, and products. Creating the

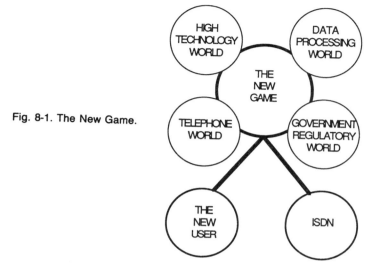

Fig. 8-1. The New Game.

information society is indeed the next frontier for opportunity and exploration.

To find this location, we have considered several interesting concepts that suppliers, providers, and users could adapt, which would enable them to play this new game a little easier, a little better, and a little more successfully, in the real world of possibilities, plans, problems, proposals, policies, processes, procedures, participating people, programs, projects, and products. For the sake of reference, we will umbrella all these concepts under the term "Top Down Planning." See Fig. 8-2.

Top Down Planning can be achieved in a firm by a series of steps to obtain:

1. Top management involvement.
2. "Go, No-Go, Rework" decisions.
3. Marketing-Technical agreements.
4. Feasibility models to minimize risk.
5. R&D-Provider-User interfaces.
6. Recursive planning activities.
7. Hand off of planning to program/project management.
8. Early network, system, product architecture/structure definition.
9. Management Planning Phases—Product Life Cycle interfaces.
10. Orchestrated multinational-multiunit planning interfaces.
11. Balancing business cycle and technology cycle.
12. Pursuing quality over the product life cycle phases.
13. Managing the pursuit of quality.
14. Achieving difficult financial risk-opportunity decisions.
15. Orchestrating business plans with strategic direction.
16. Obtaining strategic plans from business plans.
17. Funding directed research and development.

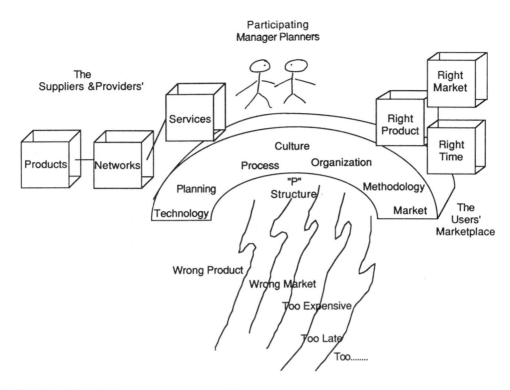

Fig. 8-2. Top Down Planning.

18. Developing people to perform successfully.
19. Obtaining Innovation.
20. Economically and effectively providing the right product, to the right market, at the right point in time.

The series of steps for playing the game, depending on whether one is the user, supplier, or provider, is outlined in the following sections.

CULTURE

Establish, as an objective, a *culture*, which fosters planning, taking the time to think, time to be creative, acceptance of risk in trying new ventures in the marketplace, expenditures on R&D to prepare for the future as well as today, reward and motivation of people not necessarily on accomplishments but on effort. The creation of an environment that uses planning processes, where ideas and possibilities are encouraged, listened to, discussed, enhanced, and acted upon.

MANAGEMENT PLANNING PROCESS

Adapt the four phase *management planning process* as the vehicle to

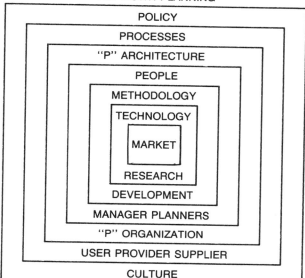

Fig. 8-3. Overlays on Overlays.

go from mission, to strategic direction, to conceptual plans, to requirements, to product's architecture and structures, to project plans, to market plans, to financial plans, to program plans, to business plans, to strategic plans.

ORGANIZATIONAL STRUCTURE

Establish the *"P" organizational structure* to facilitate the process in which market and technology opportunities become translated to programs for new products, to projects of the supplier or networks, products, and services, and to lines of business by the provider. Emphasize the planning effort, as equally as important as the implementation effort. By structuring the firm around a "P" organizational architecture to enable preproject/program planning, across lines of businesses, research, development, and marketing groups, using strategic planning groups, advisory councils, planning boards and planning teams, an innovative firm will have the right framework to work with change.

COUNCILS, TEAMS, COMMITTEES

For the planning processes within the "P" structure, establish the following *councils, teams* and *committees:*

1. Advisory councils
2. Strategic Planning Group
3. Conceptual Planners
4. Advanced Planning Groups
5. Requirement Definition Teams
6. Product Definition Teams

7. Program/Project Planning Teams
8. Phase Review Management Groups

During Development (Suppliers) establish:

1. Functional Design Groups
2. Cross Group feature/functional area committees
3. System Steering Committees
4. Integration Committee
5. Quality Group

During Operations (Suppliers/Providers/Users) establish:

1. Qualification teams
2. Benefit Review Teams

PEOPLE DEVELOPMENT

For *people* develop the following:

1. A career path matrix to technical, marketing, or management positions on a project or phased program basis.
2. Logically provide a creative, "think" office environment and if possible, physically provide separate closed offices, as well as small group discussion office "niches."
3. Provide a series of technology, planning, marketing, and finance courses internally and externally (continuing education).
4. Enable participation and attendance at conferences, round table discussion groups, technical forums across firms within the industry, and user market forums across industries.
5. Reward and motivate participating management and creative planning.
6. Provide top management leadership, guidance and decision commitments.

MARKET-TECHNOLOGY TRANSFER

Overlay the *market* transfer process and the *technology* transfer process on the planning life cycle and product life cycle.

QUALITY METHODOLOGY

Develop a *pursuit of quality* methodology to identify, establish, and review the progress of the firm's pursuit of quality.

R&D PLANNING

Establish *interfaces* with high technology research, product development planning teams, and cross industry *conceptual* planning groups, using CCITT study groups and working committees, TI, and IEEE, as well as with respected market research firms.

STRATEGIC PLANS/BUSINESS PLANS

Develop *strategic plans* based upon lines of business, or laboratory's *business plans* and *project plans* in terms of a long range program of two four year intervals or four two year intervals. Identify the market over these periods in terms of future market opportunities achieved by potential networks, products, or services of a specific architecture and structure.

PERSONNEL ALLOCATION

Orchestrate people, moving them from planning team to planning team, from project to project in the planning phases, to achieve the business plans, system plans and project plans. Balance resources by skewing the planning and implementation phases of the various projects.

DEVELOPMENT/SELECTION/PROCUREMENT

Using a *development process* synchronize the supplier's development in phases with the planning life cycle and the planning *selection/procurement* phases of the provider to achieve and provide the networks, products and services to the user.

BENEFIT ANALYSIS

Perform *benefit analysis*, reviews, reassessing designs versus operational data to determine the achievement of the desired strategic direction of the firm, as visualized in its mission. Utilize the reviews as part of a management decision system to track results of previous decisions to note success and accountability.

UNIVERSITY/INDUSTRY PARTNERSHIPS

Establish working relationships among various universities, as logical, though not necessarily physical, joint technical research institutes, as well as with industry, local government, and academic research partnerships.

GOVERNMENT RULINGS

Work with government agencies in identifying and resolving "level playing field issues" (such as future Inquiries) in order *for all to play the game.*

ISDN NETWORK ARCHITECTURAL MODEL

Using standard network architecture and standards groups, determine the U.S. version of the ISDN International model in terms of architecture, structure, interfaces, and boundaries for information transfer, handling, and processing in the U.S. competitive marketplace. See "The U.S. ISDN Network."

MANAGER PLANNERS

Achieve the above by becoming involved, participating, coaching, umpiring, refereeing, leading *manager planners.*

STRATEGIES

Establish *strategies* for playing the game. As we review the general purpose "new network game" model, we might make the following observations that could affect our future strategies:

Providers

1. Based upon their mission, strategic direction, and "strategy of the strategies", establish their Image in the marketplace consistent with their network architecture.
2. Define their network architecture around the ISDN model, as they identify its transition phases in terms of their network feature and service offerings.
3. Identify a list of "must," "could" and "wish" features, that they want to provide to the marketplace in four two year intervals or two, four year intervals, to direct their research laboratories.
4. Establish with the research laboratories a technology transfer process to review, consider, and coordinate basic and applied research activities that interface into their planning process.
5. Utilize their management planning process to address their users needs.
6. Position themselves to meet all their user's (residential, small businesses, shopping centers, office complexes, large firms, interexchange carriers, intermediaries, independents, government networks, etc.) needs by structuring to provide a total network solution.
7. Structure into market (large national/international, business clusters, shopping centers, etc.) driven entities providing the customer with a single network solution of several products from the voice, data, and video offerings, as allowed by governmental restraints.
8. Establish a short- and long-term governmental strategy game to position the firm with the right products, as the opportunity develops.
9. Identify the family of office and residential products to work within their ISDN architecture in terms of those available now and those needed in the future. Then establish working arrangements with various development manufacturers for internal or overseas markets per government rulings to achieve these products.
10. Use a technology transfer process to work with development laboratories for the next generation of products and establish standards with industry groups to interface them to the provider's network architectural vision.
11. Enter the standards arena, using T1, IEEE, open system stds, cross industry committees, and Bellcore, to move U.S. ISDN public/private net-

work standards forward and establish usage billing and numbering plan standards across industries, as well as information feature standards with data processing firms.

12. Provide joint venture relationships with numerous data processing and computer firms, to obtain necessary products and services to integrate into the network for their users. See "The Business Information Systems."

13. Provide a public data network and become an integrator of new products, as well as an internal showcase.

14. Automate maintenance and administration features to become the showcase by moving more and more functions into the network switches, as the providers become good users of their own networks.

15. Providers, users, and suppliers need to utilize roundtable discussions to work together to establish agreed direction and begin to manage change together. It will require working together, using a common planning process to manage change, to achieve opportunity in the next frontier . . . "The Information World."

Suppliers

The Suppliers are entering a unique phase in the development and deployment of technology. As one executive vice president of a digital switching development laboratory observed: "For the first time we have the technology to do 'anything.' The problem today is *defining* the 'anything' that the customer may want. The second problem is the fact that the 'anything' must now be part of a 'Network Offering,' in which its architecture and structure must fit a physically distributed integrated facility switching services environment, whose interfaces and standards must be developed with international and national agreements among numerous suppliers and providers."

In this environment, the first wave of digital central office replacements are the digital access systems to the world and clusters of central offices (as digital islands) in the rural, suburban and metro growth areas. This conversion will be completed over the 1986—94 time frame. Next, the more remote offices and those with less growth will be changed to digital over the 1990—96 time frame. However, their change out is continuously subjected to trade offs of new revenue versus system price, and maintenance costs versus the ability to provide more centralized automated maintenance. These are also considered in terms of volume discounts to change out the entire network with one or more supplier's digital systems. Unfortunately, there are numerous international suppliers competing for this market, as NEC, Ericsson, Siemens, Fujitsu, CGE(ITT), and BT(Mitel) to name just a few, join the AT&T Technologies, Northern Telecom, GTE, Strongburg, IBM(Rolm), and Rockwell information digital switching marketplace. Many others have or are developing fiber optic multiplexers, digital feature switches, local traffic control systems, distributed PBX's, cellular switches, and automated test systems.

It is now a world market with international players. Each player to play the game for the 90s must consider a wide range of strategies such as:

1. Recognize that no switch, multiplexer, or whatever can be successfully sold, as a single entity. Every device is now a subsystem or system of the network, which is evolving in shifts, transitions, or phases, per some particular vision of the manufacturer.
2. This vision from both a technical and marketing point of view should be presented to the perspective providers and users in order for them to understand the product life cycle of each of the companies' products, recognizing that they now have a five to ten year operational life, instead of forty years, as the information world evolves.
3. Each system's product must provide some relationship to the evolution of the information world, in terms of future integrated voice, data, video offerings.
4. The term "integrated" must be applied from both a technical and marketing point of view. We have seen a single 2B + D or 23B + D or NB [where B is a clear 64 kilobit channel for moving voice or data and D is a 16 or 64 kilobit channel for signalling, telemetering, or packet data] as the future loop access interface to an "integrated" switching system array of voice, data and video offerings. However, "integration" may be achieved by autonomous, functionally partitioned or functionally integrated systems, as well as by future systems based on variable bit rates (V bits) on gigabit transport mediums. These architectures and structures are transparent to the user, offering to provide an array of system offerings.
5. The array of system offerings are: digital voice switching systems, data packet switching systems, data circuit switching systems, video/wideband data megabit switching systems, nodal point access switches (remote and local) to differentiate voice, data and video traffic, fiber optic multiplexers demultiplexers, local area network entrance/exit address/protocol, code conversion pads, digital cross connects (automated), satellite to satellite data switches, mobile/cellular/personal call switching systems, local transport microwave systems, physically distributed PBX's, Business Service Units, Local Area Networks (LANs), and Metro Area Networks (MANs/WANs). These should be identified in terms of their integrated, overlaid, and extended versions that enable the network to meet new and different needs over its transition phases.
6. As systems are enhanced, moved around, or phased out during the transition period, it is important to show the role each product will play, as users are encouraged to use the new information facilities to access and exchange more and more information until traffic has built up to require new different traffic handling throughput capabilities.
7. These throughput needs should be considered from five vantage points: terminals to generate/receive information, switches to switch the information, databases (local, remote, distributed, central, on line, off line, virtual . . .) to store the information, programs to manipulate and process the information, and finally features to make the information more useful.
8. Features become the reason for a phase out, addition, redesign, new ver-

sion, or new system, as we consider moving to fast packet or burst switches in the 90s, and in the 21st century to light photonic switches with variable band widths for different usage needs.

9. Usage will be another factor, that must be identified and defined. Universal billing will be performed on usage basis, as the users use variable amounts of channel capacity. Billing must determine what systems handled how much of whose information for how long. Hence, support systems will play a major role.

10. Support will become more automated in terms of moving packets of administrative and maintenance information from devices, subsystems, and systems to determine progress, diagnose situations, recover systems, administer traffic checks, evaluate performance, and update features, especially as the levels of features extend into the enhanced value added nonregulated world.

11. The regulated versus nonregulated world considerations will determine the features, interfaces, and standards of future systems affecting the architecture and structure of these new families of systems, so they can compete effectively in both worlds with some form of commonality, and change with technology to apply new technological advances, to achieve such things as easier, cheaper human-machine interface systems in the more competitive nonregulated arena, as the regulated fades away.

12. The terms "human - machine interfaces" and "user friendly" imply that for a device or a network to be really used, it has to become an extremely easy to use tool. Only when this has been achieved in the design of the network's architecture and the structure of its systems, will the information world truly begin.

Systems will eventually move megabits and gigabytes, as larger quantities of information are made available to more naturally perform functions that are presently accomplished without the computer, such as reading a newspaper. Here, people quickly scan large amounts of information until they find the item they wish to read. Similarly, the amount of data transfer may have to change from the single item to the complete paper, to be more "user friendly."

Thus a weather eye must be out for the point, when the packet digital switch may need to give way to a megabit wideband technology. At this time, technology may meet the challenge with an entirely new emphasis, such as changing the computer's number base from binary to decimal, because the full frequency spectrum can be used in light-to-light logical switching systems, as opposed to the binary on-off states of electronic logic systems. This opens the door for an entirely new family of compilers, processors, and architectures, as one breakthrough leads to new possibilities. But only when the market has built up on today's technology to generate the megabit traffic, will this technology be needed by the users.

Hence, we have need to be looking for change, rather than being locked in to one technology, such as binary digital, as was previously done on analog. It will be an ever expanding game. Digital has a purpose; to bring the first and second wave of users into the information world, using medium speed 9600, 64K, 1.5M, 2.08M, input/output; but it may not meet the needs for the third and fourth wave, as new capacities are required to perform more complex and human friendly endeavors.

The ISDN information world, as shown in Fig. 10-22, is designed to encourage these changes, as the voice, data, and video traffic grows to the point that it is introduced into the network, through nodal access systems moving the fiber closer to the users with subsequent nodal switches under more and more user control. The network will provide new features and services, through the array of new systems, as they become available, as noted in Fig. 10-23.

Users

The users will have the deciding vote in the information world. As they delayed its entrance in the 70s, their indifference to what it could do for them may persist through the 90s. Of course, price on many occasions is the deciding factor. However, in this we become tied to the disadvantages that high technology provides. It's reduced individual device costs enables machines to provide a fantastic number of new features, but to achieve these features will require a totally new network.

Hence, we are back to the overlay game, where it is more economical to bring users into the new feature world, by stringing a special highway for them to test out their new voice, data, and video vehicles. In this manner, more and more vehicles of various types and structures are encouraged to come and use the highway. As needs are observed, exits and on ramps can be added and the highway can be expanded by adding another lane or actually rebuilding pieces and segments to handle expanding quantities and types of traffic. Finally, the initial voice network will be bi-passed by the overlay of super highways, designed for ease of use to handle large quantities of the various types of "new users," as they become quite prevalent.

Therefore, during the transition period into the information world, we must cater to these "new users" and allow them to experiment, try out new endeavors, and become comfortable with their new vehicles, so the vehicles become the tools that they cannot do without. Once this stage is reached, we are fully into the features game, where the users demand more and more integrated information access, handling, manipulating, and processing. The game will be played in the two worlds of communication and data processing. Data processing firms will provide more and more LAN protocol interfaces via nodal point CPE communications. The government will encourage more and more competition to provide ISDN universal "integrated" offerings, such as those noted in Chapter 10 at reasonable prices, not only for the large users in the metro environment, but also for the smaller users in the suburban and rural environments.

Evolution and Change

The reality of evolution and change must be understood:

- The data game was initially played by large and medium businesses using dialed-up unlimited calling local voice networks, handling analog low speed data, and by large firms on point to point leased facilities.
- Just as in the distant past when Father Strowger, the New England undertaker, developed the voice switch to eliminate excessive point to point phones, data switching will challenge LANs to replace the now too common expensive point to point lines. This causes the need for a switch to enable any terminal to talk to any other terminal with protocol conversions. This is provided by data packet switches, network entrance PADs (packet assemblers disassemblers), data circuit switches, and PBXs for local area high capability network rings, branches, and stars.
- Integrated circuit and packet switching of data will be added to voice switching systems to build up data users and provide ubiquitous service to cluster groups of data users.
- The public data switches must interface with private data networks to enable internetwork transfer of information.
- Small businesses will utilize intermediaries, public data networks, multi user "data centrex type" Telco offerings to tie into various database sinks.
- Homes will access these public data networks to provide work capabilities at home, only if priced for usage (otherwise via CATV data ports).
- Multitenant work station office complexes will use fiber and data networks to communicate with central locations. These work satellites can become quite remote, as long distance fiber and satellite systems become cheaper.
- Once data traffic has developed, then the video world for image, text, slow motion, high resolution video communication will expand first in the office and then in the home.
- Video distribution systems to homes will be provided by low speed transfer to megabit storage devices.
- Change will happen in different times for different areas, as demand and growth are encouraged for different market segments of user types and people types by the providers and suppliers.

Hence, it is not simply a question of asking the users what they want. Many times they do not even understand what is possible. Resistance by various people types is always there. Therefore, top down planning must consider the users' needs, but must also understand their resistance to change and knowledge level base. It must listen to their wants. It must give them technical possibilities. Various market research and technology visions need to be tested to determine what is possible, by using many trials here and there to see what modification, version, or twist of the feature will really be acceptable to the users. Once the users are using the new technology, then they will be better informed and more sophisticated to select various versions and request new possibilities. See "The Human Element" case study in Chapter 12.

We have seen this in the automobile marketplace, but only a few have understood it. Note the performance of the Japanese in meeting the U.S. automobile and stereo marketplace. There is a need to listen to the marketplace, which means taking time for observing and thinking. An interesting example of this is the shift from feature options in automobiles to automobiles having a fixed set of features, as part of the basic offering, at a given price. Note how foreign automobile manufacturers, such as the Japanese, are now simply playing the price game on basic packages for different types of cars, to see the highest price they can get for a particular type or model, while U.S. firms persisted in playing with low finance packages to create a demand for their cars of less quality and engine economy.

TECHNOLOGICAL RESEARCH

"The use of some scenarios is based more on the conviction that what a company becomes depends on what it does, than on what is done to it. Hence, some companies believe they can fashion almost any kind of future that they want to, within various political restraints. Whether or not a particular direction or development turns out to be profitable depends primarily on the nature of commitment that the company makes in creating that future. Thus, many scenarios are qualitative, wishful projections of the company future. There are, of course, an unlimited number of possible futures that can be prepared for any particular company." With this in mind, one might consider what has happened to many firms in the telecommunication field due to various technological changes which really were not under the control of any particular firm, except perhaps the few that participated in the breakthroughs. Many of today's technological changes were not initially considered in very many scenarios.

Much of today's "research" in many firms is simply playing with possibilities, obtained from breakthroughs of other firms, and extending them into a specific advanced development arena. There is a need for constant analysis of new possibilities between a firm's conceptual planners and the many research and development laboratories. The key to success in periods of high technological change for both the provider and supplier will be to establish this relationship using a common planning process, such as the R&D technology transfer process. As indicated earlier, this enables technology to be "somewhat driven" in a general direction and tracked, so that new possibilities can be immediately recognized. The technology breakthroughs are then more quickly moved through subsequent advanced and applied development laboratories to determine applicable architectures and structures, which can feasibly be achieved, and applied to the marketplace. In this manner, more realistic and useful scenarios can be developed, that reflect the changing technology.

MARKET RESEARCH

As indicated, we must be careful to track the users. As they become more

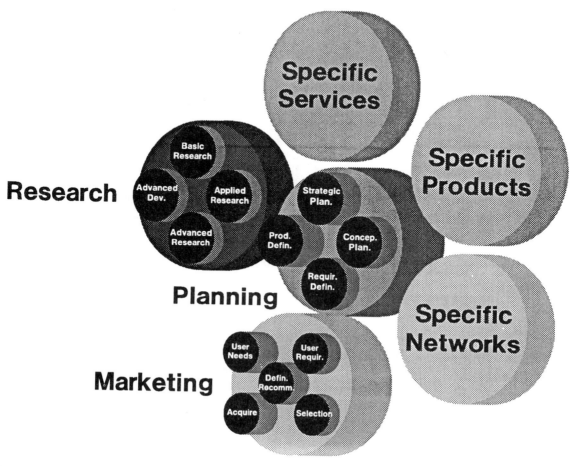

Fig. 8-4. Technology Push / Marketplace Pull.

and more sophisticated, they will want extended levels of features to enable them to work or play more efficiently. They will easily shift to using technology, that enables their machines to be more and more helpful to their endeavors. Conceptual planners should constantly use the planning process to drive many marketplace analyses to further determine what the users really want and need, as we proceed deeper and deeper into the information age. Products to be more competitive must provide features with "the twist on the twist, or a twist here, a turn there" to encourage the user to desire their product over another. Perhaps, plan old support will be the key feature in the future.

INTERNATIONAL MARKETPLACE PLANNING

The more sophisticated firms will play the game in several international arenas. By doing this, they will be able to work with different levels of maturing information users. However, this requires an understanding of these concepts:

1. "The 'buy in' is always high." The firm does not make any profit in its first offering. The learning curve is expensive.
2. No matter how backward or remote, the customer will always want the latest and best, even if they are not ready for them. Hence, the overlay game will have to be played for different market segments in a different manner for each segment.
3. The international marketplace competition will be extensive. The winners will be those who can quickly package and customize the latest and best for that particular country's market. Obtaining commonality will be difficult. Achieving an excellent level of technology transfer for various national laboratory and marketing personnel will be the major consideration for a successful multinational program.
4. The market will determine the variations and timing of various possibilities. Considerable effort must be expended, to understand the complete range of new features, that must be part of a particular country's product offerings to be successful. These requirements must then be translated into variations of the architecture and structure for new product offering before commitment to development. Note: ISDN will be offered in different phases in each country. This then will effect the commonality of the structures. It should also be understood that once laboratories are established in foreign countries, it is quite difficult, expensive, and sometimes impossible to change staffing.
5. Cross lines of business and multiple laboratories planning becomes very complex, as different countries participate in joint planning sessions. This requires a new skill of working relationships, to achieve agreements between the various nationalities. As the knowledge is transferred, each country will wish to assume control for their own country's product's versions and variations.
6. The input to the planning process activities of all the ideas and possibilities required for the different countries, will test the changeability of its products and will require a technology base, that can be used productively in many markets, as the world moves into the information society out of phase, but somewhat in step.

USERS, PROVIDERS, SUPPLIERS

First establish a management planning process to integrate users, suppliers, and providers by providing interfaces to their individual planning processes. This will enable people in different divisions, units, companies, and countries to work together through the planning process to provide new families of networks, products, and services, every four or five years on a periodic basis.

As described in Chapters 9 through 14 on the ISDN Overlay Network, ISDN

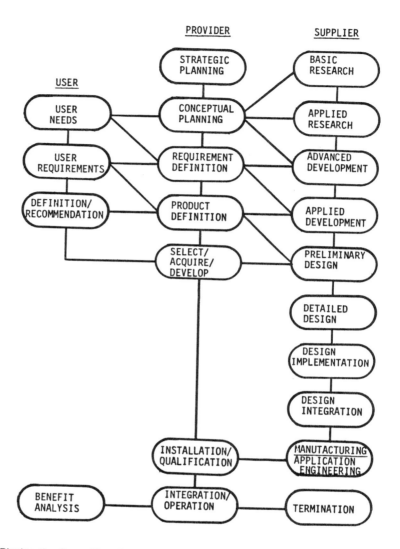

Fig. 8-5. Playing the Game Together.

Wideband Network, and the ISDN Marketplace, "to play the game" you must:

1. Per Chapter 10, establish a "rings on rings within rings" facilities strategy:
   a) Single ring
   b) Multiple rings
   c) Branch/star/spoke extensions
   d) LAN/WAN/PBX interface PADs
   e) Base/satellite nodal access switches
   f) Establish ISDN standards interfaces.

2. Establish ISDN islands strategy:
   a) Location in business sectors
   b) Location in university sectors
   c) Location in shopping centers
   d) Location in affluent residential sectors
   e) Location in multitenant dwelling clusters
   f) Location in office complexes

3. Establish interexchange networks:
   a) Voice networks
   b) Packet data networks
   c) Satellite data packet networks
   d) Wideband networks
   e) Operator and billing services.

4. Provide interLATA networks:
   a) Voice, data, video, interLATA interfaces
   b) Wideband, fiber, and T carrier networks.

5. Establish unregulated special services:
   a) 911 nationwide
   b) 911 foreign countries

6. Establish integrated digital network (IDN):
   a) Rural-Suburban, central office replacement
   b) Remote small office replacement strategy.

7. Establish access switch deployment strategy:
   a) Voice access tandums
   b) Data and video access switches
   c) Network interfaces
   d) Access modules for CKT and PKT data switches (stand alone and integrated)
   e) Operator service interfaces
   f) Signaling (CCITT #7) interfaces
   g) Usage billing functions for data and video
   h) Private network interfaces, LAN, MAN, WAN.

8. Establish metro switches (phased):
   a) Autonomous, "functionally partitioned," and "integrated"
   b) Voice, data, video.

9. Establish ring nodal/base switches:
   a) Control ring information
   b) LAN/MAN/WAN interfaces
   c) Base/satellite configuration

e) Interface info/metro switches
f) Interface home communication center
g) Interface business communication center
h) Interface rural communication centers.

10. Resolve government's "who's on first base" dilemma:
   a) Via Inquiry III establish unregulated separate accounting, colocation, interfaces, open architecture, limit-dominance/bottleneck, competitive feature offering strategy by Telco information distribution firm.
   b) Enable subsidiary services firm to perform information access, retrieval, search manipulation, and processing with whatever competitive allowed offering arrangement to achieve a "level playing field."
   c) Resolve proliferation of private network impact on future public information network.
   d) Determine quiescent state after Inquiry III/Huber report of monopolistic position of Telco's IDC's after all aspects of (a) have been implemented in terms of public information networks.

11. Resolve government Telco manufacturing restrictions:
   a) Waiver for overseas manufacturing for overseas market.
   b) Two step process to consider Inquiry III/Huber—internal vertical integration manufacturing for U.S. market—joint partnerships.
   c) Competitive supplier products for open network architecture.
   d) Interfaces determined by industry working committees.
   e) Interfaces implemented in timely fashion.

12. Telcos establish management planning process.
   a) Work with suppliers and other providers
   b) Conceptual, requirement and product definition teams.

13. Define an info switch deployment and feature strategy:
   a) Replace centrex CU and CO
   b) Voice, data and video (V,D,V) features
   c) Switch transition phases
      • Autonomous
      • Functionally partitioned V,D,V
      • Functionally integrated
   d) Establish home communication center
      • Single resident (res.) module
      • Multi res. module
      • Res. ring/access unit
   e) Establish business communication center
      • Business serving module
      • Business ring/access unit
   f) Establish services communication center

- Services server modules
- Serving access unit.

14. Establish feature packages: (See case study "Feature Cubics.")
    a) Voice, data, video offerings
    b) Price for growth
    c) Info switch serving features
    d) Telco and multiple vender service center features.

15. Establish support switch:
    a) Centralize maintenance and administration centers
    b) Customer service and billing centers
    c) Data and video as well as voice
    d) Local network controllers.

16. Integrate PABX with local area networks:
    a) Interface private nets with public nets
    b) Provide local and worldwide access rings
    c) Utilize ring nodal point switches
    d) Provide features to private nets via public switches.

17. Establish data switching satellite to satellite:
    a) International networks
    b) International protocol interfaces
    c) International billing and numbering plan.

18. Integrate U.S. ISDN to international networks:
    a) Via gateway switches
    b) Interface private networks through public networks
    c) Private networks to private networks.

19. Establish residential packet network:
    a) Move special circuits point to point to switch
    b) Alarms, meter reading, environmental controls
    c) Residential/small business.

20. Establish personal phone network within a single cell, as an extension of cellular mobile phone networks.

21. Offer user incentives to use data and video offerings:
    a) Provide polling, broadcast, alarm management, and delayed delivery at reasonable usage rates, priced to encourage growth.
    b) Separate residence's poor and subsidize via state agencies and move remainder from flat rate to usage sensitive pricing for all voice, data and video offerings.
    c) Encourage retail stores—debit card; banks—secure data packet transactions; large business—inventory control, transactions;

small businesses—inventory control, inquiry response; by offering cheap public data nets.

   d) Provide customer control to establish local configurations, private virtual nets, as well as variable bandwidth usage dynamically changing before and during the voice, data and/or video call.

   e) Develop friendly machine interfaces with user, using artificial intelligent terminals

22. Establish data processing sinks:
   a) Interfaces and programs for manipulation of databases
   b) Providing information features and services.

23. Manage the pursuit of quality:
   a) Products, networks, and services
   b) Ensure "quality networks"—reliable, safe, secure.

24. Resolve internetworking system and subsystem requirements:
   a) Develop OSI model layers' standards for code conversion, page reformatting, D channel signaling, network quality, etc.
   b) Develop "open architecture" for the info switch modules, as well as the access switch, ring switch and metro switch.
   c) Determine rings interfaces to multiple vendor terminals protocols for LANs, MANs, WANs, PABXs, base and nodal point satellites.
   d) Establish feature requirements for data and video offerings.
   e) Achieve above via roundtables, forums, and working groups across industries via T1, IEEE, and CCITT committees.

25. Change the game when necessary to meet change, and your "strategy of strategies" accordingly . . .

SUMMARY

This completes the management portion (the book in the book) of the top down planning process. The analysis moved from strategic planning of where technology, the marketplace, and society were going, to what people needed for managing change and working together to solve highly complex interrelated multidiscipline problems. It proceeded through the concepts, requirements and product description of what "top down planning" could do and should do, to your firm's actual structure.

In this manner the "top down planning" concept developed into a product, which we will call . . . "The New Information Corporation." We have seen how it consists of several processes, a "P" organization and "motivated participating people" integrated together. This was then overlaid onto the strategy of the strategy policies and business of the business operations to become an integral part of the new culture of the information world firm. The case studies in Chapter 12 demonstrate how "top down planning" helps manage change, by translating change into opportunity to achieve families of successful networks, products and services for the information era . . . This then completes our analysis of "how" to perform successful telecommunications planning.

The "visions" in the next chapter will provide a glimpse into the future by several of our industries' leaders, showing "what" providers and suppliers, working together, can achieve in the next twenty years, as they bravely explore the new frontier and push back its boundaries to achieve the information world.

Following this, we will review "what" ISDN networks, products, and services should be planned in "The Information Era" with detailed looks at the technology, the marketplace, the governmental direction, and ISDN to complete the application of "The Information Corporation" in the telecommunication-information industries.

In conclusion, the case studies and workshops of Chapters 12 and 13 are provided to assist you in determining the structure and products that you, "the manager planner", require in order to play "The Information Game" successfully.

FURTHER ANALYSES

See the case studies *Planning for the Future* and the workshop *Playing the Game.*

OBSERVATIONS: THE WORLD OF PLANNING

1. As people become more and more dependent on information, we can create information network solutions to complex problems, where the solution can create a worse problem, if the network does not perform properly. We must have a "quality" network.
2. The network solutions require suppliers to interface with providers.
3. The market solution requires providers to interface with users, and suppliers to interface with both the providers and their users.
4. People need organizations that support planning processes in order to determine what new networks, products and services they need, and how they will achieve them.
5. Firms need "people planning programs" organizations of the "P" type.
6. Orchestrating "people using processes" will greatly increase productivity.
7. Orchestrating "planned phased projects" will increase the effectiveness of management.
8. The Information Corporation has: *manager planners*—orchestrating *people*, analyzing *problems*, looking for *possibilities*, defining *plans*, using *processes*, with few *Procedures*, establishing *projects*, through new *programs* and playing the game in "The World of Planning", to achieve "The Information World of the Future" . . . The New Frontier!

Part 2

The Information Era

Chapter 9

The Information Society

Most futurists today believe that society will experience several distinct shifts over the next twenty years, each of which is a result of changes due to significant advances in the telecommunications and information processing industries. In reviewing the possibilities of the various "integrated services," that can be provided by future networks, switches, processors, and terminals, we can not help but wonder what life will be like in tomorrow's information society. This analysis attempts to provide an evolutionary picture of the next twenty years, as technology expands to meet the real and imagined user needs of the world. Trends and shifts will be addressed as realistically as possible. Our life styles and quality of life will be shown as they are affected in a manner similar to that experienced over the last 50 years as a result of the industrial revolution. Five distinct phases will be discussed in terms of mode of operation, assumptions, dependencies and alternatives based upon degree and extent of major issues and questions affecting the user's needs. For the sake of reference, the phases are called the following:

- The Preparation Period (Pre 1984)
- The Formation Period (1984-1994)
- The Transition Period (1994-2000)
- The Utilization Period (2000-2010)
- The Information Era (2010+   )

The timeframes indicated here demonstrate the gradual shifting and phasing of five distinct periods in the evolutionary growth of the information society. However, these time periods are yet to be determined in terms of extent and degree for each segment of the international marketplace, depending on the successes and failures of the providers and suppliers, as they play the game with various sophisticated and unsophisticated users, many of whom, being frightened of change, reflect hesitance, hostility, and resistance.

THE PREPARATION PERIOD

Over the 70s and 80s, those in the communications and data processing industries have read numerous articles concerning the technical possibilities and new services achievable with large scale integrated circuits. The general public became aware of these possibilities and risks with the fantastic technical feats of landing a man on the moon, followed by the space shuttle's accomplishments. In the box office, they view computer aided movies, such as *Star Wars*, and in shopping centers played computer driven electronic games. Stores like Computer World and Computer Land sprang up like mushrooms, supplying personal computers and TV games for use on home sets. Zenith and other manufacturers began to market combined phone-TV sets. Television programs picked up on marketing the future by showing pro-

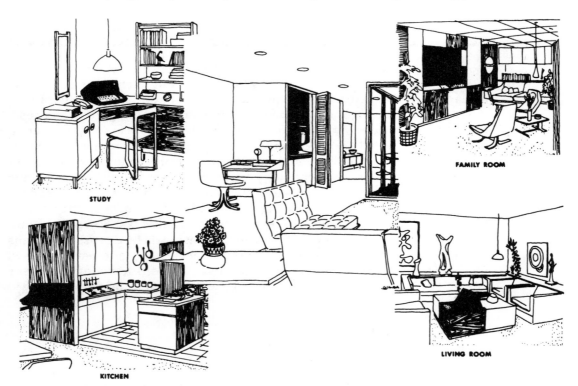

Fig. 9-1. The Home Communication Center.

grams that educated the public on Viewdata possibilities for home users. With this background of the pre-1988 time frame came understanding, a general acceptance, and anticipation of new information features and services. Large food chain supermarkets shifted to electronic checkout counters, and automobile parts store chains extensively used centralized warehouse inventory control systems. Hence, the general public became increasingly more sophisticated and ready for technological change.

During this period the telcos, specialized common carriers, and the government locked horns in an intense struggle to determine turf and future growth opportunities. Technology entered the digital world of T1, T3, fiber optics, and digital switches. Similarly, in recent years other major events have taken place to set the stage for the entrance of the information era.

History has shown that no era can begin without a real justification. We have seen need for progress, hope for opportunity, and desire for a better way of life trigger the industrial revolution. People left the farms for the cities to work on the assembly lines in order to obtain wages to purchase goods from their own assembly lines. From this came the subsequent urban sprawl, where each family acquired two cars, cities grew outward in rings, and business centers jumped to the next ring when congestion and property values became too high. We have watched New York spill over into New Jersey, which flowed into Philadelphia and onto Baltimore and Washington to become a mega-mega-metropolis. Similarly, Chicago grew to LaGrange, to Oak Brook, to Aurora, and Seattle grew to Lynnwood, to Everett, and on towards Vancouver. With this growth has come new dependencies, different needs, new problems, and new opportunities:

- Major urban highways have reached over 200% of capacity during rush hours.
- The 25-50 mile commute has become common.
- Gasoline became expensive, then less expensive, then..
- New cars became too expensive, causing artificial 2.98% loan rates.
- Executives are away from home for too numerous business meetings.
- Crime moved into the suburbs.
- Excessive drugs and alcohol use have become prevalent.
- Government complexity has increased and accountability is obscure.
- Commitment to multinational, multidivisional companies diminished, as they became too large and more impersonal.
- The high cost of living in the 90s, and the balance of trade and national debt—due to the extreme 1978-83 inflation and high 1983-85 cost of money, will greatly effect purchasing power.

Hence the stage has been set for change. Real change, not imaginary futuristic planner's dreams. The time of resistance is nearly complete.

THE FORMATION PERIOD (1984-1994)

The need for opportunity to restore quality of life, to increase possibili-

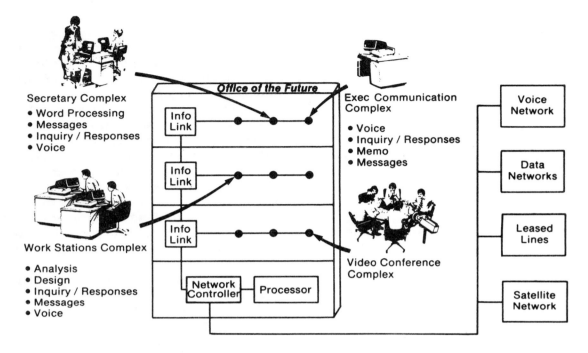

Fig. 9-2. The Office Communication Center.

ties to achieve the American dream, to have new adventures in new frontiers, is prevalent. This will be the time to awaken enthusiasm and bring about positive change with the beginning of a new era, and the end of our lost expectations. Hope exists that man will be able to control his machines and not make himself subservient to them. The industrial revolution's monotonous assembly lines, and the computers that enhance operations but regiment users, can become things of the past.

This 1984-94 time frame will be the period of the formation of powerful and versatile "overlay and integrated" networks, products, and services. It is apparent that the "Office of the Future" will be centered around total information handling PBXs that will tie internal terminals to each other, as well as to various local and remote databases. Application software packages will become dominant as word processing, mail systems, inventory control, formal cost estimating, project management, computer aided design, and computer aided manufacture programs are developed for operation on fifth generation computers that are extremely complex, but more human-machine oriented. Terminals will become more personal and intelligent, as they attempt to bridge the human interface gap. Home cable will compete against home satellite and microwave point of sight systems for more channels and services (two way) to offer to "home of the future" viewers. Similarly, the telcos will expand their digital carrier and fiber optic networks by overlaying data and video conference capabilities on the business communities. This is the period for intense activity by the providers in establishing their network of integrated services using products from the suppliers.

The catalyst for change will be economics. Throughout this period all major firms will be implementing their plans after reassessing costs of operation, mode of operation, location of operations and new business opportunities. They will turn to automation to replace people in order to cut down overall operating costs. As energy considerations, foreign trade deficit, government debt, new tax laws, and bad bank loans keep the cost of money changing, many firms may relocate to more desirable areas and tie distributed corporations together with extensive communication networks. This will cause the business communities to turn to the most economical providers of information handling features and services or have their own LAN / WAN. Society's job market will begin its major shift, as these new products and services become operational. Information management will provide more and more jobs for everyone, from the network planners to the data entry operators, as industry shifts to these local and remote computer databases. Work needs will shift from the unskilled to the more skilled in order to support these networks. School and industry training programs will emphasize information processing related studies. Service bureaus will begin to emerge for inquiry response services, as well as to perform polling for market research.

As more and more information is handled, we will see a change in call attempts and busy hour patterns. There will be a need for secure networks, as abusers of information security become a major concern. Satellite and other specialized carriers will compete with Telcos' fiber and T-carrier networks for servicing conference centers and urban ring office complexes. Many firms will use these video conferences to help cut down on executive travel and enable work locations to be closer to workers' homes, cutting their commute travel. Telcos will aggressively restructure offerings to competitively encourage users to increase volume of data traffic on their networks rather than on private leased lines or competing networks. This competition will encourage more and more "formulation" of the new integrated services networks for the "new users."

THE TRANSITION PERIOD (1994-2005)

This period will see the major shift of change on society. It is at this point that the networks will be up and operating. Users will no longer be worried about when they will have access, but will be requesting more and more new features and services. These will be "the critical years," where users begin to know what they really want and evaluate what they have and how well it is performing.

By the end of this time period, point of sales will be an accepted way of doing business. At the retail store, purchases will not just be checked for credit. The transaction will take place immediately, either from a debit card from one's bank account or a credit line. A major communications problem will be obtaining access to the right network in terms of signalling protocols, entrance codes, and security protection codes. Security of information will continue to play a significant role in the business community. A new problem will arise—the need to keep data networks up at all costs.

In the "home of the future," the TV will now be of modular design, where it interfaces on two-way channels to the telco as well as to cable, satellites, or microwave facilities, providing education, home movies, electronic mail and access to information search services, such as electronic yellow pages. However, due to economic levels, there will be gaps between the services available to various communities and various users within each community. Its feature package capabilities can be analogous to the modular stereo system market. Various information handling modules will be selected for one's home communication center on a building block basis. As users shift their mode of operation to communication rather than transportation, numerous information service industries will develop.

There will, of course, be some problems. Access to networks from some communities will be more difficult than from others. However, user enjoyment will increase as understanding and appreciation develop. This may be similar to going from crystal radio (where the early users expressed great delight in getting a distant station) to having access to many stations in the tube era. Business will follow the new media in the same way that their advertising moved from newspaper to radio to television. Their revenue will help sustain the information network's growth.

The effect on society, as a result of this transition period, will be a new mode of operation. Hopefully, it will provide an opportunity to solve many of the complex quality-of-life problems noted in the pre 1985 period. As the transition takes place, however, care must be taken to anticipate problems and minimize the impact on unemployment for the unskilled and the older employees. America needs a complete physical rebuilding of its decaying cities, bridges, and water waste facilities. Government and industry work programs can be a tremendous avenue for unskilled employment. Hence, the fear expressed in Europe about the information age and possible high unemployment should be seriously considered and resolved before this period.

THE UTILIZATION PERIOD (2000-2010)

The formation and transition periods are nearly over. By now, digital switches and fifth generation computers are quite prevalent. Digital switching has moved into its third generation design with second generation data handling features. Business strategies for all major corporations utilize integrated services offerings over networks which interconnect globally. Communications equipment is supplied by numerous international suppliers, with intense cost/feature competition. Hence, products are replaced readily on four to seven year operational cycles. Costs are depreciated by the providers over these shorter life cycles, in order to maintain competitive positions in the marketplace and not be strapped with expensive maintenance costs of upgrading older volatile programs and equipment. Distributed database management problems will be reassessed, as will access methods to the

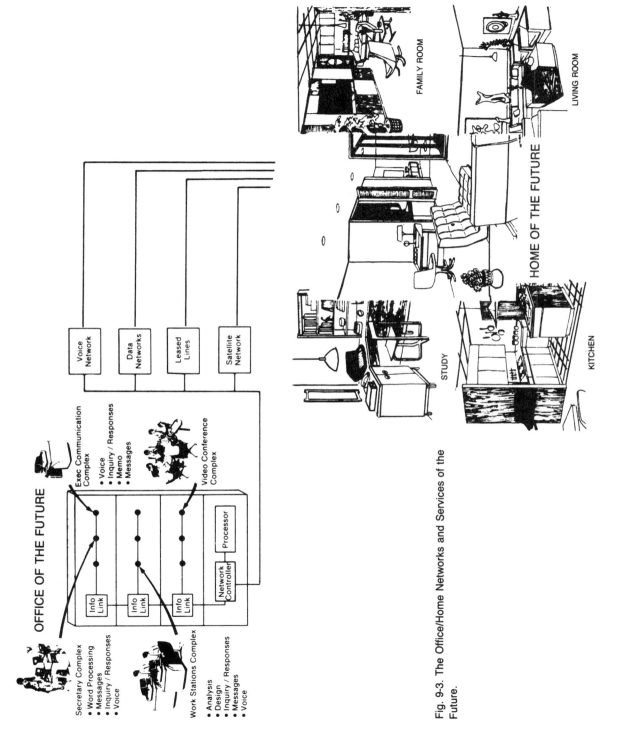

Fig. 9-3. The Office/Home Networks and Services of the Future.

237

numerous worldwide nets.

The users will find a network being used by every business, from doctors to librarians. They will become more and more sophisticated as their middle age work force, born in the mid 60s and trained on these information systems, are reaching their forties by the year 2005, achieving higher levels within the company.

Work decisions will be based on interpretations of large quantities of data, using risk probability projections. Total communication networks will offer an alternative to travel, which may provide more time at home to be with family to help solve family and community stress problems. The long lines at banks and stores should diminish, as the methods of purchasing goods and services changes. Up to this point, probably only twenty percent of the total population was affected to any major extent. However, during this period the major growth will begin, as more and more "new users" see the advantages and begin using the information networks. This second delayed shift will have an uplifting financial effect. However, it will also have a technological impact which will require adjustment and tuning, as the real growth begins to handle the large volumes of traffic and provide new services.

This will be similar to the self-sustaining shift from farms to cities in the 30s, as the people used more and more products developed in the cities. Here, as more and more users use the networks, an increasing number of services will be economically justified and become available to them, which will further increase the use and growth of the networks. Hence the years just after the turn of the century will be the real beginning of the information era, where information handling and processing become a part of our way of life and life style.

THE INFORMATION ERA (2010+   )

Obviously, this era may actually begin before or after this date, but it does appear that soon after the turn of the century, it will indeed be flourishing. Hopefully it will not be a "Big Brother" society but a healthy, growing society in which information becomes the tool of mankind and makes life a little bit better and helps people cope with the economic problems caused by previous years of waste and inefficient use of resources. If the computer becomes a tool that can cheaply and effectively help our children build a better society, then we indeed have given them a tremendous gift. The computer can enable industry to restructure, and allow companies to be relocated to the more rural areas of our country. It can diminish the extensive travel time for going to and from work. It can enable parents to spend more time with their families, and more time to get involved in their communities. It can allow smaller, closer, more functional and personal work communities to be formed by redistribution of large firms, thus helping to return work satisfaction. It can provide a more direct voice in our government and a better monitoring of our elected officials. It can allow more time for rest, relaxation and study. Finally, it can perhaps allow us time to think and enjoy the fruits of our labor.

VISIONS OF THE FUTURE

The following sections are visions of the future by several leaders of the telecommunications and computer industries.

The Changing Telecommunications Networks

By Dr. Irwin Dorros, Exec. V.P. Bell Communications Research

"A man was arrested in New York for attempting to extort funds from ignorant and superstitious people by exhibiting a device he says will convey the human voice any distance over metallic wires. He calls the instrument a telephone. Well-informed people confirm that it is impossible to transmit voice over wires, and if it were possible to do so, the thing would have no practical value." (A New York newspaper, 1865.)

"If a team of scientists, engineers, and linguists has its way, the telephone of the future will dial a number at the sound of its user's voice. Local phone lines into homes will be equipped to transmit pictures and computer data simultaneously, and phone answering machines will be so smart they will be able to pick out messages from specific individuals for playback" (The New York Times, July 16, 1985).

Despite the skepticism of the 1865 newspaper report, Alexander Graham Bell was talking over wires less than a dozen years later. We've gone from Bell's room-to-room communications to worldwide telecommunications with more than a billion circuit miles of wire and cable and 20,000 switching systems in the United States alone, making it possible for almost anybody to talk to anyone else.

Even with the break-up of the Bell System and an unresolved mix of competition and regulation, our national telecommunications network remains vigorous. It is, in fact, no longer one network, but many networks that overlay the nation. The questions now are: "Are these networks capable of doing almost anything the public wants?" "Will they be allowed to meet those needs?" "Is the technology ready?" "Is the public ready?"

It was not until the invention of the transistor, less than 40 years ago, that the information age was born—making possible the transformation of basic telephone service into the highly sophisticated telecommunications system it is destined to become. The transistor led to the development of the integrated circuit and its further miniaturization into microelectronics. These revolutionized the processing and switching of information signals from the analog, or continuous wave, mode to the much more efficient digital, or pulsed, mode. Then came the laser and optical fibers, revolutionizing transmission of digital signals by making it possible to send large volumes of information over hair-thin glass fiber strands up to 10,000 times faster than the original analog methods on copper wire. The transistor also made practical—and microelectronics made affordable—the computer, which, in turn, has revolutionized just about every aspect of telecommunication—from switching calls, to keeping track of equipment inventories, to billing the customer.

If the computer is one of the most significant influences driving telecommunications technology today, its impact on commerce and industry has been even greater. And, like a revolving door, it comes around again to affect telecommunications; the increasing number of both business and personal computers, the sheer growth in information, and the need to access databases testify to the necessity of high-speed, efficient data communications links. As we pack more functions into microelectronic chips at less cost, as lightwave communications reaches its potential and its costs, too, come down, and as computers become smarter, cheaper, and even more pervasive, the elements of technology are falling into place for whatever services the customer wants.

What are these services likely to be? The possibilities are limitless, but the networks of the future will have certain common characteristics, as seen from my viewpoint at Bell Communications Research (Bellcore). Our role at Bellcore is to look at the technology, the architecture of networks, the potential of new services and see how these elements might come together. Here's how we see the networks changing.

Future networks will be mostly digital; they will have the increased transmission capacity known as "wideband" to meet needs for new services. They will be more and more customer-controlled. And, as I will explain, they will be integrated.

But the word that first comes to mind in describing the network of the future is "intelligence." The telephone system of the future will be an "intelligent network"—able to do more things than it does today and carry more complex information. The network of the future will consist of switches that can recognize calls requiring special handling; centrally located databases containing the brains and instructions determining how each call should be handled; and a common channel signaling packet network for intercommunications between network switching points and databases. Once the intelligent network with its powerful capabilities is fully in place, it will offer many new services, providing flexible telecommunications to business and residence customers. Perhaps at some point down the road, we will be able to increase the system's intelligence by teaching it to learn by its experience. Take the call forwarding feature, for example, which many people already have today. Say I've programmed my telephone to put through calls to my office number until 6 p.m., and after that to my home number, but the computer finds that, most often, I am still picking up calls in my office until 8 p.m. The computer can learn to make a decision to override my instructions—based on statistical probabilities of my behavior in relation to its database—and try me at my office between 6 and 8 p.m. (It will, of course, guess wrong at times, but after all, once it has intelligence, it's only human.)

Another stimulating example of the use of the intelligent network may be the personal phone number—one that will be yours through life, like a social security number. Wherever you are, the telephone system would find you, as long as you have a means of inputting the nearest telephone number to indicate your new location. We could also develop a permanent national telephone number for a company with nationwide distribution centers. Unlike the standard "800" service which routes all calls to a central location, the intelligent network would route national number calls directly to the dealer nearest the caller's telephone exchange.

While these applications are still in the future, some features of the intelligent network are available today. One application is currently being tested by Bell of Pennsylvania and several other Bell Operating Companies. Known as Custom Local Area Signaling Service, it opens up a wide range of convenient custom features. It can automatically block out unwanted calls, provide a distinctive ringing signal for certain calls, send incoming telephone numbers to a display device on the customer's phone, trace calls, and redial incoming or outgoing calls.

The need to tailor telecommunications services to meet the specific needs of each customer is paramount. Many of today's large business customers have described control over their own telephone systems as a top priority. One new management system allows customers, whose calling patterns among multiple locations are constantly changing, to rearrange their own network layout to accommodate those needs. On a smaller scale, another system gives Centrex customers control over their telephone systems within a single location by enabling them to move or swap extensions, activate special Centrex features, and maintain their own directory information.

We are rapidly moving from an era of voice communications to an information era requiring both voice and data communications over the telecommunications networks. The public packet switching service will make transmitting computer data as easy as making a telephone call. Just as voice calls are distributed by a voice-switching system, this service arranges data into "packets," addresses the packets to their proper destinations (much as a voice call is addressed by the telephone number), and distributes them through a packet-switching system. But, unlike a voice call, which ties up a transmission link for the duration of that one call, packet-switched networks bundle customer data into self-contained messages, combining the packets of one call with many others. This means that the same transmission facilities can serve more customers, and the need for large numbers of dedicated lines diminishes. Although packet-switching technology has been available for more than a decade, recent rulings by the Federal Communications Commission (the first on a request from New Jersey Bell) are now beginning to make it practical for telephone companies to enter that marketplace.

Packet switching, along with the application of new transmission technology, opens the door to improve and make more cost-effective telephone-monitored services such as home information, fire alarms, burglar alarms, and utility load shedding (selective reduction in electrical power to a building when the occupants are away), as well as electronic mail, home banking, investment services, and shopping transactions.

But the ultimate goal is to merge these and other services—including voice—and transmit and switch them from one end to another in digital form, and, finally, combine them in a single path to the customer. This would give customers a single connection to the network for all their own mix of services, and make more efficient use of the network.

The innovative system that will make this possible undergoes its first commercial installation and trial in 1986 in Illinois. Known as Integrated Services Digital Network (ISDN), it is an architectural plan for networks that will integrate communications services and transport them in digital form over the same facilities—wire pairs, coaxial cables, fiber optics, microwave radio, and satellites. In addition to the potential benefit of lower operational costs, this will provide a versatile, multi-service network with standard connections to customers' equipment and international compatibility on which voice, data, graphics, text, and video signals can be sent and received simultaneously, over a single access line.

Second-generation ISDN, using higher transmission speeds on fiber optic cable, will permit full-motion high-resolution television transmission, making possible a wider range of visual uses—picture phones, video conferencing, video databases, home entertainment and sporting events—on demand. This service will be available on a trial basis within ten years. With increased transmission capacity, voice quality will improve to become similar to that of today's high-fidelity digital compact disks. And screens of text will fill up in less than a second, so that users can browse through all sorts of information as quickly as they can flip through a magazine.

Our entire social and economical framework depends upon communications, a dependence that will grow as we move further into the information age. In its evolution toward ISDN, the telecommunications industry faces major challenges in three key areas: technology, standards, and structure. The industry must meet these challenges, but how it meets them will determine the extent of the information-age benefits that are actually realized.

Technology has made competition in telecommunications possible and will continue to drive the telecommunications evolution. We need to continue reducing costs at the same time we are increasing capabilities. This demands a commitment to support long-term research and development.

The new telecommunications industry structure has a multiplicity of networks and interfaces. To provide end-to-end service to the customer, these networks must work together at their boundaries. Organizations dedicated to setting industry standards—such as the nationally accredited telecommunications standards committee sponsored by the Exchange Carriers Standards Association—provide an ideal means of developing agreements on the ways these networks will connect with each other. Significant progress is being made in this area but, for such efforts to be truly effective, all industry members need to support the process actively and constructively.

However, standards are not appropriate for all aspects of the industry. Where a telecommunications company can use internal network differences to its economic advantage, there is strong motivation not to standardize. These differences include internal network configuration, equipment quality and cost, and service and performance specifications such as quality of sound, noise, or distortion. In fact, in a competitive environment, the last thing the service providers would be likely to standardize is service quality—except for the minimum quality required for end-to-end transmission.

While technology has been, and will continue to be, the driving force behind the evolution of the networks, judicial, legislative, and regulatory policies continue to shape the structure of the industry. On their own, these policy makers have no way of anticipating new technology or the potential new services, capabilities, and economics that such technology can bring. Like the rest of the industry, our role at Bellcore is to let them know where technology is heading, and show them the benefits that can be realized, when the technology isn't held back by artificial barriers.

But whether the policies will keep pace to allow full use of the new capabilities remains a key issue yet to be resolved. Will regulators grapple successfully with the continued blurring of lines between telecommunications and information processing? And what will be the long-term effects of the changing industry structure on regulatory policies?

The Federal Communications Commission's recently opened Computer Inquiry III may determine the next step in the industry's development. Now is the industry's chance to present a coherent and compelling picture of what can be accomplished, when a truly competitive industry is able to deploy and use evolving technology to its fullest.

In the end, however, the marketplace—the customers—will decide the future of the telecommunications industry, and we must concentrate our attention on them. If we provide them with services that are too costly, too hard to use, or unresponsive to their real needs, then all the technological progress, regulatory reform, competition, and standards will mean little. The industry's challenge is to bring these elements together—the technology, the policy makers, the manufacturers of equipment, and the suppliers of telecommunication services—to focus on the needs of the customer. In meeting this challenge, we can shape networks that will truly achieve the potential of the information age.

User Needs and Network Strategies for the Nineties

By Desmond F. Hudson, President Northern Telecom, Inc.

Over the years, much of the innovation in our industry has come from the high level of interaction, interface, and cooperation between manufacturers, service providers, and end users. These dialogues, grounded in a shared focus on end-user needs and a commitment to deliver practical solutions with tangible benefits, has not only provided a fertile ground for innovation, but has also helped determine the very structure of the industry.

The rapid evolution of market needs, technology, and regulation has focussed our attention on the activities of large organizations. Because they have large resources at their disposal, and because they're aggressively innovating, they represent the largest single influence on network evolution today.

User needs today range all the way from basic voice service to enhanced multi-media communications networks that leading edge users are beginning to deploy for competitive gains into the 1990s.

The diffusion of information technology is changing the way these leading-edge organizations do business and the way they relate to customers and suppliers. Technology is beginning to influence not just their cost structures, but also their revenue streams. As a result, they have additional incentives to invest now, to gain leverage on their competition... and they're doing just that.

These organizations cross all industry segments. They include financial institutions, high-tech manufacturing, retail and wholesale distribution, higher education, transportation, and government. Their needs cross the traditional CPE, intra-LATA, and inter-LATA service boundaries. Our studies show that over 90 percent of large Centrex users, for example, operate in a mixed CPE/Centrex environment. They already know these are complementary strategies. Their vision of information networks has broadened beyond their internal needs to include their customers, their distributors, and their suppliers as well. And their need for multimedia information, especially voice, text, and graphics, is driving their network planning.

By 1990, these industry leaders will already have implemented new approaches. Their competitors, the followers, will begin to respond in the early 1990s, providing a volume market for new products and services. The enabling technologies exist today to provide what these large end users are looking for; secure, versatile, high-quality, multimedia virtual networks, over which they can have the degree of control they seek; networks with embedded services and functionality, portions of which, it makes sense to provide on a shared basis.

Let's briefly enumerate these technologies:

First of all, *synchronous fiber network systems,* which provide flexible, high-speed access and the freedom to locate functionality, are being deployed today, wherever economical.

Next, *switching and transport technologies,* to provide high-capacity, non-blocking, fault-tolerant, wide-band services anywhere in the network are available in the lab and will soon be in the field.

Third, carriers today have *network intelligence primitives,* to handle basic call set-up and manage information movement, not just for voice, but for all forms of enhanced multimedia communications.

And finally, *the feature nodes or engines,* needed to place functional intelligence anywhere required and to drive network primitives, are available or soon will be.

The bottom line is this: the technology exists to do what needs to be done. What's missing are standards and plans.

The issue before us today in delivering those solutions is not so much technology itself, but applications of technology. The technology exists to provide what large users are looking for: secure, versatile, high-quality, multimedia virtual networks over which they can have the degree of control they want—networks with embedded services and functionality.

And who are those users? What are their needs? The user community today is a different creature than it was 10 years ago. It is populated by a technically sophisticated group of people, who know how to reach out and apply new technologies in their business. What they've accomplished provides the foundation for addressing tomorrow's opportunities.

In the post-1986 era, two major challenges face all of us. The first is to do for data communications what has already been done for voice; that is, to make it ubiquitous, responsive, easy to use, and cost-effective. The second major challenge is to show how communications related applications can be used to support the business plans of end user companies. That is, to show how communications applications can enhance a company's strategic effectiveness by improving the way it handles and manages information resources. These two challenges suggest that in the immediate future we, suppliers and providers, jointly face a major discontinuity in our planning. This discontinuity is nothing less than the arrival of:

- True Multimedia Communications.
- A higher level of networking capability than exists in today's stand-alone network.
- Embedded services with new functionality for addressing the generic communication needs of users, departments and establishments.

Implementation of these newer functionalities will follow the evolutionary tradition already established by Northern Telecom. With proper planning, today's voice networks will become universal in nature, providing for voice, data, and image services. Distinctions between local area and wide area networks and between voice and data networks, moreover, will disappear over time. Computing resources will, in effect, become peripherals on the network, improving their access and efficiency. Broadband communications, from terminals to computers and between computers, will provide the opportunity for a host of new services. Control of the network and computer resources will be shared with users, each of whom will be positioned as a hub on his own virtual information network.

By and large, equipment interface standards already exist to connect network elements in an open structure. While there are variations, there is also evolution towards a single standard. ISDN is a concrete example, and a very significant step. Northern Telecom welcomes the acceptance of ISDN in the marketplace. It will help all of us realize the benefits of a multivendor environment, and it will bring order to product evolution. In concert, we are actively working to make it a reality. But, while we have hardware and network interface standards, we lack clear standards for information services in end-to-end network applications. And the absence of standards in these areas is a major impediment to the delivery of wideband ubiquitous information services to large and small users alike.

There is an urgent need to complete the service definitions and protocols of the upper layers of the OSI model for establishing service interfaces. These standards will facilitate compatibility for industry-specific services across local- and wide-area public and private network configurations.

But there is an even more urgent need to identify the basic end-to-end services themselves. Just what kinds of services should the network offer? How should they be embedded and who should provide them?

There is a general agreement on end-to-end special services where voice is concerned, but just what multimedia services does it make sense to provide on the network, and which are better left to niche suppliers? Answers to these questions are crucial to our ability to provide multimedia services across regional markets, and they are essential before vendors can afford to undertake product development. Yet no mechanism exists for deciding these important questions. A cooperative forum is needed where regional companies can resolve inter-regional marketing and end-to-end service issues. In the absence of such cooperation, there is the real risk that service in the U.S. market could become as Balkanized as it is in Europe, where fierce national protectionism has created network chaos at the expense of end users.

Different regional concepts are emerging in the U.S. market, but there is need for a consensus on how, where, and when deployment should proceed. For without that consensus, it will be difficult to achieve the early revenue potential to make deployment cost-effective. Before we can fully address these issues, however, we must come to grips with the most fundamental issue of all, the structure of our industry as it's likely to evolve.

As I see it, there are basically three potential scenarios.... *one* winner, *many* winners, and *no* winners. The first possibility is a vertically integrated, trans-U.S. structure, with little interconnection with other players. In the 5-7 year time frame, there is clearly only one player who could operate under these rules, although there may be 9 to 10 contenders. The second possibility is a number of large regional companies, with a leadership position in one region and cooperative agreements with other regionals to address trans-U.S. issues and needs; a scenario with many winners. Such a structure however, requires the mechanism I described earlier for defining, establishing, and monitoring end-to-end services. The third possibility is a multiplicity of networks, with no clear leaders in particular market or industry segments; a scenario with no winners. This is especially likely to happen under adverse regulatory conditions.

I believe the second scenario is the most likely to emerge, if the regional players are allowed to move quickly:

- To form the cooperative relationships needed to compete effectively; on a customer-by-customer or long-term basis.
- To develop needed standards in services and functionality.
- To deploy the basic network architecture and technology.
- To provide timely solutions to end-user needs.

Let me add that when there is consensus on the structure of the industry, I believe the necessary standards direction will be forthcoming. As I indicated earlier, a coordinated, well-planned strategy is critical to achieving the early revenue potential necessary for cost-effective deployment. The need for enhanced services is clear, and the market opportunity exists now; with large users.

For most telcos, business customers are the prime source of revenue. Current analysis show that business customers yielded 60 percent of large telco revenues in 1985, and projections indicate they could yield 70 percent by 1990, but they are also the revenue source most vulnerable to competition!

To protect this vital revenue source, technology must be deployed rapidly to offer networking and internetworking services; to help customers integrate their existing equipment and services in a network-based communications solution. This is the first step in creating hybrid public/private multimedia virtual networks; our competitive weapon!

And it is the basis for the longer term deployment rationale of new revenue generation; to exploit the functionality of the network in providing new information services for profit. The rate at which new capabilities are deployed, therefore, is a critical issue for carriers. The market time constant for applying these new technologies is much faster than our traditional deployment strategies. There is a very real danger, in other words, that alternative service arrangements for these leading customers will develop faster than carrier planning cycles and depreciation schedules permit new equipment to be introduced. A rapid deployment strategy, then, is essential to capturing the market opportunity and laying the foundation for longer term volume gains. It will also provide new service enhancements in the public network that could be affordable, not just to the largest end users, but to smaller businesses and residential customers as well.

Along with a coordinated plan for rapid deployment, we need an accelerated marketing plan. It must be geared to develop and exploit the market at the rate technology is deployed and can be absorbed by customers. Innovation doesn't end at the laboratory door. It's important to the marketing function as well. The end-user solutions this technology will offer are highly complex and innovative, and they demand equally innovative marketing techniques. They require a cooperative focus on key large accounts, and joint planning among users, manufacturers, and operating companies.

Let me summarize what I've said, or what I wanted to say, in case I've been too indirect. I believe the technology needed to provide a range of enhanced multimedia communications services exists today. The switching and transport technologies needed are either in deployment or emerging from laboratories. The real issue is *leadership* . . . in an innovative marketing sense:

- *Leadership* in shaping an industry structure.
- *Leadership* in setting standards for services.
- *Leadership* in resolving network functionality issues.
- *Leadership* in providing innovative solutions to customers' needs.

And that's where this network planning sessions can make a real contribution. One of the most critical issues in providing hybrid public/private solutions is network management. Virtually all customer networks exist in a multivendor environment. And our customer surveys show that among the highest-ranked network service needs are:

- A single point of control for network management.
- Common network management for voice and data networks.

In a move we all welcome, the FCC opened the way for cost-effective provisioning of enhanced network services by removing the structural separation requirements from carriers for providing enhanced services. This important decision will unlock the enormous potential of the network for providing ubiquitous, easy-to-use information services to all users. And we also welcome the FCC's endorsement of an open network architecture concept. It is one we at Northern Telecom have long advocated, and one that will ensure the widest range of network services. The dynamic network architecture provides the open network flexibility to embed these new services across the network.

Northern Telecom already offers the widest range of central office-based services available in today's market. And we have announced plans to enrich that offering with advanced meridian information services. To recognize this new level of functionality, we have renamed our network services offering meridian business services. And we have added a high-speed local area network capability as well. To define applications of these new services and capabilities, we stand ready to work in partnership with the providers and their customers. Through partnerships, we'll foster, we'll encourage, and we'll make things happen. We'll work with providers to help the user community put the basics in place and then build on them. At each step, we'll support their relationships with users to help them take advantage of technology.

I believe that partnerships such as this are the true source of innovation today. They draw upon individual strengths for the achievement of common goals. By working together, I am confident that we can build a strong secure, and profitable future; for ourselves and for those whom we serve . . . providing new and useful solutions to end user problems presented by the information age.

The Network of the Future

By Volker Jung, President and Chief Executive Officer, Siemens Public Switching Systems Inc.

The rapid evolution of telecommunications networks is driven by technology, as well as by end-user needs. As the world evolves toward the 21st Century, information and its vital concomitant—the efficient communication of information—become increasingly indispensable components of society's structure.

Current business and residential communications needs are beginning to tax existing networks. Emerging from the laboratories, however, are exciting new technologies which offer the potential for communications networks that will meet the needs of lower cost, greater flexibility, increased functionality, and vastly increased capacity.

Telecommunications network systems in the 1990s and into the 2000s will be open distributed intelligent networks offering unique applications to end-users through standard network interfaces. We look to this dramatic advancement as "The Network of the Future."

End-User Needs

Communications systems are rapidly becoming strategic tools which businesses use to compete effectively in the national and international marketplaces. Within the next decade, communications systems will become yardsticks by which the progress of entire nations may be measured. Since technology offers almost unimaginable potential for startlingly new communications applications, the needs of the marketplace will determine the structure of telecommunications networks into the 21st century.

Futurists such as John Naisbitt of *Megatrends* and Alvin Toffler of *Future Shock* and *The Third Wave* see the 21st century as characterized by the human struggle to achieve individuality in a society of homogeneity; destandardization rather than regimentation. In telecommunications this control of one's destiny equates to real-time control of resources by the end-user. Control over bandwidth, or "bandwidth on demand," and control of features via "the intelligent network" will provide end-users with the telecommunications tools needed to individualize their communications networks and solve their unique needs with customized solutions at the lowest possible cost.

With the marriage of computers and communications (see NEC's C&C concept), increased telecommunications bandwidths with application-dependent reconfigurability will be required. This technology will permit direct computer bus-to-telecommunications network interconnection, thereby providing flexible use of bandwidth for highly "bursty" communications. Such capability will use network resources efficiently while offering the end-user "bandwidth on demand," with cost reflecting the actual amount of information sent.

Video applications as well as high-speed terminals will place similar demands on the evolving network. Networks operating at speeds in the Gigabit (one billion bits) per-second domain will be prevalent, offering capabilities much like those provided today by Local Area Networks (LANs) and Metropolitan Area Networks (MANs).

Since the early 1960s telecommunications have been evolving from networks based on analog technologies designed for voice applications to networks based on digital technologies designed for both voice and data applications. During the same period intelligent Stored Program Control (SPC) switching systems emerged. These offered increasingly advanced features based on communications between SPC switching systems and databases, via Common Channel Signaling (CCS) systems. This enhanced functionality resulted in increased usage of the network, leading in turn to additional end-user requirements both in function and variety. This feedback process will accelerate as networks are further improved. Adaptable, highly functional "intelligent networks" designed with technologically advanced, feature-rich subsystems will be the key to meeting this challenge.

Technology

Just as the industrial age was founded on a solid transportation infrastructure of railroads and highways, the new information age will require an equally solid telecommunications infrastructure. This will evolve from the existing one and will be based on technological advances occurring today in our laboratories. Advanced microprocessors, memory devices, and fiber optic communications systems are three technologies driving the rapid evolution of telecommunications.

Microprocessor and memory device advances have led most visibly to the proliferation of advanced intelligent end-user terminal equipment. Fundamental examples are CAD terminals, robotics, and personal computers with enormous power. The widespread proliferation of these devices has in fact spurred the need for more advanced communications systems. Less apparent, however, is the impact these advances have had on the communications network. The evolution of the fundamental communications system from one based principally on analog technology to one based largely on digital technology, and emergence of the "intelligent network," are direct results of progress in these technologies.

With intelligent microprocessor devices deployed throughout the network, enormous processing power is unleashed for new technological solutions to existing and arising end-user needs. Exciting new switching technologies are emerging which offer the potential for truly integrated voice, data, and image networks.

Two switching techniques which take advantage of new microprocessor technologies and which are currently in exploratory development stages are fast-circuit switching (FCS) and fast-packet switching (FPS). Both technologies were developed to exploit the circumstances that in a typical voice call, information is transmitted only about 40 percent of the time, with the remaining time idle. Voice information, when digitized with existing voice compression techniques, forms bursts which are referred to as "talkspurts." These talkspurts actually are bursts of digitized voice information. Inasmuch as voice, as well as data, tends to be bursty, FCS and FPS networks are capable of carrying both voice and data applications and offer the potential of integrated voice/data networking.

Fast circuit switching is a technology which establishes and disconnects circuit-switched calls very quickly, converting each talk spurt into a packet or message, treating each much like an individual call. These spurts can then be switched along with data packets to provide integrated communications. FCS networks have the transmission efficiency associated with packet switching and the speed of circuit switching.

Fast packet switching is a technology which speeds packets across networks with remarkably little delay. FPSs are relatively simple routing devices that do not perform the complicated packet protocol functions associated with packet networks, such as error resolution and flow control. Instead, they employ an edge-to-edge protocol architecture wherein the complicated, delay-introducing functions are performed only at the edges of the FPS network.

FPS networks also employ fixed routes for each call, thereby limiting delays and delay variations. Inasmuch as only small delays are introduced by fast packet networks, packetized voice transport over FPS networks also provides the potential for integration of voice and data applications.

In addition to the emergencies of switching technologies which provide the opportunity for integrated voice/data networks, such as FCS and FPS, new switching technologies that offer dramatic increases in bandwidth also are emerging from the laboratories. Electronic switches operating at 45 Mbps are currently available. Soon there will appear 140 Mbps switching systems based on CMOS technologies.

Eventually, fast packet/circuit broadband switches will emanate to bring the benefits of integration to voice and data as well as video information. Clearly, as indium gallium arsenide components become available, speeds into the Gigabits and Terabits (one trillion bits) per-second realm will be technologically feasible by means of photonic switching, where light signals are switched without undergoing an optoelectrical conversion.

Transmission technologies also are evolving to bring sensationally greater bandwidth potential. Through single mode fiber, optical transmission systems offer the transport of virtually error-free information at extremely high velocities extending into the Gigabit world. In fact, much of the new fiber optic cable capacity currently being deployed can support optical wave division and frequency division multiplexing techniques to extend their capacity to dramatic, virtually unlimited bandwidths.

The Network of the Future

Skillful merger of the advanced switching and transmission capabilities discussed herein will develop a synergy that will form the basis for the telecommunications network of the future. Advanced microprocessor technology offers amplified network functionality through databases and intelligent feature nodes. The utility of communications networks will be sensationally improved by augmentation of the flexibility, speed, and functionality of these new switching and transmission systems with powerful signaling systems, such as CCITT System No. 7, permitting the fast and efficient transfer of information between intelligent terminal and network components.

Distributed network intelligence based on microprocessor technologies will evolve the telecommunications network from one based on fixed end-user location, with a limited feature set, to one that is independent of end-user locale and that offers a flexible, adaptable end-user programmable feature set. An open architecture will evolve through well defined standard interfaces, creating new entrepreneural opportunities for the development and deployment of new telecommunications services. The switching system would be responsible for routing calls in such a network. End-user specific profiles contained within the network will interact with public and private entities called "feature nodes" to offer individualized communications services. End users' control of their profiles will permit them to command and redefine, in real-time, their communications networks. The sum of many individualized "networks" will define what we term "The Network of the Future."

Communications networks being planned today will be capable of adapting themselves to the needs of the user with real-time precision. With such advances as broadband fast packet/circuit switching and fiber optic transmission in the loop plant as well as in the interoffice network, capabilities such as "bandwidth on demand" that are only visualized today will transcend into realities. Bandwidth on demand will allow the user to access information transport based on the application and burstiness associated with that application in real-time.

In today's communications network, the user must determine on a per-call basis where communications technology such as switch type and bandwidth will optimize that individual transaction. The communications capability is accordingly limited by the accuracy of the end-user choice as well as the technology selected.

In tomorrow's intelligent network, however, the choice will be made in real-time by the network, and will depend on the circumstances such as bandwidth and delay that are precisely related to the call at that specific time rather than at some earlier time when the call was initially selected.

Network capacity can be allocated at one moment to one application and in the next moment can be spread across many different applications, depending on individual end-user needs. Such a network will relieve end-users from the burdens and costs associated with design, administration, and maintenance of their own networks, while providing communications that meet the needs of the end-users on an application basis at the lowest practicable cost.

As can be seen, "The Network of the Future" promises tremendous opportunities. At the same time, evolving the present telecommunications infrastructure towards this network concept will not be an easy task, and will be confronted with countless intriguing challenges.

The Challenge

An efficient, user-friendly, and cost-effective distributed telecommunications network which offers the functions and flexibility discussed herein requires that well-defined standard interfaces be specified. These standards must be sufficiently specific so as to assure compatibility, yet flexible enough to promote innovation.

Cooperation among manufacturers, network providers, end-users, and regulators throughout the world is vitally necessary. We need this in order to establish a telecommunications infrastructure which promoted rapid introduction of new technology that meets a variety of vastly different end-user needs, with a network where end-user specific problems can be answered with end-user defined solutions.

252

Ironic though it may seem, definition of international "standards" is the key challenge, if not obstacle, in creating a "Network Of The Future" that will bring dazzling enhancement of end-user specific "non-standard" communications applications.

The obstacles inevitably will be conquered and the almost boundless benefits achieved. The rapid progress being made in telecommunications today is cheeringly encouraging. Integrated Services Digital Networks (ISDNs) are currently being deployed which offer many of the capabilities discussed. Innovations in technology will continue to evolve the ISDN concept towards higher functionality at lower cost. This will further increase the demands placed on networks for more powerful communications alternatives. Technological advancements offer undeniably startling potential in facing and fulfilling these needs.

A View of a Future Society Based on C&C Technologies

By Dr. Koji Kobayashi, Chairman of the Board and Chief Executive Officer NEC Corporation

In this short contribution, I will first describe briefly how the concept of C&C, that is the integration of Computers and Communications, was developed. I will then discuss a future society with an infrastructure based on C&C systems, from the two aspects of the home and the manufacturing sector. Finally, I will consider the three main problems to be solved before such a society can come about.

Development of C&C

In the keynote speech to INTELCOM 77 in Atlanta, Georgia in 1977, I presented the idea that computer and communications technologies would eventually head toward integration based on semiconductor technology. A year later, speaking to the 3rd U.S.—Japan Computer Conference in San Francisco, I used the expression C&C to sum up this concept.

In the communications field, digital technology has gradually been introduced for transmission and switching. With this technology as a common basis, the integration of the communications field is becoming a possibility. This is being done in the form of the Integrated Services Digital Network (ISDN) whose standardization is now being pursued by the CCITT.

The progress of computers has seen the single-function type give way to the multifunction, and then to the large-scale centralized processing type. Now, with the introduction of digitalized communication technology, computers have moved on to distributed processing and networking. The next step will be intelligent processing using artificial intelligence.

This development of computers and communications has been made possible technologically and economically by the remarkable progress of semiconductor devices, from transistors to ICs, LSIs, and now VLSIs.

I believe that the continued development of semiconductor and digital technologies will lead to the full integration of computers and communications, and that in the coming century these C&C systems will play an increasingly important role in the social infrastructure.

C&C Society in the 21st Century

Looking at the present rate of change compared to 15 or 20 years ago makes us realize the difficulty of attempting to predict the shape society is likely to take at the start of the 21st century. However, it may be useful to inspire us with some idea of the goal we are aiming at, to try to draw a picture of a future C&C society by extrapolating from present trends and developments. I will take two cross sections of 21st century society—the home, and the manufacturing sector.

The Home in the 21st Century

In the home, in response to the increase in leisure time and diversification of life-styles, entertainment will become more individualized with more freedom of program choice and reception time. Video and audio quality will be greatly enhanced with high definition TV (HDTV), larger screens and three dimensional sound systems. This will provide more viewer satisfaction, especially in the live coverage of sports events and concerts. Moreover, packaged information, for example, using laser discs, will include not only movies and music, but also encyclopedias, dictionaries, and teaching materials. In addition to TV and radio, videotex and teletext services will provide news, weather forecasts, regional information, and news of market conditions. The detailed information we now obtain from magazines and newspapers will be available on request from the electronic media.

At home and in one's own time, it will be possible to do one's shopping or banking, make hotel or concert reservations, to handle one's business with government agencies, and to consult the doctor.

Telecommuting will become a reality as ISDN makes possible the individual use of wide band communication circuits and as the social environment adjusts to the new conditions. Commuting time, transportation energy and costs will be cut; living patterns will be liberalized; and employment opportunities for homemakers, the aged, and physically handicapped people will increase. Productivity will increase because people will be released from time constraints and will be able to work during their most efficient time of day. In creative jobs the effects will be particularly pronounced. For mothers with young children, childcare and work will become compatible.

The Manufacturing Sector in the 21st Century

With a higher all-round level of education and quality of life, the material needs of the general public will be more complex and sophisticated. A wide variety of intelligent products tailored to the individual's requirements will have to be manufactured in small quantities and thus with high efficiency. Moreover, the manufacturer of information indispensable for intelligent products, namely, software and databases, will carry a heavy weight in production. Thus, information will play an important role in manufacturing. The customer's requirements will go via communication circuits to a design center. Here, this information will be processed to form the instructions required for manufacture and then input to the production plant nearest to the customer. There, products will be manufactured and delivered. The production process will include human-machine interactive Computer Aided Design (CAD) at the product design stage. Computer Aided Manufacturing (CAM) using computers and robots, will handle process/assembly and testing at the production plant, and customer and product information will form a database which will be used by the Computer Aided Maintenance Service (CAMS). Customers, design centers with technical information processing systems, production plants and maintenance service centers distributed close to markets, and control centers with control information processing systems, all geographically dispersed, will be integrated by C&C.

With each function integrated in a network, this C&C manufacturing system will be able to speedily make and service products exactly suited to the individual customer with both higher quality and lower cost.

An individual response design system, capable of handling personalized orders flexibly, will be developed. This will lead in turn to a design system which takes customers' conceptual demands and creates the products' specifications for them, namely, a creative design system.

Eventually, the virtual plant may be developed where the customers themselves control all the manufacturing processes via the C&C network, from submitting their design concept to receiving the finished products. Resource sharing plants may be developed, in which production facilities and materials can be effectively shared among plants and enterprises dispersed throughout the entire world.

Problems to be Solved before a C&C Society Can Come About

Before such a society using C&C systems as a base to provide a fuller and more pleasant life for all can come into existence, a number of problems must be solved.

Of the three most important, one is the problem of the human-machine interface. C&C systems of the future must be accessible to all with no need for special training. The human-machine interface must be developed to make systems easily operable by the non-expert, for example through verbal input or output by perfecting speech recognition and synthesis. C&C systems will act as high level assistants, and as such must be made to understand human intentions and demands by the development of knowledge information processing and automatic translation.

Another problem is the software crisis, already with us and becoming more acute as the supply fails to keep up with the ever increasing demand, not only for computer but also for communications software. To bring about a C&C society will require enormous amounts of new software including that for developing the C&C production system and perfecting the human-machine interface. We must analyze the present situation and institute drastic reforms of software production, management, and quality control techniques. Effective design, manufacture, and test methods will have to be developed, work practices standardized and the working environment modernized, and development and maintenance tools prepared.

The third main problem facing us is that of Transborder Data Flow (TBDF). The future society we envisage will depend on information including production instructions flowing across national boundaries through C&C networks to plants scattered around the globe. To guarantee that information—the largest production element in a C&C society—can be effectively utilized, the nations of the world will have to reach agreement on the following points: that no country will place unreasonable obstacles in the way of telecommunications, that information flow should be encouraged by lowered telecommunication charges and technical standardization, and that political or other considerations should be minimized in order that the system users will gain the maximum benefit.

Conclusions

For a C&C society to function, it must to a certain extent transcend national frontiers. To do this, to overcome language barriers and deepen mutual understanding, automatic interpretation systems must be developed. I believe that the joint international development and implementation of automatic interpretation telephone systems will be a significant milestone on the road to the C&C society.

Because C&C systems make it most efficient to place manufacturing plants close to material or human resources wherever they are in the world, the transfer of both hardware and software technologies to developing countries should happen naturally. This will have the effect of resolving the have-have not problem by shrinking the economic gap between developed and developing countries. It should also help solve trade conflicts between the advanced nations.

The C&C society of the 21st century promises to be one of unparalleled opportunity for the advancement of civilization and individual human happiness. New technologies can be abused, as we see from the recent rise of the computer criminal. However, we believe that if the moral and spiritual advances of the human race keep pace with its technological progress, the coming century will see a golden age of peace for our planet.

Technology and Network Architecture

By Dr. John S. Mayo, Executive Vice President, Network Systems, AT&T Bell Laboratories

Universal information services is an exciting goal for our industry, and for us at AT&T Bell Laboratories, it's an exciting commitment to which we have pledged our scientific and technological resources. There's no question that achieving the goals of universal information services present tremendous technical challenges, but we all believe that enormous benefits to our industry and to our customers are clearly worth the tough work ahead.

I want to share our excitement with you, by taking you on a brief journey; one that expands in scope, literally, from atomic dimensions to the entire nation. It's a journey from the laboratory to the realization of universal information services. I will bring you up to date on the key information technologies that are vital to all our progress; on the flexible new kinds of systems architectures these technologies are making possible; and on the impact of both the technologies and the systems on future network architectures.

Where is our industry today? The demand for digital services for both voice and data is high and growing. To meet this demand, special purpose overlays are being applied to the existing networks, even as those underlying networks are undergoing a rapid transition to digital.

We view Phase 1 of the course toward universal information services, as the widespread deployment of intelligent digital network elements, which have the inherent ability to grow in functionality as time progresses.

Reviewing the architectural sketch, a few elements have been added to complete the 1985 picture, shown in Fig. 9-4, although the picture is still greatly simplified compared to the multitude of configurations in service today.

The digital central office switch is the hub of the architecture, providing high functionality through sophisticated, centrex-type voice and data services. Of course this switching function itself may be distributed to remote modules in smaller central offices or at network points co-located with the customer.

Access to the switch can be over direct metallic paths, or increasingly

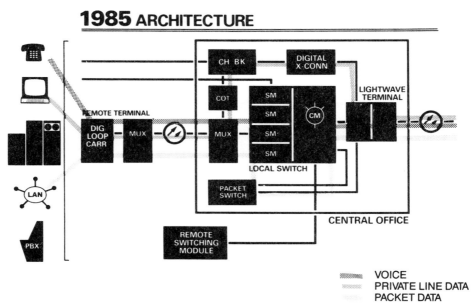

1985 ARCHITECTURE

Fig. 9-4. 1985 Architecture.

over loop carrier multiplexing systems. We have shown here an optical fiber link between the remote terminal of the loop carrier system and the switching office. This remote terminal, with intelligent digital processing capabilities, is located close to the end customer. Hundreds of such terminals are distributed in a metropolitan area. Thus they represent an opportunity to add service functionality in an economic manner as technology progresses. Exactly the same can be said for the digital channel bank and cross-connect systems shown in the central office; these can be expanded in channel services functionality through new software-based intelligence.

Between switching offices, we show a lightwave system, but T-carrier and digital radio systems will continue to play important roles. For all of these interoffice systems, the challenge is to provide very efficient transport and yet retain the sophistication to permit the reconfiguration flexibility required by a dynamically changing network.

Today's digital architecture provides different paths through the network for voice circuits, data circuits, and packet data. Different local access links are required and appear to the customer as different interfaces. Different central office gear is used on each path. Moreover, significant administrative and operational effort is required for the telecommunications provider in supporting the engineering, installation, maintenance, and billing for these diverse paths.

The second phase of network evolution sees the introduction and unfolding of ISDN. Data, voice, and signaling are integrated; access interfaces are standardized on a completely digital loop; and a rich set of new centrex functionality is brought to the end-user.

One of the fundamental features of ISDN is a small number of universal network interfaces. Standardization of interfaces gives the end user great latitude in selecting equipment to use with the network. It also has the effect of freeing the development of terminal equipment technology from a specific network configuration. We believe the natural and logical starting point for the interface between the network and station equipment is the so-called T interface, defined by the international CCITT standards for just that purpose.

The standard interfaces for the ISDN service architecture are the 2B + D and 23B + D formats. Here, of course, the building blocks are the 64Kb/s clear channel voice and data (B) channel and the full standard signaling, telemetry, and packet (D) channel.

Much of the power of ISDN is derived from the fact that it completes the delivery of local common channel signaling, a delivery process which has already begun. The rich signaling features of the Q.931 standard, utilized over the parallel D channel permit great improvements in user productivity by faster call setup, look ahead for busy, flexible incoming call screening, and so on. In fact, we use the presence or absence of Q.931 signaling as a litmus test for true ISDN products. With this signaling, a powerful new message-level dialogue is possible between the network and premises equipment, far surpassing the capabilities of today's Touch-Tone signaling.

On the architectural diagram, in Fig. 9-5, several things change in the ISDN phase shown here in 1987. Highlighting the voice, circuit data, and packet data paths, we now see a single access path from the customer into the network. This is the simplification of the interface just described. A fully integrated access link now serves the customer to either a sophisticated station set on a basic rate 2B + D link or a cluster of stations on a primary rate 23B + D path. Note that packet data is now served directly by the digital switch. Also note that the intelligent transmission terminals have been upgraded in functionality to support the ISDN interfaces.

I have also shown a separate high-speed video path through the network. This is not tied to ISDN, but in the 1987-9 time frame, we expect to see increasing demand for digital video services. We are introducing today a video system which permits full multistation color video conferencing with simultaneous graphics and audio. We expect to see widespread deployment by 1989.

ISDN offers improved access, standard interfaces, and a host of sophisticated new services. Plenty of work remains for all of us to translate ISDN's promise into reality. Why then, are we at AT&T discussing an evolutionary stage beyond ISDN?

One major reason is that it is necessary to do the planning now for the 1990s. We must anticipate the trends in technology and customer needs. We must begin the discussion of new standards needed within the industry. We must apply our research and exploratory development efforts in concert with our evolutionary view.

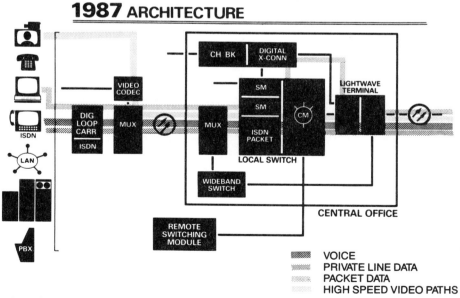

Fig. 9-5. 1987 Architecture.

259

Our view beyond ISDN envisions further integration of services into common access and transport paths. We see high rate standard ports into the network. We see greatly increased customer control of network resources so that the customer can adaptively configure virtual sub-networks to meet a particular need at a given time. We see video and high-quality telegraphics as fully integrated network services. See Fig. 9-6.

In the decade of the 1990s we see continuing robustness and yet simplification in architecture. A great deal of traffic will be carried in packet format and some of it through optical switches of cross connects. We have been doing voice packet studies in the laboratory for some time and will be embarking on a field study among AT&T locations in northern California this year. We will be taking to the field our latest wideband packet prototype equipment and evaluating both its performance and users' perceptions. We are confident that technologies such as wideband packet and optical switching hold great promise and we are proud of our leadership position.

Our architectural diagram continues to evolve. Hardware and software adjuncts to the digital central office switch increase its functionality and couple today's separate, stand-alone systems into an integrated system for universal services. The central office becomes an integrated transport node with tight coupling in the control of its elements, but with distributed functionality.

Transmission terminals continue to grow in their role of providing network interfaces. New wideband packet interfaces are shown. Interoffice transmission gateways, increasingly synchronized with the switch in a syntran-like fashion, offer flexible routing onto and from high capacity fibers. We now have

1990S ARCHITECTURE

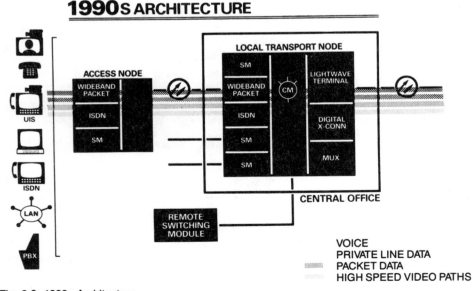

Fig. 9-6. 1990s Architecture.

both integrated access and integrated transport for the full range of services.

The loop side of the network looks increasingly like the interoffice side. Glass fibers bring high bandwidth to the doorstep of network users. Distributed microcomputers in the network respond to customer inputs and bring bit rate or bandwidth on demand, to the customers premises over either copper or fiber. There is a strong analogy here to the manner in which we draw resources, as needed, from the distribution grid for electric power, through its well-defined interface ports and according to its well-defined standards.

The powerful and distributed network of the 1990s calls for sophisticated operations support. Shown schematically is a distributed array of universal operations systems. Provisioning and network management functions respond dynamically to changing customer needs; force management directs the critical people resource; surveillance and measurement provide a self-healing network; and usage data collection leads directly to accurate and detailed billing data. Such a monumental job calls for integrated operation systems functionality in each of the network elements as well as central intelligence for overall coordination.

Customer control is available through many of the same avenues as the network provider uses for centralized network administration and operation. For instance, the distributed intelligence of the network can re-route signals, measure traffic load, isolate trouble spots, indicate current usage of particular equipment, and relay this information to either the telephone company or the customer. The key is to build the right operations capabilities into the equipment and do it with the appropriate intelligence and security in software, and with user friendly interfaces.

I have just taken you on a brief journey from the laboratory to universal information services. We can all count with confidence on the continuing richness of the power and potential of the information technologies. We can also look with assurance to increasingly flexible systems architectures, made possible by the creative and aggressive integration of these technologies with one another and with customer needs. And we can anticipate the resulting realization of ever more sophisticated and adaptable network architectures.

Achieving the goal and the benefits of universal information services will require the efforts of the entire telecommunications industry—suppliers, network providers, and end-users.

Our cooperative efforts must include the support and acceptance of standard interfaces to end-users developed in productive forums such as the T1 working groups. We as an industry must also embrace the design and deployment of robust digital network elements that will evolve gracefully toward a focussed vision of the future. Finally, there must be broad, on-going and open communications—communications among ourselves, among the entire industry, worldwide, and especially with our customers and end-users—so that we can continuously fine-tune our understanding of the evolving needs and requirements. Our industry will move the world gracefully and efficiently toward universal information services. The benefits to society will be the wide, new, exciting world of the information age.

The Future of the Information Era

By William C. Norris, Former Chairman and Chief Executive Officer, Control Data Corporation

Basic research and its innovative leading-edge technologies in a host of scientific disciplines have powered the information revolution of the past fifty years. The trends are clear, the progress inexorable. Costs, in relative terms are declining, permitting greater selectivity and interaction in information flow than ever before. Sadly, man's ability to take full advantage of the information tools at his disposal remains the limiting factor in society's ability to benefit. In the words of Alvin Toffler, "An information bomb is exploding in our midst, showering us with a shrapnel of images. New information reaches us and we are forced to review our image file continuously at a faster and faster rate."

Spurred by lower relative costs to communicate, the last twenty years have witnessed a steady decline in the size of mass audiences and a surge towards selective dissemination of information. The number of radio stations in the United States has almost tripled since 1960, with the vast majority catering to a single selected market. The circulation of major daily newspapers has steadily declined while weekly news sheets serving local communities, with information specific to them, are burgeoning. Mass circulation magazines too, are yielding to journals aimed at much smaller, special interest audiences. Network television is losing its audience share to cable T.V. which, with the aid of the communications satellite, increasingly permits more diversity of choice and the opportunity to serve specialized audiences cost-effectively.

This trend towards service to the special-interest audience is inexorable as the relative cost to transfer information declines. The ultimate special-interest audience, of course, is the single individual with his or her unique wants and needs; and today, that audience is already being served effectively in a few fields such as in education and training.

The trend toward greater information interaction is equally compelling. Information flow between remotely located parties is increasingly bidirectional, even multi-directional, propelled by low-cost microelectronic devices. The long-distance telephone increasingly substitutes for the letter. Two-way cable T.V. and information services, such as Teletext, are growing and permitting audience interaction with the T.V. program, most frequently by way of coded signals, but increasingly, particularly in Japan and Europe, with the use of audio and video channels.

The personal computer, intelligent computer terminals, video games and automatic teller machines are present manifestations of bilateral information flow between man and machine and between man and man via machine. Millions of us are learning to interact with the machine and discover that, when well-designed, it can be a very friendly, intellectually rewarding experience.

Information is useless unless it can be transformed into knowledge, which in turn becomes the agent for beneficial action. The primary key to such a transformation is the computer, which has become an integral component of the information explosion. Computers, sometimes operating cooperatively in a distributed data processing network, sometimes operating in a one-to-one interaction with the human, are increasingly able to digest the information that is exploded around us, manipulate it, associate it with other facts, and present it in forms that help the human understand its implications and apply that understanding to productive action. In other words, the computer acts as a catalyst for the transformation of information to knowledge, and it will become increasingly more adept at performing that task, as we learn to incorporate into it attributes more akin to human intelligence. Elementary expert systems, able to draw inferences from the information provided to them, analyze problems and suggest optimum solutions, already exist. Within ten years, they will have evolved to rival the ability of human experts in many fields: medicine, law and business management among them.

Education and training is one field in which all these information trends—selectivity, interaction, and the conversion of information to knowledge with the assistance of the computer are epitomized today. Technologies such as those of the computer, communications, video recording and display make it not only possible but practical and cost effective to tailor education and training to the specific needs of each individual.

These technologies, intelligently incorporated into a total education and training system, can truly result in optimum individual learning. Such a system interrogates the individual to assess the present state of his or her knowledge concerning the subject at hand. It identifies the gaps between the individual's needed and existing knowledge, prescribes and administers a course of study to close the gap, and then interacts continuously with the individual to provide the needed information until it is understood and retained, and maintains current status concerning the individual's progress.

Such a system allows the individual to progress at his or her own pace, while assuring that effective learning has occurred each step of the way. Slower learners take longer to learn, but the learning is complete for all. The individual's time is not wasted nor is his or her interest atrophied by needlessly covering topics already mastered.

Such a system is no 21st Century dream. It exists today and is in broad cost-effective use at all levels of academic learning from kindergarten to college and for training applications in business, industry and government. The system is flexible and adaptable to future technological innovations, such as those of expert systems. It is a leading-edge example, but only one example among many of the continuing trend towards selectivity, interaction and computer assistance in permitting society to cope with and maximally benefit from the information explosion.

FURTHER ANALYSIS

These visions of the future can be directly applied in *The Global Timeframe for the information society* analyses; specifically in the *The Human Element* case study and the *Another Place Another Time* workshop in Chapter 12.

Chapter 10

Information Networks, Products, and Services

This chapter provides an opportunity for us to step back and consider the ISDN Network in terms of its basic building blocks. It identifies the key aspects of the public information network that will enable it to function in the new world of private networks, valve added networks, multiple exchange carriers, unregulated offerings, governmental boundaries, minimized IDC/BOC dominance, joint offerings, open architecture interfaces (that are comparably efficient), new features, and complex "integrated services" systems. The network will be analyzed in terms of changing wideband facilities and physically distributed switching with new automated support systems, as users are provided more and more features on an open competitive basis to meet their expanding information needs.

Realizing that it is a changing game in a changing world, this analysis is supported by the case studies in Chapter 12, which provide detailed analyses of market opportunities, technical possibilities, governmental boundaries, decision processes, ISDN interfaces, and the network standards players. In a previous chapter, we positioned ourselves to play the game in terms of "top down planning" organizations and processes. Now we will play the game by defining a logical U.S. ISDN wideband network architecture and structure that providers could reasonably establish over the next twenty years, using specific new families of quality products by competitive suppliers. When it is constructed, it will enable exciting new features and services to be economically available to private and public users, as it moves us all together into the information age.

THE INFO RING: THE RING SWITCH

There has been much discussion in the ISDN planning activities on features, interfaces, standards, and switching, but nothing can be accomplished without the facility distribution plan. Indeed there is movement to have numerous cellular radio frequencies switched in cells throughout the country, as the user moves from location to location. There is also analysis to overlay a data network on the cellular network, so that the user may receive low to medium speed data in his car. (The price of the mobile terminal has dropped from $2400 in the early 80s to $1400 in the mid 80s, to a projected $700 by the 90s, to encourage more usage by small business trade organizations.) There have been new bands of frequencies provided by the FCC, which carriers and future carriers were given the opportunity to obtain on a lottery basis, with much speculation for using them in the rural environment, instead of phone lines.

With this activity came a relook at the possibilities of transport systems, that spray neighborhoods with frequencies to provide personal phones. These can also be encrypted and act as a single cell mobile system. Even electronic pagers now send a burst of data to display calling number or a brief message on their valuable limited frequencies. Of course, there are extensive microwave systems offered by new carriers to provide a point of presence and connect to either Telco public networks or private local area networks. Similarly, satellite networks are now homing directly on the large office complexes or are tying remote complexes together to form specialized private transport networks. Finally, some private and specialized carriers have elected to lease duct work from the local telephone company and insert their own fiber optic systems, while others have asked the Telco to construct a fiber optic tree network, connecting all the city's major businesses to them.

This then leads us into the world of fiber optics and its tremendous possibilities for moving megabits to gigabits of information with the potential to replace thousands of pairs of wires with a single fiber. For example, a fiber provides the ability to send the entire Encyclopedia Britannica in a few seconds, and has the ability to economically handle 6,000 conversations on a single fiber, expanding with multiple frequencies to a possible 18,000, and to many times that in the future. Hence, we need to seriously address the impact of this technology, especially as it offers the possibility for a more error free and secure transmission medium than radio, microwave or satellite.

Fiber optics also must be viewed as an economical medium for handling normal distribution plant growth. It can be utilized to extend distributed architectures of switching products for the voice, data, and video world closer and closer to the user. Its costs are decreasing, as repeater spacing extends further and further out, with decreasing connector module costs, making it more and more economical. But first, let's look at the other mediums.

Twisted Pair

As we look at Table 10-1, we see a hierarchy of transmission rates expressed in terms of the T carrier digital channel banks, where a twisted pair

Table 10-1. Channel Capacity Growth.

	Name	Rate	Channels
	(DS0)	64Kb/s	1
T1	(DS1)	1.544Mb/s	24
T1C	(2DS1s)	3.152Mb/s	48
T2	(DS2,4DS1s)	6.312Mb/s	96
T3	(DS3,28DS1s)	44.736Mb/s	672
T3C	(DS3C,2DS3s)	90Mb/s	1,344
T3D	(DS3D,3DSD,3DS3s)	135Mb/s	2,016
T4	(DS4,6DS3s)	274.17Mb/s	4,032
T4C	(DS4C,9DS3s)	405Mb/s	6,048
	(DS5).....&&		

can handle 24 of T-1's 64 Kb channels at 1.544 megabits with various framing bits for synchronization of systems. Special low capacitance wire is used for T-2 systems, which operate at 6.312 megabits transmission. However, the local loop to the customer environment is more often limited to 100 to 200 Kb. Hence, neither system is presently used there. The major benefit of twisted wire is a two way star network. Some office complexes for sending voice and data have been 6 wire systems with various techniques to reduce them to two pairs (4 wire) systems to meet the new ISDN "T" (2B + D) interface or to the two wire "U" (23B + D) interface.

Coax

Coaxial cable systems have bandwidth between 300-400 MHz and can handle 35-60 TV channels. However, the network is in place as a tree architecture, or basically one way with limited two way capability. Security is a problem since other users have access to the information. HDTV [High Definition (1200 lines)T.V.] also may have problems due to repeater amplifier noise. Coaxial can be used in star-type cluster networks, but is expensive in this arrangement.

Satellite

One-way broadcast point-to-point HDTV over satellite or packet switching (from satellite to satellite) are good long haul servers to remote locations, especially with small cheaper earth stations. These are making satellite transmission more competitive. However, some single hop and all two hop systems are not conducive for voice, due to delay, security, and echo problems for high quality.

Fiber Optics

This then again leads us to fiber optics, which provides high security, two-way capability when used in star-type networks, and high capacity in ring structures. Two semi-conductors, the light emitting diode (LED) and laser diode have been used. LEDs currently have the advantage of lower costs, but there are new possibilities for the laser diode. Fiber optics has low attenuation varying from about 3 to 3.5 dB per km. Two broad classifications of fiber for telecommunications is multi mode grade index or single mode step index. Graded index fiber transmits many modes (paths) of light through its core. Single mode allows only one path through a smaller core. The advantage of single mode fiber is a much greater bandwidth. Currently single mode systems operate at near 400 megabits per second. Systems will operate at 1 to 1.5 Gbs in the near future. Multi-mode systems generally operate at less than 200 million bits per second. Wave length division multiplexers allow different wave lengths from different sources to be transmitted over the same fiber. Devices such as passive couplers will split light from 1 into 2 or more fibers, but the limited number of these devices that can operate in series discourages fiber tree networks. Single mode fiber offers many advantages over graded index fiber (multi-mode).

Fiber optic systems, in general, operate at an integral number of DS-3 (45 mb) rates and have DS-3 inputs. New techniques for synchronization of DS-3 such as SYNTRAN, will greatly increase throughput capabilities since fewer synchronization framing and bit stuffing bits are needed. Hence the single mode fiber will become the basis for moving large quantities of information closer and closer to the user. It can tie to coax or even twisted pair in existing premises to deliver the information at lower rates.

As the distribution plant attempts to move numerous 1.5Mb/s special point to point circuits, LANs (20Mb/s), and MANs of 50 plus megabits, we can begin looking at the distribution plant from an aerial point of view and begin developing rings of usage. In the figure, rings will be tied together by multiplexors and pads, as more and more rings extend from previous rings, or are overlaid on each other. By the early 90s fiber will be overlaid down each major corridor of the cities and between cities.

Hence, there is the need for introducing nodal point access to wideband and megabit switches from remote land satellite units to put the rings under control of base switches to provide alternate routing to other rings in the event of ring failure in controlling traffic flow. As the customers contend for more and more bandwidth on a usage basis, we will see the power of the ring's megabit switches to move large transport capacities to the users on a variable usage per call basis. For example, in the video mode, it requires more dynamic capacity to send a moving hand in a picture, than to send a relatively still picture.

The ring access switch sends traffic to the internal switches. It will be the splitter switch that eventually replaces the automated mainframe and splits voice, data, and video traffic off to the appropriate network switch. In the outer areas, its MUXs and PADs become part of the distributed nodal point satellite switches to tie local area networks to MANs and WANs to the world. It can also extend features to calls within the local area networks or between local areas, when serving to integrate PBXs with LANs, as well as the major wideband networks of the future.

Hence, the ring switches of the future will evolve from the automated cross connect systems of today and the access matrixes that manage BORSCHT (Battery Over voltage Ringing Signalling Test) for current digital signalling systems, as more and more capacity is being made available to the user at cheaper and cheaper bit usage rates to encourage growth. Current switches can handle 1.5 megabit traffic, such as compressed video and computer data, but they do not handle video 45 megabit or high definition TV near 140 megabit. Hence, it will require a new family of switches, such as parallel packet switching or space division switching using CMOS and Gallium Arsenide (GaAs) devices, enabling high speed gigabit/terabit transport capabilities of 100Mb/s (with 562 Mb muxs) by fast packet, burst switches or even integrated photonic circuit switches, when photonic logic and photonic repeaters are achieved. In any event, this will be the switch for the 21st century, but the info rings will take the next 20 years to be achieved, using the single mode fiber and coax to extend information closer and closer to the user today. See Fig. 10-1.

THE INFORMATION COMMUNICATION COMPLEX

As we look at the world of Centrex, Centron, PBXs, PAXs, PABXs, Nodal Switches, Contention Systems, Concentrators, Key Systems, Multiplexors, Channel Banks, as well as Data Circuit Switches, Data Packet Switches, Programmable Pads, and Wideband 45-562 Megabit Switches, we must truly understand the direction of both technology and the marketplace, especially as we consider the switch technology evolution noted in *What's a Switch*, as switches move from physically distributed autonomous, functionally partitioned, to functionally integrated systems using VLSI, Gallium Arsenide, multiple functional processors, parallel processing, and photonics technology to provide more and more MIPS, to the 200 to 400 MIP range with VLSI functional memories at the 4 megabit level, and disk storage reaching 50 million bytes.

Home Network Needs

The marketplace has indicated that resistance to price caused PC sales to drop once governmental tax rebates were no longer available. In addition, the store owners charged for user education, even for such services as two or more hours of initial training on one's newly purchased $2500 personal computer. To expand the PC market, there is also the need to access outside database sinks, using various terminal to terminal protocol conversions. Future home communications aspects were explored, as viewtext type trials throughout the world indicated the need for cheap, inexpensive, but very user friendly terminals to enable the unsophisticated public to master input/output skills. Finally, as noted, economics always plays a deciding role, after the "vanity buyers" were finished purchasing goods as a status symbol for their homes or businesses. Many would-be buyers had difficulty justifying expensive PCs, until the price was right (similar to the mobile phone situation). Some simply wanted list access and search features provided by cheap access to inexpensive outside databases, using a limited terminal. See Fig. 10-2.

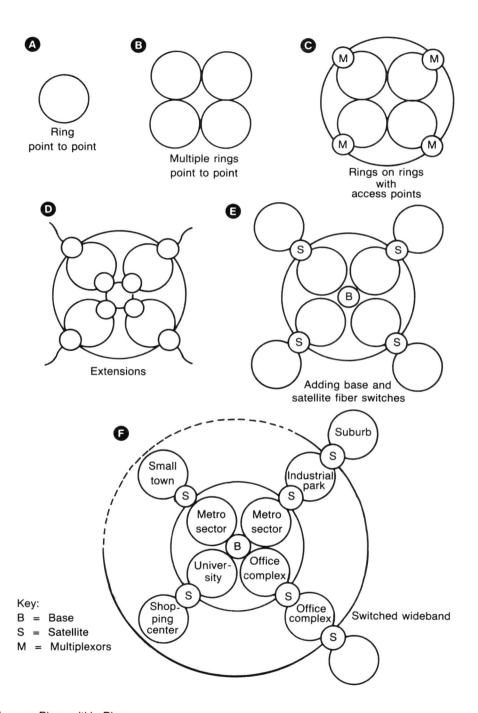

Fig. 10-1. Rings on Rings within Rings.

Key:
B = Base
S = Satellite
M = Multiplexors

269

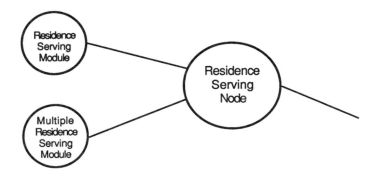

Fig. 10-2. Home Communication Center.

Business Network Needs

On the other hand, many business network purchasers were determined to obtain systems that provide total information handling in an "integrated" product, although many requirement specifications did not establish indepth, *what* information features and *how* "integrated" the product must be. As we continue our analysis of the "Who's on First—What's on Second" world (see case study), we can see that the information switch will be "Who's on First." This will become the next logical point in the evolution of the Centrex game to the data world and on to the combined voice, data, and video world. We have seen the need to provide customers their own premise systems to interface with different networks; first from a regulatory NCTE Inquiry II decision; and then for the more competitive Inquiry III environment, where nodal point (Telco provided) premise systems may be allowed to provide access for multiple types of voice and data internal network terminals to the world, using such ISDN tools as the "D" channel processor. (See ISDN reference study.)

There is another need that has become quite prevalent, as we enter the information explosion of numerous new features provided by complex and expensive software. It is the update, maintenance, and control problems to make existing systems compatible and concurrent with new features and software changes. This will be the major future need of the business community. See Fig. 10-3.

Private Network Needs

As new private networks are handled on shared public networks and switched to the world, we again return to the need for CO Centrex type offering, which may no longer be at a CO-Central Office location, but at some nodal point on an interfacing ring. Alternatively, an info switch replacing the CU-Centrex world, being located close to a centralized shopping center or business office complex is attractive in the more cost competitive small business data packet world, as an alternative offering. It can be provided by the Telco's Information Distribution Company (IDC) or by an intermediary, who

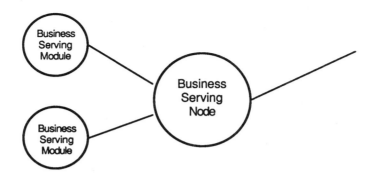

Fig. 10-3. Business Communication Center.

acts as an agent of the IDC, or by a separate shared private network offering to the local business community.

Service Needs

Finally there is the need to provide separately and/or jointly various new information services, ranging from expanded operator or human interaction information services to providing specialized data manipulation, presentation, and processing, as well as various new features in both the voice and data, as well as the video and graphic image transport arena. See Fig. 10-4.

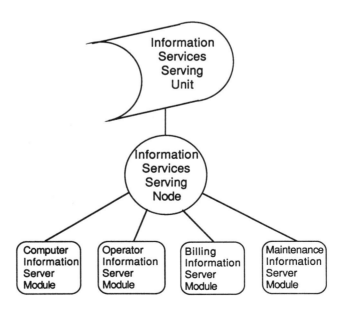

Fig. 10-4. Services Communication Center.

System Needs

As will be noted in the *What is a Switch* analysis of the internal structure of switching system evolution, and considering, where the info switch fits into the network architecture, we have a "change dilemma" in terms of extensive software features changes to meet home, business, and service world demands in voice, data, and video arenas. This requires a prudent system level architecture design to correctly position the right amount of software at the right level in the network as well as the right partition within the system structure to minimize and localize change impact on the bulk of the software.

Secondly, there is the system need to be cost effective on the customer premise, but also provide numerous new features to the customer, which can continue to grow with the other customer provided equipment.

Thirdly, there is also the need to provide more functions, interfaces and services to the hierarchy of network systems, interfacing to the metro, access, support, and signalling systems.

Finally, there is the need to encourage the public network usage by all four types of new users: residence, small business, medium business, and large business, and facilitate their usage by an expanding information ring to foster and enable their interexchange of information.

Concepts

The conceptual figures in this section show the overlays, as we build up the view of the information communication complex and position the four components into the network. One of the final figures notes the location of the info switch in relationship to the ring and metro switches. (Refined later in this chapter.)

With distributed processing, it is now feasible to achieve the interesting concept of breaking a PBX into physically distributed modules and positioning the pieces on a local area network within an office structure, a university campus, even floors of a hotel or apartment/condo complexes, homing in on a local or regionalized base unit, such as; the info switch, the metro switch, or the access switch. In looking at the serving side of the equation, we need an information serving unit to work with a remote information service serving node, which contains the specific individual services. These serving clusters can be localized with the information switch, or shared across the info and even metro switches.

As we consider the support complex, the feature oriented serving node could tie to the support center or later even tie into the signalling center. Alternatively, it could be tied to existing systems, as the adjunct processor assisting a rural or suburban complex to provide specialized feature services. However, two considerations must be reevaluated in separating it from the info switch or metro switch. One is called processing throughput capacity and handling delay, and the other is the *Who's on First* issue (see case study) of providing competitive offerings, remote from the switching hierarchy.

Architecture

The design architecture of the info switch, as shown in Fig. 10-5 indicates that the voice, data, and video features should be partitioned in order to minimize software changes. In addition, it functionalizes the access and serving functions, attempting to indicate the need for a device handler level hardware and feature oriented distributed software processor arrangement. The interface to the system, as noted earlier, is either direct or through the remote nodal access switch point, which fits nicely with the ring satellite and base access switches. In addition, the network outgoing access portion of the system could interface with the ring or directly to the tandem level access switch or localized specialized carrier facilities. The remote simplex residence and small business centers can directly home on the switch, enabling direct access to information manipulation features, especially to meet small business needs for the "office in the home."

It is also interesting to note sizing. The system should be competitive in the small PBX market, as well as the large "office of the future" by providing levels of home or office communication centers containing various degrees of localized intelligence. It then becomes the missing competitive common public business network offering to encourage private networks to use it, similarly to the earlier CCSA switches and Centrex switches. It can also be used as a co-located central office feature switch for existing rural or metro base units.

Its phases of evolution as seen in the *What is a Switch* analysis demonstrates that it can be implemented with complexes of current systems and then in the more functionally partitioned systems of the 90s. Finally, it can be provided as a totally integrated system at the turn of the century, after the data and video traffic have developed.

It can also be structured to be a subset of the metro switch (a large urban switch to be discussed later in this chapter), as a front end home/business interface, or as a "sink" service provider interface. This technology will more than likely change with that of the metro switch. In actuality, its tech-

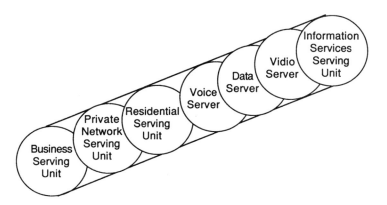

Fig. 10-5. The Information Switch.

nology may lead in the same manner that PBX technology traditionally led central office systems. It should be used as part of the ring switch structure to interface and provide features via the home and business server modules to LANs and via its base capabilities to provide them numerous shared more complex services. Hence, it then can, indeed, be a very universal switch for the forthcoming information world. See Fig. 10-6.

THE OPERATIONS SUPPORT CENTER

As we look at the network "Operations" overlay (Fig. 10-7) and consider the number of operations support programming systems and point to point support networks in place to automate the movement of just voice network support information, we begin to understand the complexity of the task of controlling these large operational databases and automating not just pieces of their operation (with numerous manual interventions), but entire functions—not only for voice, but for the future data and video world as well.

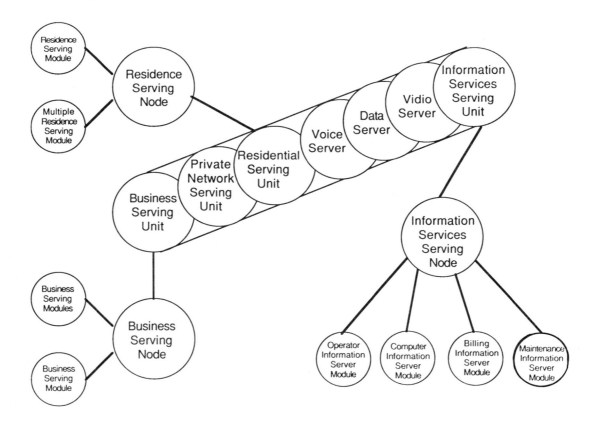

Fig. 10-6. The Information Communication Complex.

274

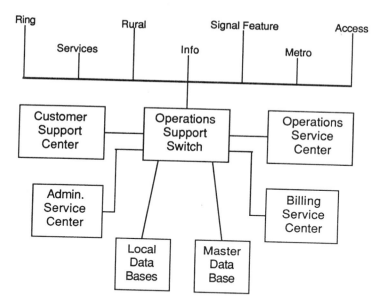

Fig. 10-7. Operations Support Center.

It is one thing to discuss providing variable bandwidth to a user, it is quite another to dynamically measure and bill the customer for variable bandwidth usage.

Similarly, networks reconfigured under customer control will require "instantaneous service" capabilities for not only the movement of voice traffic, but also data and perhaps video. Again, this requires the in-place automated mainframes, access switches or ring switches under the control of the customer service center with specific segments of the network database accessible directly by the customer. In investigating other areas, we see numerous types of information exchange between support centers and operational switching systems, such as automated maintenance information in which site dependent data is automatically updated from remote administration centers, as well as new office versions, traffic network load control information, and user "class mark" database changes, that provide classes of new services and features, as well as new feature program modules to provide new features on a group or customized basis.

Using the military weapon and control systems as an example of a major user who manipulates large complex databases and has overlaid several new systems on top of previous systems in an effort to achieve the latest in the state of the art database control, Fig. 10-7 shows the need for a support center data switch, which accesses individual operations, billing, administration and customer service centers, which control their own specific databases and interface to a master database for shared or common information.

The key to success in this endeavor is to tie, via a data packet network, the centers to each switch in the network to achieve an "on line" exchange of traffic, test, features, programs, and status information. In addition, the autonomous network switches can perform various administrative/maintenance tasks during their idle modes to assist in automating the entire network operations. The telecommunications firms have millions of instructions in programs and data in "mega databases" to provide automated operational services such as:

- TIRKS—Trunks Integrated Record Keeping System
- COSMOS—Computer System for Mainframe Operation
- FACS—Facility Assignment and Control System
- CMS-3—Cost Management System
- CAROT—Centralized Automatic Reporting on Trunks
- SCCS—Switching Control Center System
- RMAS—Remote Memory Administration System
- LMOS—Loop Maintenance Operations System
- MLT—Mechanized Loop Testing
- RCS—Electronic Equipment Records
- CIMAP—Circuit Installation and Maintenance Package
- PROMS—Provisioning Order Management System
- DAS—Directory Assistance System
- PICS—Plug Inventory Control System
- DCPR—Detailed Continued Property Record
- FAMIS—Financial Analysis Marketing Information Systems
- MTR—Mechanized Time Reporting
- TOPP—Total Operational Personnel Productivity
- UDS—Universal Dispatch System

It is interesting to note how many will have to be extended into the forthcoming data and video world offerings. Many of these programs commonly supported across the RBOCs have been written in early languages such as COBOL and will need to be restructured, and merge into the new programs, and are upgraded throughout the turn of the century. There will be no easy, inexpensive solutions. Bellcore's vision of automated support centers, working with their instantaneous services, somewhat under customer control will be important:

- OSN—Operations Systems Network. This has a comprehensive set of interface standards designed to provide universal communications across/between operation systems, telecommunications equipment, terminals and terminal users. Here, a packet switched network will tie databases to network element functions to obtain necessary traffic, testing, and monitoring data, as well as facilitate software updates and database information for manipulation by engineering or operational terminals as well as for planning forecasting and customer order control operations. Thus the network support will become fully automated without intermediate manual data analysis steps, using new programs such as:

276

- NMA—Network Monitor Analysis
- ITS—Integrated Testing Systems
- MAS—Memory Administration System

Over the years, suppliers and providers will be working with Bellcore to establish these concepts in acceptable standards (TRs) via information exchange and planning meetings (TRIFs), using individual proposals (TAs).

Hence, support systems do require complex solutions. They are presented here for understanding the need to consider their impact on any new product, network, or service provided in the public or private world of voice, data, or video systems. These complex, resistive to change, extensive, time consuming, and expensive aspects must be considered in parallel to the new technical and marketing strategies. To provide these new "supported" products, networks, and services by both the supplier and provider for the user, there is a need for cross working committees to establish an acceptable "open architecture" for these support systems, in which equipment and programming houses can provide their respective offerings. (See Pres. Hudson's vision in the preceding chapter.)

This is also not an area for new carriers and providers to overlook, as they structure their networks. Similarly, any future switching or network product of the suppliers should no longer be a "black box," that performs singular switching functions, but should be available to facilitate or assist in automating all the network support functions.

THE METRO SWITCH

The digital world has evolved from digital channel banks to the remote line units, remote switch units, and digital base units. This complex was designed as the rural/suburban switch for the 1985-95 time frame to economically replace clusters of SXS and crossbar systems and perform as a switching partner for the entrance of T (digital) and fiber optics (digital (wideband)) into the local loop and interoffice facilities. See Fig. 10-8.

However, the Metro Switch was never really defined for the urban environment until recently, due to its dependency on the market life cycle phases of the new voice, data, and video services. As a result, various efforts were made to extend the rural/suburban switch architecture to the metro environment, by using it as an adjunct collocated digital switch next to an analog switch to handle growth, as an "upside down switch" with all lines on either remote line units and remote switch units, or to meet the needs of the business sector by adding circuit data or packet data switching capabilities, or until traffic conditions warranted the next generation of technology. New feature possibilities for voice, data, and video were and still are tied to FCC and Justice decisions. This offset the ISDN trend to totally integrate switch-data processing offerings in an unregulated or detariffed world. The international picture is still evolving, as the world shifts to phases of ISDN implementation in major cities of the industrially developed and underdeveloped world.

Using this framework, we might consider the architecture and structure

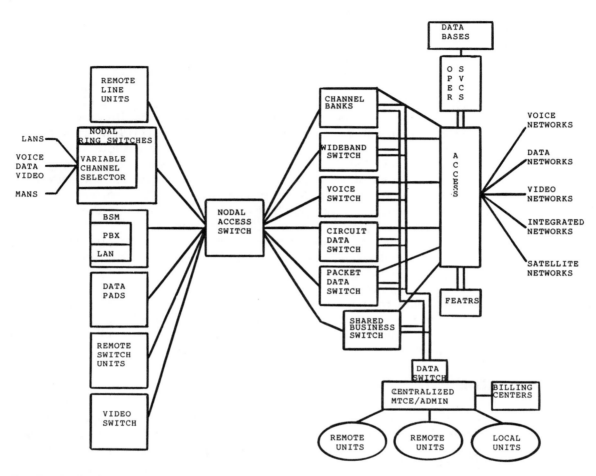

Fig. 10-8. The Network Metro Switch.

of "the missing switch—the Metro Switch" in terms of the next twenty-five years of switch evolution. It should not be viewed as a totally separate new switch offering. It is now tied to an evolving network architecture, as it has become an evolution of technology to meet an evolution of the marketplace over the 1990-2010 timeframe. Hence, it is no longer an autonomous switch. A complex changing, evolving network will determine where and how the metro switch is positioned. It will exist in a new network of physically distributed nodal point switching and processing subsystems, that are closely integrated to new fiber optic distribution facilities. These more integrated facilities, switches and data processors will consist of new architectures and structures, as follows:

1) Beginning in 1984—Digital access tandem switches

2) Digital rural/suburban switch with remote switch units, remote line units used for Metro
   - shopping centers
   - office buildings or office complexes
   - small business clusters
   - Suburban growth in one sector
   - apartment/condominium complexes
   - university buildings
3) Circuit switched data module addition or adjunct switch
4) Public data packet access switch and PAD network overlay and private data packet feature switch and PADs network overlay
5) Data packet addition modules to existing voice digital systems
6) Clear channel differentiated information content voice/data channel banks for 23B and D offerings
7) Fiber rings non-switched metro facilities
8) Video switch megabit (100 +) with sub-rate nodal switches for private or shared public networks
9) Nodal access switches to split voice/data/video traffic
10) Inter-LATA intra-state networks
11) Functionally integrated business serving modules, with physically distributed, Voice/Data LANs and MANs
12) Variable channel selector contention systems for multitenant structure's local area networks and metro area networks
13) Feature switch limited by regulation
14) Feature switch extended/enhanced, non-regulated (without information processing)
15) Rings on rings fiber with satellite nodal switches
16) Automated distributed maintenance/administration centers using data packet switches
17) ISDN islands with branches
18) Database to database overlay for local, specialized and virtual database network structures
19) "Functionalized/Integrated" remote switch units for LANs and MANs interfaced to the nodal access switch
20) Class features switch CCITT #7 Signalling
21) City mobile cellular switching with data for personal phones
22) "Fast and Burst Packet"—physically distributed nodal modules as remote switch units for local area networks
23) Variable channel selectors in fast and burst type packet mode
24) Wideband light-to-light transport only ring switches
25) Fast packet data/voice/video satellite to satellite switches with "Intelligent switch" logic seeking available paths with best error rates
26) "Work Processors" introduced to perform top four levels of OSI work functions on information exchange
27) Packetized physically distributed groupings of nodal switches for fiber rings within base architecture of gigabit switches using highly sophisti-

cated person-to-machine interfaces, usage billing system, traffic analysis anticipation and control system, and complex of data processing work processors for allowable information features

28) Light switch performing base transport only functions working from logic developed for various number based systems other than binary.

29) The Beginning of a New Era . . . 2010.

With this evolution background, we see the need for a voice, data, and video switch cluster that interfaces to remote units via a nodal point "ring" access switch on the user side, as well as to an access or gateway switch on the network side, under the control of a centralized support center, providing a new family of services, that access various databases.

Therefore, it must interface and integrate to the evolving transmission facilities, where we have seen a single mode fiber, using time division multiplexing, become a cost effective method for future integrated ISDN broadband services up to several Gb/s. We will next use wave length division multiplexing to enable additional capacity increase up to approximately six to ten channels and bidirectional transmission on one fiber. Then, coherent transmission in the future will permit up to several thousand channels. This will utilize various multiplexes and switching hierarchies, such as SONET, which covers the Synchronous Transport Signal level 1 (STS-1) to Optical Carrier level 3 (OC-3), where STS-1 signals at 49.920 Mb/s are bit interleaved multiplexed to STS-3 149.760 Mb/s from 1.664 Mb/s, 3.520 Mb/s and 28-DS1 data streams. This 149.760 mega bit data will then be multiplexed to 565 million bits per second and then to 2.26 Gb/s streams, as we enter the world of metro switched terabits where 1,000 Gb/s = 1 Terabit (1x10 to the twelfth power) and computers that reach 10 to the ninth and twelfth power instructions per second execution speeds.

Hence, the Metro Switching complex shown in Fig. 10-9 shows the structuring of several functional switches, including a new switching system called an information communications complex. The ICC unit, in an adjunct CO-Centrex type arrangement, can be accessed by the metro switch to provide numerous features.

Next, let's take a look at the several new network elements to better appreciate the role of the new metro switch and readdress the metro switch in terms of the evolution of switch architecture and the relationship between functional switches during this evolution.

THE INTELLIGENT NETWORK COMPLEX

As we move into the new world of autonomous regional operating companies, numerous long distance carriers, and many new information services, several new network level solutions have been presented by Bellcore to enable cross carrier planning to achieve interdependent offerings, such as; The "Class" family of features and 800 services. See Table 10-2.

One aspect of the proposed solution is to provide signalling to the local switches, using the CCITT #7 signalling standard, as defined for the U.S. in

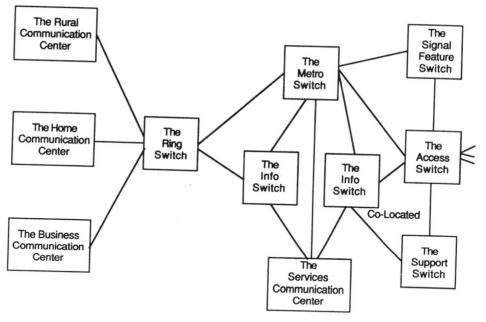

Fig. 10-9. The Metro Switching Complex.

the TIXI cross supplier/provider working committee. Signalling would be provided by inserting STP (Signal Transfer Point) centers (used to look ahead on the network to see if the destination is busy before setting up the path) into the local network architecture, as signalling gateway switches to receive the calling party identity numbers and to provide them to the local switch, perhaps through local "satellite" STPs.

In this manner the calling number is displayed and the intelligent termi-nal can perform many new features under control of the network switch, such

Table 10-2. Intelligent Network Features.

Signalling
Features
Extended features
Feature switch
Feature module

* Alternate billing services
* Area-wide Centrex
* BOC 800
* Clear channel data
* Network 911
* Network ACD
* Mobile roamer
* Voice/data transport
* Personal communications services
* Remote access to call forwarding
* Teleconferencing
* Third-party-vendor services
* Messaging service access
* Voice verification
* Private virtual networks
* Area wide Centrex

281

as translate the number to voice and announce the calling parties' name per a list look up, only transfer a specific call on a call transfer basis, or just display the calling party number with a specialized programmable ring for specific callers. The communication between terminal and switching network can be over the ISDN "D" channel. This then brings the industry to the dilemma of how smart or dumb a terminal should be, versus how much work should be performed at the network base. This then results in several types of ISDN terminal specifications, which vary, depending on the terminal sending state changes to a central controller called "functional signalling," or a more intelligent communication called "stimulus signalling" with the terminal in more control of itself. Both are needed. See Fig. 10-10.

It is then natural to use the signal systems to access remote databases for 800 type look ups, where databases are central per region or specialized carrier. In this manner, the STP talks to SCP (Service Center Points) which home on SMS (Service Message Systems) enabling access to 800 information. It has been suggested to enable the SCPs to home in on other common network databases, such as routing plans for specialized private networks to enable them to obtain alternate routing, more capacity, least cost routing, or new routes under customer control, thus making these networks more versatile or Private Virtual Networks (PVNs).

There is also consideration for using the STPs to interface with existing local switching systems and interrupt their call processing to remotely provide features on a common basis for groups or for specific individual calls on a customized feature basis. This would require access to a feature type switch, which ties into provider or vendor supported microprocessors, providing a specific family of feature offerings. Of course, the impact on traffic to

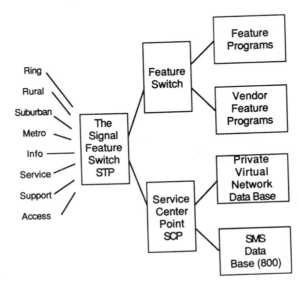

Fig. 10-10. The Network Signal Feature Complex.

282

the local switch must be protected in the event of delay in the interruption of the call processing. In this event adjunct feature modules may be collocated with existing switches to provide the more extensively used features as part of that switch offering. Alternatively, they can be provided by the info switch's service serving center. This architecture is referred to as the signalling/feature "intelligent network" (IN2) complex in the reference figures.

THE ACCESS SWITCH

As we review the MFJ, CI II and DOJ's waiver rulings (as well as the subsequent CI III considerations), which recommended that a major service offering of the local telephone companies be to provide "equal access" to the interexchange carriers, we can see a sequence of decisions consistent with this strategy. However, as we consider the events that have taken place, we note how various bypass networks have been developed to provide 2B + D and 23B + D interfaces via TI or fiber optics, directly to large business customers.

The key strategy of major interexchange carriers is to provide more than just interexchange, but an entire end user to end user "switched" network, that not only provides transport without access changes, but offers numerous features in the data and video world. This strategy includes the information services, which Inquiry II and III do not allow the RBOCs to provide. To complement this network strategy is a local area network, integrated with PBXs intelligent terminals, data processing systems, personal computers and sophisticated programming packages. This then becomes an alternative "Total C&C Solution" to "Network Access."

As a result, there has been a proliferation of local area networks by large businesses, as they built their own private networks and established direct contact with the major interexchange carriers or allowed one carrier to provide them the "Total Solution." The net result for the industry has been the absence of a "Public Information Network" other than the "Public Voice Network." In fact, some interexchange carriers refused to pay access charges, until the total public voice network was changed to ubiquitously provide equal access, even though they, in actuality, could not provide service to the more remote areas. Could this apply to data?

Therefore, with numerous customers leaving the network and new interexchange access revenues not easily forthcoming, this left the new Information Distribution Firms (BOCs) with the difficult task to reassess the "Access Game" to determine where it was going in terms of revenue, lost customers, and the new information world opportunity.

The availability of some form of public information network in the late 80s is a necessity in order to provide a competitive offering to the new "alternative total solution" for the remaining large and medium businesses. The ability to access many new information carriers for both voice and data transport and value added features must be achieved at some financial risk to a traditionally conservative industry in order to stop the migration of the voice customers to parallel "integrated" networks.

Many believe that private network providers will benefit if a "Public Information Network" does exist in which ubiquitous users (internal and external to their firm) can access their company's private LAN network, as well as enable private networks to "inter-network" with each other, through the public network.

The first phase of ISDN is noted as layers of information handling overlays in the *ISDN Concept Analysis*, case study. Here, access must now be provided in the voice, data, and video arena, in which new transport features are provided, such as bit and byte interleaving, error detection and correction, and sequencing of packets, as well as alternative international routing in the event of excessive error rates, and time of day economic trade offs to shift international data from land based networks to satellite, etc.

As will be seen in the "U.S. ISDN Network Architecture Analysis," the new data and wideband switching access features, network signalling for such services as CLASS and extended 800, as well as automated operational support are new tasks for the access switch. It must also enable new switching systems, such as the metro switch, to provide new features and handle special circuits (alarms and switched private networks) as well as the ring switches to provide more effective private "virtual" networks to business customers, as their need for bandwidth on demands increases.

In this manner we will achieve both private and public networks, with the "access switch" providing the key inter-networking feature by enabling the "Public Information Network" to access "The Information World."

THE BUSINESS INFORMATION WORLD

Workstations, office processors, business communication networks, integrated office systems, and business service offerings will play a major role in changing the business community over the next twenty-five years, to achieve a working environment in which the computer's data access, search, manipulation, and processing capabilities are readily available to the new users. The shift will occur from individual databases with single function devices with higher level languages, to integrated databases with multifunctional intelligent work stations ("the intelligent desk"). Here the office work is systemized using intra-company integrated systems and inter-company networks providing "the integrated office system," with decision making support. The environment for such an office provides for an individual's information generation, transfer, distribution, storage, and retrieval, enabling easy information filing, access, edit analysis, and presentation.

This identifies the need for multiple work stations consisting of personal computers, telephones, printers, key systems, display systems, and intelligent terminals, that are "networked" together, using the ring, branch, or star configurations in private local area networks, wide area networks, metro area networks and public information networks.

"The functional architecture of the office systems may be to utilize layers between humans and systems, and between systems and systems such as NEC's proposed application layer (office job processing, document process-

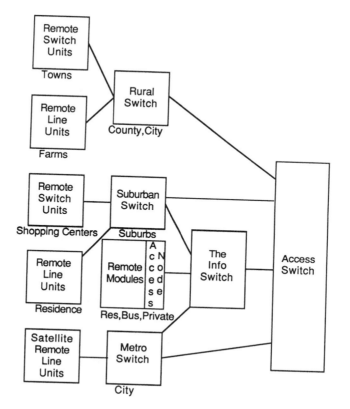

Fig. 10-11. The World of the Information Switch.

ing), software layer (such as file management, data document control, network control, math calculations, and language processing), hardware layer (office equipment and functional modules), and device (VLSI chips)."

Thus we will have numerous interfaces consisting of human interface (people/machine), software layers interfaces, software-hardware interfaces, hardware functional modules-component/device interfaces, and system to system interfaces. This results in an overlay of architectures from human to office integration to computer to information processing to communication network.

To achieve this we must first look at the various application's work activities, such as word processing, record processing, administration support, decision support, personal computing, business graphics, electronic mail, facsimile, voice mail, phone, teleconferences, electronic filing, and database access. The work stations must be capable of performing data retrieval in response to queries, requests, and instructions to enable analysis of information to achieve the creation and composition of new information, which needs processing support in the form of editing, storing, transmitting, and presenting.

Information in the form of voice, data, text, image, still picture, full motion picture, and graphics, will be supported by image processors, CTR displays, monitors, scanners, laser and dot matrix printers, optical disks, modems, writing boards, writing pads, full motion video codecs, and mobile workstations having data display and enabling order entry. As the systems are used for specific applications, we will utilize magnetic card reader/writer printers, security identification systems (eye, thumb, password, key, voice), language translators, audio responses, large image displays, impact printers (serial/line-fully formed or dot matrix) and nonimpact printers, such as thermal transfer, inkjet, and electrophotographic, as well as high resolution full graphic plasma displays.

It has been suggested to establish a "virtual office," in which office communication, office work, and decision support systems are provided by special application software packages together with basic electronic mail, file management and data processing. New office application programs will have to be easy to use, and quick to respond, in order to handle, manipulate, and process specialized feature packages. The business communication needs indicate a need for wide area communications such as world wide satellite networks to link host computers to terminals in local area networks.

Office processors (micro and mainframe) will provide for new needs, such as factory automation industrial robot, factory automation material distribution system, laboratory automation system, engineer support computer aided design system, electronic central file system, electronic billing service, electronic mail service, electronic information service, teleconference center, data processing center, work processing center and network interface to associated firms.

The future office communication networks will have to provide extensive document management systems over highly reliable, secure, wideband, high speed, communication networks, in which services are integrated and where inter-networking is achieved via new standards, interfaces and control systems. Technologies will be needed to remove terminals from having fixed channels assignment to random access schemes by enabling varying channels or bandwidths on demand on a variable usage basis. Hence, both the information processing industry and the information transfer industry now have the challenge to meet a new integrated set of user needs.

WHAT'S A SWITCH?

Rural switch, suburban switch, metro switch, access switch, ring switch, service switch, support switch, signalling/feature switch, satellite nodal switches, remote switch units—What makes them different? How about one big megabit switch that does it all? Or a lot of little switches?

When is a Switch Not Just a Switch?

A switch is not just a switch depending on its location. It does different things for different users or provides different network or support functions such as voice channel switching, data packet switching, traffic analysis, or

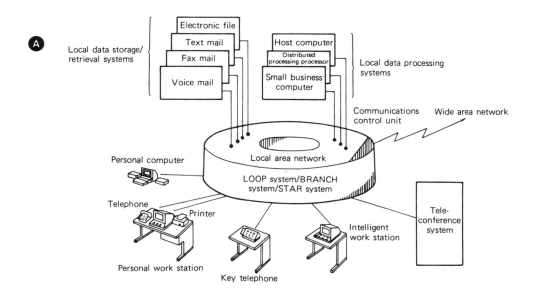

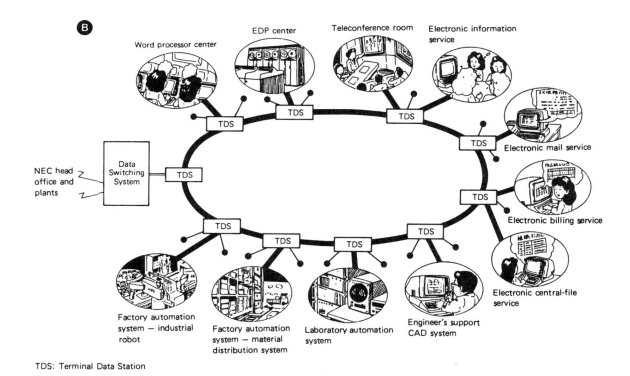

TDS: Terminal Data Station

Fig. 10-12. A) Business Functions. B) Business Applications. (Courtesy of NEC.)

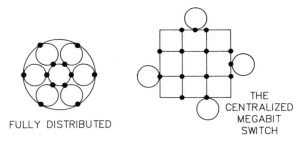

FULLY DISTRIBUTED

THE CENTRALIZED MEGABIT SWITCH

Fig. 10-13. Centralized Versus Decentralized.

alarm monitoring. As we packetize voice, we can then handle both voice and data in fast packet or burst packet switches. What affects the performance of these two structures is how long the burst of information really is. Burst switches remove the need for separate headers on each small segment of the message. Therefore, it more closely approaches the performance effectiveness of channel switches. Video information, as noted earlier, will fit nicely on wideband paths through circuit switched matrices, where the paths remain dedicated across the matrix and up for the duration of the call. The Japanese developed a model of a switch called the "super switch" in the 70s which had a separate matrix for video, as a wideband matrix, a voice channel matrix and a data circuit matrix, each with its own processor, looking like Fig. 10-14.

As we move into the data packet world, we move closer to the packet,

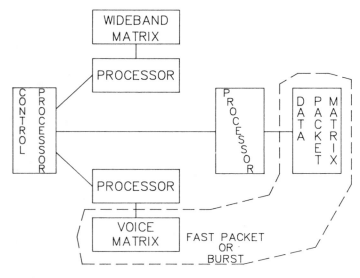

Fig. 10-14. The Super Switch.

288

store, and forward systems, where packet switches were collocated with existing switches with "nailed" (dedicated) connections across the voice switch to the adjunct data packet switch, or were positioned as separate packet switching functional modules in the same voice system. See Fig. 10-15.

As we look at the processor power and the need to extend portions of the system to remote areas, we develop structures such as that shown in Fig. 10-16.

In this configuration, we have levels of processors, depending on their work function. Processors can be exchanged for larger processors, as more and more throughput is needed, as increasing traffic, feature and support work is performed. In many configurations, this type of architecture is replaced by using a bus structure for the network and letting processors of the same power (or just two types of processors) control the working modules. The communications bus is either a separate megabit bus or paths through the network itself. Of course, as we remote segments, then the "D" channel of ISDN becomes the communication bus, as well as out of band signalling channels, which in the "T" 16K or 64K "U" form can be routed through the network to a signalling processor, or to the signalling bus directly. See Fig. 10-17.

As we then physically distribute A and B stages, it becomes questionable, as to how much work should exist on bigger processors at the remote location, especially as the switches become upside down machines with all the lines remote to the base.

As we then physically distribute A and B stages, it becomes questionable, as to how much work should exist on bigger processors at the remote was to add a digital matrix to analog systems for remote users to interface to a base system and stop the proliferation of central offices. Alternatively, the suggestion was to add an analog matrix to digital systems for local users within the one mile radius of the switch to interface to an analog switch using the existing analog twisted pairs. These two suggestions were in actuality accomplished by collocating digital base systems next to large analog stored program systems to digitally meet the needs of the local business com-

Fig. 10-15. "Integrated".

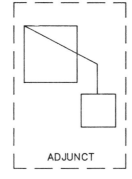

ADJUNCT

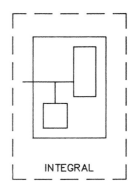

INTEGRAL

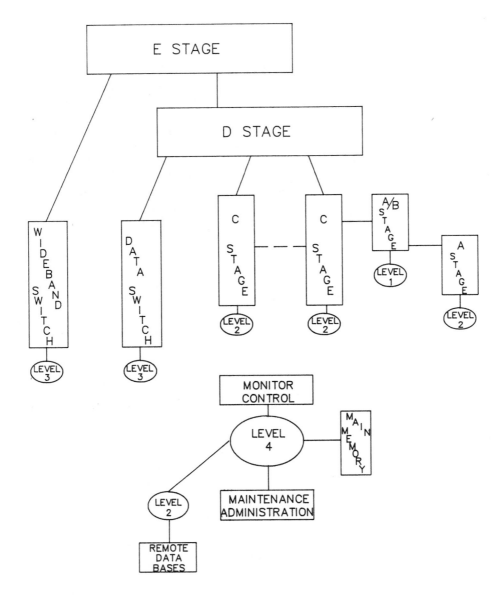

Fig. 10-16. Processor Power.

munity and pick up remote digital line units or remote switch units on a centralized base.

As noted earlier, remote switch units were initially for small towns outside the county seat to enable local calling in the town to fire departments or doctors in the event of emergencies, if the facilities were cut to the base unit or for use in the suburban/urban arena, as shopping center or office complex switches to move users to the central base for transport or to digital

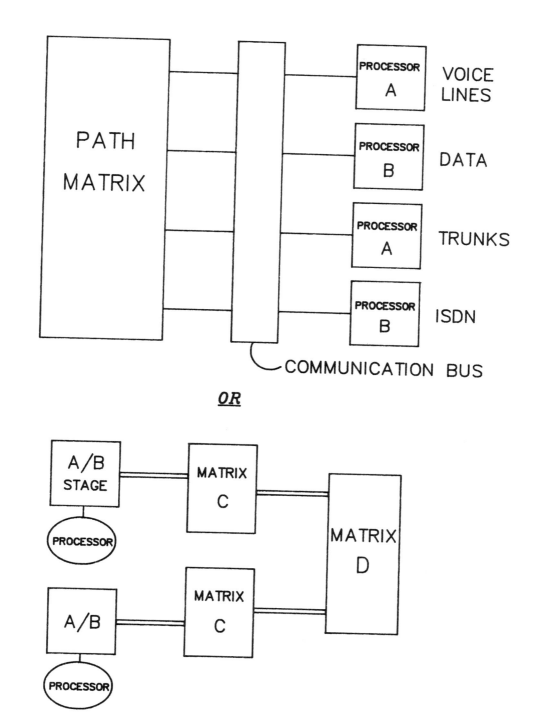

Fig. 10-17. Processor Communication.

Centrex stand alone collocated systems for special features/services.

As we introduced the users to the world of data, there was considerable confusion over the word "integrated." Providers looked for an integrated system to handle voice and data. In actuality, their internal building facilities were 6 wire or 4 wire networks. What they were really asking for was a T1 pair of multiple service offering, such as the ISDN 23B + D "U" interface or two pair "T" interfaces. This does not need to be supported by a single integrated switch, but could be handled by separate systems using a splitter to differentiate voice or data traffic and a combination access arrangement for integrating to outside facilities to the world (see Fig. 10-18). Especially, the numerous existing 4 wire facilities could home in on separate machines and just integrate outputs through dedicated channel multiplexers or the new "T" (2B + D) 4 wire interfaces.

However, some machines in the digital networks are in effect channel switchers and circuit switchers. Hence, they can nicely handle data up to 1.5Mb/s in channel switched mode, moving continuous streams of 64Kb channels. In fact, entire 1200 bit rate messages can be packaged with other 1200 bit rate messages into a single 64K channel or packaged redundantly to enable using Hamming Fire Codes for excellent error detection and correction. Some systems are natural path seekers for packet type traffic or even bursty packet (without multiple headers) traffic. As long as a very low percentage of the call mix is data traffic, the normal processor structures can handle integrated voice and data calls.

We must remember that processors today work very hard to set up a call in the traditional voice manner and will either not meet data call set up objectives or voice handling efficiencies. This is because the voice switch must be deloaded, in order to handle more data calls than it should, due to processor throughput restrictions. Hence, the next phase is to distribute the switching architecture with functionalized processors working on voice or data, but not both. Here feature software can be separately deployed for voice or data needs.

As the world becomes more complex, we can break voice calls into packets and time share voice calls with data calls, putting them on high speed switches, using the dead idle time to splice each other together. Voice can even be clipped if necessary during a high number of data calls. Supposedly, even video, which refreshes today's TV at 550 frames American/650 frames European (or 1200 frame high resolution), can have voice and data put in dead spots on very high speed megabit switching systems using parallel processors, fast gallium arsenide/silicon parallel processor logic systems called fast packet or burst systems. However, even on these systems, the software should be functionalized even though the network is not, in order to ensure that features can be added without excessive change to the total software package.

Finally, photonic switches, in which light-to-light logic decisions are made, will enable high speed channel switches to be developed for moving information through the system by splitting and combining frequencies as needed,

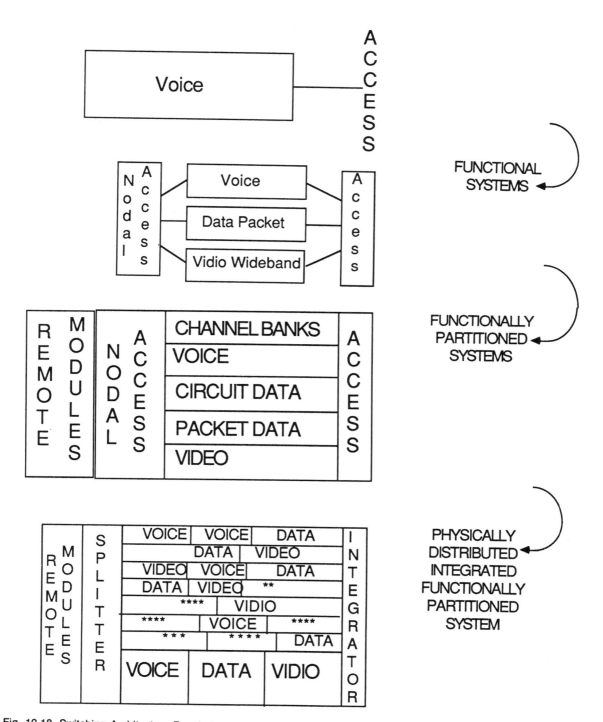

Fig. 10-18. Switching Architecture Revolution.

293

but the real breakthrough will be when the light frequency spectrum itself is used to bring us out of the binary number system to higher modulo number bases, such as decimal. For example, system logic based on presence and absence of red, blue, and yellow light (frequencies) moves us out of the binary world. Hence, by adding more frequencies, we can move to the decimal world.

Next, as we look at what a switch does during its idle time, especially with all its idle processors, we can overlay extensive maintenance and administration work on the systems to assist the operation of the network and its support. These, as well as added new revenue features such as financial analyses and access to various database lists, will change the switch to not just being a switch. However, these later type offerings are, of course, subject to "level playing field" (Case Study) considerations of Inquiry 3, 4, 5, etc.

Hence, a switch is no longer a black box, but a distributed piece of network intelligence that integrates communication, information, transfer, support, and perhaps processing capabilities and provides them closer and closer to the user.

THE PRIVATE/PUBLIC NETWORK

At issue is the public network, as more and more firms turn to owning their own specialized private network or local area network, or sharing a metro area network and/or a wide area network across a cluster of large users. Large networks have been the backbone, for economically providing the public networks, which the small and medium sized businesses utilize. Since their traffic and locations are more difficult to initially project and provide, the economic risks are greater, if there are no large users to help support the public network, such as a public switched data packet network (PSDPN), or a public packet switched network (PPSN).

Similarly, economics are achieved when gigabit traffic is moved on public networks. The more traffic, the easier it is to insert large capacity economical mediums with megabit switches. Hence, the entire traffic framework was based upon overlaying the small and medium sized business networks on the large businesses' networks.

Unfortunately, the world, per our "Who's on First" analysis on earlier government restraints, has encouraged private network growth and inhibited public information network growth. This is the reality of today and the future, even with the Inquiry III more competitive allowances for eliminating NCTE restraints. Hence, we must construct a network to meet the needs of private networks and, as economically as possible, still encourage public usage in the residential and small business arenas. There is now a new need for internetworking, as we reach the stage of everyone having their own network, but wishing to exchange information with each other, using protective passwords, codes and encryption techniques, as well as having alternate routes in the event of network segment failures or overloads to ensure that communication between vital computer systems is never interrupted. As we also move to the age of the "on line" automated computer controlled transportation traffic systems, we must remember that the reliable advantage of point-to-point was that it could not go down due to computer software switching problems. This has to be a major objective of any switched network that attempts to replace point-to-point.

A central office today has 50% of its equipment handling dedicated point-to-point "specialized circuits." Over the next 25 years, these will all be handled on some form of specialized private networks or the new public data packet or circuit networks. We have also noted the trend for LANs to be tied to PBXs, or business serving modules to provide many new features to rings of users. Hence, satellite ring controllers become natural gateway switches to the world, providing an access point for PBXs, providing business capabilities for shopping centers, office complexes, apartment/condo village residential areas. Utilizing these networks as the traffic controllers between database systems, requires a new family of interfaces and protocols, such as, the I, Q, and X series to move information from one data processing system to another. There will be the need for address codes, numerous code conversions, information reformatting, delay, and storage, as well as using store and forward techniques for insuring the correct arrival of information in the event of adverse traffic conditions.

As we discussed in "Rings on Rings within Rings," there is also the need to tie these networks together using ring structures containing satellite and base switches to access the new feature/signalling, info, metro, and access switches in order to obtain various types of shared services for individual private networks as well as access to numerous national and international networks via satellites, marine fiber or microwave facilities, enabling time of day or alternate routing considerations in the event of traffic overloads for various voice, data, video traffic mixes. All in all it has become a network to network game requiring extensive standards, such as the IEEE 802.X series protocols for interfacing protocols such as X25 (1985) and X75.

This then presents the private/public network challenge to the ISDN network architecture; to facilitate the specialized networks; to ensure that it will also provide internetworking and shared feature services on a public basis, such as various maintenance (testing), administration (billing), operations (features), and alternate routing.

By relooking at the early CCSA arrangements, where PBXs formed parallel private networks, accessed by central offices, through Class 5 (local level) switches, providing large businesses with the ability to share a separate private network, we can structure our info switches, ring switches, metro and access switches to move private network traffic on a switched basis through functionalized portions of the public switched network. In this manner common public switched info rings handle autonomous private networks, meet their internetworking needs and still provide the basis for public voice, data, video information networks. Different degrees of overlay can economically encourage information growth in the residence and small business sectors.

The alternative, of course, is to continue the direction of autonomous LANS, using PBXs to directly access VANs (Value Added Networks), such as

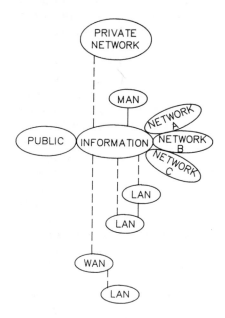

Fig. 10-19. "Internetworking".

data packet networks, and let the various VANs tie specific customers from different networks together. In any event, the choice in the competitive arena is left to the user, the economics of how it can be best achieved is left to the providers and suppliers. It will be an interesting game for all.

THE QUALITY INFORMATION NETWORK

With the integration of computers and communications, network interfaces become blurred, as more and more providers interconnect specialized and value-added networks together with the public information network. During this formation phase of the information era, we the providers, suppliers, and users should take a moment to step back and look at where we are going and what the end result should be.

Who are the "keepers" of the network? This issue must be carefully addressed, as we move from the regulated monopolistic arena to the more competitive nonregulated world of numerous private networks overlaid on a public network. To meet FCC objectives, the public network providers must ensure, via an *open architecture implementation philosophy* that there are no bottlenecks to inhibit competitive offerings. With this openness comes responsibility for all the players, both private and public.

Scope of the Network

In the standards area CCITT, TI, and the IEEE Working Committees are attempting to define standard interfaces between networks, to enable internetworking and access, as well as interface standards between users and various internal nodal points of the public network. These are sometimes referred to as the R,S,T,U, and V interfaces, as well as the D channel, and CCITT No. 7 Signaling. As systems of different degrees of quality are tied directly to the network, we must all work together to ensure that the integrity and overall quality of the network is maintained and even improved.

As systems and subsystems are collocated, perhaps within central offices, we must protect them from adversely affecting each other. In the past, multivendor aerospace system integration examples have demonstrated that RFI signals and grounding "noise" from one system can affect neighboring systems. One famous example of cross-system failures occurred when one manufacturer's ac/dc power convertors failed, causing raw ac to appear on the common dc bus going through another system's integrated circuits to ground, causing every IC in the neighboring system to short out. In the network area, we have seen the damaging effect where a fault in one system generated, via erroneous signalling conditions, call for service attempts on another vendor's system in the network. This could literally bring down the network.

Hence, as the information world is opened to new competition, we must consider future telecommunications networks' important characteristics and ensure a quality network when finished. The task is too big for just one player, but becomes the overall responsibility of all the players—the providers, and suppliers, and the new users of the new information networks.

Quality Characteristics

Quality many times is subjective, but we can all identify it when it exists. We need to occasionally step back and look at the network structure that we are attempting to achieve. In so doing, first consider the fate of the public highways in the various countries of the world. Many have not cared how they really were configured or functioned, but played with them as political toys; some have literally been dumped into a city with difficult and dangerous on/off ramps, some have two-lane tightly twisting and turning topographies, or carry too much traffic, leaving them full of ruts and holes. Others were poorly built initially, and are constantly under repair. Some have become unkept, with few visual quality characteristics, providing an unsatisfactory answer to our quest for a better "quality of life."

Similarly, we should consider the direction and goals of the changing public telecommunications-information network, as it proceeds into the future by learning from the vehicle highways. A quality network can be achieved by keeping in mind the need to achieve desirable characteristics such as:

Fault Tolerance. It must be capable of protecting itself from external and internal faulty interfaces, that could be detrimental to its overall operation. It should achieve a high degree of reliability, especially if it is to replace point to point networks, such as AT&T/BOCs Digital Data Service-DDS, which has a 99.9 percent availability, with a "switched" network. This requires redundancy, alternate routing, homing in on alternate base unity, etc. No longer can we tolerate general switch objectives of one hour down time in twenty years. We must have more realistic software-driven performance objectives and achieve hardware quality to an acceptable field support level for the first production run system. The lines should not be qualified, until the full production level reliability and quality objectives are met.

Friendly. This is still the best description of the most desirable human interface characteristic. The network should be designed to include "friendly" terminals and "friendly" terminal nodal point access to the network. For example, 26-digit dialing patterns for a feature are not friendly, answering a series of menu driven questions is a little friendlier, being able to talk and use a graphic prompter aid may be much more friendly.

Open Architecture. Enabling modular functionalization of the network, so that multiple vendors can interface their systems, can be accomplished by providing standardized communication protocols for private to public, as well as interfaces for network "integrating," as it becomes an "integrator," of numerous vendors products. However, the public network domain must be protected to ensure its availability as a ubiquitous economical alternative. Hence, access and exits must be logically identified nodal points, using the "access switches" for voice, data, and video offerings. Collocation may not be necessary as a "physical" reality, but can be provided as a "logical" possibility via megabit wideband facilities to local adjunct private networks or value added networks' nodal exit points. "Open" should not mean to reduce the availability level of the basic voice public network nor should it be used to inhibit the public information network to which numerous private and value-added networks will need a *functionally equivalent interface.* Alternatively, "bottleneck" conditions should be removed from public information network offerings in the collector arena with availability ensured in the access arena to still achieve a reasonable public network. However, if availability is removed from the public information "access" network, then the fate of a ubiquitous public information network in the future may be questionable. Hence, the bottleneck or inhibition of competitive offerings must be addressed without eliminating the basic public information network.

Instantaneous Service. This characteristic enables the network to readily provide numerous features: hook-ups, services, tests, and new network configurations, using the switching systems to assist in their network reconfigurations.

Intelligent Networks. Since physically distributed processors in large numbers are provided throughout the network, it is reasonable to enable them to work with sophisticated operational support centers, as well as engineering planning and administration centers. As various operational database information is updated and exchanged to note traffic conditions, equipment malfunctions, equipment changes, software reconfigurations, new features, and easier human-oriented work centers, they will need to be interconnected together and with the network processors via "reliable" data packet communication systems, using the basic network packet transport facilities.

Multiple Services. This includes such services as simultaneous text and voice, text and graphics, voice and graphics, parallel public-private network information exchanges, numerous new features, such as phones that talk to indicate who is calling, selectively routing desired calls, or maintenance services providing easy-to-read error rate and traffic reports, as well as polling terminals, and broadcasting information.

Internetworking Numbering Plans and Billing. Standards for private to public to private numbering plans of networks by multiple interexchange providers, and billing information, as customers move to dynamic usage of variable number of channels and bandwidth.

Office of the Future Features. Business Information handling enabling information to be reliably and securely moved around from network to network, from processor to processor, where different work is performed, such as file management, record search, documentation control, inventory control, robotic operation control, CAD, CAM, mail delivery, inquiry/response, data collection, accessing filing, searching, retrieving, manipulating, storing, transmitting, receiving, and processing of numerous databases (sinks) having different access structures, formats, codes, and systems.

Creative Support Centers. Creative work areas interconnected by standard network interfaces will enable separate centers to provide and monitor support programs and user-feature programs in a manner that enables creative competitive motivated human operated support.

Conclusion

The quality of network architectures, structures, design, and support must be paid for right up front, so as not to pay twice as much later. Providers, suppliers, and users must achieve the realization that a quality information network does cost in terms of time, effort, and money to ensure we have the right network with the right products. Achieving this will provide the right services in both the private and public arenas in a competitive marketplace. As we consider terminals, multiplexors, concentrators, nodal point switches, PBXs, switching systems, and satellite systems, quality is no longer a subsystem, system, or a single network objective-but becomes a *network of networks* objective.

A quality information network and the traditional "ilities" (reliability, maintainability, capability, etc.) can only be achieved by having a company "mission" of providing a "quality network" and a combined effort between providers, suppliers, and even users, to manage the pursuit of quality together.

THE U.S. ISDN NETWORK ARCHITECTURE

We have taken a look at the future network in our conceptual planning case study analysis *on the evolution of ISDN.* As we analyzed the impact of the "killer" technologies and new user type requirements, we noted the evolution of facilities integrated with switching, as well as the need for a new information communication complex, a metro switch, a support center, and a signalling/feature complex with integrated access to the outside world.

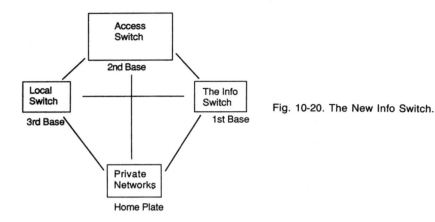

Fig. 10-20. The New Info Switch.

These elements then become pieces of a new local ISDN or ISD "L" N (where "L" means "Local") architecture presented in the attached figures. As we view these figures, we see a new local three level hierarchy of information transport and handling parallel to local/remote database management evolution, consistent with the geographical distribution of new user needs in the marketplace.

In considering the phasing of technology, as we obtain new capabilities to move megabits of information, we must synchronize its implementation with the true market and economic needs. For example, a separate 45-140 Mb wideband switch, as part of the metro switch located in ISDN islands in the information distribution firm will adequately meet the needs of the first wave of video and high speed data users. If it is provided using the fiber rings to economically move large business communication on a public switched network around the local business community with access to national and international networks, this can foster a shift from autonomous LANs or WANs to the public switched network, or at least carry private network traffic on a common public network switch, if it is inexpensively priced. This type of traffic is key to the growth of the basic network architecture to megabit switches. *We do not need megabit switches, if we do not have megabit traffic!*

As we look at the history of switching systems, they were developed when there were too many point to point lines. We will probably turn to public networks when there are too many autonomous LANs, MANs and WANs. To short circuit this and hasten the shift, the public information network should be designed to switch the private networks and provide feature growth, to encourage at least partial usage of a common network. In turn, as we look at the full spectrum of the business world, where 95% are small to medium business, we see the ubiquitous need for the type of information networks indicated in this chapter. Hence, over the next two decades, there should be a reasonable evolution first in the metro large and small cities and then in the rural and remote areas to this type of network structure. Similar structures of this type will develop across the world, as various countries' PTT telephone networks shift to meeting their major and minor cities' data and video information needs. The countries with the better networks will be able to provide many competitive capabilities for their industrial and business communities, as a "strategic asset."

The network architecture will provide for the following shifts:

- Digital voice transport offerings
- Data packet transport offerings
- Data feature transport offerings
- Medium band circuit switched 1.5Mb/s video offerings
- Wideband 45Mb/s -140Mb/s video offerings
- Integrated voice/data single point entry facilities
- Functionalized voice and data handling, billing, etc.

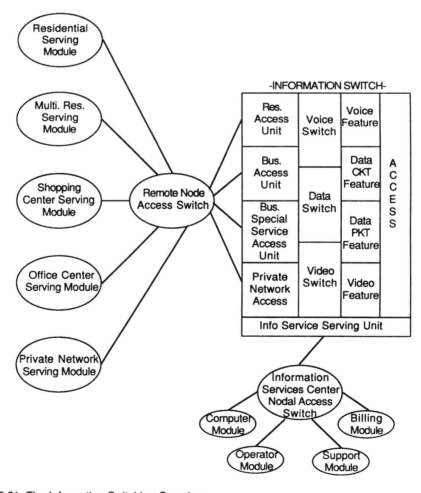

Fig. 10-21. The Information Switching Complex.

- Integrated voice, data, video transport handling on shared facilities
- Shared voice, data, video transport and billing
- Integrated voice, data, and video handling on a "usage" basis and billed accordingly.

Similarly, services will be added throughout the evolution to encourage growth of both public and private networks, enabling distributed databases to access and exchange information.

Support will evolve to become an integral part of the network switches, as processor capacity is used to evaluate situations and update the network to new configurations under instantaneous customer or operational control, as well as using artificial intelligence to assume internal dynamic control.

Advanced signalling and network information systems will be overlaid on the network to move feature type information, as well as "off network" signalling to distributed local level switches.

Processor power and memory capacity together with fiber and high level programming will be used to constantly change the network to provide more and more features from the I^3, F^3 cubics list (see case studies) using the type of systems from the S^3 cubic list, via nodal point switches identified as:

- Ring switches
- Info switches
- Metro switches
- Signalling/feature switches
- Support switches
- Service switches

As technology expands in the world of the megabit switches, with the then prevalent megabit traffic in which private LANs, MANs, and WANs are handled by the public wideband ISDN, there will be a shift to nodal point megabit transport processing structures. Here the public and private local network complexes will share distributed megabit ring switches in the local environment and access several national-international megabit land and satellite global networks.

Conclusion

In considering all the forces in motion and the direction of technology, the figures represent a reasonable technology driven-market driven (Tech-Mark) view. Of course, the marketplace will, as always, determine what features of the feature matrix will be actually needed and be successfully received. In this matter, the actual systems noted in the system matrix that economically provides these features will be determined by the marketplace in a (Mark-Tech) market driven-technology driven mode of operation. These aspects must be identified and integrated to become realistic offerings by the users, providers, and suppliers working *together*.

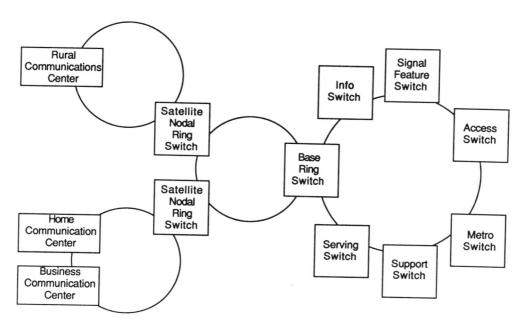

Fig. 10-22. The Ring Switching Complex.

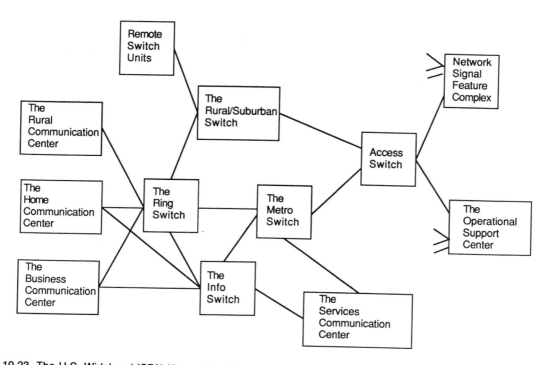

Fig. 10-23. The U.S. Wideband ISDN Network Architecture.

THE ISDN MARKETPLACE

What are the new marketplace opportunities that are made possible by the forthcoming Integrated Services Digital Network? What Services? What Features will it bring to the Marketplace? How Much Demand? When? Where?

If we sit in a quiet "think" environment and take a moment to conceptualize future marketplace opportunities by asking ourselves questions, such as If I had data network, what services could it provide? For whom? When? What will an info switch, a feature switch, a metro switch, a wideband switch, and a ring switch provide in the 1990, 1995, 2000 and 2005 marketplaces? Will the quality of life be a little better? Where? How?

To answer these questions, let's first take a look at potential new features and services. As seen in the *Feature Cubics* (I^3 Cube, F^3 Cube, S^3 Cube) case study, there are numerous new features that can be provided on many new systems located in the regulated, non-regulated, and subsidiaries of the telecommunications information carriers, as well as in the CPE and data processing firms. Assuming government rulings still ensure that information services, which process, manipulate, search, store, and access information are not provided by traditional carriers, they must still consider these features, as part of any successful offering. They may require partnerships and joint offerings between data processing and traditional carriers, but they must be provided to enable a "total solution" to the users, at least until they eventually are allowed in a Telco offering, by the Telco.

In the marketplace, we have seen an economic conservatism develop, as potential users question the value of any offering, such as a personal computer in the home in terms of initial expense, supplier support, and features that are supposedly valuable and desirable. Even more mass oriented ventures, such as viewdata or viewtext have met considerable customer resistance.

This all leads one to sit back and question. *What is ISDN? What will it provide? When should it provide it? Where and How?* Unfortunately we should also observe, that it has been left to the traditionally conservative "providers" to take new marketplace risks and play in an arena, in which they have limited experience in competitive new ventures, as well as in the new data and video information world. However, when all is said and done it remains for the providers to "provide," as they venture into the residential, small business, large business, new information world in which some of their users are as "unknowledgeable" of what they really want, as themselves, while others are "more sophisticated." This has been observed by numerous suppliers responding to RFIs, RFQs, or RFPs in which the voice features resemble the LSSGR (a multi volume set of central office features), and the data and video requirements are reduced to general statements such as "provide for data communications and eventually video."

Many have simply defined ISDN as a single plug connector of voice, data, image, and video access to N number of 64Kb channels. Numerous digital central office "class" and PBX systems were modified to provide the "T" and "U" interfaces to their systems from the ISDN users. However, when the suppliers were asked what transport and information handling features the product enabled the provider to provide to their customer, the response usually is the 2B + D and 23B + D interface or even perhaps a packet switching interface.

As we have seen from the "What is a Switch" analysis, a switch can be a single, totally integrated fast packet or burst switching unit, or a functionally partitioned integrated system of complex sub-systems. We have seen architectures of the network that will position feature switches above the entrance level of the network to interrupt/not interrupt the call handling of local switches to provide features from serving hubs, accessed by multiple "dumb" switches. Their proposals are to place adjunct feature serving modules, collocated with existing earlier systems to support new feature offerings. This has further questioned the role of the future switch.

Finally, we have seen attempts to provide customers with pieces of the switching network, as nodal point access units, using transport remote switch units. This introduced limitations to new feature growth and maintenance capabilities, as we freeze the interfaces from the switching complex.

In reviewing the ISDN feature matrix, we might conceptualize the following market opportunities. Rather than use just generic feature terms, the features must be identified in terms of potential "packaged" services for specific applications. Hopefully these "packaged features" will not restrict or detract, but simply establish a framework upon which to structure a family of offerings of many variations for various applications. In the analysis of "The New Users" case study in the marketplace, we have identified Inquiry and Response, Data Collection, Data Distribution, and Graphics, generically, as meeting the needs of 20 or so future user types, common to 18 different industries. For these needs the U.S. ISDN Network Architecture and product structure can be established to provide a public information network for transporting the voice, data, image, and video information.

However, the specific "feature features" have not yet been identified, that should be provided by the network's info switch and metro switch. In addition, the information network must also provide complex features for interconnection to private networks and access to the world via numerous interexchange carriers. In considering the marketplace, we have noticed a shift to private networks away from common public Centrex-type offerings to more "data Centrex", "integrated" facilities and switches. During this period private point to point megabit traffic will shift to private switched corporate networks, remaining in the point to point mode of operation between facilities, but forming the basis for these new gigabit information networks.

With this background of private and public networks and possible new features (case studies), it is time to take a hard look at marketplace opportunities to see what could and should be provided during the various phases of growth of ISDN in order for us all, together, to enter the information age:

Voice

1. Local calling party number display—provided first within a PAX or PBX

environment, within an office complex, on a private corporate network.
2. Local citywide calling party number display.
3. National calling party number display.
4. Duration of call timers on terminals.
5. Cost of call indicators on terminals.
6. Call waiting feature indicating calling party identity number.
7. Call transfer for selected "customer controlled" calling numbers.
8. Voice simulation indicating who is calling by translating calling number to personal name from customer supplied database list.
9. Voice storage of incoming messages within PBX and local business/home environment.
10. Voice activated phone, perhaps, initially for PBX application.
11. Personal phone.
   - single cellular home/business
   - distress indicator
   - location finder

Data
1. Debit card
   - PBX environment for retail stores access to banks
   - card access to printers or CRT's to display purchases
   - credit advances to cards for card purchases "on line"
   - security for card using eye print, voice print, finger print with password
   - security in transactions using encryption
   - security for database access and exchange of database information
2. Data user nets
   - application overlays common for many similar networks:
   - information exchange;
      - X-ray information
      - patient history
      - public health alerts
      - druggist
      - medical research centers
      - insurance firms
3. Small business nets
   - small contractors
      - ordering material
      - inquiry cost availability
      - satellite work stations
      - portable work stations
      - using data packet network
   - residential data services network
      - alarms
      - environmental control
      - using packet network

4. Information exchange services
    - Polling
        - —using data packet network
        - —polling local issues
        - —polling new products
        - —polling on legislation
        - —polling fast food stores on status of inventory for inventory control and shipment
        - —provide resulting records for analysis and graphic displays
    - Lists
        - —list searches and manipulation
        - —library research
        - —government agency services
        - —shopping center store sales advertisement (terminal/display located at entrances to malls)
    - Broadcast
        - —TV educational information channels
        - —doctors, lawyers, small business
        - —government agencies/state agencies
        - —police networks
    - Office of the future
        - —mail systems
        - —file transfer
        - —database access

Image

1. Voice/image service
    - terminals that prompt users to work with various databases
    - menu driven feature lists
    - image driven features
    - "friendly" intelligent interfaces
2. Image systems
    - 35mm slides (res.)
        - —travel
        - —new products
        - —presentations
        - —graphics
3. Specialty programs
    - financial programs
    - educational programs
    - weather programs
4. Text communications
    - text quality
    - 64Kb rate
    - one error 10^7 bits
    - error correction and detection

- sequential
- store and forward

5. Computer networks
   - access to multi-level processors
   - functional processors
   - language emulation/translation
   - graphic processors

Video/Graphics

1. Viewtext
   - graphic (video)
   - database accesses (video)
2. Interactive multiple user games
   - between users
   - between users and computers
   - between multiple users and computers
   - between teams of multiple users
3. View phone II, III, IV, V
   - 64K image
   - 1.5 megabit-compresses (slow motion)
   - 6.3 megabit-video (full motion)
   - 45 megabit-broadcast
   - 140 megabit-high resolution
4. Video conference centers
   - national network between corporate units
   - international network between corporate units
   - home digital disk entertainment centers
     - records
     - movies
     - education
     - games
   - packet networks (2.4, 4.8, 9.6, 64K, 1.5 Mb/s)
   - access to multiple databases
5. Transport quality grade levels
   - bit and byte interleaving
   - single error correction
   - multiple error correction
   - time of day best error free channel
   - retransmission
   - one error in 10^7-10^{11} BPS

As we step back and review this list of technically possible features that will have to be tailored and packaged from various marketing perspectives, we can make the following observations:

1. This set of features can be handled by overlaying voice and medium speed

data packet networks with a signalling network.

2. The network must be provided in a ubiquitous manner, which requires a public type offering in order to meet the needs of the small business community.

3. The services require access to many databases. These can only be achieved by joint partnerships between carriers and data processing firms.

4. The services must be cheap to be used. There is little desire of the users to pay an initially high terminal price, a high network access price, and an expensive per usage price. They simply will not respond to high priced offerings, unless on a selected basis. Those who have provided mail service and video text found the high resistance to first cost and high usage pricing. Hence, the user game is features, pricing, costs and volume.

5. The costs must be low for the systems and facilities, but they must be capable of handling high volume. Pricing must be in the millicents per packet to encourage millions and millions of packet exchanges for data inquiries, responses, transactions, polling and message broadcast. Systems that only handle 4,000 packets per second will soon be replaced by larger systems, as the demand builds. These smaller building block systems cannot cost mega dollars a piece, especially as several will be needed throughout a major city to handle the types of services noted and replaced as traffic builds up. The terminals must be cheap and friendly.

6. Features will require packaging, as they are translated from technical possibilities to the market. However, many features can reside on the same systems. It will usually be the packaging that will make or break the offering's success.

7. We will need the ring switch architecture to move gigabits to functional megabit metro switches to handle large amounts of data communication. Access will be via twisted pair and coaxial to residential and to business via fiber networks, during the initial fifteen years of growth. Wideband features will require the new ring distribution networks. Traditional voice switches' data traffic must be off loaded to data switches to ensure voice traffic throughput is not affected.

8. Providers will need a marketing position strategy to offer new features and services parallel to product development and network structuring strategies. This strategy must pull potential features and service into groupings of offerings.

9. The situation is one in which no one wins alone. The costs will be high to provide ubiquitous offerings, hence several marketplace options exist:

Option 1. Provide, as "regulated," an information network on a transport basis with waivers to ensure all terminals can access the limited features, which are provided in the regulated environment.

Option 2. Provide services in private networks tied to public transport access networks to handle megabits of information.

Option 3. Provide targeted offerings to segments of the marketplace, using competitive value added features provided by unregulated subsidiaries or separate marketing divisions of the Telco with competitive information firms, all serving the best market that will pay for the service.

Option 4. Simultaneous offering by several providers and suppliers to service the total area, together with several data processing firms.

Option 5. Using "Open Architecture" to enable anyone to provide any feature anyplace anywhere per Inquiry III. To remove dominance and bottleneck advantages, the Local Exchange Carrier (LEC) will compete with numerous Local Exchange Carriers for each customer.

Option 6. Provide a functional open network architecture, in which the basic network integrity is protected, but one in which value added "integrated services" are encouraged to grow.

10. Demand for a feature will depend on many variables. Today one could attend telecommunications demand modeling conferences and forums, where a recent program covered such topics as Measurement (Experimental Methods, Rank-Ordered Choice Models, Psychometric Methods); Information and Choice (Consumer Choice Theory); Estimation and Testing (Residential Choice Methods, Model Testing, Duration in Demand Analysis); Econometric Demand Models (Time of Day Modeling, Estimation of Elasticity, Toll Demand); Forecasting At Various Stages Of The Product Cycles (Diffusion Of Innovation, Demand for New Services, Issues in Time Series Analysis); Markets and Competition (Choices Under Competition, Markets and Competition, Sector Impact); Strategic Issues (Access/Bypass Demand, Organizations and Demand Analysis); Policy (Network Externalities, Benefit Measures); and Pricing (Pricing theory, Pricing Algorithm).

As we can see, as we enter a new world, "The Information World," there will be many techniques to aid us in attempting to project future demand. Ones that we should not forget are friendly, consistent features supported by price, training and service. Price it for volume, teach the new users how to use it free, give away services until the new users are no longer hesitant to use them; make the features friendly, easy to use, available, and consistent with other providers. Review the IBM computer history in the early days of the 60s to see how computer use was encouraged (user manuals were free). As we move people to spend money on a new endeavor that they currently do manually (free to them), we must price for growth, not to make money on the initial customers. Make it such a good deal that they can't afford *not* to have it.

11. Potential market groupings per customer needs and technological possibilities.

1990

- Local calling party identity
- Internal PBX message services
- Public message service
- Special interest data networks
- Office documentation management systems
- Computer networks (code conversion) (data packet)
- Terminal to terminal networks with protocol conversions

1995

- Talking "intelligent" terminals; such as voice writers
- Private office file management networks
- Office to office networks-internetworking
- Image systems
- Office view phones
- Home digital disk
- Residential alarm data packet networks
- "Smart" phones interrelating with user about incoming calls
- Instantaneous service changes
- Private to public to private network information interchanges

2000-2005

- National "Debit" card
- National data networks
- International data networks to selected cities
- Video conference centers
- View phone II, III, IV
- Parallel image/voice networks
- Computer to computer control networks
    - automated traffic
    - automated transport
    - automated banking
- International information services

THE GAME

The game should be played with integrated supplier-provider offerings for the user. Both need each other to be successful. The provider should, with several suppliers, determine its "ISDN Network Architecture," using conceptual planning teams, working with supplier planning teams, participating in

ISDN network architecture standards working committees, reviewing architecture requirements recommendations submitted by Bellcore and various other influential resources, such as CCITT, IEEE, and ANSI/T1.

By working together and sometimes separately, the provider should:

- Create a phased evolutionary strategy, in which networks evolve through various transitions, taking advantage of fiber rings satellite to satellite switching, and the new switching systems.
- Identify ISDN islands of new service offerings, in the distribution plant and overlay "switched" LANs, MANs and WANs into this arena, meeting the market needs of:

    - Office of the future complexes
    - Universities
    - Shopping centers
    - Banking, insurance, etc.
    - State networks
    - Large industry complexes
    - Hospitals
    - Hotels

- Provide joint partnerships between large national database firms, local database firms and specialized carriers to provide sinks for various types of needed information databases.
- Provide specialized data packet switches with extensive feature packages to encourage use of the data switched network such as; broadcast, and polling.
- Establish 1.5 megabit conference centers in joint providers partnerships in all major cities with price to economically encourage usage, as well as provide 100 + megabit switches for several private regional firm's networks on a shared basis.
- Encourage retail, hospital, and insurances industries to use data packet networks for inventory control, debit collection, inquiry response, interactive transactions, and remote documentation.
- Use joint partnerships between providers and suppliers for the products and networks to provide working turnkey software system packages, that not only structure internal database management operations, but provide the networks, programs, and computer systems, as a total package for the users.
- Launch a public data network in circuit and packet form, priced for growth and modified with new features, as service demands.
- Interconnect private specialized networks to global networks.
- Address LAN, MAN, WAN networks by introducing public info rings, with metro and access switches to handle private networks to provide private virtual networks on a switched basis.
- Address standards arena to resolve high level USER services, layered in

levels of OSI standards for internal and global networks "internetworking."

- To satisfy the DOJ, establish an "open architecture," "open standards," "open protocols," "open systems," "open billing," "open network route translation codes" public information network, based upon the ISDN model, that is adapted and supported by all major providers and suppliers, but ensure that all this does not impede its life.
- Provide new services into the marketplace, not waiting for customers to line up and demand, but price for growth (without the connect and collect mentality) and adjust to variations required by users.
- Provide new untested services by products that are made available from suppliers for feasibility market tests, at minimum costs, using preproduction units. These should be "beta tested" for market changes and if necessary be capable of having basic architectural changes depending upon the offering's feasibility test results.
- Establish joint market research analysis probes, as the customers become more and more sophisticated, to determine what new versions and features they require.
- Automate internal communication networks to provide administrative, maintenance, and operational "on line" control in order to provide "instantaneous service" and "on line" update of new features and programs.
- Extend national and international signalling networks to provide calling party identification to local level to enable a host of new voice services.
- Develop new architectures and standards for ring, metro, access, and info switches to replace internal architectures, as traffic develops in 5-10 year increments, such as variable usage (bandwidth on demand) network architectures.
- Develop architectures so LANs, CPE terminals and PBX structures interface to each other.
- Resolve the two major governmental concerns, collocation and interconnection for all new competitive network offerings and quickly enter a total open competitive information marketplace, using an agreed "open architecture," but provide in a manner to least disrupt the basic residential voice network, and ensure a viable public information network.
- Provide a family of cheap terminals to access data and video networks with extremely friendly human machine interactions.
- Provide the info switch and information PBXs to competitively encourage voice, data, and video information handling and access to numerous databases, lists, etc., for extensive inquiry-response and other types of services to encourage growth.
- Provide residential packet type networks to enable alarms, environmental control systems and home user access to private and public data packet networks for the home.
- Establish a usage kilobit rate unit billing structure that encourages usage and is priced for growth.
- Establish 'P' type organizational structures to utilize the management planning process, together with the technology transfer and market transfer

(user needs) processes to conceptualize, define requirements and design future networks, products and services for the information era.

FURTHER ANALYSES

To achieve our objectives, we must understand the marketplace opportunities in terms of technical possibilities within governmental boundaries using ISDN standards, architectures, and interfaces. We have now seen the iceberg sitting on the beach with all its facets emerged for further analysis and consideration. Few aspects are hidden from view. However, the problem is now one of complexity and interrelationships, as "The Game" is played. Hence, Part Four will provide a series of analyses to enable a more detailed understanding and appreciation of "The Game" by the many players of the various disciplines.

There we have:

- A Look at the Marketplace
- A Look at Technology
- A Look at Governmental Boundaries
- A Look at the Players
- A Look at ISDN Architectures, Interfaces and Standards
- A Look at the Formation Phase of the Information Era
- A Final Look at Playing the Game

These analyses together with "The Life and Death of the Public Network" case study in Chapter 12 should now be visited in light of what has just been discussed before proceeding to "The Business of the Business" workshop.

OBSERVATIONS: A COMPLEX GAME

1. The marketing opportunities require a complex supporting network.
2. The complex supporting network will be expensive to position, requiring new high capacity information facilities, switches, and data processing systems.
3. New high capacity facilities, switches, and data processing systems will be expensive to develop and have shortened life cycles, due to technological advances and new marketplace needs.
4. Technological advances must be channeled into the "ISDN-C&C" network architecture to position changing systems, subsystems and terminals with appropriately defined interfaces.
5. Interfaces are tied to "ISDN-C&C" standards, requiring working groups, technical round tables and forums between suppliers and providers to provide a host of new features and services.
6. New features and services for the marketplace must meet the needs of the new users, who must be identified, catered, coaxed, and supported to change their way of doing business and mode of living.
7. To achieve these potential features and services, they must be packaged into error recoverable "friendly" information offerings to attract the users to use them.
8. The network, its products, and its services must be provided as a quality supported offering, if it is indeed to cause a true shift in society. Otherwise, as society begins to rely on its operation, a catastrophe will cause substantial pain in becoming a true information society.

Chapter 11

The Information Era

This chapter is dedicated to the pragmatists, who wish to translate what has been discussed to actual events, issues, and problems, as well as to those who usually begin sitting in the last row of my George Washington University continuing education classes and by the last day have moved to the front row aisle seat to ask the question "How does all this theory solve my specific problem?" Of course, there are those who simply start reading from the back of the book to find something of interest to them, assuming that the best is saved for last. Finally, it is for the bottom line searchers, who skip to the end to find out if the book is worth reading.

STRATEGIES

Since the information era is progressing with time, we will address this analysis as a workshop, based on case studies of the various phases of the information era. In this chapter, we will begin with the Formation Phase, in that several case studies referenced by previous chapters have covered the Preparation Phase. As time advances, you may wish to repeat the analysis in terms of the later time period's current issues and events, emulating the steps of this workshop. An analysis which reviews several years of issues of the leading telecommunications and data processing industry magazines and research publications to perform an extensive literary search of thought provoking articles provides an excellent starting point for the data collection step of the conceptual planning phase. For we cannot think if we do not have

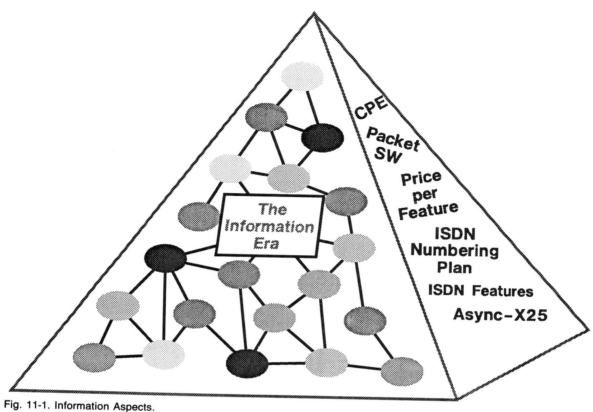

Fig. 11-1. Information Aspects.

access to timely information upon which to think and ponder. This analysis then is in the form of a five step process:

Step One: *Observations*
Data Collection: Strategies of The Formation Phase (See Reference Study)

Step Two: *Creative Thinking*
Impact: (See Case Study: Conclusions)

Step Three: *Recommendations*
Analysis: Providers, Suppliers, Users, Regulators—What is needed to achieve a competitive information era marketplace—in terms of Networks, Products and Services.(See Case Study: Recommendations)

Step Four: *Confirmation*
Comparison: Needs-Communication Perspective versus Computer Perspective

Step Five: *Strategy*
Analysis: Strategy of the Strategies

In this manner, by using "conceptual planning" techniques—to determine strategic direction in a period of intense change, we can periodically review our progress and direction to determine where we are, where are we going, what new possibilities exist, and what we should consider doing.

This analysis was performed for the 1987-1992 timetable. It moves from observations to recommendations, as investigations move from literature search, competition review, scientist roundtables, standards and shared visions to obtain the "big picture," and then identify potential ramifications and possible results, which are then analyzed to determine "strategic strategies" in terms of potential outcome.

Therefore though this analysis will be for the Formation Period, it serves as a case study for analyzing subsequent phases of the information era, and can be used as a model for conceptual and strategic planning.

THE FORMATION PHASE

As we move into a new age, it is important to occasionally look back and review its development in terms of the views, strategies, plans, and programs of the various participants to determine how far it is progressing and what new strategies may be appropriate.

In reviewing the formation phase of the information era, as noted in Part Four, it is interesting to see the various product strategies, positioning strategies, architectural strategies, ISDN strategies, information services strategies, business strategies, network strategies, market strategies, governmental strategies, and international strategies, as well as specific player's "strategy of the strategies," that formulate the entire picture.

Realizing that this is an ever changing scene, let us take a "snap shot" look at the new world of integrated computers and telecommunication several years after divestiture to see the beginning of the transformation phase and conclude by projecting several future possibilities that may result from these initial strategies and considerations.

In this manner, we should grasp an understanding of who is doing what (both suppliers and providers) in terms of: financial considerations, competitive mergers, product architectures, opportunities and restrictions after Inquiry III, to see the potential quiescent states, as well as the users' acceptance and resistance to various features, quality levels and prices. This then leads to an appreciation of the role of the planning process to better play the game.

Finally, conclusions and recommendations are presented in case studies, entitled "The Life or Death of the Public Information Network" and "The Information Game," based upon these observations of the various facets of the initial Formation Phase of the information era . . .

Needs

Seven "Needs" have become more and more apparent; as the players begin to formulate their competitive strategies to be more effective:

One: Need for an encompassing architecture, that allows the users to

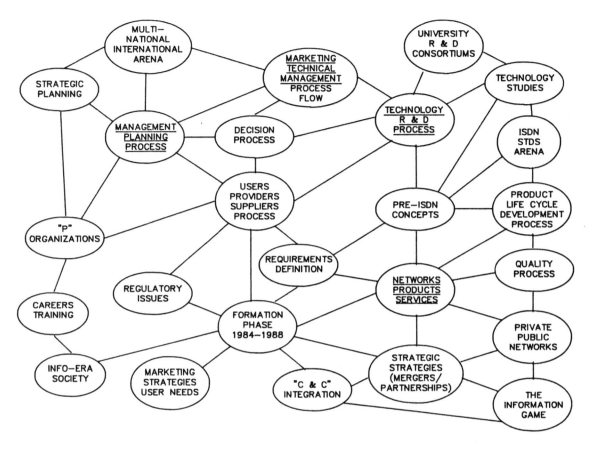

Fig. 11-2. Strategic Plans, Programs, and Projects For the Information Marketplace.

obtain many universal services, enabling the work station in the factory or office to be more and more productive.

Two:　Need to form joint partnerships for various aspects of R&D, such as: joint research at the basic and applied research level through to the advanced development prototypes. For example:

- ITT's System 12 development at its Advanced Technology Center for ITT's European BTM, SESA, STL manufacturers.
- CGE's purchase of ITT's telecommunication firms and subsequent consortium of firms.
- Midwest Technology Development Consortium between Universities in the Midwest.
- Microcomputer Technology Consortium of Bellcore, Control Data, etc.
- Race—European University and Industry R&D consortium.

319

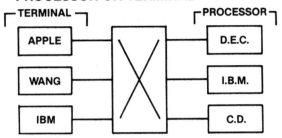

- **TO CONNECT ANY TERMINAL TO ANY PROCESSOR OR TERMINAL**
- **TO CONNECT ANY PROCESSOR TO ANY PROCESSOR OR TERMINAL**

Fig. 11-3. User Needs.

Three: Need to merge and form development partnerships to generate product lines which can be sold in several world markets, to share high cost of new high technology products. For example: GTE—Siemens merger.

Four: Need to form partnerships to construct new networks and services to offer information services to a wide spectrum of users in order to form a total national and even international network solution.

- U.S. Sprint
- U.S. VANs with France Transport
- SNET—TYMNET—TELENET.
- Video conference providers with building site owners

Five: Need to formulate networks in which all terminal types integrate. For example:

- GM MAC Demonstration of WANG. DEC, IBM, and HP terminals
- "Internetworking" protocols of LANs, IEEE 802 . . .
- Functional and stimulus terminal to network via D channel protocols
- ASYNC—X25 pads
- Protocol convertors from DEC to IBM,etc.
- U.S. Standard for word processors and International Programming Language-CHILL.
- Operating system interfaces, where the various networks support each other's operating systems by gateways, such as: UNIX, SNA, etc.

Six: Need to integrate C&C functions into user oriented systems, enabling internal LANs to interface to switched services, as well as external networks.

- NEC's C&C office systems layers, which encase levels of machine—machine—user interfaces.
- ROLM—IBM's Token Ring
- Northern Telecom's DNA—PBX'S Meridian's LAN
- AT&T's UNA-System 75/85's IDN
- Ameritech's software house providing features for its Feature Node Switch.

Seven: Need to form a C&C network/system/service package, using various C&C firms to provide a total solution, on a national as well as international level.

This then will result in three or four autonomous, complex, sophisticated networks providing offerings which users can select and utilize with the assurance that their network will maintain new features and interfaces economically with the other networks for desired services. Hence we have the communications/computer game or "the information game."

STRATEGIC STRATEGIES

Throughout the text we have discussed various strategies in terms of a driving "Strategy of the Strategies." In Chapter 2, we initially developed it around a general technical, marketing, business plan and then proceeded to look at each of these areas in more detail. By the time we had completed Chapter 8's workshop (the book in the book), we had developed our strategy for the business in terms of overlaid ISDN networks, products and services using a "P" architecture and structure to foster market planning and technology transfer, within a unit and across units.

By Chapter 9 we had a global view of the future information world which was then further supported by case study looks at various aspects of society, marketing, and technology. By the end of Chapter 10, our strategy of the strategies included more detailed plans and considerations. Finally, now we need to translate these theoretical possibilities into the day by day information game, by taking a detailed review of the formation phase in terms of strategic strategies, to consider *who is doing what, when, and where,* with a workshop for a final look at our strategy in terms of conclusions, recommendations, and comparisons, resulting in a financial positioning strategy.

As indicated in Fig. 11-4, there are actually four major strategies which encase each other to formulate the "Strategic Strategies" of the firm, based upon the marketing-technology plans (Mark-Tech) defined in business of the business plans for each of the units, as further shown in Fig. 11-5.

In reviewing the figures, we see that there are layers of strategic strate-

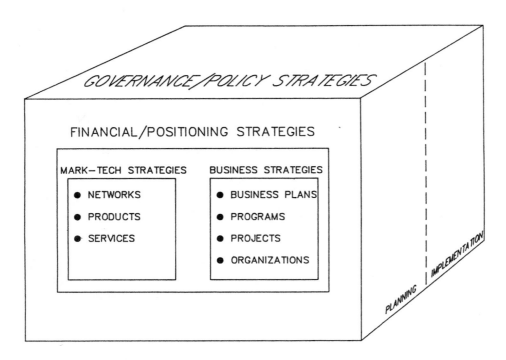

Fig. 11-4. Strategic Strategies.

gies within these four major levels. The following interdependent strategies are noted for further consideration:

Level One: Mark-Tech Strategies

1. Identify future information users by "user types" per industry.
2. View ISDN as a series of functional overlays natural to its evolution, as a network offering.
3. Consider "features" as business products and provide various "features" in the regulated and non-regulated arena with the strategy to encourage user usage.
4. Recognize that technology is changing so fast that switches can be moved or replaced in five year to seven year time frames, since the real cost is in programming support.
5. The basis for the basic public information network will be transport, using fibers that will eventually handle numerous frequencies, enabling gigabit transport, requiring a facility strategy using ring switches and fiber deployment in various rings, as essential for success.
6. Centrex will have a shortened life unless it is competitive with a business serving system, which has been identified as an "info switching complex," which provides numerous remote units to residential, small

```
.Strategic strategies
. .Governance strategies
. . .Position/financial strategies
. . . .Organizational strategies
. . . . .Operational strategies
. . . . . .Business strategies
. . . . . . .Network/product/service strategies
. . . . . . . .Device strategies
. . . . . . . . .Technology strategies
. . . . . . . . . .Society/user needs
. . . . . . . . .
. S . . . . S . .
. t . o . . t . .
. r . f . . r . .
. a . . t . a . .
. t . . h . t . .
. e . . e . e . .
. g . . . . g . .
. y . . . . y . .
. . . . . . . . . .
```

'Strategy of strategies'

strategic direction

mission

Fig. 11-5. Strategy of the Strategies.

business, large business (LANs), as well as access to information serving modules, containing feature packages.

7. Automate the operations, maintenance, and administration of the IDCs,
using packet switching, which can also serve as the data gateway access switches with data circuit switches for the public data network; enabling the information distribution company to be its own best customer.

8. Construct a network of data packet switches in the unregulated arena,
where the switch collects customers, by working directly with large and
small business (not through an agent) and providing a total integrated
solution with PBXs and Centrex offerings to the customers, using the basic public data network to access VANs and other private networks. This
is essential to enable user growth and promote usage.

9. Formulate a network architecture for ISDN, which will become part of the company's logo to identify it with the future information society. This will enable users to understand, identify, and relate to the firm. To achieve the U.S. ISDN network, its architecture must accommodate all major aspects of the voice, data, and video evolution to the 2010+ time frame, using rural/suburban digital systems, fibers, ring switches, metro switches, access switches and information switches supported by STP Centers (extended 800 services +), as well as remote residence, business, operations, and information serving centers.

10. Provide training to educate provider/supplier marketing forces to become more "information" knowledgeable to deal with sophisticated large business customers and unsophisticated (reluctant) small business customers.

11. Integrate C&C offerings on packet switching networks (#8) in the unregulated firms by providing the database management and file transfer capabilities.

12. Accept private network "LANs" as an integral part of "ring structure" and provide transport to access switches to "internetwork" local area networks, as well as to Information Switches to access Databases and Information Services.

Level Two: Business Strategies

1. Business plans, programs, projects, and organizations must now include pre-program planning of new networks, products, and services. This planning requires management decisions at unique checkpoints, as ideas move from concept to product definition to offerings, using specifically the concept, requirements and product definition phases, based upon the sixteen phase product life cycle.

2. Organization structures must be then constructed around these planning and implementation phases using appropriate joint centralized conceptual planning groups across units. Then use centralized (control)—decentralized planning groups for specific requirement definition and product definition across the involved units, perhaps making each unit a lead house for one particular area, such as packet switches, ring switches, operator services, or information services.

3. A Technology transfer process is required to enable the various vendors (suppliers) to work together with providers for the initial planning of new networks, products, and services; especially as both are faced with extensive financial costs. Suppliers need the providers and the providers' customers to help direct their efforts. This process should overlay on the management planning process phased to better direct both planning activities and achieve more directed research and faster flow to new products.

4. A user process must interface to the management planning process and the technology transfer process of the providers and suppliers to better

understand user needs and resistance in order to provide timely offerings to meet these needs and overcome resistance.

5. Business plans can then reflect different programs and products in the various planning and implementation phases; skewed in time to meet financial and human resource considerations to maximize resources.
6. In this manner we achieve "market pull" and "technology push" by "management control," with "accountability."

Level Three: Financial/Positioning Strategies

1. Usage and growth of data information services will be "the key" for long term information business success, as voice line growth levels off at 3-5% and the large business community shifts to total information services on private LANs. The public network should offer a string overlay of information services that can later become more integrated, after more traffic is fostered, requiring gigabit transport. The integrated solution in the unregulated marketplace should initially be a network offering provided "logically," but not necessarily "physically."
2. Quality will be a key trademark for success and survival in the competitive arena, as price wars segment customers.
3. "Open Architecture" of the network can be a successful strategy to enable a "level playing field" in the unregulated information services arena, but it requires a "network architecture," that ensures growth and vitality of the public information network, using "open standards" at designated interface points, such as ring switch, info switch information servicing modules, access switch, and the metro switch's "functional matrixes" (especially its switched special services matrix); finally "open protocols," "universal CCITT numbering plans" and "multi-provider billing" must be successfully achieved and financially supported by all "interconnecting providers."
4. Information computer services, or the second C in C&C, does not necessarily require the ability to write processing features in the switching "C" communication systems of the various vendors, but can be achieved by joint partnerships, shared offerings and integrated offerings with the computer firms using access protocol standards.
5. Similarly, transport features may be negotiated with suppliers in which they share in the "usage revenue" of their features, enabling fast response, and numerous new features at no financial risk by the provider to keep systems competitive, especially as the number of suppliers lines of code for systems approximate generic support limits of 3-5 million lines of code.
6. Mergers and joint partnerships among providers can ensure the universal network offerings required by large business. Similarly several suppliers can jointly provide network solutions, with each supplier providing their product's piece of the solution.
7. Database management systems will be candidates for communications—

computer partnership, as well as the super-computer firms, that provide the powerful computers that can enable large data access and data manipulation.

8. Inquiry III may result in a "ten question with ten possible answers" game, where the BOCs must prove nondominance and nonbottleneck, which may result in substantial delay, complex tariffs, limited offerings in the regulated transport with few "information services offerings," if any.

9. The financial game in the 1990s is considered a "trillion billion dollar game" (case study)—as noted in "The Formation Phase."

10. Price for growth will be key to this new integrated C&C industry, requiring the long look by both the leaders of the providers and suppliers and the business financial investment community. Once user reluctance and resistance is overcome, an avalanche of financially successful services will be achieved.

Level Four: Governance/Policy Strategies

1. By using the management planning process, the mission, vision, and strategic direction are implemented in concepts, requirements, and then products, networks, and services; which become business plans' programs and projects; which become strategic plans.

2. The life of the information industry will require a quality "public information network" for survival, as private networks "internetwork" on it, and islands of sophisticated residential and small business users utilize it. However, "standards" are key within the industry and across industries for economical success of this venture. See "The Life or Death of the Public Information Network."

3. Once these basic product planning levels are in place, "the strategy of the strategies" has achieved a platform for the "business of the businesses" to play the information game.

Conclusions

The considerations of Table 11-1 have played an integral role in helping to decide the strategic strategies of a firm. Throughout the book, the case studies and workshops in Chapters 12 and 13 have indicated how an underlaying driving force, called "the strategy of strategies," affects all the strategies, from governance to technology. This, "strategy of strategies," based upon the "mission," formulates the "strategic direction," resulting in "governance and positioning strategies," consisting of "market strategies," supported by "network/product/service strategies," composed of particular "device/program strategies," which are enabled by "technology" progress, obtained by Research and Development achievements, that meet "individual user needs," enabling society to enter its global information era.

This analysis has taken us through the "world of planning," which will indeed be an exciting, interesting, complex, international information game in "the information era."

Table 11-1. Strategic Plans for the Information Era.

1. User types

2. ISDN evolution

3. Information "cubics"

4. ISDN "feature" marketplace

5. ISDN "network" architecture

6. Technology evolution

   - Components
   - Switching
   - Transmission
   - Programming

7. Computer and communications

   Integration - "C" & "C"

8. Strategic strategies - "C" & "C"

   - Marketplace

   - Products
   - Networks
   - Services

   - Positioning

      - Shared research
      - Partnerships
      - Joint ventures
      - Mergers
      - Shared offerings

9. Management/marketing/technical processes

   - Management planning process
   - R & D technology transfer process
   - User/supplier/provider

      - Mark-tech process
      - Integration process

   - Product development process
   - Strategic decisions process

10. The information game

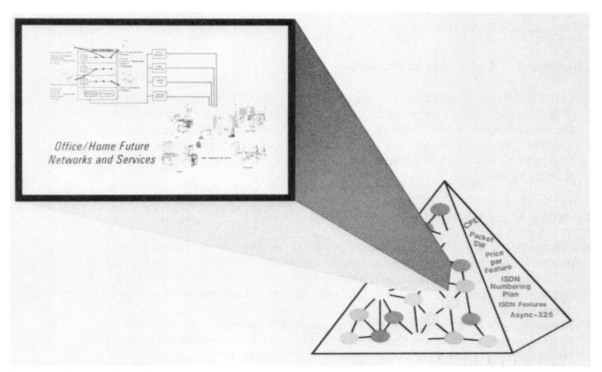

Fig. 11-6. The Information Era.

OBSERVATIONS:
THE WORLD OF PLANNING
IN
THE WORLD OF THE FUTURE

Chapter 1: Change

- The telecommunication-information industries are entering their "corridor of crises" as they merge in a period of intense change.
- It is a time to manage "change" by becoming "manager planners;" participating from the mission to the product definition; utilizing techniques that enable management, technical, and marketing to work closely together.

Chapter 2: Strategic Planning

- Strategic planning is part of a four phase preprogram, preproject, preproduct, and preservice planning activity. It must realistically establish the firm's direction within its business plans, by specifically positioning and repositioning the firm to meet the changing marketplace.
- Its underlying "strategy of the strategies" is the key driving force of the firm. This must be established in accord with technological possibilities and marketplace opportunities.

Chapter 3: Conceptual Planning

- Conceptual planning is the "missing link" between strategic planning and program planning, as the possibilities become more and more complex and the opportunities become more and more risky, expensive, and unclear.
- It is the time to think, to take the time to put together the pieces of the puzzle in a manner to see the details of the individual pictures within the "big picture."

Chapter 4: Requirements Definition

- The more we know, the more we know what we don't know. Every effective hour spent in the requirement definition phase will save several hours in the design and implementation phases and result in identifying and defining the "right product" for the "right market," that truly meets the "right users needs."
- The feasibility analyses will clarify the concepts and enhance the requirements, by establishing credibility and minimizing risk on new possibilities.
- The requirements analyses of the providers should interface and interlace with the research and development activities of the suppliers.

Chapter 5: Product Definition

- As the product's architecture and structure are more and more often contained in micro dot highly complex VLSI modules, controlled by extremely sophisticated software, the need for preproject, preprogram detailed design structuring is essential to understand the complexities of what "indeed" we are planning.
- The more detailed the architecture and structure is, the more likely we are to have a realistic program plan to achieve it with the right people and resources, within the "right" project timeframe.

Chapter 6: Planning Processes

- Suppliers' technology research and development processes can be integrated with the marketplace user needs and product selection recommendation processes via the provider's planning and technology transfer processes.
- Manager planners can utilize a family of processes around the management planning process to expand and achieve a new dimension of effectiveness, where the whole is greater than the sum of the parts.

Chapter 7: The "P" Organization

- The preproduct, preproject, preproduct, people planning programs' "P" type organization enables people to think, search, and find the right answers to the right questions, before premature commitment to wrong endeavors.
- Organizations that enable many people from multiple disciplines to work together is essential for success in a highly competitive marketplace, requiring complex solutions to complex problems.

Chapter 8: The Information Corporation

- Using the steps of top down planning, the new manager planners are orchestrating people, analyzing problems, looking for possibilities and opportunities, defining plans, using processes, establishing projects, through new programs and playing the game in the "world of planning" to achieve the information world of the future.

Chapter 9: The Information Society

- To achieve this society in which terminals tell who is calling, doctors consult with each other on data, image, and video networks, factories are automated, offices exchange document files, around the city, the state, the county, and the industrialized world, the major providers must establish with risk, feature rich quality public and private networks that access each other, using sophisticated families of new products from suppliers, requiring billions of research, development and implementation expenditures.

Chapter 10:   Information Networks Products and Services

- The ISDN network will consist of megabit switches moving information along gigabit rings, providing numerous new features and services to somewhat hesitant new users, uncomfortable with change.

- Features and services of ISDN require sophisticated and somewhat intelligent terminals, systems, and networks ubiquitously accessible in the metro communities, expandable to selected office complexes, shopping centers, universities, hospitals, small businesses, multi unit residences, affluent residences, and eventually to mass residences, where all are encouraged to generate traffic on a public information network, billed on a usage basis at prices to foster the growth of usage, by which providers and suppliers in joint ventures share in the use of their product, both making their profit on a volume usage basis.

- The game must be intensely played in the marketplace (pull), technology (push), governmental (referee), standards (agreements), and ISDN (architecture) arena to enable private and public networks to grow and interface with each other.

Chapter 11:   The Information Era

- To achieve these networks, products, and services, we must structure "P" type organizations with "planner managers," using planning and transfer processes enabling the marketing, technical, and management disciplines of the providers and suppliers to work together to provide the users with the features they need.

- To achieve a society in which automation does not cause massive unemployment, where personal privacy is not lost, where machines become tools rather than mankind becoming slaves to the machine, where people will not lose the dignity in human relationships in their business dealings with each other, where education fosters creativity, and where the quality of life is improved for all peoples of the world, as the world gets a little smaller, we must share our thoughts, concerns, hopes, and dreams, as we participate together in the international marketplaces in the information society . . . *the next frontier*

> . . . *The time is now!*

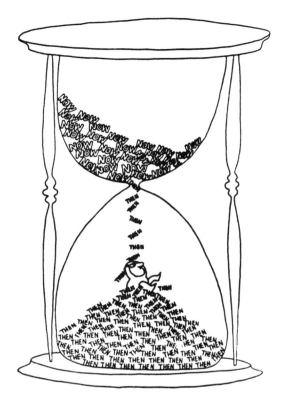

Fig. 11-7. The Time is Now. Now Never Waits.

Part 3

Case Studies and Workshops:

Information

Networks, Products, and Services

Chapter 12

Case Studies:
Where Technological Possibilities
Meet Marketplace Opportunities

In the following studies, we will see a series of "looks" at the key facets of the "figurative" information era iceberg that has now washed ashore in the violent storm of change. As we noted in Chapter 1, most of its hidden aspects and complexities are now visible for all to see and analyze. Hence, these studies provide "looks" at five of its major components to help "understand" how to break it up into manageable pieces and obtain its life supporting "water" or, more specifically, obtain successful life cycles of its ISDN "networks, products, and services."

Therefore, let's take a more detailed look at the new users of the new marketplace, critical governmental rulings, new technology, the new players, and the international CCITT and U.S. IEEE/T1/open systems ISDN game, as well as the planning, technology transfer and management decision processes, that will enable us to achieve the right information networks, products, and services for the information era.

One: Two Changing Worlds Collide

The Past: The old world of technological evolution and market control. The era of separate networks and large mainframe computers
The Future: The new world of technological change and market opportunities. The era of integrated information services.

Let us now consider "The Information Society" in terms of our resistance to change to new technology, as we review the saga of five prominent firms over their twenty year transition from one world of evolution and control to one of change and opportunity. This will demonstrate their various management styles, cultures, motivations, and achievements in terms of their effectiveness in the new high technology marketplace and the impact of change on their mode of operation.

THE IMPACT OF TELECOMMUNICATIONS AND COMPUTER TECHNOLOGY ON OUR FUTURE SOCIETY

Over the next 25 years we will see change of a magnitude comparable to that of the Industrial Revolution.

As we look to the future, we can see great changes in the area of telecommunications. These advances will establish the network upon which future generations of computers can communicate, bringing the information and technical resources of the world together. Advances in voice, data, and video communications will develop in stages, first voice, then data, then video. Some time after the year two thousand, an integrated network combining all three will become readily available. Advances in the future, based upon ever expanding technology, will be focused and directed by the consumer's needs and economic demands. The factors that contributed to the failure of the picturephone in the late 60s are diminished by today's more competitive market due to the AT&T breakup, innovations in the area of small, low cost electronics, and a willingness of people today to accept change and innovation. This analysis will examine the developments of computer technology and the telecommunications network in terms of three distinct phases.

Phase One (1985-1995) The Development Phase. During this phase technical advances will be made that will enable the computer to operate ten times faster than today's already powerful computers. Chips will be designed that have less than half micron spacing of metal substrips. (This is figuratively comparable to taking a map of every city, town, and house in America and reducing it to the size of an open newspaper.) With more compact functions, the processor chip will complete multiple operations in parallel. Since more information can be placed on a single chip, such as four million bits, the cost of memory per bit will substantially decrease. Logic elements will operate more quickly, when they are constructed of materials such as gallium arsenide.

The speed of the computer will also be increased, as the basic computer operations are skewed in such a way that many instructions of several different problems may be executed simultaneously. Computer internal architecture will consist of hundreds of functional processors, where each processor works on some aspect of the operation, such as list searches, etc. These powerful computers, linked together by data networks, will no longer be limited to the data stored within their own memory banks. These forms of integrated computer networks will be used for solving graphic and matrix type problems or searching for available information on a specific problem.

As indicated initially, there will be extensive development in the area of voice communications for home and business. Among these developments will be the wireless phone within a single area zone. Here the home or business telephone will no longer need the wire that connects it to its switching network. This phone will be compact enough to carry in a purse or pocket. Hence, within the single area zone, one will always have their telephone immediately accessible. Cellular automobile phones have also been developed, independent of single area zone limitations. As the vehicle travels, it will pass from zone to zone, with each zone switching the call to maintain a strong signal to the unit. In addition, the telephone itself will become more versatile. The users will be able to voice activate their phone. When the telephone rings, it will vocally indicate who is making the incoming call and will be able to forward specific calls, depending on who is calling to one's personal or car phone. With this service, calls will no longer be missed nor will time be wasted, waiting around for calls.

The problem of security becomes acute, when we address the area of data handling. An international data network will be overlaid on the voice network, in which packets of data will be switched and transmitted in cryptic code. Using fiber optics and satellites, parallel, competitive networks will be established, providing competing services to all areas in such a way that more features will be provided at a lower cost to the consumer. This will create a competitive pricing atmosphere to attract new users, thus stimulating tremendous growth in information services. Standard interfaces will be developed throughout the computer industry, so that most machines will be compatible with this network. In this way, the data stored in one machine may be accessed by machines all over the world. Terminals will be able to "talk" to other terminals, much the same way we use the telephone today.

As the information networks with powerful computers are readily available, there will be a reversal of the social conditions created by the Industrial Revolution. No longer will large groups of people need to work in centralized urban factories. Rather, the new telecommunications network will enable the development of 'satellite' work stations. People will no longer have to flock to large urban centers. They will be able to work in more rural or suburban areas with small satellite offices located in close proximity to their homes. These work stations will be tied to a main office by an extensive voice data network. The American dream of one owning one's own home will become a reality for a larger group of people in these more rural areas. With high housing costs in the cities, land and housing in rural areas are relatively less expensive, thus bringing housing prices within the reach of young families' incomes, as long as interest rates are reasonable. The development of advanced computer control and monitoring systems will increase the quality of life. Natural resources, especially energies, may be more efficiently used, thus prolonging the life of our planet. With monitoring and control of pollution, a more healthy atmosphere will also be possible.

Toward the end of this phase, the effects of large databases and networks created and used by large companies will be felt in society. One effect will be the establishment of a cashless society, using debt cards at retail stores to tie sales directly to the customer's bank account. There will be a proliferation of computer usage in all areas of the workplace. Automation and computers will take over many mundane and hazardous jobs. The result for society may be tremendous unemployment among unskilled workers. This must be addressed by training workers for new areas of the marketplace. However, this change will also bring about a greater job market for those with a high level of training in technology and information manipulation. Tremendous amounts of information will be available to an ever increasing group of businesses. This data will then be used in market models and financial trade off analyses for strategic planning and lines of business.

Second Phase(1995-2005) The Implementation Phase. In this phase computers will be able to solve larger and more complicated problems, as they further utilize the more distributed data networks of the 1990s. These more complex problems may be calculated using a network consisting of physically distributed, specialized computers, capable of breaking the problem into pieces and then sending the various parts to other computers that specialize in solving their specific portion. These physically distributed computers all work on their aspect of the problem simultaneously and then return the answer to the main complex. Thus, speed and capacity are increased, since the specialized computers are free to deal with specific portions of numerous problems simultaneously. The accuracy of problems can be checked, utilizing this network. Several computers can cross check output by overlapping some of the operations of the same problem on different computers. At the turn of the century, a computer will be introduced, in which the speed of calculations is vastly increased by changing from electric to light circuitry. Operations can be computed more quickly, as information is handled at the speed of light. With light switching, large amounts of data may be handled more efficiently by changing from the binary number system to a number system based on higher octal or decimal systems.

Toward the end of the second phase, there will be extensive use of high level compilers, which generate sophisticated programs, that can handle direct voice command input, as well as programs that make decisions in the form of "fuzzy logic" artificial intelligence, so that various mundane tasks may be performed under the control of these computers, such as robotically mining coal. In this second phase, a video network will be overlaid on the voice and data networks. Developments in the transmission and CRT industries will enable high resolution pictures to be displayed on screens small enough to be compatible with the portable telephones. Video conference centers will become fully developed in the business community, limiting the amount of required travel. At this phase of time the data network will extend into the home and small business market. The number of networks and services provided will drastically increase, so that anywhere in the United States and major international cities, there will be extensive facilities providing voice and data services. However, the video network will be limited to urban areas at this time.

The data network will expand to small businesses and residential areas. In the home, the need for travel will be greatly reduced or limited. Shopping, banking, and other domestic functions may all be performed throughout this network. The network will also become a tremendous tool for home learning. Small businesses will utilize the data network to access new services, such as lists of information or market analysis information. Working with low overheads, they will be able to compete successfully with large companies in the technical fields. As a result, large companies will move into non-technical areas, such as hotels or farming, where large capital, not large technical resources are required. Many college graduates will turn to small, rather than large firms for employment because of their potential for growth and advancement. This new business structure will lead to a redistribution of wealth. A large upper middle class will be formed, but there will also be a greater disparity between a larger poor class and the upper middle class due to the heightened demand for education in the job market.

The effect of McClane's "global village" will truly be seen during this phase. There will be a tremendous push to develop international markets. As first world influence spreads, and bases are established in third world nations, the telecommunications network will naturally grow to these areas to facilitate new markets. Toward the end of this phase large companies will have developed international video networks. With greatly improved communications, the need for travel will be reduced somewhat.

Phase Three (2005-2015) The Utilization Phase. During this phase of development, sophisticated intelligent computers are utilized throughout society extensively. Here we see computers freeing man from many redundant or hazardous tasks via robotic operations. Decision making or "thinking" computers, acting within carefully defined parameters, can sift through thousands of extraneous facts to provide meaningful information and conclusions, as well as performing as control systems for large, complex endeavors, such as guiding traffic flow for an entire city, running a total train system, or totally automating air traffic control.

Hence, many advances will be made within the business world, as the computer becomes a more useful tool for the user, utilizing the resources provided by the telecommunications network and human/machine advances in technology. It will be able to solve larger and more complicated problems and control major functions in society, as we enter the twenty first century.

At this point the voice, data, and video networks will reach maturity, using light switches, satellite to satellite communications, and sophisticated terminals. The total network will extend to major residential areas in the developed world and major businesses in the third world. Hence, doctors, lawyers, bankers, teachers, small business owners, and housewives will have the opportunity to economically communicate with each other, over voice, data, and video mediums to all parts of the world.

Technology will reach a critical phase in its development, when the video network moves into the home and small businesses, and the role of the computer changes from one of aiding people as they perform tasks, to one in which the computer itself is trusted to perform the large tasks mentioned earlier, such as controlling the traffic flow for large cities. People must then decide whether the computer is developing in a way that will truly advance society, or whether it is creating a sterile environment, where human interaction becomes more and more limited. If patients in a hospital are examined by computer-advanced machines, such as CAT scan, and the doctor gives his diagnosis without ever seeing the patient, then society may well decide to alter the role of the computer, favoring more human interaction.

By using the advanced capabilities of future computers and communication networks, we will have instantaneous communication around the globe, robots doing difficult or boring tasks, bionic parts for our bodies, automated car, train, and air traffic control, extensive inquiry response list services, point of sale transactions, medical databases, inventory control, shop-at-home, satellite to satellite communications, space labs, Mars exploration, weather control, and rural satellite work industries. One's mind can formulate many opportunities that are just beginning to be available to today's high school-college generation, who will be entering their mid-forties in 2009, and who have grown up in the expanding information age, as they challenge the next frontier.

—HIGH TECH WEST INC.—

A west coast aerospace firm, which we will call High Tech West Inc., was noted for many years for its electronic achievements in specialized military projects. During its period of growth, it employed up to 60,000 persons, who mainly consisted of design technologists, management, and highly skilled technicians. They constructed several interesting processes and methodologies to deal with changes in technology. They had come to the realization quite early in their development (probably due to their aerospace heritage) that the technology which made their previous work obsolete was not a threat to their existence, but an opportunity. As the cold war race heated up, causing the military to look for bigger and better weapons, this translated into more sophisticated computer controlled devices, other than airplanes. High Technology West quickly identified this as one of their best customer's needs, and shifted into providing a constant replacement of military weapons every two to four years, basing them on some new leading edge technological advantage. This led to new areas of emphasis, such as computer guidance control systems that utilized small and versatile electronics, which were extremely reliable and easy to maintain. To achieve this, the selected new technology was not the transistor, which was bulky and required large numbers of discrete resistors and capacitors, with varying failure rates and numerous wire connections. Instead, a semiconductor firm was challenged by High Tech West to provide them with a totally new device, which was subsequently called an Integrated Circuit or "IC." This was the new technology upon which they would base their future.

One of the keys to West's success was their experience gained in building large complex aircraft. Since they came from the aerospace arena, "where the plane must fly or the test pilot will die," there was considerable emphasis during the development program, to achieve a working prototype for the initial field test. The system teams to develop the product were formed early in the product life cycle to carefully break the complex design down into manageable parts. Since the military had learned to manage large forces in controllable small units, it was natural that the design architecture and organizational structure for these complex developments followed this type of format. The levels of control of military officers translated in industry into management groups within management groups, to control the development. A unique structure was developed by the more sophisticated firms, such as High Tech West, where a "Program Management" group interfaced with the customer (the military) and controlled the program through two separate groups: "Project Management," who managed the progress of the program, and "Systems Management," who controlled the technical development of the system. See Fig. 12-1.

This structure was further supported by their customers (the military), who developed a process by which they initially wrote down their requirements (needs) by working with various supplier's advanced systems teams with a Request For Information (RFI). They then asked the firms to respond with a proposal or a quote of a program that could achieve these needs. These were called a Request For a Proposal (RFP), or a Request For Quote (RFQ). The firm with the successful architecture, acceptable management team, and reasonably competitive cost/schedule program was awarded the contract.

Depending on technical complexity and time constraints, High Tech West Inc. was successfully rewarded in its cost plus, fixed cost, variable cost, development only, and pay as you go contracts. It was to West's advantage to establish a good working relationship with its customer and deliver a working prototype within a reasonable period after obtaining numerous price changes and scheduled delays for new features, during the course of the design. The customers were given several major opportunities to review the new

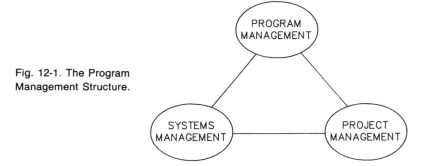

Fig. 12-1. The Program
Management Structure.

product during its development, in the form of various reviews such as the Preliminary Design Review (PDR) and the Critical Design Review (CDR). Fewer changes were acceptable for the prototype version after the (CDR), but could be incorporated into subsequent Engineering Models (prototypes that more closely resembled the production unit) or First Production Articles (first unit off the preproduction line or pilot line). Hence, there was a continuous working relationship to identify new requirements up to production and of course for subsequent versions of the product. This required an extensive change control mechanism. As technology became more and more micro dot oriented, less and less change was allowed after the CDR, but was scheduled for subsequent versions per project management control. It was this comfortable world from which the IC emerged, as a new frontier of technological opportunity, resulting in numerous military systems, such as Minuteman II and III.

Everything was fine until a civilian controller of military spending said "Though I built you, I do not have to sustain you!" Soon afterward there were no more defense contracts, and it was the end of an era. Then those same system teams who built West's complex weapon systems, were asked to take this device called an "Integrated Circuit," which was still quite expensive, and find some commercial application. When this proved futile, they decided to market their system knowledge to solve complex problems, such as the Los Angeles freeway problem, whose answer was obviously one of two choices (either get rid of the people or build a rapid transit system). Both were unacceptable to the city. In essence, there were no big programs that the political state or local governments wanted to seriously attack, so there was really little commercial work for the system teams. The net result in the late 60s was disaster, as the years of spending by the military-industrial complex drew to a close and no commercial offerings were identified.

The situation for High Tech West and other such firms was represented best by a billboard in Seattle that advertised: "Will the last engineer leaving the city turn out the lights!" Care packages arrived from Japan to northwest engineering families, causing a particularly angry U.S. senator to painfully describe the situation to fellow senators on the floor of Congress. But no one had a solution and the situation remained. Physicists delivered mail in Los Angeles, housing prices in San Diego reached rock bottom, and large firms such as High Tech West Inc., reduced personnel from levels of 80,000 to 10,000. They had great reluctance in having to let their life blood (the systems teams) leave. One of their successful military product strategies was to deploy preproject teams to define the architecture of a future project. Hence, letting them go meant no future projects. But go they did, to such places as a small sleepy college town called San Jose, and on toward San Francisco. This area later became known as "Silicon Valley."

Thus ended an era that once had worked very well for many such firms, who were unable to make the adjustment to the commercial marketplace. Some employees returned to the Midwest and East Coast, bringing the new technology with them to the more conservative commercial environments, which perhaps was the answer after all. However, this was indeed a very difficult and painful form of technology transfer!

—MID TECH TELE INC.—

Mid Tech Tele Inc. was a medium sized traditional conservative firm making telecommunication switching systems. Its customers were its sister telephone operating companies. Its holding company was preoccupied with buying up more independent operating companies or commercial electronic firms, leaving the telecommunications equipment manufacturing firm to supply whatever technical devices, they felt might be useful to cut operating companies' costs. Funds were available from a pool of resources from each operating company who really had very little interaction with the manufacturer. They were told to buy what was produced whenever and whatever.

Mid Tech's new product development centered around using the transistor to do new things, at the same time High Tech West was ploughing ahead with the integrated circuit. About the time West came up with a new missile based upon extensive software and technological advances, Mid Tech had just completed an unsuccessful field trial of a hybrid electro-mechanical transistor-wired-logic control system, using limited software. Their system was designed by loosely controlled groups of designers, with little coordinated system direction and relatively no program or project management. They had never discussed their new concepts with their prospective buyers. This was the mode of operation over the years, as one machine replaced the other. Some limited project management and system management were added to aid the development process, with little, if any market focus.

Designers did add a few new features from military projects now and then, to try on the commercial market. The project developments for Mid Tech were long and expensive, with high support costs. Since electronic machines were supposed to last forty years, like the electro-mechanical equipment they replaced, few of their buyers were overly concerned about the type of technology used, as long as capacity and performance objectives were met, which usually took several years to find out, after they had the product. Due to their long design interval, the technology had usually changed once or twice, before the machines were available. Few new features were actually developed for the provider's "subscribers." Note they were called "subscribers," not customers. Most new features were to provide more automated testing and better throughput control for the operating "providers." Market announcements described new capabilities for making the operations more efficient, not necessarily aiding the telephone company's "customers."

Hence, new services, such as data, were usually something to write in the yearly perspective and were considered as research toys. To actually offer anything other than a point to point data transmission channel was unthinkable. The mission of the firm was voice systems, not voice and data, and certainly not video. Unfortunately for Mid Tech, government rulings in the mid 70s allowed Key Systems, and Private Branch Exchanges (PBXs) that handled internal phone calls on the customers premises to be owned by the customer and attached directly to the operating company's network. This new breath of competitive air was beginning to knock on the door for attention. Too late, special customer focussed laboratories were needed, but were not available. Over the subsequent years, many new PBX firms were established, selling directly to large, medium, and small businesses. The telephone companies, Mid Tech's captive customers, lost almost all the market, keeping mainly their centrex customers, where centrex was effectively a large PBX for multiple users. As a result Mid Tech also lost most of its PBX market and kept what it could by selling directly to these new end user customers.

Although Mid Tech's strategy during the 70s was that data was not relatively important, a few of its planners did venture to large computer manufacturers, such as Hal Inc. to ask what they would need from the telecommunications supplier's equipment, as features provided by the telephone companies. Their response was that it was nice to finally be consulted, but their answer by then was simply "a line interface." With that, they would then display their families of data processing equipment with their new families of communication equipment. Their strategy was obvious, they wished to connect their new families of communication equipment directly to the network and control the entrance of their information into it.

Mid Tech Tele lost more and more sales to the competition, as its once captive telephone operating companies became more demanding. The operating companies had found, due to the PBX experience, the advantage in having the latest technology. They purchased better developed products with the recent technology from more competitive international firms. Finally, when its telephones, key systems, PBXs, modems, central office switching systems and Centrex systems were being supplied from many other venders and its subsidized funding from the telephone companies was substantially decreased, its empire crumbled inward to form a mere shell of its former self. It had successfully resisted change . . . to the bitter end . . .

—MULTI-NATIONAL INC.—

Multi-National Inc. was an international multiunit-multinational firm filled with optimism to serve unlimited international marketplaces. Originally, it was market driven. A standard product, usually developed by someone else, was modified to apply to this or that country's market. This was achieved by constantly searching for products that had been previously successful. Once found, it was not unlikely to have five of its companies in five different countries manufacture it and provide a simultaneous offering. Early in the game, a decision was made to use U.S. technology. Considerable effort was made to draw people from U.S. competitors' advanced research laboratories to build versions of their current successful new products. The formula was simple. "Follow the leader and use the leader's people to build its similar new products."

Unfortunately, this soon became an expensive proposition. The U.S. telecommunications leaders were not using the latest technology that High Tech West Inc. had used for the military. When the competitive emphasis and technical shift occurred in the late 70s from the analog world to digital, Multi-

National was unable to easily find specialists who had done it before. They then fell behind, as their new products began running five to six years behind the new leaders who began to emerge throughout the world. To counter this, Multi-National established a central laboratory in an attempt to capture the brightest and best from around the world. Unfortunately, the firm moved into the technology driven mode from the market driven mode. The technically brightest and best did not correctly identify the needs of the new marketplace.

Efforts were also made to leapfrog technologies and catch the next wave to compete neck to neck with the world leaders. Unfortunately, the company management structure did not foster planning processes or enable other management aids to exist in a very effective manner. This made it more difficult to attract skilled planners and systems team members. It took time to build up such teams internally. Usually, this occurred over several previous projects and this was not the mode of operation of Multi-National. Hence, they had numerous difficulties in attempting to follow the leader in a new competitive arena of intense technological change. Both their old and new techniques were not effective in the new marketplace. The company spent billions on R&D, attempting to reposition itself, with limited success. Eventually, after selling off many of its subsidiaries to pay for excessive (unsuccessful) R&D costs, it greatly reduced its laboratory staff and consolidated cross company marketing groups. Then its manufacturing plants attempted to obtain licenses to manufacture other companies' products, with a much more limited profit picture.

Finally, it decided to throw in the towel and quit the telecommunications and computer manufacturing business. For every system sold, it lost money trying to support it. Hence, it sold off its entire multinational family of R, D, and M firms to pay off debts and obtain capital. This enabled it to change its name and establish a new multinational family of firms in another industry, only to find that successfully changing its logo did not give it the ability to successfully handle change.

—STANDARD TEL TECH INC.—

Standard Tel Tech Inc. was a large prosperous firm accustomed to identifying direction and then using their large technical and operations base to establish it. Their monopoly world was under their control. They recognized the amount of change in technology, so they attempted to freeze the more interesting changes and build families of telecommunications products, based upon the belief that technology would have major changes every five years, under their control. By having their operating firms buy from their own suppliers, they had a built-in market for their endeavors. Unfortunately, as technology changes took place, their sheer size became their vulnerability, as technology enabled much smaller technical entrepreneurs to develop more competitive products within the five year cycle. They desperately attempted to force their operating companies to purchase internally. This holding attempt was their downfall. It was subsequently overturned in the legal arena by government requirements for more competitive purchases.

A second major problem for Standard Tel Tech was their narrow vision that the market would continue to wait for their offerings. This, coupled with their lack of emphasis on providing total communication "voice, data, and video" offerings, massed large forces from the data industry against them in the political arena, until the firm was subsequently broken into smaller pieces, with the pieces left to fend for themselves. Upon entering the new arena, each entity displayed an intense desire to play in the new game, but a new game is a difficult challenge, especially if it is being defined as it is being played.

No longer could Standard Tel's R&D laboratories singlehandedly establish international standards for new product areas. The new operating companies now had to determine what competitive products and services they should be providing to their customers, who were no longer just subscribers. No longer could the game be played by freezing segments of changing technology, but had to be played with each new technological change. Many of the new autonomous pieces decided to "manage change" using an international telecommunications network concept, called ISDN, Integrated Services Digital Network. Upon this they restructured into separate divisions and subsidiaries to market enhanced value-added services using a central research facility to work out international and national standards. Each piece, attempting to obtain a new leadership role, had to develop new working relationships across the industry and share in identifying and providing new market driven features for the information era, in order to obtain agreed standards.

—I-CHANGE INC.—

I-Change Inc. is a spin off of High Tech West Inc. and was first located in Silicon Valley, but subsequently relocated its headquarters to Washington D.C. IC established a mission statement, in the early 70s, that visualized the new information world based upon new technology, such as the integrated circuit. Over the years, they came to rely on a more detailed, directed, up to date mission statement to set the strategy of its business units to keep the firm cognizant of the opportunities afforded each year by changes in technology, market needs, regulation, and world economic shifts.

The firm's single motto "Change with Change" has enabled it to shift quickly into complex new markets. It had developed several main areas of thrust throughout the 70s, such as single chip processors, using integrated circuit VLSI technology and structured database management programming. Then it shifted in the 80s to telecommunications market research, business serving systems, and multitenant electronic office buildings to provide an array of new products and services. I-Change moved through the years collecting whatever knowledge was needed to apply to the new technologies marketplace. When one of its companies reached the phase of providing a more established but declining mature product line, Change would sell the firm with contract agreements, that its technology breakthroughs and product offerings would be available for Change Inc. to integrate into its new ventures over the next ten years. In this manner, Change had sold all but three of its operations, with considerable profit, by the 90s, and focussed its energies on new endeavors. Now, it has a large international telecommunications research planning organization and an international R&D information networks, products, and services technology review publication. Its new area of emphasis is on international technology trading centers with international technology trading firms.

For the 90s, Change has recognized and prepared for the international arena. It had developed a family of international trade centers throughout the world, connected together by sophisticated information communication networks for their tenants. Its new strategies have noted that it is not to provide office buildings that just house international trading companies, that only use the structure as an international address. Its trading centers are to provide international services to operational tenant's, such as database access to international product line searches. The centers are to be equipped with the latest of the electronic office capabilities, using distributed integrated networks, tying tenant's private networks together throughout the world. Here, we see a firm that has prospered on change in the technological arena and adapted itself to the marketplace, whatever that marketplace may be, whenever, and wherever . . .

Two: New Missions—New Strategies

—APOLLO 11—

An example of using the mission statement to establish direction was elegantly accomplished by J. F. Kennedy, when he said:

> I believe the nation should commit itself to achieving the goal of landing a man on the moon. It will not be one man getting to the moon, it will be an entire nation. We have never managed our resources on such a long range goal as going to the moon. I believe we should go to the moon.
>
> J.F. Kennedy

The following are experts from the official Apollo 11 Commentary and the president's message upon the astronauts safe return.

Apollo 11 Mission Commentary, 7/16/69, CDT 8:16, GET T-1 15/1

PAO   : Leading up to the ignition sequence 8.9 seconds. We are approaching the 60-second mark on the Apollo 11 Mission. T-60 seconds and counting. We have passed T-60 seconds and counting. We have just reported back. It's been a real smooth countdown. We have passed the 50-second mark. Our transfer is complete on to internal power with the launch vehicle, at this time. 40 seconds away from the Apollo 11 liftoff. All the second stage tanks now pressurized. 35 seconds and counting. Astronauts reported, feeling good. T-15 seconds, guidance is internal, 12, 11, 10, 9, ignition sequence starts, 6, 5, 4, 3, 2, 1, zero, all engines running, LIFTOFF. We have a liftoff, 32 minutes past the hour. Liftoff on Apollo 11. Tower cleared.

PAO   : Neil Armstrong reporting their roll and pitch program which puts Apollo 11 on a proper heading. Plus 30 seconds.

SC   : Rolls complete and a pitch is program. One Bravo

PAO   : One Bravo is an abort control mode. Altitude is 2 miles.

CAPCOM   : All is well at Houston. You are good at 1 minute.

PAO   : Down range 1 mile, altitude 3-4 miles now, velocity is 2,195 feet per second. We are through the region of maximum dynamic pressure now. 8 miles down range, 12 miles high, velocity 4,000 feet per second, and climbing . . .

Apollo 11 Mission Commentary, 7/20/69, GET 109:20, CDT 21:52 339/2

ARMSTRONG   : I'm going to step off the LM now.

ARMSTRONG   : That's one small step for man . . . One giant leap for mankind . . .

ARMSTRONG   : As the—The surface is fine and powdery. I can—I can pick it up loosely with my toe. It does adhere in fine layers like powdered charcoal to the sole and sides of my boots. I only go in a small fraction of an inch. Maybe an eighth of an inch, but I can see the footprint of my boots and the treads in the fine sandy particles . . .

Apollo 11 Mission Commentary, 7/24/69, GET 195:10, CDT 11:42 570/2

SWIM 1   : Splashdown, Apollo has splashdown . . .

PAO   : No cigars being lit up here yet. We're waiting until the crew is on the carrier. A few are being wetted in anticipation of a match, but we don't see any lit yet . . .

President's Message, 7/24/69, CDT:

NIXON   : Neil, Buzz, and Mike. I have the privilege of speaking for so many in welcoming you back to earth. I could tell you about all the messages we received in Washington. Over one hundred foreign governments, Emperors, Presidents, Prime Ministers, and Kings have sent the warmest messages that we have ever received. They represent over 2 billion people on this earth. All of them have had the opportunity through television to see what you have done.

This magnificent event illustrates anew what man can accomplish when purpose is firm and intent corporate. A man on the moon was promised in this decade. And though some were unconvinced, the reality is with us this morning, in the persons of Astronauts Armstrong, Aldrin, and Collins.

May the great effort and commitment seen in this project, Apollo, inspire our lives to move similarly in other areas of need. May our country, afire with inventive leadership and backed by a committed followership, blaze new trails.

—NEWTEL INC.—

On January 1, 1984, Newtel was formed. It originally had been part of the AT&T family of Operating Companies, Bell Laboratories, Western Electric Manufacturing Company and AT&T Long Lines. At that time, two main documents were dictating its boundaries in the marketplace; Inquiry II and Modified Final Judgement. Judge Green of the Department of Justice was orchestrating a waiver process, by which he interpreted a day to day understanding of what these two rulings meant in terms of a number of waiver requests, submitted by the new operating companies. Newtel was one of four operating companies held by New Region Tel. On Jan. 2nd 1984, Newtel was learning that its major customers were no longer committed to obtaining all their communications from it. Many of them announced decisions to own their own systems. In fact with Newtel's new freedom to do as it wanted, it found many of its customers breathing the same fresh air. With no more time for a second look back, Newtel began a long hard street fight, for the first time alone, for its survival. The first thing it had to do was to reassess what type of company it would be. Its officer's mission statement became:

> We will be a total communications firm which stands for quality and integrity. A firm which is easy to do business with, producing a long term return to stockholder's investments.

As time went on, they found that their prevailing strategies were based upon providing local voice phone service with access to the world interexchange companies, such as AT&T, GTE and MCI, etc. However, this was no longer what their major customer accounts were seeking. These customers were asking questions and making inquiries about such things as video and data switching, which Newtel was not currently offering. At that time the game plans, boundaries, and conditions were as follows: Newtel's mission and strategic direction of providing total communication was implemented in business plans that provided voice switching and special circuits to handle all other forms of communication. Their operational goals were to improve their voice network to make it as efficient as possible, using newer digital technology, and to automate their maintenance and administration using point to point hook-ups between terminals and processors.

The government had ruled that they could not offer their customers PBX (private branch exchange for internal customer premises private networks) capabilities directly, but could provide a "centrex," central stand alone switch, dedicated to serving several private networks from a central location, not on customer premises. They could offer their customers some limited features, such as dial tone, weather, time, directory assistance, and custom calling services (abbreviated dial, call transfer and call waiting), as well as high speed megabit (1.544 million bits per second), facilities. For anything differing from this, per Inquiry II and MFJ, they would have to request waivers or offer them in an enhanced subsidiary, which would be structured with no advantages from Newtel. Hence, the strategic direction was established in agreement with (pre-Inquiry III) governmental restraints. Specific strategic objectives were defined and business plans were determined to meet the large/small businesses, residential, interexchange, independent, and wholesale markets. Everything appeared to be logical.

Over the next months, Newtel formed Sub Tel One, Two, and Three; each to market their specialty, as necessary, to the same customers, but each with a different specialty—being "Product Driven." It didn't take the Sub Tels long to find that the business world did not wish to talk to them individually, but was interested in all specialties, obtained from just one source. Their customers also wanted a lot of things that Newtel could not provide, because of the MFJ and Inquiry II. Hence, they found themselves in a dilemma. Technology could now do a lot of things, the customers were quite sophisticated and wanted more than just transport communications, and Judge Green was telling them that they couldn't do what their customers were requesting in Newtel or even the Sub Tels. This was supposedly, "playing the game on a level playing field."

Pre Inquiry III

Newtel quickly moved into the strategic arena to regroup and reposition to survive. Returning to the basics, they readdressed the mission statement. One word fixed it by changing Communications to Information. Now they were specifically in the voice, data, and video business. Next, the strategic direction was modified by attacking the data issue to change strategies to include data switching with transmission from point to point, so they would be able to switch data from terminal to terminal, and from processor to processor for new integrated C&C services. Next, video and wideband graphics market needs were resolved by including megabit switching wideband services in the scope of their basic strategies. From this, the specific goals and objectives for the various business opportunities were addressed in rapid succession. These then, had to be defined in business plans, project plans, marketing plans, organizational structures, and personnel shifts, which took time. Many of the Sub Tel firms were repositioned into one firm with only "exceptionally specialized exceptions" so that one marketing group could provide any product (that was allowed per Judge Green) to their large and small business customers.

Specific strategic strategies had to be conceived, as situations were further understood. Priorities had to be established and negotiated between businesses, clarified in the courts, resolved between New Region and across sister companies, etc. Yes indeed, the game was not just "what technology could provide" but, "what does what customer want," "what are they willing to buy," "where could it be offered," and "in what type of environment—regulated or nonregulated"? Hence, the strategy game became the game of the mid to late 80s, as Newtel repositioned itself in different markets, then it had traditionally played the game, with different technology for different needs.

Open Network Architecture

As time progressed over the late 80s, it was interesting to review the new strategies and structures that Newtel had constructed, in order to survive in an intense arena of change. In the mid 80s, the FCC offered a mid course correction, by no longer insisting that new value added services be provided by a separate subsidiary, but could be provided using separate accounting.

Hence Newtel became a part of Infotel. The strategy became one of combining and separating; based on providing basic and enhanced services around an open network architecture. See Fig. 12-2.

A brief look:

1. The four sister companies, traditionally called telephone companies, each became combined but split into various divisional segments, as the telephone image was changed to the information image. Hence, NEWTEL Inc., became part of INFOTEL's Infonet Distribution Company, Advanced Info Services Company, Info Market Company.
2. Services would be priced to encourage growth in all sectors; large bus., med bus., small bus., affluent residence, etc.
3. The four newly combined and partitioned sister companies would now provide similar offerings so that the entire region would be consistent. However, innovation and differences would be allowed in order to encourage meeting the peculiarities of local markets.
4. All local market endeavors would proceed through the local division of the market firm, so no other subsidiary was dealing with Info's customers, except on an exception basis.
5. Infonet Distribution Company would offer voice, data, and video offerings, based upon an agreed regional architectural, technical vision of providing an evolving public "integrated network" "integrated services" digital ISDN. Differences between former sister companies would be in

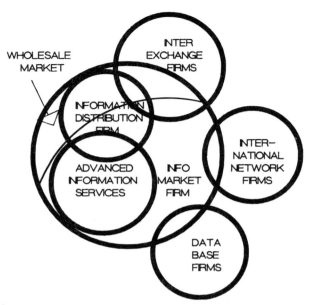

Fig. 12-2. Infotel Inc.

phasing time frames and areas of implementation emphasis. Infonet would become the network operating firm, supporting public regulated and allowed non regulated services offered by the marketing firm. In order to meet open network requirements, it would perform a direct network connect wholesale order taking role, without direct marketing, providing various pieces of the facilities for any provider to utilize.

6. Info Market Co. would offer to the customer all products in the voice, data, and video world that the New Infonet Distribution Company was allowed to provide. Thus the market company would be a collector of customers, while the distribution company would provide the network and access to the world for any firm's customers, similar to a wholesaler.

The success of the marketing company will be in structuring its separate divisions to provide for segmented markets by extending levels of value added services over the basic regulated transport services. Each division will perform the technical and marketing planning to package "Integrated Networks-Integrated Services" offerings. However, the actual provision of these offerings will be provided by the Infonet Distribution firm, the advanced information services firm, other sister firms such as the international business subsidiary of the holding firm, information database firms or information interexchange firms. The marketing firm will work out costs to obtain these services with the providing firms. In effect, this company is the marketing arm of both the Infonet distribution firm and the advanced information firm, integrating their services to offer the prospective customers a total solution to their information movement and (where allowed) processing needs.

7. The advanced information services company would provide the marketing firm's customers with the actual advanced features and services as extended information handling capabilities (that a Telco is allowed to offer in a separate subsidiary), using products from multiple vendors. This should circumvent the need for waivers or proving non-dominance non-bottleneck.

Finally, a small marketing force may be necessary to market some features that the divisional separate account regulated/nonregulated public/private marketing firm may still be restricted or delayed in offering, such as the highest level of government Telco allowed, "Integrated Services," with those from joint partnerships with information database firms or specialized private network equipment suppliers and providers.

Thus the advanced information services firm will remain for a period of time as the bridge subsidiary between deregulation and freemarket advances to provide a safety net to ensure that many potential customers, large and small, are not lost to bypass, as the BOCs wait for more competitive rulings opportunity.

8. The game would be played, as much as possible, in the nonregulated arena, all new product offerings would be provided there, except in the areas where old depreciation rates would make this uneconomical.

9. The business world, apartments, and affluent homes' new feature services would be totally nonregulated. They could be provided by a new information serving module, from a centrally shared switch.

10. All communication would be priced for volume usage of new features to encourage growth and minimize resistance to move from flat rates to usage pricing. "More for the money" would be the strategy, leaving those who simply wanted voice only, to be provided by various levels of usage packages that met local area "basic voice service" concerns.

11. International Info Inc., a subsidiary of the new regional central holding company, would be an international/national firm, where international and national network offerings would be provided to large private networks switched on the common public network. The strategy being to provide global, leading edge, instantaneous, and inexpensive feature packages to encourage the business community to utilize the common network.

12. To "spend money to make money" would be the strategy, as stockholders were encouraged to invest in the firm for a sound and stable long term investment, with the size and structure growing to provide all forms of information capabilities.

13. The information world of list accesses and data searches was closely tied to Inquiry III open network architecture decisions, which would foster a totally universal marketplace.

14. Fostering personal career goals, providing training, and enabling growth

would be the norm, as the firm invested in its people to achieve the necessary technical and marketing skill levels which would enable them to identify, define, and provide leading edge networks, products, and services for every sector of the marketplace. "Strength in knowledgeable people" was another major implementation strategy!

15. A technical/marketing organization planning process, that enabled these strategies to be achieved, by interfacing the firms with appropriate venders and research laboratories to establish standards and interfaces for multiple products, was considered essential for success.

Over time, Infotel Inc. worked out numerous strategies and agreements in establishing itself within its markets, within its regional company, within its regulated/nonregulated environment, within its competitive arena, within its universal access arena, and within its government boundaries to provide movement of information, access to information, searches for information, storing of information, manipulation of information, and processing of information.

The strategy of the strategies was to position the firm to more effectively handle change by providing, "where economically and governmentally allowed," new feature oriented information networks, products, and services to the customer, who in time would no longer view them as a telephone company, but as a leading edge information company in an unregulated open arena.

The long term growth strategy was to encourage total information usage growth by having network product offering, that provided new services, using unlimited bandwidth on demand, as cheaply as possible to keep both large and small business on the common network and eliminate bypass. Thus, "integrated services" would be provided using such products as an information switch with consumer residence/business serving modules.

"Encourage growth of information usage" would be the strategy of the strategies for future survival and success. From this specific marketing and technical strategies for each of the business unit's were subsequently identified and established. Their ideas for new product's features offerings, based upon an evolving ISDN in both the public and private marketplace were developed through planning phases, such as conceptual planning, requirement definition, and product definition. There, they further determined who they were, what exactly their product offering should be, and for whom and for what type of market it should be made. Thus they were able to resolve cross-unit conflicts before major resource deployment.

1990+

On January 1, 1990, after a six year struggle, Infotel Inc. emerged from the structure of Newtel with a more clearly defined relationship with its regional holding company and sister companies, and a crisp vision of what it was attempting to achieve in a new competitive industry in a constant, changing world; playing the game based upon change; change in regulatory boundaries, change in marketplace needs, change in technology.

Its strategy of the strategies' direction would be implemented in providing many new "integrated services" that encourage usage to grow, by using manufacturing agreements for new information systems, as well as by integrating various vendors' new systems to provide leading edge quality information services, as cheaply as possible, to encourage customers to break down their resistance to new features, obtain their satisfaction, and subsequently have high usage; by being easy to do business with.

—INFOLAB INC.—

On January 1, 1984 Infolab was formed. With the break up of AT&T, there would be a new relationship in the telecommunication industry between operating firms and lab-manufacturing companies. The people came to Infolab from previous Bell laboratories, GTE laboratories, IBM laboratories, Digital Equipment laboratories, and their associated manufacturing firms, such as Western Electric, Automatic Electric. etc. This new firm was determined to play the game in all aspects of the information arena. Hence the name Infolab. Once established, they were deeply involved in determining what to build. Many of their players had come from firms that had had established clients or captured clients for established products. Should they participate in providing products for local area networks, a new family of digital fast packet or burst type integrated exchange access switches, stand alone PBXs, data switches, distributed database systems, smart terminals, modems, or integrated nodal point switching products? As they looked at their technological capabilities, they recognized that they could do just about anything, but not everything. They could provide any product, but the dilemma was that they no longer worked at firms where, due to their size, particular area expertise, or monopoly, they could establish a leadership role, in which other firms would follow. This was especially true in the new ISDN arena for interface standards, and features between systems throughout the world.

They looked at the seven regional operating companies and independent Telcos to see what they were requesting. Many of these Telcos seemed to be looking back at them to see,what the labs had to offer. They looked around the industry and most firms seemed to be refining their current product line and telling their buyers that they could make their systems do just about anything that they would want by simply adding a module here or there, but there was no new major thrust. All were looking for new direction that had minimum risk and expenditure.

Infolab had defined its mission, strategic direction, specific objectives, in terms of general goals and objectives. In reality, they were really just opportunities, as they really did not know what the marketplace would accept. The risk was high and the management knew that the development and manufacturing of the new products would be expensive. The microdot technology in their laboratories had reached the point to question "how small is small?" If necessary, they could make less than one micron integrated circuits. These would be needed to design the next family of more fully integrated voice, data, video systems for sophisticated customers. Some managers, having gone through the problems of the picture phone, transaction phone, and viewtext, were unsure of what to do and reluctant to proceed without a solid market requirement; especially in areas of integration of voice and data features.

The cry of the times was to be market driven, but when they ventured out into the marketplace, armed with assistance from various market research firms, they did not find the customers very knowledgeable. As they asked them for services that they wished to be provided with, the immediate response by many was integrated voice, data, and video. But as they pursued this line of questioning to determine what exactly this meant, and what the buyer would be willing to pay, they saw a blank, glazed look appear in the eyes of many of these future users, who simply didn't know. Of course not all were this way, a few would describe their desires and requests, but as their list became long and specific, one could only wonder how many others would want the same.

As Infolab's people talked to the large operating companies, they found a great desire to do a lot of things, but a reluctance to do anything, because they could not meet this or that need of their customers by an offering acceptable to both justice and the FCC. They were initially locked in this form of analysis, until the final decisions of Inquiry III and the Huber report. During this period, there was one successful approach that was being pursued by many manufacturers. It was to develop a system and simply keep adding devices to it to create a little island of offerings and then gateway the interfaces to the world, using existing standards and interfaces, selling to both the regulated and unregulated markets. With these constraints, Infolab swam in a sea of unknown direction for several years attempting to understand the strange new world, where technology could do "anything," but no one could define the "anything," that was really wanted or allowed.

After the FCC and justice decisions in 1987-8, allowing the telcos to better compete in information interexchange arenas with fewer restrictions requiring waivers, on March 31, 1988, after several major product failures, Infolab made its move to survive. Something had to be done to tie strategic objectives down to realistic market-based business plans. They recognized that the visualized game, as it could be played, was only one half the story. They could have an exciting "strategy of the strategies," but without it being used to structure the "business of the business," it was meaningless. There was a need to be able to tie the market to the technology and to the strategic direction in terms of realistic products and services. There was a need to work with their potential customers and agree on needs, as well as establish networks, standards, and interfaces for future products between other laboratories, so all could have a "piece of the action." As it was, everyone was standing knee deep in opportunity with no place to hang their hats. Nothing was firm, everything was possible. This was almost as frustrating, as the previous world, where only little changes were possible. It was like turning a kid loose in a candy store and saying "You can have anything that you can carry, in a bag with a large hole in it."

With these lessons learned, Infolab launched a planning process, sometimes working separately, sometimes working jointly with prospective customers, fellow laboratories, and manufacturers, to establish a series of phased product offerings to cultivate and build acceptance in the marketplace and to foster a customer desire to use more and more new technical possibilities, as they were made available.

They decided to use the three-phased planning process to develop their technical analyses from basic and applied research studies to advanced and applied developments. They used the process to work with the future buyers and users, to tie technological opportunities to desired specific product offerings. Concepts were further identified and refined in their requirement definition phase using existing and proposed standard arrangements. They participated in the CCITT and U.S. forums, such as TIDI, to obtain ISDN network architecture agreements, remembering how the cassette tape became a standard by giving its patents to the industry. They established an "open systems architecture" for their new product line to which any manufacturer could design and interface their product.

During the product planning phase, they were able to structure their products to provide several new families of features over several future versions. Their products had project plans based upon carefully structured system plans, phased to a reasonably understood market. These projects were defined in business plans, which were subsequently reassessed against the strategic direction, causing some repositioning of the "strategy of the strategy" and of the time phasing of various strategies with new emphasis on others, thus making their planning and strategies realistically tied to the actual "business of the business." Next, they established joint planning partnerships with providers and/or other suppliers to help minimize risk.

By 1994, Infolabs had a family of successful new products with two other new families in different phases of their planning and development lifecycles for specific types of new users, using a relatively easy to use technology/marketing (marktech—techmark) planning and transfer process, that ensured continuous success in the marketplace.

—CENTRAL RESEARCH INC.—

In this era of intense technological change, many groups were banding together to sponsor joint research and development efforts to obtain technical guidance and technical assistance for mutually owned software systems, hardware techniques, and patents. In reviewing possibilities of what could or could not be provided, each owner questioned what such and such a facility could achieve in terms of strategies and processes for technology planning and transfer. How would the laboratory meet the needs of multiple owners? How will the owners work with each other, as well as with several laboratories on future endeavors?

In this environment, Central Research was established. After its first year, it solicited views to help establish better relationships with its owners/clients to become more effective. Here is one such view:

As the industry moves into the new information era in a divested, regulated/non-regulated, basic/enhanced feature world of multiple financial opportunities with the freedom of choice, we players are asking ourselves basic strategic questions: "What R&D do we want? What will it cost? What are we willing to pay for? What are we getting now for what we are currently paying? Is it worth it? If not, what parts are acceptable? What are not? How much are we really willing to spend? How do we review current research and indicate what we want?"

In reviewing R&D's needs in areas such as:

- Applied Research
- Network Planning and Architecture
- Support Systems
- Information Systems
- Market Needs Research
- Vendor Interfaces and Standards
- Mathematical Modeling and Support
- System Verification

we may find some analyses effective and useful and some not so effective and useful. In asking "what do we really want?," the answer may be that we do not want to give undirected funds to any research laboratory not under our direct control. In turn, the laboratory may view its own mission as becoming the best leading R&D laboratory in the world, to meet the needs of its many owners. Unfortunately, the owners, the buyers of their new technology, have few technical planners to specifically define what they want. Some can readily see what they don't want, and some are learning quickly.

A strategic crash on control of research programs will usually occur between multiple owners. However, without confrontation on control, the owners can shift to the role of the knowledgeable buyer. In the stamp and coin collecting industry, it is called "cherry picking." Instead of buying the complete collection, one only buys what is desirable at a particular point in time and price, and then goes searching for other cherries. Occasionally, one may make a contract with the original party to obtain a special type or particular group of cherries.

This can put the R&D firm in a very difficult situation, of having to continuously anticipate a changing short term market or be stuck with long range undesirable goods (research). In addition, if the marketplace becomes tied to economic decisions and political destinies, the view of the purchaser may become increasingly short term. We have heard more than one purchaser of R&D exclaim, "Why spend for the future?," especially when the attention of today's firms are on today's performance. On the side of the laboratory, they may question how to keep long term employees, if projects are constantly cancelled half way through the R&D life cycle due to the fluctuating interest of the buyers and subsequent shaky funding.

In addition, how do they move people from project to project, especially when the buyers' emphasis may shift within applied research from some particular field of expertise to a different area requiring different expertise or even from applied research to advanced development to applied development to development to support. To balance this, the laboratory may turn to the marketplace to resale its R&D or at least further utilize areas of experience for new research for different outside buyers. Also, it may endeavor to obtain a X% general research, Y% contracted specific research mix from its owners and outside purchasers. However, parties who sponsored the original research may object to outside groups benefiting from their expenditures, especially if they are their competitors.

Finally, the FCC/DOJ government agencies view's must be considered, as well as relationships with vendors, and of course the impact of changing technology on the world telecommunication community. Here we find the government initially leery of any possible monopoly considerations that may give a firm or group of firms a competitive edge. Hence, every joint Telco R&D analysis must usually be visible to the world and "concurred" by the government agency. Over time, changes to this view will allow joint manufacturing efforts by suppliers and the Telco providers as well. Many vendors may prefer to deal directly with each buyer to sell their goods and not be "OK'd" or "KO'd" by a central laboratory. Other vendors may believe they have the right technical solution, but have limited funds to deal with all the buyers separately, and may wish to be "approved" by the central laboratory in order to hopefully obtain later sales. The more technology impacts industry and the more affordable it becomes to all nations of the world, it makes the international and national standards committees more and more needed, especially in the interface and exchange of intelligence for new features, products and services. Hence, the more dependent the owners are in obtaining these standards, the greater the need to use the central laboratory to achieve them.

In this framework, each of the owners must ask themselves the question of control and payment. The more they assume individual non-shared control over their own destiny, the more they must really be willing to pay for it. Technology is expensive. Anticipating the future is expensive, being a leader rather than a follower is expensive. They must also ask themselves how they will obtain the technical ability to truly identify direction and define the products, networks, and services they need. Hence, they need a strategy on how they are going to play the technology transfer game, and if they elect to play it themselves, they must staff their firms with the right players.

Therefore the owners, the providers of information networks and services:

1. Need to begin understanding and defining the direction of their own networks, products, and services, especially the overall architecture.
2. Need to upgrade their internal staffs to be able to become knowledgeable buyers.
3. Need to understand the marketplace needs and not just have others do the market research. The real knowledge is not obtained in the report,

but in the process of the investigation.
4. Cannot afford to support undirected research and development, and must work closely with the planning of its activities.
5. Need a strategic network architecture plan for participation in the regulated, unregulated, enhanced arena.
6. Do not need to "cherry pick," but need to establish a reasonable four year program with laboratories, that supports their internal program plans.
7. Each of their business units need conceptual, requirement definition, and product definition groups to work with multiple vendors and laboratories, such as Central Research.
8. Need to be in control, but in "knowledgeable" control. Since they are responsible to their stockholders, they need to separately establish their own destiny, and use common research facilities such as Central Research to achieve it, realizing that technical knowledge can be shared, as in Japan, but individual success is in effectively using it. Knowledge is power.

In considering such a supporting research laboratory, we note that:

1. A common research laboratory in a start up mode needs active direction from its owners to adjust and tailor its programs to their needs.
2. There will be conflict, as multiple owners attempt to direct the laboratory in different directions.
3. The management of the laboratory cannot afford to provide undesirable programs to the owners. The more the programs are not considered relevant, the less interested the owners are in funding all the R&D efforts with a blank check.
4. The more comfortable and sophisticated the buyer, the less willing to pay for guidance. However, many times this is a fleeting position, because the really knowledgeable buyer realizes that a little knowledge is a dangerous thing, and that technological knowledge has a short life span.
5. Many times the above lead to "cherry picking" programs, where the short term look dominates. Then the structure of the lab changes from R&D to D.
6. Software costs are totally underestimated, usually by a factor of five, unless advanced planning and structuring is performed. Benefits are obtained by developing software, using "leverage" money from multiple owners, on common shared projects.
7. A laboratory that exists in a state of changing direction due to different emphasis of multiple owners, will cause a fight for control between lab management and owners. (Usually ends with continuous replacement of lab management.)
8. Staffing of laboratories to obtain quality output demands job stability and visible career paths. In a laboratory of continuous change, the best personnel will leave, or not come to the laboratory.

9. R&D is expensive—very expensive. It should be 5-8% of sales in a high technology game, and it could be as high as 10-12%.
10. No single laboratory can cover all the aspects totally, especially where small entrepreneurs can provide extremely sophisticated autonomous software systems.
11. Once we think we have a firm grip on technology, we lose it to breakthroughs that greatly affect broad areas. However, the direction, if carefully planned using applied research, is usually understood with enough lead time to effectively position ourselves with future changes and shifts.
12. Grid lock must be broken where: technology today is waiting on applications, which are waiting on policies, standards, user acceptance, and the definition of new networks, which are waiting on seeing what type of future R&D advances will effect current benefits of today's technology . . .
13. Government initially imposed numerous restrictions on common developments, but have separated out planning, definition, and prototypes as acceptable areas for common efforts. Subsequent Inquiry rulings will reassess manufacturing for foreign competitive local markets by Telcos, as well as local manufacturing, once an open network is achievable.

These thoughts may lead to the following strategic objectives and goals:

1. A central laboratory could help resolve multiple national architectures with international laboratories to establish "open network architectures and structures," that are consistent with the needs of the providers, by assisting in standardizing interfaces for multiple suppliers. Achieving this would make such a laboratory a great asset for its owners, if they quickly capitalize on this achievement.
2. Identifying phases of network architectures and structures for various transition periods, as technology changes to meet market needs more economically and effectively, would enable long range planning of families of new products.
3. New emerging technical possibilities and network structures need to be identified early to foster further investigation of their possibilities.
4. Market needs should be carefully identified and established by the owners to provide the basis for guidance to direct further areas of research.
5. A planning process for interfacing the market analysis of the users by the providers to the technology investigations of multiple laboratories, such as Central Research, is not only necessary, but essential for all parties to be successful.

This type of recommendation and others were used by Central Research to restructure its mission, goals, objectives, limits, and reviews, as it began working more closely with its owners, to perform more "directed" specific R&D programs and projects such as:

1. Establishing International ISDN standards

2. Defining ISDN Networks in terms of overlays and phases of access, features, and integrated systems.
3. Producing fast packet, burst, wideband, and photonic switching architectures and device studies.
4. Investigating the integration of support system's software into network system architectures.
5. Performing studies of various vendor's architectures and structures and determining their quality characteristics.
6. Providing studies on various transmission and switching materials, as well as friendly machine-human interface systems.
7. Defining future ring access systems to differentiate voice, data, or video transmission and route them to the appropriate metro and info type switching systems, as discussed in Chapter 10.
8. Coordinating research across several universities, on topics such as artificial intelligence.
9. Defining possible future customer needs (features) and identifying for all in the telecommunications industry, where in the regulated/unregulated structure they could be provided.
10. Modeling new software languages for building features from common functional program modules.
11. Modeling new packet, circuit, integrated distributed network architectures, as well as new ISDN network standards to determine inconsistencies in structure and definitions.
12. Qualification testing of various manufacturing systems and inplant component quality inspections.

—INTERNATIONAL TECHNOLOGY TRADE CENTER—

While there had been talk of a world technology trade center in the past, nothing really moved forward. Several proposals were unveiled to the media in the early 80s. Interest was aroused, but no one was successful in bringing together those interested—developers, technology firms, international traders, trade organizations, and state governments into a unified effort to really get the idea off the ground.

Then, Change Inc. took an aggressive role and recommended that an international technology trade center be an integral part of the midwest states new international marketing plans and economic development efforts. In 1987, legislatures of five midwestern states established with Change Inc. a permanent 13-person governing body for the project. The Technology Trade Center Board was charged to oversee and manage programs and services to promote the growth of international trade in the midwest. The new board was authorized to finalize the negotiations for the development and construction of the center. On July 4, 1988 the Technology Trade Center Board and Change Inc. finalized their development agreement concerning the development and organization of the Trade Center. The agreement called for development financing to be finalized and construction to commence by June 1, 1989.

The $70 million financial package was put together in late October 1988. Ground was ceremonially broken on May 30, 1989.

The Trade Center would have approximately 1,000 people working in it, employed in technology research, technical database services, and technology export management, as well as international finance, sales and marketing, communications, and language translation. The impact will be significant in new export sales, job retention, and in job creation.

The Trade Center will help technology firms achieve international trade objectives in a variety of ways. Primarily, it will be accomplished by bringing people together. Simply put, it will be a one-stop-shop for buyers and sellers, a place to establish trade contact, a place to obtain information, and a place to get trade services. These three things; contacts, information, and services, would be provided in many different ways.

High technology and computers are becoming growth industries. Their economic future will, in a large part, be a function of this increasing international business and effectiveness of trade promotion and marketing. Centrally located, it can serve states such as Arizona, California, Colorado, Florida, Illinois, Massachusetts, Minnesota, New Jersey, New York, North Carolina, Texas, Virginia, and Washington, who are leaders in super computers and computer technology, electronic equipment, office automation, and data communications. Their marketing efforts will be global. Services available will include financial advice, governmental and administrative assistance to help with regulations and red tape, translation and interpretations services. Communications facilities will link sellers with buyers worldwide. Display space will showcase products, companies, and services. A contact clearinghouse will be provided for buyers, sellers, and visitors. Trade is based a lot on person contact. Today's visitor may be a trading partner tomorrow.

Specific elements will include:

- Exhibit space for specific products and services.
- A fully coordinated information and resource center to take advantage of the hundreds of foreign trade delegations going through the Trade Center each year.
- Office space for trade associations and associated organizations.
- Corporative office space for smaller or start-up companies with shared tenant services.
- A publication and distribution point for a worldwide directory for incoming trade tours, foreign companies, publication of a worldwide newsletter, and a listing of major shows, exhibits, and similar events around the world.
- A starting point for world trade groups and foreign delegations wanting first hand information on locally made products.
- A technology trade education seminar program through private companies, and various university and college offerings.
- Technology Trade Center research services, including high technology market research, technology trade analysis, and technology database.

- A Technology Trade Center locator service and clearinghouse for buyers and sellers.
- A Technology Trade Center public relations/promotions outreach program for the industry.
- A Technology Trade Center conference and seminar facility with language translation and interpretation services for meetings and conferences.
- Technology incubator space for new projects or initiatives, with emphasis on the expansion of future encouraging opportunities for midwest high tech products.
- An information and issues clearinghouse or referral office.

It is an exciting array of services and options. Each needs to become a regular part of how industry conducts and expands its international technology trading business.

Contacts will be made with foreign governments and foreign trading companies, concerning their setting up "technology-trade marts" for their products and import needs.

This future technology trade mart could be used by foreign trading groups to serve a large part of the U.S. market. Not only are they looking to sell their products, but to buy and find investment opportunities. Trade is a two-way street and the world is increasingly becoming interdependent economically.

Tenants

The Trade Center will be a great resource, in part, because of who the tenants are. They will be the lifeblood of the trading activity. The tenant mix is a major factor in achieving the one-stop-shop objective. The tenants will attract people to come to the Trade Center. An individual tenant will benefit from the traffic generated by the other tenants.

Technology Transfer Institute

The Institute will be the integrated element of the Trade Center. It is the glue that will make the Trade Center the single stop for international technology services. A single private or public organization, acting alone cannot do all things or be all things. The Institute is an umbrella organization, a coordinator and facilitator. The charge of the Institute is to help streamline the transaction of technology trade and to promote technology trading activity through its broad-based international technology trade services, programs, and activities.

The Technology Trade Institute will consist of six operations:

- Technology Information Center
- Technology Trade Club
- Technology Exhibits
- Technology Education

- Technology Research Center
- Global Information Networks

The Technology Information Center will be the place to call for information. It will offer not only trade reference materials, but technical personnel, who can help you get answers to your questions. They will steer you in the right direction so your time can be spent on using the information, not on trying to find where to go and whom to ask. In addition, it will be connected to the major private and corporate libraries and computerized databases.

The Information Center will be the place where you can call to find out what international activities are taking place, what foreign delegations are in town and how you can contact them.

The Technology Trade Club will be the hospitality arm of the Trade Center. This private member club will offer an ideal setting for business meetings and entertainment. In addition, its U.S. and international locations will be the setting for receptions, luncheons, and dinners in honor of foreign visitors and trade delegations.

The Technology Exhibits will offer exhibit and display facilities to showcase products and services. The exhibit facilities will be integrated into the lobby as a marketing center.

The Technology Education programs will provide an extensive array of seminars, short courses, conferences, and language training, to meet the diversity of needs.

The state-of-the-art telecommunication-information services will be provided through a shared tenant system. This will allow tenants, whether they are a one-person operation or a full floor operation, the same basic high quality and economically price service.

As you can see, the Trade Center will offer specialized types of trade support programs not available elsewhere. The level and type of service will be user oriented. Flexibility will be important as trade needs change or as new opportunities arise, they can be dealt with as a matter of course. New programs and approaches will be tried and others dropped. It will be the center of change.

Three: Integrating Marketing and Technology

—TOP DOWN PLANNING FOR THE NEW USERS—

As we in the telecommunication area become extensively involved in proposing, designing, and building new worldwide digital integrated services, networks, and products, it is important to constantly reassess what "user needs" must be met. The term "integrated service" means many things, de-

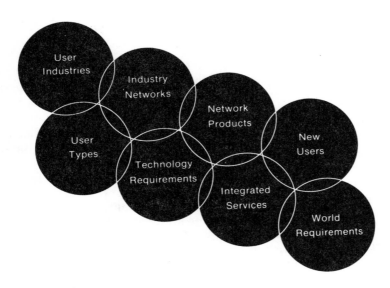

Fig. 12-3. User Industries.

pending on one's perspective. This analysis addresses the issue from a "needs" basis. It attempts to step back and take a "big picture" view of evolving new user requirements in terms of their transport technical attributes' impact on terminals, switches, networks, and services.

Today, many firms are planning products for the new information age. The timing appears to be for the early 90s rather than the end of the 70s, now that the information handling satellites and local networks are being implemented, digital islands of fiber optics and digital switches are being inserted into the local plant, and the PTTs, BOCs and IDCs are placing special emphasis on new services in order to obtain more revenue. However, now is also the time to take a very careful review of the anticipated new users and identify them in terms of their immediate needs, their modes of operation, and their technical characteristics.

We have been through this type of thinking in the 70s only to find that, for numerous reasons, new users did not emerge in the quantities which were originally envisioned by the planners and developers. This then is a top down planning look at the new users and their immediate and future integrated services needs in terms of transport requirements for network products. It is time to redetermine who the new users really are and what they need. This analysis will use a different methodology than that of the blindfolded men in the child's fable, hopefully with better conclusions.

User Industries Networks

A review of eighteen major industries and groups provides an excellent basis for understanding the new users. Each group can be analyzed in terms

366

of its projected future telecommunication networks. They can be reviewed for information handling, transmission, and processing needs.

The following list is representative:

- Banks
- Federal Agencies
- State Government
- Education
- Investment Firms
- Entertainment
- Insurance
- Transportation
- Small Business
- Law Agencies
- Manufacturing
- News/Magazine
- Wholesale/Retail Stores
- Information Services
- Health Care
- Home Communications
- Operations/Utilities
- Large Business Complexes

As discussed in many trade articles, each of these groups will need, over the next ten years, new integrated voice, data, and video networks and services. Various firms within these groups will develop specialized information grids, such as shown in Fig. 12-4. These will emerge in phases, as the company's user resistance decreases and usage expands.

In Fig. 12-4, combinations of local and remote computer banks are tied together over switched or leased facilities. The networks are composed of class level switches, PBXs, concentrators, MUXs, local controllers, and intelligent terminals. In reviewing many of the specific networks for each major group's firms, it is interesting to see that each has a particular configuration, which overlays on this type of general grid, but emphasizes one or two special aspects more than others.

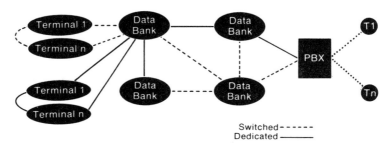

Fig. 12-4. Industry Networks.

User Mode

Further understanding is achieved by reviewing the network's user's mode of operation, not only for voice features, but also in terms of total information flow.

Mode of Operation—Categories

- Interactive—inquiry/response (single or sequence) (I/R)
- Data Collection—Polling/Sensing (DC)
- Data Distribution Networks (DD)
- Interactive—Remote Access/Time Sharing (RA/TS)
- Remote Display/Documentation (RD/D)
- Interactive—Graphics (G)
- Transactions (T)
- Video Conferencing (VC)
- Voice (V)

For example, the investments and securities information network's users would perform the following tasks using one or several of the modes of information transfer shown in Table 12-1.

The users of this industry will be performing the types of information handling, transmission, and processing functions shown in Table 12-1. A similar analysis can be performed on each major group, using selected representative firms. The tasks for each of the groups can then be sorted by mode to obtain a cross view of users from each industry. It will show, for example, all of the industries and groups who may be performing inquiry response tasks, graphic type tasks, etc.

Technical Requirements—Attributes

Next, the mode of operation of the users can be translated into these kinds of telephone characteristics over an accepted range of values:

- Connect time
- Holding time

Table 12-1. User Tasks and Modes of Operation.

Tasks	Modes of operation
Inquiries	I/R
Buy/sell transactions	RD/D,T
Portfolio monitoring	I/R,RD/D,VC
Remote to central transactions	T
Central to stock exchange transactions	T
Central to remote billing	RD/D,T
Internal paperwork transactions	RD/D,T
Research survey monitoring	DC
Information to broker	DD

- Attempts
- User facility location
- User error rate tolerance
- Terminal device speed
- Encryption

From this, various types of specific technical users are identified. They are obtained by making permutations of these requirements over a range of values. Not all permutations of users exist, at least in any reasonable quantity. The next step is to determine what user types will realistically be prevalent, if a cost effective integrated services network is available to meet their needs.

For example, a user type, who is in a broadband graphics category and has an extremely low holding time, generating an excessive number of attempts, and having an extremely sensitive error rate tolerance will possibly not be found in any group. On the other hand, an inquiry/response user type, generating greater than normal POTS (Plain Old Telephone Service) traffic, with an average error rate tolerance, over low to medium speed terminals will most likely be present in all groups.

Range of Values

The range of values becomes an important issue in identifying the new users. The range can be related to traditional POTS values, in terms of equal to, less than, or greater than normal. Similarly, error rate tolerances, transmission speeds, etc., can be broken down into two or three broad ranges of values to enable a clear division among user types.

- Connect Time   (Normal POTS, instantaneous)
- Holding Time   (Less than, normal, greater than POTS)
- Attempts   (Less than, normal, greater than POTS)
- Error Rate Tolerance   (Low, med, high)
- Terminal Speed   (Less than 2400-low, less than 9600-med, greater than 9600-high.)

User Types

Each category has several distinctive types of users. These types are characterized by their attributes range of values. It is interesting to note that not all the permutations exist. Hence, it is necessary to crosscheck each possible combination against the real world.

User Type = f(User Category (Attribute (Range)))

(User types are a function of user category ,which is subdivided over a range of specific technical values for particular attributes.)

An example of how we can analyze each category's user types is demonstrated by this representative process analysis for determining Category 1 Inquiry /Response User Types (I/R).

Definition

The inquiry/response data user makes a single inquiry or sequence of inquiries to determine the status of a remote file. As noted in the attribute values, the single inquiry will normally require fast connection and only hold for several seconds. The I/R user will, in general, operate on the 4 kHz network switched (dial up or packet) or private (for fast connects). The I/R call volume will be very large; as indicated by the large list of I/R users from each industry group. See Table 12-2.

Category 1 Attributes

The attributes associated with this category were carefully investigated. Three main attributes were used to identify potential users (connect time, PBX/local exchange facility, and terminal device operation speed). This

Table 12-2. Category I Users.

Federal-state info exchange	Manufacturing
Inventory control	Book distributors
Planning	News/mag info transfer
Marketing	Research staff operations
Purchasing	Entertainment
Legal	Theater setting
Logistics	Performance bookings
Field maintenance	Medium/business
Accounting	Wholesale-orders
Utility, oil, tele, power, gas	Food industry distribution
Distribution control	Drug business order/customer bill
Control (planned)	Inventory control for chain stores
Records	Hotel/motel reservations
Maintenance clusters	Auto rental chains
General message operations	Home communications
Air, rail, car transportation	Time sharing accounts management
Travel agencies inquiry	Shopping selections, remote
Customer control	University accounting
Operations control	Civil defense
Maintenance control	Red cross network
Logistics control	Political organization nets
Personnel control	Government services
Payroll/accounting	Health care
Hospital patient files	Insurance-hospital claims
Hospital med records	Hospital equip control
Hospital staff control	Dr-education (remote) files
Dr-consultation files	Remote test reports
Information services	Library files for inquiry
Lib-distrib info exchange	Library-to-home/bus terminal
Library-to-home	DP info services (statistics)
Education	University file-student statistics
Remote student grading	University library files
	Stock market inquiries

Table 12-3. Inquiry/Response Attributes.

Facility	TDOS	Connection time	
		Normal	Inst
Internal to user	Low	1	2
(PABX,PAX)	Med	3	4
External to user	Low	5	6
(Class exchange)	Med	7	8

resulted in eight possible user types, as shown in Table 12-3. As the applications for each were examined, some were eliminated as not existing in this category. The final user types for each category are described by the following analysis which determined, from the eight possible Inquiry/Response user types, shown in Table 12-4, those that are realistic.

Three main attributes generates six distinct user types. These attributes are:

1. Connect time (normal POTS, instantaneous)
2. User facilities location (internal, external)
3. Terminal device operation speed (Low < 2400/Med < 9600/High > 9600)

Category 1 Possible User Types

The user types all have the following same general requirements: on-line, medium error tolerance with retransmission, attempts greater than POTS, initially analog later digital, initially private and switched—later publicly switched, holding time less than 3 minutes—normally less than 1 minute.

The number refers to a position in Table 12-3. Every chart has eight (8) positions, one for each user type listed, showing the relationship between connect time, terminal speed, and error rate tolerance. Table 12-5 shows the user types and their network attributes.

Table 12-4. Possible User Types.

Attribute	Single	Sequence
Connect time	Instantaneous	Normal (N)
Holding time	< N	N
Attempts	> N	> N
(N = POTS)		
User facilities location	Internal(I)/	Internal(I)
	External(E)	External(E)
Connection facility	P/SW	SW
Operation mode		
(RT = realtime)	RT	RT
Error tolerance	Medium	Medium
Terminal device operation		
speed (TDOS)	Low/med	Low/med

Table 12-5. User Types and Network Attributes.

User type	Network attributes
1	PABXs with low speed input devices.
2	Economical concentrators replace the need for this user type's PABX requirements.
3	Normal PABX port if the line quality can transmit at less than 9600 rate.
4	Internally hardwired to computer ports and can be captured by a PABX port, if the PABX can provide fast conections and medium speed trunks. This type will not be switched unless the PABX connect time is decreased and the switching network can pass up to 9600 bits/sec at reasonable error rates.
5	Acoustic coupler type user on the Telco's present switched network. This user type will grow to be very large. This will effect processor capacity and offset traffic load projections for telephone offices. These users will go from voice data to data in the future, which will further effect switch capacities. They are currently geting a free ride on unlimited local "call pack" offerings and inward WATS facilities, where use of these facilities is much more than initially estimated.
6	A fast connect, low speed transmission, local exchange facility is unwarranted for this user type.
7	Requires up to the 9600 rate of transmission available on the present trunks that are on the present exchanges.
8	Requires a fast exchange connection using medium speed trunks, presently is on the private point-to point network. Hence, this user requires a fast non-blocking switch, but will not be switched unless the exchange connect time is decreased and the trunk/matrix switching transmission network can pass up to 9600 bits/sec.

General Conclusions

- If the switched networks are upgraded to handle requirements of the user types 8 and 4, then the large private distribution type network can be switched and need not be on expensive private lines (point to point).
- Cost for this I/R type of call should be a function of call duration or amount of bits rather than a flat 1 minute rate.
- Traffic patterns generated by these lines and trunks will be inconsistent with previously established voice traffic patterns.
- Volume of calls and transactions for the 1990s is the most difficult to predict. Gross statistics can be given for major groups. Projections are usually made by extending a trend, relating to another industry, or by curve fitting. Otherwise, the consumer demand curve must be determined, using an extensive list of specific products soon to be available to the consumer. Since information transfer is a new industry, which is not independent, but has a definite cross-elasticity relationship to the computer industry, transmission medium, terminal market, and programming language advancement, it is too early to project by macro-econometric models. Some have chosen micro-economic techniques, such as; demand forecasting. (See "ISDN Marketplace.")
- Demand for past services has mostly been technology driven. Companies determined the products for the user. The user did not initially demand them, until learning about them.
- Market driven services can greatly increase usage. This is further noted

by the fact that computer usage breeds computer dependency, which breeds more computer usage. This increase in usage and sharing of costs brings down costs which increases usage and user demand. In addition, if hard copy can economically replace oral communication, many persons such as doctors, druggists, police officers, etc., will switch from this type of oral conversations (voice data) to data conversations. This will decrease the volume of voice communications and further increase the number of data transactions.

The New Users

As noted in Table 12-3, the user types are simply possible permutations of users over a range of technical values for each mode of operation. They must be overlaid on each industry or group and be identified as a reasonable possibility. In this way, the many possibilities are reduced to only realistic types.

However, some of their requirements may be so extensive that the timeframe for their actual existence may not be until the third or fourth phase of their industry's network's evolution. Alternatively, they may exist today, but not in the near future.

This approach will enable extensive lists of new users to be identified for each industry. As the analysis progresses, the number of similar user types from each industry can be determined. However, these will not be numbers of potential customers for marketing to project sales, but merely profiles of users. For example, the number of banks in the USA that have remote tellers that perform inquiry/response functions of a particular type will not be quantified. However, the analysis will identify the number of realistic inquiry/response user types that are common in each industry. Their needs are met by a particular network, product, or service. (Later more extensive marketing sampling and projection models can provide quantities for sales projections.) In other words, if you are a bank in New York, these are your transport "Needs," but how many banks in New York that will pay for meeting these needs in 1990, 1995, 2000 is not identified.

New Users Impact

The new users of the networks and products, who will utilize the home communications centers and offices of the future, are for the most part less than twenty or so distinct user types, that can be realistically identified by performing a detailed top down planning analysis of this form. The following are recommendations on the types and timeframe of integrated services that the suppliers of telecommunications products should include in their network products, so that the providers of these services will be able to meet the needs of the new users.

In reviewing Table 12-6 of these new users, we may come to the following conclusions that affect the type and timeframe of the evolution of the in-

Table 12-6. User Types.

User type/category	Attributes (range of values)				
	Attempts	Connect time	Holding time	Error tolerance	Data speed
Interactive/time share					
Type 1 (remote programming)	< N	N	> N	L	L/M
Interactive remote access					
Type 1 (remote batch processing)	N	N	> N	L	L/M
Interactive TS					
Type 2 (remote programming)	> N	F	< N	L	M/H
Interactive RA					
Type 2 (remote batch processing)	> N	F	< N	L	M/H
Remote display/doc'mt					
Type 1 (facsimile)	> N	N	< N	M	L/M
Type 2 (printing)	< N	N	> N	M	M/H
Interactive graphics					
Type 1 (computer graphics)	< N	N	> N	M	M/H
Transactions					
Type 1 (bank network)	> N	F	< N	L	L/M
Type 2 (stock exchange network)	> N	F	< N	L	M/H
Type 3 (wide band users)	< N	F	> N	L	M/H
Voice inquiry					
Type 1 (reservations)	> N	N	N	M	- - -
Inquiry/respone					
Type 1 (credit check)	> N	N	N	H	L/M
Type 2 (auto parts inv.)	> N	N	N	M	M/H
Type 3 (airline reservations)	> N	F	< N	M	M/H
Data collection					
Type 1 (retail inventory control)	> N	N	< N	H	L/M
Type 2 (gov't status network)	> N	F	< N	L	M/H
Data distribution					
Type 1 (motel network)	> N	N	< N	H	L/M
Type 2 (police network)	> N	F	< N	H	L/M
Type 3 (medical network)	> N	N	< N	L	M/H
Type 4 (news network)	> N	F	< N	L	M/H

tegrated services network phases:

- For PBX and local exchange type applications, many new user types would be satisfied with a fast connect, medium speed transaction system. The network and processors must handle a greater than normal volume of call attempts, that have less than normal holding time duration.
- Extreme wideband users will be more economically handled on private lines until their number increases or until video conferencing on separate wideband switches over digital pipe networks is economically available to handle them.
- An error rate of one error in 10^7 would probably be acceptable for most data user types with the exception of air traffic and long transaction computer-to-computer users.
- The 9600 bit rates or less will easily handle many of the new users during the first phase of their evolution into the information world.
- The 64K or multiples of it will handle most data users over the next ten

years of their growth (1990-1999), until variable bandwidth on demand (channel or bit rate) is required.

- Inquiry/response user types will exist extensively in all major industries, as they generate single and multiple inquiries in various modes of voice, voice/data, and data communications.
- Terminals will be switched through PABXs and local offices rather than point to point. Industrial private networks will increasingly use more and more switched terminals to reach numerous local and remote data banks.
- Transactions, data collection, and data distribution with inquiry/response user types will greatly increase traffic on communication switches and facilities, as retail stores go to the debit/smart card point of sales and "online" inventory controls.
- Due to excessive volume, transactions for some industries' users (such as banks) need not be circuit switched, but could be handled by packet switches or facilities, that are controlled and selected by variable channel selectors or contention systems.
- Circuit switched systems and packet switched systems will continue to compete for a large number of similar user types, who are transparent to the medium except for response time, security, and block size. These three requirements will be crucial, as longer calls may favor burst switching over fast packet switches.
- Traffic patterns generated by data users will be inconsistent with previously established voice traffic in terms of attempts, time of day traffic peaks, call duration, and area concentration.
- WATTS and unlimited local calling will have to be seriously addressed to economically move data users to separate non-regulated integrated services networks.
- Protocol, connect time, error rate, grade of service, data tariffs, barred access, three attempt limit, polling, retry, code conversion, multi-address calls, direct calls, short clear down, and data collection transport services, as well as list processing, word processor reformatting, and file management, are features that are greatly dependent on understanding these new user types and their technical requirements.

This methodology could be further applied to each individual business or home communications market area to identify, which of the twenty user types will be most prevalent for their application. Such an analysis should consider the following points:

- Home computers that are unable to communicate with large external databases will have limited growth. The future trend will be towards interactive access to several types of external databases, i.e., obtain information on stock exchanges, airline reservations, weather, initial retail transactions from the home, etc. These connections may require only low speed facilities, or a residential type public data packet network.
- Office of the future users must first see an extensive human factors analy-

sis to ease the human-machine interface problems, before there will be widespread acceptance of office automation.

- Governments may wish to encourage tax incentives to subsidize the formation of large topical public databases that can be economically accessed and administered, so that new users can access new information networks from more remote locations. This will help relieve demand for new, bigger roads to handle rush hour traffic and encourage rural growth.
- Internal country requirements must be carefully identified in terms of what the new users will expect and how the initial information overlay networks can be economically provided to encourage growth. The overlay networks must be provided in phases over the next decade. Waiting for user demand to justify the overlay networks will not encourage sufficient growth on a cost effective basis.
- Growth of usage will also be dependent on gateway switching exchanges to enable users to access multiple networks, both internal and external to a country. Standards must be identified and adopted before real growth can be expected.
- The business community will lead the residential use of databases and networks and will bear the initial cost for overlay network facilities. Hence, business communications, centers that truly solve the problems of inventory, electronic mail, information access (reservations, stock market),etc., using easy human interfacing, should be the next development step for future integrated services.

In summary, the home communications center and the business communications center (office of the future) that have been described in trade journals over the past fifteen years can indeed become a reality, as the overlay and wideband phases of the ISDN network are completed in the 90s . . .

—TOP DOWN PLANNING FOR NETWORK OF THE FUTURE—

Today's competitive marketplace can best be served by understanding the network that will support that marketplace.

History

Today we are all aware that the total telephone industry is undergoing a tremendous transformation. Since the late 60s, data handling devices have been interconnected to the telephone network and major forces began demanding change in all facets of the industry. As the technology changed from transistors to large scale integrated circuits, new products became available to help the traditional carriers increase their productivity by changing their mode of operation from electromechanical switching systems and manual operator boards to more computerized systems, that better utilize the total network. Three major forces (technology, competition, and new business computer users), united to push the telephone common carriers into recognizing the economic advantages of changing from a carrier of voice communication to a provider of integrated voice, data, and video communication services.

During the early 70s, there was intense controversy of the form, direction, magnitude and time frame of the transformation into the use of integrated services. Would there be a great number of wideband video users or medium speed data users? Would its direction be over analog or digital switches and facilities? If the transformation was to use digital transmission, would it be digital in the local plant, as well as toll? These types of questions were of major concern.

ISDN Overlay Networks

However, in the mid 70s the pattern became evident. The late 80s and 90s would be the years of major change and innovation. Telcos subsequently re-evaluated their planning programs to delay their major switching system conversions until the 80s, to take advantage of the digital technology. It was also an opportunity to begin upgrading outside plant in order to meet digital "noise" requirements. In anticipation of this change, the telecommunications industry had been scrutinized from every aspect. Competitive manufacturers began preparing to provide new equipment in the switching, transmission, terminals, testing, billing, routing and operator services areas. They attempted to find every alternative way for using the latest technology. Numerous technological advances were moving their product's design quickly into the digital world. These products were based upon structures and architectures, that were implemented by using stored programs on extremely powerful physically distributed processors.

Hence, we arrive in the nineties with an exciting realm of new possibilities for products and services. No longer is the marketplace dominated by only traditional suppliers, each with their own uncontested product line. As we have seen by the exit of ITT, the marketplace is an arena of intense struggle of old and new suppliers attempting to provide the equipment that best meets the needs of the users (be they the local subscriber, the Telco's business customer, the private network customer or the Telco itself). Thus, the initial emphasis of successful suppliers must first be to identify the evolution of the network and then the systems and products that fit the network and its user's market requirements.

Voice Systems

As a result of the first phase of this analysis, manufacturers, suppliers, and Telcos are introducing digital switching and digital transmission facilities into the voice network at the lowest concentration point using a "physically" distributed base-satellite network structure.

This distributed network is seen in Fig 12-5, where remote line units (located on poles or in huts) bring subscribers to remote switching units located in small offices or suburban areas. These subscribers are then brought into a sophisticated base unit control system (located at the urban local or lo-

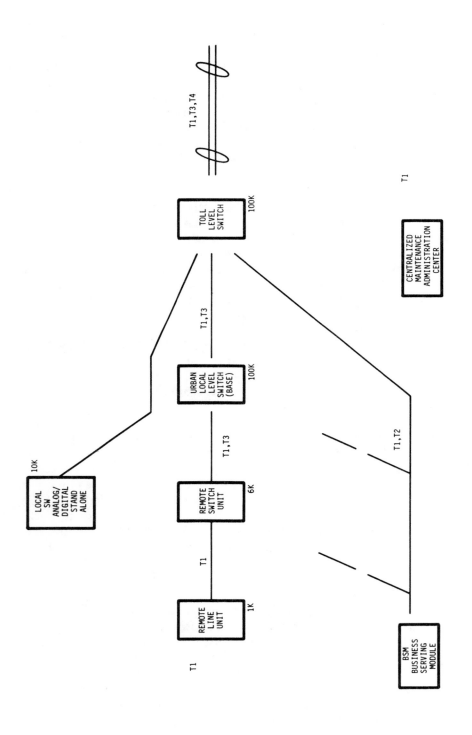

Fig. 12-5. IDN Integrated Digital(Voice) Network.

378

cal/toll 4/5 level office). Alternatively, remote line units interconnect directly to base units. In this manner, a digital island can be formed using the natural toll area cluster to upgrade older offices, offset directional growth and upgrade outside plant. In addition, stand alone analog or digital switching systems within the cluster can interlace at the toll level or access switch. This integration allows for needed early office conversation to digital to take place independent of the future ISDN integrated wideband services 1996 + concept (see Chapter 10).

Figure 12-5 also shows two other areas, that can benefit from the digital technology. They are the business services module (BSM), the former PBX application, as well as the centralized maintenance and administration center (CMAC). The BSM will meet the needs of the private users, while the CMAC will address the future needs of the changing Telco itself. Both of these areas are under intense review and change. Similarly, the Telco is just beginning to realize the need for another way of doing business in terms of controlling, maintaining, administrating and planning the large switch/facilities plant. This will be reflected in the new extensive centralized (with distributed work stations) maintenance and administration centers.

Currently, other new areas of interest are beginning to surface: smart terminals, digital subscriber loop, data features, digital data packet switching, BSM data features, automated main frame, and fiber optics. However, in attempting to logically fit these considerations into this new network, we have seen many limitations, inconsistencies, and contradictions. The basic question continues to arise and must be re-addressed: "What type of network can best meet these changes?" One can again see the need for a top down network solution rather than a bottom up device or system change answer. Hence, there is the need for the big picture to be even bigger. The more complete perspective view should include the individual phases of the network evolution.

Data Systems

Figure 12-6 overlays the specific capabilities of data switching (up to 64K synchronous data rates) on the new digital or older analog switching systems, to complement the BSM system. Similarly, the CMAC system is enhanced with a data switching function to allow it to communicate to any point in the network or to distant data banks. It is interesting to note that, depending on the size of the local switch and the build up of the data users over the 80s and 90s, the office at the local level nodal point can *switch* instead of concentrate users to the higher level. In the normal application, the local/toll (4/5 level) office becomes an access switch or a gateway to the private and specialized common carriers, as well as the interface point to the traditional common carrier's new data networks, which may be used to provide the future non-regulated services. Here, also, is a natural point for interfacing protocols, code conversions and providing billing. Similarly, non-regulated services, such as data message processing and data message storage could be performed by specialized systems at this point, once government rulings

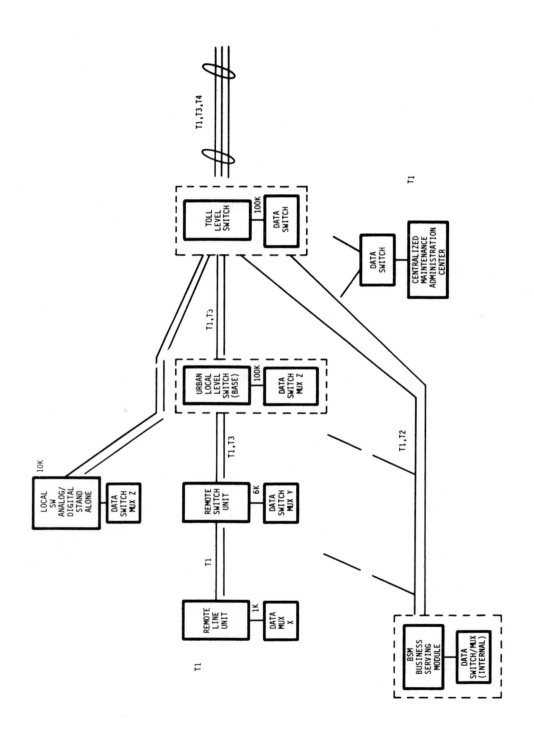

Fig. 12-6. Data Overlay on IDN of Fig. 12-5.

enable Telcos to provide information services, or through joint competitive data processing offerings (see Chapter 10 on the info switch).

Terminal/Loop Overlay

Figure 12-7 overlays the smart terminals, digital terminals, wideband systems and the digital subscriber loop on the evolving voice and data network.

Notice how this overlay of wideband data and video networks enhances the ISDN. It shows how separate switching matrixes and integrated transmission can be accomplished using new facilities such as fiber and T carrier on adjunct switches, controlled by main switches. Again the local/toll (4/5) point or access switch appears to be the switching nodal point with multiplex units located at the lower levels to distribute the information. Obviously, the growth of the wideband users will be different from other data users. It is reasonable and necessary to provide this type of pre-wideband ISDN structure now in order to encourage participation and growth through the 90s, until they reach maturity in the twenty first century.

In reviewing how the smart terminals, digital voice terminals, and digital subscriber loops are overlaid on the network, it becomes apparent that these networks and systems will support the intelligent terminals of the future. It can also be seen, where the digital subscriber loops support their interfaces to the networks. Thus, intelligent devices will be able to move both voice and data information simultaneously on effectively two networks, that provide the new feature options noted earlier. In addition, wideband terminals can interface directly to the adjunct wideband network, which will provide them high speed data or video services. An ISDN family of "T" and "U" standard interfaces will be universally available to integrate the transmission of voice, data and video from the user.

ISDN

Much can be observed by reflecting on Figs. 12-7 and 12-8 of the integrated network and seeing how all three networks overlay together to form the complete picture. It is evident that this structure will enable the user to move his intelligence in many forms and formats such as: voice, packet data, synchronous 2.4K, 64K, N64k and/or variable bit rate data, wideband data or video. This network will meet various modes of user operation such as voice, voice inquiry, interactive data, inquiry/response, transactions, data collection, data distribution, remote display, documentation, interactive graphics, image and video.

In order to realistically understand the user requirements, it helps to review the future user's communication networks, as was performed in the previous case study for the following industries: banking, investment, wholesale/retail, insurance, law agencies, city/state government, federal government, manufacturing, operations/utilities (such as the Telco itself), transportation, health care, information services, education, news/magazine,

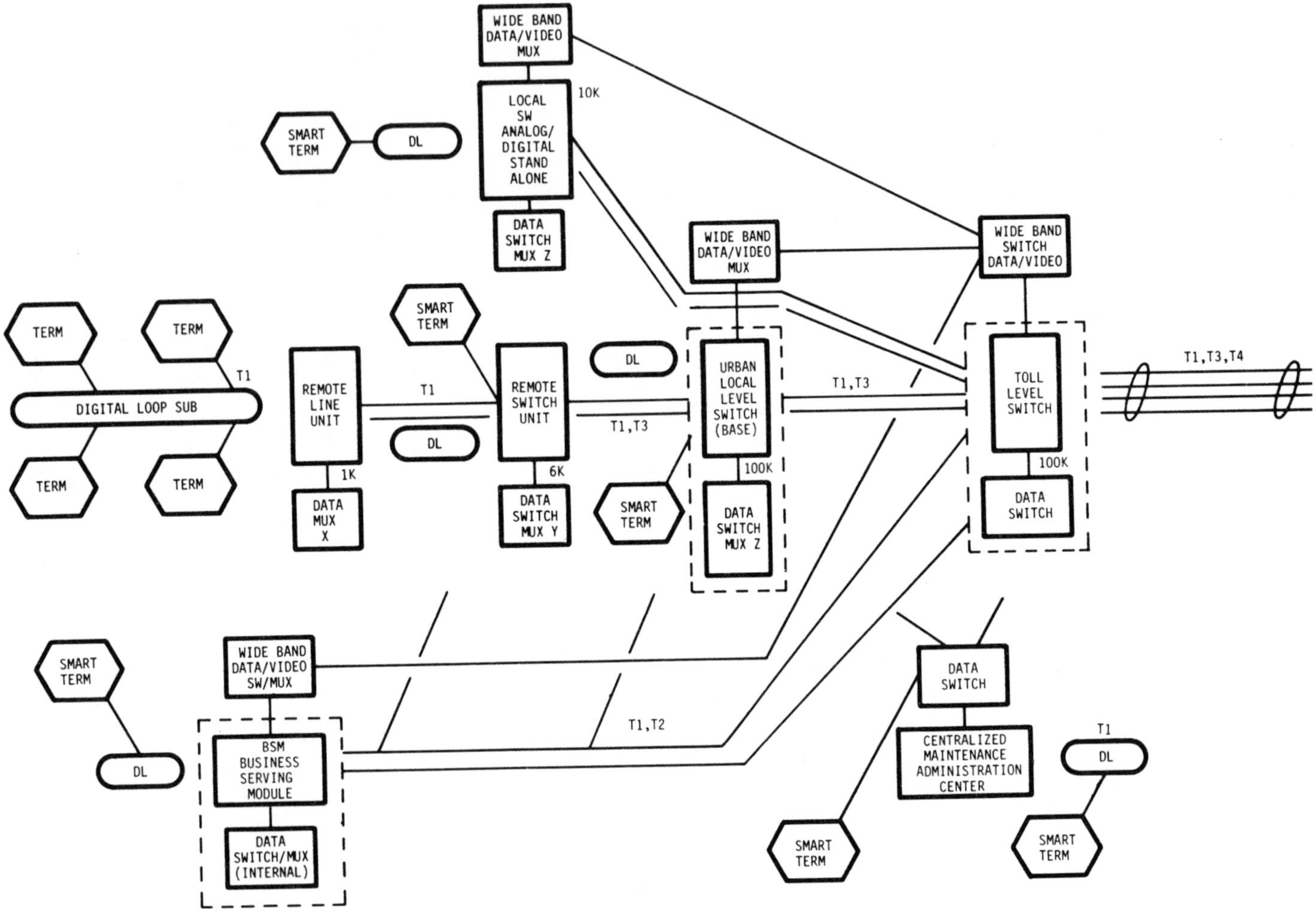

Fig. 12-7. Wideband Overlay on IDN of Figs. 12-5 and 12-6.

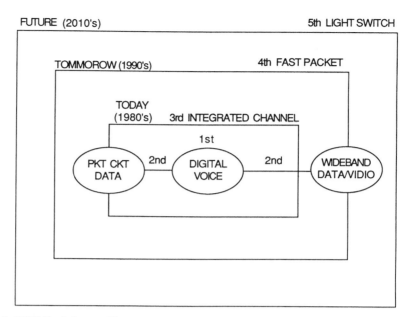

Fig. 12-8. ISDN Evolutionary Phases.

entertainment, small business and the home. Future communication needs can then be translated for the 90s into specific telephony requirements such as: transmission rates, error rates, reliability and quality of service, number of attempts, holding time, connection time, operation mode (real or store/forward) etc. which directly affect the network. Subsequent specific values for these attributes establish the requirements for the ISDN.

Conclusion

In summary, the "new users" noted in the preceding study can, in time, become a reality, as the ISDN local network is completed. Presently, many corporate and research offices are preparing to have intelligent terminals on a per employee basis. Similarly homes are beginning to have interactive systems using personal computers and to use the television for Viewdata and interactive games. Thus the foundation for an ISDN network is being laid for their interconnection to extensive data handling external networks. In addition, the Telco's are preparing for the change with their new financial revenue restricting effort to remove unlimited calling at local level and to have unit bit rate pricing on all services (voice, data, other, etc.) via regulated and non regulated network offerings.

Therefore, there will be considerable changes in telecommunications mode of operation in the 90s, and with that change, tremendous opportunity exists for the suppliers of the new telecommunications information equipment and the providers of the new services.

—WHY DO CONCEPTUAL PLANNING?—

All companies do some form of Conceptual Planning, such as, enhance or re-apply a current product; recommend a new product to meet the competition; or respond to a request. This may require considerable formal complex analysis and difficult high risk decisions. Hence, more and more companies are being forced to perform more indepth planning in order to survive in tomorrow's marketplace. The case for planning can best be shown by reviewing AT&T's role of recent years. See Fig. 12-9.

1970-1977 Planning Position in Terms of Technology Evolution and Marketplace Situation

- No. 1, 2, 3 ESS Common Control Stored Program analog switches are to replace SXS and Crossbar Central Offices through the 80s and 90s.
- No. 4 ESS Digital Switches are to replace 4A toll centers.
- Processors are becoming more powerful in smaller sizes.
- Telco's begin to upgrade their toll facilities to handle T Carrier.
- Competition moves into terminal key system and PBX market.
- Toll market has small parallel specialized carriers.
- Inflation is rising and adversely affecting cost of capital.
- Anti-trust suits are in process by Justice Department.
- Cable is being overlaid parallel to voice network in medium size towns.
- Provide trial transaction network to move data.

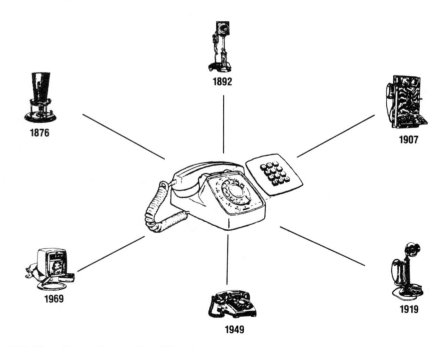

Fig. 12-9. Evolutionary Approach to Planning.

- Sell dimension PBXs with two tier pricing.
- Plan to launch new ATC data network hopefully in the 78-80 timeframe.
- Resist anti-trust cases in court.
- Request tariff increases on WATTS and local plant.
- GTE and Northern Telcom announce plans for local digital switches with remote switch units to replace smaller offices.
- GTE announces plans to create digital islands and interfaces to network through 4/5 toll centers.
- Rolm, Mitel, and Datapoint announce new family of PBXs.
- SBS announces plans for parallel satellite wideband network.
- Xerox announces plans for their PBX data network.
- Nippon, Hitachi, and Siemens announce plans to build plants for digital switches in the U.S.
- ITT sues for a share of supplying to AT&T's "captured" market.

1978 to 1983 AT&T's Planning Position and Market Strategy

- Try to settle anti-trust suit with Justice Department so that they can compete in the opening information market.
- Divest a few Telcos in highly regulated areas with older equipment lines.
- Restructure market to cater to non-regulated user.
- Provide non-regulated specialized services network.
- Remove features from switches to support features on feature/cost basis.
- Sell terminals (voice) back to subscribers and launch new voice, data, video terminal market.
- Remove unlimited local, WATTS and call pack service.
- Tariff on unit call pricing for all voice and data calls.
- Develop local digital switch with remote line unit and remote switch unit.
- Introduce fiber optics in local office plant.
- Begin design of a voice data PBX.
- Settle all existing suits, such as the ITT suit.
- Design extensive centralized Maintenance and Administrative software programs.
- Begin automated main frame development.
- Provide more extensive satellite system for voice and data.
- Develop cellular mobile radio call services.
- Provide a fiber optic lightwave cable between Europe and U.S.
- Sell support programs in outside market.
- Provide No. 4 ESS in international marketplace (Taiwan) to be followed by Local Digital No. 5 ESS with RSUs and RLUs.

1984-1986 Aggressive Positioning

- Divest Telcos Jan. 1, 1984.
- Keep Bell Labs, Western Electric, as Advanced Technologies.
- Establish an information systems firm to later combine with Advanced Technologies.

- Provide Digital Class 5 (local) voice switching systems with remote switch units (RSUs) and remote line units (RLUs).
- Develop #1 PSS (first data packet switch).
- Develop personal computer.
- Provide smaller data packet switch offering.
- Integrate data on #5 ESS in circuit (later packet) switching mode.
- Develop new PBX, handling alarms and special services.
- Market advanced technologies products directly to Telcos and Telcos' customers.
- Obtain international market agreements with Phillips.
- Develop marine fiber with high capacity.
- Manufacture 256K bit memory chips, research 1 million - 4 million chips.
- Define a more competitive long distance pricing strategy.
- More involved participation in International CCITT Standards arena.

1986-1996 New Planning/Market Strategy

- Provide 45-120 megabit wideband switch.
- Provide 1.5 megabit wideband packet switch.
- Provide next generation UNIX personal computers.
- Provide specialized packages of information service for hospitals, CAD/CAM etc.
- Design 1 million/4 million memory chip devices.
- Integrate data packet switching on voice switches.
- Research Fast packet (voice/data/video) switching models.
- Research Photonic light switch models.
- Design 2.2+ Gigabit rate transmission systems.
- Provide competitive feature offerings to, sometimes within, telco boundaries with ISDN interface.
- Present Universal Services vision.
- Market voice, data, video networks, products, and services.
- Encourage usage of their new universal service network in a totally open competitive arena.

1986-8 Summary

- Shift to new factory industrial computer applications. PC terminals with UNIX for internetworking supported by "C" language were considered by design shops as excellent and by some Universities as a good educational support tool. Their terminal in color was clearer than IBM, but many users use the Macintosh as the alternative to IBM. Hence, they shifted to Olivetti partner to provide new products.
- The "T" and "U" interfaces were added to the number 5 ESS to meet the McDonald Oakbrook Illinois field test for ISDN interface.
- Telemarketing type services were provided using ISDN "D" channel operator signaling from number 5 ESS.
- The clear channel transmission systems were introduced using out of band

signaling to identify type of traffic such as voice, data, video that is being transmitted.

- Systems 75 and 85 were introduced, where systems interconnect directly to local area networks for voice and data traffic.
- System 75 will handle protocol interface and code conversion to enable private networks to have different terminals talk to each other and interface to the world using X25, X75 packets, etc.
- A 4,000 Data Packet Switch was developed for information services and the Telcos. It initially had high quality transport features, but limited extended data handling features.
- A circuit switched data network at 56K was established with the RBOCs to use CCSA links and the I ESS to enable dial-up 56 Kilobit customers to access their 56K network.
- A digital cross connect switch was developed to automate facilities. However, the next generation must enable the Telco to obtain the advantages of Gigabit rings, for dynamic usage.
- The universal service network advocates integrating switch access, splitters within their system by first providing petitioned and then integrated voice/data handling capabilities.
- SDS 4 ESS will be their node for providing software defined services (SDS), above the network to enable RBOC customers to bypass Telco.
- New York Tel and other Telco's were asked to provide a fiber tree within the local network to their 4 ESS systems throughout the business communities.
- The Ku ground to satellite transport frequencies for commercial/university/government buildings access the number 4 ESS's by bypassing ground facilities completely.
- Attempt to become the private systems contractor for government networks and effectively establish CCSA type wideband ISDN private networks within the BOC's for the government.
- Planned 4 ESS's for the Far East, China, Taiwan, Korea, etc. to be followed by 5 ESS's using digital multiplex transmission systems.
- Addressed the public information market by first attempting to enable customers to access menu driven systems, but government decisions reduced offering to a non-menu service.
- Provide total "solutions" to the private network customers, such as: turn key hospital systems.
- Dropped network 1,000, also called the "ACS" and "NET 1" data network, when Ford Motor Corporation dropped Beta test.
- Dropped shared tenant services (STS)—ShareTech venture between IS and United Technologies.
- Initial attempts with Phillips were unable to obtain British Telcom Network Switching sales in price competition with European firms.
- EDS (Data Systems) joint venture, initially for GM (General Motors) for integrating network and computer services, also, has government and commercial customers, using an integration of joint marketing, working with

EDS has been a good access to Federal contracts.

- A consortium of seven major European computer manufacturers, the X1 Open group, chose to standardize its operating system software on UNIX System 5 giving the AT&T standard a good deal of European momentum in the commercial marketing place over IBM.
- Reach out for RES has been joined by PRO America for Small Business and Megacom and Software Defined Network Systems for large users.
- Sales forces of AT&T Communications and AT&T Information Systems has been consolidated into a single customer selling unit which is subdivided into basically four business groups.
  - BMG-Business Marketing Group—for 80 plus line customers.
  - GMG-General Marketing Group—for under 80 line customers.
  - SMG-Special Marketing Group—for joint ventures and partnerships such as EDS, Olivetti and "Quoton Systems."
  - NOG-Network Operations Group
  - AT&T IS and AT&T Communications will have separate accounting procedures to prevent cross subsidization with 92,000 people in IS and 118,000 in Communications such that BMG has 33,000, GMG has 72,000 and SMG only has several hundred and 21,000 are in support organizations. Their charter is to integrate operations into a one stop shopping sales force for computers, PBXs, local area networks, enhanced services, long distance telephone services, etc. But, the question remains, after the boxes of people are slid over here and there, "who will do strategy and planning in the shops, and what will it be?"

As indicated, this type of conceptual planning affects strategic product and tactical plans. It has risk, but attempts to make AT&T a formidable opponent in the competitive marketplace of the 90s, rather than use the limited planned evolution of the early 70s. This case example illustrates the complexity and need for continuous "conceptual planning."

—CONCEPTUAL INFORMATION RINGS—

A creative thinking methodology using rings of information to formulate the concept or vision, by projecting from the known to the unknown is as follows:

Steps

1. Define initial circle of functional areas of consideration.
2. Identify for each functional area subfunctional areas.
3. Develop relationships between subfunctional areas.
4. Identify dependencies and time phasing.
5. Define a new list of sub topics which are identified by relationships (3) and dependencies (4) in reference to the topic under study.
6. Make observations and draw conclusions from sub topics concerning

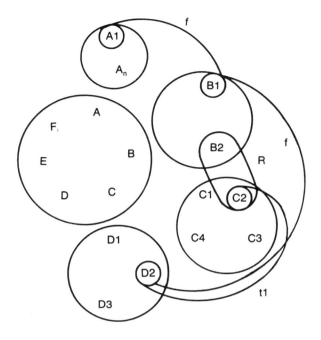

1. Establish primary ring
2. Establish secondary rings
3. B_2 and C_2 are related
4. $D_2 = f[B_1(A_1)]$, where: D_2 is dependent upon B_1 which is dependent upon A_1
5. Define new sub topics, where:
   $$T_1 = C_2 \times D_2 \text{ where}$$
   $$D_2 = f[B_1(A_1)] \text{ and } C_2 = R(B_2)$$
6. $O_1 = T_1 + T_2$
   $$O_2 = T_3 \times T_4$$
   $$O_3 = C_1$$
7. New concept $= O_1 + (O_2 \times O_3)$

Fig. 12-10. Thinking Rings.

main topic in terms of conditions, variables, dependencies, differences relationships, extensions, possibilities, and applications.

In Fig. 12-10, the sub topic T_1 is determined by condition C_2 and D_2, where D_2 is dependent upon B_1, which is dependent on A_1 happening first.

Steps (continued)

7. Determine big picture, new concept or vision where $V = O_1$ or (O_2 and O_3). Here either O_1 or both O_2 and O_3 must be true.
8. Step back and note impact of catastrophes, major events, new technologies, economic shift, wars, etc. on big picture.
9. If necessary based upon step 8 revisit step 1 thru step 6 for alternative big picture best/worst case scenarios.
10. Note market, technology and economic research areas, which need to be further pursued.
11. Let the vision sit for a while and then revisit the analysis to consider new insights after other investigations are completed from step 10.
12. Finalize the concept by attacking its assumptions and performing "then what" analyses. If it stands up, the concept is a viable candidate for further analysis.

Conceptual Thinking

Several innovative techniques have been developed, enabling one to conceptualize new possibilities. One seminar used the example of "different thinking" by asking the participants to write down all the functions and items associated with a restaurant. Then pick one item and remove it. Note what type of restaurant business could you have without for example a menu, or waiters, or parking, etc. It is interesting to note how functional and subfunctional arenas can be developed, using this simple technique.

WHAT WILL BE REALISTIC NEEDS OF SOCIETY

FOR TELECOMMUNICATIONS AT THE TURN OF THE CENTURY?

Twenty planners participated in a conceptual planning information era round table discussion on the subject, by first taking a look at the amount of change achieved in the last twenty-five years, in order to appreciate the next twenty five.

A Past Look, Twenty-Five Years Ago

- The integrated circuit was just being developed for commercial application after initial use on Minuteman II.
- No. 1 ESS, an analog central office system, was just going into full scale production runs, based upon transistor technology.
- Life was basically slow, an appearance of small town atmosphere prevailed even in big cities—but this changed to rioting as racial unrest and Vietnam unrest prevailed.
- College students were filled with new society ideas to change the world.
- Gas was cheap—big cars were "in"—(later gas was expensive causing big cars to be "out," then gas prices dropped and big was back "in").
- Energy conservation was not the issue—cheap electricity—usage was to expand everywhere, especially as the world went to nuclear power.
- Crime in big cities was not a major concern.
- Computers were just being used in accounting/payroll applications.
- Environmental issues, high divorce rates, trash on TV, super inflation, etc., were yet to come.
- Telecommunications meant the telephone or a fax machine.
- FCC was just beginning to question rate of return and profitability on interstate services.
- Space program was just getting underway, the slide rule was still used by engineers, satellites were just being launched.
- Most operations were manual or used various analog feedback control systems.

The next effort attempted to look at the future, to really see what major shifts are taking place.

A Future Look, (Twenty-Five Years From Now?)

- Information will be everywhere—computers will be used to shift and sort information and provide recommendations—this is where artificial intelligence in a first level application will be of assistance.

- Personal movement in large metropolitan areas will be a problem.
- Personal movement in rural areas will not be a problem, but high energy costs could return, causing more restrictions on travel.
- Technology must provide a user benefit to be really used.
- New poor—a split in the system to a two world society—the educated and skilled, who have opportunity—those that do not.
- People will use home as an extension of the corporate world:
  - working at home, if they drop out of corporate world during gaps such as to raise children
  - working at home, as areas of their employment are automated by robotic or computer functions
  - working at home, when tired of corporate life or design of large complex systems
  - working at home to supplement income
  - working at home to have freedom to own one's company for more challenge and reward

- Some people do not want to work at home—need more social relationship—will work at satellite work centers ringing metro areas, or located in rural work area communities.
- Will no longer change as technology changes—must have new good features as reason. "How small is small?" Two 1 megabit chips are as acceptable as one 2 megabit chip.
- Choice will still prevail but will be tempered with compromise. There will also be a shift back to take it or leave it packages, that are cheaper.
- Larger personal and government debt will cause buying power to weaken, as homes with both parents working are strapped for cash, as new products with multiple features are priced on a per-feature basis.
- Voice input to computers will be available to ease communications.
- World competition for everything will be the times.
- Third world rich, and third world poor, will want different goods having different needs.
- Unemployment in Europe will have to watch America's answer to unemployment, which will be more willingness to move, change industry, and take self education, versus more and more social programs.
- New products will be the answer to unemployment as the information world opens up many new possibilities, but products will be more automatically built, causing shift to automated flow operations from assembly.
- Shorter work week to employ more may be necessity, after a reduction of work force by early retirement incentives.
- Baby boom will generate new generation of babies, care for the elderly will be a major industry, baby boomers will be in the 45-55 age group with new product needs, as well as new service needs such as community child care facilities in home community or condominium/town house complex.

- Value systems will perhaps be reestablished by large senior group or by baby boomers as family problems become extremely severe due to the tensions of both parents working, both traveling, taking care of the child problems; causing people to ask "where are we really going?"
- Judgements and decisions will be made by using more and more data.
- Desire to see the big picture.
- Holograph or full image views may be used in such applications as education and product design.
- Simulated experiences to fully understand situations may become useful.
- What society is really willing to pay for will be communication that is universally available to provide full services, as cheap as possible, so it becomes a tool for business survival.
- Food and natural resources will be major assets, as farms are bought up by large multinational or foreign firms, or as joint partnerships with city folks.
- Technology itself will be sold as a commodity.
- Space will be a new laboratory for manufacturing new goods.

A Look at Today

The price of oil has dropped below 15 dollars a barrel. Interest rates returned to a single digit. The U.S. dollar was devalued 33% against European currency after a 75 to 126% rise. Trade deficits became out of line. Foreign stocks became attractive. European and Japanese partnerships occurred. Interest rates became desirable. Stock market index doubled in one year and then gained and dropped over 100 points a day. Firms retired or laid off 25% of management. Numerous telecommunications firms fall out, and joint partnerships occurred. Users did not respond quickly to expensive new data features.

Conclusion

These potential economic realities will demand more preprogram, preproject, preproduct/network/service planning for survival and success in the future's more competitive international marketplace.

Now what does that mean to strategic telecommunication planning requirements and opportunities in terms of future goals and objectives?

Goals

1. Participate in an International Network offering.
2. Universal, single plug available for total information exchange.
3. Must be cheap as possible to enable volumes of usage.
4. Must become a tool to help business become successful, and not an obstacle.

Objectives

1. Obtain international interconnect standards to enable new product in-

teractions and access to the world.

2. Network must be non-restrictive on bandwidth to promote all forms of usage.
3. Interface must be user friendly to promote usage—this does not mean a complex arrangement.
4. Position technology solutions in the marketplace:
   — create needs in market for technology
   — utilize technology to solve real identified needs
   — identify need for new technology from market needs.
5. Providers must perform a major role in planning the products, that they will want to provide.
6. Money must be leverage in numerous expensive opportunities—leveraged money will be essential in financing new ventures, that will have greater risk, due to the need to foster markets—causing many joint ventures, and joint research projects, but not necessarily acquisitions . . .
7. Technology must be flexible and feature friendly (easy to use) to extend its already short life. Providers must be ready to change to new products as necessary to remain leading edge and competitive in the marketplace, but not change for change sake.
8. Successful suppliers will have the image of having leading edge products, that fit into a total network offering, and successful providers will provide a network, offering total information services.

Four: The Features World

—INFORMATION CUBICS—

The information world has opened up a new game for telecommunications—the feature game. No longer are we simply concerned with technical operational features, such as network attempts, connect time, holding time, and signalling systems. We now have several users: the provider, the provider's customers, interexchange firms, intermediaries, the private network customers, etc.

To visualize new needs, requirements, and opportunities, we can look at this new world in terms of several three dimension cubics. See Fig. 12-11. In effect, it is a four dimensional problem, which can best be seen by two three dimensional views. The new requirements are like a bottle of champagne. See Fig. 12-12. The bubbling features have been bottled up for many years waiting for an opportunity to escape. The divestiture breakup has shaken up the bottle and released the cork, enabling them to fizz out! As they begin to emerge, various corks have been reapplied to the bottle, such as the MFJ (Modified Final Judgements), the conclusions of Inquiry II, waivers, and open architecture considerations. The strategies of AT&T and IBM, as well as the

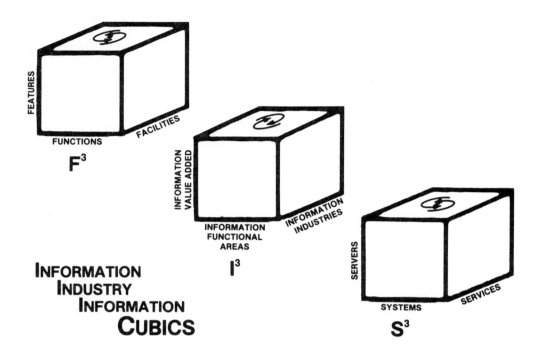

Fig. 12-11. Information Industry Cubics.

CCITT and TIDI ISDN standards have attempted to control the flow and direction of the new energy and life that has been breathed into the world of telecommunications, especially as it integrates with the world of data processing. Finally, Inquiry III sets a "mid course correction" to enable the Telcos to participate in the formally very restricted CPE (NCTE) interface world. Earlier inquiries were used, as a delay tactic, for non Telco players to prepare for the game.

It is indeed a new game, where the whole will be greater than the sum of the parts, as the two giant industries join together. There was a definite "Pop" on Jan. 1, 1984, when divestiture took place. Since then, there has been a flow of smaller "Pops," as bubbles of opportunity begin to flow and burst into new ventures. Indeed it is the time for a party—so let's play the game and see what kind of party it will be.

First we must ask ourselves: "What kind of game will it be?" "Where will it be played?"

Figures 12-13 and 12-14 indicate that it will be a world of many new features that will be provided by many new systems. It also notes that the game will be played on at least three, if not more arenas; the customer provided equipment (CPE) market, the new subsidiaries of the new seven regional Telcos, and the new nonregulated divisions (after Inquiry III) in what we will call the basic information distribution firms (the former BOCs). Though this

394

Fig. 12-12. It's Time For an ISDN Features Party!!

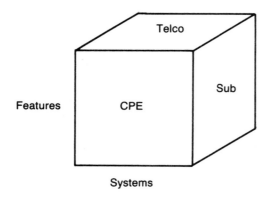

Fig. 12-13. What Features Where?

appears to be a reasonably complex three dimensional problem, we will see how another dimension called functional areas, further complicates the picture.

As we look at where we wish to play the game, we must constantly drop back to strategic strategies, determining, what is the business of the business. Never in the decades of defining, designing, supplying and providing new products have we seen such an involved overlay of special requirements to meet the concerns of the government (Inquiries, MFJ, Waivers, and then mid course new freedoms etc.), for meeting the needs of potential new customers, who are not yet really customers, for a new industry, that is just beginning. Yes, it's a challenging world, for those who dare to play the game.

We will see that requirements are not only greatly linked to strategic direction, but to the strategy of the strategies of various teams playing the game.

The Big Picture

They say a picture is worth a thousand words. The bigger it is the better.

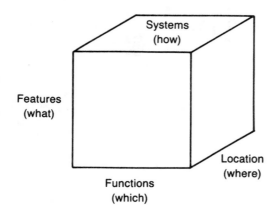

Fig. 12-14. The Business of the Business.

396

The F³, I³, S³ cubics are big pictures, that show the many facets of the new game. Let's pause and take time to understand these views, from every angle and perspective we can: First, from afar to see the forest and then up close to see the beauty and complexity of each tree.

The Feature Game

Figure 12-15 shows the future voice, data, video, text, and image world in terms of features. The vertical axis breaks features into six groups, as it extends through several levels adding more and more value to the service:

I/O. This level is the terminal area, where any form of input/output (I/O) device may be connected to the network. No longer are the dial pulse and touch tone telephones King and Queen. Terminals must meet not only voice, but also data and video needs. Depending where the game is played, terminals can also be the interface point to private networks, or new data networks, where local area networks (LANs), private branch exchanges (PBXs), key systems, computers, printers, modems, and concentrators exist.

Basic. These are the traditional transport features, such as plain old telephone service (POTS), as well as new transport needs for data switching and wideband switching. Here data can be switched on circuit switches, packet switches (packet, fast packet or burst) or megabit wideband switches. See "A Look at Technology" in Part Four.

Level 1 Extended Information Transport. In this case, more and more capabilities are added to the transport of information. As noted, custom calling and extended custom calling features are available, as well as a new family of transport features for various grades of service, levels of maximum error rates, and different types of protocol conversions. Here also, transport considerations for security and levels of quality would be available as offerings above the basic level. Note that the new family of class features, based upon receiving the calling party identification number are available here. The case study "Transport Feature Features" lists numerous possible features for those who may wish to further consider them.

Level 2 Extended Inquiry. As we enter the new information era, there will be a great need for inquiry response interactions. See "A Look at the Marketplace." Information will be moved by remote data distribution and data documentation systems. This "F³" figure indicates an extended world of new service offerings, as information is requested and exchanged from various sources and sinks.

Level 3 Extended List Access Services. Not only must we access lists, but we must be able to search through masses of information. Only then will the computer be a tool for society. Using more and more artificial intelligence, it will acquire mountains of information and search through it for relevant data.

Level 4 Information Processing Services. Here the information found in level three is processed, analyzed, manipulated, and prepared for presentation. At this level the computer is able to truly solve complex problems by using its fully developed multiprocessors' capabilities, operating at several hundred millions of instructions per second (MIPS), preparing answers to ques-

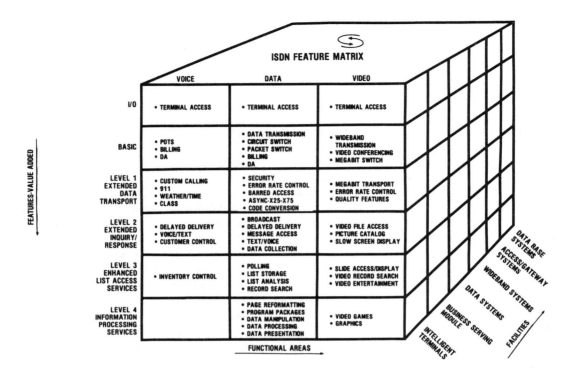

Fig. 12-15. Features/Functions/Facilities — the F_3 Cubic.

tions in real time applications (weather, control systems etc.).

We can see the type of work that becomes more and more useful, as well as complex, as we progress through the various levels. The providers of database services will use numerous versions of new families of product offerings. The government will devise many playing field questions, such as "How will the Information Distribution Companies be able to provide for the masses on a public common carrier 'integrated network' offerings?" "How much will their subsidiaries or unregulated divisions be providing to more sophisticated customers on an enhanced value added offering. How will the feature be competitively offered (no longer where it is offered)?" These issues are further discussed in "Who's on first?", "A level playing field," and "The government's playing field," as well as "Inquiry III."

The third dimension, the right axis, shows the complexity of what system should have what features. Here intelligent terminals, business serving modules (from the extended PBX or info switch, that is located in shopping centers, office buildings, large apartment complexes), data systems (circuit and packet), 1.5, 45, 120, and 564 megabit wideband systems, 2.2 gigabit facilities, access gateway systems (to voice, data, and video interconnect networks), and database systems will become the new information networks systems. Thus, the strategy of the strategies is to twist and turn the features or requirements to position them in these various systems. However, before this can take place effectively, we must further understand the game. See Fig. 12-16.

I³, shown in Fig. 12-16, is essentially an F³, but instead of determining what systems should provide what feature, it considers how we will offer what feature. Here, we address the future of the distribution firm (in its regulated and non regulated arenas per Inquiry III), the Telco marketing subsidiary or division, database information centers, and the customer provider equipment (CPE), such as intelligent terminals. For example, the future features to be provided in a data switch should be carefully understood in terms of providing them in the regulated distribution company, the nonregulated distribution company (with separate accounting procedures), the Telco subsidiary, or as CPE nodal switches. With future Inquiry III, IV, and V decisions on freedoms, for playing the game in the value added, information, and manufacturing world, the arena will become more of a public network versus private network business, requiring decisions such as: "What unit will provide what services and features for basic public transport?" In so doing we must also consider what the user needs and wants, today and tomorrow, as the marketplace develops for the extended features. This type of investigation should become an integral part of the equation that determines one's strategy of

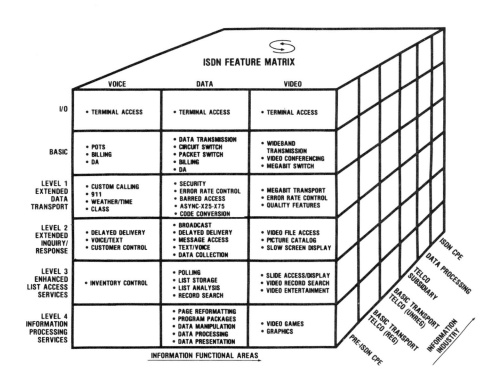

Fig. 12-16. Information Cubic — I₃

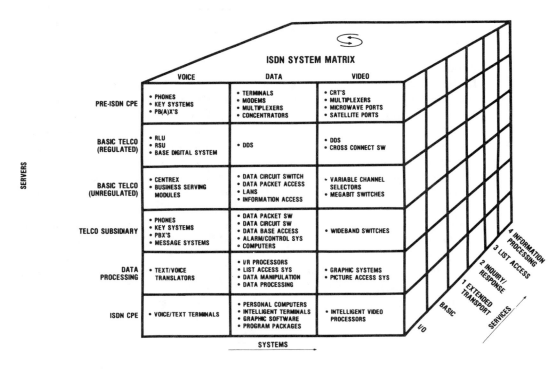

Fig. 12-17. Servers/Systems/Services — the S_3

the strategies, as we position our business of the business. Indeed it has become a four dimensional problem:

1. What functions (Voice, Data, Video).
2. What Level of features (IO, Basic, 1,2,3,4).
3. Provided by what system (Data, Wideband, Access . . .).
4. How, in what arena (Distribution Co., Subsidiary, Data Center . . .).

The two different third dimensions of the problem, noted in the I^3 and F^3 cubics, become the vertical and horizontal axis, in the S^3 cubic shown in Fig. 12-17, showing the servers; from Pre-ISDN CPE, through the Telcos, their subsidiaries, and data processing firms, to the ISDN CPEs of intelligent customer terminals and nodal point switches. The center horizontal axis displays new potential systems for voice, data, and video functional areas. The depth axis will now be the features, noted earlier, for each functional area in the I^3 and F^3 cubics.

It is this future world, in which the users, providers, and suppliers must play the new game under the challenging and changing rules and guidelines of the FCC and DOJ. It is the world where, if one wants to win, much must be totally understood in order to position one's firm in a specific area, with the right product, or the right service. This can best be demonstrated by again considering the "packet switch" for the "new data networks." For the collection arena it can be positioned as a public network first level switch in the unregulated Telco with separate accounting or in its fully market oriented advanced services subsidiary unit, as a specialized common unregulated network, or even as a shared private network offering, where it can interface to the "office of the future" internal networks of large businesses, shopping centers, and clusters of small businesses.

There it can provide an unlimited, continuously changing, enhancing, and expanding array of new features, that are not delayed through the waiver processes or limited by Inquiry III. However, it could also be a public data network second level switch, used as an access switch to the world. Here it could exist in the basic transport Telco in an unregulated portion of the firm, with separate accounting to ensure facilities and switches are not subsidized by the local voice plant, enabling direct interfaces from private local networks to more global data interexchange carriers.

Alternatively, it could be in the regulated portion of the Telco, enabling universal access by all, but with only a limited set of transport features, with additional features, perhaps, still provided on a waiver basis, tariffed or detariffed (depending on existing governmental restrictions, which come and go), or it could be the network entrance level switch of a special carrier. As noted, synchronous conversion pads can now exist in the basic Telco. Initially, they were marketed from the subsidiary, until later governmental decisions. Hence, the Access System may in actuality provide limited enhanced features, but will mainly provide basic transport to the new inter-connect interexchange international data networks to the world.

The S^3 cubic shows that not only for packet switches, but also for other numerous opportunities, the task is to map the right feature into the right system located in the right server. This is the "Masters Game" for the players of "the strategy of the strategies!"

—THE GOVERNMENT'S PLAYING FIELD—

Before Inquiry III, many constraints existed. We must understand them in order to see how changing governmental decisions have affected and will continue to affect our strategies. Basically the MFJ, Inquiry II, and the waivers established the following framework and structure for playing the game, supposedly, on a level playing field. The basic telecommunications network, as it moves voice information, can be subdivided into local communities of interest called LATAs (Local Access Telephone Areas). These communities can talk to the world through access vehicles called access switches. One or more must exist within each LATA. The world networks will be provided on an open competitive basis by interexchange interconnect companies (ICs), such as AT&T, MCI, and U.S. SPRINT, for long distance calls.

Initially, calls between communities of interest on a local basis must also be handled in a competitive arena by interLATA transmission firms. Subsequent to divestiture, the Telcos may be able to perform this interconnection. However, the calls within a community of interest (IntraLATA) no matter how big or small it may be (some LATAs cover an entire state; others cover only a single city) are within the boundaries and jurisdiction of the existing telecommunications provider (Telco) be it a Bell Operating Company or one of two thousand or so independent companies, the biggest of which is GTE. (Bell Operating Firms serve 87% of the phones; GTE 11%, and 1 - 2% are served by the remaining 1999 enterprises of which Continental and United are the largest.) With this division, local operators can handle local calls, and long distance operators in the interexchange firms can handle long distant calls. They may wish to contract among themselves about who really handles whom. Similarly, billing of calls within the LATAs are the business of the local telecommunications company. It may continue to do the billing for the interconnect firms, if they so desire on a contract basis. The yellow pages went with the local telephone companies, as long as they are not electronic. Thus, if the Telcos were to ask themselves "What are their products?", "What is their business of the business?" they may have identified it, as follows, on Jan. 1, 1984:

1. Local calling within a LATA for voice calls.
2. Directory assistance on local calls.
3. Billing for local calls.
4. Credit card local calls and operator assisted local calls.
5. Special services circuits for moving information on special tariffs (state regulated charges) for data information calls, on which the facilities utilize different modems, requiring different types of conditioning of lines and trunks to improve performance.
6. Via waivers, they could provide time of day, and weather information, as well as 911 information to local city emergency agencies, such as calling party, priority on calls to emergency center, and information on the caller (name, address and zone location information).
7. Yellow pages.
8. Access to interexchange carriers to the world for voice calls.
9. Access only to databases—no manipulation, look up, retrieval, storage, reformatting, or processing of information.
10. Centrex—a stand alone system to service many autonomous private internally switched networks of large and small business customers from either a CO or CU location (in a central office or out near the customer's premises but not on the customer's premises, until post Inquiry III).
11. Custom calling features for residences and small businesses (abbreviated dialing, call waiting, three way calling).

Before the 1986 correction, they were allowed to provide the following offerings in a separate subsidiary, where the people, buildings, resources were on an independent accounting basis.

The subsidiary or subsidiaries could:

1. Sell telephones directly to customers.
2. Provide PBXs directly to customers to develop their own internal net-

works, within their own premises. If they existed on the customer's premises, either party could own them.

3. Provide all forms of telecommunication systems, such as modems, concentrators, PBX voice switching systems, data circuit and packet switching systems, and video switching systems.
4. Sell mobile telephone terminals.
5. Provide specialized billing.
6. Perform joint ventures with data processing and other providers of new information services.
7. Provide an integrated total telecommunication solution to the customer, where they become, in effect, prime contractor and combine other firm's offerings, to obtain the right total solution for the prospective customer, but the selection of interexchange carrier was only to be performed by the customer. Similarly, information processing must be provided or selected by the customer.
8. Perform all necessary protocol conversations and value added services that anyone else was able to provide to move information. However, they could only access information, not store, search, manipulate, or process.
9. Design, structure, and implement private local area networks and switching arrangements for private customers on their facilities.
10. Provide a centrally located (not on Telco premises) common switch for handling multiple private networks.

This then established the boundary lines for the new playing field, a new set of rules, and identification of the type of players. However, as we noted earlier, the game was further defined and changed as it was being played. During the initial years, several major problems developed in which the Department of Justice's (DOJ) Judge Green made decisions concerning waivers requests from each Bell Operating Company (BOC) to provide this or that new service. The BOCs could not manufacture their own products, nor could they provide any enhanced new services without obtaining waivers. In fact, at one point the Judge was concerned that they would not offer weather, time, and 911 information and encouraged them to file waivers.

Various BOCs addressed the problem differently. Some attempted to obtain waivers for everything and play the game in the basic telephone company, the others attempted to establish functional subsidiaries for particular areas such as:

1. A firm to provide data switching.
2. A firm to provide mobile telephone.
3. A firm to provide PBXs.
4. A firm to sell terminals.
5. A firm to wire buildings.

However, the marketplace did not respond to the numerous single product firms having various unknown names. They wished to do business with a single known entity to establish their network. Unfortunately, this was not allowable for the basic Telco, which we will call the IDC (Information Distribution Company), and it lost many of its major customers. Waivers were requested for the basic telephone company (the ICD) in order for it to better distribute new types of information. Initially, it may be allowed to perform data switching as a new service, if it complied with a waiver request to identify how many potential customers would be charged what amount for what new services, before the game was even carefully considered. Hence this form of regulation was simply an academic exercise at the user's expense.

It was allowed to perform the necessary data X25 protocol conversion to X75 protocol in order to tie local data networks to national and international networks. However, it was initially restricted from performing asynchronous to X25 conversions to enable various types of terminals to easily connect to the network. (Various manufacturers, such as AT&T Information Systems and IBM would provide nodal point conversion systems for office buildings of terminals or whatever.) Subsequently, the IDC basic distribution firms were allowed to provide the conversion with separate central office systems (PADs), but were not allowed to market this capability, except through a marketing subsidiary, based on common circuit charges that it charged others.

The marketing subsidiaries that sold telephones were eventually allowed to sell other terminals, such as computers. So as the game was played, the Telcos were allowed to provide more products, but in actuality the removal of restrictions was a little late in coming. As pressure built up, as they lost more and more large customers, the Telcos repositioned themselves into several major entities. One entity, called an Information Distribution Firm, was to provide the major basic network complex, serving residential and business customers and providing access to the world.

A second entity was to market all forms of information services and products to the major medium and small businesses and affluent residential markets. It would become the main marketing wing of the company, where many of the small satellite units would collect under its wing. (See Newtel case study.) Of course exceptions initially existed, where the distribution network firm would enable specific interfaces to its centrex or transmission capabilities, because it must offer to all, what it offered to its marketing firm.

However, the marketplace would still determine the future, as new, more extensive products became available. For example, who would utilize a shared "voice only" system, if they could own a system which performed their financial budget calculations for them? Thus the marketplace desired versatile systems, or at least a network of systems, to meet their changing needs, with extended value-added "Integrated Services."

Technology is also facing a dilemma. The world is quickly moving to new expanding private voice, data, and video information systems. Now these can be provided by totally separate communication networks in terms of facilities and switches or they can become more and more publicly integrated. As we noted, we are in a time of change, where megabit switches can handle megabit traffic from fiber optic type facilities. Megabit traffic occurs when we combine all three forms of communications: voice, data, video. Hence, the emergence of a new network concept called Integrated Services Digital Networks (ISDN) was based upon eventually providing an integrated voice, data, and video offering, in which the user would have a single plug connection to the world, and obtain ubiquitous services everywhere. These factors (both market and technical) are inconsistent with the separated, value-added, waiver-ridden, nonuniversal network offerings view provided by Inquiry II.

The Government recognized this dilemma, as AT&T, Special Carriers, and Cable companies bypassed the Telco distribution companies, leaving fewer and fewer customers for a common public network. The small and medium businesses in remote areas would suffer, due to limited services, as would those who required basic telephone residential service, as their service prices would go up substantially, with less services ubiquitously available.

This dilemma was addressed over the years as Inquiry II decisions would give way to Inquiry III (see "A Level Playing Field"), until a fully competitive arena develops, as the marketplace for total information services matures per the Huber report. The section "Who's on First, What's on Second?" in Chapter 13 further analyzes this development, based upon key decisions.

—FEATURE FEATURES—

Let us take a hard look at the new world of features and consider their possibilities for specialized carriers, the Telco, the Telco's subsidiaries, private networks, the public data network and the new private/public data network providers. First we should consider the technical, marketing, and social observations made as a result of analyses, such as the one presented on "the new users." They were as follows:

Mark-Tech (Marketing and Technical) Observations

- New changing traffic patterns for data users and traditional voice will require phasing new networks and products every five years.
- Home computers must be able to interface with the outside world.
- Office of the future growth depends on friendly human-machine interface.
- Data networks should provide fast connect—medium speed, greater than normal volume attempts, and less than normal holding time.
- Initially extreme wideband users will require parallel separate networks.
- 9600 bit rate is optimum for first phase.
- 64K bit rate or multiples of it is optimum for 2nd phase.
- Extensive inquiry/response user types.
- Terminals must be switched.
- Retail stores are a key to increase in transaction and data collection user types.
- Extreme high volume multipoint transaction industries, such as banks, are key to packet networks.
- Block size, delay, and overhead is a major consideration for circuit versus packet, or fast packet versus burst data networks.

- Common access databases must be economically available to encourage user growth.
- Gateway switches to multiple networks must use standard interfaces.
- The business community will lead residential.
- Quality of life will improve, as we attain the information era, but we must ensure that instantaneous information does not harm society in terms of personal freedoms; causing the need for information access blockage, passes, audit trails and transfer security.

Hence, we see an initial need for a medium speed network for economically moving data at reasonable error rates, using fast connect systems, that can handle greater than normal volume of attempts, as the basic backbone requirements for new data networks. There have been families of packet data switches and circuit data switches developed to meet these needs, as well as an effort to integrate them into digital voice systems. However, at this point we should make some observations:

1. To be more successful, the new data networks should provide a full range of new data features.
2. To overlay data capabilities in present voice systems can drastically affect the throughput of voice systems, which were structured to handle voice and not data, especially complicating software structures and interfaces.
3. Access splitters should be autonomous from voice switching systems, so that the providers are able to obtain separate data systems from different vendors than voice systems or change outdated systems easily as traffic increases.
4. Functionalizing systems will enable better software/hardware design.

Data Features

Data networks will be developed over the 90s, as six major markets are developed. During this time there will be reconfigurations and new strategies, as the possibilities, problems, and advantages of various structures are reconsidered, as usage expands, by the following type providers:

1. A Telco public "data collector" network to enable residence, small business, satellites of large business, or medium size self contained residence or business complexes to interface locally with each other or with specialized databases with limited features.
2. A Telco public "data access" network to enable a resident, a small business, a small office complex, or a large business complex's local area network to access the new world of long distance data carriers, such as Telenet, and Tymnet.
3. A Telco unregulated subsidiary data collector network to enable financial, retail, wholesale, professional, and industrial groups to access numerous databases (sinks), with extended features.

406

4. Private network for medium to large businesses to enable local area networks with central switching to move internal data traffic.
5. National and international networks that provide second and third level hierarchical switching to move data to any world community of interest.
6. An overlay private network on the public data network for first and second level data switching, interfacing to the third level data international and national networks. Here the public data network enables numerous private networks to ride on it in a piggy back manner, where they remain autonomous from the rest of the data community except from those, with special access codes to interface to them. (In the same manner as public voice facilities and switches across the states handle large private voice networks for major businesses, such as IBM, General Electric and General Motors.)

These data networks will offer the features shown in Table 12-7 to transport information, as well as provide value, as they move information. This will enable the types of services shown in Table 12-8 to be offered. The networks that provide these features to enable new services, will have to consider the network parameters shown in Table 12-9. These parameters will have various operating values or range of values that are being determined throughout the world in CCITT working committees.

PBX Features

We must be aware that features are constantly changing and evolving. For example in the mid 70s, PBXs were developed with feature packages of twenty to fifty features by small groups of three to four designers. In the 80s, those same PBXs have nearly one hundred and sixty to two hundred features supported by groups of 30 to 60 application programmers. The new feature

Table 12-7. Data User Needs.

Broadcasting	Call back (Automatic)
Delayed delivery	Redirection of calls
Packet interleaving	Speed/format transforms
Byte interleaving	Multiple lines
Bit interleaving	Incoming calls barred
Code conversion CCITT codes	Abbreviated address call
Polling	Packet switching
Inquiry facility	Re-try by network
Three attempt limit	Store and forward
Low error rate	Short clear-down
Data collection service	Manual/automatic calling
High grade service	Manual/automatic answering
Standard interface	Data service classes
Data tariffs	Direct call
Access to lease lines	Network to subscriber interface
Duplex facility	Barred access
Bit sequence independence	Remote terminal identification
Short set-up	Multi-address call

Table 12-8. Service Applications.

Service applications	Peak bit rates Kb/sec
Energy management	.3
Slow facsimile	1.2
Low speed data entry	1.2
High speed data entry	9.6
Home information systems	9.6
Communicating home computer	9.6
Remote job entry	9.6
Inquiry response	9.6
Point of sale verification	9.6
Audio/graphics conference	9.6
Fast facsimile	32/64
Electronic mail	64
Communicating word processors	64
Integrated work stations	64
Electronic filing system	64
Timesharing	64
Batch processing	64
Communicating minicomputers	64
Computer interactions	64
Voice communications	64
Compressed video	1.544 Mb/sec
Mainframe interactions	1.544 Mb/sec
Variable graphic-video	64K to 90 Mb sec

"physically distributed" PBXs will completely redefine the PBX architecture. Table 12-10 shows an example of PBX voice transport features to demonstrate the amount of past change.

Voice/Data/Video Features

Over the next fifteen years, we will see an integration of features, where for example, a voice command will trigger a data message to be generated, or a data text message will be translated to voice. A data message will be able to change a display system, during a voice conversation, so that both parties can interactively change a text image that they are both seeing and discussing. Similarly, a video file may be displayed during a voice conversa-

Table 12-9. Data Network Parameters.

Transfer time	Format structure
Rate structure	Network synchronization
Route selection	Data call processing modes
Network interface	Transmission limitations
Speed conversion	Network signalling
Class of user services	Call clear-down time
Category of error rates	Call request time
Type of network switching	Numbering plan
Overall grade of service	Inquiry handling
Overall quality of service	Usage recording

Table 12-10. Basic PBX Features and Services.

Alphanumeric display for attendant position
Attendant camp-on
Attendant CCSA access
Attendant console (maximum 2)
Attendant control of trunk group access
Attendant controlled conference
Attendant flash over trunks
Attendant lockout
Attendant position (2 max.)
Attendant transfer—all calls
Automatic callback busy/don't answer (station to station calls)
Automatic callback—busy (station to trunk)
Automatic night service switching
Automatic queuing to attendant position
Broker's call
Busy lamp field
Busy verification of station lines
Call forwarding—all calls
Call forwarding—busy and don't answer
Call forwarding—busy line (DID)
Call forwarding—don't answer (DID)
Call hold
Call pick-up
Call waiting service
　Attendant call waiting
　Terminating call waiting
　Distinctive tone signals
Calling number display to attendant
Calls waiting indication at attendant position
CCSA access
Class of service display to attendant
Code calling access
Code restriction
Conference calling
Contact monitor
Controlled outward restriction
Controlled station-to-station restriction
Controlled termination restriction
Controlled total restriction
Data restriction
Date display on console(s)
Diagnostics—automatic
Dial access to attendant
Digital clock on attendant position
Direct department calling (DDC)
Direct inward dialing (DID)
Direct outward dialing (DOD)
Direct termination of miscellane-

ous circuits on attendant position (paging)
Direct trunk group selection (DTGS)
Directed call pick-up
　Hold-for-pick-up option
Distinctive ringing
DTMF and/or DCKP on attendant position
DTMF calling
DTMF to dial pulse conversion
Dump and load of customer data
Executive override
Flash for attendant
Flexible numbering of stations
Foreign exchange (FX) access
Fully restricted station
Identified trunk group
Immediate audible ring on attendant handled calls
Immediate ring
Incoming call identification (ICI)
Indication of camp-on
Intercept treatment
　Attendant intercept
　Intercept tone
Interposition calling
Interposition transfer
Inward restriction
Line lockout with warning
Listed direction number (LDN) service
Loudspeaker paging
　Direct access by attendant
　Dial access
　Multizone
　Priority paging
Main/satellite service
Manual originating line service
Message waiting (audible)
Message waiting (lamp)
Miscellaneous trunk restriction
Multiple listed directory numbers (LDN)
Multiple access codes for a single trunk group (10 max.)
Music on hold
Music on attendant position hold
Night console position
Night service
　Fixed
　Flexible
Night station service—fixed service
Night station service—full service
Origination restriction
Outgoing trunk call back
Outgoing trunk camp-on
Outgoing trunk queueing

Outward restriction
Power failure transfer—station
Priority queue
Privacy and lockout
Radio paging access
Recall dial tone
Recorded telephone dictation access
Remote access to PBX services
Remote administration and maintenance (hardware option)
Re-ring from toll (on toll terminal)
Reserve power (hardware option)
Room audit
Room status
Rotary dial calling
Route advance
Serial call
Sharing (4 tenant)
Shared attendant service
Single digit dialing (non-conflicting)
Single digit dialing (conflicting)
Speed call
Splitting
　One-way manual splitting
　Two-way manual splitting
　One-way automatic splitting
　Two-way automatic splitting
Station hunting
　Terminal hunting
　Circular hunting
　Secretarial hunting
Station message detail recording
Station message register service
　Electronic storage and display
　Internal charging
Station override security
Station-to-station calling
Straightforward outward completion
Switched loop operation
Tandem tie trunk switching
Termination restriction
Threeway conference transfer
Through dialing
Tie trunk access
Timed reminders
Toll restriction
　Battery reversal
　0/1 access
　Multi digit
Toll terminal access
Total "do not distrub" display
Total "message waiting" display
Total "room status" display
Traffic data collection
Traffic display to customer
Transfer into busy

Table 12-10 continued.

Trunk answer any station	Trunk-to-trunk connect	Wake-up service
Trunk group busy indicators on attendant position	Trunk verification by station	WATTS access
Trunk status Field	Uniform call distribution	

tion. This interconnecting and interlacing of voice with text and with video will offer a new world of requirements for simultaneous parallel network operations, but this does not necessarily initially require fully "integrated switches," but more fully "integrated facilities." See "When is a Switch not a Switch."

Hence, the game becomes extremely interesting and exciting, as the ISDN feature matrix of I^3 is mapped on possible system products indicated in S^3 (see the case study on information cubics), especially as regulatory considerations that greatly affect where the game can be played, change. It is interesting to allow one's mind to wander over the ISDN feature matrix shown in Table 12-11 and consider one's "strategy of strategies" on where and how you would wish to play the game.

—ISDN REQUIREMENTS AND QUESTIONS—

The top down planning for ISDN networks in the previous case study "The Network of the Future" described a possible network evolution from an ana-

Table 12-11. ISDN Feature Matrix.

	Voice	Data	Video
I/O	Terminal access	Terminal access	Terminal access
Basic	Pots Billing DA	Data transmission Circuit switch Packet switch Billing DA	Wideband transmission Video conferencing Megabit switch
Level 1 extended data transport	Custom calling 911 Weather/time Class	Security Error rate control Barred access Async-X25-X75 Code conversion	Megabit transport Error rate control Quality features
Level 2 extended inquiry/ response	Delayed delivery Voice/text Customer control	Broadcast Delayed delivery Message access Text/voice Data collection	Video file access Picture catalog Slow screen display
Level 3 enhanced list access services	Inventory control	Polling List storage List analysis Record search	Slide access/display Video record search Video entertainment
Level 4 information processing services		Page reformatting Program packages Data manipulation Data processing Data presentation	Video games Graphics

log voice network to one providing integrated services. The network is made possible by rapid advances in electronic technology (especially in integrated circuits and fiber optics). However, the successful realization of the concept will only be achieved by those suppliers that fit systems and services to the requirements of the network's users. With the introduction of digital switching comes the concept of distributed switching and control; first in the form of remote switching terminals and then ultimately in the customer terminal itself. These changing network structures can only be justified on economic grounds, by providing traditional services at lower cost, and by providing new services not now practical. Thus, new markets are created. The perceived value a user will have for these new services is not obvious. It is clear that many questions remain to be answered before a viable marketing strategy emerges.

We have seen that ISDN is a comprehensive information network for the future, which will make powerful new information services available at dramatically reduced costs. Driven by user demands and fueled by technology, the path to the ultimate integration of all information processing and delivery in the year 2010+ will be an evolutionary one. Such an evolution will be plausible, when logical mechanisms for change economically determine the stages of development. This has been described as a sequence of phases, each providing further and more comprehensive integration of information services to an everwidening audience of users.

In order to be certain of providing "Future Safe" designs for ISDN, the network view must be supported by detailed analyses of all aspects of information use and delivery. These detailed analyses are identified by a sequence of issues and questions that require investigation. They are divided into five major areas: systems, transmission, switching, terminals, and marketing. The issues and questions of these areas overlap and are sometimes redundant, but all express the network problems from different facets, that enable us to obtain a more complete picture of its complexity.

The following are some of the issues and questions that have been addressed in the 80s. They require an answer in the requirements definition phase, before proceeding to the product definition phase, for specific products for the future integrated services networks.

Questions and Issues

- Who are the users? What are their characteristics? How many users are there? Where are they located? What services do the users want? How much will they pay? Do users really need simultaneous voice and data service? Why? What type? How? What does "integrated" really mean to them?
- What are the new services? When can the services be available? How big does the market have to be to justify each service? How much does it cost to provide each service? Does the cost match the user's perceived value?
- Who provides the services? Will the Telco only be allowed to provide the local communications path? How will the Telco be in the service business? To what extent? As cable and other carriers provide local communication paths, what happens to the LATA concept? Will regulation reappear?

- What needs are going to control the network evolution? How are existing services supported? What is the impact on current value-added networks? What should Inquiry IV allow in terms of information processing, access, search manipulation etc? After Justice's Huber recommendation free BOCs then what?

Network Evolution and Requirements
- How will ISDN phase one overlays and ISDN phase two wideband evolve and what new products and services will be offered differently . . . in each phase?
- How will the public versus private, and voice versus data versus video issues of maintenance and administration services of the network evolve? Will they continue to be centralized, and if so, how?
- What open network architecture standards are required for the network and constituent parts? Who will lead the standard setting bodies (FCC, EIA, CCITT, CEPT, TI, IEEE, ANSI, USITA, REA, BELLCORE, TELCO, OSI,IBM, DEC, WANG . . . etc.)? How will the U.S. ISDN be different from the world ISDN?
- How and where will information be processed in the network? Where is transparent information transmission and delivery required?
- Will network facilities and services be designed to meet European, as well as North American requirements? If so, at what cost?
- What are the synchronization requirements of the network and how are they related to the voice requirements? What are the permissible error rates, end to end, for voice and data calls? What about reliability of data networks?
- Within the network, is voice and data integrated? If so, at what stage (subset, facility, switch level, etc.)? Do they really need to be?
- Will low speed data streams be sub-rate multiplexed for transmission through the network? If so, how will this be accomplished and how will the multiplexing control information be sent to the demultiplexing points, especially on new integrated wideband transport/switch structures?
- What are the data rates within the system? How will wideband data be handled? What role will fiber optics, that can handle many wavelengths, play in the evolution of the network?
- How will the existing copper analog facilities be integrated into the network, until replaced by digital fiber?
- How will private networks coexist and integrate with the public network?
- How will Huber's Geodesic Network be achieved?
- How will secure communications be implemented? Where will encryption/decryption be performed? Audits? Access codes . . .?
- When and where will we need fast packet and burst switches?
- How much customer control is really needed?
- What about a "feature switch" separate from the network? How much should it really interrupt call processing? To what extent should its "feeder switches" be dumb? IN2?

Switching and Transmission Requirements
- What are the advantages and disadvantages of packet, circuit, fast packet,

and burst switching? What impact will the chosen techniques have on the future evolution of the network?

- Will there be separate data and voice switching and transmission systems?
- What new measurement and occupancy requirements are needed for an integrated network?
- What will the security block requirements be for data and integrated voice/data systems? Will the voice system security block requirements change? How intelligent must the home terminal be and still be inexpensive enough to encourage mass purchasing?

User Service Demands

- How will the integrated terminals of the future evolve? Will the terminals in the home be offshoots of the terminals in the "office of the future," or will they evolve due to different requirements?
- What services will be required and when? How much will the user be prepared to pay for these additional services?
- Due to high cost of personal computers, will mass users want cheap terminals that interface with network centralized time shared programs?

Traffic

- To what extent (degree) shall services be integrated in the digital switch of today; without mixing of traffic and merely sharing the same equipment, or with traffic mixing and complete functional integration?
- To what extent will traffic integration of different services affect the grade-of-service in the digital switch?
- If integration of services in a digital switch of today is not acceptable, may an adjunct switch be used for data, in series, with a nailed-through connection through the switch, or in parallel with the switch? Does the decision depend on the size/traffic of the switch, or on the data switch? What is the role of the incoming access automated main frame switch?

Switches

- In the case where an adjunct data switch is used in parallel with the switch, shall voice and non-voice data be split at the switch, at the remote switch unit (RSU), at the remote line unit (RLU), access nodes or elsewhere?
- Shall future digital switches be designed to accommodate all types of data services in an essentially non-blocking manner? Must the network always be up with highest reliability and redundancy? Should growth be by new modules or new switching systems?
- What type of digital switch is preferable—a channel switch, circuit switch, packet switch, fast circuit switch, or burst packet switch (adjunct switch)? See "What is a Switch and A Look at Technology."
- What future features, both voice and data, will cause programs to change? How is the software affected?
- Determining stimulus versus functional terminal—network information ex-

change requires understanding how intelligent both areas will become . . . Where? When? Simultaneously?

- Will future light switches work in higher number systems, instead of binary? Modulo N number base? When will new languages be developed to support this? When will light-to-light logical decisions be made? When will traffic be at the level requiring this expanded level of technology? Will photonic switching just be used to switch fibers till the middle of the twenty first century?

Integrated Service Switching

Telecommunication switching for the various forms of information services has developed along different lines. For digital telephones, a synchronous, circuit-switched network has been adopted. For most other forms of data communications, synchronous, store and forward, or computer-based message/packet switched networks have been adopted. In the past, various types of switching equipment have been developed and optimized for their intended applications. Reviewing past developments, the extraordinary advances in digital switching technology demonstrate that the existing communication networks will eventually be combined into a single, Integrated Service Digital Network (ISDN). It is visualized that the ultimate ISDN will accommodate all forms of data services. There is a need to complement existing plant, practices, regulatory issues, etc., as they change over the future time frame. Switching systems are anticipated to go through a three phase evolution from current adjunct voice and data systems to fully integrated wideband future systems, to super wideband. The studies in this network area must take these phases into account.

The digital voice switches can handle non-voice data on a circuit switched basis, but not in an optimal manner. It appears that the bandwidth/channel utilization will be inefficient; the processing times may be excessively long; the software program must differentiate traffic to handle voice or data, etc. Thus, important questions arise, relating to integrated service switching, and must be addressed.

Today each communication network employs its unique signaling system/protocol to affect communication between its users/terminals. Some signaling systems are compatible, while others are totally incompatible. In order to achieve any degree of integration of service in a network, agreement must be reached between the users/terminals on the network, as to the choice of the signaling system/protocol, as well as the network itself being or not being transparent to their choice of the signaling system/protocol. Likewise, agreements on interfaces and standards for system parameters have to be reached, such as X25, BX25, CCITT #7, extended #7, D channel protocol, faster D rates, X75 and X75M . . .

Terminals

There are a number of issues, problems, and questions which must be

414

resolved with respect to the terminals, that will be used in the local ISDN. Since the functions of the terminal equipment (used here to include both voice and data equipment) are determined, as noted earlier, by user needs, many of the areas to be studied are market and/or product definition oriented, rather than technical. The issues are broken down into five areas: General issues related to all terminals, basic telephone devices, voice plus data devices, higher speed data terminals (64 k + b/s service), and wideband (1.5 M + b/s) terminals.

General Issues

- When will it be ubiquitously possible to achieve an ISDN 2B + D type standard "Basic" "T" interface for all types of terminals via network terminal interface (NT) and terminal adapters (TA)? Will this interface be different in North American and European markets?
- What data rate should be available for what uses in the subscriber loop? How should n x 64 = k bits be used between the terminal and the switch?— "U" "Primary" Interface.
- What protocol should be used between terminal and switch considering technical aspects and human factors for various degrees of stimulus and functional signalling? (This relates to call initiation, termination and ringing, concerns for both voice and data services.)
- What portion of the terminal's facilities must be independent of local power? What techniques can be used to accomplish this?
- What sort of maintenance strategy should be employed? (Self test capabilities, tests from central office.)
- How should regulations concerning CPE premise location equipment ownership affect the network structure requirements for adding new features and automating tests from a central base? Especially after Inquiry III changes on NCTE and ownership requirements.
- Who is responsible for security functions? Is security necessary for voice? What technique should be used? How close to the user? What international access codes or tokens shown be used?

Basic Telephone Devices

- What are the minimum features required in the basic residential voice terminal? Will it be on a cheaper non enhanced copper network with business on another?
- Will rate increases be permitted based on the improved transmission quality of the digital subscriber loop and voice terminal? To what degree? Will there be two networks one basic copper and the other enhanced digital full service?
- Is it necessary to have multiple parallel connected voice and data terminals? How many . . . three? What techniques could be used to provide the "extension phone" function?
- How can the "human engineering" of the voice terminal be improved with the digital subset?

- To what degree should phones talk to the user?
- What will the terminal of 2010 + be?

Voice Plus Data Terminals

- What combinations of features and services are desirable in the home and business environments?
- What data rates are required for the various services and features?
- Is simultaneous voice and data transmission really required; and to the same or different terminals? When?
- Should data transmission be transparent to the user?
- To what degree should the voice terminal and data terminal be physically integrated? For ISDN 2B + D, where (D = 16K), 23B + D where (D = 64K)? What sort of data port should the terminal provide? How do we optimize the human factors in an integrated voice/data device?
- Will there be levels of services and transparencies based on price?

High Speed Data Terminals

- What data rates are required? 23B + D? N(23B + D)? When? Where?
- Who should perform code, speed, and terminal-to-terminal protocol conversions (the user or the network)? Where? For what price?
- What degree of network control should the user have?
- Where should page reformatting be performed?

Wideband Terminals

- How and where will video conferencing be used?
- What bandwidth is required for acceptable picturephone service 56k,1.5M,45M,140M, . . .? At what price . . .?
- How and when will entertainment TV and stereo be introduced? How will it tie into the data capabilities of the digital subscriber loop? HDTV?
- What services other than video and audio can be offered on a wideband network? What type of terminal equipment do they require?
- What about variable bandwidth for a video transmission from 64K to 140 megabits?
- Will the future users require variable channel selectors to allow many terminals in the office or home contend for bandwidth?
- How will it be priced to encourage growth?

See "A Look at Technology" and "A Look at the Marketplace," in the reference section, Part Four.

—REQUIREMENTS DEFINITION PHASE METHODOLOGY—

Each phase could be defined to a detailed "How to" level, and used as a check list for activities, tasks, and decisions. Realizing that this is not necessary for every phase, these details are defined here for this particularly important phase to demonstrate how to understand user needs and translate them into the right solutions. As systems became more and more complex, there is the need to aggressively pursue, understand and define requirements, to obtain strategy decisions by early management involvement and commitment. This analysis will further demonstrate, how a history log of changing requirements, conclusions and decisions could be developed to track the project progress for later review by using a decision support system.

During this analysis we will see when and how technology specialists interface with marketing research to better understand the user's specific needs. *Together* they will be better able to define the detailed requirements and specifications by clearly identifying the features, products, and services that are needed by the new users. Further feasibility tests, new studies and measurements may be required to support the requirements. The resulting requirement specification report will contain both marketing and technical conclusions, that can support each other when reviewed together, obtaining quicker approval by management.

Task Procedures

The flowchart in Fig. 12-18 shows the various paths that move the analysis through the requirements strategy—specification steps. Each task step may be performed or omitted, as shown, depending on the complexities of the issues being addressed. The net result will be a clear requirement, strategy defining the status, needs, and basic preliminary requirements, which are further defined in a detailed requirements specification, which may subsequently be revised and modified to further refine the requirements per review decisions.

Requirement Definition Phase Tasks

Task 1: Determine Status

- Perform baseline measurement, compare to existing and planned networks, products, and services available in industry.
- Review mission and objectives in light of financial situation, capabilities, current problems and deficiencies.
- Identify limits and dependencies, based upon early warning systems, reviews, audits and benefits received from previous endeavors.
- Conclude analysis with a status analysis.

Task 2: Identify Needs

- Perform market research to identify user needs per specific types.
- Based upon status, analyze impact on each major endeavor.
- Perform measurements, if necessary, of sensitive systems to clarify current capabilities.
- Project needs for future networks, products, services using market research and technology research activities.

417

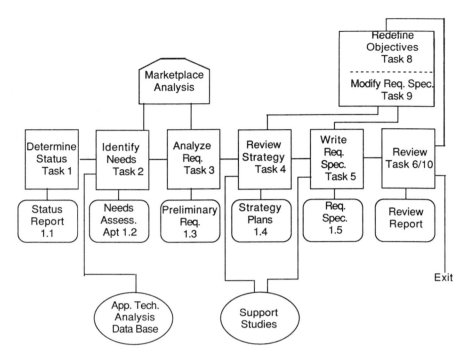

Fig. 12-18. Requirement Phase Tasks.

- Determine time-frame for utilization of systems' features.
- Identify priority and economic limits of projected needs.
- Identify additional or new studies for marketing and technology.
- Identify needs based upon these considerations.

Task 3: Analyze Preliminary Requirements

- Review the status report, needs report, and market and technology measurements studies.
- Provide an initial list of requirements.
- Analyze list in terms of real needs that can be economically justified.
- Structure list in terms of mandatory, necessary and desirable.
- Phase and place a priority on the items noting limits, risks and areas of cross usage.
- Recommend feasibility tests, where necessary.
- Review "requirements" with potential "users."
- Finalize with a preliminary requirement analysis.

Task 4: Strategy Analysis

- Review status, needs and preliminary requirements' reports with management.

- Request if necessary more information from market research or a technology feasibility analysis.
- Establish a logical strategy between involved players and management.

Task 5: Write Requirements Specification

- Utilize preliminary requirements report and strategy report.
- Determine specific features' requirements based upon new available feasibility data from market and technology research.
- Resolve trade off decisions, as much as possible, or identify alternatives for consideration in product definition phases.
- Review requirements with potential users.
- Modify existing specifications, as required in the review phase (Task 6), and redefined objectives (Task 8); via the modification analysis (Task 9).

Task 6: Review

- Perform review of the requirements specification.
- Base exit criteria on ability to meet identified needs.
- Approve, hold or terminate report, redefine objectives, or return to areas needed for modification (Task 9).

Task Descriptions

Status Analysis Task

To perform this task, a requirements definition team is established. Their analysis can be performed for numerous reasons, such as conceptual planning proposal, baseline flag, early warning system flag, review or audit of a particular project or program, change of a competitor's product, project or program, leading indicator flag, project tracking flag, request for assistance, new market research data, or major technology change.

A status report is completed during this analysis, even if this task has in effect been performed during a proceeding audit or review. It is important to understand the current status in terms of: entrance reason, baseline status analysis, leading indicator status analysis, asset inventory status analysis, applicable market and technology research studies conclusions, objectives, assessment, schedule, resources, limits, and features.

Needs Analysis Task

During this task a clear concise picture of the needs is determined. It is important to focus on the specific needs that further analysis will attempt to resolve. Many times we do not necessarily address the most important need(s), but later must suspend efforts and retrack. Too often, we solve the wrong problem or meet the wrong need.

Preliminary Requirements Task

There is a fine distinction between requirements and needs, which is best

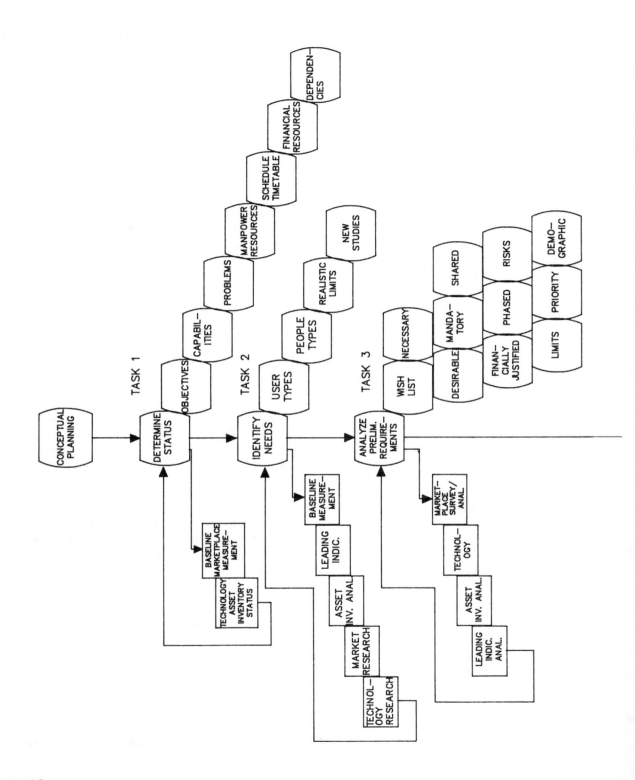

420

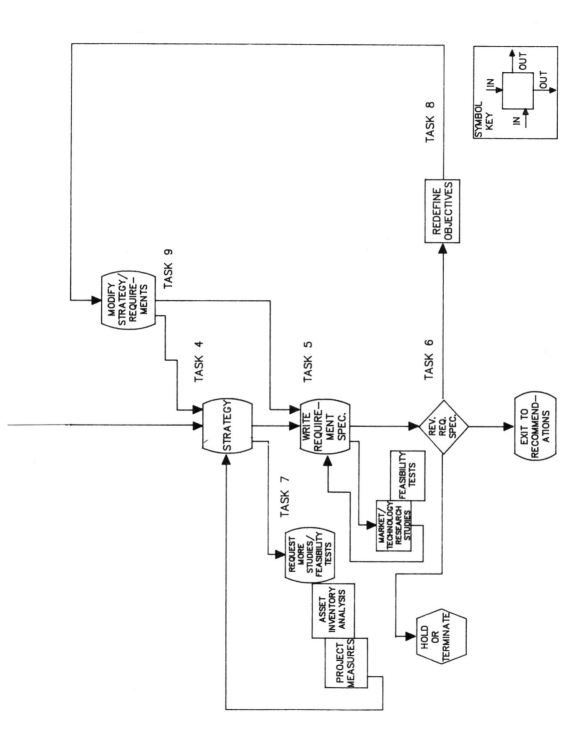

Fig. 12-19. Requirements Analysis Tasks.

421

understood by the word "commitment." The purpose of this task is to further analyze the needs in terms of this emphasis, as well as to clarify them. For example, the extent and degree of the requirements will be analyzed to establish realistic limits before going to the strategy task.

Furthermore, needs for use in several different products may help collectively to extend a requirement's cost limit on resource expenditures. Hence, these trade-off considerations should, if possible, be identified, before entering the strategy analysis task. Once strategy direction is established, the requirements can be further analyzed and resolved.

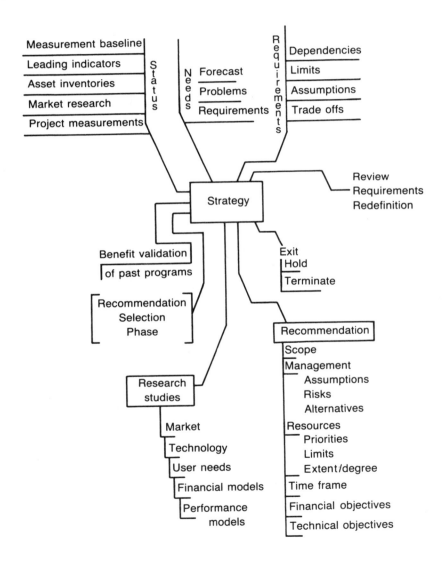

Fig. 12-20. Requirements Strategy.

The "preliminary requirements" analysis will summarize these considerations and recommendations for the strategy analysis. Even if the recommendation is to delay or terminate the phase, exit will be made to the strategy task for the decision. There, other overriding management strategies may determine different limits and resource trade-offs. This analysis will indicate the assumptions, limits and trade-off decisions considered in arriving at the recommended requirements. It must indicate all the needs and their cross need dependencies in order to fully show the scope of the need.

Strategy Analysis Task

Depending on the complexity of the requirement analysis and how much interaction and support the study teams require, this task may be combined with the review, but works best, as a separate task before defining the detailed requirements specification. As can be seen from the more detailed figure, this step is extremely critical. It can become a major decision point in the process, crucial to success. This, along with the review task, prepare management for the final product definition phase review. They form the planning apex, where previous studies, audits, and analyses come to a conclusion and new direction is established. These are the points where all aspects and facets of the financial, technical, and policy issues must be coalesced into a reasonable, logical, and economical strategy. Hence, responsible management must participate here to the extent necessary to ensure management's objectives can indeed be achieved and to set clear direction. Otherwise the next steps and phases will be performed in the atmosphere of uncertainty of management's position and commitment. This may cause understaffing and misdirection. Strategy will be determined by reviewing the conclusions from the status, needs, and requirements (preliminary) tasks, as well as, analyzing past programs benefits. This will result in one of three courses of action:

1. Exit, hold, terminate
2. Request for supporting studies, such as market, technology, user needs, financial models, performance models
3. Recommendation: scope, assumptions, risks, alternatives, priorities, limits, extent/degree, time frame objectives, financial objectives, technical objectives, and concerns.

Conclusions are noted on a summary report with supporting management references attached. These may include internal memo's or minutes to strategy meetings, as well as any letters requesting additional studies and the results of these studies.

This strategy will be revised at least two more times. At each instance, a new summary report should be completed. It should reference the others with cross reference dates. This provides a management history record of the strategy proceedings.

Requirement Specification Task

The requirements' specification task analysis consists of four major loops,

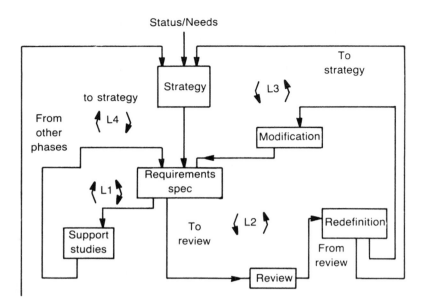

Fig. 12-21. Requirements Analyses Loops.

as shown in the accompanying figure, until the requirements are completed and accepted. One is through the support studies to provide further data analysis and insights needed to define the requirements. The second is via the review step, from which requirement areas are redefined. The third is via the review—strategy redefinition cycle to redirect efforts or reestablished objectives and direction. These changes will result in new requirements. The fourth is from other phases such as the verification, recommendation or selection phases, which may require new strategy considerations, that affect specific requirements. (This, of course, is the least desirable due to loss of time and expenditure of resources. However, if necessary, it is important to force a return to the requirements phase, where strategy and requirements can be reanalyzed correctly, not in an improper environment.) When the requirements are finalized, and approved they will be released for the product definition phase.

Requirement Specification

A report form should be used together with the detailed requirements specifications. It may be necessary to use the form several times before obtaining a successful review. At each point the specification should be attached with any new changes, comments, conclusions, etc. Thus if a particular support study is requested, it should be noted with the responding study's conclusions and attached report. Similarly, if redefinition of direction is established, a report is attached and summarized. Alternatively, if requirement modifications are needed, these are noted in the attached report and

424

subsequent changes in the requirements should be made in the specification and reflected in the Table of Contents and Executive Summary.

Review Task

The purpose of the review is to ensure that management, marketing, and technical personnel had an opportunity to consider the requirements specification from all angles. The strategy objectives should be met, as well as the market and technical limits. A report form should be used to summarize the decisions and provide an accompanying report. The form should note the following information: "go" reasons, concerns, limits, observations, and conclusions; "no-go" reasons, concerns, limits, observations, and conclusions; redefinition recommendation reasons, concerns, program objectives, and limits; and finally exit criteria, including concurrence statement, and signatures.

Technology Studies, Market Studies

Appropriate Research Labs may be requested to perform supporting analysis to help resolve, clarify, or establish various performance, structure, economic, test, or support requirements, as well as provide a tentative feasibility product architecture and structure. Further market and user studies may also be requested. These studies may be performed in parallel to the requirements specification or the requirement analysis may wait for their results. The study reports are attached to requirement specification in order to ensure that the information is not lost for later reference. Note that the product definition phase may begin before the requirement phase is concluded to provide more extensive supporting architectures and structures, than feasibility studies.

Redirection/Definition (Subtask)

All major problems, concerns, inconsistencies, inefficiencies, unresolved, unclear, uneconomical, unrealistic, unachievable, unlimited, unfeasible, impractical requirements should be identified as early as possible. The purpose of the review is not only to perform a "go, no-go" function, but to detect these issues and cause reanalysis loops to be activated. The final strategy should note new needs, modifications, and redirections.

Modification (Subtask)

Requirements that are to be modified or new requirements to be added are specifically identified before revisiting the requirement specification task.

Requirements Report Forms

A single page form per task such as in Fig. 12-22. In this manner, a history log is maintained to track the history of evolving requirements. These forms become a part of the program history log (even if the attached referenced reports are not kept active).

UNIT NAME: _____

PROJECT NAME: _____

PROGRAM NAME: _____

REFERENCES: _____

UNIT
STRATEGY
REPORT
FORM   1.4

CODE #: _____

DATE: _____

UNIT REP: _____

PROJECT REP: _____

UNIT
SUPPORT
TEAM: _____

UNIT STRATEGY   SUMMARY

[RECOMMENDATION _____

SCOPE _____

MANAGEMENT _____

ASSUMPTIONS _____

RISKS _____

ALTERNATIVES _____

RESOURCES _____

PRIORITIES _____

LIMITS _____

TIMEFRAME OBJECTIVES _____

FINANCIAL _____

TECHNICAL _____

CONCERNS] _____

MANAGEMENT TEAM: _____

MANAGEMENT
REFERENCES _____

EXIT _____

HOLD: _____

TERMINATE: _____

REQUEST FOR SUPPORTING STUDIES/CONCLUSION

MARKET _____

TECHNOLOGY _____

USER NEEDS _____

FINANCIAL _____

PERFORMANCE _____

Fig. 12-22. Task Review Reports.

Summary

All the forms of the requirements specification phase "package" the analysis and conclusions reached in the process of achieving satisfactory requirements. These are available later, if the phase is re-entered from the conceptual planning, or product definition phases, or where results are revisited in the benefits verification phases.

During this phase:

- Needs research, base line measurements, and asset inventory analysis play a major role in determining user's status and needs.
- Leading indicators will help management establish a more "realistic effective" strategy.
- Strategy will be a key controlling directive to scope the requirements and benefit objectives.
- Requirements will be more consistent with management goals, because of early management strategy involvement.
- The review process can identify inconsistencies between the requirements and strategy.
- The review can achieve early hold or terminate decisions (due to a clearer understanding of needs, strategy and requirements), before prematurely launching programs, or even performing on extensive product definition phase.
- Management involvement and interface points are identified in this process, where the strategy and the review become logical common management participation points, while the other tasks are logical team participation points.
- Exit to the next phase reflects a management acceptance and a "second look commitment" to the program, if it meets strategy objectives.
- The forms will provide an excellent history log of management considerations and decisions, for the product definition commitment review with top management.

—THE TRILLION BILLION DOLLAR DECISION—

Figure 12-23 is an example of a series of multimillion dollar decisions, some of which were incorrectly made, resulting in a very expensive trillion billion dollar "technical" decision. Now history has a chance to repeat itself with a second trillion billion dollar "marketing" decision. Let us pause for a moment to review the first and learn from it, in order to better address the second.

The First Trillion Billion Dollar Decision

In going from step by step or crossbar switching systems to stored program control, the eastern and midwestern telecommunication field was greatly lagging behind the military/aerospace west coast industries. In 1963, west coast firms were putting their money on distributed control missile weapon

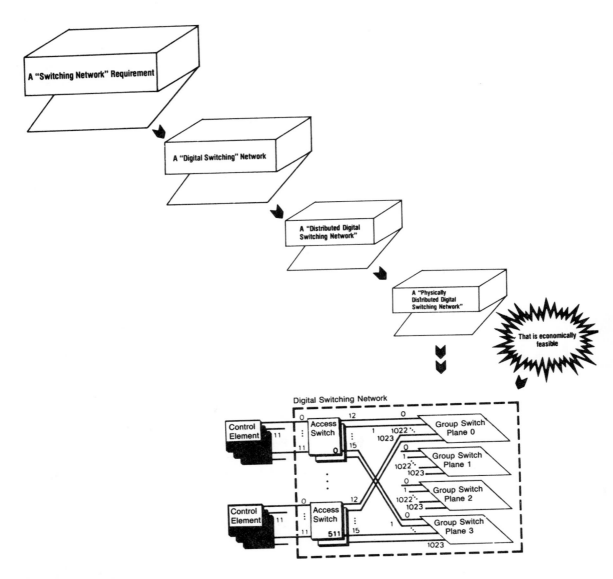

Fig. 12-23. The Expensive Requirement.

systems, based upon new micro integrated circuit technology. Bays and bays of systems were being reduced to drawers, containing multiple processors, using sophisticated software control programs, remotely working under layers of centralized control systems. At that time telecommunication systems used germanium or silicon transistors, with 50% of the work performed by wired logic (not software computers). These were then replaced by internally designed special purpose processors, requiring special languages, whose software was designed by non programmers.

There was an extensive learning curve, as stand alone telecommunication systems, though more reliable, tracked similar problems previously encountered by stand alone large main frame commercial computer systems. Little knowledge was gained or wanted from the leading edge military—aerospace systems. Since, as noted earlier, the systems were only designed for the Telco, not the Telco's customers, feature packages were mainly to interface with existing electro mechanical systems, various transmission systems, or to enable the systems to be non attended. Extensive reliability requirements required the design to be exercised by numerous internal maintenance sanity check programs to ensure its integrity. Using the mentality of following the cow paths to make roads, systems were only designed to replace the previous electro mechanical systems (small, medium, or large) on a one to one basis. (Even in 1985 a small central office was replaced at a cost of 400,000 for only 400 lines.)

Much discussion centered around, how large was large, because of concerns such as: The building could be bombed, affecting too large a customer base; or the vault in the basement of offices could handle limited amounts of lines and trunks. Systems never reached their models' projections, because electronic systems were really "attempt limited" on how many calls they could effectively handle, especially as the call mix (the type of calls) changed, requiring additional specialized work by the systems.

Little consideration was given to new features for the customer. Eventually a series of non user friendly customer calling features were offered, of which, only two had limited success. Call waiting did not even tell the caller, with a different ring, that the called party was indeed busy—forcing that party to interrupt his or her conversation in the fear that the person calling would be unaware that there was someone at home. Note the "Else condition" action—the type of ring; not very friendly from a user needs and requirements point of view!

The suppliers first provided a family of analogue stand alone software controlled systems, but resisted moving to the integrated circuit technology until the late 60s, early 70s. Then they moved to the integrated circuit technology with more extensive software control and scanning techniques, but still analog, resisting the new digital technology. Next, the systems did become digital, but were still stand alone with only remote line unit concentrators, homing in on the central system.

Next they had distributed control systems for functional parts, but only within a central stand alone system. Finally, a few manufacturers initially made the major shift to "physically" distributed digital systems in which pieces of the network stages were moved to replace previous stand alone systems by forming clusters, homing in on a central base, becoming digital islands. However, data switching was still ignored, as well as providing integrated voice and data facilities to the customer. This then required a new family of separate systems and new versions of existing systems, still with little initial requirements and design allowance for: video piggy back systems, automated cross connect systems, separate feature systems, more customer control systems, etc.

As indicated the design of these past systems has been a rough evolving path with four major shifts—one to store program, the second to digital access systems, the third to "physically" distributed local digital systems, the fourth to data packet systems. All in all, these have been a series of expensive multi million dollar decisions, with limited return on investment, not counting millions of lost revenues due to lack of new features or delayed features, and not counting the break up of AT&T due to attack by computer industry for not meeting network data needs, not counting extensive maintenance and training costs to keep up with drastically changing systems. These costs and replacement costs for hundreds of thousands of several million dollar central office systems became the first trillion billion dollar decision.

Perhaps this could have been considerably less, if R&D laboratories had taken the time to utilize a better strategic, conceptual, requirement, product definition planning process to really identify and understand the requirements in terms of the right technology. Perhaps, they might have gone back and readdressed the overall concept and have come up with new requirements without building all those new types of systems. Perhaps we all could have "leap frogged" at least one new type or version—perhaps?

The Second Trillion Billion Dollar Decision:
The Year 2,000 Marketplace

We must truly understand the needs that an ISDN trillion billion dollar family of systems will meet in order for it to be successful economically! In previous sections, we have considered several views of the future. At this time let us attempt to understand how to obtain a profile of the market in terms of current statistics, trends, observations and feature possibilities. Many analyses are available from research firms, where they all review each other's projections and attempt to add their particular twist or view of the future. Most analyses attempt to segment the market by types of industry such as finance, banking, manufacturing, accounting, insurance, medical, etc. Next they consider their annual sales volume, (non profit, less than 10 million, 10-100 million, 100-1,000 million, 1 billion+); also by annual telecommunication budget (less then 1 million, 1-10 million, 10-100 million, 100-1,000 million); as well as by types of telecommunication equipment (voice, data, video, special services etc.). Some have attempted to segment by geographical distribution such as rural, suburban, metro or intercity, intracity, interstate, international, or even intra/inter building complex etc.

These considerations have been used to provide various matrices of information from actual to projected, such as: noting the amount of intrabuilding, intracity, intrastate, international traffic each industry generated for various types of communication (such as from local area networks, or for various bit rates (300 bits/sec., 1200, 2400, 4800, 9600, 19.2K, 1 mega, etc.) for various applications from electronic mail to terminal to terminal traffic. By analyzing this information observations may be made, such as: that the bulk of the terminal users prefer at least 9600 bit rates and that the large businesses prefer 1-20 million bit local area networks rings of switched services. Relationships can be established across industries to determine common needs and expenditures, such as, for data packet switches. Understanding of technology opportunities can be determined, such as: What is their view of ISDN?, What will it really do for them in 1995, 2000? Next, their demand for various services can be challenged for changing from basic telephony through packet switching to handling electronic mail, wideband data, facsimile, full motion video, videotext, alarms and slow screen video in terms of various user perspectives.

However, in actuality these studies, though necessary, should only be an input to our consideration and challenged by a "doubting Thomas." For example, in many instances, price is sometimes a misunderstood and underestimated factor. If video in the office could be available at $25 per month for 10% of one's calls, it could be very desirable. A mobile phone for $2500 is one thing, a mobile phone for $700 is something else, or a $29.95/month rental . . . to trigger usage.

Also, as seen earlier, understanding people types is important in considering features in terms of their understanding of a feature, their wanting it for social reasons, being a leader, being a follower. All these factors can assist us as part of our investigation of feature needs.

Other considerations may help us identify the truly needed key features. Futurists have attempted to give us a glance into the future in terms of today, by indicating "big picture shifts," socially, geographically, economically, politically, morally, by age group, etc., such as noting:

1. A shift from 10,000 working at home, to 10 million by the year 2010.
2. Bell weather states having major growth, such as Florida, Texas, and California.
3. 20% of Florida's population are over 65 yrs old.
4. New England is embracing the information technology.
5. Resistance to the information age will be over by 1995.
6. U.S., Japan, Germany, and France will be major players in the global economy in the 90s.
7. High tech backlash will cause many to return to nontechnical industries, as too much automation takes place; such as robots in supermarkets versus family butcher.
8. Economic shifts, such as long periods of prosperity due to new industries in information, telecommunications, and robotics.
9. Integration of TV with telephone, with computer, with megabit memory disks. Move to reality simulated movie type games.
10. Shift to decentralization—no longer need for large production line work forces of industrial revolution, but will return to cities for arts, conventions, banks . . .
11. Yuppie—baby boomers moving into middle class, less middle manager positions, more concerned about future retirement funds, etc.
12. New wave has different value systems than previous baby booms.
13. More violence and gangs in major cities, due to a "why not" attitude, since little is offered by family, church, and state programs.

14. Poverty increases, as unmarried mothers attempt to care for children on single, sometimes limited income. Unskilled workers will have fewer job opportunities in the information age. The third world technology gap is keeping them from real economic growth opportunities.
15. Deregulation continuing in the more competitive areas, but with protection clauses.
16. Shift to entrepreneurship, because lack of opportunity for innovation in large firms, desire to buy technology from smaller, more innovative firms, ability to provide super programs from garage shops of homes, need for recent graduates to fulfill higher expectations.
17. Management style will be to solve more complex problems by pushing involvement further and further to those anywhere within the organization who have the solution.
18. Information will be analyzed by computers to aid management, but still require their intuitive decisions.
19. Firms will relocate satellite work groups to any location in the world, where inexpensive or "quality" conditions exist.
20. States attempt to establish new work opportunities using the information industry as the basis . . .

Observation

Technology will continue to be a driving force. For example, the struggle between analog and digital systems will give way to medium speed ISDN overlays followed by ISDN wideband digital networks, as technologists see more and more opportunities for megabit switches and transmission systems. However, the users will again determine the marketplace, as they selectively choose and reject various features, preferring the more and more intelligent.

Fortunately, or unfortunately, we are in their world of likes and dislikes, as we move from needs to wants. For example, consider the changes in the automobile throughout the last 50 years; as it changed from providing basic transportation; to having tires that did not blow; to windows all around that were not buttoned; from seats in the trunk, called rumble seats, to no back seats in sports cars; from large type gas guzzlers, to small box efficiency cars, to sporty smooth looking vehicles; to cost per feature to flat price per feature packages, to financing games, to . . .?

As we move from transportation to communication, from providing new highways to providing new forms of communication vehicles, we should also consider how our transportation road system developed from the single two lanes with a few cars to mega-super highways of six to eight lanes, to rings around cities with layers of internal rings with various cross-spokes. (Note that at rush hour even these are not enough.) We may wish to consider these ideas, as we determine our marketplace views of what features will be required at the turn of the century; where, when, how, and for what next trillion billion dollar family of ISDN systems? Meeting what requirements? Providing what features for what users in the future marketplace?

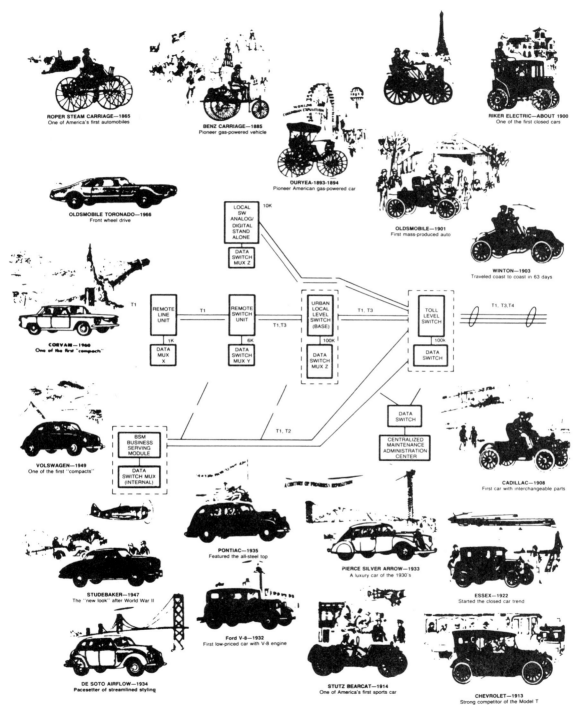

Fig. 12-24. Telecommunications Instead of Transportation.

Five: The Network Game

—ISDN—

In order to perform the "right" analysis during the product definition phase to achieve the "right" architecture and structure, for future networks, products and services for the 90s and beyond, we must take a moment to understand and appreciate the architecture, structure, interfaces, standards, boundaries, features and phases of the internationally agreed ISDN (Integrated Services Digital Network) model. It is important to consider these facets in terms of the following points:

1. The players—who they are.
2. Where they play the game.
3. The guidelines under which they play.
4. What they have accomplished. What ISDN is today.
5. What will ISDN be is the future.

To achieve this we are analyzing ISDN throughout the text in terms of:

- ISDN definition.
- ISDN organizations and standards' players.
- The I series recommendations.
- The OSI reference model.
- The ISDN USER Interface Model.
- The CCITT recommendation series.
- ISDN market, costs, and governmental boundaries conflicts, as well as its impact on the providers and suppliers.
- ISDN architecture—structure—features.
- The ISDN features and services game in the information world.

ISDN Definitions

Integrated Digital Networks (IDNs). A combination of *digital transmission* and *digital links*, that use *integrated digital transmission and switching* to provide digital connections, between two or more points to facilitate telecommunication and possibly other functions.

Integrated Services Network (ISN). A network that provides or supports a range of different telecommunication services.

Integrated Services Digital Network (ISDN). An *integrated services network (ISN)*, that provides integrated switch and facility *digital connections (IDN)* between *user-network interfaces* in order to provide or support a range of different telecommunication services.

Descriptions

According to CCITT Working Group XVIII: "The main feature of an ISDN

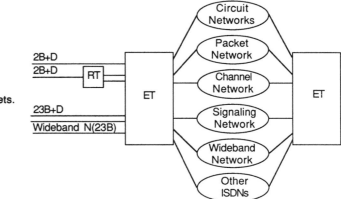

Fig. 12-25. ISDN Network Facets.

is the support of voice and non-voice services in the same network. A key element of service integration for an ISDN is to provide a limited set of multipurpose user/network interface arrangements, as well as a limited set of multipurpose ISDN bearer services.

"ISDNs support a variety of applications including both switched or non-switched connections. Switched connections in an ISDN include both circuit-switched and packet-switched connections and their concatenations. As far as practicable, new services introduced into an ISDN should be arranged to be compatible with 64K bit/s switched digital connections based upon a 2B + D, 23B, . . . where B is 64K b/s and D is 16K or 64K bps.

"An ISDN will contain intelligence for the purpose of providing service features, maintenance and network management functions. Its intelligence may not be sufficient for some new services and may have to be supplemented by either additional intelligence within the network, or possibly compatible intelligence in the user terminals.

"A layered protocol structure should be used for the specification of the access to an ISDN. Access from a user to ISDN resources may vary depending upon the service required and upon the status of implementation of national ISDNs.

"ISDNs may be implemented in a variety of configurations according to specific national situations.

"ISDNs will be based on, and evolve from telephony IDNs by progressively incorporating additional functions and network features including those of any other dedicated network, such as circuit-switching and packet-switching for data, so as to provide for existing and new services. The evolution towards an ISDN digital end-to-end connectivity will be obtained via plant and equipment used in existing networks, such as digital transmission, time-division multiplex switching and/or space-division multiplex switching.

"The transition from an existing network to a comprehensive ISDN may require a period of time extending over one or more decades. During the transition period arrangements must be developed for the interworking of services on ISDNs and services on other networks."

The ISDN Standard Players

The CCITT (Consultative Committee on International Telephony and Telegraphy) is one of the seven organizations of the International Telecommunications Union (ITU), headquartered in Geneva, Switzerland. The ITU is an agency of the United Nations. As an international treaty organization, it promotes voluntary compatible telecommunications interconnections among its member nations. It contains governmental groups, Scientific or Industrial organizations (SIO), and recognized private operating agencies (RPOA). It has many working committees that publish their agreements at a Plenary Assembly every 4 years. These agreements comprise standards groups, which work with the (ISO) International Standards Organization.

In the U.S.A. membership in the CCITT is handled through the Department of State's Office of International Communications Policy, Bureau of Economic and Business affairs, having five groups, including study group A: Regulating Matters, study group D: Data Transmission, and an ISDN Working Party. Most of the United States' input to CCITT is through the Commerce Department's National Telecommunications and Information Administration (NTIA), who with its sub-group ITS (Institute for Telecommunications Sciences) assists the Department of State, which sets the office policy in U.S. International Telecommunications. Working committees of ANSI's TI, sponsored by ECSA, have become the major U.S. ISDN working group to formulate a U.S. ISDN position across BOCs and U.S. manufacturers, giving its recommendations to the Department of State.

In CCITT, a major group addressing ISDN is Study Group XVIII: Digital networks. Data Communications are handled by Study Groups VII and XVII. Signalling is covered by Study Group XI. Contributions can be made to CCITT through approval of each CCITT study group. They come from individual members or national groups, such as ANSI (American National Standards Institute), or the EIA (Electronics Industry Association), as well as ad hoc groups, established to support the CCITT US approval process or by their members working through TI DI or their firms' international subsidiaries, by working directly on CCITT study groups. These methods are used by many large corporations, who are more interested in participating to understand what is coming, than waiting for the final agreed standard interfaces which are documented every four years in book with different colors for different years. (See Reference ISDN study.)

Current information is exchanged in the working committees, where new concepts, ideas, and requirements are submitted, considered, expanded, and enhanced. The IEEE (Institute of Electrical and Electronic Engineers) has sponsored ISDN symposia, which have influenced and accelerated interest in ISDN in the U.S. and establish their 802 area network LAN, MAN, WAN, standards, which they then recommended to ANSI.

In the 80s, the FCC recognized possible conflicts between their competitive regulated/nonregulated marketplace vision of a "level playing field" and the direction of totally integrated services networks. In early 1983 they asked in a Notice of Inquiry for views and comments on possible conflicts with integrated ISDN and their view of separating enhanced services, value added networks and CPE NCTE. This eventually lead to further inquiries and reviews of the MFJ, (Modified Final Judgement) with subsequent more integrated decisions. In 1986-7 Inquiry III considerations, they decided to look more at the service to ensure that it was competitively offered, and to worry less about where it was offered, leaving the battlefield of CPE equipment, NTI and NT2 interfaces to the technical arena. This allowed them to concentrate on financial and marketplace restrictions, such as using non regulated separate accounting, once non dominance and non bottleneck marketplace conditions were satisfied. Hence, as the Huber report noted, the changing U.S. government's decisions must be constantly analyzed in terms of changing international ISDN decisions to determine the actual direction of future U.S. ISDN networks, products, and services.

Standard Organizations and Standards Work

This government recognition and intense standards activities by numerous CCITT, and TI (US) working committees set the stage for monitoring, understanding, and determining the future ISDN network, over the 90s. See "A Look at the Players."

The I Series Recommendation Model

According to Working Group XVIII; "As ISDNs evolve from IDNs (Integrated Digital Networks) for telephony, there are many features which are specific to the ISDN, such as user/network interfaces aspects, which are related to the user perception of the ISDN (e.g., service related capabilities), network related aspects, which are variants of, or complementary to those pertinent to the telephony IDN, interworking aspects between the ISDN and dedicated networks, reference models for protocols and for network architecture.

"Since an overview of essential ISDN characteristics and recommendations concerning ISDN would attract a wide range of interest, the relevant information will be made available in one CCITT volume. To cover these aspects Study Group XVIII, in its coordinating role on ISDN matters, proposed that CCITT establish a new recommendation series, the I-series. This new series would contain recommendations related to overall network aspects, as well as user related aspects and protocols. For some of the recommendations in the I-series, Study Group XVIII was responsible for other recommendations of the I-series, other study groups of CCITT would be responsible to resolve." (See "A Look at ISDN.")

As indicated, an ISDN is generally understood to be a network evolved from the telephony IDN, that provides end-to-end digital connectivity to support a wide range of services, including voice and non-voice services, to which

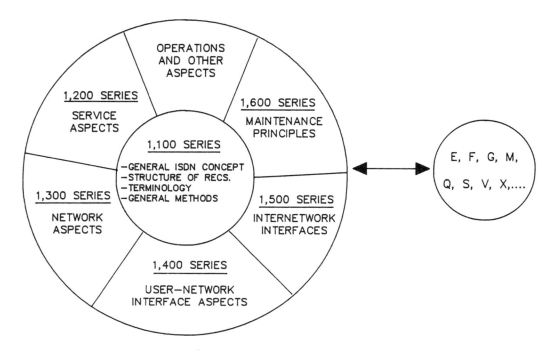

Fig. 12-26. ISDN "I" Series Chart.

users have access by a limited set of standard multi-purpose user-network interfaces.

This concept required a family of CCITT recommendations. Therefore, the I-series was defined in a single volume for the users containing the following information:

- The concept and principles of an ISDN
- Service capabilities
- Overall network aspects and functions
- User-network interfaces
- Internetwork interfaces

The I-series recommendations will provide principles and guidelines on the ISDN concept, as well as, detailed specifications of the user-network and internetwork interfaces. They will furthermore contain suitable references so that the detailed recommendations on specific elements within the network can continue to be developed in the appropriate Recommendation series. See I Series reference study.

The OSI (Open Systems Interconnection) Reference Model

OSI was described as follows by a working committee: "The International

Organization for Standardization (ISO) has been working since 1976 to produce standards to promote the free interworking of information systems via communications known as Open Systems Interconnection (OSI). The term OSI qualifies standards for the exchange of information among systems that are 'open' to one another for this purpose by virtue of their mutual use of the applicable standards. 'Openness' does not imply any particular systems implementation, technology or interconnection means, but rather refers to the mutual recognition and support of the applicable standards.

"It was realized that to successfully tackle such a wide-ranging area of standardization, a structured breakdown of the task was required. This has been provided by defining a Reference Model for OSI, which is structured into 7 layers namely the application, presentation, session, transport, network, data link and physical layers. This reference model provides a conceptual and functional framework, which enabled international teams of experts to work productively and independently on developing standards for each layer. The activities of ISO have since consisted of a number of parallel activities to define the reference model, which has now been approved as an International Standard, and to develop standards for the individual layers.

"CCITT decided to adopt a reference model for Public Data Network Applications and there was collaboration between ISO and CCITT to ensure that the two models were consistent, resulting in the I.200 series.

"Over the period 1960-1980, only computers or devices of the same manufacturer and model could communicate with one another, due to the unique signal structure and format built into each machine. Even with identical source and receiving machines, a 'handshaking' routine had to be pre-established for proper communications.

"The problem of connecting machines of different manufacturers, which used different formats, speeds, etc., remained an engineering research activity. Under the continuous pressure of increased data transfer and higher speed requirements, development of worldwide standards for data transmission were initiated by several organizations. Much has been accomplished, and many manufacturers are attempting to make their equipment and devices conform to these rules, but standardization is still in an evolutionary stage.

Scope

"The ISO version of the OSI reference model is applicable to all user to user communicating systems, which are 'open' whether using public or private communications facilities.

"The CCITT version of the OSI Reference Model is restricted in application to user to user communicating systems, which communicate over a public data network, either alone or in tandem with one or more compatible networks. The CCITT networks included leased lines, circuit switching and packet switching and the use of the Telex Network for data are also considered. The user in this context may include internal administration users (e.g., for communicating operations and maintenance information).

"In 1978, ISO Technical Committee 97 established a new subcommittee,

SC 16, on Open Systems Interconnection. SC16's task was to develop a reference model, whose architecture would serve as a basis for all future development of standards for worldwide distributed information systems. Once the architecture had been determined, existing standards were to be analyzed to determine whether they met the requirements of the reference model and, if not, what changes were needed to bring them into alignment.

"In addition, areas that lacked standards were to be identified and development action taken where appropriate.

"In June 1983, the work finally resulted in the approval of ISO *International Standard 7498* and *CCITT Recommendation X.200*, which specify the basic architecture of Open Systems Interconnection (OSI). As these two approached publication, the texts were completely aligned. There were no technical differences and very few editorial differences.

In March 1983, the British Department of Industry announced its support for application of OSI as a national policy in the United Kingdom. In the U.S. the National Bureau of Standards has contributed to and supported the ISO Reference Model since 1979. France has adopted OSI as "ARCHITEL," and many other countries are pursuing similar lines.

"In its Master Plan, the American National Standards Institute (ANSI) X3 Committee requires that all related standards work be based on the OSI reference model. Every related ANSI standards project must identify how it will ensure consistency with OSI.

"The new work in CCITT for Integrated Services Digital Networks (ISDN) is also incorporating the principles of OSI. CCITT is developing standards for a worldwide switched digital telecommunications system, that will support most of the familiar services (voice, data, facsimile, electronic mail, video, etc.). Newer requirements emerging from the ISDN work will be reflected back to the OSI architecture in the form of additions, enhancements, and adjustments to ensure its continuing evolution, such as: the Transport and Session layers.

"The OSI reference model is a layered hierarchical structure of communication peer protocols. It is the base for coordinating future standards efforts. The model defines the functions of each layer, interlayer communications, and the protocols used for peer communication.

"The approach was to use a layered architecture to break up the problem into manageable pieces. Three levels of abstractions were explicitly recognized; The architecture provided by the model itself, the service definitions and the protocol specifications.

"The OSI Architecture defined a seven-layer model for interprocess communication that is constructed from the concepts of relations and constraints. These concepts were used as a framework both for coordinating the development of layer standards by OSI committees, and for the development of standards built on top of OSI. The OSI Service Definitions represent a lower level of abstraction and define in greater detail the service provided by each layer. A service defines the facilities provided to the user of the service, independent of the mechanisms used to accomplish the service.

"The OSI Protocol Specifications represent the lowest level of abstraction in the OSI standards scheme. Each protocol specification defines precisely what control information is to be sent and what procedures are to be used to interpret this control information. The protocol specifications represent the most stringent design guidelines placed on implementations built to conform to OSI standards.

"Products can satisfy the much weaker constraints imposed by the reference model, but still may not be able to communicate with open systems. There can be many options at any layer, that conform with the OSI model but may not allow intercommunication.

"SC 16/WG 1 was charged with developing formal description methods for defining the protocols so that they could be implemented unambiguously by users all over the world. (See 'The Standard Players.') The method within WGI, currently being applied to several hundred protocols, was initially developed by ICST."

Principles of Layering

Partitioning is a common method for developing structured solutions to complex problems and is the technique used in the reference model. According to this technique each system is viewed as being logically composed of a hierarchy of subsystems, containing one or more entities or functional units. Subsystems of the same rank collectively form a layer of the OSI reference model.

ISO 7498, the document describing the basic OSI reference model, is divided into two major sections. The first of these describes the elements of the architecture; these constitute the building blocks used to construct the seven-layer model. The second describes the services and functions of the layers.

In the OSI reference model, communication takes place among application processes running in distinct systems. A system is considered to be one or more autonomous computers and their associated software, peripherals, and users that are capable of information processing and/or transfer. Although OSI techniques could be used within a system (and it would be desirable for intra- and inter-system communication to appear as similar as possible to the user), it is not the intent of OSI to standardize the internal operation of a system.

Layer

A conceptual region that embodies one or more functions between an upper and a lower logical boundary within a hierarchy of functions.

Layering is used as a structuring technique to allow the network of open systems to be logically decomposed into independent, smaller subsystems. A layer, therefore, comprises many entities distributed among interconnected open systems. Entities in the same layer are termed peer entities. Protocols are examples of peer entities.

```
SYSTEM A            SYSTEM B
┌─────┬─────────────────┬─────┐
│     │  HIGHEST LAYER  │     │
│     ├ ─ ─ ─ ─ ─ ─ ─ ─ ┤     │
│     │                 │     │
│     ├─────────────────┤     │
│     │  (N+1) − LAYER  │     │
│     ├ ─ ─ ─ ─ ─ ─ ─ ─ ┤     │
│     │   (N) − LAYER   │     │
│     ├ ─ ─ ─ ─ ─ ─ ─ ─ ┤     │
│     │  (N−1) − LAYER  │     │
│     ├─────────────────┤     │
│     │                 │     │
│     ├ ─ ─ ─ ─ ─ ─ ─ ─ ┤     │
│     │  LOWEST LAYER   │     │
│     ├ ─ ─ ─ ─ ─ ─ ─ ─ ┤     │
│     │ PHYSICAL MEDIA  │     │
└─────┴─────────────────┴─────┘
```

Fig. 12-27. Layers.

The basic idea of layering is that each layer adds value to services provided by the set of lower layers in such a way that the highest layer is offered the full set of services needed to run distributed applications.

Another basic principle of layering is to ensure the independence of each layer by defining the services provided by a layer to the next higher layer, independent of the way that these services are performed. This permits changes to be made in the way a layer or a set of layers operates, provided

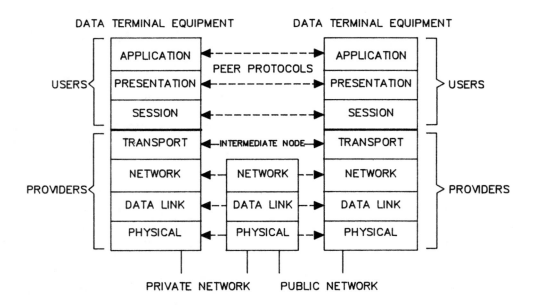

Fig. 12-28. Private/Public Layers.

442

they still offer the same service to the next higher layer. This technique is similar to the one used in structured programming, where only the functions performed by a module (and not its internal functioning) are known by its users. Therefore, each layer uses the services of the next lower layer, plus its own functions to create new services, which are made available to the next higher layer.

The 7-Layer Model

The general principles of a layered architecture have been described above and to apply these principles to the OSI environment a number of criteria may be used in performing the partitioning of the system as follows:

1. The first criterion relates to the number of partitions defined. There should be a sufficient number of partitions such that each partition of a solution can be easily comprehended. At the same time, there should not be so many partitions, that the task of describing and engineering the system will be difficult.
2. Boundaries should be selected such that similar functions are located in the same partition and unrelated functions are in different partitions. This usually minimizes the number of interactions across the boundary and results in simpler boundary descriptions.
3. Boundaries should be selected to permit flexibility in a structured manner. A partition should be defined, where alternate technologies exist or are foreseen. This permits these technologies to be introduced, without affecting other partitions. A boundary should be selected to coincide with present standards or procedures, so existing equipment is not made obsolete and an evolutionary plan can be developed. The boundaries should be selected such that the functions performed by a partition can effectively contribute to the solution by minimizing redundancy, and so optional functions can be inserted or bypassed; thus ensuring that the total solution is cost effective, yet still structured.

The application of the criteria described above has led to the identification of seven layers, which are briefly described below.

The basic elements of the OSI Reference Model serve as the building blocks for constructing the model of interprocess communication. In OSI, interprocess communication is subdivided into seven independent layers. Each (N)-layer uses the services of the lower (N-1)-layer and adds the functionality peculiar to the (N)-layer to provide service to the (N+1)-layer above. Layers have been chosen to break up the problem into smaller problems, that can be considered relatively independently. The seven layers are as follows:

Physical Layer. Layer 1 provides the mechanical, electrical, functional, and procedural characteristics needed to establish, maintain, and release physical connections between the network termination and the exchange.

Data Link Layer. Layer 2 protocols provide reliable transmission over a single data link including frame management, link flow control, and the link initiation/release procedures.

Network Layer. Layer 3 provides the control needed for call establishment and clearing through the switching network nodes.

Transport Layer. Layer 4 provides end-to-end control signals from user terminal to user terminal across the network (e.g., network acknowledgment or received information).

Session Layer. Layer 5 establishes, maintains, and terminates logical connections for the transfer of data between processes. Examples of session layer services are dialogue control, message unit flow control, and segmentation of message data units.

Presentation Layer. Layer 6 provides data formats and data information, if needed. Examples of presentation layer services are data translation, data encoding/decoding, and command translation for virtual terminals.

Application Layer. Layer 7 is the source of data, usually consisting of services which process data (i.e., data are combined, converted, calculated and processed to create new data). Airline reservations and on-line banking are just two examples of possible user applications.

Physical Layer

The physical layer has various characteristics to activate, maintain and deactivate physical connections for bit transmission between data-link-entities. A data circuit is defined as a communication path in the physical media between two systems together with the facilities necessary in the physical layer for the transmission of bits onto it. A physical connection may be provided by the interconnection of data circuits. A physical connection may be point-to-point or multi-point and allow duplex or half-duplex transmission of bit streams.

Data Link Layer

The data link layer provides the functional and procedural means to transfer data between network entities and to detect and possibly correct errors that may occur in the physical layer. Typical data link protocols are High-level Data Link Control (HDLC) for point-to-point and multipoint connections and IEEE 802 for local area networks. Data Link protocols and services are very sensitive to the physical transfer technology. In the upper layers, only a limited number of protocols are specified per layer, but this is not the case in the lower layers. To ensure efficient and effective use of various transfer technologies, protocols designed to their specific characteristics will be required.

The data link layer allows exchange of data link data units over a data link connection. The size of the data link data units may be limited by the relationship between physical connection error rate and the error detection capability. The functions of the data link layer include:

- Data link end-point identities if required for multi-point.
- Maintenance of sequence integrity.
- Data link connection establishment and release.
- Data link connection splitting onto several physical connections.

- Data unit delineation (e.g., frame detection).
- Sequence control.
- Error detection.
- Error recovery and reporting to network layer unrecoverable errors.
- Flow control.

Network Layer

The network layer provides independence from the data transfer technology and provides relaying and routing. It masks from the transport layer all the peculiarities of the actual transfer medium, so that the transport layer need be concerned only with the quality of service and its cost, not with whether optical fiber, packet switching, satellites, or local area networks are being used. The network layer also relays and routes data through as many concatenated networks as necessary, while maintaining the quality of service parameters requested by the transport layer.

Therefore, the network layer provides the means to establish, maintain and terminate network connections and the functional and procedural means to exchange network data units over network connections. It provides to the transport entities independence from routing and relaying considerations as-

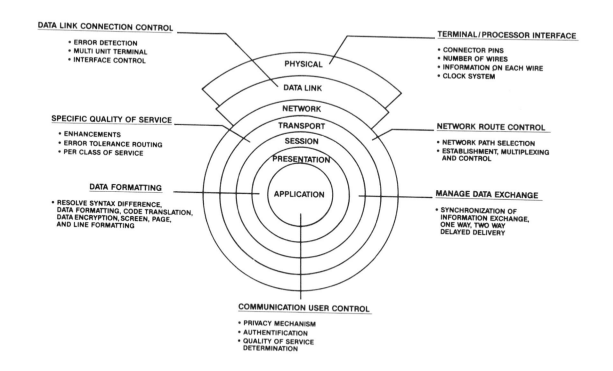

DATA LINK CONNECTION CONTROL
- ERROR DETECTION
- MULTI UNIT TERMINAL
- INTERFACE CONTROL

TERMINAL/PROCESSOR INTERFACE
- CONNECTOR PINS
- NUMBER OF WIRES
- INFORMATION ON EACH WIRE
- CLOCK SYSTEM

SPECIFIC QUALITY OF SERVICE
- ENHANCEMENTS
- ERROR TOLERANCE ROUTING
- PER CLASS OF SERVICE

NETWORK ROUTE CONTROL
- NETWORK PATH SELECTION
- ESTABLISHMENT, MULTIPLEXING AND CONTROL

DATA FORMATTING
- RESOLVE SYNTAX DIFFERENCE, DATA FORMATTING, CODE TRANSLATION, DATA ENCRYPTION, SCREEN, PAGE, AND LINE FORMATTING

MANAGE DATA EXCHANGE
- SYNCHRONIZATION OF INFORMATION EXCHANGE, ONE WAY, TWO WAY DELAYED DELIVERY

PHYSICAL
DATA LINK
NETWORK
TRANSPORT
SESSION
PRESENTATION
APPLICATION

COMMUNICATION USER CONTROL
- PRIVACY MECHANISM
- AUTHENTIFICATION
- QUALITY OF SERVICE DETERMINATION

Fig. 12-29. OSi Design Architecture Model.

sociated with the establishment of network connections. The functions of the network layer include:

- Routing and switching.
- Network connection establishment/clearing.
- Multiplexing of network connections onto a data link.
- Error detection and recovery based on error notification from data link layer.
- Sequencing.
- Flow control.
- Normal and expedited data.
- Path purging procedures (reset).

Transport Layer

The purpose of the transport layer is to provide reliable and transparent transfer of data between end systems, thus relieving the upper layers from the task of providing reliable and cost-effective data transfer. In some cases, the boundary between the transport and network layers represents the traditional boundary between the carrier and the customer. From this point of view, the transport layer optimizes the use of network services and provides additional reliability over that supplied by the network service.

The transport layer optimizes the use of resources according to the type and character of the communication. The transport layer enhances the quality of the network service (e.g., cost reduction by multiplexing, reliability by error recovery, re-establishment of virtual circuits after failure etc). Specific enhancements of the quality of service may be achieved by means of optional functions within the transport layer according to the quality of service required. The functions of the transport layer may include:

- Mapping transport address onto network address.
- Transport connection, establishment/termination.
- Quality/class of service selection.
- Multiplexing transport connections onto network connections.
- End-to-end sequence control, flow control, error detection and recovery.

Session Layer

The primary purpose of the session layer is to provide the mechanisms for organizing and structuring the interactions among application processes. The mechanisms provided in the session layer allow for two-way simultaneous and two-way alternate operation, the establishment of major and minor synchronization points, and the definition of special tokens for structuring exchanges. In essence, the session layer provides the structure for controlling the communications.

It provides the means necessary for cooperating presentation entities to organize and synchronize their dialogue and manage their data exchange. The functions of the session layer include:

446

- Session connection establishment/termination.
- Quarantine service.
- Dialogue control.
  - One way.
  - Two way alternate.
  - Two way simultaneous.
- Session connection synchronization.

Presentation Layer

The primary purpose of the presentation layer is to make application processes independent of differences in data representation, i.e., syntax. The presentation layer protocol allows the user to select a "presentation context;" this may be specific to an application (such as a particular machine representation), or to some standard or canonical representation. OSI users may use an existing context or define their own for registration with ISO. The presentation layer represents information to communicating application entities in a way that preserves meaning, while resolving syntax differences. The presentation layer adds the following facilities:

- Data syntax transformation.
- Data formatting.
- Transformation of presentation image definition.
- Syntax selection.
- Selection of presentation image definition.

Examples of presentation layer services are:

- Code translation.
- Data compression.
- Data encryption.
- Command translation (virtual terminals).
- Presentation format (screen, page, line).
- Data structure.

Application Layer

As the highest layer of OSI, the application layer does not provide services to any other layer. The primary concern of the application layer is with the semantics of the application. All application processes reside in the application layer. However, only part of the application layer is in the real OSI system, i.e., those aspects of the application process concerned with interprocess communication (called the application entity). SC 16 developed the Common Application Service Elements that provide common procedures for constructing application protocols and for accessing the services of OSI. SC 16 also developed three application protocols of general interest (virtual file, virtual terminal, and job transfer and manipulation services), as well as OSI application and system management protocols.

As the highest layer in the reference model the application layer provides a means for the application process to access the OSI environment. All specifiable parameters of each OSI environment are made known to the OSI environment via the application layer. The layer provides all services directly usable by application processes. In addition to information transfer such services may include:

- Identification of communication partners (by name, address, definite description, or generic description).
- Determination of availability of communicating partners.
- Establishment of authority to communicate.
- Agreement on privacy mechanisms.
- Authentication.
- Determination of cost allocation.
- Resource adequacy determination.
- Quality of service determination.
- Selection of dialogue discipline.
- Identification of constraints on data syntax.

Protocols

Working groups within CCITT have defined protocol as follows:
"Protocol is a formal statement of the procedures that are adopted to facilitate communication between two or more functions in the same layer of a hierarchy of functions.

"Access Protocol is a defined set of procedures that is adopted between a user and a network to enable the user to employ the services and/or facilities of that network.

"User-User Protocol is a protocol that is adopted between two or more users in order to facilitate communication between them.

"Therefore a protocol is the set of message exchange and format rules, that the peer communicating layers use to control and synchronize their communication functions. The functions performed by a layer are reflected in the services provided by that layer. Functions may be either centralized, or they may be distributed, using the peer-layer protocol for communications and synchronization. A layer, therefore, need not have an associated protocol, if all of its functions are local and its only communication is through its services to adjacent layers. Distributed functions, however, need a communication mechanism to transport their protocol messages between their peer-layer modules. Thus, each layer in the structure must present a communication function service to the layer above it.

"The communication services capabilities discussed earlier will, therefore, become the concerns of the protocol supporting that communication mechanism."

The following protocol elements will appear in many protocols. These factors have been observed over the years by numerous communications consulting firms. They are based upon the earlier military and university data networks' experiences, such as 465-L, 480-L, AUTODIN and ARPANET, one such firm noted them as follows:

1. Addressing: The specification or representation of the name of the source and the destination of information.
2. Error Control: The detection and recovery from errors introduced by the lower-level communication mechanism.
3. Flow Control: The management of the flow of information from the source to the destination.
4. Synchronization: The control and knowledge of the state of each peer half-layer by the other half, so they may remain in a consistent state and avoid deadlock.
5. Circuit Management. The connection and disconnection of message paths or circuits in circuit-oriented communication mechanisms.
6. Sequencing: The management of an ordered, sequential flow of information.
7. Message Management: The segmenting and reassembly of messages and the management of buffers.
8. Priority: Providing differing degrees of service through the communication mechanism.
9. Switching or Routing: The selection of a path from source to destination and the method for determining that path.
10. Security: Providing secure communications.
11. Accounting: Providing a mechanism for accounting for the use of network resources.
12. Performance: Achieving specified levels of performance, given the characteristics of the underlying available communication mechanism.
13. Robustness: Continuing to operate and be available when nodes, links, or other resources fail.
14. Information Representation: The management of the format, code set, size, etc., of the information transferred through the communication mechanism.
15. Interleaving: Inserting messages with other messages, usually on a channel basis, such as; voice,voice, data,voice . . .
16. Interlacing: Intermixing bits, bytes and channels from different messages in the bit stream.

The Basic Access (2B + D) contains a D-Channel 16K for signalling and packet data. (In the Primary rate interface the D channel is 64K.) The D-Channel enables the terminal to request various services through the use of a set of three layered protocols, defined by the I series of CCITT Recommendations as:

- Layer 1; CCITT 1.430
- Layer 2; CCITT 1.441 (or Q.921)
- Layer 3; CCITT 1.451 (or Q.931)

The layer 1 protocol defines the physical characteristics of the multidrop interface, provided by a network termination device. This protocol includes the timing and electrical parameters of the 2B + D access. Layer 1 also provides contention resolution, which allows multiple terminals connected to a single network termination to send messages on the D-channel.

The layer 2 protocol (LAPD) is a bit-oriented data link protocol that includes three major functions. The first is message frame processing, which converts messages between a serially transmitted format and a CPU memory data structure. The second is procedural processing, which provides error control and flow control of message traffic in the D-channel. The final function is terminal identifier management, which provides the capability to distinguish between the message traffic for different terminals.

The layer 3 protocol defines the content of messages in the D-channel, and provides the capability for negotiating for services via the exchange termination. This protocol includes services, such as B-channel call control (basic telephone calling features), as well as data-oriented services, such as packet switching and telemetry via the D-channel.

As more and more protocol signalling messages are exchanged on the "D" channel designers are shifting "packet data" out of the D channel to the "B" channel as well as emphasizing the 64K signalling rate.

ISDN User/Network Interfaces

ISDN has been defined by working groups in terms of services and interfaces, as:

The main feature of an ISDN is the support of a wide range of service capabilities, including voice and nonvoice applications, in the same network by offering end-to-end digital connectivity.

A key element of service integration for an ISDN is the provision of a limited set of standard multipurpose user/network interfaces. These interfaces represent a focal point both for the development of ISDN network components and configurations and for the development of ISDN terminal equipment and applications.

An ISDN will be recognized by its service characteristics available through user/network interfaces, rather than by its internal architecture, configuration or technology. This concept plays a key role in permitting user and network technologies and configurations to evolve separately.

Interface Applications

Some examples of ISDN user/network interfaces are identified corresponding to:

1. Access of a single ISDN terminal.
2. Access of a multiple ISDN terminal installation.
3. Access of multiservice PBXs, or local area network, or more generally, of private networks.

4. Access of specialized storage and information processing centers.
5. Stimulus and functional signalling protocol between terminal and network intelligence.

In addition, depending on the particular national regulatory arrangements, either ISDN user/network interfaces or internetwork interfaces may be used for access of:

6. Dedicated service networks.
7. Other multiple services networks, including ISDNs.

Interface Recommendation Objectives

User/network interface recommendations should allow:

1. Different types of terminals and applications to use the same interface.
2. Portability of terminals from one location to another (office, home, public access points) within one country and from one country to another country.
3. Separate evolution of both terminal and network equipment, technologies, and configurations.
4. Efficient connection with specialized storage and information processing centers and other networks.

User/network interfaces should be designed to provide an appropriate balance between service capabilities and cost/tariffs, in order to meet service demand easily.

Interface Characteristics

User/network interfaces are specified by a comprehensive set of characteristics, including:

1. Physical and electromagnetic (including optical) characteristics.
2. Channel structures and access capabilities.
3. User/network protocols.
4. Maintenance and operation characteristics.
5. Performance characteristics.
6. Service characteristics.

In the definition of the interface protocols a layered functional specification method is applied, using an OSI-type of reference model, suitably adapted to allow for the specific requirements of an ISDN.

Interface Capabilities

In addition to the multiservice capability, an ISDN user/network interface may allow for capabilities such as the following:

1. Multidrop and other multiple terminal arrangements.
2. Choice of information bit rate, switching mode, coding method, etc., on a call-by-call or other (e.g., semi-permanent or subscription time option) basis, over the same interface according to the user's need.
3. Capability for compatibility checking in order to check whether calling and called terminals can communicate with each other.

Reference Configuration

The reference configurations for ISDN user/network interfaces define the terminology for various reference points and the types of functions that can be provided between reference points.

The number of different interfaces is kept to a minimum. The ISDN recommendations defines a limited set of channels, channel structures, and possible access capabilities for the ISDN user/network interfaces. A distinction is necessary between the channel structure supported by the interface and the access capability supported by the particular network, access arrangement.

An ISDN user/network interface defines the functions of the components used in conjunction with ISDN user/network interfaces. Figure 12-30 shows the reference configuration and optional configurations. This figure is meant to include the possibility of bus (multidrop) architectures at T and also bus, ring and star architectures at S.

The reference configurations figure apply for the specification of "interface structures" for ISDN user-network physical interfaces. Interface structures are composed of "channels." A channel represents a specified portion of the information carrying capacity of an interface. Channels are classified by "channel types" (e.g., a B-channel which operates at a bit rate of 64 kbps and a D-channel which operates at one of two currently defined bit rates 16K, 64K as described further below). Channels are combined into interface structures. Channel types and interface structures are defined in the I series recommendations [1.412]. An ISDN user-network physical interface at a reference point S or T complies with one of the standardized interface structures.

A family of user-network interface structures have been standardized. They are limited in number and multi-purpose so as to allow (1) terminal equipment with a wide range of capabilities to use the same interface, (2) terminal portability i.e., any ISDN terminal can be plugged into and operate over any ISDN network interface, and (3) separate evolution of customer and network technologies.

The "basic" interface structure is composed of two 64 kbps B-channels, which can be used independently, and a 16 kbps D-channel. The total bit rate of the interface structure is 192 kbps with a total user data rate of 144 kbps. The "primary rate" interfaces can have several channel structures based on combinations of B (64 kbps), HO (384 kbps) and H11 (1.536 Mbps) and the requirement that a controlling 64 kbps D-channel exists either on the same or another physical interface. The total bit rate of one of these interface structures is 1.544 Mbps with total user data rate of 1.536 Mbps.

The Functions are defined as follows:

ET-   Exchange Termination
LT-   Line Termination
NTI-   Network Termination 1:
       Level 1 Functions only (line transmission termination, interface termination, timing, power feeding, and level 1 maintenance functions). These are intended to be simple functions associated with the proper physical and electrical termination of the network.
NT2-   Network Termination 2: Level 2 and 3 protocol handling functions may be included (switching, statistical multiplexing, physical distribution/concentration, maintenance functions at level 2, and others). PSBX's, terminal controllers and local area network gateways are examples of equipment which provide NT2 functions. In some cases, the NT2 functions may be null.
NT12- Combination of NT1 and NT2 functions.
ST-   Subscriber Terminal equipment (T2)
T1-   Terminal type 1: An ISDN user terminal equipment complying with ISDN interface recommendations, such as future digital telephones and data terminal equipments (DTEs). T1 may also provide connection to other user terminal equipment.
T2-   Terminal type 2: A user terminal not complying with ISDN interface recommendations, such as existing terminals (e.g., X.21).
TA-   Terminal Adaptor—Interface and protocol adapting functions to make a T2 terminal connect to the ISDN interfaces.

Therefore for Fig. 12-30, the physical interfaces are defined as follows:

V —to exchange interface
U —Subscriber Line—2 wire 23 B + D where D = 64K
T —ISDN user interface—4 wire 2B + D where D = 16K
S —ISDN user interface;
R —Non-ISDN user terminal interface

ISDN user interfaces S and T correspond to different user configurations or national conditions. When the NT2 Functions are null, S and T are identical as an objective.

The user ISDN Access Channels are defined for the following bit rates:

    D —16KBS, 64K.
    B —64KB/S
  B + D —80KB/S
 2B + D —144KB/S
NB + D —1.544KB/S U.S.

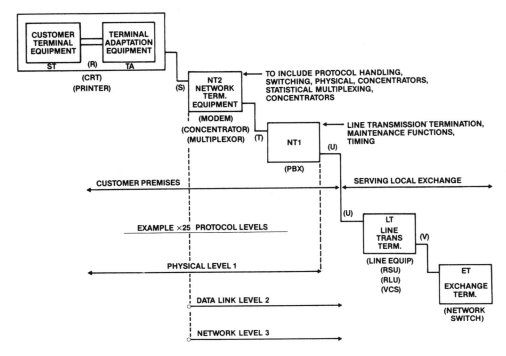

Fig. 12-30. ISDN User/Network Interfaces.

Where the D Channel will Carry:

- B Channel signaling
- Telemetry information
- Low speed interactive data

Summary

1. The terminal Equipment (TE) functional grouping is associated with functions at layer 1 and higher layers of protocol. Examples of equipment which perform TE functions are digital telephones, data terminal equipment and integrated workstations. The Terminal Equipment Type 1 (TE1) functional grouping is associated with functions belonging to the functional grouping TE and also associated with an ISDN user-network interface structure.

2. The Terminal Equipment Type 2 (TE2) functional grouping is associated with functions belonging to the functional grouping TE and associated with an interface other than an ISDN user-network interface structure e.g., CCITT X-series interface, CCITT V-series interface or a proprietary interface.

3. The Terminal Adaptor (TA) functional grouping is associated with functions that map the TE2 functional grouping into the TE1 functional grouping.

4. Reference prints are abstract locations of interface between functional groupings. The interface between the NT1 functional grouping and the NT2 functional grouping is at the T reference point; the interface between the NT2 functional grouping and the TE1 functional grouping or the TA functional grouping is at the S reference point; the interface between the TA functional grouping and the TE2 functional grouping is at the R reference point.

5. The Network Termination 2 (NT2) functional grouping is associated with functions at layer 1 and higher layers of protocol. Example functions are multiplexing of connections at layer 2 and/or layer 3 and routing at layer 3. An example of an equipment which performs NT2 functions is a three terminal interface unit for voice, data and data . . . or perhaps a PABX . . .

6. The Network Termination 1 (NT1) functional grouping is associated with functions at the bit level (layer 1 protocol) such as bit multiplexing and functions such as the proper physical and electromagnetic termination of the loop.

"**User-to-network aspects:** The objective of user-to-network standards is to provide a limited set of ubiquitous interface specifications for voice and data services.

"Currently, two interfaces are defined—basic access and primary rate access.

"Both interfaces use B-channels and D-channels. The B-channel is a 64 kilobit-per second (kbit/s) circuit switched channel used for voice or data. The D-channel is a message-based 16-kbit/s or 64-kbit/s channel used for

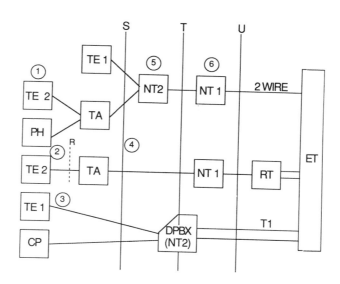

Fig. 12-31. CPE/Terminal Interfaces.

signaling and packet-switched data. The primary rate interface may also use HO and H1 channels (384 kbit/s and 1536 kbit/s).

"To denote reference points at which the limited set of standard interfaces may be defined, standard reference configurations, depicted in Diagrams A and B, have been developed.

"For basic access, the interface reference points are as follows:

R-Existing interface specification covering, for example, RS-232.
S-ISDN terminal or terminal adaptation interfaces, characterized by four wires, 144 kbit/s (2B + D) user rate (192 kbit/s including overhead), and up to eight terminals on a bus.
T-Normally, the T-reference point is the same as the S-reference point for basic access; however, if an optional network termination (NT1) is provided on basic access, some differences are possible.
U-U.S. standard currently under study; field trials will use two-wire echo canceller hybrid with AMI line code at 160 kbit/s.

"For primary rate access, the interface reference points are as follows:

R-Same specifications as basic access.
S-Same specifications as basic access.
T-Four wires; in North America, 1544 kbit/s (23B + D + overhead); in Europe, 2048 kbit/s (30B + D + overhead); point-to-point only.
U-Primary rate transmission system: for example, T1.

"**Network aspects:** Network standards are required to connect calls between two ISDN interfaces or between an ISDN interface and an existing network interface. These standards address:

- connection types, which define the types of connections necessary to route calls across the network between ISDN interfaces;
- a numbering plan, which is necessary to accommodate voice and data terminals and to interwork with existing numbering plans;
- interworking, to define interworking and compatibility requirements with existing networks and services, such as voice services and packet data services;
- network signalling, including mapping between ISDN access and network signalling systems; and
- as necessary, new network protocol and architecture models.
- OA and M operations, administration, and maintenance aspects.

"**Services aspects:** The three types of ISDN services—bearer services, supplementary services, and teleservices—will each need standards:
"Bearer services define the type of service the user requests. Examples of bearer services include 64-kbit/s circuit-switched voice and 9.6-kbit/s packet-switched data.

- Supplementary services are those supplementary to bearer services, such as conference calls, call transfer, and closed user group.
- Teleservices include such applications as telex and videotex."

WHAT CONSTITUTES A NETWORK, SYSTEM, OR PRODUCT?

Too often, a device becomes a sub-system, a sub-system a system, or a system a network, as a concept evolves from an idea to a product. As we move to physically distribute technology and intelligence closer and closer to the user, it is especially important to utilize a formal planning process with phase reviews, that analyze all aspects of the design from the architecture to the support systems. The design review can identify inconsistencies and different strategic viewpoints, for a particular product or product version in its ability to provide features, meet new application requirements, and achieve performance objectives.

This is an example check list, provided by Dave Lawsen, an advanced systems research expert, of items, that should be reviewed during the four major design reviews of a switching system product. Each review will cover the same items in greater depth. The risk is reduced at each review, as more items are finalized. During the product definition phase, many items may only be identified, but by using a consistent list for each review, management can easily tract the programming and/or hardware development and keep abreast with their impact on original Conceptual and Strategic Planning strategies.

A design review provides an opportunity to obtain a common and accepted level of understanding by management and product development teams of the following:

Specifications

Requirements
System Effectiveness
Generic Functions
First Applications
Future Features

Objectives
Product Costs
Development Costs
Performance
Market Applications
Market Penetration

Architecture
Hardware Functional and Subfunctional Level
Software Functional and Subfunctional Level

Fault Detection and Recovery Plan
Maintenance Plan (Diagnostic and Repair)
Administration Plan
Database Plan
Serviceability Plan
Call Processing Plan
Traffic Engineering Plan

Structure
Hardware Packaging Plan
Hardware Configurations
Hardware Interconnections
Redundance
Programming Languages
Program Constructs
Operating System
Database Management System
I/O Control
Application Software
Interconnections
Data Models
Performance Allocation
Extensions

Support Systems
Hardware Development
Software Development
Configuration Management
System Management
Customer Application Engineering

Documentation/Information System
Requirements
Objectives
Documentation Plan
Information System Plan
Education/Training

System Requirements

System Effectiveness
Reliability and Availability
MTBF (Mean Time Between Failures)
MTTR (Mean Time To Repair)

458

MDT (Mean Down Time)
Performance
Capacity
Delay
Response

Generic Functions

Environmental
Temperature
Humidity
Mechanical (Shock, Floor Loading, Dimensions)
EMI
Radiated power
Radiation Tolerance
Electrical
Power, Ground
Transmission
Line/Trunk Carrier Group
Signalling
Metering, Charging, Billing
Statistics
Traffic Measurements
Plant Measurements
Number Plans, Routing, Screening
Features

First Applications

Features Signalling
Human/Machine Communications
Line/Trunk Testing
Remote Operations and Maintenance

Objectives

Product Costs

Competitive Comparisons
Exchange Models
Cost Models
Start-Up Costs
Manufacture Volume Expected Each Year
Support Costs

Development Costs

Hardware
Software

Integration
On Site for First Applications
Field Support, First Year
Configuration Control
Program Management
Support Systems
Lab Models

Performance

Capacity
Response
Delays
Overload
Traffic Engineering

Market Applications

Access
Local
Toll
Tandem
Data
PABX
Information Systems

Market Penetration

European
North American
Asia/Pacific
Latin America
Product Introduction
Phasing Out Other Products

Architecture

Hardware

Network
Clock
Power/Ground
Tone and Announcements
Interconnections/buses
Lines
Trunks
Service Circuits
Ring Supply

460

Peripherals
Test Facilities
Processors and Memories

Software Major Components

Operating System
I/O Control
Database System
Call Processing
Maintenance
Administration
Metering, Charging, Billing
Traffic and Plant Statistics

Fault Detection and Recovery Plan

Redundancy Plan
Reliability Allocation Plan
Security Blocks
Failure Modes
Fault Detection Methods
Fault Handling
Verification
Sectionalization
Isolation
Recovery

Maintenance Plan (Diagnostics and Repair)

Replaceable Unit
Removal from Service
Diagnostics
Repair
Verification
Restoral to Service
Routine Tests
Demand Tests
Resolution Objectives

Administration Plan

Human/Machine Communications

Input Messages
Output Messages
Remote Operation and Maintenance
Billing Data Output

Traffic Data Output
Plant Data Output
Database Administration
Extensions
Change Control (Modifications, Patches, Program Loads, etc.)

Database Plan

Data Definitions
Data Operations
Data Access
Data Administration
Redundancy, Distribution, Error Recovery
Physical Organization

Serviceability Plan

Hardware Changes
Software Changes
Field Patches
Updates
Reloads
Record Keeping

Call Processing Plan

Objectives
Partitioning, Functions
Interfaces
Data Models
Call Scenarios
Fault Detection/Correction (Audits)

Traffic Engineering Plan

Network Load/Blocking Characteristics
System Resources
Service Ckts. Memory Blocks, Queues, etc.
Under Failure Conditions

Structure

Hardware Packaging Plan

Chips
PCBS
Subrack Assemblies
Racks

Cabling, Interconnections
Noise Shielding

Hardware Configurations

Model Exchanges
Options
Floor Plans

Hardware Interconnections

Bus Plans
Cabling Plans
Power/Ground System
Tone and Announcement Distribution
Clock Distribution
Alarms
Protocol Interfaces

Hardware Redundancy

Failure Modes
Switchover
Replacement
Restoral

Programming Languages

Problem Oriented
High Level
Assembly
Test
Database

Program Constructs

Process
Procedure
Region
Data Scope Rules

Operating System

Process States
Scheduling, Preemption
Timing
Processor Control Block (Descriptor)
OS Primitives

Data Management System

Distribution
Access Methods
ID
Structure
Data

Data Models

Logical Models
Physical Models

Performance Allocation

Program Size
Execution Time

Extensions

Modules
Processors
Memories
Features

Support

Hardware Development

Requirements
Objectives
Architecture
Implementation
Availability
Security
Recovery

Software Development

Requirements
Objectives
Performance
Architecture
Implementation
Availability
Security
Recovery
Archiving
Purging

Configuration Management

Requirement
Objectives
Generation Breakdown
Nomenclature
Change Control
Architecture
Implementation
Availability
Security
Recovery
Archiving
Purging

System Integration

Lab Models
Configuration Control
Lab Test Facility
Repair
Logs
Availability
Plan

Customer Application Engineering

Questionnaires
Order Estimating
Order Processing
Customer Data Processing
Program Generation
Installation
Customer Documentation
Acceptance, Proof of Performance
Qualification

Documentation/Information System

Requirements

User Needs
Organization, Partitioning of Information
Rules for Preparing
Technology Transfer
Education/Training
Type/Amount
Support

Objectives

Use
Modifications/Updates
Access, Availability
Costs

Documentation Plan

Hierarchical Structure
Contents
Formats, Templates
Nomenclature

Information System Plan

Objectives
Requirements
Architecture
Implementation
Availability
Security
Recovery
Updates
Archiving
Purging
Access
Performance

Education/Training

Courses Needed
Course Preparation
Course Presentation
Modifications, Updates
Refresher Courses

—PRODUCT DEFINITION METHODOLOGY—

During this phase, extensive problem analysis is performed based on the requirements specification to define a network, system or service to meet its specifications. A sequence of tasks is performed to develop the product specifications. These may be verified by a benefit model to support the final recommendation. This recommendation consists of one of the following for a particular network product service.

- Obtain a particular type of off-the-shelf Product.
- Define a new architecture and structure.

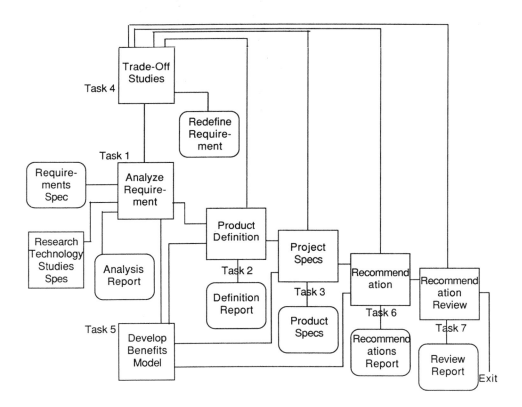

Fig. 12-32. Product Definition Methodology.

- Modify an existing one to meet this architecture.
- Initiate New Research to obtain a feasibility model.
- Wait for the next technology shift.

Tasks

A detailed methodology of analysis can indicate tasks, such as those in Fig 12-33, as guidelines for performing a complete product definition phase.

Task 1 Analyze Requirements Specification

- Review strategy, requirements, reviews.
- Request further studies.
- Develop benefits model—requirements.
- Clarify features, performance, cost, schedule, interfaces, objectives, and definitions.

467

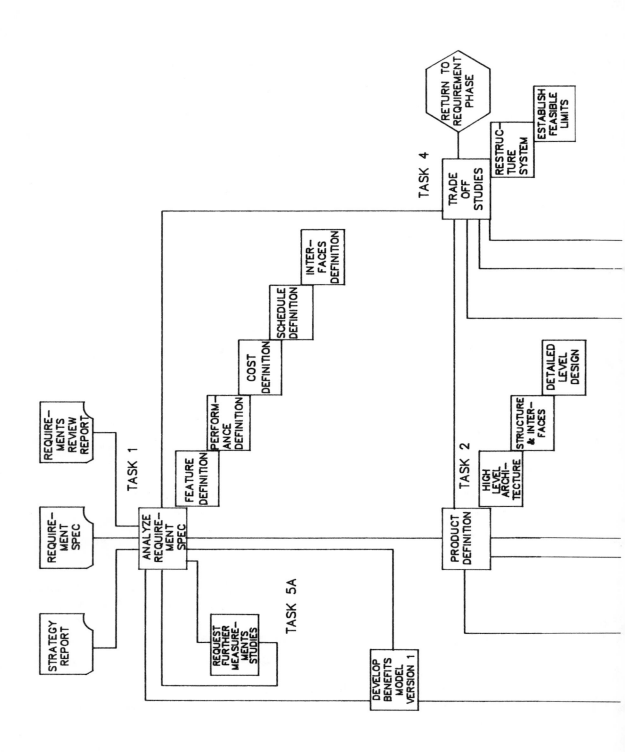

468

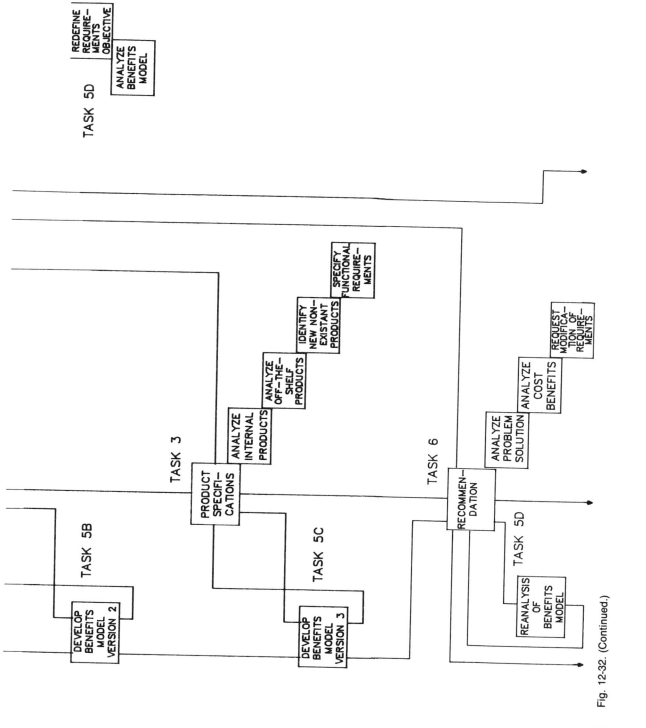

Fig. 12-32. (Continued.)

469

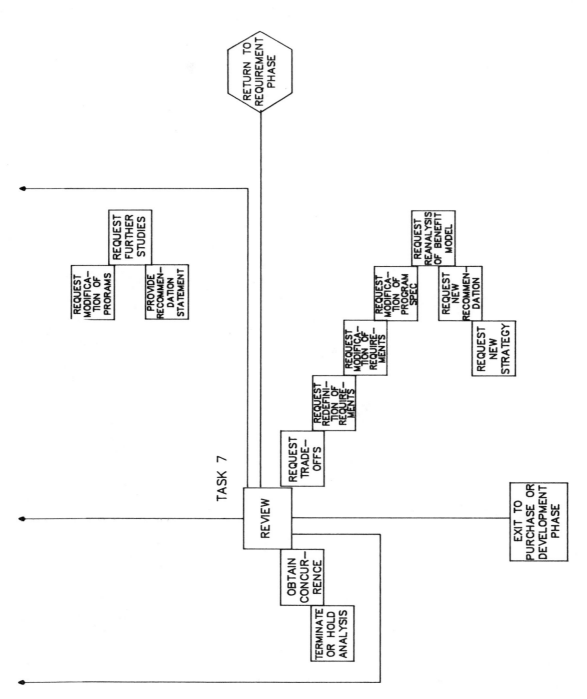

Fig. 12-33. Product Definition Tasks.

Task 2 Network System Product Definition

- Define High Level "System" Architecture
- Define Hardware/Software Architecture
- Define Hardware/Software Functional Structure and Interfaces
- Establish Programming Architecture and Structure Design, Test, Manufacturing, Operational and Support functions.
- Extend Major functional areas into subfunctional building blocks.
- Resolve Functional—Sub Functional Area Structures and Interfaces

Task 3 Product Specification-Program Definition

- Define product specifications for system/subsystem, hardware/software architecture, and function, and subfunctional area structures. Identify structures interfaces and support systems.
- Establish feasibility models and trade off studies
- Define benefits models per requirements per program
- Establish market plan, project plan, financial plan, manufacturing plan, support plan, and program plans.

Task 4 Trade-Off Studies

- Analyze benefits Models
- Redefine Requirements Objectives
- Restructure Network System Product Service Objectives
- Establish Feasible Cost/Performance Limits

Task 5 Feasibility Benefits Models

- Technology Feasibility Analysis
- Requirement Models
- "Top Level" Architecture Models
- Detailed Level Structure Models
- Market/Financial Models
- Analysis of Benefit

Task 6 Recommendation Analysis

- Analyze Problem Solution vs. Problem
- Analysis of Costs benefits
- Request Further Studies
- Request Requirement or Program Modifications
- Provide Recommendations Statement

Task 7 Review Analysis

- Review Requirements—Program Spec
- Request Trade-Offs, Requirement Models, New Feasibility and Benefits Analyses
- Establish New Strategy or Recommendations

- Obtain Concurrence
- Return to Requirements Definition Phase
- Exit to Development or Selection Phase
- Terminate Analysis

Conclusions

- The requirements and the high level architecture-structure and interface levels of the proposed program can be recursively analyzed in trade off studies against the feasibility and benefits models until an acceptable program specification is achieved.
- Further measurement studies or research studies can be made during this phase to help establish the requirements and program.
- The review process will be an effective point for involving decision making management to obtain commitment of the company's resources.
- Requirements have been clarified in terms of possible architectures and structures.
- Realistic program/project plans are established to achieve the desired network, product, or service.

—WHO'S ON FIRST—WHAT'S ON SECOND—

Where and how the major Telcos will offer new value added features is of major concern to Users, Suppliers and Providers, as well as Governmental Agencies. (Refer to The Governmental Impact On Integrated Service Networks.) Providers of telecommunications networks, as well as database services are impacted by the MFJ, Inquiry II and Inquiry III limits and boundaries for providing information: search, retrieval, manipulation, and processing.

Timely data handling transport value added features, as well as the various voice value added features are affected by these rulings and have been subject to waivers, depending on where they are to be offered. The players in the game must consider present and potential rulings, as they review its impact on the evolution of U.S. ISDN to determine: where they wish to provide various forthcoming value added features in order to obtain the desired services from the most appropriate architecture and structure of their business units.

However, before the game can be played by the individual players, let's take a moment in this analysis to review the game, as it is now defined in the late 80s realizing that it is a moving target, that will change over the 90s, as the various players position and reposition themselves. It is important to understand the situation, in terms of where areas overlap, complement or conflict with technology, the ISDN network model, the new information users needs, the competitive marketplace, and governmental decisions, in order to better appreciate the overall direction and its ramifications.

Prior to Inquiry III the situation is analogous to Abbott and Costello's "Who's on First" review, so let's take a deeper look at "Who's on First." Consider a baseball diamond configuration as noted in Figs. 12-34 and 12-35.

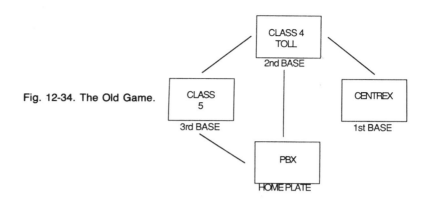

Fig. 12-34. The Old Game.

There have been many problems and proposals for playing the new "information world game." In this configuration, the private networks remain at home, at home plate, as a switched or non-switched local area network, whose data users communicate to and from each other within it. They can access the world or other data users directly via leased circuits or through the public data switching network, when provided as an access point, at 2nd base. The private network may have remote users at satellite locations, such as third base, where data pads are available for performing asynchronous protocol conversions to X25 ISDN protocol. These users' data traffic will be handled by the data switch at 2nd base and forwarded down to the local private data switch at home plate. Alternately, the Telcos subsidiary may provide a data switch, at first base, as a shared private network offering, where multiple firm's users are switched. There, it meets the data handling needs of the small to medium large businesses. This collection switch will enable the users to communicate locally, to remote users at satellite work locations, (such as, at 3rd base), to the world (directly from 1st base), or through the public data network at 2nd base.

Prior to Inquiry III, if the data switch at 2nd base was located in the regulated world, it was only allowed to provide X25-X75 protocol conversion with waivers in order to interface with long distance networks. Additional transport or handling features for the switch must go through the waiver process. However, the more independent subsidiary's data switch at 1st base will be allowed to provide the same data handling features as that at home plate, except for information processing features other than information access. If any processing is to be performed, this can only be done, as the figure notes, at the adjunct data processing firm in right field.

Similarly, if any value added features are to be added to the voice switches, these can only be provided with waivers in the switches at 3rd or 2nd base, or at a separate feature switch, located in left field. The left field offerings may be provided by the Telco base distribution firm, in which waivers are needed for the value added offerings, or they may be provided by a separate Telco marketing subsidiary's advanced network services provider, where

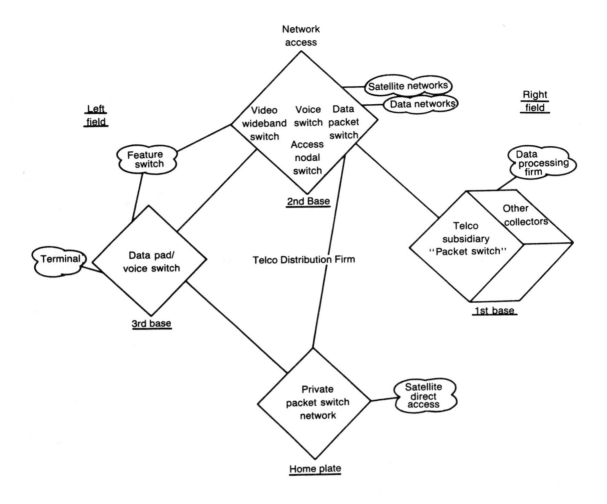

Fig. 12-35. The New Game.

all, except information processing features, may be provided without a waiver. However, in the latter case, processing can be individually achieved by selected joint partnerships. [Note that the DOJ, as a result of FCC encouraged open architecture networks and the Huber report, reassessed these earlier restraints in a recommendation to Judge Greene.]

This completes the big picture of the playing field, except for one qualification to make it level, which is that wherever the Telco subsidiary exists, another nonTelco firm may also exist. In fact N number, in order to enable total competition. This was the state of the playing field after a few first year adjustments; as it was played with only a vague understanding of the direction of technology and needs of the marketplace.

During pre Inquiry III years, the players were having difficulty playing the game. As the game was being played, more and more rulings and boundaries were beginning to be questioned in terms of their reasonableness in allowing the players to even play the game, such as:

The Data Game Rules and Considerations:

1. If the Telco tries to play the data game in an unregulated arena, must it be played in the Telco subsidiary? This was later changed so it could be played in an unregulated portion of the basic distribution company with separate accounts on a waiver basis. Alternately, if the data switch existed in a nonregulated portion of the Telco, to what extent could the offering be detariffed ? The original ruling was a regulated tariff offering.

2. If the Telcos elect to play the game only in separate marketing subsidiaries in an unregulated arena, then there still will be the need to provide equal access to all local data switches, because the Telco's sub cannot receive preferential treatment, even if it has the only value added features being offered by the Telco. Hence, how can this be economically provided by a local public data network, especially for the small resident or small business user?

3. If the Telco wished to provide a synchronous protocol conversion to X25 (ISDN standards) for customers, interfaced with its public data switch (at 2nd base), this feature could only be marketed by the subsidiary or some other firm once the subsidiary marketed it, per pre Inquiry III. Note that:
   A) The Telcos may be required to locate stacks of converters in their central offices.
   B) Technically preferable, the conversion should also be performed in the data switch or integrated voice/data switches and not only in an adjunct unit, to reduce costs.
   C) A new interface needs to be established to interface the conversion unit with each switch.
   D) If conversion is performed for the subsidiary (at 2nd or 3rd base), then the circuit to the sub must be provided at the market price as other data circuits to other private networks (such as 3rd to home). Thus increasing costs.

   Hence, the customer for the public data network, if the conversion is performed at 3rd base, must pay for a circuit from 3rd to 2nd. Thus, the customer is paying for mileage, as the Telco hauls his traffic here and there to economically handle it on a shared system. This will encourage conversion on customer premises or at least at a nodal switch in an office building or a shopping center local area networks.

4. Value added features can only be provided after waivers. They will therefore always be delayed, if at all allowed. Note, the long delay before the Telco could provide Async- X25. This does not make a public data network, a first choice for those who wish to have a constant stream of new features, such as code conversion, etc . . . To provide a full range of current features, the Telco must have two offerings: an access switch in the Telco distribution company (2nd base) with pads (3rd or 2nd base), and

another switch and pad offering in the Telco subsidiary with the full range of constantly changing, current, enhanced, value added, allowable (non-data processing) features.

5. However, once the Telco has a public data access switch, it will enable large private networks to bypass its own feature data switch offered by its sub (1st base). This encourages large customers to own their own data switch and other intermediaries to exist at 1st base with the Telco subsidiary.

6. Due to the above the sub will lose a good number of major customers. Hence, the Telco loses the ability to offer at many ubiquitous locations, both public data network access, as well as current features to the medium size business community, which usually rides piggyback on the networks offered to large business customers, such as the old CCSA network. This was a private voice piggyback shared system offering specially conditioned switched circuits. It was used initially by large and then by medium size businesses.

7. Growth for a new network will usually only happen if it is ubiquitous. A public network solution implies a network that is more or less universal. It will be severely limited (due to a lack of a large customer base) to grow as a universal offering. Instead of something for everyone, it will be a little for a few.

8. Costs of resulting private networks will be passed on to each firm's customers, as the costs of doing business in the information world. Costs incurred by the Telco for interfacing to many first level private networks, at 2nd base, in the regulated environment will become part of the regulated rate base costs, with limited real revenue due to loss of feature revenue and threat of total bypass, if prices become high enough for a reasonable profit.

The Voice Game Rules and Considerations

Voice network features have been suggested to be in a separate switch, in left field, using STP centers (network signalling transfer message switches) to communicate with the internal voice call handling programs of the voice switches at 3rd and 2nd base. The concept being, that any local voice switch can interface to a common feature switch to provide the customer a feature. It may not have the feature capability due to its technology obsolescence, delays in waivers, costs of obtaining features in all systems, etc. However, as this concept develops, the following must be considered:

1. If this feature switch (left field) provides the features that are value added, a waiver is required, if the switch is provided by the basic regulated Telco. During waiver negotiations, the feature may not be allowed or only portions may be provided (example extended 800 service, its main

feature was to be list directed menu driven; however, it was only allowed if the user already knew the phone numbers on the list).

2. A feature switch cannot have features for both the Telco and its separate subsidiary/company in the unregulated arena. So to have a complete offering, the Telco is forced to provide a feature switch at 1st base, as well as in left field, or at least at 1st base to be competitive.

3. If the Telco's feature switch only exists in the sub, at 1st base, the local offices must allow equal access to other intermediary's voice feature switches, which may also be located at 1st base.

4. Suppliers' switching systems without features will lose the competitive marketplace edge. Conversely, the supplier of the feature switch must obtain interfaces from all the other switch suppliers. Hence, if a suppliers' switch does not have new feature capabilities, (assuming the provider is not looking for their system to provide any features other than transport) this does not make it a very special offering to the marketplace. So if it is not different from anyone else's, at a billion dollar R&D cost with other firms supplying a similar system, *why build it*?

5. This will slow the introduction of new features to the voice world.

6. This will encourage large and medium users to obtain new features via the PBX, BSM (Business Serving Modules), or CPE (Customer Provided Equipment) market.

Final costs for having double switches in both the voice and data world will greatly affect universality of offerings by the Telco from either its basic distribution or advanced services subsidiary for both voice and data extended features offerings. See "A Level Playing Field." In fact, there may not be a subsidiary on first at all, especially if it is a rural environment where, in fact, no one may be on first. In the metro arena, the subsidiary will not be alone on first. Hence, we must ask the question "Who's on first?"

Table 12-12. The Allowed Game.

	I/O	Basic	Level 1 extended data transport	Level 2 extended inquiry/ response	Level 3 enhanced list access services	Level 4 information processing services
Voice	Terminal access	Pots Billing DA	Custom calling 911 Weather/time Class	Delayed delivery Voice/text Customer control	Inventory control	
Data	Terminal access	Data transmission Circuit switch Packet switch Billing DA	Security Error rate control Barred access Async-X25-X75 Code conversion	Broadcast Delayed delivery Message access Text/voice Data collection	Polling List storage List analysis Record search	Page reformatting Program packages Data manipulation Data processing Data presentation
Video	Terminal access	Wideband transmission Video conferencing Megabit switch	Megabit transport Error rate control Quality features	Video file access Picture catalog Slow screen display	Slide access/display Video record search Video entertainment	Video games Graphics

Table 12-13. The Systems Game.

		Voice	Data	Video
Pre-ISDN CPE	I/O	Phones Key systems PB(A)X's	Terminals Modems Multiplexors Concentrators	CRT's Multiplexors Microwave ports Satellite ports
Basic Telco (Regulated)	Basic	RLU RSU Base digital system	DDS	DDS Cross connect switch
Basic Telco (Unregulated)	Level 1 Extended Data Transport	Centrex Business serving modules	Data circuit switch Data packet access LANS Information access	Variable channel selectors Megabit switches
Telco Subsidiary	Level 2 Extended Inquiry/ Response	Phones Key systems PBX's Message systems	Data packet switch Data circuit switch Data base access Alarm/control system Computers	Wideband switch
Data Processing	Level 3 Enhanced List access Services	Text/Voice translators	I/R processors List access system Data manipulation Data processing	Graphic systems Picture access system
ISDN CPE	Level 4 Information Processing Services	Voice/Text terminals	Personal computers Intelligent terminals Graphic software Program packages	Intelligent video processors

Six: Using the Processes

Any process can be further defined, as a methodology, and then as a detailed procedure. However, experience has indicated that most managers, planners and designers wish to play the game their own way, with the result that it is more important that the basic process be understood. Then the execution of it is left to the "manager planners" to determine what particular methodology is really best for their situation. No two situations are the same, nor do they last very long.

Over the years many versions of various types of planning processes and detailed methodologies have been defined, as guide lines for all to see and understand. The more that users, suppliers, and providers use common processes to interface with each other, the better their relationships will be. However, in many cases, the methodologies can quite successfully be used as check lists to ensure that various aspects have been covered during the implementation. As we move more and more into a world of change, rigid, detailed methodologies may not enable creative expression, and they may become too restrictive. In this framework, the case studies will show several methodologies that are "versions of versions," developed over the past twenty years, from those originally defined for developing the large military systems of the 60s, based upon the systems approach. They attempted to establish a common interexchange of information.

Experience has shown that in using methodologies, they should be available for all to see, but not necessarily rigidly followed. On the other hand, if they are not seen or understood, everyone will participate independently. This may diminish the overall process, so that it is not really a tool or aid. It should be noted that the Japanese, and others who have been successful, have indicated that one key to their success has been the effective participation at all levels by all types of people. This can only be achieved, if all are using a commonly understood process with a methodology and/or procedure guideline or checklist, available for all to know and understand.

What is especially important then, is flexibility and availability of the process itself. Therefore, the readers are encouraged to take the time to study the processes, overlay them on their current situation and sketch out a methodology to fit their situation and environment. These case studies, "System Definition Stage," "Product Development Methodology," and "An Overall Methodology for Meeting Programming *User Needs*" are examples of extending the processes to one's particular application, using more detailed methodologies to fit one's own environment.

—THE SYSTEM DEFINITION STAGE—

We all know the fast pace of our complex marketplace, so today's management must apply much restraint and skill in order not to prematurely commit their company to an unfinished product. It has been seen over and over, that a product which is hastily defined and allowed to evolve throughout its development and manufacturing period, will result in one that has high redesign time, abnormal maintenance problems, extended site activation time, numerous manufacturing modifications, little market glamour, a short life cycle (for both planning and sales) and a poor rate of return on capital investment.

This applies particularly to the competitive telecommunications market. A switching system must be marketable. Today, there are few unsophisticated customers who buy without questioning products that are overly expensive or not maintainable. To obtain desirable characteristics in a system, requires careful consideration of its application and conceptual requirements. Then its specific feature requirements must be recursively analyzed with the various potential basic design architectures and structures, until one is found that successfully meets application, cost, size, capacity, and reliability needs.

Before a system leaves its definition stage, each of these factors must be carefully analyzed by a product team. In order to satisfy the requirements adequately, especially when they conflict and cause alternate configurations of the design, the right human resources need to be assigned early to the analysis. They are called "the product team." The team is composed of representatives from the various disciplines. They can be assigned, once the product has successfully passed the preliminary conceptual planning analyses. At this point, top management is willing to commit more of their company's resources to obtain a detailed, complete analysis of the product, before full commitment to development. This period, called the system definition stage, consists of the advanced product proposal, detailed requirements, and product definition phases. The keys to success are sufficient time to perform the analysis, and the right people.

This time frame for the product team's analysis is analogous to holding back an aircraft from taking off a carrier flight deck, until its engines are straining to go. Holding it back appears to lose valuable time, but once it is let loose, it is quickly high in flight and requires very little runway. Similarly, if a small number of market and product specialists can initially adequately define and structure the product, it can then subsequently be built with a minimum amount of capital expense and delay.

The Five Stages of System Evolution

We all have seen that a system of any degree of complexity undergoes five distinct stages of evolution. They are as follows: the system definition stage; the system development stage, the manufacturing stage; the field operation stage; and the system review stage. The purpose of this study is to take a closer look at the importance of the system definition stage. The reference process shows all five stages in perspective to each other.

The System Definition Stage

In reviewing these stages, one can see that the system definition stage of a system's evolution is by far the most critical stage, because it is at this time that a system is flexible to change, to be molded into a system which is marketable, manufacturable, and maintainable. It is at this point that the cost trade-offs for various versions and configurations can be applied to make the system truly economical. The work in the subsequent stages of a system's development is dependent upon the results of the definition stage. These stages must, of course, be successfully completed to obtain the desired product. However, even if they are successfully completed, but if the original guidelines were wrong, the final product will not be financially successful. The following is a viewpoint for successfully completing the system definition stage, which is performed by three analyses.

Network/System Planning Phase

After the initial concept has been established, it is essential to work the ideas into a well thought out proposal, which requires others to join the planning activity. During this first phase planners from the product team assist the original conceptual planners in further defining a future system's basic application, requirements, and concepts. Its technical feasibility, application, and cost are determined by applied research and marketing. During this analysis of the marketplace, sufficient market research is performed to ensure that this is indeed the best system or systems, that the company should be building. Areas of agreement and support or non-support will be determined to

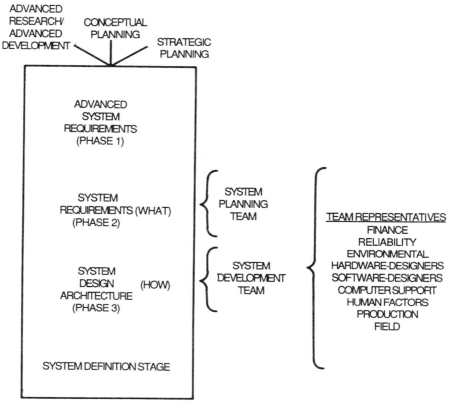

Fig. 12-36. System Definition Stage.

enable management to have sufficient information to proceed or stop the project. The end result of this phase will be a high level product requirements specification document, that defines the system and its application. This will be called the advanced system requirements' specification. or advanced product proposal.

Requirement and Product Definition Phases

Once management has given the firm's review approval go ahead, the next two phases are carried on simultaneously in a highly interactive mode. It is during this time that two groups of system specialists are brought together to define the detailed system requirements. The requirements (what) will be defined by the advanced planning staff and the detailed design of the system (how) will be determined by the development system staff. This analysis period is assisted by the potential program manager, who along with the systems specialists will be responsible for completing the design of the system. They are supported by the planning, applied research, and marketing staffs.

Product Team

As noted earlier, the talents of many personnel are utilized at various times in this small group called the product team. They are: system specialists, finance, marketing, legal, reliability, maintainability, human factors, manufacturing, field support, and software support representatives, as well as the project management personnel, who will be responsible for schedules and milestone commitments.

Much money can be saved by doing a good job at the system definition stage. It is very costly in the long run, if a minimum or mediocre specification of a system originates from this product team and is handed to a development team of 100 people to build the product. The product is soon found to be inadequately defined and specified and must be redefined and respecified. The result is chaos as 100 people wait for various problems to be solved quickly. It has happened, where good development managers find their people waiting around to have their jobs redefined, or in some worse cases, where detailed design must be stopped and started over. Thus, the product team should not be put under intense pressure to define a system in a week or two weeks. They should be allowed a sufficient period of time to define the correct system requirements. If the system requirements are nebulous such as: "We want a maintainable, fast, reliable system that meets various general objectives," how can a subsequent system be carefully defined? The end result will be that the system is defined and then redefined and redefined until it evolves into a system that meets a set of more specific detailed requirements, that are quite different from the original general requirements.

Hence, the product team must be given full company backing to allow them immediate access to any type of information needed or any particular personnel, that will aid them to totally define the system. Once the system requirements are identified, then the team will proceed to the detailed description of the appropriate system or systems. In doing so, various configurations will be reviewed in terms of features, cost, size, speed, capacity, architecture, maintenance, reliability, modularity, logistics, components, testing, installation, and field maintenance. When a system has been objectively considered in terms of these requirements, then it can be said, that the appropriate trade-offs have been made in order to arrive at the most marketable system. Hence, no latent surprises.

Advantages

Once the system is completely defined, it will not be necessary to re-evaluate major philosophies during the development stage. All major equipment and programs will be known in advance of the development stage, so that personnel can be assigned. No longer will twenty begin a project that expands into 200, when the initial estimate was 100. Once a product, defined in this manner, enters development, more realistic PERT schedules can be developed by project control and closely monitored. All divisions of the company can be notified, well in advance, of the amount of their input and time needed by the project, so that they may schedule it into their normal work load, or utilize an alternate source.

Another advantage is that a realistic program plan can be developed on the management level, because management will be able to project a more realistic duration of the system development, once it leaves the planning stage. This plan can also encompass total company operations such as marketing, sales, field support and manufacturing. Maximum resource utilization will result. In addition, personnel can see themselves involved in a growing mature company, as they move from level to level in system to system. However, it should be emphasized that the period of the system definition state can be lengthened or shortened drastically, depending on corporate backing. Hence, the total time frame to conceive and produce the product is greatly dependent upon top management involvement.

Results

Three documents should be produced during the system definition stage. The first is a singularly small but complete document approved by management indicating their agreement of the need of a particular type of product. For example; an electronic PABX is needed that handles viewdata and facsimile, processes computer data terminal traffic, and provides normal telephone service. A time frame for this product is given to indicate when the product is needed. Of course, it should be noted that this report is from the Product Planning and Marketing divisions and hence should indicate sufficient lead time to realistically develop the product, if the company is stable and mature in its long range planning. Then, with top management approval, the product team is brought together to produce, with whatever help is necessary, the second document, which is a detailed specification of the system requirements.

In defining this document, marketing research personnel play a major role to help establish the limitations of the system. Should it be: size A or size B, features X or Y, short lived or long lived, maintainable or throw-away?

Since they are to market the system, when the system is available, there will no longer be any disgruntled comments that they have to sell this "thing," because this "thing" is what they themselves have indicated that they want to sell, in the early planning.

In addition, finance personnel review the system in terms of projected market and rate of return on invested capital, required to build the product. They relate this investment against other investments of the company to ensure that the maximum rate of return has been considered. (Of course, the product may be built for other reasons, such as to keep the competition out, etc.)

Once the detailed system requirements specification is completed, the final phase of the definition can be completed. Here the Product Team completes the third document, which is the system definition document. This effort has, usually, been going on in parallel, but behind the detailed requirement analysis. Various design personnel are brought in early to assist in determining the mechanics of the system to ensure that the planning requirements of what the system is intended to be, are consistent with the real world problems of building and designing the system. It is refreshing for both parties to obtain a practical and theoretical compromise. Also, the development team will have had a direct say in the definition of the system for which they will have personal responsibility to develop. The manufacturing personnel are brought into the conferences to ensure that the system is indeed manufacturable. The human factors personnel ensure that the system is appropriately designed for maintenance personnel and the customer. The talents of the system analysts can be utilized to consider trade-offs of system configurations to analyze the various architectural costs versus capabilities. The packaging and mechanical designers ensure that the system is not a "kludge" and that the field personnel are appropriately consulted to ensure that the design is indeed maintainable. No more will the field complaints be such that Systems has again come up with a "Rube Goldberg" invention.

Reliability is best defined properly at the beginning. No longer, for example, are the customers of future telecommunication information systems satisfied with a general requirement of 2 hours down time in 40 years, when the system turns out to be inoperable for 30 seconds every week at the most critical times, causing operators to re-establish hundreds of calls. Note how, during the mid 80s in France, a software traffic routing problem, that only surfaced during peak loads crippled their data network for several days. They might prefer a longer single outage at one time. Early consideration of reliability provides an opportunity for the marketing representative to consider marketable advantages of the various degrees of reliable systems to ensure that the company does not produce a "Gold Plated Cadillac," when a "Bug" is really what is marketable, or vice versa.

Therefore, the system design specifications should reflect the experience obtained on past systems in arriving at the appropriate hardware and software limitations. It is very difficult under the best conditions to determine which portion of the machine should be hardware and which portion should be software. Also software normally requires support software backup requirements, that must be carefully considered and provided. One system may require a compiler that would take several years to develop, while a different system, requiring a simpler assembler, may be a better trade-off. In turn, hardware configurations must consider available technology over the life of the system. If a system requires 5 years to develop and if the component technology is changing at a 2-3 year rate, there is a source of supplies problem, that must be considered and circumvented. In addition, the spares required for the various hardware configurations may or may not be expensive to stock. This is where, in the past many companies have lost their profit in trying to maintain expensive systems at annual field costs, that the customer is not willing to pay. Hence, these types of system decisions are made before the design phases begin.

Ten Checkpoints for Evaluating System Costs and Marketing Potential

Every system needs checkpoints to ensure that appropriate company personnel are satisfied, that this is indeed the system their company can produce at a reasonable profit. The checkpoints occur as follows:

1. After the advanced systems concepts and product market research identification phase.
2. After the initial detailed system requirements are defined.
3. After the system design specifications are determined, which normally change the system and its requirements recursively until agreement is reached.
4. After the company's project control PERT (or equivalent) schedule is signed by all affected company divisions.
5. After the preliminary design review.
6. After the critical design review.
7. After the engineering model test period.
8. After the first production unit field qualification test.
9. At the one year review date after production has begun.
10. At the two year review date after production has begun.

It is interesting to note that four of the checkpoints occur before, during, or just after the system definition stage. This gives management ample opportunity to consider the profit possibilities of this product, before any major financing is required, to do detailed design and build the system. In this way the company does not find itself in a salvage type operation of putting more capital on a high risk chance of recovering initial investment.

Conclusion

In summary, this analysis has attempted to show the role of the product team approach and the techniques for product conception and definition that make up the system definition stage of a five stage process. This methodology was developed from the concepts presented in this book for a present day telecommunications company's application and environment.

A Five Stage Process

System Definition Stage

Phase 1 - Long range planning concepts/requirement document and marketing survey.

Phase 2 - Detailed requirements specification of the system

Phase 3 - Detailed definition specification of the system with functional and subfunctional partitioning.

System Development Stage

Phase 1 - Detailed definition of hardware black boxes (Interface signals defined, hardware defined)
- Detailed definition of software program modules, (Calling sequence, parameters passed, database)
- Detailed definition of support equipment needed for design test, manufacturing test, site activation, and field support at the site level
- Detailed definition of support software program modules for compilers, translators, assemblers, simulators, test programs, etc.
- Ordering of required components for system hardware

Phase 2 - Design and test phase of the system hardware-software and test equipment (on-line and off-line, subsystem-system testing in controlled environment)

Phase 3 - Labs evaluation

Phase 4 - Eng. model site activation/test period

System Manufacturing Stage

Phase 1 - First production model field site test

Phase 2 - Modification changes to production run

System Field Operation Stage

Phase 1 - System in-house acceptance test period

Phase 2 - System site activation and acceptance

Phase 3 - System maintenance on site, centralized maintenance facilities, and factory levels

System Review Stage

Phase 1 - 1 year review point of system operation to ensure it meets present and future requirements goals from a design, maintenance, and customer viewpoint.
- Suggest versions of system to meet extended requirements
- Define modifications to system requirements document, system definition specs, and component specs.

Phase 2 - 2 year review of system after first field site

Phase 3 - 5 year review of system after first field site

—PRODUCT DEVELOPMENT—

The following example methodology identifies the type of tasks performed for the various phases of a product development and the type of analysis performed during each phase.

Product Development Preliminary Design Phase

During this phase the project is staffed in accordance with the development plans, that were defined and concurred by top management in the preceding planning phases. Here, key personnel will move from the definition to the development phase to ensure an orderly transition occurs with maximum information exchange and minimum redefinition.

This phase has two basic steps. During the first, the top level hardware and software architecture and structure is finalized against all the details of the requirements in trade-off analyses. Next each functional area for both hardware and software is specified to handle the set of functions, derived from the detailed requirements, that are specifically identified for its resolution.

The result will be a completed top level and functional area design, sup-

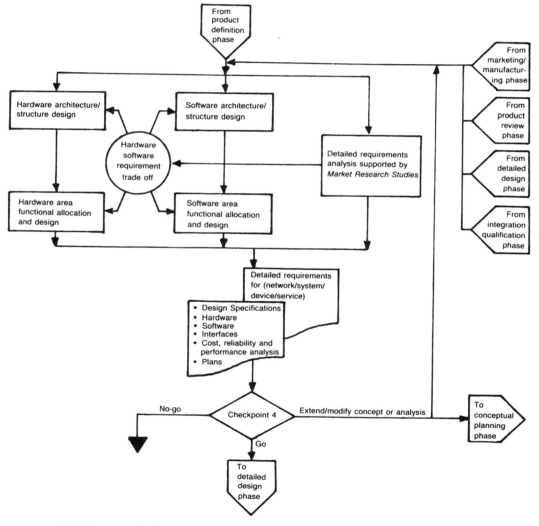

Fig. 12-37. Preliminary Design Phase.

ported by interface control documents between hardware and software, and among software functional areas for both control and data exchange. Parallel to these design documents will be a description of the detailed requirements expressed in terms of specific functions for each design area.

Enter Phase From: Product definition phase, detailed design phase, market/manufacturing phase, product review phase, integration/qualification phase.

Basic Objectives: To design the product against all of its requirements by completing the top level architecture and structure and its functional hardware and software areas' design.

Dependencies: Requirements baseline, further market research, applicable technology, manufacturing capability.

Activities: Top level design per requirements, software/hardware areas functional allocation and design per functional requirements.

Personnel Skills: Project managers, system planners, system specialists, software analysts, hardware designers, software designers, configuration management, quality control, test planners, technical writers.

%Calendar Time of Life Cycle: 15 to 25%.

%Cost of Life Cycle: 10 to 20%.

Analysis Considerations: Overall structure, subsystem structure, functional area structure, features, reliability, modifiability, manufacturability, cost, security, privacy, risk, confidentiality, performance, quality assurance, make-or-buy.

Tools and Methods: P&E, structured analysis and design; information retrieval systems, flowgraphs, decision tables, simulation models, artwork documentation (text/graphs), configuration management tools, CAD, breadboards, sensitivity analysis, communication networks between development sites.

Measurements: Phase duration, person-months required, documentation pages, number of lines of pseudo-code or PDL statements, defects found during review, actual vs. plan, % of known technology in solution.

Quality Methods: Design inspections, feasibility models, test plan inspections, design audits.

Phase Review: Checkpoint 4 project management preliminary design review to ensure that the top level and functional area allocation and design specifications meet all the functional requirement's objectives.

Exit Criteria: System design review team approval, software functional area design review team approval, hardware functional area design review team approval, preliminary design review (PDR) approval by management, customer, and user.

Phase Outputs: Top level design document, detailed functional requirements document, hardware/software functional area design specifications, interface control documents, functional area test plans, measurements plan, training program plans, qualification plans.

Configuration Management Baseline: Establish functional baseline; establish qualification plans.

Product Development Detailed Design Phase

During this phase each functional area's subfunctions are identified and specified. Hardware design specifications are defined together with software module specifications, database layouts, and transfer algorithms and interfaces. Requirements are clarified and modified to complement these design specs. Some basic design studies are performed to verify algorithms, performance objectives, hardware principles, packaging restraints, etc., using breadboards, prototypes, and computer simulation models. This all results in having finalized requirements and detailed design specifications.

At completion, these documents are reviewed by project and system management for their concurrence before implementation. This is called the critical design review. From this point on, no new requirement or major ar-

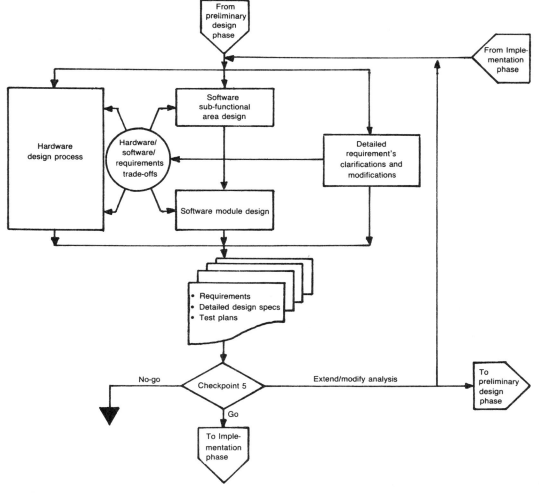

Fig. 12-38. Detailed Design Phase.

chitecture changes are anticipated or considered without schedule impact. Realistically, during implementation, the design may need to be modified to meet cost or performance objectives, but these changes are kept to a minimum by forcing all major issues to be resolved in these earlier phases.

Enter Phase From: Preliminary design phase, implementation phase.

Basic Objectives: To complete the detailed design specifications of the product and perform studies to ensure all hardware-software concepts are feasible.

Dependencies: Functional baseline, functional detailed requirements, top level design, functional area design.

Activities: Hardware/software sub-functional area design per functional requirements, feasibility studies.

Personnel Skills: Requirement specialists, system analysts, hardware designers, software designers, technology specialists.

% Calendar Time of Life Cycles: 10 to 25%.

% Cost of Life Cycle: 15 to 25%.

Analysis Considerations: Structure, features, interfaces, performance, reliability, changeability, security, privacy, confidentiality, risk, human factors.

Tools and Methods: P&E; simulation models, flowgraphs, decision tables, structured analysis and design, data analysis, breadboards, prototypes, information retrieval systems, computer aided design tools, measurement tools.

Measurements: Phase duration, person-months required, documentation pages, number of lines of pseudo-code or PDL statements, inspection and review defects, actual vs. plan.

Quality Methods: Design inspections, test plan inspections, design audits, model execution.

Phase Review: Checkpoint 5 management critical design review to ensure requirements and design are consistent with overall objectives, commitment point for management to enable project to complete its development process.

Exit Criteria: Critical design review board approval.

Phase Outputs: Requirements document, completed design specifications, feasibility analyses supporting design, test plan, qualification plan, approval for project to enter implementation phase, alt. decision to retain project in development phases or terminate project.

Configuration Management Baseline: allocation baseline.

Implementation Phase

Two major activities take place in the implementation phase. The hardware and software is physically implemented and unit tested. It is during this phase, that the functional area's design is completed as software modules are coded, and hardware circuits are designed and built. Inconsistency tradeoffs between modules or circuits are performed against functional requirements. Then they are unit tested and reviewed to verify that their operation is in concurrence with their functional requirements. It may be necessary to modify requirements to finalize design techniques or restrictions.

Once completed, they are reviewed by an internal review process. Then they are available for the program, subsystem and system build/test integration, where the product takes its formal shape. Each unit separately enters this phase, as its schedule directs. The exit point is simply an internal milestone per functional unit. Rework may be required in an iterative loop back through the detailed design or even preliminary design process, depending on the severity of the problem. However, though some corrections are anticipated, they should occur only in a small number of instances.

Enter Phase From: Detailed design phase, integration/qualification phase.

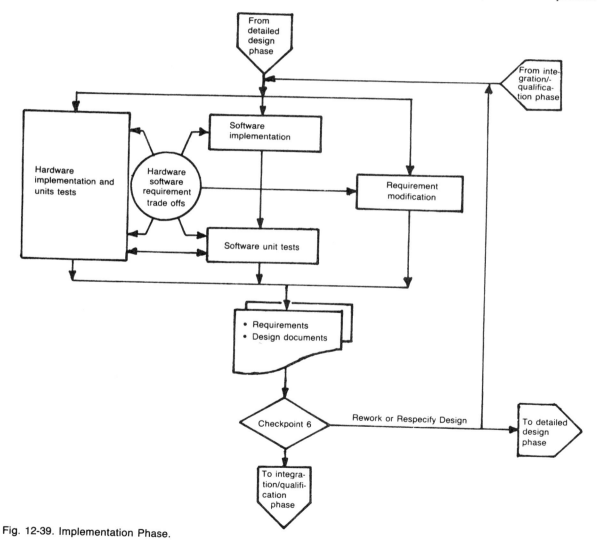

Fig. 12-39. Implementation Phase.

491

Basic Objectives: To implement hardware and software design and test unit areas per modified requirements.

Dependencies: Functional requirements, top level design, functional area design, subfunctional area design, support programs for design and testing.

Activities: Design implementation, functional unit testing.

Personnel Skills: Requirement specialists, system designers, hardware designers, software analysts, software designers, software programmers, test engineers, hardware packagers, quality assurance, technical writers.

% Calendar Time of Life Cycle: 25 - 40%.

% Cost of Life Cycle: 25 - 50%.

Analysis Considerations: Structure, features, interfaces, performance, reliability, manufacturability, security, privacy, confidentiality, risk, human factors.

Tools and Methods: Reusable functions, support programming systems, support test vehicles, computer aided design tools, information retrieval systems, measurement tools, programmer's work bench, design and code inspection.

Measurements: Phase duration, person-months required, coded statements by programming language, documentation pages: number of lines of pseudo code or PDL statements, inspection and review defects, actual vs. plan.

Quality Methods: Code inspections, test plan inspections, test case inspections, unit testing, correctness proofs, desk checking.

Phase Review: Checkpoint 6 internal technical review of each functional unit area's documentation, test and inspection results for completeness.

Exit Criteria: Acceptance of code and unit test results by technical management.

Phase Outputs: Completed coded functional units and supporting documentation, completed hardware circuit design, functional unit's test results.

Product Development Integration/Qualification Phase

During this phase functional areas are integrated into subsystems, which, depending on complexity, are integrated into systems, networks, and the final product. This integration-verification-validation process proceeds in an orderly series of intergrations, beginning with the unit tests, performed in the implementation phase. Depending on the complexity of the integration, there may be a need for special integration site centers or in-house test centers.

Once the program, prototype, engineering model, or network testing is complete and corrections or enhancement modifications are finalized in the design and the requirements, the product is ready for production. The first production unit is then qualified in a formal procedural review, that ensures the design meets the requirements. This completes the product development phases.

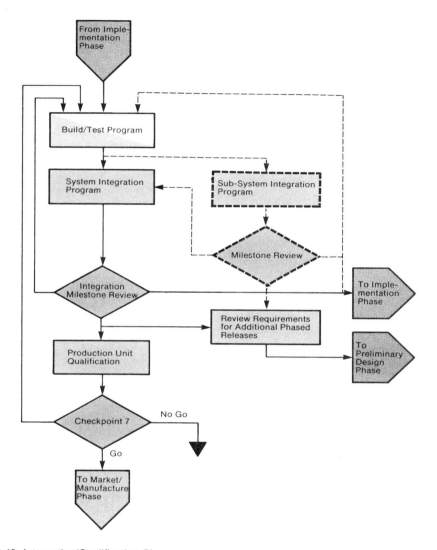

Fig. 12-40. Integration/Qualification Phase

Enter Phase From: Implementation phase.

Basic Objectives: To perform subsystem and system level integration, to qualify first production unit.

Dependencies: Integration test plans and procedures, acceptance test plans and procedures, qualification test plans and procedures, functional baseline.

Activities: Subsystem integration, system integration, product qualification.

Personnel Skills: System specialists, hardware designers, software designers, hardware and software test engineers, quality engineers, maintenance personnel.

% Calendar Time of Life Cycle: 10 - 20%.

% Cost of Life Cycle: 10 - 25%.

Analysis Considerations: Functions, interfaces, performance, reliability, maintainability, human factors.

Tools and Methods: Support test vehicles, prototype engineering model, test data reduction tools, test case generators, test library control systems.

Measurements: Phase duration, person-months required, number of test cases, number of test runs, defects found, documentation pages, actual vs. plan, number of defective test cases, number of redundant test cases, MTBF of qualified model.

Quality Methods: Integration testing, test plan inspection, test case inspection, fault reporting, qualification testing.

Phase Review: Integration milestone review by systems management, that product has successfully passed integration tests, checkpoint 7 qualification by quality management, that product's design functions are in accordance with its requirements.

Exit Criteria: Integration review team's acceptance report, qualification review team's acceptance report, concurrence by management.

Phase Outputs: Integration report, qualification report, rework non-acceptance report.

Configuration Management Baseline: First production unit's qualification.

Market/Manufacturing/Operations Phase

During this phase, the product is manufactured and sold through its marketing sales program. Customer application engineering (CAE) is performed to apply the product to various applications, that are consistent within its basic design capability. However, new version requests are also made for more features and capabilities than those provided in its original objectives. If redesign is required to meet these new requirements, customer design engineering (CDE) will be performed by recycling through the complete development phases to qualification. After this is accomplished, these new product versions can be marketed and manufactured.

Enter Phase From: Integration/qualification phase.

Basic Objectives: To manufacture—sell product/provide service to users, to receive customer applications (CAE) or customer new design (CDE) requests from users, to perform customer acceptance procedure.

Dependencies: Manufacturing program, sales program, competitiveness of product in the marketplace, functional baseline, 1st production unit qualification.

Activities: Product sales/manufacture, customer application engineering, customer new design requests review, perform user acceptance procedures, maintenance and operations procedures.

Personnel Skills: Manufacturing, sales, test engineers, application engineers, marketing, education.

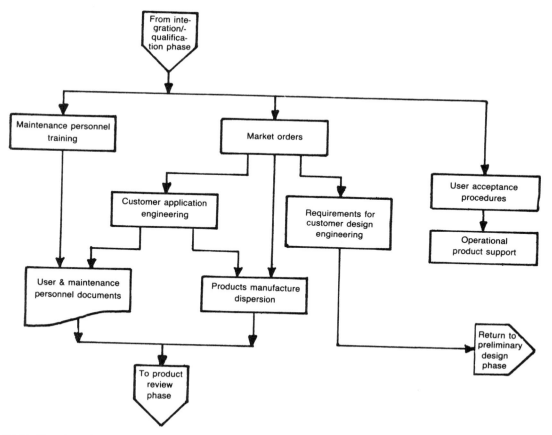

Fig. 12-41. Manufacturing Phase.

% Calendar Time Life Cycle: 5 - 10% (segmented development work in manufacturing phase).

% Cost of Life Cycle: % Variable (can be equal to the total development costs).

Analysis Considerations: Adaptability, changeability, modifiability, testability, marketability, cost reduction, human factors.

Tools and Methods: Test vehicles, inventory control systems, computer aided design tools, configuration control systems, automated change control process, automated customer documentation, maintenance training vehicle, maintenance tools, diagnostic, testers, administrative tools, error analysis, performance analysis, reliability analysis, cost analysis.

Measurements: Phase duration, person-months required, new and modified coded statements, operational defects found, actual vs. plan.

Quality Methods: Fault reporting, acceptance testing, code inspection.

Phase Review: Sales reviews, manufacturing process reviews, customer application reviews, customer new design requests reviews, customer acceptance test reviews.

Exit Criteria: Product review, termination.

Results: Products, user documents, maintenance training and test documents, customer application engineering (CAE), customer new design requests for further engineering (CDE), market segmentation, penetration and version application marketing plans.

Product Review Phase

Once the product has been manufactured and marketed, measurements are performed on its performance and operation. A formal review should be performed at various points in the manufacturing cycle, normally on six months or yearly intervals, to determine if the product is performing to its requirements. This will indicate if its requirements need redefinition, or if its design needs modification to correct operational problems. This review and analysis should continue for the life of the product on a periodic interval basis, until it is determined that the product should no longer be supported by the firm. At this point, the product completes its life cycle and is terminated in its final termination phase.

Enter Phase From: Market/manufacture phase.

Basic Objectives: To review product (network/system/program/device/service) to determine its operational effectiveness in the marketplace in terms of performance and competitiveness.

Dependencies: Measurements, performance, reliability, sales, costs.

Activities: Product performance review.

Personnel Skills: System planners, system designers, market analysis, financial specialists, manufacturing specialists, field support specialists.

% Calendar Time of Life Cycle: 1% (segmented intervals over manufacturing life of product).

% Cost of Life Cycle: 1% (over manufacturing phase).

Analysis: Performance, reliability, efficiency, usability, integrity, marketability, human factors, customer response.

Tools and Methods: Information retrieval systems.

Measurements: Phase duration, person-years required, defects, review of all estimates against schedules and make recommendations, actual vs. plan, defect removal efficiency.

Quality Methods: Fault reporting.

Phase Review: Checkpoint 8 management periodic review point for analyzing performance of product.

Exit Criteria: Review reports.

Phase Outputs: Performance report, design modification report, termination recommendation report.

Configuration Management Baseline: First production product baseline.

Termination Phase

A product that is to be terminated is reviewed to determine the extent of required support for existing products in service, in terms of maintenance,

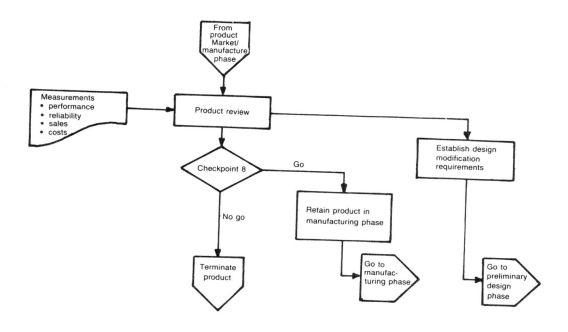

Fig. 12-42. Product Review Phase.

parts, etc. A post-mortem review is held to determine the advantages and disadvantages of various activities, performed during the product planning, development, manufacturing and field support phases. This is documented for future project analysis in a termination report.

If the product is to be maintained for an extended period of time, periodic reviews are performed until all support efforts are completed. The final status and disposition of resources is provided in a completion report.

Enter Phase From: Product review phase.

Basic Objectives: To terminate marketing/manufacturing process, to initiate, if required, any maintenance or plant support effort for product existing in service, to perform the review.

Dependencies: Measurements, support costs.

Activities: Product termination.

Personnel Skills: Field support, parts maintenance support.

Analysis Considerations: Performance, reliability, costs.

Tools and Methods: Information retrieval systems, inventory control systems.

Phase Review: Checkpoint 9; periodic review to determine point of completion.

Exit Criteria: Termination report, field service support, maintenance, parts, completion report.

Phase Outputs: Termination report, completion report.

This generic development process was developed by this author at North

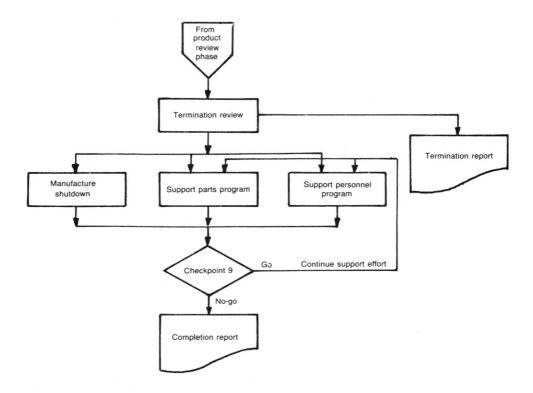

Fig. 12-43. Termination Phase.

American and GTE over fifteen years, in an effort to separate work functions on switching development projects, in a manner similar to that utilized by the North American and Boeing aerospace firms during the Minuteman development era. It was subsequently presented to ITT, as a vehicle to influence numerous worldwide software projects. ITT subsequently adapted a more extensively detailed sixteen phase process for its computer industry. Portions of the process were published in a series of well received articles in *Telephony and Engineering Magazine*. In addition, it has been used as a case example for five years at George Washington University Continuing Education Program. At Northwestern Bell, this author has used it to identify work relationships with Bellcore, Bell Labs, GTE, Siemens, Erickson, NEC, and other equipment suppliers. The Midwest Technology Development Consortium of Governing Agencies and Universities have considered it for assistance in tracking their R&D programs.

A director of a French company once noted; "It does not really matter how many phases are used, as long as the firm has a visible accepted product life cycle process for all to see, use, and relate." Hence, these processes are provided as generalized models, developed over 25 years, and analyzed by many firms, which the readers may wish to utilize in developing their own

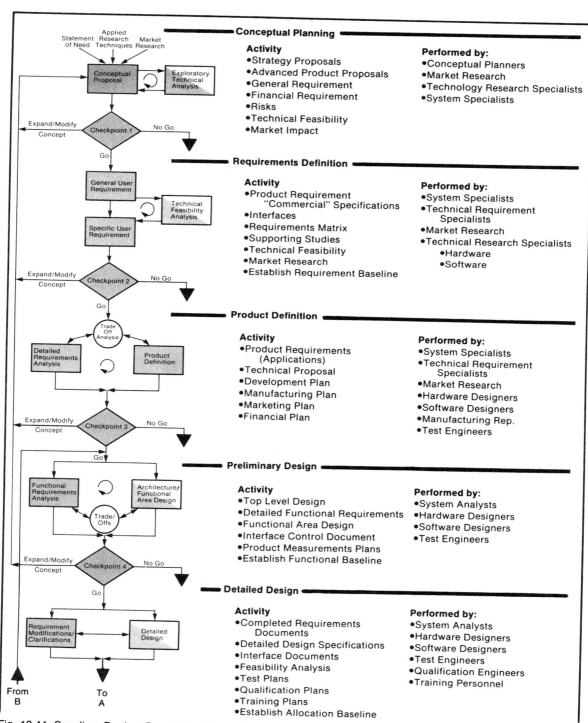

Conceptual Planning

Activity
- Strategy Proposals
- Advanced Product Proposals
- General Requirement
- Financial Requirement
- Risks
- Technical Feasibility
- Market Impact

Performed by:
- Conceptual Planners
- Market Research
- Technology Research Specialists
- System Specialists

Requirements Definition

Activity
- Product Requirement "Commercial" Specifications
- Interfaces
- Requirements Matrix
- Supporting Studies
- Technical Feasibility
- Market Research
- Establish Requirement Baseline

Performed by:
- System Specialists
- Technical Requirement Specialists
- Market Research
- Technical Research Specialists
  - Hardware
  - Software

Product Definition

Activity
- Product Requirements (Applications)
- Technical Proposal
- Development Plan
- Manufacturing Plan
- Marketing Plan
- Financial Plan

Performed by:
- System Specialists
- Technical Requirement Specialists
- Market Research
- Hardware Designers
- Software Designers
- Manufacturing Rep.
- Test Engineers

Preliminary Design

Activity
- Top Level Design
- Detailed Functional Requirements
- Functional Area Design
- Interface Control Document
- Product Measurements Plans
- Establish Functional Baseline

Performed by:
- System Analysts
- Hardware Designers
- Software Designers
- Test Engineers

Detailed Design

Activity
- Completed Requirements Documents
- Detailed Design Specifications
- Interface Documents
- Feasibility Analysis
- Test Plans
- Qualification Plans
- Training Plans
- Establish Allocation Baseline

Performed by:
- System Analysts
- Hardware Designers
- Software Designers
- Test Engineers
- Qualification Engineers
- Training Personnel

Fig. 12-44. Suppliers Product Development Overview.

499

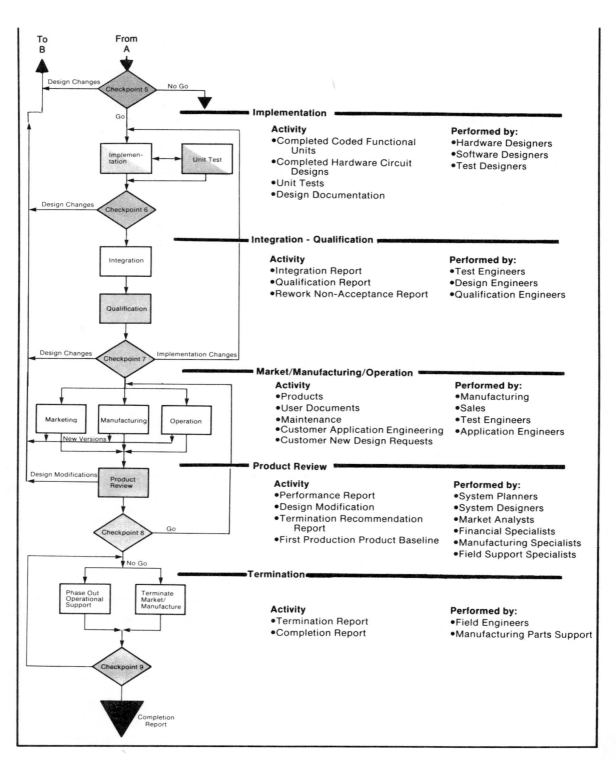

To
B

From
A

Design Changes — Checkpoint 5 — No Go

Go

Implementation

Activity
- Completed Coded Functional Units
- Completed Hardware Circuit Designs
- Unit Tests
- Design Documentation

Performed by:
- Hardware Designers
- Software Designers
- Test Designers

Implemen-tation ↔ Unit Test

Design Changes — Checkpoint 6

Integration - Qualification

Activity
- Integration Report
- Qualification Report
- Rework Non-Acceptance Report

Performed by:
- Test Engineers
- Design Engineers
- Qualification Engineers

Integration

Qualification

Design Changes — Checkpoint 7 — Implementation Changes

Market/Manufacturing/Operation

Activity
- Products
- User Documents
- Maintenance
- Customer Application Engineering
- Customer New Design Requests

Performed by:
- Manufacturing
- Sales
- Test Engineers
- Application Engineers

Marketing | Manufacturing | Operation

New Versions

Product Review

Design Modifications — Product Review

Activity
- Performance Report
- Design Modification
- Termination Recommendation Report
- First Production Product Baseline

Performed by:
- System Planners
- System Designers
- Market Analysts
- Financial Specialists
- Manufacturing Specialists
- Field Support Specialists

Checkpoint 8 — Go

No Go

Termination

Phase Out Operational Support | Terminate Market/ Manufacture

Activity
- Termination Report
- Completion Report

Performed by:
- Field Engineers
- Manufacturing Parts Support

Checkpoint 9

Completion Report

500

R&D product life cycle process to overlay on a marketplace process to identify and resolve users' needs.

—METHODOLOGY FOR MEETING USER NEEDS—

The following is a general six phase methodology that identifies the tasks for understanding user needs, establishing requirements, selecting alternatives, making a recommendation and providing the solution to assist a unit of a multi unit firm to improve its software designers' (users) programming productivity with the right support programming aids.

This is a general process which can be applied to any situation, where we wish to understand users needs and provide them with the right product, network, or service. It also indicates a decision support system in which decisions are documented with brief, one page reports to enable subsequent tracking and reanalysis as products and services are moved to the marketplace.

Programming Technology Transfer Phases

Requirements Specification Phase

During this phase specialists interface with users to better understand their specific needs. Together they define the detailed requirements and specifications to clearly identify the programming, processes, methods, measurements, training, tools, systems, and standards that are needed. Further measurement analysis may be required to support the requirements. The resulting requirement specification report will be the conclusion of this analysis, once approved by user.

Activities:
- Specific product problem analysis.
- Thorough requirements analysis and specification.
- User involvement in the specification of requirements.

Exit Criteria:
- Requirement specification report.
- Requirement specification user concurrence statement.

Definition and Recommendation Phase

During this phase, extensive problem analysis is performed based on the Requirements and Specifications Report. The trade-offs will be carefully analyzed in terms of benefits, resulting in specific recommendations such as: economic justification; the selection of off-the-shelf, the utilization of a modified version of another division's program, the development of a program, or delay for further measurements. Once the recommendations are reviewed and concurred by the user, they form the basis for initiating a support program.

501

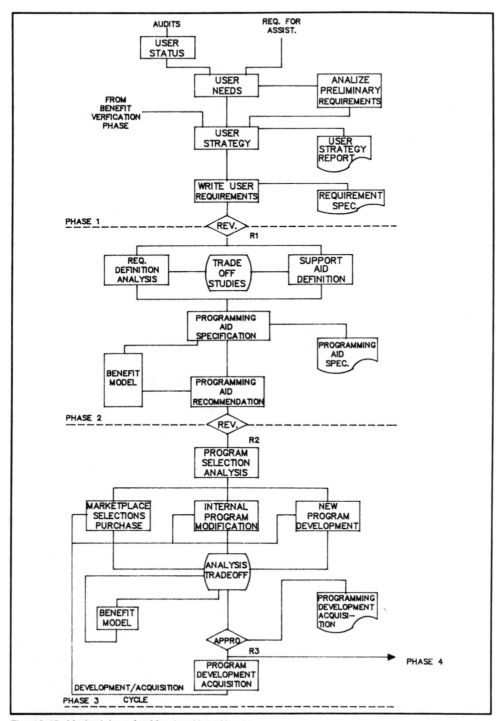

Fig. 12-45. Methodology for Meeting User Needs.

The exit criteria from this phase will consist of the recommendations, benefit analysis report, support plan and user concurrence statement.

Activities:
- Problem analysis based on the requirements specification.
- Problem solution.
- Recommendation of programs, methods and tools.
- Cost benefits analysis.

Exit Criteria:
- Recommendations and benefits analysis reports.
- Support plan.
- User concurrence statement.

Selection/Development/Acquisition Phase

During this phase, the software support program is selected from alternatives and acquired. It may be simply to modify existing programs, purchase one from an outside vendor or prepare internally a particular program, measurement, method, tool, standard, or process.

Activities:
- Assistance in acquisition of program, method, tool, standard etc.
- Development, assistance and support.

Exit Criteria:
- Product ready to install.
- Supplier contracts.
- User concurrence.

Programming Installation and Qualification Phase

During this phase the required software or software support aid is installed. Its error-free operation is determined by a performance qualification test performed on location.

Activities:
- Implement problem solution.
- Installation of the tool or method.
- Testing of the tool or method.

Exit Criteria:
- Operational qualification of product.
- User concurrence.

Programming Integration and Service Phase

During this phase the programming aid is installed and integrated with other programs. It is tested to ensure that the aid is functioning at the level expected and that it does indeed meet its requirements. Support documentation and maintenance is obtained to help ensure the program will be continually operational.

Activities:

- Integration of technology into environment.
- Enhancement of method or tool if necessary.
- Operational review.

Exit Criteria:

- Operations Report.
- Unit Concurrence.

Programming Benefits Verification Phase

Data is obtained during the program's initial period of operation (6 months/1 year). After a sufficient period of performance, a review is performed to ensure it does meet the needs of the user. All aspects are reviewed in assessing the worth of this expenditure. Reviews subsequently occur on a periodic basis as required until termination.

Activities:

- Review of performance.
- Verification of benefits.

Exit Criteria:

- Benefits Verification report.
- User Concurrence.

The Decision Methodology

Hence the process contains a decision methodology to facilitate, document, and track decisions in working with the customer to transfer the right technology. (See Table 12-14.) It meets the following objectives:

- A report per task.
- A decision report form per task.
- Not every task need be performed, only those established by strategy.
- Should enable tasks to be revisited as the analysis is pursued.
- Past decisions can be easily analyzed.
- A typical task may require additional studies to be completed before the task's decision.
- The methodology should prevent prematurely leaving a task without adequate studies to support the decision.
- Provide a record of decisions and agreements, which also becomes a history log.
- Each report is a decision.

Table 12-14. Phase Reports.

Phase	Phase task reports
Requirements Phase	Status report Strategy report Needs report REQ spec report Prelim REQ report Review report phase 1
Recommendation Phase	REQ analysis report Program spec report Support programming def report Recommendation report Trade-off studies report (benefit & model) Review report phase 2
Selection/Development/ Acquisition Phase	Program selection analysis report External marketplace selection acquisition Internal program analysis strategy report report Internal new design report Trade-off studies report (benefit model) Internal program modification report Program selection approval report phase 3
Programming Aids Installation Phase	Management envolvement report Tool qualificaiton test procedures - test report Management review-mod report Installation process, method, measurement, Installation plan report tool report Tool in house inspection report Review report phase 4
Integration service Phase	Integration plan report Integration acceptance test procedures/test report Operational service log report Operational service performance analysis report phase 5
Benefit verification Phase	Data collection form report Benefit analysis report Benefit verification analysis report Benefit verification recommendation report phase 6

—MANAGING THE PURSUIT OF QUALITY—

The terms "quality," and more specifically "programming quality," are universal and widely interpreted by companies involved in the various aspects of producing programming products. In order to successfully manage "programming quality," each of the quality characteristic's specific objectives must be carefully defined and then pursued at each phase of the programming product life cycle. This study was developed with Henry A. Malec, a computer and communication's quality specialist, to address the pursuit of quality based on the concept of a quality level index system integrated with the programming product life cycle phase activities and reviews. This process is called "quality prisms." It can be used by quality management to produce the most cost effective "quality program."

This concept will also enable a comparison of different products within the same company or between different companies. This can be achieved across a wide range of products for many unique applications, utilizing different programming languages. "Quality prisms" can also be used to integrate hardware quality and software quality for an assessment of total system quality. However, this analysis will mainly concentrate on programming quality

Table 12-15. Degree of Effort Matrix.

	0	1	2	3	4	
Planning	No activity	.General high level REQ.	.Specific detailed REQ definition	.Highly complex REQ definition & support model	.Difficult/complex REQ definition & prototype	
Design & test	No activity	.General architecture consideration .General test & measurement program	.Detailed arch/structure impact .Lanaguage impact .Test program extended	.Extensive arch/structure structure consideration tailored language/operating system/man machine interface impact etc. .Code walk throughs .Detailed documentation .etc.	.Separate quality teams to verify design .Detailed test facility .Extensive qualification test plans & procedure	E x t e n t
Integration/installation	No activity	.General quality management program .Acceptance test .Nominal change control quality program	.Extensive qualification test plans & procedure to verify characteristics .Above nominal quality requirement verification testing	.Quality teams formed.Detailed: Quality configuration control release program .Extensive data collection, verification and analysis	.Specialized quality integration/manufacturing/installation programs to ensure achievement of quality characteristics by separate quality organization	o f e f f o r t
Service	No activity	.General quality tracking & redesign program to achieve quality objectives/requirements	.Formal data collection & analysis program to verify quality objects .Quality redesign effort	.Detailed measurements data analysis and modeling program to verify high level quality objects .Extensive redesign to obtain quality	.Extensive measures/modeling, vigorous data analysis and specialized tests to ensure high level achievement of detailed quality requirements-extensive change program	
		First level of quality	Second level of quality	Third level of quality	Fourth level of quality	
			Degree of effort			

506

for specifically telecommunications products. You may wish to briefly examine Table 12-15 before further reading in order to establish familiarity with the concepts of "extent" and "degree" in the pursuit of quality.

Introduction

The major objectives of quality management are to assure that a selected quality level of a product can be achieved, on schedule, in a cost effective manner. Today's management must make extremely complex strategic decisions to achieve balance in schedule, productivity and the cost of quality.

This analysis will describe a conceptual approach for the quality management of programming products called "quality prisms." If formally implemented, it can establish a program to pursue quality objectives early in a product's life cycle and identify the necessary design, test, and monitoring effort required to achieve the desired level of quality in the final product. "Quality prisms" are based on quality characteristics and the extent and degree that they are implemented.

Therefore, "quality prisms" is the proposed management tool to be used in planning, designing and testing of a product to enable it to meet desired goals. In developing a quality management system, the product's life cycle phase reviews provide the reference base for tracking the achievement of quality objectives. For reference, the life cycle phases for reliability and maintainability management are:

- Concept, Requirements, and Definition Phases (Plan).
- Design and Development Phase (Design/Test).
- Integration and Installation Phase (Integrate/Install).
- Operation and Maintenance Phase (Service).

The "extent of effort" that a given quality characteristic has been implemented in a product increases with the number of life cycle phases, where this quality characteristic has been properly addressed. The "degree of effort" varies from "no activity" to a "high level of activity" for each individual life cycle phase. An example of extent and degree is contained in Table 12-15. Thus, the "quality prism" concept based on "extent and degree" can be tailored to fit a corporation, a group of companies, an individual company, a group effort, or even an individual effort. Other applications include competitive product assessment and long range quality planning.

Quality

Programming quality for this analysis is defined as the achievement of a selected level of quality characteristics *(ilities)* within the boundaries of the cost, schedule, and productivity, as established by management for the product. In practice, the extent of the pursuit of quality (emphasis) can change with respect to the specific product application environment. Different perspectives of quality have been presented over the years. Recognition is made that different levels of quality are acceptable for various applications and types of products. However, past history shows that a product which does not achieve its required quality objectives, will have numerous unplanned costs. The "delicate balance" of quality and cost is conceptually shown in Fig. 12-45 and discussed in detail throughout this analysis. It will be graphically shown how a product, that progresses uniformly through pre-selected quality levels throughout its life cycle phases, attains its cost goals and meets its quality objectives.

This analysis presents a conceptual process for defining and ensuring the achievement of desired quality objectives (pursuing quality). A product can have quality emphasized at one or all phases of its product life cycle (planning, design/test, integrate/install, and service). These are referred to as the levels of extent, that quality is pursued. The degree to which quality is emphasized at each phase level can become increasingly rigorous and expensive. For the sake of discussion, this analysis has four possible degrees of effort (from no activity through a high level of activity). Before beginning a project, these levels of pursuit should initially be established for each desired quality characteristic. Actual selection can vary, depending on a firm's commitment to that particular quality characteristic. This is demonstrated here by using figurative examples and models. The objective of this analysis is to provide a conceptual framework called "quality prisms" for quality management to consider. It enables planning, implementing, and monitoring within a company or companies of the quality characteristics of their products.

The Characteristics of Quality

Different products generally have differing sets of quality characteristics from a quality characteristic tree. Primary quality characteristics can be listed in terms of "ilities," such as: maintainability, portability, reliability, testability, understandability, usability, changeability, and reusability. These have all been discussed in depth in numerous articles, with the exception of changeability and reusability.

Changeability is becoming a major requirement for telecommunications products, as more and more voice and data integrated features are required in future versions of these programming products. Similarly, reusability has recently been highlighted in the business applications programming product area, as a possible key to improved quality, productivity, and lower costs.

However, it is essential to note that to date, the realization of the "ilities" has not been entirely satisfactory. No one has developed a universally acceptable reliable measure. For example, consider the "portability" characteristic. Several recent operating systems are called "portable," but usually each computer's version in practice is different and not interchangeable. Testability is even more nebulous and subject to conflicting claims and costs. Similarly ease or use (usability) is hotly contested. The concept of "quality prisms" described in this article will hopefully allow the "ilities" to be considered in a more regimental and defined perspective as part of a rigorous quality management system. Quality characteristics must be initially identi-

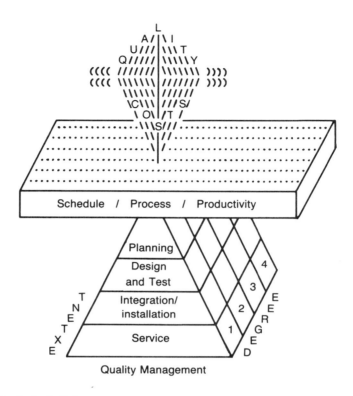

Fig. 12-46. The Delicate Balance.

programming planning phases and then tracked through the developmental phases. Thus, quality management becomes an integral part of the programming life cycle process. This planning effort for achieving each desired characteristic's objectives can be modeled using a quality level index system described later in this analysis.

The Objectives of Quality

A recent article in the Harvard Business Review stated that, "No longer just an afterthought, the management of product quality determines market success." A product's life cycle has key decision points at each major phase in the planning and development of a product. This provides a management vehicle for establishing and controlling the extent and degree that the "ilities" are identified, quantified, and achieved for each phase during the product's development, as management vigorously addresses their quality objectives. If the product life cycle phase reviews emphasize schedule or productivity over quality, then the delicate balance will falter. Hence, to be more competitive and successful, the objectives of quality need to shift from the traditional measuring of a physical entity for conformance to the implementation of a quality analysis at each phase in the product life cycle.

Management emphasis to implement a very specific quality process, such as defined here, will enable realistic achievement of their quality objectives.

The Costs of Quality

In general for the programming product, the higher the level of quality the lower the costs of the operation and maintenance phase. The programming industry has traditionally required large maintenance organizations to correct defects and add new features and changes. A typical phase-cost curve is presented in Fig. 12-47 showing the increased costs to correct defects in the later phases of the product life cycle. In this example the vertical axis is non-linear. It has been seen where firms, whose past developments effort took five to ten programmers for the initial programs, now have thirty to sixty programmers supporting and adapting these earlier designs.

Degree And Extent of the Pursuit of Quality Throughout the Life Cycle

As a product is planned, developed, tested, and placed into service, it should achieve predefined quality objectives at each phase level. The characteristics of quality are initially identified and then measured to ensure achieve-

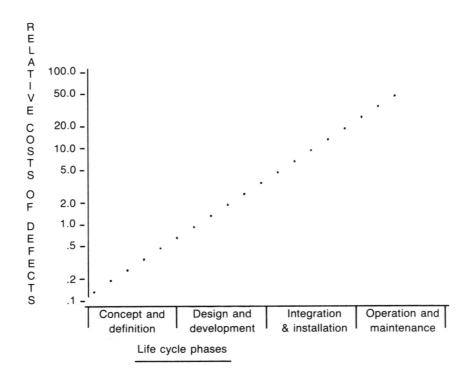

Fig. 12-47. Increasing Costs.

510

ment. Any attempt to emphasize a different or new objective or characteristic at the end of a product's developmental life cycle is usually quite difficult, costly, and substantially impacts schedule (if it can be achieved at all). Hence, this analysis is proposing a fresh look at quality by continuously managing the desired degree of quality throughout the life cycle. Initial planning by quality management will provide a matrix such as Table 12-15 for each desired quality characteristic. For this conceptual example, the extent of the pursuit of quality is considered for only four generalistic product life cycle levels (phases)—planning, design, integration, and service. The degree of quality within a level is simply noted as one, two, three or four (maximum). Hence, if a firm is seriously interested in having a particular quality characteristic of a product, they must carefully determine for each phase (level) throughout the life cycle, the degree to which the characteristic should be achieved.

In reviewing Table 12-15, we can note the following:

1. Each quality characteristic can have a matrix similar to this matrix with a specific quality program tailored to the firm's products.
2. The "quality effort" is extended to each level of the product life cycle (phases) to the firm's desired degree.
3. For each level, as the complexity and difficulty of a characteristic requirement increases, the degree of intensity of the test and verification program effort increases.
4. This matrix will change for each characteristic in accordance with company emphasis.
5. Traditionally quality levels of a product will correspond to degrees of effort. However, this matrix extends the effort to all phases of the product's life cycle.

As an example for using the matrix shown in Table 12-15, a characteristic such as reliability may be targeted to reach a service two level, where throughout its design it orderly achieves each progressive planning two, design two, and integration two level. These indicators are tied to the proper major phase review points of a product's life cycle process. For most characteristics, the planning level should be achieved after the preliminary design review (PDR), the design level after the development phases or at the critical design review (CDR), the integration level after integration at the qualification testing, and the service level during the operational service reviews.

Now quality management can apply this matrix to each characteristic in a manner depending how critical it is for them to ensure achievement of the characteristic. A key system may be satisfied with ten mishandled calls per week, while a PBX may be satisfied with five mishandled calls per month. These objectives may cause quality management to define a planning two, design two, integration two, and service two program for the key system and a more extensive planning four, design three, integration three and service three program for the PBX.

In this manner the quality characteristics are clearly identified by detailed

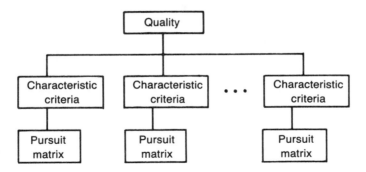

Fig. 12-48. Pursuit of Quality Program.

criteria which scope and limit their requirement objectives. Once these goals are identified, then a quality program can be determined that defines the required specific definition, design, tests and measurements efforts. No longer are nebulous measurements made against vague objectives at the service period of a product's life cycle in a last minute attempt to improve quality.

The key to identifying the proper "quality criteria" is to categorize levels of criticality for various programming objectives. Once this has been accomplished, then the actual criteria values can be established. For example, there is a method for quantifying the occurrence of software bugs. However, their manifestations in the systems operation are detrimental, as each manifestation could cause a failure event. The key is to categorize levels of criticality for bug manifestations and estimate their probability of occurrence and distribution. Table 12-16 presents a quality criteria benchmark that can be pursued at each of the four life cycle phases. The degree to which a particular quality characteristic is targeted and the extent in which it is pursued, will, of course, be governed by system requirements, market factors, and costs.

Hence, there is a need for the "quality process" to establish the required pursuit program of quality characteristics early. If a particular quality characteristic is not pursued at the planning level and design level to a reasonable extent, then at the subsequent service level a maximum degree of four may not realistically be achieved. Conversely the more uniformly and consistently a quality characteristic is pursued, the more achievable and figuratively stable is the characteristic. This is graphically reflected for a single characteristic in Figs. 12-49 through 12-51 where the quality item is shown as stable, unstable, or extremely costly to stabilize.

In Fig. 12-49 an optimum trade-off of stability and productivity is portrayed. The base of the prism is secure, supporting the platform by properly balancing quality versus costs.

In Fig. 12-50 the pressures of schedule have established an unstable prism to support the platform. In this example the decision was made to send the product into the field at the service one level, even though it initially had reached a more extensive degree of quality three at the planning level. (Con-

Table 12-16. Quality Criteria Program.

Bug manifestation rate	Defect removal rate	Level of criticality	Fault	
			Type	Characteristics
4 per day	1 per month	5	transient	errors come and go
3 per day	1 per week	4	transient	errors are repeated
2 per week	1 per month	3	transient or catastrophic	service affecting
1 per month	2 per year	2	transient or catastrophic	system partially down
1 per 2 years	1 per year	1	catastrophic	system stops

siderable effort to define quality objectives at the planning phase, but no follow up.)

Figure 12-51 presents the extremely costly view of upgrading a programming product in the field to the level of service four (after passing the first three levels only to the first degree). Note the increasing amount of time and effort to achieve service one, service two, or service three. Service four in this example is usually very difficult and expensive, if not impossible, to achieve. The measured productivity on such a product will most likely be very low.

Example

An excellent example of the need for this type of quality management process occurred many years ago. The lessons still apply today. An automated

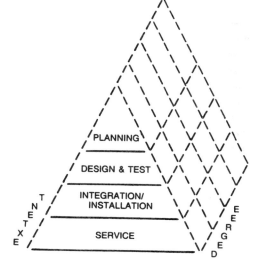

Fig. 12-49. Stability in Quality and Cost.

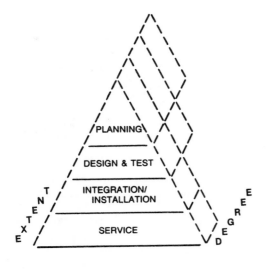

Fig. 12-50. Instability due to Scheduling Decisions.

program was proposed to generate from 160 fields of input data per customer, a centralized data base, that would control a table driven wired logic system.

It was estimated to require thirteen weeks of design time to construct the table generator using a nominal amount of computer support time. A representative of the design group was assigned to define the input/output requirements for this support program and verify its operation. The program was initially written in assembly language. It was later redesigned and split

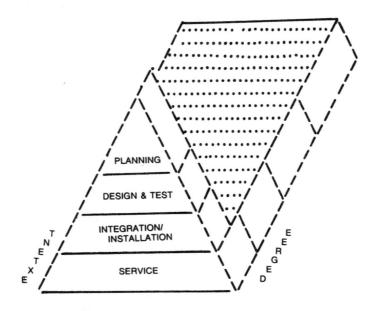

Fig. 12-51. Extremely Costly Programming Product.

into three separate programs, written in a high level language. These could then be separately designed, verified and maintained. The main consideration became the verification process. An input/output test was written to check the extensive program paths. The project dragged into a year, as verification testing attempted to meet a zero defect objective (imposed after the initial design had been completed). Costs increased and the schedule became critical as the customer became impatient (Fig. 12-51).

As the program began to function more successfully, it became a serious question deciding the degree of testing required for verification. Confrontation developed between design and marketing over the commercial release of the program. Without agreement on the required amount of degree, the testing continued. Eventually the customer became disillusioned and turned to another firm to provide the table generator. Had a clear quality management decision been made at the planning phase and tracked throughout the development on: the degree of error free "verified" operation; the quality characteristic objectives for its design architecture and structure; the language required for changes, etc., then a more realistic projection (and control) of schedule and people could have been achieved. It may have required several releases to the customer as the program designs and operation were verified to a predetermined extent within the various life cycle phases. In conclusion, there would have been a more satisfied customer and supplier.

This example offered an excellent opportunity to first determine the type and amount of quality desired. Once this was accomplished, then management could have constructed a quality process, in terms of the extent and degree of each desired characteristic with a realistic compromise between schedule, resources and the design activity to achieve it. In this case many of the "ilities" were subsequently more critically identified, such as changeability, usability, maintainability, and reliability. These considerations could have been translated into the initial requirements for structural design, program segmentation, extensive documentation, type of language, as well as amount of code walk through, subfunctional tests, amount of error acceptable at first release, depth of verification reviews, etc. From this form of planning, the "quality prisms" could have been established to define the extent and degree (such as service two, service three, or service four) to which each of these characteristics should have been pursued in terms of project cost restraints, depending on user willingness to pay and wait for a quality product.

Achieving Stability in the Pursuit of Quality

A figuratively secure prismatic base for the programming product was presented in Fig. 12-49. This security is developed through execution of an extensive quality program as progressively shown in Figs. 12-52 through 12-54. A product's quality objective is usually composed of more than one characteristic. Previously those have tentatively been noted as maintainability, portability, reliability, testability, understandability, usability, changeability, and reusability. Thus, quality management can extend the support prismatic structure to a greater depth, than to just one quality characteristic.

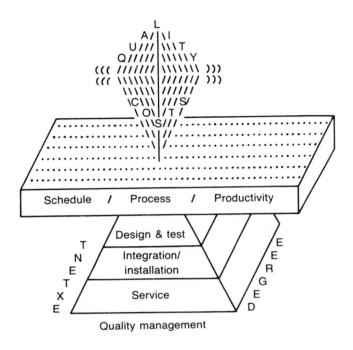

Fig. 12-52. The Delicate Balance—Planning Completion.

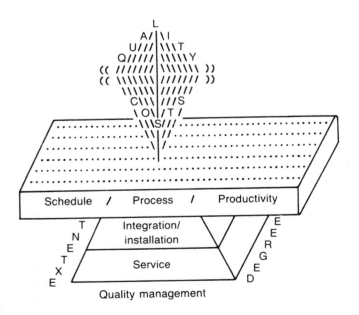

Fig. 12-53. The Delicate Balance—Design and Testing Completion.

516

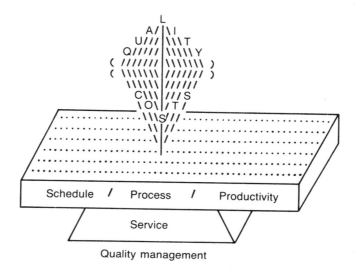

Fig. 12-54. The Delicate Balance — Integration/Installation Completion.

In practice, several "quality prisms" will be placed together to achieve a firm quality base.

It may be desirable to have a product developed that has reached the service four level for all of the fore mentioned quality characteristics. However, realistic schedules and productivity goals must be considered in terms of costs. These considerations establish the need for vigorous quality management overall life cycle phases to selectively balance the various possibilities. It would be very non-supportive, expensive, and time consuming, if quality management established the structural combination of individual characteristic quality prisms, as graphically presented in Fig. 12-55. Unfortunately this is the case for too many products. Quality management would do better to

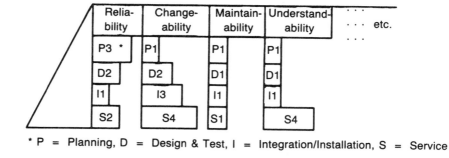

Relia- bility	Change- ability	Maintain- ability	Understand- ability	· · ·
P3 *	P1	P1	P1	· · · etc.
D2	D2	D1	D1	
I1	I3	I1	I1	
S2	S4	S1	S4	

* P = Planning, D = Design & Test, I = Integration/Installation, S = Service

Fig. 12-55. Example of Poor Quality Management.

517

Relia- bility	Change- ability	Maintain- ability
P3 *	P2	P3
D3	D2	D3
I3	I2	I3
S3	S2	S3

*P = Planning, D = Design & Test, I = Integration/Installation, S = Service

Fig. 12-56. Example of Good Quality Management.

establish a more consistent supportive structure, like that represented in Fig. 12-56.

The figurative result of this effort is shown in the solid cost effective base of Fig. 12-57.

Quality Management Process Matrix

If quality characteristics are established, monitored, measured and verified throughout the life cycle, then a realistic balance can successfully be achieved between quality costs, schedule and productivity. However, it will require an active quality management process to establish and track these indicators. An example of such a quality management index level process is presented in Table 12-17 to quantify the extent and degree of effort to achieve a desired level of quality. This table can be used as a programming product quality worksheet (PQW), as well as both the characteristic survey data collection instrument (DCI) and part of the final quality prisms planning document (QPPD).

As discussed, a quality management team must establish the degree of quality, that a particular quality characteristic must reach throughout its life cycle. They may use specialized support tools, measurements systems and specific product quality standards in pursuing their desired quality objectives. The following is an exemplary point system, which gives a quantitative refer-

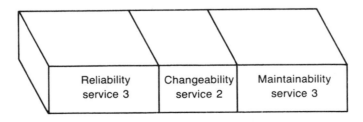

Fig. 12-57. Example of Solid Cost Base.

518

Table 12-17. Example of Quality Management Process Matrix.

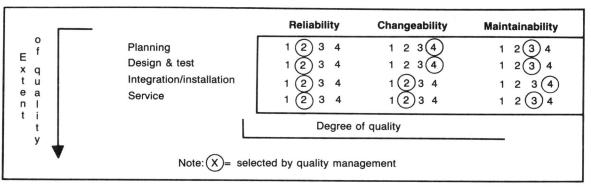

	Reliability	Changeability	Maintainability
Planning	1 (2) 3 4	1 2 3 (4)	1 2 (3) 4
Design & test	1 (2) 3 4	1 2 3 (4)	1 2 (3) 4
Integration/installation	1 (2) 3 4	1 (2) 3 4	1 2 3 (4)
Service	1 (2) 3 4	1 (2) 3 4	1 2 (3) 4

Extent of quality

Degree of quality

Note: (X) = selected by quality management

ence for the pursuit of quality effort. This can become the basis for trading time versus costs to reach specific quality goals. Of course, a firm's Quality Management will define their own point system. However, for discussion purposes, this example point system will serve as an illustration.

If a single characteristic quality effort has progressed through all four levels, as well as through each level's maximum degree, then it has accumulated a maximum of $4 + 4 + 4 + 4 = 16$ points. If another characteristic's effort has moved through the levels only at $1/2$ of its maximum degree, then it has accumulated $2 + 2 + 2 + 2 = 8$ points. If it reached $3/4$ of the maximum degree of effort on all levels, it has $3 + 3 + 3 + 3 = 12$ points. Management can now assign a reference value to the pursuit of quality for a programming product. This is shown in the simplified example in Table 12-18.

For this example the total $= 8 + 12 + 13 = 33$ out of a possible $16 + 16 + 16 = 48$ or 69%. (In more general terms, this can also be referred to as an overall level three quality effort in the 50% to 75% range.) Note that the real indication of the quality objectives will be the magnitude of the X/Y (33/48) values. The greater the X and Y values, the more the characteristics have been pursued to a deeper degree. The greater the X values the more stable the structure has become and the more quality objectives the programming product has achieved.

Carrying this type of analysis over all eight characteristics (8x16), a maximum of 128 points is possible. Products that approach this level of effort will have a considerably more stable structure than those that are only based upon a 16 point single character structure. The X% quality reference number should also be qualified by a factor number to note how many characteristics were actually used. This could be shown as 69%/Q3 or 33/48/Q3.

Finally, some characteristics will have more complexity and require greater costs in order to be achieved than others. Thus a weighing multiplier (WM) can be used, which will help to equalize the quality characteristics. Weighing multipliers for the above example are demonstrated in Table 12-19.

For this example the total $= 10 + 28 + 19 = 57$ out of a possible $20 + 40 + 24 = 84$ which is 57/84/Q3, 68%/Q3, or a level three/Q3. This three part programming quality ratio (PQR) can be used for reviewing quality

Table 12-18. Example of Pursuit of Quality.

Extent of quality	Quality characteristics effort		
	Reliability	Changeability	Maintainability
Planning	2	4	3
Design & test	2	4	3
Integrat/Install	2	2	4
Service	2	2	3
Total points per Available points	8/16	12/16 (75%)	13/16 (81%)
Total		33/48/C3 (69%)/C3	

across programming products within a project as a more quantitative reference for cross referencing their quality costs to quality objectives.

Summary

A quality management process matrix (Table 12-17) has been presented for pursuing quality throughout a programming product's life cycle. It relates the pursuit of quality characteristics effort to the product definition, design, testing, and service monitoring phases. In practice, actual implementation of this approach will require selection of languages, code walk throughs, type of testing, etc., to be specifically defined to reach service two, service three, or service four quality levels. From this the schedule impact and the cost of quality can be projected and monitored. Perhaps these concepts can be fur-

Table 12-19. Example of Use of Weighing Multipliers.

Extent of quality	Quality characteristics					
	Reliability		Changeability		Maintainability	
		WM		WM		WM
Planning	2 × 1		4 × 2		3 × 2	
Design & test	2 × 1		4 × 2		3 × 1.5	
Integrat/Install	2 × 1		2 × 3		4 × 1	
Service	2 × 2		2 × 3		3 × 1.5	
Total points per Available points	10/20 (50%)		28/40 (70%)		19/24 (79%)	
Total			57/84/C3 (68%)/C3			

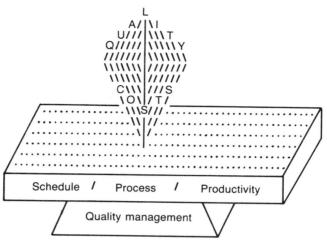

Fig. 12-58. Achieving the Delicate Balance.

ther developed over the years into a measurable standard relationship between planning one, design one, integration one, and service one and the degree of reviews, walk throughs, tests, measurements, etc.

This process will also help management to identify the extent and degree of the pursuit of quality across products of competing companies or internal corporate divisions. Of course, until such a standard is developed, the quality management team will subjectively assign values and multipliers as noted in the Table 12-17 (programming product quality worksheet), and relate them to their own acceptable degree of documentation, code walk through, module tests, etc. However, though they are subjective, these are extremely useful in establishing individual product quality effort goals. By translating this concept of "quality prisms" to planning, design and test considerations, that balance schedule and cost against quality objectives, management will now have a more reasonable opportunity to pursue and successfully achieve the extent and degree of "desired quality" for their products.

Seven: Planning Applications

—DESIGN COMMITTEES—

A specific methodology for working committees and design reviews, which has been perfected by the aerospace industry and is currently being used by other telecommunication design houses is shown in a five step program that describes the movement and exchange of ideas across Requirements Groups, Logical System Design Teams, Physical System Design Groups, Design Control Committees and a System Product Control Committee. Vari-

Table 12-20. Analyses Relationships.

	Requirements	Logical system functional structure
Purpose	Identifies a realistic set of requirements with brief descriptions and priorities.	To identify functional areas which partition a general structure that meets referenced requirements.
Relationship	Provide "Release Package" schedule target for other steps.	Recursive trade off analysis of general structures that meet base requirements.
Action	Provides requirements which are the base reference point for the design and System/Product Engineering control committee.	Provides general structure for functionalized design area studies (i.e., data base bus, line terminal, etc.).
Output	A complete set of formal requirement documents.	High level system structure identified with base requirements.

ous aspects are noted in Table 12-20 in terms of purpose, relationships, actions, and outputs, as the design progresses from a document, that clearly identifies all features in terms of feature package releases to the resulting switching system of a communications product development program. Figure 12-59 notes the need for cross relating these features to a logical design architecture to see the impact of each feature in each appropriate design area. From this, an actual "physical" detailed system design structure should emerge, which meets these "logical" system descriptions and addresses each of the major expanding or limiting feature requirements of the user and provider.

To achieve this structure, the figure notes the design control committee approach that continuously monitors each major area of consideration. Here, either a system specialist, responsible designer or design manager should chair a committee containing representatives from each affected design team. The committee can meet as needed throughout the design phase. The chairperson from each committee is also a member of the main system/product design control committee, which has its own chairperson.

The purpose of this system level committee is to cross tie the efforts of the individual working committees to avoid conflicting decisions. It also responds to requests for new features that enhance the system.

It should be noted in the Fig. 12-59 that there are three special committees that continuously track the hardware/software/support structure. They keep the system control committee updated with the present version of the system. Members of these three committees are usually managers of the respective design teams. Major new system requirements should recursively go through all the steps, while lesser feature changes can be added directly

Phsyical system structure	Design control committees	System/product engineering control committee
To provide a specific HW/SW structure that meets the base requirements.	To control the specific design areas and ensure that base requirements are met.	To provide, control, and resolve cross-committee design problems.
To provide the agreed structure that logically meets the target feature/requirement upon which are based the design trade offs.	Provide forum/focal point for each design team to participate in resolving common design areas requirements	Provide a forum for tracking the system design and a focal point to resolve design conflicts.
Provide a specific structure for the design.	Resolves specific design issues across design groups. and ensures that design structures meet base requirements	Provides immediate resolution and exposure to cross-committee design conflicts
Detailed system design structured.	The specific designed circuits/programs of the responsible individual design teams.	Control of the design structure and interface decisions.

in the last step, unless these changes begin to seriously change the intended configurations.

Thus, this simple little addition to the "P" structure enables people to better participate and exchange information. It has been proven to greatly enhanced traditional design approaches by ensuring that major features and common design considerations are constantly addressed throughout the design.

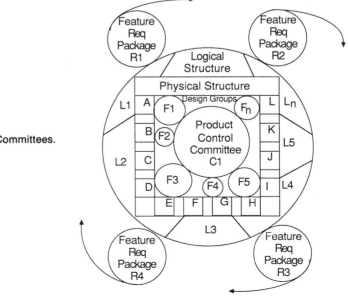

Fig. 12-59. Design Committees.

—MULTI UNIT PLANNING—

"In order to cost effectively compete in the North American marketplace in the 90s, we must integrate the strengths of the multiple units." It is easy to observe the obvious, but more difficult to achieve a delicate balance. Much of what is said in this analysis has already been considered; but it provides a somewhat unique perspective on the products, organizations, processes, and strategies necessary to achieve this objective from a centralized/decentralized perspective.

Product Needs

As we all know, the marketplace opportunities are more competitive and non-monopolized in business arena of the common carrier. There will be tremendous growth, as the shift takes place from analog voice to integrated digital voice and data. The business communications systems market, consisting of key systems (16, 32 lines), PBXs (60, 120, 1000, 4600, 9600 lines), local digital voice and data networks (MUXs, switches), specialized common carrier switches, intelligent terminals, digital phones, fiber optics, and private networks (Tandem and PBX switches) for Fortune's top 100 firms, has become internationally competitive. To succeed, a multinational firm must draw upon experience and from past products in each of the its multiple units and get them to work together to build versatile multi-faceted network service/switching products to support the new data and voice public information networks, as well as achieve PBXs and nodal point access systems for separate private networks, such as the banks, oil companies, etc.; where the stand alone versions of these PBX systems, supported by digital phones, intelligent terminals, and key systems, with "turn key" computer software application packages, will be attractive to hospitals, shopping centers, apartment complexes, etc.

Task forces of system planners from multiunit firms have only recently begun to note their cross dependencies and need for coordinated advance development analyses, requiring specialized shared knowledge in programming, transmission, networks, protocols and terminals. These analyses must also be supported by trade off studies, dependent on market research (features and limits), performance models, financial models and pricing/tariff analyses.

Organization

In reviewing mode of operations, scope of view, depth of capabilities, level of aids, management style and organizational structure, there is much discussion and analysis of the advantages and disadvantages of centralized versus distributed research and development. Perhaps the answer is in the following organizational structure:

- Centralize the advanced planning, applied research, and advanced development functions (not necessarily physically but logically coordinated). This

524

will maximize the strengths of talented specialists in:
— Program planning and product planning.
— Product structure.
— Product feasibility models.
— Support tools for management, design, languages, design aids, test, support, manufacture automation, and documentation.

- Decentralize the development, manufacturing support, and field support functions to areas where units are currently located, to support manufacturing facilities, or to geographical areas, that attract the design labor market and obtain more economical building costs.

At these unit's development design centers, teams perform:

— Program and project management.
— Product architecture/structure—applied design.
— Produce product engineering prototypes.
— Design first release features.
— Support product application design.
— Provide application packages.
— Extend and customize support tools for design, manufacture, and field support.

The centralized functions could logically (not necessarily physically) consist of:

— Market research group.
— Product definition system arch/structure teams containing hardware/software, transmission, traffic, network, operating systems, management tools, models, advanced languages, test vehicles, manufacturing software, and manufacturing hardware representative specialists.

The Strategy

The marketplace drives the products, which drive the organization. Hence, the new products are identified by a market-product driven organization, that has two major functions. One is to determine feasible products, the other is to develop manufacturable products, not as a traditional product development group, but as an advanced planning laboratory with knowledgeable systems, hardware, and software designers, who will develop new designs to encompass many new features, and integrate individual products into an integrated network offering.

In order to prevent having architecture designs that are not acceptable to the unit's designers and to utilize the expertise of the unit's lead designers, they should be members of preproduct definition teams that establish the initial architecture. It is interesting to note that the central "feasibility model" need not be totally completed before unit design can begin. In many instances, both might run in parallel, with knowledge gained from one influencing the other, as both the unit and central locations perform their particular type of preproject analyses.

In this manner, the units acquire the knowledge of the centralized expertise and common support tools and methods. Therefore, the centralized facility is now a living facility and simply not transferring support to a unit to answer design questions.

Later, a central unit support group can assist the unit in the transfer of technology, methods, and tools. A process should be utilized, which breaks the program into planning and development phases with specific checkpoint reviews for management to monitor the flow through the various labs in accordance to the product plan.

This should achieve an effective organization such as one which:

— Coordinates product planning across North American units via conceptual planning analyses.
— Identifies specific products for the North American marketplaces.
— Establishes requirements definition teams to perform preproduct system architecture design, and review and clarify requirements.
— Establishes feasibility model design teams with hardware designers and programmers to develop a common test model.
— Provides coordination between central planning, unit program and project management, and applied and advanced research laboratories.
— Maximizes unit's development progress.
— Provides the most effective methods and tools to the units for management, design, test, manufacturing and support.
— Achieves a versatile family of telecommunication-computer products developed and supported by maximizing skills across units using the best methods and tools available.

These can be accomplished by centralized (logically not necessarily physically) product planning, advanced research (studies), and advanced development (feasibility models) activities, integrated with the distributed unit's development (engineering model), manufacturing, and field support activities.

—UNIVERSALITY OF THE MANAGEMENT PLANNING PROCESS—

To demonstrate the versatility of the planning process, let's take a brief look at how it can be universally applied to achieve such things as social programs. In the 90s, social organizations' structures must be as efficient and streamlined as possible, to effectively handle the magnitude of concerns that our increasingly complex world will provide. For the "information society" to succeed, such organizations must be able to responsed to new forms of human issues and needs, as the world gets closer together. In addition, many who retire early, due to the tremendous automation changes of the twenty first century, will be encouraged to continue to use their skills in the planning and implementation of many large scale social action programs.

Hence, the emphasis will be to provide a functional organization, that

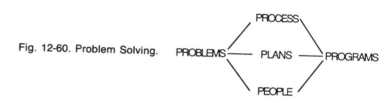

Fig. 12-60. Problem Solving.

utilizes collective talents to meet and respond to the needs of others. These new social "programs" can address issues on a national and universal basis with other internationally concerned groups. Major social objectives will be achieved by organizations having:

1. A process that enables an orderly flow from problem identification to program planning, to program implementation, to program review, to program termination.
2. A problem solving oriented organizational structure, that identifies problems, provides plans, implements programs, and reviews programs.

A successful process enables people to identify problems, define plans, and implement programs. It can best be described as having six distinct phases with a review after each phase by a review steering committee, who either terminate the effort, request rework and modification, or recommend its continuance to the next phase of its development or operation. The phases are as follows:

Conceptual Planning

During this phase the "why" and "why not" questions are asked by conceptual planners, ad hoc planning councils, and social program directors. The causes as well as the effects are identified with possible plans and programs for resolving them. The results are documented as strategic long/short range plans for specific problem areas.

Problem Definition

During this phase all the "whats" are identified to ensure that all facets of the issues are understood concerning the particular need, problem, or concern under review. The scope, time frame of need, priority, areas of concern, cost, risks, and requirements are clarified, as much as possible, to help prevent entering programs prematurely, before fully understanding what the problem solution should provide.

Program Planning

During this phase, by utilizing the talents and skills of advisory specialists, program directors, and council representatives, the detailed plans for providing a problem-solving program are conceived and finalized. They specifically define position, policy, organization, solution, method of implementation, and checkpoint for monitoring progress. The results are feasible program plans to meet the needs and requirements that were identified in the problem definition phase.

Program Implementation

During this phase the responsible program director(s) and their staff implement program plans. This effort is ongoing until a review determines that the program is no longer needed. To accomplish this the program director may wish to utilize the talents and skills of advisory councils and working committees.

Program Review

During this phase all programs that are currently active are reviewed on a periodic manner (6 months to year basis) to ensure that they are meeting the original objectives and requests, for which they were instigated. Their review should be by a cross representative steering committee to ensure a complete full scope analysis occurs that reviews all aspects.

Program Termination

Here a program is completed and formally terminated. A program may initially only shift from the active mode to the support of previously initiated currently ongoing activities, before final conclusion of all efforts.

Return Paths

Return paths to preceding planning phases exist to modify and clarify the concept, problem, or program plans. Similarly, a return path occurs between the implementation phase and the formal program review phase after periodic reviews. If necessary, there may be a need for new planning during the implementation phase. In this case, depending on the magnitude, it is best to return back to the conceptual planning phase and repeat all three planning phases to ensure all requirements are considered.

In conclusion, the process enables an orderly flow from problems to plans to programs to reviews by utilizing the right people at the right point in time. The process indicates checkpoints for management review and decisions. It emphasizes the conceptual planning-program planning phases as the key points for early management involvement in establishing strategy and plans, that are consistent with the organization's mission.

This organizational architecture should contain the following key personnel utilization elements:

- Description of a process for identifying needs and forming action programs to resolve them.

- An organization that supports the process and enables top down partici- pation in the planning phases.
- An organization that utilizes the talents of the various specialists in the planning process.
- An organization that enables the program directors to utilize interested volunteers in implementing action programs.
- A check and balance system which enables a steering committee of chair- persons and representatives from advisory councils for program planning and implementation reviews.
- An organization of a small conceptual planning group to conceive long and short range programs for consideration.
- A director of program planning with a small staff, who controls the pro- gress of identifying needs, conceiving solutions, defining plans, and es- tablishing programs.
- A director of program implementation, who is responsible for coordinat- ing resources for all the program directors' program implementation plans.
- Program directors, who are responsible for implementing programs using their staff, advisory committees, and working committees.
- A director of program review, who is responsible for establishing a steer- ing committee to review each phase of "the process"—conceptual plan- ning, problem definition, program design, and program implementation until program termination.

In Summary

This "architecture" indicates specifically the phases of the process: who does what at each phase, who controls the flow through the phases, and who coordinates the phase reviews and program reviews. It provides the follow- ing feature points:

- Management has a checkpoint after each phase to determine if they are ready to proceed into the next phase.
- Needs, concerns, possibilities, opportunities, and problems are fully un- derstood before they require a management commitment to develop detailed plans.
- Escape routes are available at checkpoints. If changes, adjustments, and modifications are required, loop backs are provided to go back to concep- tual planning, problem definition, or program planning from any phase. Alternatively, the study or program can be terminated at that phase with- out any further expenditure of time and money.
- Before a program is launched, complete plans are required. This prevents premature entrance into programs during which purpose, direction, objec- tives, costs, etc., are seriously requestioned.
- Big picture, long/short range plans, full scope planning help put things into perspective and enables the planning of programs that seriously ad- dress the cause instead of the effects.
- Needs, problems, and requirements are further refined, modified, etc., as

they are analyzed through the three planning phases (conceptual planning, problem definition, program planning), reducing risk.

- Plans can exist in preceding phases before the program planning phase, in order to better understand the impact of needs and problems on resources. However, it is not until this phase, that complete realistic detailed plans need to be defined and finalized.
- Program management plans are provided with program plans for complete review at the final planning checkpoint before commitment to program implementation.
- The director of program planning controls the progress of a potential program through the planning phases to ensure it is not lost in committees in problem definition planning.
- Budgets can be traded-off against different programs and normal operating expenses in a more realistic manner, once conceptual plans and several program plans are completed.
- The talents and skills of the directors of program planning and implementation will greatly affect the success of this structure, as well as the cooperation of the councils.
- Review's "go, no-go" decisions can be performed at the right point of the process.
- The review steering committee consists of representatives and chairpersons from each major area of concern. Cross-area requirements can be discussed and resolved, in order to ensure a program's success.
- Volunteers can find a working committee in the area of their choice to assist program directors in implementing programs.
- Programs can be "phased in" to accommodate personnel and funding restraints.
- Talents of specialists can be used in an effective manner, to provide their expert assistance in problem definition and program planning.
- People can begin to play a more active role in the information society by participating in the phases that their interests and capabilities best meet— problem defining, program planning, program implementation, program review, or problem solving.

—PARTICIPATING MANAGER PLANNERS—

As we all know that with a change from a totalitarian, authoritarian, or even a benevolent dictator type organization to a more democratic, participating structure, we have now opened the door to a new set of problems. This latter case requires people working together for the common good of the company, as they share their many different views in working groups, cross lines of business committees, advisory councils, and planning boards. The Manager Planners must ensure that these groups function smoothly with the many different types of personalities. They must be able to participate together to arrive at acceptable conclusions and recommendations for their strategies, proposals, product definitions and programs.

This is no easy task but must be successfully accomplished if the new complex network's architectures and structures are to be properly identified, using numerous people from various disciplines. Similarly, management review teams must work together to obtain decisions and commitment for these highly complex new products. Assuming we are not dealing with people who are using "base" motives, who can only be removed or bypassed as road blocks, we are simply faced with the situation of understanding people and working with their different personalities. One laboratory went so far as to employ a psychiatrist to determine why their committees could never achieve any progress. In most cases, it is not necessary to go to that extreme but one company did employ a multi million dollar per year master sales person to teach the management how to deal with people more effectively in moving ideas to accepted programs, by working with many different people.

Henry Biggers, a marketing specialist who is an outstanding people specialist, noted that people have personality traits which must be recognized and effectively handled to complete a transaction. In his workshops, he discusses how to work with various types of people. This brief set of his observations help identify the complexities of "working together and obtaining agreements:"

1. "Know the players, the decision maker(s), the key players who are on our team, neutral or against.
2. Assess their fears, point out benefits, request their expertise and assistance.
3. Acknowledge all involved, and share recognition and benefits.
4. Remember the objective is to convey understanding, obtain acceptance, and achieve action and commitment.
5. Knowing beforehand (where possible), who the real decision makers are and who the potential decision breakers are, helps you defuse problems. Recognize the "buy in" influentials for your proposal:

   — The Specifier: One who states the required. product or service.
   — The Constrainer: One who limits how much can be spent.
   — The Voter: The member of a group who is permitted to participate in the decision.
   — The Information Supplier: One who gathers factual data for others.
   — The User: The unit, person, or agency for whom the product is actually produced.
   — The Buyer: The person who actually places the order.
   — The Vetoer: Ultimate authority, who may refuse to accept the conclusion of others.
   — The Kibitzer: One who volunteers unsolicited opinions.
   — The Screeners: People who influence what information may go through to the other buying influentials.

6. Selling the concept, proposal, or product definition to management requires:

—Understanding need.
—Showing benefit.
—Creating conviction.
—Achieving desire.
—Obtaining agreement.

7. Understanding that "no" may mean different things, it could mean:
   —I don't understand.
   —I want more information.
   —I'm not sure the price is right.
   —I don't believe the benefits outweigh the costs—Prove it!
   —I want more time to consider the proposal.

8. Deal with "difficult people" and balance their mode of operation without changing them or fighting them, by accepting them, recognizing them, separating them, and separately defusing them; by (depending on the type): using direct firm statements, questions, giving them documented data, showing superior knowledge, giving them a way out, not responding, helping them, being assertive but not to a direct fight, surfacing their attack by questioning if they meant it, getting peer or group pressure, dealing with them when you are ready, coping, showing that you are serious by breaking meeting to resume later, etc. Each is dealt with differently, once recognized. The key is in identifying the twelve most prevalent types of difficult behavior, which are the most obstructive to progress.

The Bulldozers. Very positive. Will not tolerate argument or interference with their plans or programs. Do, in fact know it all. Are right most of the time. Often in positions of authority. Cannot abide ambiguity or uncertainty. Will not accept other's opinions. They are, of course, sometimes wrong. When they are, disaster results. They will blame failure on subordinate or anyone else. You?

The Hot-Air Know It All. Tells stories based on fragmented knowledge, as if they were the absolute truth and the whole story. They are not con-men; they are not out to deceive. They confuse plausibility with actuality. Above all they seek respect. They love center stage and will often "take over." They are not as often in positions of power or authority as bulldozers. Unlike bulldozers, being right is not bedrock with them. Being respected is their bedrock.

Remember that most often they are not in positions of authority or power. In such cases, you might simply want to tolerate them; even be amused. But when they are in positions of power and authority, they can cause real problems, when their sketchy knowledge is presented as the full picture.

The Clams. Remain totally silent or unresponsive, when their response and communication is needed. Sometimes maddeningly so even when a project or their jobs may be at stake. May be in a position of authority, your boss for example, who refuses to tell you why he/she removed you from a certain project, or a customer who will not tell you what he is thinking or what they like and dislike about your proposal. May of course, also be a subordinate, who clams up when discussing a problem, or a neighbor who remains totally silent when you want to discuss say, his or her barking dog. Breakdown in communication. Stagnation of problem or project or sale. A complete lack of movement.

The Too-Nice People. Promise anything and everything for the short term benefit, i.e., your approbation. Their promise will frequently exceed your requests. Very congenial. Bend over backwards to make you happy, but never follow through. Make promises and commitments in good faith. But these are often undeliverable and therefore unfulfilled. To the extent that you or your group are dependent upon them to meet a schedule or a deadline, you will almost surely be disappointed.

The Complainers. Complainers are people who find fault with almost everything and everyone and do it most of the time. They are not to be confused with people who have a legitimate complaint and need your help. Complainers are not problem solvers. They expect someone else to do something else about it. Their view of the world is that they have absolutely no control over it. Their style is to accuse. They are guiltless, they are perfect, and they are powerless. They derive satisfaction by placing the blame for ills and evils on others and by comparing their "goodness" to other's "badness." Bear in mind that distasteful and tiring as they frequently are, they may also serve a purpose by bringing you important information you might otherwise not have had.

The Negativists. People who habitually find absolute and "good" reasons as to why an idea will not work. They use terms such as: "It's no use trying, we tried that last year, forget it, they'll never let us do it." If you ask them, "Well then, what should we do?" They respond with "Nothing, there's no way to deal with that problem." Looking for ways out is anathema to the negativist. Be sure to differentiate between these people and negative analysts who consciously search for unplanned effects that might result from a given course of action and then plan for ways to evade or minimize those effects. Negativists are easily able to depress and immobilize an entire group. Bear in mind, there is a potential for depression in all of us. Understand they are not by intention obstructionists. They honestly believe that the blocking forces are out of their or the groups' control. They see these forces as immutable barriers rather than as obstacles that might be gone around. Like complainers, they are convinced that they have little power over their lives. They believe that people in power cannot be trusted (not as often true in complainers).

The Indecisives. A person may be indecisive because he/she does not yet have all the facts needed, or because of factors and pressures, which he/she cannot or will not discuss with you. These include, but are not limited to: Pending policy decisions, financial problem, conflict between two or more courses of action, pending events (internal). This does not really describe indecisive people, as much as it does situations, which cause indecisiveness.

The Procrastinator. Motives are usually hidden even from oneself. Finds it very distasteful to make decisions per se. Not just some of the time, but almost always. Reason: In making any decision he/she is forced to deny one person or one idea in favor of another. Cares a great deal about people. Finds it very hard to rebuke anyone or deny anyone. Therefore finds it easier to stall in hopes the problem will go away. Procrastinators have a strong sense of honesty. They cause problems: To the extent they do not confront problems and deal with them, they cause more, not less, tension within themselves and certainly with those who are directly involved. Alternate ways of getting the job done are not seriously considered. Those dependent on a decision lose interest and commitment.

The Hostile Aggressor. Important to note that hostility and aggression are not the same thing. Aggressiveness is associated with pushiness and stems from a desire to change things to the way the aggressive person sees them and believes they ought to be. An aggressive person may be selfish and egotistical, yet not hostile. An aggressive person may even be caring. They think their way is best and that you need their help. Hostility on the other hand may be silent as certain clams. These are three different ways in which hostility and aggressiveness combine into very damaging (to you) behavior and how to deal with them. The behaviors are:

The Locomotive. They come out charging (sometimes even physically). They are abrupt, intimidating and overwhelming. They tend to attack not only what you've done, but also you. Their manner is accusatory, contemptuous. Often however, they maintain an attitude of civility while being unrelentingly critical and argumentative. Pushing their victims into unwilling agreement. The latter type is more difficult to deal with than the charger. He/she is more often in a position of authority. And it is sometimes difficult to tell the difference between useful, well intended persistence vs. out and out hostile attack. The clue is that civil or violent, the characteristics are the same: (a) abrasive and personal and (b) preemptively begun before the facts you want to present are even laid out.

The power they possess does not evolve from the validity of their attack, but from the usual response of their victims: confusion, fear, frustration, flight or acquiescence. These reactions prevent the victim from dealing coolly or sensibly with the situation. Locomotives have an on-going and urgent need to prove to themselves (and to everyone else) that they are right, that the business would make serious blunders without their intervention: They have a strong sense of what everyone else should do. They are contemptuous of others' feelings and rights. Plus they have acquired confidence from the very fact that they have become so adept at destroying others. They value aggressiveness and confidence, but delight in demeaning others. They perceive this as enlarging their own sense of superiority. In short they are driven by a need to show how right they are. They expect others to run from them, but when they do they become non people. Use words and phrases that are assertive, but do not imply an attack: "I think I disagree with you, In my opinion, In my experience." Be prepared for their friendships and accept it. They like to be accepted by strong people.

The Sniper. Takes pot shots, but maintains a cover. Will make asides to the group, while you're working at the blackboard. They use innuendoes. They employ nonplayful teasing. Their attacks are powerful enough to hurt, but are accompanied by non verbal signals that say "pretend that what I'm doing is okay or neutral or that you don't hear me." The sniper has learned to use the rituals and social constraints in which the victims participate, as a cover. Like the locomotive, snipers have a strong sense of how others ought to think and act. But because of their belief in their superiority, they find it extremely difficult to see things from another's perspective. They often have unrealistic perceptions of the realities of the situation under discussion and the power of the victim to make the changes in the first place. When their expectations are not met, their strong motivation to be "right" results in even more cutting attacks; often not on the problems, but on the object of their scorn who should be punished. Snipers are usually not in a position of power or control vice versa their victim. If they were, they might come out as Locomotives. If the situation (social and pecking order) permits, they too can come out fighting, though not always. Often they do not have the fighting skills nor do they really want to be in charge and held responsible for results, as is the case with locomotives.

The Tantrum. Give it time to run down. Try to get a break—then resume the meeting.

In conclusion: deal with each type separately in a manner to achieve the overall objective and enable a long term relationship, don't win the battle, but loose the war—take the long view look. Attend "working together" skills courses to understand the fine art of handling various types of people to achieve the concept, proposal, and product definition, with management's commitment and action.

It is not an easy game, but the satisfaction can be great, as all disciplines are orchestrated to play at their full potential, *together*, to achieve the "right" network, product, and service.

Eight: Playing The Game

—RESTRUCTURING INTERNATIONAL MARKETS—

Before deciding to not play the game in the U.S. with System Twelve, by closing down their U.S. System Twelve development, and then selling their entire telecommunications operation to France's CGE, ITT made the following repositioning moves for their European front, as noted by one industry observer:

Brussels, Belgium—ITT Europe Inc., faced with mounting competition from overseas suppliers with the liberalization of European markets, launched a "Pan-European" product strategy, making sweeping changes in marketing and product responsibilities of several ITT companies in Europe. The move followed a similar step by ITT in the United States to bring all ITT's business-system products, from computers to PBXs, under one ITT business systems group.

Under the plan, key ITT companies were made "Lead Companies" in the development of certain products and in the research of other technologies. Those companies include Standard Electrik Lorenz AG (SEL), of West Germany, Bell Telephone Manufacturing Co. (BTM), of Belgium, ITT Face Finanziaria of Italy, ITT Austria Gmbh of Austria, and Standard Electrica S.A. (SESA) of Spain. For example, SEL, one of the chief telecommunications equipment suppliers in West Germany and the second supplier of switching equipment to the Deutsche Bundespost after Siemens AG, was made lead company for large PBXs, responsible for product development of large PBXs. The designation follows SEL's development of ITT's System 12 digital central-office switch into a large PBX, called the System 12B or BSC 5600. On the research side, because of its forte in fiber-optics and broadband ISDN, SEL would lead research into those areas by all ITT companies.

As Europe's telephone administrations (PTTs) begin to look outside their traditional supplier base for systems and as markets become liberalized, many outsiders were finding new sales opportunities. BTM, for instance, had always been a powerhouse in Belgium. But the Belgian PTT has said it wants to open its market to competitors. "Where we've been used to selling to PTTs over the years, with the advent of market liberalization, we've had to develop a new type of sales force." Said ITT Europe's president, "We've got to attack our end-user business on the level of an ITT business. We're going to take all of our products across Europe with the full strength of ITT behind it."

ITT's Pan-European, or "Transnational" product strategy, was the responsibility of the ITT Corporate Vice President and ITT Europe Inc. Director of Market and Product Management-Telecommunications and Electronics, whose team of 39 was to coordinate the marketing efforts of all the ITT Europe companies, which together accounted for about $6.3 billion in sales in 1985 with 53.6 percent in telecommunications. The Director also had "dotted-line" responsibility for the telecommunications and electronics marketing teams in each of the ITT Europe companies. In the United States, ITT Corp. management, "pulled together" Qume Corp., the Information Systems Division, ITT Courier Terminal Systems Inc. and ITT's Business and Consumer Communications Inc. into a single Business Systems Group. "We're doing the same thing in Europe. We've come up with the concept of lead houses, as we try to assemble a Pan-European product line," the Director noted during an interview in his Brussels office. "SEL might be particularly good at large PBXs. SESA was particularly good at telephone subsets. Another unit like our acquisition in Denmark, Christian Rovsing [A/S], had excellent data networking capability."

In the old days, each company enjoyed a high profile in the home markets, such as BTM in Belgium. But that situation, while successful, didn't do enough for ITT in terms of promoting the ITT name across Europe and other markets, where the company either operates or is seeking greater penetration, the Director further noted that "Our strategic planning told us we could not come close to competing in the business systems market in Europe. It also told us that a competitor with a cohesive strategy would be much more attractive," he said, "A bunch of people have come in where this type of transition has happened—in spades. You're condemned to be a niche vendor. That might work if you didn't have anything with which to begin. But if you start from a position, as a leading supplier in a country and then go into niches, you have nowhere to go."

He indicated that the new strategy could accomplish three things. First, each company can become a full systems supplier of such products as digital PBXs, data terminals, telephone subsets and networking systems and software, without having to become a full systems manufacturer; they can draw off other houses for products as needed. Second, companies such as FACE, a key-system supplier to Italy's SIP, can sell from a position of strength by capitalizing on the ITT name. Third, ITT's global image will become the ultimate beneficiary from the new marketing plan. Such a profile is needed if the company wants to compete effectively with such companies as Siemens AG, West Germany; LM Ericsson Telephone Co., Sweden; Olivetti, Italy; Northern Telecom Ltd., Canada; and probably most significantly, AT&T partnerships with Holland's N.V. Philips and Olivetti, he indicated. IBM's 70 percent computer market share in Europe is enough to give any systems marketer the religion. "In Europe we have 15 percent market share in PBXs," he said. "I see IBM-Rolm, as a tough strategic competitor, as well as the Japanese."

Some examples of lead house responsibilities include:

- BTM: digital packet-switching product development, and on the research side very large scale integration (VLSI) components.
- ITT Austria: product development of small PBXs, particularly the BCS 5200, a hot-selling small PBX with a 40 to 800 line capacity.
- SESA: telephone subsets development. SESA is ITT's largest subset manufacturer. As a lead research house, SESA will take top responsibility for how the ITT companies approach software development.
- Standard Telefon og Kabelfabrik A/S (STK), Norway; medium-sized PBX development. STK designed the BCS 550, which can be used by companies with multi locations to link other similar PBXs in a distributed network.

In addition to the capabilities of the lead houses, he cited investments in such companies as Computer Technik Muller GmbH, a 49 percent owned SEL affiliate, and Holland Automation International, which was 37 percent owned by ITT Nederland B.V., as two companies with software and systems capabilities that will help further ITT's penetration into the banking and insurance markets. He admitted that in some cases company pride might cause a unit to be somewhat protective toward products of its own development. But he said the new approach is being done for the benefit of all companies, and will not require too much adjustment. For many years ITT companies have been used to working together through a "general relations agreement" under which each company pays into a research and development pool according to its sales and can draw from all research done by the ITT companies.

On the sales side, a company that has a leading position in a certain country will take the lead sales role, regardless of whether the unit is the manufacturer or the product lead-house. Every unit has been asked to evaluate its performance and "where required, to bring in the kind of talent to sell systems to end users, to make sure the proper emphasis is made on selling rather than on administrative support functions." (Communications Week)

—JAPANESE—AMERICAN JOINT VENTURES—

Nippon Telegraph and Telephone Corp. recently said it will form a joint venture with IBM's Japanese subsidiary to offer value-added network services in Japan. It also announced agreements with AT&T and Nynex Corp. to exchange information and personnel. NTT president Hisashi Shinto, who signed the agreements with AT&T and Nynex, was in New York and Washington to discuss NTT's privatization and its equipment procurement plans. The actions by Japan's largest telecommunications company came as pressure mounted in Washington for protectionist legislation.

In Tokyo, NTT and IBM Japan Ltd. signed an agreement in principle to form a joint venture that will develop a value-added network (VAN) in Japan. The VAN will provide computer-to-computer communications and other enhanced services to business customers, and will use IBM's Systems Network Architecture (SNA) and NTT's Computer Network Architecture (DCNA). The network will be based on IBM's Information Network offering in the United States. The VAN to be provided by IBM Japan/NTT will compete with another value-added service that IBM Japan is expecting to offer, and with yet another VAN that IBM is planning to offer in a joint venture with Mitsubishi Corp. and Cosmo 80 Ltd., both of Tokyo.

It will also compete with a network from Japan ENS Inc., a Tokyo-based consortium that includes AT&T and major Japanese electronics and financial companies. IBM's joint venture with Mitsubishi and Cosmo 80, called Advanced Systems Technology Development Inc., will also base its offering on the IBM Information Network. NTT and IBM Japan will own equal shares in the new venture. In addition to network services, the company will provide information processing services and software products. IBM Japan and NTT are developing ways to interconnect their network architectures, following a study completed last year that indicated that the two protocols could work together.

NTT will bring to the venture its expertise in communications and will contribute personnel, while IBM will provide systems and applications software, network management and information processing capabilities as well as marketing. The deputy general manager of NTT's New York office, said IBM Japan and NTT agreed in principle to form the joint venture. NTT, which is being transformed from a government owned monopoly into a private corporation as part of the deregulation of telecommunications in Japan, also signed agreements with AT&T and Nynex.

These agreements include the exchange of information and personnel, but do not represent any purchases of equipment. The Japanese company has increased its negotiations with U.S. suppliers since its privatization began on April 1, possibly because of pressure from the U.S. government. But the spokesman denied that NTT was bowing to U.S. pressure in making the agreements. "We want to learn about each other's networks, exchange information and understand what others are doing," he said. He added that the agreements are not intended to lead to any supply contracts. NTT expects to complete its own information network service by 1995, but will offer digital computer-to-computer and facsimile services to business customers in Japan soon. He said the company is converging its network from analog to digital, based on demand from customers (Communications Week).

—IBM LOOKING TO THE FUTURE—

Michael Schrage of the Washington Post noted: "When IBM's chief financial officer discusses his company's business and the nation's economy, in the late 80s, he acknowledges a certain irony. On the one hand, the world's largest computer company is worried about the rise of the service economy and the decline of America's manufacturing base—a decline contributing to what could be International Business Machine's first back-to-back yearly earnings drop since the Great Depression."

"We can't be an economy that's based on selling hamburgers to each other." On the other hand, he concedes, the company with $50 billion a year in revenue is fast developing a service economy of its own. Where IBM once depended mainly on hardware price cuts, salesmanship, and customer support to drive its business, the company now is counting to an unprecedented extent on its software and services sector to rekindle growth and profitability.

"There is substantially more emphasis on value-added services and software at IBM today, than a few years ago," said an IBM marketing vice president. "We're more willing than we were in the past to be a full-service supplier to our customers."

"This may be heresy coming from an IBMer, but the future of this business is going to be as a service business," noted a vice president of strategy, requirements, and quality assurance for IBM Information Services.

The numbers reveal that software and services, growing at more than a 30 percent annual clip since 1982, have already become a significant share of IBM's revenue. In 1983, less than 20 percent of the company's revenue came from software and services. Just two years later, they contributed more than 23 percent.

During the first six months of 1986, software and services climbed to nearly 30 percent of corporate revenue—an unanticipated level that was expected to drop, once IBM hardware sales picked up.

The rise of IBM's service economy reflected important structural changes going on throughout the data-processing industry as well as IBM's efforts to reposition itself as a full-service supplier.

The customer's focus has changed. Instead of just automating the back office, customers are now asking, "How do I use computer systems for strategic advantage?", and that's making software and services more critical!

It also is a tacit acknowledgement that the future of IBM's revenue growth and profitibility depends more on the creation of new high-margin businesses than simply selling more computing power to more customers. IBM apparently believes that, in the future, it will get better margins from service software than from hardware.

The company consequently is reorganizing and investing heavily in what might be called the "three Ss" of the information industry: Software, services, and Systems integration.

While IBM always has been involved in these areas to some extent, the company now appears to have adopted them as areas of strategic importance rather than just tactical efforts designed to boost its hardware sales.

IBM has been most aggressive in software, creating a software Independent Business Unit (which is how the successful IBM Personal Computer got its start), forging alliances with other software companies and dramatically expanding its software investment.

Before 1980, IBM had less than a quarter of its development dollars in software, but in the late 80s almost half of the development dollars were then in software.

These dollars go into everything from the operating systems that run the giant IBM mainframes to applications software, such as spreadsheets that run on personal computers.

Currently, the multibillion-dollar applications-software industry is fragmented into hundreds of markets and thousands of companies, covering the spectrum of applications from database management systems to so-called artificial intelligence programs. There are no clear leaders in the field, and the largest software companies see revenue at the $100 million mark—pocket change for IBM.

Yet IBM recently has moved quickly to establish a presence both in the applications market and in the software tools used to build applications.

The company is trying to use its dominance in operating systems as a cornerstone upon which to build its strength in applications.

It was noted by an industry watcher that strategic products, which were obviously targeted at the independent software market, such as the DB2 [a database software product] would indeed capture "market share" from independent software companies, because it was a very good product.

Conceding that there is no way it could write all the applications, IBM is turning itself into a software distributor, offering to sell top-notch software packages through its global-distribution network. The company signed a distribution agreement with Hogan Systems, a banking-software company, that many in the industry see as an important step by IBM to position itself as key software supplier to specific industry segments.

Yet some are dubious about IBM's ability to wring significant growth out of the applications market, saying, "I don't see a lot of markets where IBM has the opportunity to make substantial headway. They have not done well yet in applications markets, they're playing catch-up."

IBMers of course disagree, noting "We have 1,500 packages out. In the aggregate, they've been financially successful."

While IBM is moving to gain market share in applications software, it has moved to boost revenue from its operating-systems software. The company raised prices on its mainframe-software licenses by more than 12 percent.

One analyst projected that IBM mainframe customers could be paying double their current rates for such software by the early 90s. However, the increases partly offset IBM's hardware price cuts, consequently, IBM's price per unit of computing power has not been falling as sharply as it once did. One watcher observed, "The cost of software is going up, because the price of people is going up. The real problem isn't software development—it's maintenance and service. You won't see the extent of price declines in software that you do in hardware. This creates a potential problem. If software prices remained so high as to slow down the rate at which the total price for a system dropped, customers may be inclined to seek a substitute."

Consequently, IBM is faced with the challenge of balancing its needs for higher margins for software and the risk of giving its customers an incentive to look elsewhere for computing power.

While software was a strategic cornerstone for IBM, the company moved into the service arena as well. IBM offered customers a data network called "Info Express," which allowed users to do business and exchange documents electronically. IBM had "several hundred" customers on the network as one way it sought to "add value" to installed computers.

More traditionally, IBM offered human services such as consulting to its large customers—indeed, IBM worked with outside consultants to help advise customers on their computing and information-processing strategies.

The most dramatic example of this will ultimately be in the "systems-integration" arena that in the late 80s was dominated by companies such as H. Ross Perot's Electronic Data Systems, a subsidiary of General Motors Corp, who spent several billion dollars acquiring EDS and Hughes to become a leading edge manufacture at the turn of the century.

"In the early 90s systems integration will become the hottest area in technology" an analyst noted. Essentially, systems integration is the creation of customized information processing systems that link disparate types of hardware, software and communications systems. While IBM had done systems-integration work for the federal government, it wasn't until the mid 80s that it set up a "complex-systems" integration group and won large contracts from companies such as United Airlines and Hospital Corp. of America.

It's an interesting phenomenon, because for 25 years they had denounced this sort of thing as unworkable and a risk the customer shouldn't take.

"What IBM was saying was that continued automation required a new level of integration beyond their historic lines of business." One IBMer noted, "If you had told the people in early 1980 that IBM would be doing this in the early 90s, they would have laughed."

"We moved to systems integration because that's what the customer wanted," said an IBM vice president. "The task is now to educate its customers that IBM can be more to a customer than just a hardware and software vendor, and that it can do it in a cost-effective way."

For example, IBM indicated that it was now willing to incorporate computers made by competitors into its systems-integration contracts. Asked if IBM had offered computers made by archrival Digital Equipment Corp., a new vice president noted, "Not yet, but I just got here." That joking response reveals a sharp dilemma for IBM—to what extent will the company insist on using its own equipment when supplying customers? Can customers believe IBM will be looking after the customer's best interests in recommending a hardware package? "They may have the broadest product line," noted an analyst, "but it isn't always the best."

If IBM does sell competitive equipment, a software house noted, "you're kind of starting to eat your own children by reducing your hardware content . . . It's an interesting trap." Yet, for competitive reasons, IBM has to move into the multibillion-dollar systems-integration market.

"IBM is going this route reactively because it sees competition. It sees the Martin Marietta and Lockheeds coming into their pea patch. They know that complex computer based solutions are the ones you'll make the most money on," indicated a Washington analyst.

However, one concern that IBM and other systems-integration companies face is that big companies may seek to create such systems themselves rather than contract them to outside companies. If that happens, the opportunity for huge multimillion-dollar contracts dramatically declines.

Still, Perot of EDS, noting the future, said, "IBM is a hot outfit. When they enter the market, they will stimulate the market. I wish them all the luck in the world, except when they're competing with EDS."

Nine: The Formation
Phase of the Information Era

—THE HUMAN ELEMENT—

"Where are we going? I don't know, but we'd better decide, as we won't know we've gotten there, when we've arrived!"
—Dr. Doolittle

The human aspect of the information era iceberg has shown itself, after the initial mad dash to achieve information handling products. The following questions and statements have surfaced as providers, suppliers, and users took the initial steps of their complex and hazardous journey into the information society:

• "So where are the customers for the information era?"

- "Who is going to pay for all the new network possibilities?"
- "How many customers for these new services will we have in one year?"
- "I don't see very many people demanding this new feature!"
- "ISDN is only a network, what new packages of offerings will obtain revenue from it?"
- "We must recover all our costs from new revenue in four years."
- "Look what happened to the Personal Computer (PC) market. Who really wants new technology?"
- "All the hoopla is over, now we must get down to business and be market driven!"
- "Training? You must pay extra for training on your PC—$90 for a two hour course! You only have just a few technical questions? Well, I really am not technically able to answer any detailed questions. To get an answer you must talk to our technical support group and they charge by the hour!"
- "We should automate and become a showcase, but no financial manager really wants to push to it."
- "I wish everything was left alone, as it was before the government got involved—all I see is a slightly lower long distance bill (2%), but a higher local bill (14%) and less service."
- "What features should our data switch provide? Isn't transport enough?"
- "We need to have our own private network to control our costs."
- "Is anyone interested in providing a data network for us doctors to share radiology information quickly, but cheaply? IBM and GE say they want to provide us the application software, but how about the Telco's public data network?"
- "How do we get the universities in the Midwest to access our Cray II super computer to increase usage, and share its power to smaller schools? Who will provide a data network throughout the region?"
- "Who is going to manage and coordinate an 'open architecture' network? Working with only the current voice access firms requires an extensive effort!"
- "My job is to keep my job with the company. Why take risk, what will it gain me in offering this new product, which may fail?"
- "It takes time and resources to plan a new offering . . . why should I spend today's profits to make my successor successful?"

As we step back from the rush to success and assess our progress, we must be careful to truly understand why things are happening and not just what is taking place. Too often the solution becomes the old "no market" or "not enough customers" cliche answer to account for the lack of anticipated growth of the information users. So let's consider what is happening in terms of the users, the suppliers and the providers.

Users

- The *Mitaka Experiment* in Japan by NTT has shown many shortcomings of moving from pure technical possibilities to undesirable offerings. For example, remote doctor analysis is good for some things, but requires additional physical information from the patient to enable a good analysis. The doctors felt limited by the inability to touch the patient. Similarly, the desire of the housewife to get out of the house and shop, as well as the restrictiveness of ordering things by remote terminals that require careful prethought before calling the store, was not desirable. Some solutions were to provide more sensors for the patient and a simple advertisement search menu for the housewife, indicating sales and showing available merchandise.

- The French viewtext offering has reached 2.8 million Minitel customers, in contrast with 600,000 U.S. subscribers to over two dozen U.S. videotex services, because in France, the users did not have to worry about the terminal purchase and had an established need to access telephone numbers. Then, once in place, other services were being overlaid on the established network at minimum cost per feature. Finally, the smart card or debit card for retail/bank trade will later subsidize the network.

- As noted in previous analyses, the dust on the newly purchased PCs is primarily due to a lack of customer training. Users resisted the added cost of training in favor of just not using the PC or selling it in the resale market. Free training and healthy customer relationships should have been established, similar to the stamp and coin collecting business. These hobby store owners answer thousands of questions to educate their "regulars," who then come back again and again to buy products on a "regular" basis. Instead, PC sales increase dropped from 82% to 24% to average 8%, in the 1984-88 time period with limited real growth in support software.

- High speed FAX in Japan met a true need. This was due to the complexity of transmitting thousands of different types of characters. As a result, the high speed fax, if priced correctly (less than $3,000), can become a tremendous value added service (1 million sets in four years). However, this is not necessarily the case for other countries, such as the U.S., with its 400,000 old terminals.

- The Notre Dame bookstore on the Saturday morning of a game has people lined up to go in and buy something with a Notre Dame logo. To achieve a constant large demand, week after week, year after year, the offering must have and maintain a touch of class, quality, and excellence to maintain customer interest or it will just fade away, like the hula hoop fad.

- Resistance to change can be overcome, if the offering meets a true need and if it is priced to encourage growth. Others will follow once the path is established, then many more will use the road, when it is finally available, if it is economically attractive, and if the vehicles that we need to ride it are not too expensive.

- Mistakes are expensive—as users become stuck with products that don't meet their expectations, don't work, or have limited quality. This drives many back to traditional providers, as they again are willing to pay for quality and service. Too much growth by a new offering, that causes its poorer service can be its demise.

- Users were quite ignorant as to what they really wanted from the new data networks. Initial systems were needed, that enable different types of equipment to communicate to each other, transparent to the user—but this was not what was provided.
- The driving force of large business users was a desire to tie all the locations of the firm together on a personal "unlimited," "fixed cost," "owner controlled," "responsive to owner," "new features defined by owner" network, in a point to point, switched mode over ring buses, that move data as well as video, with the basic voice information. This led to the proliferation of "private networks." However, this left the problem of tieing them together to the public network providers, who initially did not see this as an opportunity, leaving it to DEC, IBM, WANG, etc.
- Choice has become a problem, as many overwhelmed users give the decision making to consultants to determine what is economically best for them and later to manage their network system or service. As the complexity has grown, so has their resistance to "playing the game."
- Few firms offer the users inexpensive new services, everything has quite a high price tag on it. For example, cellular phones at $2,500 were not a bargain. Even at $700, they were expensive. Look at the history of VCRs. Initial upfront prices for small business is everything—at least until the desire for usage is established. Look at the initial price of dial-up 56 kbt service. It is very expensive now, but in a few years . . .
- ISDN field trials in the mid 80s only offered a 2B + D or 23B + D data/voice transport connection, but few "feature features" were offered to encourage actual new data application usage and growth.
- Balancing quality and price has been discouraging in the Telco's efforts to promote true growth. A regulator chairperson from the New England area observed that it is essential to have control over prices to be able to effectively play in the information marketplace.
- Providing ubiquitous offerings, for a data packet network in which users in remote locations could access databases, is not the initial interest of any telecommunications provider newcomer; especially as the big business umbrella base is lost. Hence, the accepted solution of the users is to only locate firms in traditional urban environments. Thus, these possibilities do not promote rural growth, but hamper it.
- Users were not truly coaxed to enter the new information world, where costs were high and few features were provided. Viewtext attempted to compete for "on TV time" versus the "off TV time." Few really inexpensive databases were established initially for the masses, because the network access and transport costs were prohibitive.
- By 1986, users were beginning to decide what they wanted, as noted in the Wall Street Journal: "Smart office buildings clearly aren't for everyone. Even though security checks can be installed, many concerns simply don't like the the idea of loading their corporate accounting, client contracts, or list of daily phone calls into a system used by dozens of other companies.

   "That's confidential information, and with the shared tenant system, it was going to be passed around to other people," noted a representative of a Denver law firm, that recently moved into a "smart" downtown office building. The firm decided to buy its own $150,000 phone system rather than hook up to the shared PBX, and ended up saving money.

- But experts noted that even if a company chooses a "dumb" building instead, it still should make sure the building will be able to handle future communications needs. For instance, does the new building have enough space for equipment rooms and telephone switch closets for a PBX? Is there enough space between floors to put in a LAN or other network?

- "Dozens of companies are moving into great buildings, with beautiful architecture, that are supposed to last them 40 years," observed a Houston communications consultant, "Instead, those facilities are technologically obsolete in five."

Suppliers

- High Tech became High Cost. A memorable quote as 1600 people were laid off when a firm terminated a too late product was:

   "With the large number of expensive people on the project, we could not afford to have them standing around breathing, while considering how to redesign a new product with different features."

   Better be the "right" product, for the "right" market, at the "right" time. The "right" time is the *first* time!

- In the 70s, planners structured a distributed switching product with remote switch units to meet the needs of the rural/suburban and limited urban environment. The world suppliers rushed to build the product; many suppliers delayed while overcoming their resistance to digital and few took the time to truly plan the next family of product offerings. Today many simply wish to extend the life of their single existing product to the integrated metro market . . . However, there are now questions of its size, as its 3-4 million line software programs become more and more a major concern. Especially as the market seeks the $150 equipment line cost objective.

- "Open Systems Standards" and joint "C&C" product partnerships may be the key to success, as more and more suppliers begin to team up or work together. The industry can learn from the original cassette people, who gave their patent away, so it would become an industry standard of which everyone could provide (especially cassette) and make money on the growth of the cassette tape recording/playing industry.

Providers

- Telecommunications customers have not been given a sophisticated sales force. There are a lot of sales persons with a great deal of energy, but few who truly understand the technology enough to provide good technical solutions and who are able to identify new features and services to meet new user needs.

- Sophisticated consultants for large business users were unable to obtain reasonable solutions from most public providers, so they encouraged large firms to obtain their own network, as well as small businesses to band together on a shared network.
- Private IBM type integrated token rings, ring buses, advanced Ethernet and sophisticated PBXs are becoming the answer to the business community, as big business moves off the Network to private LANs, MANs and WANs.
- "Open Architecture" as requested by the FCC, that enables anyone to connect anyplace at anytime, will have to be scoped to be practical, otherwise too much of a good thing can be so complex that no one has anything anyplace anytime. Standards must be resolved for ports of entry, billing must be adapted for multiple providers, and maintenance support must be resolved to ensure network quality and to prevent congestion. Coordination costs must be pooled to manage the network to ensure that usage and growth of the common network is achievable. Otherwise it will simply become a large confused arena in which no one wishes to participate, while the real game is being played elsewhere, in the private LANs, etc.

Military

- The voice and data networks of the 70s, which achieved the military "L" systems, Autovon, Autodin, and "hot line" networks were built with the technology of the 60s. There is a desire to update these networks with the technology of the 90s into more integrated voice, data, video networks, especially for the new C^3 (communications, computers, command and control) applications. This update will spawn new technological advances, that will carry over into the commercial world, as non-military versions are marketed to the business community. So it may be the military application, that drags the resistant commercial business world into becoming global "information" networks.
- Terrorism and fear are two unplanned motivating forces, that bring the world closer together, as western countries unite to resolve the terrorism problem by sharing information on new global data networks, creating the information world.
- War—this factor is always prevalent in an unstable world, as the Middle East, Africa, Central America and Asian trouble spots occur due to terrorism, or war-like attacks on neighboring countries. This may drag super powers into conflict, requiring extensive information networks. Even if war does not truly occur, the fear of war causes a desire to achieve a state of preparedness, which will require substantial information exchange.

Governments

- In reviewing plans of thirty of the major governments of the world, most talked of going to the ISDN information world; but to many, this simply meant a digital voice switch, an expensive data network, and an ISDN 2B + D interface. Few talked of levels of "C&C" integrated program solutions.

- The traditional integration of telecommunications and postal systems by non-technical governing bodies, where decision making positions were political, greatly limited many countries from moving quickly into the information era. They simply wanted cheap telephone service, that subsidized the postal system, and enabled levels and levels of bureaucratic positions, as the governing body. However, a few countries such as France have sought a leadership role, such as in data input/export to Europe, to achieve a major edge over the other countries.

Complexity

- As initial human resistance is being overcome in the marketplace, the real game will be played in the complex arena of standards, which must be identified, defined and acquired to achieve the ISDN [Overlay (phase I), C&C Integrated (phase II), Wideband (phase III), and Photonic (phase IV)] information networks of the future. This requires congenial working groups to successfully resolve access and interface protocol standards.

Office and Factory Automation

- Management of technology has become a major world leadership question, as governments move to establish technology innovation, technology transfer, and technology management centers between various military divisions, universities, and industry firms.
- Resistance to factory automation and expensive start up problems have been identified, as numerical control equipment, computer-aided design, and robotics are being integrated, using GM and Boeing MAPs/TOPs manufacturing type programs to coordinated design/purchasing/factory inventory control/production line control/customer orders/management production PERT programs to enable production lines to shift to large and small quantities of different types or versions of products.
- A project in the Technology Management Office, and Advanced Technology Centers of Pennsylvania, commissioned by the Office of Trade Adjustment Assistance, International Trade Administration, U.S. Department of Commerce noted the following effects of foreign technology impact on the machine tool, electronic components, and medical devices industries, showing the human element's resistance to change:

"The major finding of the project was that in a majority of cases, U.S. manufacturers have ignored the argument that new technologies produce higher quality products faster and cheaper, and have hesitated to adopt modern manufacturing techniques. For all the publicity and advertising dollars spent in promoting these new processes, small companies are puzzled about their use and their benefits. For the most part, only very large corporations are implementing some of the advanced manufacturing technologies and even they are proceeding at a slower-than-anticipated pace.

"The problem is not one of the availability of technology. In fact, the technologies presently available appear to be far ahead of the ability of U.S. industry to implement. Rather it primarily concerns a human element—introducing people to new systems and achieving acceptance. One major finding is that management is confused by, and generally not knowledgeable about, advanced manufacturing technologies' advantages and capabilities. As a result, they are ill-prepared to implement them effectively, even when these technologies are acquired. Compounding the problem is also the traditional organizational resistance to change. Foreign competitors, particularly Japan, appear to be using more of these technologies and appear to be more willing to adopt advanced processes in their production systems. By concentrating on yields, quality, and delivery times, industry analysts indicate that the United States and Western Europe are looking at yesterday's solutions to manufacturing problems. The Japanese have essentially resolved these issues and are now moving to computerized production control. In this respect the Japanese also appear to have the advantage in that most of their computer based manufacturing technologies use compatible controls, while U.S. companies, attempting to automate, struggle to interface equipment developed by a variety of manufacturers using their own computer controls.

"There is no secret to the existence of modern manufacturing techniques and the competitive edge that will inevitably belong to those who apply them effectively. Conversely, those who do not apply them will just as inevitably be placed at a competitive disadvantage. Industry experts claim that technology can account for as much as a 60 percent productivity increase.

"However, the new technologies are only a tool, a computer-aided way to do the things always recognized as necessary to run an efficient factory. If management is not running an effective factory, no amount of computer automation is going to help. If the industrial engineering is sloppy, if the standards are loose, if the layout is poor, if the production planning and control systems are not up to the standards of today's best practices, if the product designs are inefficient—then simply computerizing the manufacturing process is unlikely to help substantially."

"Discussions with industry experts indicated that the following conclusions to the project are representative of U.S. industry:

— U.S. industry is using very little of today's advanced manufacturing technologies, a circumstance which has affected the ability of some industries to compete effectively with overseas competitors.
— Today's advanced manufacturing technologies are often complex and not easy to implement.

New computer based technologies used in the manufacturing process are becoming increasingly sophisticated and often require a high degree of engineering and scientific expertise to be implemented effectively. In fact, the technologies presently available appear to be way ahead of the ability of U.S. manufacturers to absorb. Despite the marketing rhetoric used by equipment manufacturers, the introduction of new technologies in a plant is also often a difficult process, which does not take place overnight and requires commitment and dedication on the part of management. More often than not several months will pass before productivity improvements, resulting from the use of technology will be noticed, and many firms report that in fact productivity decreases may occur during the implementation period. Technologies such as MAP, may take two years simply to implement.

In instances where new manufacturing technologies have been implemented by industry, they have far too often been applied inefficiently. As a result, potential productivity gains have not been realized. This inefficient use of new technologies has usually resulted because, for the most part, they have been acquired without regard to their role in an overall manufacturing strategy. Unlike marketing or financial plans, which most companies generate annually, less than 10 percent of the firms surveyed had developed a plan for the acquisition or use of computers or technology in their companies. This lack of planning has created "islands of automation," sophisticated technologies acquired at random, scattered on shop floors with little regard to their overall role in producing a better product. This has done little to increase the competitiveness of firms and in many instances has in fact created problems, which have had a negative impact on productivity.

In addition, as opposed to the Japanese producers, who have a reputation for exquisite execution and use of advanced technologies and techniques to strive for their goal of manufacturing products with zero defects, U.S. manufacturers are apparently willing to settle for somewhat less than the best. Far too often, using many of the same technologies as their overseas competitors, U.S. companies are happy to settle for marginal improvements over their previous production techniques, without exploring or extending their equipment to its full capabilities.

Although the acquisition of new technologies is a capital investment decision and financing can often be a problem, the major reasons companies do not use advanced manufacturing technologies is because they do not understand them, find them too confusing, and are intimidated by them. U.S. industry tends to be overly concerned with short term results and returns. Investment in technology does not produce immediate returns and should be considered a long term investment. Thus it is often difficult for companies to justify automated equipment, using traditional payback formulas.

Companies surveyed generally required a 2-3 year payback period, whereas Japanese firms do not generally place inflexible requirements when investing in new technologies. As a result, the use of new technologies by many U.S. companies is considered a risk rather than an investment. The use of higher levels of more sophisticated manufacturing technologies will not necessarily make a company more competitive. Despite evidence to the contrary, a large number of small- and-medium-sized manufacturers perceive themselves as using advanced manufacturing and state of the art technologies. Small and medium sized manufacturers do not appear to be aware of the fact that they are competing in a global market and are not taking any anticipating action to compete against foreign competition. In developing a program to help companies use advanced manufacturing technologies, there are not readily available, enough criteria to determine those firms that are more likely to implement advanced technologies:

The initial analysis, which primarily included small and medium-sized businesses, ranging in size from $500,000 to $50 million in sales, found no discernible patterns as to which companies were more likely to be receptive to implementing new technologies. Some observations, which may shed some light on the types of firms more willing to adopt new manufacturing technologies, however, can be made as a result of the audits conducted.

In general, the study found those firms with fewer than 50 employees and being run by the founder, or by older management, to be less likely to be interested in investing in computers or other technologies.

Management in these firms were entrenched in conducting business in a particular way and were not looking to change, particularly since many of the businesses would likely be sold or closed when current management retired. In strategic terms these companies had no long term objectives, therefore there was no reason to invest for the future.

In cases where management displayed some curiosity, they had little opportunity to investigate alternative manufacturing techniques. For the most part they were preoccupied with the daily problems of getting their product out the door and had extremely limited in-house engineering capabilities available to look at new technologies. For many the acquisition of a PC for the front office and accounting functions was considered a quantum leap into the age of technology. Interestingly, there were also a number of well run, profitable concerns, that were simply not interested in growing any larger than a $250,000-$500,000 level, turned business away, and were not interested in investing in new processes.

There were, however, three distinct exceptions to this pattern. The first of these concerned companies being run by the sons of the original owners or by young management. These individuals appeared to be much more interested in introducing new technologies, that could help the firm in the long run. The second exception pertained to the tool and die industry, where it was observed that there were a number of young engineers starting or taking over businesses, and acquiring state of the art technologies such as CNC machining centers, lasers, EDM and CAD. Interestingly these engineering entrepreneurs were forsaking the use of computers for front office functions, as not being important to the operation of their businesses. The third exception, where management was very interested in a new technology, occurred in instances when there was an easily identifiable market niche that a company could fill by using new techniques to manufacture a particular product.

The one common element in these companies was a management interested in future growth and development of the firm. Particularly intriguing was the fact that for these companies the financing of new technologies did not seem as an overwhelming problem. They somehow managed to make the necessary investment, in some instances even where they had to give up part of their pay to invest in a technology that they felt was needed. Larger companies, particularly publicly owned firms, were generally hampered in the acquisition of new technologies, because all investment decisions were scrutinized for short term returns. Unless a particular technology was easily justifiable, or the president of the company was behind a project, the investment was not likely to be approved. Some firms also indicated that investment tax credits, enacted to encourage capital investment, were considered to be "accounting techniques" and often did not translate into new technologies on the shop floor.

A final observation from the study was that the firms that appeared to be most affected by not using technology, were privately owned, medium-sized companies averaging approximately 130 employees, primarily in the metal working industries. These firms had neither the economies of scale required to invest in advanced technologies and compete with large manufacturers, nor could they effectively compete with smaller firms which had specific market niches. As a result, those firms, which were often very labor intensive, needed the greatest amount of assistance in implementing modern manufacturing techniques and overcoming human resistance to change, if they are to survive."

User—Supplier Concept Review

As technology reaches the point where it provides numerous possibilities that are in reality bounded by true market needs, we can reach a reasonable balance by offering the users an opportunity to become a "beta" test site for a new product offering. This "beta test" enables users to participate with the supplier on an experimental basis in which the product may have several operational flaws. The user will obtain the product at greatly reduced cost by an agreement to accept the product over a test period, to expose the product's limits and work out its problems. What's in it for the users as they critique the product? Usually this enables them to find out what they like and dislike about a new product without a severe financial commitment; for example: the Westinghouse experiments on early picturephones. Note the supplier did not pursue picturephones, but Westinghouse wanted to keep the experimental system due to their improved operations.

Concept Phase

The initial step in the user-supplier relationship can be successfully achieved by inviting the perspective users to work with the supplier at the conceptual planning phase to review the concept, critique its application, expand its features, identify its worth, and solidify its need.

As we move into the information era, supplier concepts can be tested on sophisticated and unsophisticated users by group presentations, to obtain general overall opinions followed by individual discussions to carefully listen to specific user concerns and comments. The secret is to obtain a dynamic imaginative, knowledgeable, recognized and respected user to bring together a cross section of representative colleagues. If the busy users are encouraged to participate, by future partnerships on reduced cost beta test products, the suppliers may be able to save substantial R&D costs, obtain early internal management commitment and more easily be able to identify the "right" requirements for the "right" product, with minimum expense and shortened developed cycle.

Recently, Dr. Chandler, a dynamic leader for a Minneapolis group of radiologists and doctors, gathered a group of doctors to participate in a conceptual review of a potential joint product offering to their profession by GE and IBM. It was quite interesting to see that many of the observations were exactly the same as those made by the doctors and housewives that participated in the 40 million dollar Japanese Mitaka experiment. These opinions were obtained without spending the 40 million dollars. This is a prime example of a "Danka Experiment," the "What if, then what" think analysis of the conceptual planning phase.

User Concerns

As we consider the human element impact on the future of the information era, let's review the doctors' comments and critique of a new technology to assist their mode of operation . . .

- Concern for dependence on a technology, which if it does not work will prevent normal successful operation, is a key resistance factor.
- Resistance to believe protection can occur on security of patient information, so no law suits and violation of patient-doctor privacy occur.
- Desire to receive information such as x-rays from remote locations, so they could better advise how to handle patient.
- Need to fill the CRT quickly—10 seconds or less was emphasized over 1 minute slow scan, but concern of prohibitive costs of transmission preventing economic feasibility.
- Need to access several databases within and external to the hospital to construct changing patient profile status, as well as access historic information.
- Resistance to typing—input/output must be some form of simple graphic aid /with voice recognition to really get doctors to use it.
- Instantaneous data was threatening to some doctors. They enjoyed walking around the hospital with time to think and talk to other doctors—similar to results of the housewife experiment in Japan.
- Conversational interaction programs enabling a series of think-action steps could help solve intimidation problem of CRT, as well as levels of sophisticated interaction programs to help doctor's analyses of information.

- Parallel traditional "hard copy" to carry is still desirable—reluctant to give up the old way of life immediately.
- Distributed systems versus Distributed "Integrated" Systems must be resolved to obtain integrated solutions.
- Business will change as specialists become more valuable, networks become more productive, specialists with networks are more effective, and specialists without a network are no longer specialists!

The Human Element Cycle

- Need for technology discussions—resistance—time to digest—further questions—gradual use—technology change to occur—phases of acceptance as confidence level increases—strong demand for new features—facilitates greater usage.
- The supplier must be willing to work with the "human element cycle" over a reasonable long period to diminish resistance to change. Doctor's recommendation was not to respond to Wall Street bottom line to achieve short term success or they shouldn't enter the business. As one expert said, "Lemons ripen in two years, fruit bearing trees in seven."

Choice and Complexity

User selection of information technology, such as the Data Switches versus the LAN Ring, Bus, Loop configurations are compounded by the complexity of offerings, as noted by the following extensive options and facets example:

1) LAN Standards and Protocols

- Are becoming highly complex and require a device composed of hardware and software to interconnect.
- Require network interfaces called a network controller, device handler, network adaptor, or communications server.

2) Sophisticated Standards

IEEE 802, Ethernet, coax/fiber, baseband, bus, CSMA/CD, token bus (map), broadband, twisted pair/fiber, etc.

3) High Level Protocols

XNS	— Xerox Network System, office automation, defacto std.
TCP/IP	— ARPA-DOD internetworking file transfer standard or integral part of UNIX 4.2 BSD.
SNA	— IBM System Network Arch for wide area networks evolving to meet APPC (LU6.2), DIA, DCA.

ISO	— International standards also adopted by GM MAP and Boeing TOP.
MAP	— Manufacturing Automation Protocol of General Motors defined by IEEE 802.4.
TOP	— Technical and Office Protocol of Boeing supporting IEEE 802.3, with various application protocols.
DECNET	—
DNA	—
C&C	—

4) *Performance*

- Terminal to Host
  - bursty small packets
  - fast response no delay interaction
  - screen fill time

- Host to Host
  - large packets
  - fast transfer

- Switched versus LAN
  - shared resources
  - switched terminals
  - distributed control
  - file transfer
  - interactive graphic terminal
  - file management

- User interface features
  - names
  - access control
  - port contention
  - routing codes
  - billing
  - multiple processing
  - parallel processing
  - network management (throughput control)
  - testing, error rate control

- Security and access control, audits, protection, keys, passwords, etc.
- Sophisticated levels of support people to achieve reliable operation.

5) *Internetworking*
Bridge, Router, Gateway, etc.

6) Physical Interfaces

RS232 to 19.2K, 422 or V.35 to 64K, 449, IEE 488

7) Multi Business Interfaces

IEEE 796

8) Protocol Interfaces

Async, Bisync, SDLC, HDLC, X25, X21bus, SNA

9) Value Added Carriers Interfaces

Telenet, TYMNET, Uninet, etc.

10) Integrated Voice and Data

Baseband, Broadband, Wideband, "T", "U"

11) Facilities

Twisted pair, coax, fiber

12) Access Layered Protocol for peer to peer interfaces

DEC to IBM to Wang to NEC to . . .?
Unix System V, APPC (LU6.2), DIA, DCA . . .?

Yes, indeed, there are many many variables and choices. The result of these complex choices is to drive the users (in the above case doctors) to firms that choose and provide for them personal computer networks (IBM, DEC, Wang) and independent local area networks or to use equipment providers, such as IBM to provide a special purpose network for a specialized application (such as the hospital—doctor HMO network)—with cost of doing business passed on to patients, hopefully achieving savings to hold down costs. Many users will be more effective and successful by leaving the choice of network to the specialists, and the decision on services to themselves.

The Formation Period

As noted here, the "real world" is a process of overcoming resistance by understanding, coaxing and supporting, as well as pricing and effectively advertising. Doing various things the wrong way can many times scare prospective users.

Suppliers have similar "human element" resistance as demonstrated in one case in the hiring of new college graduates. Even though they were familiar with operating computers and electronic equipment and had a basic background in high technology, if the job looked too complex, it could scare them away. One firm took potential applicants around the facilities and showed them highly sophisticated complex areas of which they would have responsibility. However, the applicants would subsequently turn them down. A more successful approach was to indicate that the new employee would initially be part of a team working initially under a knowledgeable veteran. After a few months of employment, the once frightened employee would be asking for more and more technical challenges and opportunities.

Theory "F"

"Theory Z" by W.C. Ouchi has popularized the notion of Japanese management supremacy. However, *Inc* magazine has carried a feature article on "Theory F" where "F" is "fear" and subsequent "frustration" in the Japanese workforce of the 80s.

Here, "the human element" problems of the supplier's management was discussed openly and frankly, noting a loss in creativity and motivation in the new generation of management, as their expectations of upward mobility were diminished, when corporate growth slowed appreciably and as they felt they had no place to go outside the large corporations to obtain desired financial success and security. The article discussed how large firms no longer generated enough executive positions to satisfy ambitious young "sarariman." Its interviews of young management noted:

- The only executives who reach the top of Japanese companies are those who succeed at every step in their careers.
- Many of the people who make it in these companies are extremely tough.
- Rivals try to give them enough rope to hang themselves.
- The choice for an executive who fails is a one way ticket to oblivion in some remote subsidiary or early retirement.
- During the 60s and 70s double digit growth rates created enough positions, but not in the 80s.
- Just as diminished growth is curtailing new opportunities, firms are being inundated by maturing members of the enormous baby boom generation.
- 66% of the 1985 college graduates will obtain the rank of "bucho" or division manager by age 54, but by 2000 only 17% will have the same advancement potential.
- Small and entrepreneur businesses do not provide much of an escape valve. Although medium and small companies constitute 99% of all private enterprises and employ 83% of all private sector employees, most are small retail operations or subcontracting firms tied by quasi-federal links to the giant companies.
- They pay 20% less in salaries than larger companies and rarely offer the same level of health benefits, subsidized houses, vacations, lavish travel, entertainment accounts, lifetime employment guarantee (that attracts the most qualified college graduates), and private pensions tied to company service.
- The term of being "nothing" outside the confines of the corporation causes the Japanese executive to view the company not only as a guarantor of a certain life style but the ultimate arbiter of one's own self-esteem. The

company is everything. One has a tendency to ignore reality, just works, forgets one's family and loses one's identity in the corporation.

- A mistake can put an executive on a "trial of suffering" in which he (or she) is passed over for promotion, utterly trapped, or have a pathetic non-functional job until retirement: These madogiwa-zoko or "window-side managers" can be seen in almost any corporate office reading newspapers at their empty desks, stoically whiling the hours.
- Another common trait for these "Kacho" section managers that are passed over for top posts at the major corporations is a transfer to one of the parent corporation's host small affiliated companies. This on the surface looks like a promotion, but is in effect a sham with pay cuts and little chance of success. Because Japan is basically a village society, the unity of the group and the tendency to exclude outsiders are very strong. Hence the transferred executive would be a "gaijin" (foreigner) under whom people would not work efficiently.
- Displaying "Gamian," the Japanese virtue of suffering without complaint, is the greatest challenge to maintain a level of enthusiasm, work hard, be ambitious, but realize the reward may not be there and become old along the way.
- Management by consensus is in actuality under the power and control of the limited few top management. The others work under compliance due to fear of loss of advancement.
- The new generation of college graduates known widely as "shirake sedai" or "reactionless generations" seem to lack both the loyalty of the 60s generation and the nonconformity of the 70s baby boomers. They have decided to lower expectations and play along with the system.
- The analysis noted that top corporate executives were disturbed about a generation, that seems to displace fear with apathy. Faced with tremendous competition from Korea, Taiwan, and other emerging Asian countries, they realize that they cannot rely on organizational skills associated with low cost manufacturing, but must rely instead on the creative abilities of their employees. They observed that this new generation can execute, but can't come up with new solutions and ideas. One indicated: "They are just like goldfish, they open their mouths and you feed them information."

Observation

What has been observed as unique for Japan is of course not unique for American corporations as experienced in the lost expectations, goals, and dreams of management of the 60s and 70s as well as the concerns and desires of today's "yuppies."Instead of "sarariman" concerns, one does not have to go to Japan to recognize the switch from Theory "F"—Fear and Frustration— to Theory "A"—Apathy. This human element must be addressed everywhere in the world to enable the supplier's people to truly play the game of creating, designing, and supplying the new information products, networks and services for the new users.

What is needed during this formation period is a new structure for corporations that enable their people to participate more effectively with true motivation, such as: the "P" organizational structures that support the management planning process, in which planning becomes an integral part of the product life cycle, where planning activities are rewarded even though results will be long term and difficult to be subjectively measured in the short term, but will enable corporate growth to return with new exciting products.

This loss of creativity of large firms has blossomed in America in the movement to obtain smaller firms, which (once successful) are then purchased by the larger firms. This has become a short term solution, as results have shown an inability of the larger firms to truly capitalize on these new purchases. Hence, this is not the solution to the human element of the corporation.

Conclusion

What is recommended then is a corporation based upon resolving "the human element" of the providers' and supplier's people, as they resolve "the human element" of the potential users of their products and services. We have much to learn in this formation period, as firms begin to realize the need for understanding the complexity of "the human element," as the essential "key" to unlocking the door of the information era . . .

"I may not know where we are going, . . . but I do know that where we are now is not where we want to be!!"

—An Information User

Ten: Conclusions

—THE LIFE OR DEATH OF THE PUBLIC INFORMATION NETWORK—

This analysis will provide two views of the future of the public information network, based upon conclusions drawn from observations of the strategies of the players, noted in the reference section. From these conclusions, recommendations may be proposed for the suppliers, providers and user's consideration, as they play in this ever changing game of change. In the 1988-94 timeframe, we will have indeed reached a crossroad in terms of future networks, products, and services, that will (can) be achieved during the formation phase of the information era.

The Death of the Public Information Network

The public information network could fail for the following reasons:

- Telco Can Not Provide:
  - InterLATA connections without third party.
  - ASYNC-X25 protocol conversion without extensive tariff fillings with re-

strictions on circuit charges, where conversion takes place, as well as extensive tariff delay on other offering.
  — Code Conversions. They will take similar extensive tariffs and delay; causing protocol and code conversion to be provided in terminal or nodal access switch.

- Telco must demonstrate proof of non-dominance and non-bottleneck. This will extensively delay, limit or inhibit any competitive offering, as the competition object, leaving proof to Telcos.
- Delay of entrance into Information Services World, until all access arrangements are available.
- Depreciation rate on life of equipment needs to be 5 to 7 years to economically provide new equipment to increase capacity of network and provide new features.
- Extensive tariff costs—Extensive connection monthly rates, distance rates, installation and usage rates drive customers to "dark fiber" and "Ku satellite" bypass.
- Telco or sub's inability to search lists for data that does not require processing, just look up, is hurting information era services for small business/residential users.
- Inability to write system requirements for needed hardware and form competitive partnerships, without having court cases to prove non-competitive advantage, again causing substantial delays in all offerings.
- Inability to define software requirements for joint R&D partnerships for needed services, without court case will also inhibit usage of public network and encourage private networks.
- Need for data networking, such as PC-PC file transfer, high network fault tolerance, single point of contact for network management of voice/data transfer and protocol conversion, end to end digital switching over high capacity circuits, movement of high speed digital facsimile; public to private LANs and WANs interface to route and control . . .
- Need for ISDN standards before any major firm can provide public network services other than ISDN physical layer and data link layer offering; interim solution is LANs and WANs that are extensively designed as individual networks with gateway access software to meet some of the user's "networking" needs today.
- Mentality of Telco to charge extensive prices for new offering rather than price to what is needed to stimulate growth; Telco will need to encourage new markets, such as France's give away terminal concept to promote extensive use of viewtext.
- Need for Non-LAN cluster customers (small business) to access data networks and obtain data services at common nodal points, such as info switches at reasonable circuit prices.
- Time is working against Telcos, as they attempt to first define and then ensure "open architecture," "open standards," "co-location," "equal access" and provide "new feature tariffs" in order that anyone can connect

to the network to provide anything, anywhere, at anytime, before being allowed to actually compete on the "level playing field" in the information services arena, themselves.

- Competitive arena has begun to mean choosing to serve selected user concentrations having different economic capabilities, rather than sharing the costs or averaging them across various geographic locations. Hence, it is no longer a game of ubiquitous offerings for everyone, but a game to provide services to the biggest group of customers, having the ability to pay and concentrated together to reduce costs.
- Extensive tariffs encourage large users to develop their own networks. To form their large networks, users attempt to pull in neighboring groups of other users, which are located in common geographic clusters. This then leads to mutual partnerships to share the network among several large users. Once these networks are up, they then resell their services to other smaller users, leaving fewer public network users.
- Once the private network is in operation, users' private network managers are very in tune and responsive to their own needs. Aggressive firms have decided to make the network part of their strategic competitive positioning program, as they extend it into their factories, to automate the flow of their production lines, so the lines can process multiple products (GM). Also, the network linkage to remote plant locations enables factory system designers to distribute the assembly among several plants more effectively. These, then, require network flow control of information to be shared among numerous sites. This pushes the firm into local area networks internal to its various plants by connecting together by private network facilities. Next by using switched tandem arrangements, this enables users on these networks to interface with users in their many support plants. Hence, separate switched LAN networks emerge outside the public network and also do not use the shared CCSA type arrangement, where numerous larger firms piggybacked on the existing network.
- Emergence of the second "C" in "C&C" (Communications and Computers) outside the public network occurs, as new private LANs develop, in which software packages are defined for interfacing MacIntosh, IBM PC, WANG, DEC, etc., terminals to each other, via their LAN, as well as enabling remote systems to access the various mainframe operating systems via UNIX System V and talk to each other over various standard architectural interfaces.
- Need for Conformity on basic service offerings to the masses by all the RBOCs, but the inability of RBOCs to discuss with each other market offerings, at least until they are available.
- Newspaper loading dock analogy. A colleague once observed what happens when vendors are allowed to deliver papers, as well as deliver papers to the deliverers by accessing the loading dock, have access to machines that generate the papers, have ability to locate their printing presses next to existing presses and generate portions of the paper, obtain ability to price their portions cheaper than the full paper, provide only the more interesting portions of the paper, and thus have their presses multiply and

eventually move to a new location with customers (readers) from the original paper. This causes higher costs to be carried by original paper suppliers due to a half empty building and delivery trucks or idle equipment, generating half the original information to half the original readers, causing economic inability to provide future new readers with the new types of information they will want at original prices.

- High costs of new systems to provide new services for large groups of people, as R&D costs climb and climb. The more ubiquitous the group, the more features the new system must support; requiring hordes and hordes of expensive software programmers, supporting up to 4-5 million lines of code. Hence, new complex systems must share the costs of planning, design, and support, causing new features to be expensive and time consuming to obtain; especially as suppliers attempt to obtain a bigger base of providers, that would desire a new feature.

- High tech sophisticated users require high tech sophisticated networks, products and services, which can not necessarily be readily and timely provided by people who are not in tune with the new technology, especially as the technology is tied to another industry, such as computer features by communication people, or communication features by computer people.

- User resistance to change by masses will delay high yields as various people types must be coaxed to participate, and many small firms must be economically encouraged to move their information on the new networks. Hence, a need to offer numerous new features to attract users, but features will be expensive. However, FCC and DOJ restraints, even after Inquiry III, will still require a collector switch in the unregulated arena perhaps by separate sub, as well as an access switch to the public network and an access switch to the world, requiring three or at least two separate switches for one new service investment, which a LAN can achieve using a single switch. Hence, this requires double the investment by the Telco, even though the user resistance will still take time to overcome for real growth and return on investment.

- Controversy over any investment in the unregulated arena by those users, hoping to keep the network on a flat rate, large calling area, cheap basis, resisting any nonvoice expenditures.

- Need to charge on a volume basis to encourage information (voice, data, video) network usage; but this requires machines and facilities designed and available to move gigabits of information economically; and billing on a throughput bases, that encourages growth of volume and handling by several providers.

- Need to disperse many of these systems, at the same time in a large area to encourage usage by small businessmen, as well as residential customers.

- Residential users desire for extensive bandwidth for color video—at cheap rates to compete with cable, but unwillingness to pay higher costs for quality, switched, non-multiplexed facilities, that enable multiple services. This conflicts with economic advantages of ubiquitous offerings and leads to specific area offerings.

- Entrance of courts to resolve technical boundaries, usually in a compromise fashion that results in long delays and decrees that prohibit the basic Telco from playing in the competitive arena, using common usage technology to economically share service advantages, as well as causing extensive legal costs.
- Complex technical decisions on trade offs, being made by non-technical financial oriented upper management, attempting to satisfy short term view of Wall Street analysts; have moved firms into a financial game not necessarily based on logical technical long term view; making firms vulnerable to foreign competition, such as the Japanese.
- Inability of Telco marketing to achieve the capability of creating a market for a new service; due to earlier conditioning and programming of providing a new service only when the customers have developed a long history over several years of demanding a particular service. Many times, almost grudgingly, Telcos have been coaxed into providing a new service, which, of course, made a great deal of revenue shortly after being in service.
- Willingness of traditional providers to wait for suppliers, such as Bell Labs and AT&T, to identify, design, develop, and provide new services in new systems, rather than take risks themselves and assist in directing suppliers with new requirements for new products.
- Unwillingness of Telcos to lead the way in office automation and enter the information age; while factories have taken the lead with new factory automation, using information networks to support and control production facilities.
- State commission role over separations and tariffs, as well as, unregulated boundary conditions can be short sighted in favor of keeping short term voice costs down to the determent of long term voice costs, as well as conflict with FCC over competition rulings over future of local monopoly.
- Participents' desire to keep doing what they did in the past in arenas, where Telcos performed very well (inside a closed protected well defined arena); unfortunately this is a new world, in which there are no longer any real boundaries or any real protection from aggressive competitors.
- Unreasonable ruling from commissions catering to John Q. Public, making Telco providers the escape goat for numerous limiting restrictions by "non-level playing field decisions."
- Inability to position and form a point of defense has left the Telcos ineffectively utilizing its resources and defending itself from competition in the local public voice network; adding transport data capability, but *not* providing feature packages, that LANs or internal (CPE) nodal point access switches provide. This causes shift of users to LANs/WANs private networks over the public; resulting in a decreasing shrinking voice network with a limited data network. This does not foster a growing living public information network, as networks go private, shared private, and direct to new interexchange carriers that support numerous types of PC and PC to computer information exchange.

- CPE ruling, that initially prohibited Telco from locating equipment on customer premise, encouraged growth of LANs and inhibited growth of Telco data networks. Changes by CI 111 were quite late in the game, as many firms formed their own LAN. Recent study indicated that for those having 10 or more terminals, 60% had a LAN by 1986 and 100% would be part of a LAN over the 1988-96 period.
- Financial communities, banks, and stock exchange's, private secure networks; airline's high speed error free networks; encripted military-contractor networks; super computer-university networks; large multi-unit private networks like GM, IBM, etc, have now developed "integrated" voice and computer transport offerings, using every conceivable network vehicle, such as; satellites, microwave, dark fiber, T1, etc., and have been removed from the operating usage revenue base, upon which Telco's could build ubiquitous networks for residential/small business services in the data world.
- VANs, Value Added Networks, have captured a sophisticated segment of the users wishing to access databases. They have begun to enable "inter-networking between VANs" to provide a broader base.
- International VANs will be the next key to local VAN's successful growth, as VANs attempt to provide "Global Network" offerings.
- Electronic databases will be the publisher's business, as large publisher's purchase databases and database management firms, while Telcos are inhibited from these purchases and involvement.
- Cellular networks across the RBOCs were initially inhibited and delayed by justice rulings, limiting RBOC positioning as interexchange cellular carriers within the U.S. (not necessarily outside the U.S.).
- Terminal market and CPE nodal point access switches initially removed from basic Telco offerings have tended to further isolate Telco from customer needs and ability to understand and meet new "networking" demands of tying PCs together and LANs together, etc.

The net result of all this has been to encourage the public network providers in the local areas to:

1. Provide access to any interexchange and interLATA carrier.
2. Do not provide single point of contact network solutions.
3. Stay out of data information world except for point to point transport or non interaction switching, such as circuit switching or transport only packet switching.
4. Provide wideband (video) transport, but at expensive tariff rates; encouraging bypass to video conference sites directly to/from interexchange carriers.
5. Lose large business base, and up to 50% of small business base.
6. Continue to transport data to users at low rates; using data over voice.
7. Delay ISDN offerings due to limited economic incentives or provide it only to business areas, as access transport networks.

8. Remain only in the residential, small business—voice business.

The resulting public Telcos will be too big to be supported by its shrinking revenue. Hence, a need for downsizing and streamlining of people with less emphasis on change for the sake of change of technology for providing information services ubiquitously. Hence, many geographical areas will remain analogue, be sold as a bad revenue source, or changed to digital only to cut or reduce maintenance and operation costs, with more automated systems and facilities.

This leaves the growth of numerous LANs continuing with an ever increasing need to be interconnected, but no central public network, upon which to interconnect. Hence, other countries, as noted in the observations, are taking other approaches to deregulation during the formation phase of the information era.

The Life of the Public Information Network

The public information network could succeed for the following reasons:

- New life, no AT&T control, new data features, new products, new partnerships to share risk and cut costs, as the world gets a lot closer: GTE, NEC, RBOC, IBM, NTT, ATT, Plessey, BT, Mitel, ECMA, etc.
- Services switched—as a business.
- Upside down switch controlling remote digital local loop; systems open to competition with new services; not just controlled by one source, first step into the information era.
- Realization of loss of business to LANs; they are here to stay, as users wish to control their information; new need for "networking networks" of computer products. This becomes a new business opportunity, as a transport integrator.
- Bellcore, ANSI, and IEEE are in place to support industry groups to establish "open architecture" and "open standards" for various layers and levels of the OSI model; to perform a lot of cross providers—suppliers coordinating work.
- Once RBOCs have defined their new network architectures, suppliers can fit new products; so there is dialogue between RBOCs and suppliers to determine best architecture for both to be successful.
- Once agreement of direction is established, financial commitments from suppliers and providers can be reached; a lot of legal decisions can be removed, reducing Washington's role to border patrol, overseers, or watch dog instead of day to day judgments.
- Large businesses are free to use their planning process and determine their own networks products and services. This will push technology to the limit, as new territories of the new frontier are explored. These expeditions, when successful, will be followed, moving the frontier to new boundaries.
- Need for the public network to tie the LANs together will become more and more evident, as more firms are unable to achieve their goals due to

internetworking dilemma, which only a public network can achieve.

- BOCs will find their pricing game the most critical element, that is inhibiting real growth, as they continue to lose business. No longer can a user pay all the connect and usage costs just to move a 9.6K or 64K of data. New pricing will then encourage growth.

- BOCs will find fiber can move a lot more information than they originally visualized, as thousands of frequencies can be sent in a single fiber. Thus giving more pressure for wideband communications using dark fiber. Then BOCs will be forced to counter in the gigabit world with competitive offerings, otherwise they are bypassed by fiber in their own conducts. Hence, BOCs enter the world of gigabit switched interconnected networks in order to survive.

- Once BOCs come to terms with the new multiple networks and meet the change with gigabit movement; priced economically to encourage more gigabit growth—we all enter the world of gigabit traffic; if the BOCs construct an architecture, that promotes growth, enabling LANs to enter here and there on the public info rings to talk to each other. The public network rings then become analogous to major local interstate highways, with main streets in cities; leaving the special subdivisions, shopping complexes and factory sites to the LANs. Realizing that some users will use trains to bypass the highway or ride special buses on the streets, Telcos should structure the network for interconnecting and meeting all forms of all types of user's needs.

- Computers will be the name of the game, as users want more and more access to databases. Hence, communications will interface more and more with computers in a natural evolution, using service nodal point systems and front ends of the computers, that will compete with PBXs and Centrex systems to provide control of information for office building complexes, as well as small business computer traffic . . . hence growth.

- BOCs will construct a new growing network, in which they will transport different forms and types of traffic—for example: analog voice, digital voice, packetized voice, async data, sync data, circuit switched data, packet data, burst data, wideband video, wideband voice/data/video/ and burst voice/data/video . . . data growing from 3% to 30% to 50% by 2010.

- Competition will enable 10% of voice traffic to be subsidized. Resolving the survival phone "dilemma." The era of unlimited voice communication at a fixed rate will be gone. Hence, for a reasonable incremental cost, a large amount of voice, data and video information would be transported at a fraction of today's costs. (Indeed isn't this the case of most commercial goods. For example from 1960 to 1985 the cost of goods went up a factor of five and labor a factor of three; by using the computer which has increased a factor of 100 over this period, we can reduce costs substantially by using these new processors to perform work other than accounting.)

The firms in the communications-computer information industry are entering an exciting era of new growing business, as each industry expands, employing numerous new players with new skills, enabling society to advance a step closer to making the machine a tool of mankind to make life a little better for men and women, enabling them to better address the realities of family, community, government and society to improve our overall quality of life; as we all work on the formation phase, on an international level, of the information era, as the various geographical societies begin to move closer to interface and interlace, as we "internetwork" together, in the Global Information Society.

Eleven: Recommendation

—THE INFORMATION GAME—

From the proceeding observations and conclusions, we may formulate the following recommendation and considerations for the suppliers, providers, users and regulators, as they play the information game:

- Cannot afford billion dollar machines in a market of intense change, except for systems that grow with change or can be functional, segmented, and changed out, every five years or so.
- Can form partnerships, such as GTE-Siemens, but may spend much on coordinating and agreeing to project, so delays and extensive costs occur—need a planning process.
- May be better to cross-license to manufacture and customize someone else's system for U.S. Market, rather than joint R&D partnerships such as CDE and CAE partnerships.
- Central laboratory—several firms joined together for designing a prototype can be beneficial. Each firm repackages product for individual countries' markets, and perhaps even share in total sales in all markets.
- Must form cross industry partnerships between communications and computers to provide software to enable communications systems to "network" computers and provide higher levels of OSI feature packages, such as encryption, and page reformat.
- Software packages will become a joint venture opportunity, as suppliers enable other software houses to provide and support beneficial software packages for their product's users.
- Providers will need an ever changing array of new features from a supplier's product—one technique is to enable providers to use a set of primitive instructions and write their own programs. An alternative is to form application partnerships with the supplier for fast response, supported software and share in the usage revenue from features used by the provider's customers.

- The users must prepare facilities and spend more to be ready for the future networks, such as building fiber wiring which does not limit their future capabilities by short term financial solutions, (note GM new plant network decision). In the same manner, the Telcos and Interexchange carriers spend money on local and long distance plant. For example, a building for doctors can be just an office building, or it can be a real aid to being a successful doctor if wired properly for "information exchange."
- The ability to "obtain someone who did it before," rather than internally develop and transfer from within-technology or marketing skills. Of course this will always be attractive in certain situations, depending on the skills needed and the type of individual. As the industry becomes more and more competitive, however, those who actually design and support the systems should become an integral part of the firm.
- The market must be closely tied to the technical, with numerous "beta" tests, using prototypes. Shared ventures with various providers will be necessary to encourage growth in the complex high risk new information marketplace.
- Suppliers must recognize the change to "different types of networks" for their products.
- Data manipulation, access, interexchange, processing, formatting, presentation, and storage will become integral functions of systems, which will no longer serve just as "black box" transport systems.
- Suppliers must develop planning into a strategic weapon for achieving success in the war on development and support costs. The proceeding analyses have described processes for managing R&D and establishing technical direction, consistent with the marketplace. Each supplier needs to apply this thinking to their own particular planning and transfer processes in their unit, division, multidivision, multinational environment.
- Need to use applied research, as a marketing tool to understand change in technical direction long before it effects the market and develop a technical transfer program to timely use new technology possibilities in the marketplace, by using a formal R/D technology transfer process to work with several laboratories, universities and even governmental agencies.
- Need to change with technology for long term positioning. Some changes are necessary, for example; an "integrated" system can be achieved by first using separate systems, then partitioned systems, using new packet systems, and later the future wideband matrixes, in which the many frequencies that can exist on the same fiber can be switched.
- Not all aspects of the market need be covered, but whatever is should be distinguished from the rest by being the best.
- Total network solutions can be established by using products from several firms—all of the same quality level, packaged together, jointly.
- Billing and routing will become the major factors in any movement of data, using instantaneous selection of most economical "international" route, where vendors sale capacity, as it is available, at different rates through the day.

- Growth in volume will be essential to both private and public networks, requiring charge out, movement and provision for more and more capacity, computer power, and features in new systems.
- Automatic support will be key to success, as systems of the 90s use the artificial intelligence of expert systems for self analysis and friendly flexible human interaction.
- Training of support people is critical, as complexity increases, to maintain good field user support.
- Increasing support by using second party support centers will be an economical necessity; perhaps a business for a provider in a separate subsidiary.
- Understanding technology is the key where packet transfer leaves off and wideband takes over in terms of new fast packet, burst, phase shifted and frequency division techniques, enabling economical marketable features.
- Provider fiber deployment strategy is essential to suppliers. Supplier multifrequency fiber switching technology is important to providers for long term picture: perhaps sharing supplier's technology research with provider's market research.
- Users are and must become more sophisticated, as well as utilize system/network design and support specialists to assist them in using the right technology for their needs. Hence, the growth of a new "USER Network Planning" industry.
- User network planning must support both data processing and communication within a division, responsible for both endeavors.
- User information management must consider both information movement and processing as a required key strategy for becoming more competitive in their markets; like cars instead of horses; air flights to meetings instead of phone; text with phone instead of mail; automatic file management and multiuser accesses instead of file clerks; and video conference instead of travel, etc.
- Providers must price for growth and establish revenue sharing arrangements with suppliers to obtain new features that encourage network usage.
- Providers must work with suppliers to identify degree and extent of new features in terms of quality, friendly, maintainability, customer controllable, etc.
- The regulators must enable the BOCs to develop quick response information networks, that integrate private networks together or their will be no public information network to regulate.
- Inquiry III leaves the BOCs in a time consuming position of proving nondominance and non-bottleneck. The regulators and BOCs must resolve this dilemma so features can be provided quickly to the public information network without delay.
- The public information network might exist in several states:

  — Regulated to supply those in economic need with voice service over a "limited voice" network.

- Unregulated but monopolistic to ensure a common information transport network exists.
- Unregulated shared public information services offerings, such as info switch as local data Centrex offering.
- Unregulated shared private to public to private networks for special purpose users.
- Combination of all of these in overlaying areas of operations.

- The game is international and must be played accordingly, recognizing internal constraints within each government arena, in terms of political, social and economical limits, as well as the capabilities, resistance and needs of the colloquial users.
- The ISDN world is a vehicle for movement through the maze of interfacing supplier's product's "open standards" and provider's "open architecture" network. It should be defined by sharing, as necessary, internal visions in order to obtain common standards—requiring a "game with a game" strategy.
- Suppliers must work with providers to determine technical aspects for future products such as:

  - When current digital switches should be capped. Many have 2-4 million lines of code supported by 500 to 1500 programmers!
  - Where the public data network should be provided—as part of existing digital voice systems, as separate adjunct systems, as part of extended feature switch, as part of STP switch, as part of access switch to the network, as part of access switch to the world, or as part of a separate value added network?
  - How wideband networks can be extended to move clusters of customers directly to large wideband switches, using rings of multiplexors of 64K, 1.5M, 45M, 140M, 564M, 2.2G b/s channels to gigabit switching clusters, that provide variable bandwidth on demand and alternative routing on fibers for survivability.
  - What role the 1980-89 Digital Switch has in the 1996-2010 metro environment; especially as an adjunct switch with remote switch units throughout the metro community with the analog local exchange systems that handle voice traffic within 1 mile of the central office; versus the new "information metro switch."
  - Which maintenance and administration strategies are to be used for automation of networks in terms of metro switch, ring switch, information switch, feature switch possibilities, as well as existing digital rural and suburban switches?
  - Should voice/data traffic multiplexors and splitters be integrated within voice Class 5 and Centrex Systems to access data Packet switches to provide an "integrated" offering, or should a separate new "integrated" system be provided? Or both in time phases?
  - Could providers define an acceptable time frame for replacement of current product lines for new gigabit network systems?

In summary— *Why* should *What* features be provided by *What* systems, *Where* in the network architecture *When?*

The financial game of mergers with various partnerships should be determined in terms of an overall network market structure, not only by the high internal costs of doing business. If indeed there may be a better way of doing business at half the cost, existing firms may be able to perform much better given the opportunity to plan products better. Simply purchasing firms that may have an existing needed product or doubling the size of R&D staff may not be the answer. Consortiums may need to be established to formulate an entire end to end network/system/feature package in which different firms with different expertise provide various pieces of the picture and share in the cost and revenues of the entire solution.

Market solutions of "throwing products into the marketplace and seeing which ones take" is also not the answer, especially as the initial users are left to live with terminated product lines having limited support and few enhancements; removing "good will" from their view of the firm.

Training and support partnerships will play a major role, as providers attempt to provide numerous complex products to users. Providers will form partnerships with suppliers, who will provide the best maintenance and support package.

The universal information network will require numerous standards to interface to private networks (LANs, MANs, WANs). These standards will require "commonality of offering" agreements across RBOCs, specialized carriers and interexchange carriers throughout the world, using BELLCORE, IEEE, ANSI/TI, CCITT, ECMA, etc., groups. Care must be made to obtain agreements much faster than the four phase CCITT process of going from working drafts to recommendations. This may cause country gateways, but today's marketplace must be met by overcoming time consuming delays for full universal agreement. However, standards need to be a priority, with give and take at the bargaining tables and sharing of architectural plans to obtain the interfacing agreements.

Database access from public networks will be key to information era, as security, protection, encryption, entrapment and access technique's are resolved enabling "intelligent" computers to search through information for answers.

Cost and price averaging, usage pricing, variable bandwidth capacity pricing, bit rate or throughput pricing, feature packages and pricing for growth will be the marketing game of the 90s to encourage return to the public network, as private network costs increase for individual networks, compared to shared public networks.

Risk and decisions—both of these factors have been missing from suppliers and providers over the 70s and 80s. Even the change to digital world was only taken with numerous protests over the great personal courage and pain of the network architecture planners. Change must be accepted. Decisions must be made without all the answers. Processes such as the management planning process must be used to minimize risk; but risk must be undertaken, especially to develop a public information network, when many users are already on their own or shared private networks.

Users need to respond to opportunity and share in the risks and rewards of obtaining many new features and services, that will change their current mode of operation and way of doing business, realizing that the change to the information era will enable them to be more productive and competitive in the marketplace, by enabling their office, design, and marketing workforce to be more effective. This acceptance of change for new inventions and techniques has been a key to America's past success in world social growth.

Management, technical, marketing, and financial must begin to use a planning process enabling them to plan ahead and capitalize on using technology leads time to reestablish order and control; as time can become a formidable asset when it enables them to move into the marketplace with the right array of products and services in a world of "predictable" change.

Internetwork information interexchange using global access codes will require resolution during the formation period, before the real transition phase of the information era can begin.

Unemployment of unskilled workers and shift in number, type, and skills of educated workers will require reassessment of work force, as many leave for less technical career and those more technically skilled enter.

Programming will reach 90% of product costs as microtechnology reduces large systems to microdots; and work functions are performed on super computers, using high level specialized languages.

Distributed processing must address throughput problems, as well as reliability, error rate tolerance, and feature processing, as user traffic builds up, by using physically distributed processing throughout the network and more distributed processing within a system.

Database management expert systems that store, search, and retrieve information from multiple sources will require a new level of standards for automated entry and analysis, not requiring human interface entry.

The future of world power will no longer only be in military capability, but in economic capability. This will be directly proportional to the extent and degree of having inexpensive universal information access, transport and processing capabilities.

The desired result (bottom line) of these recommendations is to obtain a shift in organizational structure from implementation to one which emphasizes planning, as key to survival and success in the information era.

Today, both suppliers and providers must work together to determine networks, products, and services for the providers and the providers customers, as they participate in the highly competitive information arena of the 1990s. As new products' research and development costs approach the billion dollar mark, as more and more firms compete for the sometimes elusive market, as technology advances change rapidly, obsoleting earlier designs, it is necessary and mandatory to formulate a logical network architecture, which embraces technical changes, marketplace needs and regulatory/non-

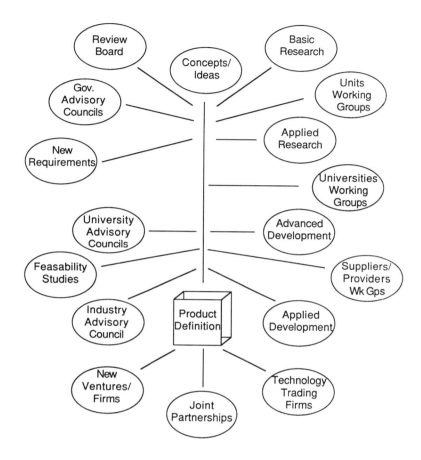

Fig. 12-61. Transfer of Technology to the Marketplace.

regulatory conditions in terms of conceptual possibilities that are achievable over the next twenty years, as we enter the information era together.

Twelve: Tech-Mark — Mark-Tech

— TECHNICAL POSSIBILITIES MEETING MARKET OPPORTUNITIES —

Over the next twenty years, the technology game may be played as follows:

• Video switch fabrics are likely to remain separate from voice and data, but will share facilities under common network control.

- Multi-rate switching will occur, where multiple numbers of 64Kb/s channels are switched in parallel.
- Statistical switching, such as burst or fast-packet will integrate voice and data users to current switches and later integrate a range of voice, data, image and graphics services on a single shared network, but not necessarily video, until gigabit rates are economically available.
- Switching crosspoints in today's systems can handle 1.5 MB/s but not the higher speeds of 45 Mb/s for full motion quality video. VLSI chips for space division or time space time switching of 100 + Mb/s will be building blocks for wideband switching systems.
- Wideband services for internal sophisticated work stations and video displays will require: 64K, 1.5M, 6.3 M, and 45 Mb/s rates.
- Operation systems will require strategic plans for simplifying operations for the more integrated facilities/switching digital environment, using the switching systems to help automate operations, maintenance and administration functions.
- SS#7 as defined in TIXI will become the backbone for numerous new stimulus and functional terminal features requiring the D channel processors and signal transfer point (STP) to play a major role in the signalling, as well as the 700, 800, 900 features world, perhaps using a two level hierarchy of STP type signalling centers in the local plant.
- Voice/data integration of POTS, PPSN (Public Packet Switched Network), and PSDS (Public Switched Digital Service) will be provided to the customer on ISDN 2B + D (16K) or 23B + D (64K) but will not necessarily be handled by a completely integrated switch.
- Public packet switching networks (PPSN) will be overlaid on existing facilities providing ASYN to X 25 conversions for analogue interfaces.
- Integrated network access (INA) will provide digital connectivity between local distribution plant and interoffice facilities via digital cross connect systems or "nailed up" (dedicated path) digital switches.
- Integrated special services networks will handle special services or switched channel circuits.
- Wave length multiplexing of possibly 10 wave lengths to eventually 100 will drastically change our information world, as more and more cheaper facilities are achieved through the fiber as single mode fiber is placed throughout the plant.
- Optical networking will be based on synchronous building block families of 45 Mb/s rates to handle 140 Mb/s high resolution video to provide transmission capabilities of over 2.2 Gb/s.
- Digital service nodes or digital islands will be constructed as hubs to serve pockets of the business community with integrated facilities for voice, data and video offerings. They will be connected together using optical networks, MANs, LANs, and wideband ISDN access systems.
- Local area networks will be interconnected by point to point links and distributed switching using shared broadband transmission medium metro-

metropolitan area networks.

- Metropolitan area networks using fiber technology and folded ring star topology will be defined via 802 standards.
- Intra LATA services will require access to 700, 800, 900 and ICs private virtual networks. IntraLATA competition will extend equal access to Intra LATA as well as Inter LATA toll traffic.
- Inter LATA services will require access to network databases and operation systems.
- Personal computers will need to access viewtext and other outside databases increasing network usage.
- Computer Inquiry III may enable both customer and provider to own terminating equipment on customer premises, as long as both can enter the network as part of "open architecture" agreements.
- Customer control of private networks and access from private to public using digital (channel and bit) cross connect systems will be more and more desirable.
- Private virtual networks (PVNs) enabling customer control in real time of variable usage of voice network will be needed.
- Intelligent network services may be provided using STP centers within the local area to access various databases enabling new features to be provided universally and consistently within the area.
- Consistency across RBOCs for similar services will be desirable and necessary.

The marketplace must now determine which of the above technical possibilities are realistic marketing opportunities that should indeed be implemented, in the form of the specialized feature packages, noted throughout the preceding sections. It is now time for marketing to play the game and pull society into the information era, reinforcing the push from technology, but reversing the leadership role from Tech-Mark to Mark-Tech, as:

- Multi-firm shopping complexes will require significant communication enrichments in the form of "retail information services" to achieve the "store of the future."
- Touch sensitive screens, graphics, and text displays of selected menus, high resolution graphics, and three dimensional images, as well as text to voice using speech synthesis, speaker recognition (selected and multiple user), and speaker identification verification will be used in various combinations to greatly enhance the exchange of information and achieve the "office of the future."
- Factories will be *automated* using internal intelligent work stations as nodes of internal information networks, integrating product engineering design with the factory, as well as overlaying marketing production orders with factory production control and purchasing and integrating, inventory control with parts control, quality testing, support vendors, and sister plant order control; thus transforming themselves into the "factory of the future."

- Information services in the home, such as "friendly" directory assistance, home security (fire/police), on line catalogues, remote energy management, directories of goods and services, personal messages, information request and retrieval, home banking, education, and entertainment become economically available for the masses, creating the "home of the future."

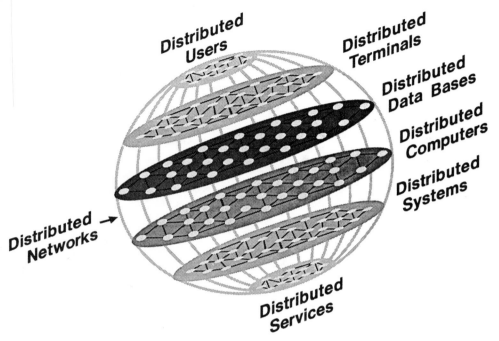

Fig. 12-62. Huber's Geodesic of Distributed Information.

Chapter 13

Workshops

ONE: WHAT IS THE STRATEGY OF THE STRATEGY?

After reviewing the key points made throughout Chapter 1 and Section one of Chapter 12, it is interesting to study the case histories of the five firms to determine their specific strategies and consider how they adapted or did not adapt to the new marketplace, as the old world collided with the new. It is important to learn from the past in order to appreciate the finer points and subtleties, that expand a casual observation into a realistic application of theoretical strategies. They say we must either learn from history or relive it. We should not only avoid having to relive it, but in learning, we should obtain new data from which to derive new approaches and new techniques. This will enable us to apply these lessons from the past to successfully meet future situations and opportunities. With this in mind, a brief series of questions and topics have been identified to consider, reflect, discuss, and contemplate in order to help develop future strategies on how to play the game.

Questions

1. What one line statement best describes each of the five companies? What common word should be in each one line statement?
2. Why did High Tech West Inc. decline, when it lost its best customer?
3. What steps should Mid Tech Tel have performed to prevent its destruction?

4. How can Multi National regain a position in the marketplace?
5. What are five basic strategies that the lost leader companies should have to retain some form of leadership role in providing telecommunications/information networks, products, and services?
6. What is the tool that Change Inc is using to be effectively changing? How long should it keep its mature product lines in periods of high change?
7. Why take the time to build a new business? Why not acquire the ones needed? Especially in a period of intense change?

Strategy Topics

1. Describe the degree and extent of possible new technologies' impact on firms (such as the cases) in the 1990, 2000 and 2010 marketplaces, in a manner similar to the impact of technology shifts of 1960, 1970, and 1980. Note where your firm should play the game.
2. Define a planning process that will be needed in order to participate in the 1990 - 2010 period of technological and marketplace changes.
3. Describe the role of the manager planner in this new environment for each of the following areas: top management, strategic planning, market research, systems analysis and design for both the R&D labs and the telecommunications provider's lines of business.
4. Establish your own strategies for playing the game.

A brief "vision" of the next twenty five years of the world of computers and telecommunication was provided as a framework to assist you in developing your strategies. As other chapters are analyzed, you may wish to revisit this framework and refine your analysis, so that when all sections are completed, you will have completed your specific strategy, on how you wish to play the game, such as: with what business strategies, with what mode of operation, with what processes etc. This, then, will be your "strategy of the strategies."

TWO: STRATEGIC THINKING

Now that we have developed an understanding of strategies and processes and reviewed three different, but interdependent companies' strategies in the case studies, let's consider the following questions to see how each firm's strategies affects the other's business programs, projects and products.

1. What would be specific goals and objectives for the Infonet Distribution Firm in today's environment?
2. How can the Marketing Firm's planning groups for advanced services work with Infolab? How should they all together, or separately, work with Central Research, to define network interface standards, identify new features, establish new products, determine quality objectives, obtain quality assurance, and define international information networks?

3. How can Central Research become a profit center? Should it? How much applied research versus applied development is needed? What should its key offerings be to its owners? How should it be a national resource?
4. How can Info planners become proficient in technology to define and direct research endeavors? To what extent? To what degree?
5. How big should Central Research become in relation to Info? to Infolab? to Infonet? In terms of being a national resource?
6. How interrelated are the mission, strategic direction, specific goals, objectives, and business plan for Info, Infonet, Infolab, and Central Research? How should they work together?

To further understand how a firm's mission and strategic direction unlocks tremendous new opportunities in technological change and focuses the energies of the firm on the game, let's look at the Section on the International Technology Trade Center, to see how a joint venture in the 90s between several states and Change Inc. could develop a large international technology trade center. Let us assume that you have just been appointed on an advisory council to the board of directors of the center. You represent a commercial firm, that may be interested in using the center.

After reviewing the background reference describing the center's future possibilities, identify its mission, goals, and objectives, in terms of its underlying "strategy of the strategy." If the center is to be different from any other office building, what should be its driving positioning strategy? Finally, what products should it really offer the world? As we go into the information era, what should be its business of the business?

THREE: A "DANKA" EXPERIMENT

1. The first study is an analysis of the new data and video users in terms of user types, that are consistent across industries. The section described the marketplace of people types for various market segmentations, determined by personal characteristics and demographics. How would you integrate the two approaches? In terms of "user types," how would you address the next two marketing strategies after market segmentation, which are market targeting and market positioning?
2. What key conclusions concerning the evolution of ISDN networks can you determine? What will be the life of future switching systems? How important will distributed subsystem architectures be? What do the dashed boxes (Fig 12-7) imply in terms of future "integrated" wideband facilities and switches? (Chapter 10.) Can you see how the trend to the one plug connector is established by ISDN "overlays" that increase network usage of voice, data, or video calls?
3. What should AT&T have been doing in the 70s to head off their break up? Consider their offerings for business data networks.
4. How does this analysis of market "user types" give you quantitative estimates for various functional areas? (See "A Look at the Marketplace.") What should be done next to feel more comfortable in understanding

future opportunities and to minimize risk?

5. What will be the realistic needs of society for telecommunications at the turn of the century? In order to ensure that we are not in a "tulip mania" situation, if possible perform "difference thinking" or an information ring session with others, using them to help you determine your vision of the future. Then you may wish to return to your "strategy of the strategies," to reassess, modify, and enhance it.

FOUR: A TRILLION BILLION DOLLAR DECISION

What telecommunications features will be truly needed in the 90s and at the turn of the century?

To properly identify the network's features, products, and services, we must understand the marketplace in terms of "why?" various things may be needed. Only then will we be able to truly define the business communications systems and home communications systems required for the office of the future and home of the future. As noted in the case study, "The Trillion Billion Dollar Decision," there are many possible features, but an improperly identified one can carry a high price tag. Hence, we must take a more in depth look at the world, in which they will exist, to determine the major key features, that will be successful in meeting real needs, in terms of the following questions:

What features? For whom? When required? Where? How? Why? In other words, "*Who* wants *what when, where, how,* and *why*?"

FIVE: WHO'S ON FIRST, WHAT'S ON SECOND?

As we review the general purpose "New Network Game" model, we should consider the following specific questions, effecting our future strategies:

1. To have orderly growth in the information world, it is essential that a coordination committee (IEEE, TI, State Department), perhaps chaired by the Computer Manufacturing Associations, Bellcore, etc. will become the standard group for establishing the new ISDN-C&C network architecture standards, based upon the U.S. version of ISDN, due to our regulatory/non regulatory arena changes. By working with data processing, network systems suppliers, the various RBOCs, independent Telcos, interexchange, and intermediaries, how could this take place?

2. Should the Telco distribution company become the central network "data information" access point? . . . even for business data customers, who wish to bypass the Telco?

3. With the removal of the separate subsidiary requirement by the FCC in the late 80s, how can the Telco and a new/different Telco Subsidiary compete in the changed marketplace to handle medium to large businesses, clustered in shopping centers and downtown areas, who wish new, extensive, non-delayed data features and access to local databases for data manipulation and processing?

4. Will large customers return back to the Telco for internal systems, once they have moved off the network, as they integrate their communication networks deeper and deeper into their operations as these larger firms move to automate their functions? Will their use of the Telco distribution company to manage outside networks prevail? Once they have achieved company to company satellite connections, will they use land networks for secure traffic backups? What happens to the small business community?

5. Will small business wait for the Telco to provide basic data transport features? Will data intermediaries skim major medium business customers, leaving rural, remote individuals, or islands left for the basic Telco?

6. Will information search, manipulation, preparation, and processing be part of every major information service? In order to do such things as polling and broadcast data handling services, can the network distribution firm obtain waivers, to be able to handle meter reading or alarms on a public data switched network? Will future Inquiries change DOJ information services restrictions, once open architecture is achieved? (Note DOJ Huber based information freedoms.) Could extended data features be provided in an unregulated portion of the distribution firm or the Telco subsidiary, when allowed? How can the Telco's network meet Inquiry III collocation and interconnect considerations to enable open competition?

7. What impact did Inquiry III's open architecture and CEI have on Inquiry II as the network emerges, fragmented to meet the needs of residence, small, medium business owners? The Geodesic Network?

8. Per Inquiry II, government regulators for networks became the driving force to determine the location of features. This required the Telco to have two machines one for limited basic transport, interfacing to many adjunct feature switches, such as protocol conversion units or through STP centers to feature switches. Will new traffic conditions develop as these transport switches either route to or wait for feature switches to perform their call handling function? Should there be stand alone feature switches, if so what type? Offering what features? How did Inquiry III resolve these concerns?

9. Will the feature switch/system become more and more a PBX, BSM (See Info Switch) or the new Centrex? Will this system have difficulty establishing standards with all network switches? Will calls probably be routed to it for service, rather than interrupting basic call handling on the network central office system? Will feature switch access be an option of the Users, similar to their access carrier to the world? Will billing become a major work function on a per-feature basis?

10. Where should the NCTE line interface boundary be for network channel terminating equipment? Where should level three and level four systems be located?

11. What impact will the OSI levels have on the architecture of systems with distributed switching and databases, in terms of providing various types of new features?

12. What standards other than protocol standards are necessary to enable the U.S. network to proceed, in an orderly manner at the higher levels?

13. Inquiry II questions have led the Government to Inquiry III—which changes the rules of the game to such an extent that in fact it is a completely different game in which the government was now more concerned with "how—marketwise" rather than "where—technically."
    — Concerned with how [requiring open competition] new Telco offerings are provided, but not being overly concerned with putting artificial boundaries on where it is offered, such as ownership on customer premises.
    — Ensuring collocation and interconnection on all open competition services provided by the Telcos.
    — Enabling competition from Telco through unregulated separate accounting, using "open architecture" and "CEI" concepts.
    — Opening the door for ISDN.
    — Achieving Huber's Geodesic Network.

Therefore, let's take a moment to relook at "Who's On First" and assess what is different due to Inquiry III and the Huber report, and then determine for yourself how level the playing field really is and where the holes are. Then revisit your "strategy of the strategies."

SIX: MANAGING THE PURSUIT OF QUALITY

As we consider the reference case study "Managing The Pursuit Of Quality," we should ask ourselves, how we could achieve our desired levels of quality, in our particular networks, products, or services, by using the suggested approach, together with the other processes, identified within the section. We should also consider how we can achieve these objectives on schedule at reasonable costs, using specific methodologies, organizations, and aids. Consider the following questions:

- Does quality cost schedule?
- What major changes are needed to put the management planning process in place in most companies?
- How can planning groups be established across lines of businesses to achieve conceptual, requirements and product definition phases?
- How detailed a methodology would you or your group agree to follow?
- What aspects of this quality process can you adapt to your environment?
- How should "development decision" processes or a "user needs" processes, as identified in the case studies, be actually implemented? As a detailed methodology? In your firm?
- Reassess your "strategy of the strategies" in light of all these processes and determine how you wish to achieve "the delicate balance."

SEVEN: RESTRUCTURING THE FIRM

Assume that you are responsible for recommending restructuring of a multiunit, multidivision, multinational telecommunications firm located in New York City, with several specialized laboratories, situated around the Tri Cities Area, throughout the United States, Europe and the Far East. (See case study; "Multi-National Inc.") Each of the units is responsible for a separate product line, such as terminals, modems, switches, fiber optics, etc. As the network becomes more integrated, each has need for the other, with some form of central technical planning and marketing.

What should the firm do to provide an aggressive entrance into the information era marketplace? How should it be structured? Where?

EIGHT: PLAYING THE GAME

Indeed there are really two issues: the "what" and "how." Neither can be achieved without the other, which is the reason for "the book in the book" to bring management together with marketing together with technical, to achieve "Mark-Tech" and "Tech-Mark" opportunities and possibilities!!

Now is the time to review the steps outlined in Chapter 8 and consider "how" you want to play the game, with what new processes, organizations and people considerations, to successfully achieve these future networks, products and services.

Next, the "what" will be further analyzed as the Chapters 9 and 10 provide the big picture view of the direction of U.S. ISDN, the ISDN Marketplace, technology, Governmental decisions, and the direction of the information society to assist you in finalizing your analysis. Chapter 11 consists of a five step workshop to consider the formation phase of the information era in terms of your particular "strategy of the strategies," consistent with your strategic direction.

NINE: ANOTHER PLACE, ANOTHER TIME

Projecting the future in terms of scenarios of possibilities is in reality only step one of a six step process.

Step One

Here, each aspect (voice, data, and video) should be differently time phased in its application, depending on economic conditions, availability of wideband transmission facilities, geographical cultural requirements and users' acceptance.

Step Two

Once a logical framework of possibilities has been identified, we should then develop a more complex "realistic" scenario based upon phasing, within the phases, of voice, data, and video applications for rural, suburban and urban locations of the home, office, and factory in the industrial and the non-industrial major and minor cities of the world. This would be a logical next step in achieving a more extensive look at the information society.

Step Three

As will be noted in Chapter 11's analysis of the formation period, test experiments are conducted over this period to determine specific variances of user needs, as well as user acceptance of various potential information features possibilities; for example, the eighty million dollar information age Tokyo suburb "MITAKA" experiment by Nippon Telegraph and Telephone Co. demonstrated the limitations of remote video doctor patient interactions, without the doctor's ability to touch the patient, as well as the lack of features to overcome user resistance by meeting real needs, once the information network became available.

This step should be performed in terms of "what if" and "then what" conceptual analyses of human needs, resistance and acceptance to potential information society possibilities in order to better establish boundaries, conditions and variances of its applications.

Step Four

Should take a detailed look at the economic picture of the world communities over the next twenty to forty years and overlay various models of industrial, third world and fourth world possibilities, based upon social, power, leadership, economic and technological changes for each major segment of the world arena.

Step Five

Cost and price should not be overlooked or underestimated. They are essential and must be overlaid on the various world marketplaces in terms of promoting growth, using the latest advances of technology, taking into account that the initial technical capabilities of the inhabitants may be substantially limited; as technology possibilities meet the marketplace opportunities based upon the economic realities noted in the next sections, in terms of both the private and public environments.

Step Six

At this point we can step back and look at these analyses and time phase them to the different world market segments and indicate percentage (%) of possibilities of occurrences (for example, a doctors' information network, banks' transaction network, retail stores point of sales/inventory control network for specific major and minor cities in the various segments of the world communities).

In the future more timely reference studies will be available to assist in formulating a Feature/Location/% Market Penetration matrix, such as:

1. Econometric study of the world society based upon recursive iterations of an advancing information society.
2. Study of the effect of the various pricing and promotional tactical deployment strategies, providing packaged potential features to geographically and social-economically different marketplaces.
3. Study of economic impact of hundreds of transmission frequencies in the

single mode fiber conduit in terms of potential technological advances of super computers, high level programming languages using high level number base systems, artificial intelligence enabling decision making and talking interactive computers, cheap gigabit memory storage, etc. that will enable extremely cheap ubiquitous information access, transfer and processing.

4. Study of human technology/feature needs and limits, as noted in various test experiments based upon specific types of technology, marketplace features and user cultures.

5. Study of international market applications in terms of different unique cultures, political governments, developmental levels, environmental limits, as well as feature variations for each segment of the world marketplace.

Of course these studies can only be superficially addressed here in a brief workshop, but should be considered in your analyses. They are interdependent and will develop, as we experience the formation phase in the international arena. Perhaps they should be left for another book in another place and another time.

TEN: THE BUSINESS OF THE BUSINESS

During this analysis we have "played the game" from both a technical and a marketing position by identifying the initial phases (Overlay, Integrated, Wideband and Photonic) of the potential ISDN Network Architecture and its marketing opportunities. The complexity of the game has been unmasked, in our series of "analyses." Hopefully, they have been sufficient to show the need to aggressively participate in these interdependent arenas.

It is appropriate now to take a moment to review your "strategy of the strategies" and translate it into more specific "business of the business" strategies for your firm, division, department or group in terms of potential programs, projects, products, and services. Hence, it is now the time to determine the specific technical and marketing aspects of "the game."

ELEVEN: NETWORKS AND SERVICES OF THE INFORMATION ERA

Reviewing Chapter 11's five step process, compare the strategies noted in step three with your own particular underlying basic driving strategic strategy, developed throughout the text's workshops in terms of events, issues, conditions, problems and opportunities of the current period. Perform step four by comparing your strategy with those of the major suppliers and providers, currently involved in the computer and communication marketplace, and then perform step five as a series of "what if" and "then what" scenario analyses, considering regulatory changes, potential technology advances, and market shifts.

In this manner, you have attempted to develop an architecture to handle change, determine a regulated/deregulated strategy to meet the concerns of FCC, DOJ, State commissions, resolve the private network to public network dilemma, ensure conformity of offerings, interconnect to world ISDN networks, integrate C&C to achieve office and factory automation, provide new information services to the home, and encourage growth and usage of the new information networks by integrating exciting new terminals to numerous new database services to achieve an orderly platform for the formation of the information era.

Once this analysis is concluded, risk should be minimized to increase your strategy's chance to survive in the C&C industries' "Corridor of Crises," and compete successfully in the "Global information era."

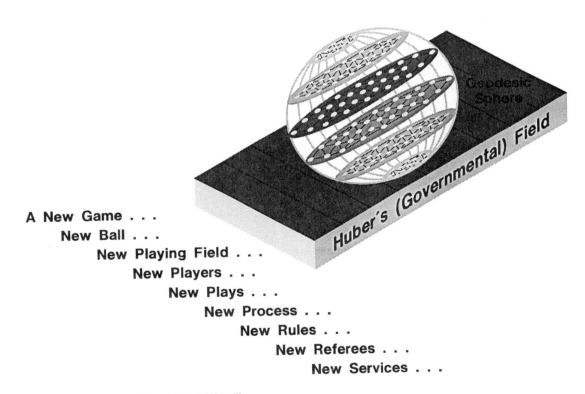

A New Game . . .
New Ball . . .
New Playing Field . . .
New Players . . .
New Plays . . .
New Process . . .
New Rules . . .
New Referees . . .
New Services . . .

Fig. 13-1. Time to play a little Huber "G" ball!

Part 4

References

Chapter 14

The Information Game

It is truly a game—an Information Game—to see who will be successful in working their way through the maze of aspects of the information pyramid to access its inner chamber, containing the treasures of the information era, consisting of a trillion billion dollars of new revenues and sales from the "right" information networks, products, and services. The following is a "big picture" review of several of the key aspects of this Information Game. To survive in its first period of play and be able to master this constant game of change, we need to take several detailed "looks" to better understand its goals, rules, players, boundaries, and equipment. This includes analyzing the more competitive and dominant player's strategies for their forthcoming information networks, products, and services. To be successful, we must become competent with the new technology, sensitive to the new information user's needs, and cognizant of the government "what, where, and how" boundary lines for value added services, in order to be the successful "master players" of the new "Information Game." See Fig. 14-1(A).

One: A Look at the Standards Players

As noted throughout the text, the standards game will determine the

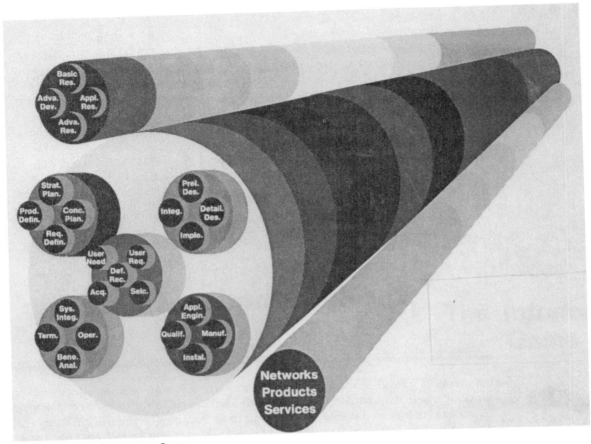

Fig. 14-1(A). The Information Game.

future of ISDN and the information world. It is an intense arena where suppliers, providers, government, and users must work together to resolve tremendously complex inter-networking: access, numbering plans, protocol and routing issues, etc. Here is a brief look at who is playing the game and where it is being played.

Standards are developed when contributions are accepted by consensus and incorporated into working drafts. Of those contributions, derived from the technical discussions from the various participants that are accepted, most go through a process of editing before being approved.

The standards formulation process originates at a national or subnational level. Before a standard becomes accepted, it must filter through a public review process of evaluation. Standards may be developed specifically for national or for international purposes. When standards are being formulated for the U.S., they must be accredited by ANSI. Within ANSI, there are three methods to formulate an American National Standard. First, a standard can be developed by any accredited organization, such as IEEE and EIA, that has agreed to follow ANSI's procedures. Secondly, any Accredited Standards Committee, for example X3 or T1, can formulate an American National Standard. Lastly, any general interest group, such as the Department of Defense, can submit to ANSI a draft standard, that they developed under their proceedings. Other general interest organizations are trade, professional, technical, consumers and labor groups.

Standards submitted to international standards organizations can proceed, along different paths, depending on which international body the standard is referenced. When a contribution is sent to CCITT, it must first be sent to the appropriate U.S. CCITT Study Group for evaluation and approval. When sent to ISO (International Organization for Standardization), a U.S. Technical Advisory Group (TAG) will submit the contribution as the representative of the United States. For example, ANSI X3S3 is the U.S. TAG for ISO Technical Committee 97 - Subcommittee 6 on Data Communications.

Contributions may also be sent directly to international standards organizations on issues, that are under development both domestically and internationally. Typically, the intention of doing this is to alter the international standard to assure consistency with national requirements.

KEY STANDARDS COMMITTEES

ANSI is the primary national standards forum. It accredits and coordinates national organizations, such as Committee T1, that develop standards for telecommunications systems. ANSI oversees standards committees in the preparation, processing, approval and distribution of proposed standards. ANSI has formalized procedures to ensure "open representation" and "due process" in working committees, such as consensus in decision making and appeals for any committee actions in question. T1 is ANSI's largest accredited committee, with 200 or so member organizations. T1 was formed in February 1984 due to the recognized need to provide an industry-wide forum to develop interconnection and interoperability standards. With the divestiture of the Bell System, the Federal Communications Commission (FCC) expressed concern that a void has been created within the industry with respect to telecommunication standards. The Exchange Carriers Standards Association (ECSA), representing 95% of the telephone subscribers in the U.S., proposed the establishment of T1 as a public standards committee open to exchange carriers, interexchange carriers, manufacturers, vendors, user groups and government agencies. With the overwhelming support of the telecommunications industry, the ECSA proposal for the formulation of T1 was accepted by the FCC.

T1's charter describes its functions as: "the development of standards and technical reports related to interfaces for US networks, which form part of the North American telecommunications system." T1 also develops positions on related subjects under consideration in various international standards bodies. Specifically, T1 focuses on those functions and characteristics associated with the interconnection and interoperability of telecommunications networks at interfaces with end user systems, carriers, and information enhanced service providers. These topics include switching, signaling, transmission, performance, operation, administration and maintenance aspects. Committee T1 is also concerned with procedural matters at points of interconnection, such as maintenance and provisioning methods and documentation, for which standardization would benefit the telecommunications industry. T1 is composed of six technical subcommittees and working groups with the following five work programs:

- Carrier-CPE Interfaces (T1C1)—Deals with interfaces between customer premises equipment (CPE), including private networks, and the networks of exchange, interexchange, and other carriers.
- ISDN (T1D1)—This subcommittee is concerned with all aspects of Integrated Services Digital Network (ISDN) services, user-network and network-network interfaces, and administration. T1D1 will prepare positions on ISDN matters for submission to the U.S. CCITT/CCIR Study Groups and other standards organizations.
- Internetwork Operations, Administration, Maintenance (OAM), and Provisioning (T1M1)—Deals with basic network management; OAM system interface languages and telemetry; Man Machine Language (MML); ordering, provisioning, and restoral procedures; preventative testing and maintenance; billing data interchange; automatic transmission measuring systems; and network tones and announcements.
- Performance (T1Q1)—This subcommittee develops end-to-end network performance standards with due consideration for the allocation of performance parameters among exchange, interexchange, and customer portions of network connections. Performance parameters will be defined, as well as measurement techniques.
- Carrier-Carrier Interfaces (T1X1)—Deals with interfaces of exchange carriers (including cellular carriers) and interexchange carriers. Projects include equal-access and mid-span interconnection, common channel signaling and synchronous DS3 formal and network synchronization.

The T1 subcommittees and their areas of responsibility are:

T1C1—Carrier/Cpe Interfaces
 T1C1.1—Analog Interfaces
 T1C1.2—Digital Interfaces
 T1C1.3—Special Interfaces
 T1C1.4—Editorial

T1D1—ISDN
 T1D1.1—ISDN Architecture and Services
 T1D1.2—Switching and Signaling Protocols
 T1D1.3—Physical Layer

T1M1—Internetwork Operations, Administration, Maintenance and Provisioning
 T1M1.1—Internetwork Planning and Engineering
 T1M1.2—Internetwork Operations

T1M1.3—Testing and Operations Support Systems and Equipment
T1M1.4—Administrative Systems

T1Q1—Performance
    T1Q1.1—4 kHz Voice
    T1Q1.2—4 kHz Voiceband Data
    T1Q1.3—Digital Circuit
    T1Q1.4—Digital Packet
    T1Q1.5—Wideband Program
    T1Q1.6—Wideband Analog

T1X1—Carrier/Carrier Interfaces
    T1X1.1—Common Channel Signaling
    T1X1.2—Exchange/Interexchange interfaces
    T1X1.3—Digital Network Synchronization
    T1X1.4—Hierarchical Rates and Formats

T1Y1.4—Specialized Subjects
    T1Y1.1—Specialized Video and Audio Services
    T1Y1.2—Specialized Voice and Data Processing
    T1Y1.3—Advanced Technologies and Services
    T1Y1.4—Environmental Standards for Central Office Equipment.

Committee X3—Information Processing Systems

X3 was formed in 1960 and has 50 or so member organizations. Two of its technical committees of particular interest are X3S3 on Data Communications and X3T5 on the Open Systems Interconnection. As well as developing US standards, X3 determines the topics for new work projects, and contributes to development of international standards.

Technical Committee X3S3—Data Communication

X3S3 is concerned with protocol-oriented data communications standards. This includes responsibility for developing the service definitions and protocols for the lower four layers of the OSI Reference Model (Physical Interfaces, Data Link, Network and Transport). The task groups deal with questions of planning (coordination of development), system performance, interface protocols, reference models and transmission speeds.

X3—Information Processing Systems

X3S3—Data Communications
    X3S3.3 Network and Transport Layer
    X3S3.4 Data Link Layer
    X3S3.5 Quality of Service
    X3S3.7 Public Digital Network Access

X3T5—Open Systems Interconnection
    X3T5.1 OSI Architecture
    X3T5.4 Management
    X3T5.5 Application, Presentation and Session Layers.

SUMMARY: WHO'S WHO IN OPEN SYSTEMS INTERCONNECTION

ISO—International Organization for Standardization (Geneva).
Worldwide association of the national standards-setting groups with primary responsibility to create OSI standards through its Technical Committee 97 for Information and Data Processing.

ECMA—European Computer Manufacturers Association (Geneva).
Technical group consisting of main computer companies in Europe including IBM, DEC, HEWLETT-PACKARD, ITT, and Burroughs. Sets own standards, which become basis for ISO standards.

CCITT—International Telegraph and Telephone Consultative Committee (Geneva).
Worldwide group of national PTTs and private telecommunications companies. Sets norms for telecommunications and suppliers input for ISO standards setting in OSI.

ANSI—American National Standards Institute (New York).
American standards-setting organization. Administers ISO work on OSI standards and represents U.S. viewpoint in ISO work.

IEEE—Institute of Electrical and Electronics Engineers (New York).
American industry association. Provides basic U.S. industry recommendations for ISO standards.

ITSTC—Information Technology Steering Committee (Brussels).
Newly formed group to coordinate European efforts on function OSI standards, integrating work of both CEPT and CEN-CENELEC.

CEPT—European Conference of Post and Telecommunications (Bern).
Group of all European Telecom administrations. Given main technical role for telecommunications in new European Community (EC) standardization effort.

CEN-CENELEC—European Committee on Norms-European Committee on Electro-technical Norms (Brussels).
Group of European national standards-setting bodies plus major industry manufacturer and user groups. Given main standardization role for computers in European effort.

SPAG—Standard Promotion and Application Group (Brussels).
Association of 12 European computer makers that have agreed to cooperate on OSI standardization under EC sponsorship. Provides technical recommendations to ITSTC.

EC—European Community (Brussels).
Key European cooperation organ. Seeks strong harmonization of telecommunications standards, especially OSI. Is also pushing strict procurement rules to force wide OSI use.

Table 14-1. Major Standards Organizations.

Organization	Type	Committees	Typical functions performed, standards/data interfaces
ANSI	Trade Business	X3 information processing systems X3S3 data communication X3T5 open systems X3T9 I/O interconnection T1 telecomm. T1D1 ISDN	X3 66 ADCCP RS 232C RS 449 RS 423
EIA	Electronics Ind. Associates	TR (voice, data, video)	Component STDS Subsystem STDS
ECMA	European Computer Manufacturing Assn.	TC9	ECMA-40 HDC
CCITT/ITU	International Telephone Consultative Committees of ITU International Telecommunication Union Public/Private Telephone Companies, Scientific Organizations, Governments, Telecommunications Agents		I series, Q series V series, X series CCITT signalling systems R1, R2, #6, #7
		Study group I	Definition and operational aspects of telegraph & telematic services, teletex, facsmile
		Study group II	Tele operations Quality of service
		Study group III	Tariff principles
		Study group IV	Transmission, maintenance of integrated circuits
		Study group V	Electromagnetic protection
		Study group VI	Protection and spec of cables
		Study group VII	Data communications networks (X.30, X.31)
		Study group VIII	Terminal equipment
		Study group IX	Telegraph networks
		Study group X	Telegraph networks and terminals
		Study group XI	Telephone switching and signalling
		Study group XII	Local telephone networks
		Study group XIII	--
		Study group XIV	Telematic services and networks
		Study group XV	Transmission systems
		Study group XVI	Telephone circuits
		Study group XVII	Data communications over telephone networks
		Study group XVIII	Digital networks (I-series)
USCCITT		Study group A	Regulatory matters working with CCITT I, III, and SMM
		Study group	Telegraph operations working with VIII, IX
		Study group C	Telephone operations working with II, IV, V, VI, IX, XI, XII, XV, CMBD, GAS 3, 4, 5, 7, 8, 9
		Study group D	Data transmission working with VII, XVII
		ISDN working group	Working with XVIII and III, VII, VIII, XI, XVII

Table 14-1. (Continued.)

Organization	Type	Committees	Typical functions performed, standards/data interfaces
		Special groups	Special groups dealing with specific technical issues: SMM: mobile maintenance service LTG: other telephony users CMBD: circuit noise and availability GAS: special autonomous groups that prepare information
NTIA	National Tele-communications and Information Admin.	ITS	T1
NBS	National Bureau of Standards	ICST (Institute for Computer Services and Technology)	FIPS 100/Federal Standards 1041 (X25 STD) FIPS Federal Information Process Standards MIL- STD's—XXX
DOD	Department of Defense	Transport Control Protocol comm.	TCP-4
IBM	International Business Machines	SNA committee System Network Architecture	
BNA	Burroughs Network Architecture	BNA	
DEC	Digital Equipment Corporation	Digital Network Architecture (DNA)	
NCR	National Cash Register	Distributed Network Architecture (DNA)	
AT&T	American Telephone & Telegraph	UNIX operating system architecture	
NUA	Network USERS Assn.		
ISO		TC Technical Committees SC Sub-committees TC97 TC97 SC 6 SC 16 sub-committees working groups (WG) Examples for SC (16) WG (1) architectures WG (4) systems mgmt WG (6) Transport/system layers for TC 6 WG 1 data link layer WG 2 network layer WG 3 physical layer	HDLC (High Level Data Link Control Protocol) OSI Model DP 7498 reference model for open systems interconnection levels
ECSA	Exchange Carriers Association of US Telephone Companies Sponsors ANSI T1	T1	
CBEMA	Computer and Business Equipment Manufacturing Association Trade Assn. of Computer and DP Equipment Manufacturers Sponsors ANSI—X3	X3	
IEEE		(LAN STD groups, MAN STD groups) internetworking or internetworking at network layer on MAC bridges	IEEE 802 MAC protocols 802.3, .4, .5, .6
Bellcore	Bell Communications Research	TA/TRIF/TR	TR-008 TA-303
OSC	Open Systems Committee	Standard/interface committees	
ONAF	OPEN Network Architecture Forum	Standard/interface committees	

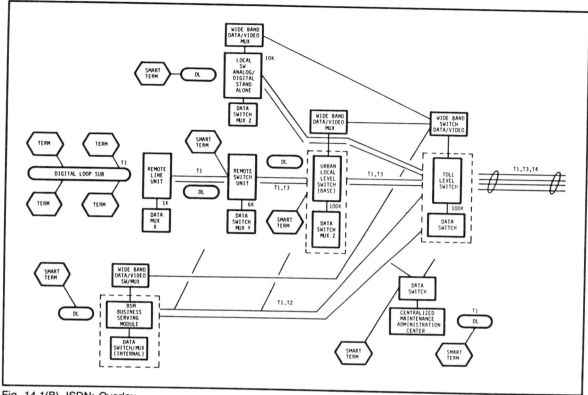

Fig. 14-1(B). ISDN: Overlay.

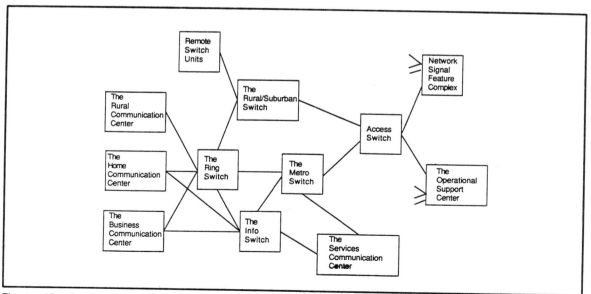

Fig. 14-1(C). ISDN: Broadband/Wideband.

Two: A Look at the International ISDN Game

Per CCITT working groups, "Integrated Services Digital Network" (ISDN) is an all digital network, that provides cost-effective, end-to- end digital connectivity to support a wide range of voice and nonvoice (e.g., data) and video services, to which users have access, by a limited set of standard multi-purpose, user-network interfaces.

CCITT has been actively working on a set of urgent study items on ISDN matters. The majority of the work was carried out in Study Group XVIII, which produced the I-Series Recommendations. Study Group VII participated in the ISDN work by preparing X-series Recommendations, such as X.30 and X.31, for the support of circuit mode and packet mode data terminals on an ISDN. All the I-series form the basis for the international as well as the national ISDNs, that will be developed and deployed over the next century.

An ISDN is assumed to evolve from a digital telephony network by progressively incorporating additional functions and network features so as to provide existing and new services. It is specified to allow interworking with services on existing and future networks.

ISDN services are categorized into two groups: Bearer services, which are the capabilities for information transfer between two ISDN interfaces involving layers 1 to 3 of OSI Reference Model, and Teleservices, which are both the low layer and high layer functions to provide full communication capabilities (e.g., CCITT defined Teletex service). In previous Study Periods, CCITT has concentrated on the bearer services, which are further classified into two groups: circuit mode services and packet mode services.

One of the major advantages of ISDN is to offer the wide range of services through few standard interfaces. A focus of ISDN work done in CCITT to date is the definition of ISDN user/network interfaces. The Recommendations define a Basic interface and a Primary interface rate. Across each interface, a channel structure is defined.

A B-channel is defined to be a 64Kbps channel for carrying end- to-end user information, such as voice or data. A D-channel is used to carry signaling information for the ISDN circuit mode bearer services. The D-channel may also carry low-speed packet data or telemetry. The bit rate of D-channel depends on the type of interface.

The basic Basic interface structure provides two B-channels and 16 Kbps D-channel. The Primary interface structure provides 23 B-channels and a 64 Kbps D-channel. In Europe and Australia, the Primary interface will have 30 B-channels due to different digital transmission standards. See "A Look at Technology's—Digital Transmission."

For example—"CCITT Study Group VII has developed Recommendation X.31 for the support of packet mode terminals accessing packet switched public data networks through ISDN interfaces. X.31 defines two scenarios for the support of such terminals that conform to X.25: minimum integration and maximum integration scenarios. In the minimum integration scenario, the packet switched calls are handled transparently through the ISDN, whose only function is to provide a physical connection between the X.25 terminal and the packet switch. This type of access is offered over the B-channel. In the maximum integration scenario, the packet handling function is provided within the ISDN. Packet mode access over both B-channels and D-channels is possible. Once the physical connection is established between the X.25 terminal and the packet handling function in the ISDN, virtual calls can be set up using X.25 packets level procedure. For both scenarios, the support of packet mode (i.e., X.25) terminals through ISDN interfaces requires a Terminal Adaptor (TA) at the customer premises. The TA handles all the ISDN signalling and interface protocols toward the network, as well as any necessary rate adaption."

ISDN working committees document their findings and interface with other CCITT working groups using the following documentation series:

A Series   —Organization of the work of the CCITT.
A.21   —Collaboration with other international organizations on CCITT defined telematic services.
F Series   —Telegraph and "telematic services" operations and tariffs.
G Series   —General characteristics of international telephone connections and circuits.
G.702   —Vocabulary of pulse code modulation (PCM) and digital transmission terms.
G.705   —Integrated services digital network (ISDN).

GENERAL STRUCTURE OF THE I-SERIES RECOMMENDATIONS

Part I—General

I. 110   General structure of the I-Series Recommendations.
I. 111   Relationship with other Recommendations relevant to ISDN's.

Part II—Service Capabilities

Part III—Overall Network Aspects and Functions

Part IV—USER-Network Interfaces

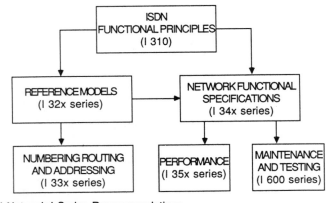

Fig. 14-2. ISDN Network I Series Recommendations.

Q Series General Recommendations Relating to Signalling and Switching in the Automatic and Semi-Automatic Services

V Series Data Communication Over the Telephone Network

X Series Data Communication Networks, Services and Facilities, Terminal Equipment and Interfaces

Message Handling Systems

| X.411 | Message Transfer Layer |
| X.420 | Interpersonal Messaging User Agent Layer |

After each assembly the study groups are assigned answers and questions to resolve over the next four years. There are then several levels of agreements, as these recommendations move to become a fully supported recommendation to be voted on every four years in the CCITT Plenary assembly, the results of the assembly are documented in a series of volumes of various colors for different years of assembly, such as the "blue" books for the 1988 to 1992 period. For reference, here is the table of contents for the "red books" after the Eight Plenary Assembly:

Volume IV

IV.1 — Maintenance; general principles, international carrier systems, international telephone circuits. Recommendations M.10-M.762. (Study Group IV)

IV.2 — Maintenance; international voice frequency telegraphy and facsimile, international leased circuits. Recommendations M.800-M.1375. (Study Group IV)

IV.3 — Maintenance; international sound program and television transmission circuits. Series N Recommendations. (Study Group IV)

IV.4 — Specifications of measuring equipment. Series Recommendations. (Study Group IV)

Volume VIII

VIII.3 — Data communication networks; interfaces. Recommendations X.20-X.32. (Study Group VII)

VIII.4 — Data communication networks; transmission, signalling and switching, network aspects, maintenance and administrative arrangements. Recommendations X.40-X.181. (Study Group VII)

VIII.5 — Data communication networks; Open Systems Interconnection (OSI), system description techniques. Recommendations X.200-X.250 (Study Group VII)

VIII.6 — Data communication networks; interworking between networks, mobile data transmission systems. Recommendations X.300-X.353. (Study Group VII)

VIII.7 — Data communication networks; message handling systems. Recommendations X.400-X.430. (Study Group VII)

Volume IX

— Protection against interference. Series K Recommendations. (Study Group V). Protection of cable sheaths and poles. Series L Recommendations. (Study Group VI)

As current products are interfaced to the ISDN world and future systems are considered, working groups will be essential to resolve ISDN Network connections, internetworking, numbering plans, clear channel (data handling) digital requirements, architectures, standards and interfaces.

INTERNATIONAL ISDN REFERENCE MODULES

In working study groups many people throughout the world have developed the following models to identify issues and work areas. They utilize the CSI levels and USER interfaces described in section five, as they play the game to establish standards to enable internetworking of multiple International ISDN's and various types of networks. Hence, it has indeed become a Network game of high interest and properties.

As any planning book is used as a reference guide, the brief description of the models are included for subsequent reference by the more technically involved reader. They do, however, demonstrate (using a quick skim of this material) the complexity of the world of requirements and need for active participation in the ISDN Game.

ISDN Architecture Functional Model

This architecture functional model is not intended to require or exclude any specific implementation for an ISDN, but only to provide a guide for the specification of ISDN capabilities.

Definitions

Reference configurations are conceptual configurations useful in identifying various possible arrangements to an ISDN. Two concepts are used in defining reference configurations: *reference points* and *functional grouping*.

Functional groupings are sets of functions which may be needed in ISDN arrangements. In a particular arrangement, specific functions in a *functional grouping* may or may not be present. Note—specific functions in a functional grouping may be performed in one or more pieces of equipment.

Reference points (R, S, T, V) are the conceptual points at the conjunction of two functional groupings. In a specific arrangement, a reference point may correspond to a physical interface between pieces of equipment, or there may not be any physical interface corresponding to the reference point. Physical interfaces, that do not correspond to a reference point (e.g., transmission line interfaces), will not be the subject of ISDN Recommendations.

ISDN Reference Configuration

The general ISDN reference configuration is divided into three parts:

- Customer network
- Local network
- Transit network

Recommendation I.411 describes more precisely the reference configurations for ISDN user/network interfaces, which Recommendation I.412 specifies the channel structures to be used at reference points S and T. An ISDN connection is seen by a user from the user/network interface at reference point S or T.

The local network includes the set of equipments located in the connection area of a local exchange, including NTI. It mainly comprises the local access and the serving local center, including line termination (LT) and connection related functions (CRF). The functional grouping CRF may include functions such as exchange terminations, switching, control, network management, operation and maintenance, etc. It corresponds to one (or more) exchange(s) and possibly other equipments, such as multiplexers or concentrators or electronic cross connect equipments. It is understood that all functions referred to in the functional grouping CRF do not have to be performed for all connection types. As an example, only network management functions would be performed in the case of a non-switched 64K bit/s connection type.

Reference point V divides functional groupings line terminal (LT) and connection related functions (CRF). The transit network is the set of equipments used to interconnect all local networks.

Overall Architecture of an ISDN

A basic component of an ISDN is a network for circuit switching of end-to-end 64K bit/s connections. It will be named circuit-switched part of an ISDN. Depending on national situations this network may or may not handle other connection types, such as packet switching. However, ISDN subscribers could be provided only with ISDN packet-switched services in the case of a hybrid user access arrangement.

Architectural Model of an ISDN

These are the seven main switching and signalling functional components of ISDN as far as ISDN connection types are concerned:

- ISDN local connection related functions (CFR) (e.g., user/network signalling, charging);
- Narrow band (64K bit/s) circuit switching functional entities;
- Narrow band (64K bit/s) circuit non-switched functional entities;
- (The identification and definition for 8, 16, 32K bit/s switched or non-switched functional entities is left for further study.)
- Packet switching functional entities;
- Common channel inter-exchange signalling functional entities, for example, conforming to Signalling System No. 7, CCITT signalling system specification;
- Broadband switched functional entities;
- Broadband non-switched functional entities.

These components need not be provided by distinct networks but may be combined as appropriate for a particular implementation.

Higher layer functions implemented within (or associated with) an ISDN may be accessed by the means of any of the above-mentioned functional entities. Those functional entities could be implemented totally within an ISDN or may partly correspond to dedicated networks. Both cases may provide the same ISDN bearer or alpha service (see Recommendation I.200 on services) and comply with the same Hypothetical Reference Connections (HRCs).

In the case where packet services are provided on the D-channel, the local center will have to perform some functions related to packet handling, and may even provide packet switching functions where appropriate.

In all cases circuit switching and common channel signalling functions will be performed by ISDN local centers. During the early stage of ISDN, packet switching functional entities may be located in the exchanges of dedicated public network for data, designed in conformity with CCITT I-series Recommendations.

Also the set of circuit switching functional entities may comprise a terrestrial IDN evolved from the present telephone network, as well as satellite system switching networks.

Local Network

The local network comprises:

- transmission line systems, including network termination;
- remote multiplexers and switching units;
- a local serving center.

The digital local serving center is understood as a set of functional entities, some of them being specified by CCITT Recommendation. Depending on national conditions a local exchange complying with an international Recommendation may be implemented in a unique centralized equipment or distributed in a set of separate sub-equipments, some of them being remotely located.

Functional entities NTI and NT2 may be integrated within the same equipment or separately by a physical interface at reference point T. In cases where a complex customer installation is provided with more than one basic access, a basic channel structure may be used which could be downwards multiplexed into a multiplexed channel structure at the primary or intermediate bit rate. Another possibility consists in using a primary rate channel structure at T reference point. Depending on the actual access capability and on transmission considerations, an intermediate bit rate transmission system could be used downwards.

Transit Network

The transit network could be homogeneous. In this case, the same digital links and the same digital switching nodes are used to set up communications for all the services offered to a customer; the transit network could also be non-homogeneous. In this case the same digital nodes are used to set up communications for a part of the services offered to a customer, while specialized functional groupings are used for the rest of the services.

Functional Aspects of ISDN
Circuit Switching in ISDN

Circuit switched connections are carried by B-channels at the ISDN user/network interfaces and switched at 64K bit/s by the circuit-switching functional entities of ISDN.

Signalling associated with circuit-switched connections is carried by D-channels at the ISDN user/network interfaces and processed by the local exchange. User-to-user signalling is routed through the common channel signalling functional entities.

User bit rates of less than 64K bit/s may be rate adapted to 64K bits before switching in ISDN. Moreover X1 circuit-switched data services will be provided by data network to which the user gains access by means of an ISDN connection.

Non-transparent applications such as telephony applications of ISDN circuit-switched capabilities may also employ non- transparent transport channels (e.g., packetized voice, digital speech interpolation). Channels at 8, 16 or 32K bit/s may be used in the transmission part of the network; they may be used to carry non-transparent connection types, e.g., suited to a virtual 4 kHz channel. They may also be used in cases where 64K bit/s channel (B-channel at S or T reference point) carries user data streams at bit rates lower than 8, 16 or 32K bit/s respectively.

Connection types at higher bit rates could also be provided by this network on a semi-permanent basis. Switched connections at these bit rates could also be provided by broadband switching functional entities.

Packet Switching in ISDN

Packet switching functional entities of an ISDN may be centralized in a set of specialized switching nodes or distributed and integrated with the 64K bit/s circuit switching features within the exchanges forming part of the basic transit network. Both implementations are regarded as fulfilling ISDN requirements. Protocols used between these nodes should conform to the CCITT X-series Recommendations. Packet-switched services are routed to the packet switching functional entities of an ISDN.

A number of methods may be used to access packet-switched services in an ISDN. One group of methods accesses services via a B-channel. A second group of methods accesses services via a D-channel.

Methods which could be used are:

1. B-channel packet access
   — Circuit switched through a local exchange to a dedicated PSN,
   — Circuit switched through a local exchange to a packet network that is part of the administrations' ISDN,
   — Packet-handling functions provided within the local exchange;
2. D-channel packet access
   — Processed through a local exchange to a dedicated PSN,
   — Processed through a local exchange to a packet network provided by the administrations, using CCITT recommended or an internal network protocol,
   — Packet switching the local exchange.

High Layer Functions (HLF)

Provision of "higher layer functions" could be made either via special nodes in an ISDN belonging to the public network or centers operated by private companies and accessed via ISDN user/network or internetwork interfaces. Some features—such as mailing boxes—encryption—will be used on a very large scale and the relevant functional entities could be implemented within the exchanges themselves. For both cases the protocols used to activate such features should be identical and integrated with the general user procedures defined for the activation of ISDN communication services.

Relationship with Specialized Networks

It is important to note that the introduction of ISDN capabilities into a network requires a massive development effort. Consequently, administrations or RPOAs will be introducing various ISDN functions successively over a course of time. For example, the 64K bit/s circuit-switched capability may be introduced initially, followed later by provision of packet switching features, and so on.

An ISDN will therefore have to interwork with a set of various specialized networks or terminals in order to:

1. provide ISDN connections to non-ISDN terminal equipments (TE2);
2. provide a non-ISDN terminal equipments (TE2) connected by means of a terminal adaptor (TA) with access to non-ISDN services provided by a dedicated services network; ensure that an ISDN terminal connected to ISDN interworks with a non-ISDN terminal connected to a dedicated network.

ISDN CONNECTION TYPES

The ISDN may be described by a limited set of user-network interfaces (refer to Recommendation I.411) and a limited set of ISDN connection types to support the telecommunications services described in the I.200 series of Recommendations. This Recommendation identifies and defines these connection types insofar as they relate to the provision of particular network capabilities for an ISDN. The basic lower layer capabilities of an ISDN (refer to Recommendation I.310) are represented by a set of ISDN connection types. This Recommendation should be considered in conjunction with other Recommendations in the I- series, with particular reference to Recommendations I.120, I.210, I.211, I.310, I.320, I.411 and I.413. For definitions of terms used in this Recommendation refer to Recommendation I.112.

Basic Concept of ISDN Connection Types

An ISDN provides a set of network capabilities which enable telecommunication services to be offered to a user (refer to I.200 series Recommendations). An ISDN connection is a connection established between ISDN reference points (see Recommendations I.310, I.410 and I.411). Thus an ISDN connection is a physical or a logical realization of an ISDN connection type. Each ISDN connection can be categorized as belonging to a connection type, depending on its attribute values.

Function Associated with ISDN Connections

Any ISDN connection involves an association of functions to support telecommunication services. Three sets of functions are required:

1. Connection means, including transmission and switching.
2. Control functions and protocols, including signalling, flow/congestion control and routing functions.
3. Operations and management functions, including network operations, network management and maintenance functions.

Applications of ISDN Connection Types

Four situations have been identified thus far to which ISDN connection types apply:

- between two ISDN user-network interfaces, i.e., between S/T reference points. (Note—There may be a need in certain cases to differentiate between the S and T reference points. This is for further study.)
- between an ISDN user-network interface and an interface to a specialized resource.
- between an ISDN user-network interface and a network-to-network interface.

In (overall) ISDN connections involving several networks, each network provides a part of the connection and may be categorized by different attribute values. In such cases, the characterization of the performance for the overall ISDN connection is for further study.

ISDN Connection Types and Their Attributes

Attributes and Their Values

ISDN connection types are characterized by a set of attributes. Each attribute has a set of admissible values. The definitions of these attributes are given in Recommendation I.130. The attributes which are associated with ISDN connection types have a similarity to those used to define telecommunication services in Recommendations I.211 and I.212. However, the two sets of attributes differ in several important aspects. For example:

- ISDN connection types represent the technical capabilities of the network and are a means to ensure defined performance and interworking between networks. Telecommunications services supported by the ISDN are the packages offered to customers and the definition of their attributes is the means to standardize the service offerings worldwide.
- Quality of service and commercial attributes are relevant to telecommunications services, whereas network operations and maintenance attributes are relevant to connection types.

Where there are two or more S/T interfaces, different values of the access attributes may occur at each interface. Values need to be specified for each channel of the interface structure. The role of the access attributes in determining connection types is for study. Interfaces to network specialized resources and to other networks are for further study.

ISDN PROTOCOL REFERENCE MODEL

The objective of the ISDN protocol reference model is to model information flows, including user information and control information flows, to and through an ISDN. It is based on the general principles of layering given in the X.200 series of Recommendations, but it is recognized that many of the entities and information flows modeled here do not consist of Open Systems (in the X.200 sense). It is also recognized that the signalling protocols currently recommended by CCITT (e.g., Signalling System No.7 (Q.700 series)) and D-channel protocol (Q.900 series) are layered and it is a matter for further study how these protocols and this model should correlate.

A fundamental concept for protocol modeling is based on the principles of layered communication defined in Rec. X.200 (The Reference Model of Open Systems Interconnection (OSI) for CCITT Applications). The OSI Model was originally conceived for data communications, while the ISDN is conceived to support multi- service types of communications, including voice and video applications. The OSI Model therefore needs to be applied judiciously in order to effectively represent the ISDN-specific features not encountered in current data networks. With these features, a wide range of communication modes and capabilities can be achieved in the ISDN, including the following:

- Circuit-switched connection under the control of common channel signalling.
- Packet-switched communication over B, D and H channels.
- Signalling between users and network-based facilities (e.g., information retrieval systems such as Videotex; operations databases such as directory).
- End-to-end signalling between users (e.g., to change mode of communication over an already-established connection).
- Combinations of the above as in multi-media communication, whereby several simultaneous modes of communication can take place under common signalling control.

With such diversity of ISDN capabilities (in terms of information flows and modes of communication) beyond those of data networks, there is a need to model all these capabilities within a common framework (i.e., reference model). This would enable the critical protocol architectural protocols and associated features.

Relationship with Recommendation X.200

The protocol reference model, interface structures and protocol reference configurations are defined by layered structures based on and using the terminology of the reference model for Open Systems Interconnection (OSI) for CCITT. Applications (Recommendation X.200). The layer identification used in Recommendation X.200 is limited in this Recommendation to the use of layer numbers.

The following ISDN needs have not at present been considered in the X.200 series of Recommendations.

- Information flows for out-of-band call control processes, or more generally, information flows among multiple related protocols.
- Information flows for selection of connection characteristics.
- Information flows for re-negotiation of connection characteristics of calls.
- Information flows for suspension of connections.
- Information flows for overlap sending.
- Information flows for multi-media calls.
- Information flows for asymmetric connections.
- Information flows for network management (e.g., change over and change back) and for maintenance functions (e.g., test loops).
- Information flows for power activation/deactivation;
- Interworking.
- Switching of information flows.
- New layer service definitions for non-data services.
- Application to other than end-systems, e.g., signal transfer points (STPs) and inter-networking points.
- Information flows for multi-point connections.
- Information flows for applications such as:
  - Voice (including A/u law conversion).
  - Full motion video.
  - Transparent.
  - Telex.

The functions and procedures described in the Q-series of Recommendations for access and network signalling in general conform to the principles described in this Recommendation. Certain features, however, in particular facility procedures and user-user signalling, will require study.

The seven layers of the protocol structures represent even distinct ordered partitions. Each layer exhibits specific properties and features in respect of its relationship both with adjacent layers and with more general aspects of communications. Each layer offers a specific layer service or set of layer services to the layer above.

The functions of each layer and the service offered by each layer are defined in general terms in the Recommendations of the X.200 series. Detailed specification of layer services and protocols are the subject of other Recommendations.

In order to construct the ISDN protocol reference model, a fundamental generic protocol block has been identified. Such a protocol block can be used to describe various elements in the ISDN user premises and the network (e.g., terminal equipment (TE), signalling point (SP) and signalling transfer point (STP), etc.)

ISDN FUNCTIONAL PRINCIPLES

As described in Recommendation I.120 an Integrated Services Digital Network (ISDN) is a network providing end-to-end digital connectivity to support a wide range of telecommunications services.

The standardization of ISDN by CCITT is centered on three main areas:

1. The standardization of services offered to subscribers, so as to enable services to be internationally compatible.
2. The standardization of user-network interfaces, so as to enable terminal equipment to be portable.
3. The standardization of network capabilities to the degree necessary to allow user- network and network-interworking, and so to achieve 1 and 2 above.

The I.200 series of Recommendations has identified the range of telecommunication services to be offered in an ISDN, namely Bearer and Teleservices, and the attributes characterizing these services. The I.400 series of Recommendations describes both the functional and technical aspects of user-network interfaces. This Recommendation defines the network capabilities to support services via this interface in terms of Network functions. A network functional description enables a decoupling of services and network capabilities, and allows an implementation-independent approach.

The transition from an existing network to a comprehensive ISDN may require a period of time extending over one or more decades. Therefore the design of an ISDN will be evolutionary, adding capabilities in a flexible and modular form. An ISDN may therefore be expected to provide an open-ended set of functional capabilities able to accommodate new needs as they arise at acceptable cost.

During a long intermediate period, some functions may not be implemented within a given ISDN. Also specific arrangements should be used to ensure compatibility with existing networks and services. An ISDN should also give access to existing services and interwork with existing networks and terminals; in some countries this situation is likely to exist even in a very long term.

ISDN FUNCTIONAL CAPABILITIES

To achieve the functional objectives the ISDN functional description has been designed to:

• Define the overall characteristics of the ISDN.
• Be implementation independent and place no constraints on national net-

work architectures beyond the network and interface standards given in the I-series of Recommendations.

- Take full account of the constraints of existing dedicated networks.
- Support the layering protocol concepts defined in Recommendation H.211 and I.320.

The ISDN functional description defines a set of network capabilities which enable Bearer and Teleservices to be offered to customers (see Recommendation I.210). The services require two different levels of ISDN capabilities viz:

- The low-layer capabilities relate to the Bearer Services.
- The high-layer capabilities together with the lower layer capabilities relate to the Teleservices.

In addition, operation and management capabilities are required to support both Bearer Services and Teleservices. ISDN functional capabilities can be further defined as follows:a) Low-Layer capabilities—the set of low layer functions (LLT), pertaining to layers 1-3 of the OSI reference model which provides the capability for the carriage of user information over an ISDN Connection. These functions include:

- Basic Low Layer Functions (BLLF)—these functions support the essential Layer 1-3 requirements of ISDN Connections. BLLF may be further subdivided into two sub-types, namely:
  — Connection Control and Management Functions—these functions are needed for the control and management of connections in the network, e.g., signalling functions for the establishment and release of connections, maintenance functions performed during a connection.
  — Other Connection-Related Functions—these functions comprise all BLLF other than connection control and management functions necessary to provide the connection, e.g., switching and transmission functions.
- Additional Low-Layer Functions (ALLF)—these functions support, in addition to BLLF, low-layer requirements of supplementary services (e.g., call forwarding, abbreviated dialing). These functions are not always required in the provision of ISDN connections.

Functional Description of Interworking

A key element of service integration for an ISDN is the provision of a limited set of standard multi-purpose user-network interfaces.

The I.400 series of Recommendations describes the characteristics of user-network interfaces for the following cases:

1. Access of a single ISDN terminal.
2. Access of a multiple ISDN terminal installation.
3. Access of multiservice PBXs local area networks (LANS) or, more generally, private networks.

4. Access of a non-ISDN terminal.
5. Access of specialized storage and information processing centers.

In addition, considering that the evolution to a comprehensive ISDN will take place over a long period of time interworking with existing networks as well as other ISDNs will be necessary. These cases include:

1. Access to existing telephony network and to dedicated networks (e.g., packet network, telex network).
2. Access to another ISDN.
3. Access to service providers outside the ISDN.

The ISDN user-network interfaces or internetwork interfaces may be used in the above cases. The definition of internetwork interfaces is necessary for these arrangements for interworking and administrative requirements.

Interworking with other networks or other ISDNs requires the provision of Interworking Functions (IWF); either within the ISDN or in the other network or in both. These functions would ensure interworking between different protocol and user procedures.

Within a country or geographical area, an ISDN connection may consist of an interconnection of several networks, each of which supports the attributes of one or more ISDN Connection Types (as defined in Recommendation I.340).

Basic Architecture Model

A basic architectural model of an ISDN shows the seven main switching and signalling functional capabilities of ISDN:

- ISDN local functional capabilities (e.g., user-network signalling, charging).
- 64K bit/s circuit switched functional capabilities.
- 64K bit/s circuit nonswitched functional capabilities.
- Packet switching functional capabilities.
- Common channel interexchange signalling functional capabilities.
- 64K bit/s switched functional capabilities.
- 64K bit/s nonswitched functional capabilities.

Three: A Look at the Governmental Game

If we were to put on our conceptual planning hat and step back and look at the current governmental situation of inquiries, waivers, strategies and players and postulate what the final quiescent state should be, "where all will benefit," the following scenario may come to mind, but first a few postulates:

First Postulate. The conflicting directions of the public information network and the private information networks must be resolved if indeed the broad spectrum of ultimate users will benefit from ISDN.

Second Postulate. There are no easy solutions, such as; "open architecture," "collocation," "internetworking," FCC "Competitized features and USER Interfaces," that can easily be identified to easily resolve the First Postulate.

Third Postulate. The playing field can never be level as long as there exists extensive delay in offering new features by attempting to ensure the game is competitive for everyone all the time.

Fourth Postulate. A competitive marketplace implies a totally unregulated, uncontrolled arena with no governmental intervention, a compromise is the identification and control of the boundaries of the arena in which a competitive marketplace can exist. The "where" and the "how" for both the technical and market arena.

PRE-INQUIRY 3 BOUNDARIES AND LIMITS

As we look at the potential of the evolving ISDN network architecture in terms of present and future marketplace possibilities, as it was originally encased within the boundaries determined by Inquiry II and MFJ waivers, we see an early decision to attempt to keep the playing field level by ensuring that the full resources from the Telcos are not left unchecked to provide numerous information services in the marketplace. This was especially true if they tended to inhibit competition by controlling interfaces or limited new parallel network structures; if they limit new features by resistance to participate; if they use voice communication funds from the regulated monopoly to support new ventures offerings; if they raise the rate of basic services to raise capital to participate in the new information arena; or use their position of network controller to time phase offerings to their best advantage and limit others.

There were political constraints and compromises to please other forces in the arena, such as: ensure the Telcos can not go into the electronic yellow pages, by ensuring the Telcos cannot perform information searches, retrievals, manipulations or processing. To limit direct sales to the customer, to ensure their traditional market presence could not become an advantage, especially in the new terminal arena and local networks for office buildings, etc., they were initially required to provide interfaces to CPE equipment and only sell traditional basic voice phones. However, they could market new value added feature terminals directly to customers via a subsidiary.

This thought process extended into the world of data switches, where even data transport basic features, such as, terminal interfaces were initially considered value added. Hence, asynchronous to X25 protocols required waivers with such numerous restrictions that conversion systems had to be provided by the transport distribution firm but marketed by a subsidiary. Interfacing circuits to the various systems must be costed and priced, so that the customer paid for "WHERE" conversions were performed. If they were handled on a common basis in a distance office for efficient operations, the users would have to be charged for the circuits. The whole customer ownership problem broke down when it came to testing what was at the end of a line, from the common network maintenance center. Even the location of nodal point systems on customer premises, such as extensions of Centrex to connect university customers more economically at distributed switching concentration points to enable them to enter the network on wideband facilities, were not permitted, unless customer owned.

As a result of these economic limitations, a considerable number of the major customers of the Telco began to establish their own networks; especially with the conflict on "integrated" technology capable for providing a single 2B + D or 23B + D (1.544 megabit) connector to the customer to handle voice, data or video needs.

Clearly the basic public network was not meeting the needs of the large customers. As noted in the "Who's on First" analysis, the Telcos did respond, after several years of delay with data switching functional systems in the subsidiary, and with network access functional data switches in the distribution company. However, many large customers simply bypassed the collector and tied directly to the access systems and complained about the limited number of features that could be provided. There was also limited motivation for the Telcos to provide access Pads at remote offices to enable one or two remote customers to access their company's private data networks.

Features became an interesting problem when new system capabilities, for "off line" information searches and processing could perform all types of services for a private network and none for the public network customers. The result was substantial effort by the Telcos to meet private network bulk volume needs, but there were few feature offerings to the small and medium businesses, who usually ride piggyback on the large networks. There also were few, if any, services to the residential market, with the exception of perhaps an alarm packet network joint relationship, with a few database firms. All these factors resulted in loss of business, increased rates for basic voice services and substantial layoffs of operating personnel to keep costs down for a dwindling market.

However, it did enable the entrance of new competition and serious consideration of new services, such as; data switching and the array of new features, as noted in the Feature Matrix of the "ISDN Marketplace Analysis." Unfortunately, only a limited number of these features were actually allowed to be provided by the distribution firm in the mid-80s and none of the information services by the subsidiary.

As a result, the information world did not advance very quickly. Terminal manufactures still could not have terminals talk to each other, unless they did so through CPE network interfaces. This then lead to Inquiry III, where the government indicated that it would prefer to stop worrying "where" new services were to be provided in the network and concentrate on the "how." Their objective was to ensure that whatever new services were provided, they would enable competitive offerings and that no new services would inhibit others from being offered, due to monopolistic controls. This then left the door open for locating the data packet switch in the basic Telco to provide many new features, without extensive waivers such as terminal to terminal transport protocol conversions. However, it must be provided by an unregulated portion of the firm, using separate accounting methods to ensure all offerings were competitive, as well as enable "functional" collocation of competitive equipment to increase the number of more competitive offerings by all involved and provide the ability to easily interface to the network, through an "open architecture."

Considerations also took into account the AT&T ability to bypass local distribution plants to major accounts and the Cable TV ability to pass data in their local networks. The local network was not necessarily a monopoly anymore. Hence, the local distribution firm should be allowed to be more competitive. In terms of manufacturing capabilities, Telcos could build prototypes per Inquiry II, but not manufacture. A few specialized waivers were requested to enable them to manufacture outside the U.S. for sales to foreign markets. Similarly, they requested the ability to provide outside specialized carrier networks in foreign countries. Many initially thought that Inquiry III was to readdress some of these concerns to make initial offerings more competitive. It did not address them all, but did provide a "NEW PROCESS" to consider them.

This background of a somewhat unlevel "level playing field" for everyone, forced many to turn to private networks. This formed a new world of numerous private networks, with no public information network, still requiring access points between private networks, so particular customers on different networks could talk to each other.

Now lets take a look at what concerns Inquiry III initially attempted to address and how it proposed to resolve them.

INQUIRY III

The proposed decision framework for Inquiry III is a two step process. It first diagnoses the situation in terms of a matrix of questions and then establishes a series of action options for implementation of "where" boundaries and "how" limits. The providers participate during the first step to identify and negotiate whether or not they have a competitive, dominant, bottleneck position for each new service offering. During the second step the providers must attempt to resolve concerns by ensuring that they enable any and all other competitive offerings in the forms of interfaces, collocations, open architectures, or direct accesses simulating collocation, as well as using separate accounting and competitive pricing techniques. This results in the game of "10 Questions," which determine the selection of 1 of 5 alternative paths, each of which having a sequence of actions with several options for each action. Hence, for 1,000 issues this could become 10,000 Questions and 10,000 Actions.

The real problem will be achieving politically acceptable answers to the questions, as more and more players enter the arena desiring to provide alternative networks. One variable that has not been addressed is time. For every action, there is a series of resulting changes that then require new actions. For example, if providers cannot provide specific features, the network will decline or will not develop. Hence, a dominant position today can drastically change in time due to a decision to enable an alternative action to affect these positions, such as the potential of a public data packet network depends on the extent and degree of new information services provided. A governmental feature by feature acceptance review approach, delaying offerings, may cause no one to benefit from achieving a universal Public Information Network, due to the lack of availability of the Public Data Packet Network, which no one will want due to its limited or delayed features.

As we address solutions, such as; collocation, interconnection and open architecture as alternatives to the bottleneck, we must be careful that boundaries still exist to protect the basic network itself. In other words, it may be necessary to limit competition in various areas to ensure that, indeed, there is a resulting basic network, upon which everyone can benefit and provide new products and services. See the following "Inquiry III" analysis for further considerations.

INQUIRY III—THE 10,000 QUESTION AND ANSWER GAME

We shall examine this topic in light of a broad FCC Regulatory Direction, given by FCC chairman Mark Fowler in a May 1985 interview with USTA, "Generate a telecommunications industry model that will allow for transition to an environment similar to that envisioned for the broadcast industry— i.e., FCC regulation from technical standpoint and removal of all other rules," which translated into the explicit FCC goals: to simplify the industry structure, allow the efficiency of structural integration, reap the benefits of competition, as well as the benefits of technical integration. The following goals are also implied: to ultimately move exchange carriers from tariff, rate-of-return regulation to regulation by the complaint process, and replace regulation with competition.

These goals provided the regulatory framework for Computer Inquiry III (CI-III), which had the following advantages as viewed by the Commission:

- Eliminates need for structural separation.
- Better focuses regulator resources (i.e., on potential for abuse of "bottleneck" control).
- Allows non-competitive ancillary services to be treated as regulated basic service.
- Encourages competition which allows for movement towards deregulation.
- Less reliance on definitions.

This results in two major changes for CI-II:

- Regulation based on degree of market power and not the function performed.
- Protection against abuse of market power through accounting distinctions instead of separate subsidiaries.

Hence, the broad FCC proposals replace CI-II's basic versus enhanced (value added) unit of measurement with a new CI-III yardstick, which first differentiates communications, ancillary to communications, and non-communications. It establishes various degrees of regulation:

- Title II (Regulate Rates and Rate of Return).
- Title I ("Regulate" through complaint process).
- Total non-regulation.

The degree of regulation of ancillary to communcations would be based on the following considerations of the service:

- Dominance
- Competition
- Bottleneck

Finally, this will minimize the Inquiries II structural separation requests and as one person said "All the 'Subs' will go away."

This will supposedly move, but not remove, the original "basic" communications boundaries, which rigidly established it between CPE and Enhanced in terms of NCTE on the CPE side and Network Processing on the Enhanced side and changes the Inquiry II NCTE boundary, moving it into the ancillary with the following categories and classifications to help differentiate the boundaries.

Categories

Service categories will remain the same, but new treatment of offerings within some categories is proposed:

- Communications Services are today's basic services and the commission proposes no changes in treatment.
- Services Ancillary To Communication include "enhanced services" and the commission proposes to regulate this category, as a function of market power of dominant carrier.
- Non-Communications Services are not regulated but commission states protection against cost impact on rate payers may be warranted.

Classifications

Certain classifications would be established to administer new framework:

- Carriers and NonCarriers, where carriers provide "basic" service, and non-carriers do not provide "basic" service.
- Dominant and non dominant carriers, defined by the Commission's competitive common carrier proceedings; there may be further regulatory distinctions among dominant carriers.
- Competitive and Non Competitive Services.

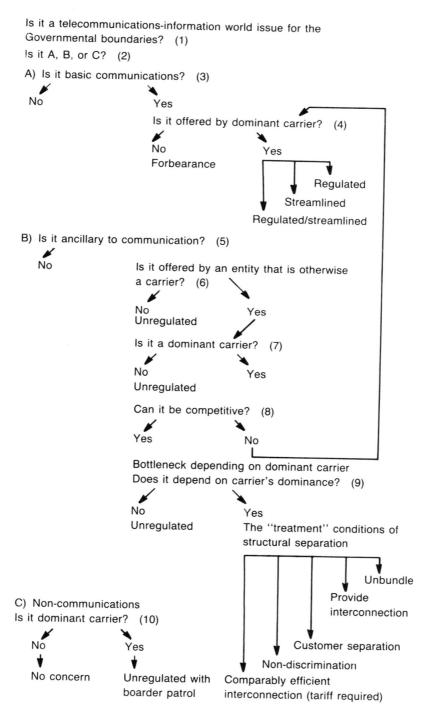

Is it a telecommunications-information world issue for the Governmental boundaries? (1)

Is it A, B, or C? (2)

A) Is it basic communications? (3)

No   Yes

    Is it offered by dominant carrier? (4)

    No   Yes
    Forbearance

          Regulated
        Streamlined
    Regulated/streamlined

B) Is it ancillary to communication? (5)

No

    Is it offered by an entity that is otherwise a carrier? (6)

    No   Yes
    Unregulated

    Is it a dominant carrier? (7)

    No   Yes
    Unregulated

    Can it be competitive? (8)

    Yes   No

Bottleneck depending on dominant carrier
Does it depend on carrier's dominance? (9)

No   Yes
Unregulated   The "treatment" conditions of structural separation

                Unbundle
            Provide interconnection
        Customer separation
      Non-discrimination

C) Non-communications
Is it dominant carrier? (10)

No   Yes

No concern   Unregulated with boarder patrol   Comparably efficient interconnection (tariff required)

Fig. 14-3. Ten Questions.

Controlling Control

The Commission sees three forms of possible misconduct by carriers with "bottleneck" control:

- Preferential treatment (e.g., pricing, availability) for its own offerings
- Misuse of its advance knowledge of network improvement and modifications
- Misuse of customer information

To prevent this the Commission would impose:

- Comparably efficient interconnection
- Accounting delineations
- Disclosure

To help differentiate and identify dominance for basic service or bottleneck conditions, a series of questions will be asked to identify possible actions, such as:

1. Are there economies of scale or scope which would tend to preclude competition? If so, it is regulated "basic" service. If not, degree of regulation depends on competitor's ability to utilize/interconnect to any "bottleneck" facilities.
2. Does the carrier control "bottlenecks" needed by competitors to compete? If not, it is treated as non communications service. If so, protection against anti-competitive conduct may be required.

Game of Ten Questions

This then results in "A Game of Ten Questions" in the form of a decision tree, (Fig. 14-4) so that answers to the questions then determine a logical set of treatment actions.

Game of Answers

The "treatment" is determined by a matrix of alternative paths (Fig. 14-5) in which several actions options are proposed for each alternative path, where each action option has several variables, which are cross dependent on other action option variables.

This then leaves "the decision" of what to do as the "The Ten Answers Game" following the identification of the alternative path by "The Ten Questions Game" between providers and the Governmental decision makers. Hence, we have a two step process.

Initially, the process will be used to determine answers for 4 pending questions:

- Protocol-type processing

Action options	Alternatives					Examples of options variables
Title I regulation	A L T.	A L T.	A L T.	A L T.	A L T.	Y/N
Title II regulation	# 1 "L	# 2 "L	# 3 "R	# 4 "W	# 5 "A	N/Y
Cost separation	I K	I K	E D	A I	D J	Separate accounting/ tariff justification
Separate personnel operations marketing	E O T	E P R	E F I N	V E R	U N C T	Joint/allocation contract
Enhanced servicers collocation permitted	H E R	O T O O	E A	F O R	T O	Permitted/ conditionally
Unbundle local loop interoffice	C A R R	C O L O	S B A S	C O L O	B A S I	Bundled/ unbundled
Comparably efficient interconnection	I E R S "	R D E R "	I C	C A T I O N	C	Tariff/ compensate for loop/ efficiencies/ bundled vs. tariff

Fig. 14-4. Ten Answers.

- Voice Message Storage
- Interconnection
- NCTE

Noting that the new ISDN "T" interface 2B + D or "U" interface 23B + D has a "D" signalling channel for enabling terminals to talk to the Network System, the FCC through early requests for comments on ISDN has recognized the power and future direction of the world to integrate voice, data and video on switched facilities by sending control information on the the "D" channel. In addition, this "D" channel and the CCITT #7 signalling channel will enable levels of terminals, from dumb to intelligent, to talk to levels of Network controllers and processors to provide many new features and services.

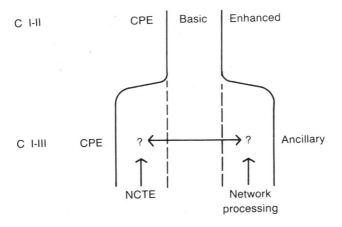

Fig. 14-5. CI II to CI III.

ISDN is defined to provide: end-to-end digital transport (economy, technology, performance), integrated access (services, flexibility, reduced costs), and a small family of standard interfaces (wide range of terminal equipment, independent evolution, portability).

Technology merges with the marketplace to enter the world of customer interaction, providing storage devices to enable restructuring of the network, and code and protocol conversions, as various signalling and message systems attempt to communicate with each other, as well as adding and deleting of information, as information is being moved through the network.

This then opens the door for new information services that can be provided by the Telco, other than customer access for network control. In this arena the Telco then meet head on with the electronic yellow pages issue or the ability to do inquiry/response searches in the world of lists. Finally, when Telco's address the issue of page reformatting to enable the network to translate information by manipulation so one terminal can talk to another, the public network has then entered the last door of the information world which is to "information processing," which has met great resistance in the political world of vested interests.

However, who would really want an info switch which does not provide information access, inquiry/response data search, data manipulation and

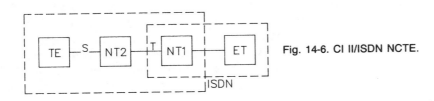

Fig. 14-6. CI II/ISDN NCTE.

processing, on a "public information network," when they can have them on a "private network" basis? The private systems can do transport as well as these new information features—hence, the C&C industries enter the world of Inquiry IV.

If we consider the approximately 1,000 issues that the FCC will have to address (where an issue is a voice, data, video feature, facility, switch service, or location) and play the 10 Questions-10 Answers Game, we will have to consider 10,000 Questions and possibly 10,000 Answers, for a new set of issues that change on a yearly basis, becoming more complex after the initial 1,000 are addressed. In considering these ramifications, we must seriously consider the Four Postulates of "The Level Playing Field" and address the issue of time. Will there be enough time to play the game and still achieve a competitive arena?

Thus, one should step back and ask the following type of questions on the initial proposal, describing the new rules of the game, to determine if the Inquiry III game should even be played, and for whose benefit?

- Does the proposed framework move in the correct direction?, or; Do the new definitions create even more pitfalls and industry uncertainty?
- How dependent is the FCC's framework on mandatory standards for all types of interconnection? If dependent, can today's standard mechanisms be counted upon?
- Are the FCC's conditions for structural integration achievable?
- Should all embedded services be considered in the "Communications" category or should they be tested against the framework and potentially moved to "ancillary" and deregulated?
- Does the framework lead to further deregulation?
- Can the FCC criteria for a framework stand the test of application?

HUBER REPORT

In January 1987, Peter Huber was contracted by the DOJ to provide a review of the situation three years after divestiture. His analysis was based on his vision of a *Geodesic Network* which supports vertical integration of the players, allowing the BOCs everything but interchange until the "local monopoly" issues are resolved. DOJ recommended this to Judge Greene.

POST INQUIRY V

After Inquiries III, IV and V, we will hopefully have established a competitive arena that looks something like the following:

1. All Telco business offerings are in an unregulated arena.
2. Usage pricing on all voice, data, video calls and services.
3. Subsidies protect the poor, retarded and non-profit charities to ensure their reasonable local calling at reasonable rates, such as a 10% of the resident traffic.
4. With the exception of #3, deregulation of the residential market, but

monopolistic protection of the base.

5. Continued monopoly on local residence voice network to ensure a national base, however, no monopoly on value added services for local networks. Hence, option to have a traditional voice phone on the basic network or a value added phone on anyone's network.

6. No restriction on "Transport Related" information services by Telcos, as long as they are provided by using separate accounting of unregulated Telco or subsidiary.

7. No restriction on value added features provided by subsidiaries, as long as there is no restriction or inhibition of being offered by other firms or parallel networks.

8. Ability to interface any system to access systems to world network through interfaces which are determined by outside Telco standards committees, such as; CCITT, T1, etc.

9. Fast implementation response requirement to interface standards, as part of ubiquitous service offering to maintain local monopolistic access network for voice, data, video transport.

10. Depreciation rates of 5 years for switches and 10-15 years for facilities.

11. Effective collocation achieved by access loops to gateway switches.

12. Manufacturing of equipment by Telco allowed as long as an "open architecture" enabling any manufacturer to interface to any other piece is achieved and competitive network purchases from multiple suppliers is ensured. However, limits are imposed on "open" to determine how much "open" and still have a base network.

13. Facilities will be costed and priced to charge the Telco's subsidiaries, whatever is being charged to the competition for value added offerings.

14. Telcos plant including poles and conduit are maintained and supported by the Telco, who can lease out at reasonable cost rates capacity, consistent with similar Telco service offerings, but other firm's work crews are not allowed physical access to the plant to ensure security of network.

15. Governmental protection, where necessary, to qualify the above to protect the integrity and universality of the ubiquitous transport services of voice, data and video offerings, to ensure a basic public information network is ubiquitously available.

16. Ability to market products and services, in areas of other regions.

17. Ability to locate equipment on customers' premises or sell portions of network equipment to customer will enable a better response to the marketplace need with various pricing structures for full feature packages to attract growth.

18. Ability to utilize resources of a central national resource type research laboratory and cross industry working committees to ensure the common telecommunications network is efficient and versatile to support new features, establishing "open," but not damaging, interface standards and network architectures on which the providers and suppliers will achieve their New Networks, Products and Services, that will meet the NEW USERS' needs.

Four: A Look at the Marketplace

First we need to generate a list of users and identify them as to their feature and service requirements; resulting in a listing of potential users per potential services. Next, these users need to be overlaid on the telecommunication environment to identify information handling requirements per user type. The result will be a look at network capabilities, that have to be acquired in order to meet the user's needs and a time frame, in which they should be available. Hence, we will have an indication of facility, switch forms and configurations, that are required to satisfy the marketplace.

The following fifteen step methodology is performed to help ensure the validity of this analysis:

Step 1 — Determine all possible types of industries and groups, that will be generating data traffic over time frame 1990-2010.

Step 2 — Obtain all available data growth projections for these industries and groups.

Step 3 — Determine all data applications within each industry and group.

Step 4 — Determine all possible categories of data handling. Then reduce to the least number of independent categories, such as inquiry/response, data collection, data distribution.

Step 5 — Relate applicable categories to each industries' subgroups.

Step 6 — Determine a visual aid of each major industry in terms of Step 2 information and Step 5 applications. Note switched, private, or hardwired present transmission modes.

Step 7 — Recursive analysis of Steps 3, 4, 5 and 6 until most reasonable results are obtained.

Step 8 — Sort from Step 5 list, a listing in terms of categories, that shows applicable industry subgroups per category.

Step 9 — Determine a listing of attributes (connect time, holding time, etc.), that further describes each category.

Step 10 — Determine a range of values for each attribute that relates to the users needs for each category.

Step 11 — Determine the various types of users for each category as defined by various attributes with various ranges.

Step 12 — Recursive analysis of Steps 9, 10, and 11 to determine each categories' user types, using the most descriptive attributes and these attributes' range of values.

Step 13 — Relate all possible user types for each category to real world possible users noted in Steps 8, 6, 5 and 3. Eliminate the not applicable (NA) user types.

Step 14 — Coalesce all categories' user types for the PABX and Network equipment to determine any overlaps and general similar requirements.

Step 15 —Determine observations, conclusions, and recommendations
throughout the analysis.

This analysis attempts to realistically evaluate the forthcoming data customer's needs for the 90s and their effect on the telephone industry in order
to determine what should be the future telecommunications network capabilities. Overdesign is as bad as underdesign in these competitive times.
Hence, this report has evaluated the detailed data needs of users in 18 major
industries and groups. Twenty-six meaningfully distinct user types were determined by realistically relating them to potential users. Twelve of these types
apply to an internal user facility, such as a PABX system. The other fourteen
user types have outside communication needs, that are satisfied by network
switching systems.

Some of the following observations were made earlier in the case study
"The New Users" but are noted here for easy reference:

- For "PABX" data user types, this analysis notes that 9 of the 12 user types
  would be satisfied with a fast connect, medium speed matrix/transmission
  system. There will be a need for the 3 wideband users, wideband circuit
  matrix nodal systems or a PABX switched LAN matrix [2000 + systems can
  be integrated circuit or burst/fast packet if the local facilities are in place].
  The system must handle a greater than normal volume of call attempts that
  have less than normal holding time duration.
- For "Network" data user types, we find that 10 of the 14 user types would
  be satisfied with a fast connect, medium speed system capable of handling
  a large volume of low holding time calls having greater than normal call
  attempts. The extreme wideband users will be more economically handled
  on point to point networks until their numbers increase or until economical wideband switched networks are available to handle them, when overall traffic in information has developed.
- Market research firms have not considered all industries or all the possible
  users for each industry. However, even so, their approximate projections
  indicate around 300 billion transactions within the business community.
  These figures may be 50% too low or 25% too high, but they do indicate
  the birth of a new industry.
- It should be noted that before this large list of data users becomes a reality, four major problem areas must be resolved.
  —It will take numerous cost-reduced friendly terminals to become avail-
    able to attract large volumes of data users.
  —Acceptable software programming for the data processing computer
    (which is now mainly payroll/accounting oriented) to handle the time-
    sharing, remote inquiry/response, data collection and data distribution
    requirements will need several years for development. In this area an Air
    Force data communication system took approximately four years longer
    than expected.
  —A large number of potential customers are noted. There are indeed many

customers within each group whose data needs are immediate. However, before the full volume of data customers will rush to use data terminals, the normal customer resistance to new technology and new products must be overcome. This requires time and education. Price will encourage use if the new network services are priced for growth—high volume, but low initial return on investment.

—In order to meet the competition from competitive networks, common carrier facilities will have to be upgraded. This upgrading will require considerable expenditure on data during times of substantial voice growth. Also, due to FCC decision delays and economic problems, competitive networks will not be a reality until approximately the mid 90s. The result will be a slower realization of publicly switched data handling networks than initially visualized.

- The analysis notes that data traffic will be generated by users of the seven categories noted below. The list is ordered to indicate decreasing volumes of traffic:

  —Inquiry Response
  —Transactions
  —Data Collection
  —Data Distribution
  —Remote Documentation and Display
  —Remote Access/Time-Sharing
  —Graphics

- Although the volume from each industry is not known, it is significant to observe the number and type of industry subgroups that will be generating each category's data traffic
  —The three main attributes, which generated eight distinct possible user types for each category were:
    a. Connect time (normal telephony, instantaneous)
    b. Terminal Device Operation Speed (TDOS) (Low, Med, High)
    c. User facility location (internal, external).
  —Not all possible user types existed. Only 26 were actual "real world" candidates.
  —Fifteen of the twenty-six user types will generate calls having less than normal voice holding time and greater than normal voice attempts.
  —An error rate of one error in 10,000,000 bits would probably be acceptable for most data user types with the exception of long transaction (computer to computer) users.
  —Private line user types will go to private switched networks until either the telephone company or new common carriers economically provide fast inexpensive connect systems having medium speed (9600 bit rate) trunks, with a medium error rate (10^7).
  —Many of the inquiry response, data collection, and time-sharing users are getting a free ride on unlimited call pack, WATTS flat rate pricing offer-

631

ings, because they use these facilities much more than initially estimated.
—Traffic patterns generated by data users will be inconsistent with previously established voice traffic patterns, causing many problems during the initial growth years, requiring early replacement of switching systems every 5 years.
—Cost for data type calls should be a function of bit rate usage and priced for high volume growth.
—Concentrators, multiplexers, modems, keyboards, printers, display devices, must be integrated together via new interface standards or the network will never be achieved in the 90s.
—Inquiry response and data transactions has such a large rate of growth, that processor capacity will be affected.
—The high cost of data transmission for time-sharing is inhibiting its present growth toward more and more powerful conversational systems. An offering of billing only on transmit time and an automatic droppage from the network when idle would be attractive, this can be provided by data packet switching and bit rate billing.
—Some store and forward offering would be attractive to broadcast, distribution, and transaction users.
—Present facilities are hurting facsimile operation due to line errors and low speed capabilities.
—Graphics, computer to computer transactions, and some large remote access calls require a wide bandwidth, but their volume will depend on meeting sophisticated, friendly, human machine interface needs, using economical fibers.
—Data traffic will be replacing voice traffic throughout the 90s as doctors, law agencies, retail/wholesale orders, etc., switch from verbal orders to hardcopy.
—Data manipulation, formatting, filing and processing will be the key parallel industry, before data "handling" transport is successful.

SUMMARY

1. The effect of the forthcoming gradual shift from voice conversations to voice and data conversations will be to load network switching systems to capacity during the business day. This will downgrade service causing many unsatisfied voice users. More and more data users will migrate to competitive networks. This will eventually require the telephone companies to provide facilities to handle both voice and data traffic more efficiently. Since this must be done before or after the fact, it will be good strategy to do it before and encourage growth by offering many new features.

2. The data users will not be in full volume until a medium speed (9600 BPS-64K bps), medium error rate (1 error in 10^7 bits), fast system connect, and publicly switched network is readily available at economical cost. The time frame for these networks appears to be in the 90s. Thus

the full impact of data will be felt in the 2000-2010 time frame with a gradual build up from 1990.

3. The analysis noted that the majority of data users for this time frame have the following technical requirements:

—Fast system connect; CCITT recommends a 100 ms connect at 2400 to 9600 bit/sec. signalling rate.

—Capacity to handle a large volume of calls from numerous data terminals with less than normal holding time.

—Initial 9600 bit rate outside plant transmission facility with selective areas having multiples of 64K bps capability.

—4 kHz network upgraded to handle initial 9600 bps data traffic.

—One error in 10^7 bits transmitted for 99.9% of the calls at 9600 bps, will be required to move from point to point to switched facilities.

—Data will require sub 64K channel rates of asynchronous up to 2400 bps, and synchronous rates of 2.4, 4.8, 9.6, 64K and N64K bps.

—Distributed switching systems capable of CCITT 2B+D, 23B, NB interfaces with computer ports and terminal ports, using new "D" channel processors for signalling and information exchange.

—Some store and forward nodal point access capabilities.

The Marketplace

General information and terms used for this analysis concerning user industries, user categories, category attributes, attributes range, user types, user terminals, and volume of users are as follows:

• User, industries, services, facilities, etc., were divided into 18 major groups. Each group has a further breakdown into subgroups. No extensive effort was made to ensure all possible subgroups were included. This is not a full market survey made by a team of market forecasters over the next twenty-year period. However, by personal visits with members of each of the major industries, a good sample has been coalesced here as a database for our analysis.

• User categories—Major general grouping of data/video data communication users.

User Category 1—Interactive-Inquiry/Response (IR) (single or sequence)—such as: reservation systems for air travel, hotels, and theaters.

User Category 2—Data Collection Systems (DC)—such as: weather, surveys, and stock exchange.

User Category 3—Data Distribution Networks (DD)—such as: news media, stock status, and civil defense.

User Category 4—Interactive Remote Access/Time-Sharing (RA/TS)—such as: remote batch, computer aided instruction, education usages, and research problem solving.

User Category 5—Remote Documentation and Display (RD)—such as: high speed facsimile.

User Category 6—Interactive Graphic Systems (Graphics)—circuit design, car design, and building design.

User Category 7—Transactions (Trans)—such as: computer to computer messages and bank teller to computer transactions.

- Categories Attributes (Range). These attributes further define various users within each category. Each attribute has a range of values. The attributes (range) are as follows:
  - —Connect time (normal POTS (N), Instantaneous)
  - —Holding time (<N, N, >N)
  - —Attempts (<N, N, >N)
  - —User facilities location (Internal, External)
  - —Connection facility (switched, point to point, hardwired)
  - —Operation mode (real time, store forward)
  - —Error tolerance (low, med, high)
- User Type—Each category has several distinct types of users. These types are characterized by the attributes and range of values of the attributes. It is interesting to note that all permutations do not exist. Hence, it was necessary to cross-check each possible combination against the real world to ensure its existence.
- Volume Calls and Transactions for 1990-2010. This is the most difficult to predict. Gross statistics can be given for major groups based upon various projections. However, one should realize, that a projection is usually made by extending a trend, relating to another industry, or by curve fitting. Otherwise the consumer demand curve must be determined, or a review must be made of future products, that will be available to the consumer. Since it is a new industry, which is not independent, but has a definite cross-elasticity relationship to the computer industry, transmission medium, terminal market, and programming language advancement, it is too early to project by macro-econometric models.

  Some have chosen micro-economic techniques such as demand forecasting. There is another concept; that companies determine the products for the user. The users do not initially demand them, until they learn about them. This is further noted by the fact, that computer usage breeds computer dependency, which breeds more computer usage. This increase in usage with more user demand, will usually depend on pricing strategies, such as, . . . "Price for Growth!"

  In addition, if hard copy can easily replace oral communications many persons such as doctors, druggists, police officers, etc., will switch from oral conversations to data conversations. This will decrease the volume of voice communications and further increase the number of data transactions.

  Since this analysis is for the conceptual planning phase, we will apply best judgement to determine future technical requirements. Later when technical trade-offs are solely dependent upon the accuracy of these figures, a more detailed market analysis will be required.

USER ANALYSES PART 1

Here, each major industry or group heading is broken down into its constituent subgroups. Each subgroup has been analyzed as to which user categories are applicable and this data is presented in the User Category column following each subgroup title. The various user categories are listed before the main analysis.

It is interesting to note the length of the total list of subgroups presented in this section. This list attempts to include all subgroups that will be present for the 1990s.

User Categories

USER Category 1—Interactive-Inquiry/Response (Single Or Sequence)
USER Category 2—Data Collection-Polling/Sensing
USER Category 3—Data Distribution Networks
USER Category 4—Interactive-Remote Access/Time Sharing
USER Category 5—Remote Display/Documentation
USER Category 6—Interactive-Graphics
USER Category 7—Transactions
USER Category 8—Video
USER Category 9—Digitalized Voice

Industries and Group's Tasks	User Categories
100 Banks	
101 Teller Trans	1,7,8
102 Remote Teller Trans	1,7,8
103 Credit Verification	1
104 Check Clearing	3
105 Remote Branch Bank Trans	1,5,7,8
106 Remote Account Monitoring - Bus	1,5,8
107 Remote Account Monitoring - Res	1,5
108 Credit Billing and Control	2,5,7
109 Federal Reserve Trans	
110 Bank-To-Bank Trans	1,5,7,8
111 Bank DP Service	4,8
112 Retail-Bank Automatic Trans	5,7
113 Checkless Trans	5,7
200 Investments and Securities	

201	Inquiries	1
202	Buy/Sell Trans	5,7
203	Portfolio Monitoring	1,5,8
204	Remote-To-Central Trans	7
205	Central-To-Stock Exch Trans	7
206	Central-To-Remote Billing	5,7
207	Internal Paperwork Trans	5,7
208	Research Survey/Monitoring	2

300 Retail Trade

301	Credit Ref Checks	1
302	Central Distribution	7
303	Store-To-Store Inventory Control	1,2
304	Central Billing	2,7
305	Management Info Exchange	1,2,3,8
306	Bank-Retail Trans	7
307	Mail-Order Business	1,5,7
308	Freight Handling	1,5,7

400 Insurance (Car, House, Life, Health)

401	Credit Ref	1
402	Policy Trans	5,7
403	Remote Inquiries-Customer	1
404	Timesharing Business for DP	4
405	Claims	1,5,7

500 Police/FBI/State and Fed Law Agencies

501	Crime Monitoring	2,3,5,8
502	Criminal Files and ID	1,2
503	Auto Thefts/Files/Accidents	1,2
504	Drug Files	1,2
505	Agency Communication	3,5,7,8
506	Licenses Files	1,2
507	Missing Persons, Theft, Etc.	1,2

600 City/State Government

601	Operation Communications	1,3,5,8
602	Operation Communications	1,3,5,7,8
603	Taxes (Wage, Real Estate, Sales, etc)	1,2
604	Health and Welfare Trans	1,2
605	City and County (Birth, Death, Disease)	1,2
606	Legislation Operation	1,2,8

636

607 Judicial Operations · · · · · · · · · · · · · · · · · · · 12,8
608 Road Construction/Maintenance · · · · · · · 1,2,7
609 Licenses · 1,2,7

700 Federal Government

701 Legislation · 1,2,3,5,8
702 Judicial · 1,2,3,5,8
703 Defense · 1,2,3,5,7,8
704 Social Security · 1,2,3
705 Statistics · 1,2,3
706 Internal Revenue · 1,2
707 Health and Welfare · · · · · · · · · · · · · · · · · · 1,2
708 Patent · 1,2
709 Library · 1,2,
710 Federal-State Transactions · · · · · · · · · · · 1,2,3

800 Manufacturing

801 General Transaction · · · · · · · · · · · · · · · · · · 1,2,8
802 Cluster Corporate Trans · · · · · · · · · · · · · · 2,3,5,7,8
803 Internal Corporate Trans · · · · · · · · · · · · · · 2,3,5,7,8
804 Inventory Control · 1,2,3
805 Planning · 1,4
806 Marketing · 1,3,5,7
807 Purchasing · 1,2,5,7
808 Personnel · 1,2,5
809 Legal · 1,5
810 Logistics · 1,2,3,7
811 Field Maintenance · · · · · · · · · · · · · · · · · · · 1,2,3,7
812 Design-Hardware · 4,6
813 Design-Software · 4
814 Design-Support-Facilities · · · · · · · · · · · · · 4,6,8
815 Accounting · 1,2

900 Operations (Utility,Oil,Tel,Pwr,Gas)

901 Distribution Control · · · · · · · · · · · · · · · · · · 1,2,3
902 Control Planning · 1,2,3,4
903 Records · 1,2
904 Maintenance · 1,2,3,7
905 Cluster-General Message Operations · · · 1,2,3,5,7

1000 Transportation (Air,Rail,Car)

1001 Travel Agencies Inquiry · · · · · · · · · · · · · · 1,7

1002 Customer Control	1,2,3
1003 Operations Control	1,2,3,7
1004 Maintenance Control	1,2,3,7
1005 Logistics Control	1,2,3,7
1006 Personnel Control	1,2,5
1007 Billing/Collection Control	2,7
1008 Payroll/Accounting	1,2

1100 Health Care

1101 Hospital Patient Files Status/Med	1,2
1102 Insurance-Hospital Claims	1,5,7
1103 Remote Documented Orders	5
1104 Hospital Med Records	1,2,5
1105 Hospital Eqp Records	1,2
1106 Hospital Staff-Dr/Nurse Control	1,2
1107 Dr-Dr Communications	8
1108 Remote Dr-Patient Communication	8
1109 Dr-Education (Remote) Files	1,2,5,8
1110 Dr-Consultation Files	1,2,5,8
1111 Remote Test Reports	1,3,5
1112 Remote Test Monitors	2

1200 Information Services

1201 Library Files for Inquiry	1,2
1202 Library-Library Info Exchange	3
1203 Library-Distributors Info Exchange	1,3,5
1204 Library-Distributors Trans	7
1205 Remote Book Review Service	5,8
1206 Library-To-Business Terminal	1,5,8
1207 Library-To-Home Terminal	1,5,8
1208 Library Micro Dot Book Reading	8
1209 DP Info Services (Statistics)	1,2,4,8
1210 DP Walk-In Remote Computer Service	4
1211 Canned Application Programs	4,6
1212 Research Remote Computer-Exchange	4

1300 Education

1301 Computer-Student Remote Time Share	4,6
1302 Computer-Research Faculty Prob Sol	4,6
1303 University Files/Student Bills	2,7
1304 University File/Student Statistics	1,2
1305 University File/Student Grading	1,2
1306 University Library Files	1,2

1307	Computer-Computer Language Share	4
1308	Computer-Tutorials Via Remote Terminal	4
1309	Computer-Tutorials Via Local Terminal	4
1310	Testing Via Remote Terminals	4
1311	University Accounting	1,2
1312	Book Distributors	1,7

1400 News/Mag Info Transfer

1401	General News Syndicate Bulletins	3
1402	Remote Printer	3
1403	Customer Bills	2,7
1404	Distribution Control	2,3
1405	Advertising	2
1406	Reporter-Staff Info Exchange	2,3
1407	Research Staff Operations	1,2

1500 Entertainment

1501	Sports Setting	1,2
1502	Theater Setting	1,2
1503	Performance Bookings	12

1600 Medium/Business

1601	Wholesale-Orders	1,7
1602	Food Distributions For Restaurant	7
1603	Food Industry Distribution	1,2,3,7
1604	Drug Business Order/Customer Bill	1,2,7
1605	Inventory Control For Chain Stores	1,2
1606	Hotel/Motel Reservations	1,2,3,7
1607	Auto Rental Chains	1,2,3,7

1700 Home Communications

1701	Time Sharing Accounts Management	1,4,7,8
1702	Shopping Selections, Remote	1,8
1703	Student Calculations	4
1704	Newspaper Bulletins	3
1705	Electronic Mail	3
1706	Remote Work	4
1707	Remote Education	4

1800 Misc.

1801	Organizations Bulletins	3

1802	Civil Defense	1,2,3
1803	Red Cross Network	1,2,3
1804	TV Transmissions	3
1805	Political Organization Nets	1,2,3
1806	Government Services	1,2,3
1807	Postage Messages Special Delivery	3,5
1808	First Class Business Messages	3,5
1809	First Class Home Mail	3,5
1810	Computer-To-Computer Data Banks	3

USER ANALYSIS PART 2

This is a cross reference for the subgroup list of part 1 above, relating these subgroups to user categories 1 thru 8. Though volume figures are not available for each user category, it attempts to show the number of users for each category by listing the applicable industries and the type of usage (tasks) within the industries, so as to provide a basis for extrapolating volume.

User Category 1—Interactive-Inquiry/ Response (Single or Sequence)

100	Banks (First National Bank)
101	Teller Trans
102	Remote Teller Trans
103	Credit Verification
105	Remote Branch Bank Trans
106	Remote Account Monitoring-Bus
107	Remote Account Monitoring-Home
110	Bank-To-Bank Trans
200	Investments and Securities
201	Inquiries
203	Portfolio Monitoring
300	Retail Trade
301	Credit Ref Checks
303	Store-To-Store Inventory Control
305	Management Info Exchange
307	Mail-Order Business
308	Freight Handling
400	Insurance (Car, House, Life, Health)
401	Credit Ref
403	Remote Inquiries-Customer
405	Claims
500	Police/FBI/State and Fed Law Agencies
502	Criminal Files and ID
503	Auto Thefts/Files/Accidents
504	Drug Files
506	Licenses Files

507	Missing Persons, Theft, Etc.
600	City/State Government
601	Operation Communications
602	Large City Communications
603	Taxes (Wage, Real Estate, Sales, Etc.)
604	Health and Welfare Trans
605	City and County (Birth, Death, Disease)
606	Legislation Operation
607	Judicial Operations
608	Road Construction/Maintenance
609	Licenses
700	Federal Government
701	Legislation
702	Judicial
703	Defense
704	Social Security
705	Statistics
706	Internal Revenue
707	Health and Welfare
708	Patent
709	Library
710	Federal-State Trans
800	Manufacturing
801	General Transactions
804	Inventory Control
805	Planning/Design (CDE)
806	Marketing (CAE)
807	Purchasing
808	Personnel
809	Legal
810	Logistics
811	Field Maintenance
815	Accounting
900	Operations (Utility, Oil, Tel, Pwr, Gas)
901	Distribution Control
902	Control (Planned)
903	Records
904	Maintenance
905	Cluster-General Message Operations
1000	Transportation (Air, Rail, Car)
1001	Travel Agencies Inquiry
1002	Customer Control
1003	Operations Control
1004	Maintenance Control
1005	Logistics Control
1006	Personnel Control

1008	Payroll/Accounting
1100	Health Care
1101	Hospital Patient Files Status/Med
1102	Insurance-Hospital Claims
1104	Hospital Med Records
1105	Hospital Eqp Records
1106	Hospital Staff-Dr/Nurse Control
1109	Dr-Education (Remote) Files
1110	Dr-Consultation Files
1111	Remote Test Reports
1200	Information Services
1201	Library Files For Inquiry
1203	Library-Distributors Info Exchange
1206	Library-To-Business Terminal
1207	Library-To-Home Terminal
1210	DP Info Services (Statistics)
1300	Education
1304	University File/Student Statistics
1305	University File/Student Grading
1306	University Library Files
1311	University Accounting
1312	Book Distributors
1400	News/Mag Info Transfer
1407	Research Staff Operations
1500	Entertainment
1501	Sports Setting
1502	Theater Setting
1503	Performance Bookings
1600	Medium/Business
1601	Wholesale-Orders
1603	Food Industry Distribution
1604	Drug Business Order/Customer Bill
1605	Inventory Control For Chain Stores
1606	Hotel/Motel Reservations
1607	Auto Rental Chains
1700	Home Communications
1701	Time Sharing Accounts Management
1702	Shopping Selections, Remote
1800	Misc. Organizations
1802	Civil Defense
1803	Red Cross Network
1805	Political Organization Nets
1806	Government Services

User Category 2—Data Collection-Polling/Sensing

100	Banks

108	Credit Card Billing and Control
200	Investments and Securities
208	Research Survey/monitoring
300	Retail Trade
303	Store-To-Store Inventory Control
304	Central Billing
305	Management Info Exchange
500	Police/FBI.State and Fed Law Agencies
501	Crime Monitoring
502	Criminal Files and ID
503	Auto Thefts/Files/Accidents
504	Drug Files
506	Missing Persons, Theft, Etc.
507	Missing Persons, Theft, Etc.
600	City/State Government
603	Taxes (Wage, Real Estate, Sales, Etc.)
604	Health and Welfare Trans
605	City and County (Birth, Death, Disease)
606	Legislation Operation
607	Judicial Operations
608	Road Construction/Maintenance
609	Licenses
700	Federal Government
701	Legislation
702	Judicial
703	Defense
704	Social Security
705	Statistics
706	Internal Revenue
707	Health and Welfare
708	Patent
709	Library
710	Federal-State Info
800	Manufacturing
801	Manufact. Transactions
802	Cluster Corporate Trans
803	Internal Corporate Trans
804	Inventory Control
807	Purchasing
808	Personnel
810	Logistics
811	Field Maintenance
815	Accounting
900	Operations (Utility, Oil, Tel, Pwr, Gas)
901	Distribution Control
902	Control Planning

903	Records
904	Maintenance
905	Cluster-General Message Operations
1000	Transportation (Air, Rail, Car)
1002	Customer Control
1003	Operations Control
1004	Maintenance Control
1005	Logistics Control
1006	Personnel Control
1007	Billing/Collection Control
1008	Payroll/Accounting
1100	Health Care
1101	Hospital Patient Files Status/Med
1104	Hospital Med Records
1105	Hospital Eqp Records
1106	Hospital Staff-Dr/Nurse Control
1109	Dr-Education (Remote) Files
1110	Dr-Consultation Files
1112	Remote Test Monitors
1200	Information Services
1201	Library Files For Inquiry
1210	DP Info Services (Statistics)
1300	Education
1303	University File/Student Bills
1304	University File/Student Statistics
1305	University File/Student Grading
1306	University Library Files
1311	University Accounting
1400	News/Mag Info Transfer
1403	Customer Bills
1404	Distribution Control
1405	Advertising
1406	Reporter-Staff Info Exchange
1407	Research Staff Operations
1500	Entertainment
1501	Sports Setting
1502	Theater Setting
1503	Performance Bookings
1600	Medium/Business
1603	Food Industry Distribution
1604	Drug Business Order/Customer Bill
1605	Inventory Control For Chain Stores
1606	Hotel/Motel Reservations
1607	Auto Rental Chains
1800	Misc. Organizations
1802	Civil Defense

1803	Red Cross Network
1805	Political Organization Nets
1806	Government Services

User Category 3—Data Distribution Networks

100	Banks
104	Check Clearing
300	Retail Trade
305	Management Info Exchange
500	Police/FBI/State and Fed Law Agencies
501	Crime Monitoring
505	Agency Communication
600	City/State Government
601	Operation Communication
602	Large City Communications
700	Federal Government
701	Legislation
702	Judicial
703	Defense
704	Social Security
705	Statistics
710	Federal-State Info
800	Manufacturing
802	Cluster Corporate Trans
803	Internal Corporate Trans
804	Inventory Control
806	Marketing
810	Logistics
811	Field Maintenance
900	Operations (Utility, Oil, Tel, Pwr, Gas)
901	Distribution Control
902	Control Planning
904	Maintenance
905	Cluster-General Message Operations
1000	Transportation (Air, Rail, Car)
1002	Customer Control
1003	Operations Control
1004	Maintenance Control
1005	Logistics Control
1100	Health Care
1111	Remote Test Reports
1200	Information Services
1202	Library-Library Info Exchange
1203	Library-Distributors Info Exchange
1400	News/Mag Info Transfer
1401	General News Syndicate Bulletins

1402	Remote Printer
1404	Distribution Control
1406	Reporter-Staff Info Exchange
1600	Medium/Business
1603	Food Industry Distribution
1606	Hotel/Motel Reservations
1607	Auto Rental Chains
1700	News
1704	Newspaper Bulletins
1705	Mail Electronics
1800	General
1801	Organizations Bulletins
1802	Civil Defense
1803	Red Cross Network
1804	TV Transmissions
1805	Political Organization Nets
1806	Government Services
1807	Postage Messages Special Delivery
1808	First Class Business Messages
1809	First Class Home Mail
1810	Computer-To-Computer Data Banks

User Category 4—Interactive-Remote Access/Time Sharing

100	Banks
111	Bank DP Services
400	Insurance (Car, House, Life, Health)
404	Timesharing Business For DP
800	Manufacturing
805	Planning
812	Design-Hardware
813	Design-Software
814	Design-Support-Facilities
900	Operations (Utility, Oil, Tel, Pwr, Gas)
902	Control Planning
1200	Information Services
1210	DP Info Services (Statistics)
1211	DP Walk-In Remote Computer Service
1212	Canned Application Programs
1213	Research Remote Computer-Exchange
1300	Education
1301	Computers-Student Remote Time Share
1302	Computer-Research Faculty Prob Sol
1307	Computer-Computer Language Share
1308	Computer-Tutorials Via Remote Term
1309	Computer-Tutorials Via Local Term

1310	Testing Via Remote Terminals
1700	Home Communications
1701	Time Sharing Accounts Management
1703	Small Student Calculations
1706	Remote Work
1707	Remote Education

User Category 5—Remote Display/Documentation

100	Banks
105	Remote Branch Bank Trans
106	Remote Account Monitoring—Bus
107	Remote Account Monitoring—Home
108	Credit Card Billing and Control
109	Federal Reserve Trans
110	Bank-To-Bank Trans
112	Retail-Bank Automatic Trans
113	Checkless Trans
200	Investments and Securities
202	Buy/Sell Trans
203	Portfolio Monitoring
206	Central-To-Remote Billing
207	Internal Paperwork Trans
300	Retail Trade
307	Mail-Order Business
308	Freight Handling
400	Insurance (Car, House, Life, Health)
402	Policy Trans
405	Claims
500	Police/FBI/State and Fed Law Agencies
501	Crime Monitoring
505	Agency Communication
600	City/State Government
601	Operation Communications
602	Large City Communications
700	Federal Government
701	Legislation
702	Judicial
703	Defense
800	Manufacturing
802	Cluster Corporate Trans
803	Internal Corporate
806	Marketing
807	Purchasing
808	Personnel
809	Legal
900	Operations (Utility, Oil, Tel, Pwr, Gas)

905	Cluster-General Message Operations
1000	Transportation (Air, Rail, Car)
1006	Personnel Control
1100	Health Care
1102	Insurance-Hospital Claims
1103	Remote Documented Orders
1104	Hospital Med Records
1109	Dr-Education (Remote) Files
1110	Dr-Consultation Files
1111	Remote Test Reports
1200	Information Services
1203	Library-Distributors Info Exchange
1205	Remote Book Review Service
1206	Library-To-Business Terminals
1207	Library-To-Home Terminals
1600	Medium/Business
1700	Home Communications
1800	General
1807	Postage Messages Special Delivery
1808	First Class Business Messages
1809	First Class Home Mail

User Category 6—Interactive-Graphics

800	Manufacturing
812	Design-Hardware
814	Design-Support-Facilities
1200	Information Services
1212	Canned Application Programs
1300	Education
1301	Computer-Student Remote Time Share
1302	Computer-Research Faculty Prob Sol

User Category 7—Transactions

100	Banks
101	Teller Trans
102	Remote Teller Trans
105	Remote Branch Bank Trans
108	Credit Card Billing and Control
109	Federal Reserve Trans
110	Bank-To-Bank Trans
112	Retail-Bank Automatic Trans
113	Checkless Trans
200	Investments and Securities
202	Buy/Sell Trans
204	Remote-To-Central Trans

205	Central-To-Stock Exch Trans
206	Central-To-Remote Billing
207	Internal Paperwork Trans
300	Retail Trade
302	Central Distribution
304	Central Billing
306	Bank-Retail Trans
307	Mail-Order Business
308	Freight Handling
400	Insurance (Car, House, Life, Health)
402	Policy Trans
405	Claims
500	Police/ FBI/State and Fed Law Agencies
505	Agency Communication
600	City/State Government
602	Large City Communications
608	Road Construction/Maintenance
609	Licenses
700	Federal Government
703	Defense
800	Cluster Corporate Trans
803	Internal Corporate
806	Marketing
807	Purchasing
810	Logistics
811	Field Maintenance
900	Operations (Utility, Oil, Tel, Pwr, Gas)
904	Maintenance
905	Cluster-General Message Operations
1000	Transportation (Air, Rail, Car)
1001	Travel Agencies Inquiry
1003	Operations Control
1004	Maintenance Control
1005	Logistics Control
1007	Billing/Collection Control
1100	Health Care
1102	Insurance-Hospital Claims
1200	Information Services
1204	Library-Distributors Trans
1300	Education
1303	University File/Student Bills
1312	Book Distributors
1400	News/Mag Info Transfer
1403	Customer Bills
1600	Medium/Business
1601	Wholesale-Orders

1602	Food Distributions For Restaurant
1603	Food Industry Distribution
1604	Drug Business Order/Customer Bill
1606	Hotel/Motel Reservations
1607	Auto Rental Chains
1700	Home Communications
1701	Time Sharing Accounts Management

User Category 8—Video

100	Banks
101	Teller Trans
102	Remote Teller Trans
105	Remote Branch Banks Trans
106	Remote Account Monitoring—Bus
110	Bank-To-Bank Trans
111	Bank DP Services
200	Investments and Securities
203	Portfolio Monitoring
300	Retail Trade
305	Management Info Exchange
500	Police/FBI/State and Fed Law Agencies
501	Crime Monitoring
505	Agency Communication
600	City/State Government
601	Operation Communications
602	Large City Communications
606	Legislation Operation
607	Judicial Operations
700	Federal Government
701	Legislation
702	Judicial
703	Defense
800	Manufacturing
801	Design Transactions
802	Cluster Corporate Trans
803	Internal Corporate Trans
1100	Health Care
1107	Dr-Dr Communications
1108	Remote Dr-Patient Communication (Limited)
1109	Dr-Education (Remote) Files
1110	Dr-Consultation Files
1200	Information Services
1205	Remote Book Review Service
1206	Library-To-Business Terminal
1207	Library-To-Home Terminal
1208	Library Micro Dot Book Reading

1210 DP Info Services (Statistics)
1700 Home Communications
1701 Time Sharing Accounts Management
1702 Shopping Selections, Remote

USER ANALYSES PART 3

In this analysis, each individual industry or group should be pictorially presented in a single drawing. All of the subgroups making up the industry or group should be shown with their relationships to one another and their type of interconnection (either point-to-point or switched). It should be noted that users designated as point-to-point or private in the 80s may become publicly switched in the 1990s.

USER ANALYSES PART 4

Table 14-2 shows the 26 distinct user types which were generated by this analysis. Included in the table are the values of the attributes for each type with references to the original category(s) and User Type number.

Table 14-2. User Types.

General user type number	Related category numbers		Facility	TDOS	Connect time	Error tolerance	Holding time	Attempts
1	IR	1	Internal	L/M	N	M	N	>N
2	*DC,DD	1				H	<N	>N
3	RA/TS	1				L	>N	<N
4	RA	1				L	>N	N
5	RD/D	1				M	<N	>N
6	DD	2			F	H	<N	>N
7	Trans	2				L	<N	>N
8	IR	3		M/H	N	M	N	>N
9	RD/D	3				M	<N	>N
10	Graph	3				M	>N	<N
11	IR	4			F	M	<N	>N
12	*DC,RA/TS	4				L	<N	>N
13	IR	5	External	L/M	N	M	N	>N
14	*DC,DD	5				H	<N	>N
15	TS	5				L	>N	<N
16	RA	5				L	>N	N
17	RD/D	5				M	<N	>N
18	DD	6			F	H	<N	>N
19	Trans	6				L	<N	>N
20	IR	7		M/H	N	M	N	>N
21	DD	7				L	<N	>N
22	RD/D	7				M	<N	>N
23	Graph	7				M	>N	<N
24	IR	8			F	M	<N	>N
25	*Trans,TS,DC, RA	8				L	<N	>N
26	*Trans,DD	8				L	>N	<N

*Multiple entries indicate types with exactly the same attribute values exist in more than one

Five: A Look at Technology

Let's take a "big picture" review of the world of technology to better assess the direction of new networks, products, and services, realizing of course, that technology is a moving target, changing at an accelerated rate, providing technical possibilities to cause more and more change in the marketplace. This is an example of the type of data, that conceptual planning activities draws upon during "danka experiments" or "thinking" sessions.

These definitions, relationships, observations, and conclusions are collected from many sources too numerous to mention, and are brought together here to provide a common technology understanding framework for communication. Seventy-five percent of any business is terminology. Real progress is made when "thinking" people are truly communicating. Communication requires using commonly understood terminology. Hence, these terms have been defined by experts in the field, who have attempted to clarify our terminology in order to enable us to truly address the real issues, problems, and applications which are the remaining portion of the job. This is only a brief list of commonly used terms today. Perhaps some organization would venture to put together a more complete list and keep it up to date for all of us to reference, as we play the constantly changing telecommunications information game.

ANALOG SWITCHES

Stored program systems providing over 700 features, enabling local lines within a 1.5 mile radius to economically home on the switch in an analog mode. Some systems are being used as tandems to access the world, providing equal access features, many applications have co-located digital systems to handle business digital traffic and extend the life of the analog systems, as the local plant changes to higher digital residence-business mix.

ARTIFICIAL INTELLIGENCE

The language for the fifth generation computer will probably be built on LISP or Prolog A-1 languages, using new VLSI technology, that will allow different computer architectures and softwares, that provide significant intelligence or expertise in a variety of different domains. Developments in logical programming, object oriented programming and various exploratory programming concepts will play a major role in shaping the fifth generation software. Some of major subtopics under Artificial Intelligence are: Cognitive science, expert systems and fuzzy logic.

BANDWIDTH ON DEMAND

Variable channel selectors that contend for bandwidth either in call set up or on a dynamic basis during the call. A structure in which voice and data

652

calls share a number of channels for a variable amount of time.

BORSCHT

Battery, Over voltage protection, Ringing, Supervision, Coding, Hybrid and Test access are all considerations of the hostile environment of the local plant, which digital systems must interface. There has been some concern, as we move to the electronic terminal, that there is still need in the plant for a constant battery to keep the line resistance from increasing and effecting transmission.

BROADBAND/BASEBAND

Broadband transmission technology was developed from the CATV (Community Antenna Television) and the cable television industry. It has the capability of simultaneously carrying data, voice, video and many other applications. It is typically very high band, 300 MHz or better, or over 1.5 megabits and characterized by very low error rates. Broadband LANs use a bus topology since transmission on a broadband cable is unidirectional, bidirectional communication is obtained by either: splitting the bandwidth and using a re-transmission point (header) at one end of the cable to receive with one set of frequencies and re- transmit with the other; or, using a two cable system.

Baseband transmission uses a digital signal which is more appropriate for LANs in which the primary application is data. Baseband is a broadcast technology and each signal uses the entire bandwidth. Devices share the channel based on some means allowing the station to obtain channel access, baseband transmissions provide a wide bandwidth up to 50 MHz baseband.

Access control refers to how a device establishes control over a channel in order to transmit. Broadband channels are allocated on the basis of frequency either on a dedicated basis or by request. Access control of base band systems has received a great deal of attention in recent years. Both polling and contention systems are used for access. Polling methods can be used on both ring and bus topologies. Contention techniques are for bus technologies only. The most prevailing polling techniques are distributed; some form of token passing is viewed as most efficient.

BURST SWITCHING

An alternative to fast packet, where destination user information is stored on the switches along the route for the duration of the call. Each switch extends the information through the header and a flag is attached at the end of the burst to signal the end. Hence, a limited number of headers and trailers, thereby increasing throughput, and minimizing overhead.

TASI was designed to handle voice signals at a fixed rate, in burst switching the whole network is time shared and a variety of signals operating at different bit rates can be transported in an integrated way. This is achieved by combining the concept of multi-slot circuit switching with the time sharing of the network, for example, different bit rates can be carried on different routes. This potentially can meet a wide range of bandwidth needs.

In burst switching the bit rate on the network links is matched to the bit rate of the source and sinks. Voice and video samples have higher priority than data so their bursts may have the first chance at resources in case of contention. Clipping can occur due to non availability of idle channels. In these cases, data is buffered and stored to avoid voice or image degradation due to excessive clipping. Call blockage can be introduced to limit network congestion.

CBXs/LANs/PBXs

The LAN market proposes both a threat and an opportunity for PBXs. It is not attractive to deploy two internal networks: PBX for voice and LAN for data. PBXs, designed for voice calls with long holding time, are not well suited for short data calls and the spasmodic transmission bursts. The Computerized Branch Exchanges (CBXs) use the star topology to support both voice and data, using some form of distributed control to allow facility sharing. CBXs have more limited bandwidth, about 64 kHz, than LANs. They are suitable for terminal to computer information exchange, where computer to computer communications usually requires greater than 64 kHz. CBXs and LANs have roughly the same distance range and each can support about the same number of devices.

PBXs can take advantage of existing twisted pair wiring within a building where LANs probably goes to fiber or coax. In the long term, the two technologies may become more alike as each tries to incorporate the features of the other. Standards within the industry for LANs and MANs, etc., are being established by the IEEE 802 committee covering inter-networking, joining LANs and MANs, logical link control, medium access and physical specifications, including Xerox's CSMA/CD as a standard for medium access and physical specifications. Although the LAN is most frequently privately owned, interconnection is needed to other facilities using a variety of architectures to provide a gateway for LAN inter-connectivity. A host or switch is required to provide the necessary software for reliable transmission and this host may be part of a LAN or a separate special purpose processor, perhaps dedicated to the act as a gateway server.

CHANNELS

US-DS1 has capability of 24-64K b/s channels at 1.544 Mb/s; European has 30-64K b/s channels at 2.048 Mb/s. Most switches are designed for 2.048 internally and then stepped down to interface to the T1 (DS-1) rate for the North American market. Problem in sending data is requirement for clear channels, that can handle 0 patterns without losing framing, require "clear channel" DS-1 capable of moving voice and data and identifying (recognition) the type of traffic.

CIRCUIT SWITCHING

Uses a fixed number of channels, usually 64K b/s, and does not utilize or take advantage of the burstiness of the information. Can be used as gateway switches to handle clusters of packets from packet switches or alternatively as a constant circuit data path offering within voice digital switches. Can handle redundant data to increase error correction capabilities to achieve higher error rates than one bit error in 10^7 bits.

CLASS

The Bellcore name for a new family of features based on receiving call party identity number in local LATA where, for example, terminal identifies the calling party by name using translation of local database or just displays calling party number. Can transfer only selected calls as a function of who is calling.

CLASS 4

Toll level systems at the Class 4 level provide access to the world, billing and operator services using TSPS operator-type systems, such as 4ESS, #3GTD, DMS-200, etc.

CLASS 5

Class 5 systems are local level digital switches, sometimes called digital base-satellite switches having remote switch units and remote line units that home on the base, such as; #5ESS, #5EAX, DMS-100, NEX, etc.

COGNITIVE SCIENCE

Cognitive science is the study of what and how the human mind functions in an attempt to simulate it through the use of computers. Some experts feel that artificial intelligence's most important implication may turn out to be not computer programs but rather the ability to understand how people think and in turn help them to do it better. It has been said that AI should eventually provide insights into how to learn, how to remember better, how to improve exploratory faculties, and even how to extend creativity. The real results will be a new kind of understanding of ourselves; an understanding that is ultimately more valuable than any program.

COMPUTERS

Fourth generation computers have reached the end of the road with sequential ("Von Neumann Processor") processing techniques, one instruction at a time, obtaining the capability of Millions of Instructions Per Second (MIPS). We have entered the fifth generation parallel processing world with VLSI (Very Large Scale Integrated) logic circuits, that can perform between 100,000,000 to 1,000,000,000 logical inferences per second to provide symbolic processing. Processing power is doubling every two years or so, as indicated by the following observations:

- Super computers reach several hundred MIPS.
- Commercial business computers handle 25-30 to 50 MIPS.
- Super mini's achieve 4 or 5 to 10 MIPS.
- Personal computers perform 1 to 5 MIPS.
- Large frame, high end, are tied to micro frames, to low end micros, to achieve relational database management systems requiring new standards, data formats between micros and mainframe.
- Computer half life 3 years obsolete by 6.
- Processors are constructed using CMOS (complementary metal oxide) or ECL (Emitter Coupled Logic), enabling a single process to reach speed limits of about one Nano second—in the future VLSI single chip may contain as many as 5 to 10 million components.

DATA STORAGE

The cost of memory is reducing to milli-cents per bit, as memory systems are drastically reduced in size, achieve short access time and a tremendously increased capacity. This is causing a revolution in physically distributed systems that no longer need to share databases. There is a re-evaluation of the initial partitioning of the switching network, as VLSI logic memory increases from 256K to 1 Meg to 4 Meg, where processors work with active databases in an associate memory, that no longer needs to be constantly refreshed from central memory databases.

The hierarchy of memory systems can be classified into: primary, secondary and tertiary storage levels, as well as a cache memory between primary memory and central processors. The cache is a high speed access associate memory for working data. Primary memory is basically a VLSI array of logic chips replacing core memory. Secondary memory is a drum or disk; while tertiary storage is a magnetic tape, used as backup, usually not on line.

- Floppy disks are reduced from 8 inches to 5.25 and smaller.
- Single sided and single density are at 200K bytes.
- Single sided and double density are 400K bytes.
- Double sided and double density are 500K bytes.
- Hard "intelligent" Winchester 5.25 inch drives are capable of 10 to 30M bytes.
- Optical disks store several gigabytes can transfer 5 megabits with 50 microsecond access (eraseable in the future).
- Emerging technologies like magnetic bubble, charge-coupled devices, electron-beam-addressable, thin film, vertical recording, and magneto-optics are under investigation.
- Diskette format, file conversion, data transfer, work stations are being standardized.

DIGITAL SWITCHING SYSTEMS

Time division digital systems provide the following advantages over space division analog: direct interface to digital carrier systems enabling the conversion to move closer and closer to customer, ability to decrease the amount of wiring by increasing bandwidth, providing noise-immuned transmission across the switch, handled by a switching matrix whose components costs are rapidly decreasing, as well as A to D and D to A conversions. Digital prove-in over analog was only 10%, but long term picture is deciding factor for integrated voice and data facilities and switches, and new maintenance and testing techniques.

DISTRIBUTED ARCHITECTURE

Distributed Architecture is one in which functions of the system are distributed to various word processors either locally or physically removed, using high capacity mega and gigabit transmission medias to exchange information.

DISTRIBUTED CONTROL ARCHITECTURE

Numerous mini-computers and sophisticated micros work together to sequence the call through various processing state changes, such as; providing dial tone, receiving incoming digits translating to determined route, selecting path to route, pulsing route control information to next switch, providing special announcements, switching call to outgoing trunk or local phone and providing local ringing. These work functions are time shared among many calls in different states, using distributed processors having partitioned and layered software to enable sophisticated autonomous levels of processing and accessing of central databases for "class mark" information (user dependent information) or local databases for specific functional work data.

DISTRIBUTED PBX

Decomposed PBX into physically distributed units, used to move information traffic along branches of a star or portions of a ring in a local area network configuration to achieve office of the future type network complexes.

DVMs

Data Voice Multiplexers that enable low speed data to be sent on voice facilities, so that the data calls can split at exchange access points to packet networks or value added VANS.

EMI (ELECTROMAGNETIC INTERFERENCE)

They will become a problem as more and more systems are co-located, requiring shielding to prevent radiation and susceptibility protection requiring better grounding separation to earth ground.

EXPERT SYSTEMS

An expert system is one of a class of computer programs designed to address problems normally thought to require the talents of human experts. Fuzzy logic is a concept aimed at bringing the reasoning done by computers closer to that done by humans by using graded or qualified statements about objects belonging to fuzzy sets. A fuzzy set does not have precisely defined membership but rather objects are assigned grades of memberships. Expert systems are a class of computer programs that have the ability to advise, analyze, categorize, communicate, consult, design, diagnose, explain, explore, forecast, form concepts, identify, interpret, justify, learn, manage, monitor, plan, present, retrieve, schedule, test, and tutor.

They are designed to address problems normally thought to require the talents of human experts or specialists. The domain now in which the expert systems work is usually pre-defined and very narrow in scope. The structure of an expert system attempts to imitate the manner in which human specialists arrange and infer from their knowledge base. They are driven by a database made up from either a set of "if then" rules or a set of frames or schematic nets. A frame is a model representing an object using certain standard characteristics or relationships to other objects. Frame organization generally results in more concise knowledge base, which allows generalizations upon groups of objects. Schematic net is a graphic representation of an abstract relationship where nodes represent objects and links represent relationships. The computer program is written such that it must examine the state of a problem in each step of the decision process and react appropriately.

There are several fundamental components in most expert systems, these are reasoning mechanisms, searching mechanisms, natural language interface and explanatory mechanisms. Reasoning mechanisms use backward chains, consisting of moving from conclusions back to facts to support them. This is done by predicting unobserved conclusions and looking for facts to support these conclusions. The second mechanism is forward change or data driven reasoning in which one reasons from the facts to conclusions. Forward chaining mechanisms gather initial data and then establishes which hypotheses are plausible explanations of this data. Forward chains have no provisions for stopping if the initial evidence does not lead to any conclusion. For this reason, most expert systems are backward chains. The third alternative is to use a combination of forward and backward chains, as searching mechanisms utilize the minimum amount of time searching for a solution.

There are two methods generally used by expert systems to search for a quick solution. The first of these is called the Generate and Test Method. This process consists of generating all possible solutions to a problem then testing each to eliminate those that fail to meet the constraints. The second type of search mechanism, specific to the domain of the problem at hand, is used to describe the search and reduce the amount of competition in this domain. Specific information is generated in the form of rules of thumb for that area of expertise. Natural language interface for the user interface is critical to the acceptance to any system. The natural language system is one that accepts questions and commands and responds to them in the users natural language. The natural language interface will make computer power available for portions of the population, that are either unable or unwilling to learn a formal computer language.

Consummate Pattern Directed Modules (PDMs) have been developed to cope with change. Expert systems programs are generally a loosely organized collection of PDMs that can detect situations and respond to them. A PDM is a single separate independent unit which is meaningful within the domain of task for which it is designed. Systems based on PDMs are relatively easy to develop. There are two basic types of expert systems that make use of PDMs. The first of these is called a pattern directed inference system (PDIS). This is composed of PDMs, data structures and exact system. A PDIS works by breaking large complex problems into small independent sub-problems. The second type of system, which is by far the most common, is the rule base system (RBS). The Rule Base System is made up of PDM called rules each of which has a separate antecedent and consequence. These rules often have a form of a logical "if then" statement. Some of the rules are merely statements of facts, while others are absolute rules of thumb, called heuristics. Expert systems do not have the ability to learn from experience as human experts do. Software shells are the basis for which systems are written, however, most expert systems today are merely prototypes.

FAST CIRCUIT SWITCHING

Network responds to bursty traffic, but puts numerous headers and tails on sequential fragments of the message. Call assembly and disassembly is achieved by fast signaling medium, such as Common Channel Signaling (CCS).

FAST PACKET SWITCHING

Is closer to conventional packet switching than burst switching in the sense that it applies the basic techniques of packet switching in which the transmission facility carries short packages for many different users. In contrast to conventional packet switching, virtual connections can be made to transmit all packets through the same route. For a call in this manner, switching nodes would not normally process the header information of a packet other than routing instructions. The drawbacks are that each packet carries a header and the bandwidth for user information is reduced by 10% or more. This reduction in bandwidth is more than in burst switching and it introduces preferential delay for packets of the same burst of information, where elastic buffers with time sampling would smooth out the dispersion to improve the quality of voice signals, where the effect of delay on speech is usually spread over a larger number of calls on the facility than burst. Packet switches today are using the X25-X75 type protocols to move information throughout their networks, with asynchronous to X25 achieved using programmable PADs (Packet Assemblers-Disassemblers).

FUZZY SYSTEMS

Fuzzy sets members are assigned grades of membership 1 representing full membership and 0 representing full non-membership. The grade of membership is subjective independent upon contents on which the object is being used. These fuzzy sets are operated upon using fuzzy logic, a type of logic that utilizes faded qualified statements rather than ones that are strictly true or false. The results of fuzzy logic are not as precise as traditional logic but cover a broad area. Fuzzy logic and fuzzy sets have several advantages over conventional methods. They value their rigidity inherent in traditional mathematics and computer science. They simplify the transition between the flexibility of human reasoning and the rigidity of digital computation. They also allow the description of systems too complicated to be fully understood in terms of exact mathematical relations. Probably most significantly fuzzy sets allow the computer to stimulate the use of an important part of human intelligence called common sense. Most common sense knowledge exists in statements that are generally but not always true. These are statements, such as usually, most, or almost always.

HDTV

An emerging proposal for improved quality television makes use of a digital format known as High Definition Television (HDTV). This is planned to be a totally new television format, which will not be compatible with the existing NTSC standard. One recommended system is based upon an 1125 line, 60 Hz field picture format, with 2:1 interlaced fields, and 1290 active picture samples per line. The system will reproduce pictures with twice the vertical and horizontal resolution as the best television studio pictures presently obtained. The quality of HDTV rivals that of 35mm film. HDTV is also not compatible with existing NTSC signals. The bandwidth required is very great. An HDTV system requires a bit rate of 800 Mb/s. Because of this, one channel can fully occupy a current top of the line single-mode optical fiber or direct broadcast transponder.

HRTV

One proposed method to increase the quality of television is High Resolution Television (HRTV). HRTV makes use of an analog format that is compatible with existing standards. The bandwidth required for HRTV is twice that required by traditional broadcast TV, i.e., the bandwidth required is 12 MHz.

The prospects for HRTV are good. It has the advantages of combining high resolution and compatibility with existing TV bandwidth requirements. If an existing television is used, six of the available twelve megahertz are used, in the conventional way. If HRTV is desired, all 12 MHz are available for this use. Most Community Antenna or cable television (CATV) systems have the capacity for 50-100 6 MHz channels, much of which is left idle due to a lack of programming. With HRTV it would still be possible to have 25-50 channels, each with a much higher quality.

HIGH LEVEL LANGUAGES

Enable segmented partitioned programs, where sub-level work modules perform common cross program work functions, enabling structure design to partition systems in hierarchical levels, using layers of software to talk between levels. Work functions are broken down into manageable reliable units; thus enabling faster design and testing of program with minimal number of standard sub-program access interfaces.

INTER-NETWORKING

CI-II has encouraged a proliferation of private networks. Now the Local Area Networks 2-20 megabits, metro area networks 50 + megabits, and wide area networks require interface standards such as IEEE 802.X series and switching capabilities such as PBX or ring switches for inter-networking and local access.

LANs

Local Area Networks is a communication network used to connect disparate technical devices spanning the distance from several tens of feet up to 1 or 2 miles, usually linking devices within an office building, factory or campus, designed to have bandwidth usually over 1 Mb/s, with high reliable, low message transmission delays, using recognition access codes to identify devices. In selecting a LAN there are various choices to make in terms of topology, allocation mechanism, access control, transmission medium and the nature of the service.

Space, time and/or frequency division multiplexing are used to divide the LANs transmission capability into multiple channels. Space division multiplexing allocating wires for individual users, is found in star networks only and it represents the least efficient use of wideband transmission medium. Both frequency and time division multiplexing are effective ways of sharing a wideband channel. LANs, that modulate the signal and use frequency division multiplexing (FDM) to create multiple channels, are broadband systems. Such systems may also use time division multiplexing (TDM) to further allocate channel capacity within the FDM channels. The TDM system simply divides the channel into time slots and access control determines how a device acquires control of time slots. TDM systems are baseband systems. Topologies may use either broadband or baseband, but the point-to-point characteristic of ring topologies are best matched to baseband transmission.

Three kinds of transmission are used in LANs: twisted pair, coaxial cable and optical fibers. Twisted pair can support data rates of up to 10 Mb/s for short distances. This medium is acceptable to electrical interface and may produce unaccepted error rates due to electronic interference in some circumstances, but is the cheapest. Coaxial cable consists of single insulated cable with an outer sleeve. Most baseband systems use 3/8 inch cable while most broadband systems use 1/2 inch cable to support the greater bandwidth. Coaxial cable is also subject to electrical interface to a much lesser degree than twisted pair. Optical fibers are the newest transmission medium being offered for LANs. This is the technology that is still being researched and developed. It offers the potential for being high bandwidth medium with near zero interference and errors. Another advantage of fiber is that it provides the very high security; a drop in signal level occurs as unauthorized taps are made. LEDs are cheaper, presently more reliable but provide narrower bandwidth than laser sources.

LANs generally require additional software, additional layers of protocol to be usable. IEEE's open systems interface reference model structures around the OSI seven layers. The LAN products provide the first 2 or 3 of these, the physical layer covers the LAN physical specification and network access and the digital link layers provided the nature of service. The third layer, the network, has the principal functions of routing and congestion and control. LANs which provide congestion control at the physical level and which use a broadcast rather than a point-to-point transmission provide network layer functionality. Additional layers of software to meet the requirements of other layers are required outside the LAN to provide operational systems.

LSSGR

Industry-wide accepted BOC requirements specification for Class 5 level features, standards and interfaces, should identify sequence of feature steps and always be kept up-to-date with new features for the voice, data, video world, as well as eliminate older less wanted features or those no longer required. It is used as an input for future products requirement specifications.

MF/DTMF

Multi-frequency signaling between systems in MF mode and between terminal and system in DTMF mode, using high/low bands of frequencies. Will be replaced by out of band CCITT #7 signaling systems and "D" channel signaling in time.

MICROPROCESSORS

Going from 16 bit to 32 bit control, with 16 bit data bus; to 64 bit microprocessor; changing from single user PC/MS-DOS to multi- user XENIX or System 5 networking, going from dumb to intelligent terminals containing, 4 MIP processors and 256K-4 Meg memory chips, at prices closer to $1,000 (1990 dollars), using human friendly "ICONS" or a Mouse interface. The availability of powerful microprocessors that address megabytes of data, make speech recognition using Artificial Intelligence, AI programs, will enhance the use of PCs.

MULTI-RATE SWITCHING

To handle buckety or bursty data, bandwidth on demand needs and full motion video require variable megabits. To handle degrees of movement there will be varying usage demand during call handling, requiring usage billing and variable channel selectors.

MULTI-SLOT CIRCUIT SWITCH

Provides multiples of 64K b/s channels in parallel using several channel paths, as needed, during call set up. These channels are restructured at the output of the switch to restore to a higher bit rate of signal.

NAILED CONNECTION

Direct held up path across matrix usually to an adjunct processor to perform some type of work function, such as data packet switching.

NETWORK ARCHITECTURE OF THE INFORMATION WORLD

We have taken a look at the future network in terms of a conceptual "integrated" architecture analysis. An integrated architecture will integrate the architectures of various network systems into an overall architecture, which allows them to work together. This is different from distributed design architectures and open architectures.

OPEN ARCHITECTURE

This a term being used to indicate a competitive world in which network interfaces are identified, enabling Private Networks, VANS, Intermediaries, CPE, etc., to interface to the traditional public network, local loop facilities and access switches, as well as enabling various vendors systems to tie together, using standard interfaces to provide various new features and services. In this manner the network can grow in a competitive manner. However, we must be very careful to understand the impact of these objectives on the actual structuring of systems, it must take into account both distributed and integrated architecture concerns and enable various subsystems to interface to the system complex.

OPTICAL REMOTE SWITCH UNIT

It is connected to the digital base unit via a fiber optic loop. Though it is capable of providing many of the Remote Switch Unit functions, it is not intended to be a sophisticated and survivable unit. Hence it is placed in locations that do not require survivability.

PABX (PRIVATE AUTOMATIC BRANCH EXCHANGE)

Has capability of automatically, without operator assistance, establishing call within a community of interest and capable of enabling calls to access the outside world with or without operator assistance, homing in on the Class 5 or Class 4 network systems.

PAX (PRIVATE AUTOMATIC EXCHANGE)

Has the capability of automatically, without operator assistance, establishing calls within a community of interest, such as a factory but not the outside world.

PBX (PRIVATE BRANCH EXCHANGE)

Capable of establishing calls to the outside world with local operator assistance.

PBX/LAN

Fourth generation PBXs interface to high speed digital LANs and wideband networks to tie host computers to terminals, as well as terminals to each other, using interfaces meeting RS 232C interfaces for data terminal equipment and data communication equipment. In fifth generation structure as physically distributed systems move "n" number 64K b/s channels of voice/data information using "T" and "U" CCITT interfaces.

PCM HIERARCHY

- TV coder (9 bit) requires 46.3 Mb/s.
- Original picturephone coder (3 bit) requires 6.3 Mb/s.
- 24 D channel bank (7 bit) requires 1.5 Mb/s (T1).
- 4 T1s require 6.3 Mb/s.
- 7-6.3 (T2) requires 46.3 Mb/s (T3).

PPS

Throughput of packet switch in packets per second will expand from 1,000 to 10s of thousands to eventually megapackets.

PPSDN

Public Packet Switched Digital Network utilizing packet switches and programmable pads (packet assemblers and disassemblers) to interface various asynchronous and synchronous terminals to X25 local interfaces and X75 outgoing inter-networking interfaces, such as, TYMNET, TELENET, etc.

PACKET SWITCH

Breaks message into segments, puts a header and tail on the message to "package" from 256 to 1,000 characters. Routes packets to destination and assumes error control of messages as it moves them through the network, as well as ensures their order of delivery. It enables numerous packets to share a facility.

PHOTONIC SWITCHING

The switching of information bearing photons (light) from one photonic interface to another requiring multiplexing, de- multiplexing and circuit switching in all optic switching systems. Photonic switching also has the potential to overcome the problems associated with high speed electronic switching, such as jitter, delay, skew, radiation, mutual reduction, parasitic capacitance and susceptibility to electromagnetic fields. The ultimate switching speed in photonics will be three orders of magnitude higher than the highest speed achieved in electronic switching.

This is accomplished by using such technologies as mechanical switches to transfer light from one fiber to another by moving a fiber or light reflecting surface, electro-optic switches, where an electronic field is used to change the index or refraction of optical materials thereby accomplishing switching, as well as bi-stable devices in which optical control signals are used to alter the characteristics of light. However, at this point in time, light to light interfaces will still be investigated over the 90s before economic reasonable breakthroughs are achieved allowing technology to move from the applied research arena to the development world.

PROTOCOL

Packets of information are handshaked between various machines by talking to each other in a protocol (manner) which acknowledges reception of messages, asks for exchanges, etc. Today's packet switches use X25 CCITT protocol as being the ISDN standard where X25 1984 and X25 1985 added many necessary capabilities to the format to make it an acceptable international standard for most situations. Other protocols exist as noted in the various Q and X series of CCITT.

PULSE AMPLITUDE MODULATION

In Pulse Amplitude Modulation (PAM) the amplitude of a pulse carrier is varied in accordance with the value of the modulated wave. The value of each instantaneous sample of the modulated wave is carried to modulate the amplitude of a pulse. Signal processing in time division of multiple terminals often begins with PAM, with further processing before transmission.

PULSE CODED MODULATION

Pulse Coded Modulation (PCM) is when only certain discrete amplitudes of sample sizes are allowed. When the message is sampled in a PAM system, the discrete amplitude nearest the true amplitude is sent. Representing the message by a discrete and therefore limited number of signal amplitudes is called quantizing. It does introduce error in restructuring the wave caused quantization noise. For example, 7 pulses yield 128 sample levels or 8 yield 256. The amplitude of the original continuous wave is then determined by one of 256 levels and transmitted as an 8 bit code.

PULSE DURATION MODULATION

Pulse Duration Modulation (PDM) referred to as pulse length modulation or pulse width modulation is a particular form of pulse time modulation. It is modulation of a pulse carrier in which the value of each instantaneous sample of a continuously varying modulating wave is caused to produce a pulse of proportional duration.

PULSE MODULATION

In "Pulse Modulation" systems, the un-modulated carrier is usually a series of regular recurrent pulses. Modulation results from varying some parameter of the transmitted pulses, such as amplitude, duration, shape, or timing. Though the baseband signal may be a continuous waveform, it will be broken up by the discrete nature of the pulses. It has been convenient to specify signaling speed or pulse rate in "bauds." The speed in "bauds" is equal to the number of signaling elements or symbols per second. The baud denotes pulses per second in a manner parallel to hertz denoting cycles per second.

The continuous waveform is sampled at regular intervals and at a rate of at least twice the highest significant message frequency, so the samples contain all the information of the original message.

PULSE POSITION MODULATION

Pulse Position Modulation (PPM) is a particular form of pulse time modulation in which the value of each instantaneous sample of modulated wave varies the position of a pulse relative to its un-modulated time of occurrence.

REMOTE LINE UNIT

This is the initial A and B stage of a digital switching matrix, controlled by microprocessors, enabling 96 lines to concentrate and/or multiplex on up to 4 T-1 digital 24 channels and home on remote switch units or digital bases.

REMOTE SWITCH UNIT

This is the 4000 to 8000 line remote A, B and C stages of a switching network, enabling large clusters to home in on the base unit from a remote area, such as; small towns tied via T carrier or fiber optics (DS-3) to the county seat, where a main digital base unit, capable of serving 20,000 lines (including lines of remote switch or remote line units), is positioned.

The Remote Switch Unit will be capable of surviving in the event the umbilical is cut to the base and provide local translations, establish a 48 hour billing tape and even interface to other RSUs or another base unit. The RSU is sometimes called the "Class 6 Switch."

SOFTWARE

Cost 65-85% going to 90% system costs, moving to higher level languages, such as ADA (Department of Defense), "C," Pascal, Chill, PL1; structured software enabling functionalized partitioning; future fourth generation languages take the best features from Ideal, Mantis, and Natural; artificial intelligence (AI) uses lisp or versions or dialects of lisp languages, such as Vax LISP, common LISP, franz LISP, unix based LISP and Prolog. Prolog is a logic programming language, which uses assertions about logical relationships between data elements to achieve a program rather than specifying how operations should be performed on data. It treats predicate logic, as the basis and uses an automatic theorem provider to drive or interpret the language, thus expressing programs as logical formulas verified automatically during execution. Operating systems, such as DOS, VAX, and Unix are moving to a PC-XENIX, a unix type operating system, as well as System 5, and XENIX System 5 is the candidate for next operating system standard, perhaps for mainframes, minis, and micros.

SPEECH CODING

Speech coding is the sampling of an analog voice signal with a subsequent representation of this sample in digital form. Ordinary speech coding requires a bandwidth of 46K bit/s. This is because sampling is currently done at a rate of 8,000 bps and 8 bits are required to encode each sample. One speech coding is analytical synthesis, which makes use of voice compression techniques, such as: Adaptive Delta Modulation (ADM), Adaptive Differential Pulse Code Modulation (ADPCM), and Adaptive Predictive Coding by Adaptive Bit Allocation (APCAB). These are methods of reducing the original voice bandwidth of 64Kb down to 16-32,000 bits per second. Later they are re-expanded back to their original bandwidth and transferred back to analog form with accurate reproduction of the original voice wave form! This type of system is capable of pronouncing only pre-analyzed sentences or words, but has the advantage of sounding quite natural, as the original voice signal is reproduced.

SPEECH RECOGNITION

Is the acceptance and understanding of verbal input by computers. The majority of current speech recognition technology is based on pattern match. Pattern matching is a technique in which information about the acquistic characteristics of each word in the devices vocabulary is stored within that device. When a word is input into the device, the input words characteristics are compared to a set of stored characteristics closely match, then the closest match is the recognized word. The information about the acquistic characteristics of a word is derived from a frequency analysis of samples of speech input.

The most common methods of frequency analysis for speech technology are analog analysis, digital filtering and linear predictive coding. Analog zero crossing analysis consists of dividing the speech signal into two frequency regions and then detecting the zero signal amplitude points to provide estimates of major resonant frequencies of the spoken word. In digital filtering, the analog signal is first converted to a digital signal before being sent through a digital filter to determine the component frequencies. Linear predictive coding is a method of encoding the voice signal based on engineering models of human voice track.

Many available speech recognition systems use analog or digital filters to extract speech characteristics. Speech recognition can be classified in terms of speaker dependent, speaker independent, isolated word and continuous speech. Most devices or systems have average vocabularies of 50-75 words. Some systems have the ability to have multiple sets, each having a small number of words that can be swapped in and out at a rapid rate resulting in an unlimited vocabulary. Speaker independent recognition systems have the ability to recognize, accept and respond to a fixed set of words spoken by a wide range of speakers not requiring the training system, as would be required in the speaker dependent recognition systems. The major barrier standing in the way of large vocabularies for speaker independent continuous speech recognition is the need for large amounts of data and processing capability.

Many systems today employ speaker dependent isolated word recognition with a few being able to handle continuous speech recognition. Speaker dependent is beginning to be offered. Speech recognition will become more tolerant of environmental conditions such as background noise and changing speaker characteristics. Small vocabularies, speaker independent continuous recognition will become available, as well as systems that employ graceful means of correction through incorporation of knowledge based on procedures leading us to the voice activated typewriter, voice to text dictation, and interactive microprocessor control systems for human interface.

SPEECH SYNTHESIS

Speech synthesis is the simulation of human voice through the electronic reproduction of words or sounds. Artificial speech is composed of words, syllables, or pieces of words called phonemes, that have been stored in digital form and are later recombined to form words. Phonemes are the smallest units of speech that distinguish one word or utterance from another in a given language. Speech synthesis systems contain "dictionaries" made up of collections of words, syllables, phonemes, or some combination of these elements. These systems also contain collections of linguistic rules that govern how the aforementioned units of speech are combined and pronounced.

The amount of computer power required in a system is determined by the size of the dictionary stored and the number of language rules used. Various systems use different "units" to make up their dictionary. Some use full words and pronunciation lists, while others make use of pieces of words such as syllables and phonemes. When smaller units are used, the number of units required is reduced and less storage is needed, but a larger set of rules and amount of calculations is required. For example, in the English language, only 43 phonemes are required for the combinations necessary to produce any word in the English language. These 43 phonemes would require a small amount of storage, while it has been estimated that roughly 5 megabytes of storage would be required to store a pronunciation list including each individual word of the entire English vocabulary. However, a system that synthesizes speech purely from phonemes would need a much larger rule set and more computational power to properly combine these phonemes, than would a system storing a pronunciation list for the entire language.

Regular synthesis systems memorize phonemes, syllables of words, or occasionally entire words, and combine them according to linguistic rules to simulate speech. Voice Synthesizers are basically made up of three component chips; the synthesizer controller, a data memory programmable read only memory (PROM), and a speech synthesis large scale integration (LSI) chip. Current technology can simulate the individual resonant frequencies found in human voice, but can only approximate the combinations of those frequencies that occur when humans speak. Therefore, synthesized voice does not sound completely natural.

SWITCH CONTROL

System level control may be shared across N + 1 processors or reside in duplicated or triplicated system level monitor/control processors. Switching modules for front end (A or B stage) can be "usage limited," in some cases "attempt limited." In "attempt limited" conditions the processor capability is not enough as calls are blocked and re-tries occur. Thus, the amount of work can go up exponentially causing overload. Usage is usually a problem of network loading in which the amount of time a call occupies the channel, such as what portion of a hundred seconds (CCS) or portion of an erling, where an erling is 36 minutes. Voice systems are usually designed for three to five calls per hour for the home and 10 to 20 for business, where a home call can average 4-6 minutes and work calls 3 minutes. Exchange switches at a Class 5 level, that accommodate 150,000 lines and 15,000 trunks (line is customer side, trunk is outgoing network side of switch) usually support 300,000 busy hour calls: or in total tandem (trunk to trunk, office to office) environment 550,000 busy hour calls for 100,000 trunk switching are provided by similar switching arrangements.

SWITCHING MATRIX

Non-blocking digital design between time and space stages where high usage trunks interface with non-blocking design and low usage lines have some form of concentration such as 4:1, 6:1, 8:1, usually through an access stage, enabling interface to hostile loop plant environment facilitating BORSCHT functions. (Many types of switching arrangements exist such as TSTST, TTSSTST and TTSTST arrangements, as signals are handled in time or space mode.)

SYNCHRONIZATION

Time division multiplexing of several different signals to produce a higher speed system can be accomplished by a selector switch that takes a pulse from each incoming line in turn and applies it to the higher speed line. The receiving end does the reverse. The main problems involved are the synchronization of the several pulse streams so they can be properly interleaved and the framing of the high speed signal, so that the component parts can be identified at the receiver. Both of these operations require elastic stores, called data buffers, due to delay variations of incoming lines to the framing and synchronization operation of the multiplexing unit. Hence, digital signals cannot be directly interleaved in a way that allows for their eventual identification, unless their pulse rates are locked to a common clock. Because the sources of these digital signals are often separated by large distances, their synchronization is difficult. Synchronization methods which can be used are: (1) master clock, (2) mutual synchronization, (3) stable clocks, and (4) pulse stuffing.

TASI

In TASI (Time Assignment Speech Interpolation) the network resources are time shared on a one link basis.

TSPS

Operator service position systems in which clusters of operators, some local, some remote, will handle segments of a call as needed for credit cards, operator services, etc. etc., sometimes called TOPS and other names by various vendors, located between 5 and the 4 level, as an adjunct system in the path of the call.

TELEVISION

There are three types of television technology: NTSC, High Resolution TV, and High Definition TV. Most broadcast television systems make use of a 6 MHz bandwidth. The basic broadcast television in use in the United States today is referred to as NTSC (National Television System Committee) television. NTSC is a standard which specifies a 525 line, 60 field analog system with a video bandwidth of 4.2 MHz. An NTSC system is one in which there is an NTSC signal into the system, and an NTSC signal out of the system. In most video services, the NTSC signal is supplied at some interface, after which it may be digitally encoded, analog encrypted, or otherwise altered for transmission to a second point. At the receiving interface, the signal is then converted back to an NTSC analog signal.

TEXT TO SPEECH

An important, and the most used, subset of speech synthesis is the conversion of text to speech, which involves computer generation of electronic speech based on translation of textual input. Since the input is in the form of computer readable text, a knowledge of linguistics must be applied to the speech before the actual waveform is generated. This includes interpretation of punctuation, non-alphabetic characters, stress patterns, and non-standard pronunciations. Text to speech systems are currently being used in the area of Computer Aided Instruction (CAI). Advances in semiconductors will enable the 64K bandwidth requirement to be reduced to 9.6K, enabling speech synthesis information to be handled by the existing network.

TOKEN PASSING

In token passing access, a token circulates around the system and a station wishing to transmit takes possession of the token and follows token possession with transmission. Enhancements to token passing has included allowing multiple transmission slots (slotted rings) instead of a single token and insertion of large data packets (register insertion rings). All these methods depend upon a station waiting until it receives a signal that tells it it is free to transmit. With contention methods of access, a station attempts to transmit whenever it has something to transmit. The most used contention technique is carrier-sense multiple-access with collision-detection (CSMA-CD). Here a station first listens to find out if a device is transmitting and after retransmission, detects collision and attempts some kind of back off procedure to stop transmission and try again at a later time. (Similar to the trunk glare problem as two offices seize the same trunk.)

TOPOLOGIES

The topology most used for LANs are primarily bus or ring architectures, as broadcast technologies with all messages going to each station with each station responding only to the messages addressed to it. Alternately, a third topology, the star, is used in some LANs, but is most common as a PBX feature. A new technology CBX (Computerized Branch Exchange) is under development in the PBX world. These systems are designed to incorporate LAN capabilities into PBXs. With distributed control, multiple devices attempt to transmit with a central control. With central control, a single device controls when each device is permitted to transmit. Thus bus and ring topologies are most frequently characterized by distributed control. A main advantage of distributed control is that a number of devices affected by failure of the control device is minimized. The bus type topology represents a single physical medium in which many devices can connect by using passive taps, all messages are transmitted past each tap, each station copies only messages addressed to it. This creates a topology that is insensitive to station failure and is a strong advantage for bus topologies.

A ring topology connects multiple devices in a circle or ring with transmission flowing in one direction around the ring. Each station receives transmissions from the station before it on the ring and re-transmits to the next station. Because the failure of any station could bring down the whole ring, safeguards must be built in to bypass failed stations. The ring topology is considered to be well suited to fiber optic technology. Light fiber transmission requires, at present, point-to-point transmission. The re-transmit required at each station in a ring matches the fiber characteristics. A third topology is the star, in which all devices are connected to a common point. Stars are a non-broadcast topology and may have either central or distributed control. With central control, the central node may poll each station to determine if it wishes to transmit. With distributed control the central node simply acts as a switch. Since the PBXs or CBX's main function is to act as a switch, distributed control is a natural direction for CBX LANs.

VANs

Value Added Networks exist where special features, such as access to database information, is achieved over various types of network arrangements such as packet networks.

VLSI

Very Large Scale Integration is achieved using emitter coupled logic, high speed, high power CMOS with speeds of 100-200 million b/s, and gallium arsenide with speeds of several Gb/s. VLSI chips are the building blocks for super computers.

VOICE COMPRESSION

Voice compression is the conversion to a digital voice signal and then to the original analog signal for playback. Voice compression uses an actual digital recording of the voice and is not a form of synthesis.

VOICE RESPONSE

Voice response systems are those in which recorded prompts guide users through a given process. These systems respond with one or a fixed set of messages, played back under software control in response to a user's actions. These responses can be either digitally recorded voice or actually synthesized voice.

VOICE STORE AND FORWARD SYSTEMS

Voice store and forward systems are the type used in many voice mail systems. In these systems, the users can create, store, send and retrieve voice messages, they are capable of continuously changing sets of messages, as they employ real time encoding compression and storage of the user's message.

WIDEBAND SWITCHING

Those that exceed 4K or 64K bits per second can be handled by existing machines up to 1.544 megabits. Wideband switches then switch information up to 140 megabits in the ISDN world of HO 384Kb/s and HI of 1.544 Mb/s and then on to 45 megabits, 140-300 megabits for high resolution TV systems and broadcast video (NTSC) of 45 Mb/s. Wideband switches using VLSI technology enter the world of giga rates within the switch fabric to move hundreds of mega rate calls.

Six: A Look at the Formation Phase

As we move into a new age, it is important to occasionally step back and watch it develop in terms of the views, strategies, plans, and programs of the various participants to determine how far it is progressing and what new strategies may be appropriate.

FINANCIAL STRATEGIES

- The Telco construction and revenues 1986 picture was; $65 billion revenues for BOCS, $18 billion for Independents (up 5%), with a 20 billion construction program (15 billion Bell and 5 billion independent) up 2 to 4%. Total 1985 net income for RHCs (Regional Holding Companies) revealed all time high of $7.5 billion.
- RHC's revenues for 1985 come from: subscriber stations (39.8%) Interstate Access (24.1%) Intrastate Access (7.3%), MTS (10.7%), WATS (2.7%), Directory Sales (3.7%), Billing (3%), other 8.7%.
- AT&T's market service dropped to 83.3% of growing market of 40.7 billion (1983) to 48.5 billion (1984); but AT&T themselves see their market service as 69.2% (1983) with BOC 15.5% of 45.6 billion going to 64.3% (1984) with BOC 18.5% of 51.6 billion. MCI's 1983 $203 million earnings goes to $59 million in 1984 due to their spending on future long distance customers, as it changes from 1 billion in revenues to a 2.8 billion in revenues in two years.
- The information era must continue to ensure employment and income for many governments of the world, especially to support the postal systems and maintain governmental regulatory agencies.
- Intra-Lata packet switching tariffs in Connecticut in the mid 80s were as follows: Access channel for 9.6k b/s access costs $120/month and $550

to install; access to 56k b/s costs $275/mo and $625 to install; protocol change for X.25 or X.75 interface is $210/mo for 9.6k/s; $1,210 for 56k b/s plus $500 installation. Add per call charges and time of day based usage charges from $.30 to $.50 per kilo packet - expensive? - leads to BYPASS?

- Post office closes Electronic Computer Originated Mail (ECOM) with 1984 losses at 100 million.
- Strategic partnering is the game of the 90s.
- Depreciation rates of equipment have been considered in terms of using FCC's "Equal Life" method from 40 year to 20 year to 12 year to 7-8 years. A key issue over which depreciation method accurately reflects costs of ageing equipment, in a high tech arena, where computer equipment is obsolete every two-four years and uses a 7-8 year depreciation rate versus similar telecommunication equipment using much longer rates. State regulators have resisted revenue rate increases based on faster depreciation methods of FCC. Hence, a jurisdiction issue over policy making occurs, especially as telecommunication equipment approaches computer equipment 7-8 year rates.
- Telecommunications equipment imports by the United States in 1984 exceeded exports by $608 million. In 1983, the U.S. imported $1.2 billion and exported $790 million with a difference of $400 billion; while in 1978, the U.S. imported $233 million and exported $388 million. Hence, Congress pushed Japan to encourage U.S. purchases, such as: The NTT-IBM VAN. However, there is a resistance to purchase based upon lack of quality American products.
- IntraLATA calls generate 9.6 billion in 1984 revenues. InterLATA calls provided 40 billion with the following distribution:

AT&T	85%
MCI	5%
GTE Sprint	3%
300 other	7%

- Switch costs rose to 500 million-1 billion, requiring 10-15 billion in sales to be profitable. Ten competitive firms would require the whole world market for voice systems; at this ratio, the current number of firms would require 175%.
- Linkups, partnerships, mergers, shared research, joint ventures, and takeovers are the game of the 80s and 90s as indicated throughout the analysis. For example, the following have been noted:
  —Linkup:

    SNET's Comnet and Tymnet's Van

  —Partnerships:

Britain's Plessey Telecommunications and Office System LTD. and Stromberg Carlson Corp.—AT&T and N.V. Phillips—CIT-ALCATEL and Thomson Telecommunicators—Siemens Communications Systems, Inc. and GTE Communications Systems

—R&D Pool:

Siemens, CIT-ALCATEL, Plessey and Italy's ItalTel—IBM and Industrial Networks for factory local area networks—Concord Data Systems to supply MAP (Manufacturing Automation Protocol) products to DEC and Honeywell—MacIntosh and Northern Telecom PBX.

—Joint Ventures:

GTE and France's Thomson-CSF were awarded a 4.3 billion (which could grow to 15 billion over 10 years) contract from the Army for Mobile Subscriber Equipment (MSE).

—Take Overs and Buyouts:

GEC attempted to take over Plessey with 1.73 billion buy out; Plessey then counter proposed to buy out GEC's System X digital central office operation.

—Mergers:

GTE Sprint and United Telecommunications formed U.S. Sprint from 1,100 miles of fiber, 2 million customers and 1.3 billion dollars 1985 revenue of Sprint, and U.S. Telecom's $350M revenue ($230M to GTE to balance the deal) with 4,700 miles of fiber and 14,000 of future fiber operating in 1986. This will provide a point of presence in every local access and transport area (LATA) with target of 23,000 miles of fiber.

BUSINESS STRATEGIES

- The price game has more and more competition for the same marketplace as demonstrated by:

Switching	1980-85	10% drop
PBX's	1980-85	30% drop
Key System	1981-85	50% drop

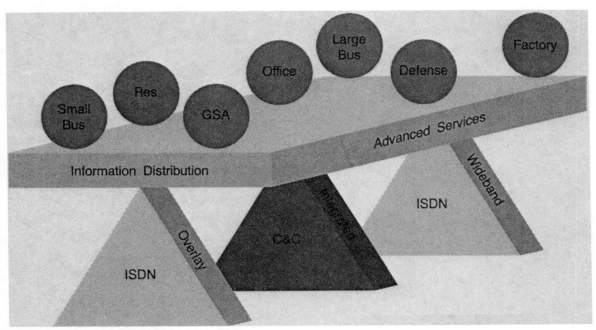

Fig. 14-7. C&C — The Pivotal Point.

- Pricing wars will be based on: services without cost sharing, cost per feature, and sharing of revenues from pooled sources. This will begin a new phase of offerings, once networks are available with these new services from the various vendors.
- End to End service with numerous feature packages will be the major strategy of value added and enhanced providers. The Telcos must also have this freedom in order to be at all competitive.
- Resale packages for small business customers, who do not wish to deal with both the local and long distance carriers will be a growing business, as the alternatives become more and more complex.
- BYPASS—Local telephone company revenues lost to BYPASS $230 million in 1984, 340 million in 1985, with a typical example of New York Telephone Company projected to lose $67 million in 1985 and $110 million in 1986.

  Many new providers are users of their own network who wish to supply circuits to other users such as Teleport Communications, a joint venture of Merrill Lynch & Co. and Western Union Corp. It erected satellite earth stations on land developed on Staten Island by the Port Authority of New York and New Jersey across New York Harbor from Wall Street and lower Manhatten to link 30 large buildings in lower and mid-Manhattan using its own fiber optic lines. The types of bypass that can occur are as follows:

  "On-Site Bypassing. A customer bypasses local telephone company circuits between facilities at a site or at nearby sites by direct transmission of signals between the facilities (usually coordinated by a PBX), thereby avoiding a local call charge.

Facility or Local Bypassing. A customer bypasses the local telephone company switching center (the local loop) by connecting the customer's PBX or single line directly to a long-distance carrier, thus avoiding switched access charges.

Service Bypass, Special Access Lines, Private Lines, or Tariff Shopping. A customer leases a private line—a circuit for the customer's exclusive use from the local to reach a long-distance carrier at the local switching station, paying leasing costs rather than switched access charges.

Resale. Lines are shared by several customers, whose calls to the long-distance carrier are routed by an independent owner of equipment that connects users with the access line. The owner pays lease fees to the phone company, and the customers pay use fees to the owner.

Total, Pure, or End-to-End Bypassing. A customer bypasses the local telephone switching center and a long-distance carrier by transmitting a signal directly from one site to a distant site with his own or leased equipment, avoiding both switching access and long-distance charges.

In addition to these technical classifications, analysts speak of economic and uneconomic bypassing from the phone company's point of view. *Economic bypassing* refers to the case when a less-costly (to the user), nontelephone company connection is priced lower than a more costly telephone company connection. *Uneconomic bypass*, however, refers to a more costly, nontelephone company connection that is cheaper (to the user) than the equivalent telephone company connection, which is priced artificially high because of regulations."

- The FCC allowed AT&T to sell customer premise equipment without using a separate subsidiary by using an accounting plan.
- Who owns wire on the commercial premises?—Telco, telephone customer on the property, or building owner, after amortization period of nine years or less? Telcos must grant right to access the wire, as long as no damage to network occurs.
- Due to 1 billion dollar costs for GTD#5, #5ESS, and System 12 requiring 400-500 programmers to maintain systems at costs of $50 million, as generic lines of code approach the 3-5 million mark, many suppliers such as GTE and Siemens form joint partnerships to share the costs for the next product development, as estimates approach the $2 billion figure to obtain the next generation of switching.
- In 1985-6 the pricing war began in earnest, as more and more fiber routes became available and more and more firms saw BYPASS as an alternative. In some cases digital routes are not yet available for example from Duluth to Mpls./St. Paul, MN. The future of private point to point networks versus switched data public networks using expanded enhanced Centrex type data/voice switches will be based upon economic decisions similar to CCSA Networks, as well as feature decisions. But for any real usage by small busi-

ness, communication costs must be considerably reduced and more simplified.

- Merges of Networks such as Lightnet with United Telecommunications and GTE Sprint with United Telecommunications will occur until at some future point their may only be one or two major alternative networks to AT&T, using fiber and satellites, in which many firms share their excess capacity. Growth plans will initially be over the major city to major city corridors.
- France's smart card with Bull's 8 kb/s chip will have 12 million cards in circulation used mainly for point of sale (POS) purchases and electronic banking, as well as pay telephones and medical identification supported by 300,000 card readers, while Mastercard invests $500,000 to test 50,000 Bull cards in Washington and a two chip card made by CASIO of Japan in Florida.
- AT&T's custom offerings strategy may be to entail electronic mail to provide financial information from Quotron Systems Inc.
- NTT—Japan's Nippon Telegraph and Telephone Corp. indicated concern for using American products, which were frequently riddled with random defects, that are found in less important components and could have been caught with better quality control; as they reconsider $140 million U.S. product purchases (only 6% of their Telcom equipment buys).
- Uneconomic bypass inherent in usage sensitive NTS—Non-traffic Sensitive Costs will be a major issue in determining the usage sensitive National Exchange Carrier Association's Carrier Common Line (CCL) pool charges for terminating switch access minutes, WATS and 800 service access line costs; as various proposals for flat rate transitional fixed charge on Interexchange Carriers (IXC's) originating Busy Hour Minutes of Capacity (BHMC), as well as U.S. West's proposal for a two rate element to recover the IX carrier portion of NTS revenues (a transitional line charge, as a monthly per line charge and a terminating usage charge collected on terminating minutes of use (except 800 service).

POSITIONING STRATEGIES

- What was the cost of doing business is becoming a source of competitive advantage and profit, as firms use information to be more effective in the marketplace.
- Highly complex voice networks have begun the slow process of merging with the primitive networks connecting data.
- IBM acquires Rolm, sells SBS to MCI and purchases 18% stock in MCI, as well as a joint venture with NTT for a Japan VAN.
- British Telcom, 50.2% privately owned, has a single long distance competitor, Mercury Communications. There are 600 VANs, but BT controls (owns) the wires inside the buildings that interface PBX's. 1985 revenues of 8.4 billion will earn 1.8 billion before taxes. Mercury intends to reduce error rate using fiber optic rings to send information in two opposite directions to destination to provide the information with the lowest error rate.
- Japan converted Nippon Telegraph and Telephone (NTT) into a private com-

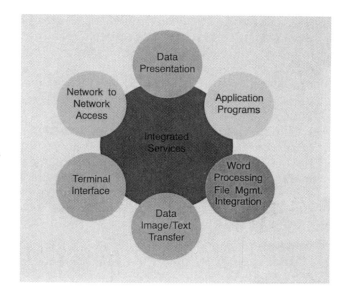

Fig. 14-8. Integrated Services.

pany and enabled "General VANs" to be essentially free from regulation. The VAN market in 1990 may range from Y30 billion to Y200 billion with 170 general VANs competing, using suppliers: NEC, Fujitsu, Hitachi, and OKI as well as IBM.

- There initially are five alternative long distance carriers, one of which Hughes Communications has 20%.

- Japan is experimenting with a Model System of their Information Network Systems (INS), a version of ISDN in Mitaka and Musashino where 550 homes use digital telephones, digital TVs, high speed facsimile and data terminals to exchange voice, text, graphics, as well as still and moving pictures.

- West Germany has a three phase program based upon ISDN to first provide 2B + D switches and transmission systems, then a universal connecting device on user's premises as phase 2, and in 1990 the integration into ISDN of broadband services at 2 megabits/sec and 140 mb/sec with cable television distributed separately. They have developed an experimental broadbase (140 mb/s) integrated network to demonstrate feasibility called Bigfon (breit bandages integriertes glas farsar fernmelde ortsnetz (a broadband, integrated fiber optic local telecommunications network) for 320 customers in seven cities: Berlin, Hamburg, Hanover, Dusseldorf, Stuttgart, Nuremberg, and Munich.

- France's packet-switching network—TRANSPAC transmits 500 + billion characters a month as part of a videotex system in which France pioneered a computerized telephone directory, in which terminals (Minitels) were provided to customers free or at extremely reasonable prices ($100). Theory being that increased usage will more than pay for subsidized terminals in three or four years. The DGT has over 50% of central offices digital and provides satellite data transmission to 30 ground sites, as an overlay network.

- Italy—SNET—The SOC Finanziaria Telefonica, a major holding company, will work with the PTT with more control, as they transform to the digital world in which, by 1990, 25% of the countries' local switching offices will be digital.
- China—Numerous firms such as AT&T, as well as RBOCs wish to participate in a planned eight fold increase in telecommunication capability by 2000.
- Pacific Telesis to offer nationwide call paging capabilities and operate cellular radio facilities throughout the United States by acquiring for $430 million Communications Industries, Inc. and selling its equipment manufacturing units, an activity forbidden by divestiture. However, Greene did not initially believe that RBOCs should provide competitive services in other RBOC's regions. Huber and Justice recommended otherwise.
- Turbulent years.

  — DSC—14 million loss in first quarter 85 after GTE cancelled order for SPRINT of 72 million in tandem systems.
  — Control Data lost 300+ million.
  — U.S. Postal Service closed electronic mail (ECOM) which processed 1 million messages a week—loss could be as much as $1/message.
  — Bellcore audit disagreed with 110 million spent on such things as testing of product quality and applied research.
  — EXXON lost 100 million plus on EXXON Office System unit.
  — IBM's SBS was losing 100 million a year and still required billion dollars for a land fiber network, this lead to an MCI purchase.

- AT&T and British Telecommunication announced they would sell rooftop to rooftop private satellite links, initially, using Intelsat's Transatlantic Satellites.
- Ameritech purchased a software house, Applied Data Research, for $215 million.
- British Telecommunication purchased Mitel.
- AT&T and Electronic Data Systems (General Motors subsidiary) formed a joint venture to sell private data networks.
- Martin Marietta bought 25% of Equlorul Communications to together sell satellite networks.
- GE and RCA firms with a total 1985 sales of $36.7 billion made merger agreements, that would combine Data Communication's 24th and 25th largest vendors to achieve a combined data services and data equipment sales of 1.9 billion; including GE's Value Added Network (GEISCO) and RCA's competitive Value Added Network RCA CYCLIX communication.
- Twelve long distance lightwave plans including telecommunications firms railroads and banks call for a 6 billion dollar investment by 1990. Five ventures including AT&T Communications, MCI Communications, GTE Sprint and FiberTrak (Southern Pacific+) plan to have national networks with 7 other ventures having regional networks. Just one pair in the 16 single mode fiber pairs can handle 6,048 voice conversations at once at 417 Mb/s. The

typical cable will have 144 pair, while the initial needs call for only 12 to 96 pairs. Technical advantages should cut costs in half within six years with costs dropping below $1 per unit mile with repeaters at 25 mile spacing. The NY-Washington corridor will have MCI and ATT fiber; as MCI plans an 18,000 mile fiber network perhaps by 1987 and AT&T a 10,000 mile network by 1990.

- France's Transpac Network will provide access to an international transit node for CSC Computer Science's INFONET (VAN) to link data packet lines between U.S. and France.

- MCI purchased Western Union International in 1982 from Xerox for $195 million, which grew to 23% of international message traffic in 1985.

- AT&T Skynet (Satellite Bypass) will support direct lines to AT&T at digital transmission T1 data rates and connections from satellite to AT&T terrestrial network via Accunet T1.5 with up front installation charge of $25,000, site prep $12,000 to $50,000, recurring monthly lease cost about $4,000 to $5,500 and transmission capacity one way charges of $900 for 56K, $1,000 for 64K, and $9,000 for 1.5 Mb/s (usage sensitive pricing). This works out to be in California, equivalent to a 100 mile T1 access channel charge. By interfacing the 64K channels to AT&T Central Office and the 56K channels to DDS and by adding some sub-T1 interconnection options and slightly lowering earth station costs and transmission costs, Skynet could become a formidable competitor to the local exchange companies, as a ubiquitous way to handle customer data to and from the switched AT&T long distance network.

- Future fiber networks if all built could expand present AT&T 1 billion circuit miles network seven fold, providing three to five times the capacity. Several regional networks have banded together to form National Telecommunications Network (NTN) to provide a forum to work out technical and business problems of interconnecting separate networks. Alternately such partnerships as Lightnet and U.S. Telcom's agreement for one to build 2000 miles of the other's 3,500 mile network and buy some of the pairs. Others like the Fibertrack may put networks on hold until more capacity is needed, and new special purpose network needs are identified.

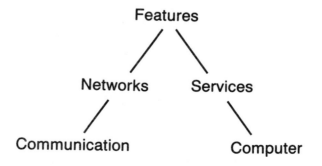

Fig. 14-9. Information Features.

- McDonnell Douglas to spread global coverage of its U.S. value-added network service, TYMNET, Inc. signed an agreement with local telephone companies in Japan for joint development and reportedly was working with British Telecommunications PLC. Its aim is to provide a global facility for sending orders, invoices and other documents as bursts of electronic data between computers.
- France has elected to use V.26Ter (third) rather then V.22 bis (second) for document transfer between business; requiring those outside France to use Transpac packet-switching network for connection to their network on international calls.
- AT&T ended 1985 with Megacom, Software Defined Network, Private Line Tariffs 9, 10 and 11 along with the removal of the FCC need for its separate subsidiary for the provision of CPE under Computer II.

PLAYERS STRATEGIES

- Japan Communications will send up a Hughes HS-393 with 32 transponders in December 1987 and a second for data at a cost of 300 million to sell service in competition with NTT (Nippon Telegraph and Telephone Corp). Space Communications Corp. will use Ford Aerospace satellites to also compete inside Japan.
- AT&T and Harris Corp. to file for a very small operative terminal network, where a business user with 300 to 1,000 sites could save at least $750 million per month over 1986 leased lines costs or private line costs at $1,250/M for 500 sites providing 128K to 1.544 Mb/s. This enables point to multipoint video and data distribution; using a KU-band network designed by Bell labs. This will complement AT&T's widely used SKYNET C-band service.
- Europe's Information Technology Steering Committee (ITSTC) unites work by CEPT (The European Conference of Post and Telecommunications) and CEN-CENELEC (European Committee on Norms—European Committee on Electro Technical Norms) defining local network's X.25 implementation. Their work is supported by SPAG (Standard Promotion and Application Group) an association of 12 European computer and telecommunication firms. They work on formulated ISO (International Organization for Standardization) protocols such as those for level 6 and 7 which received recognition from (ECMA) European Computer Manufacturing Association of which American firms such as IBM and Digital Equipment (DEC) are members, where both supported the OSI open systems interconnection standards.
- BOCs began providing ISDN 2B+D: with Wisconsin Bell's Siemen's voice/data ESWD PBX switch, that can be used by any customer including, Centrex; Illinois Bell with an ISDN #5ESS test with MacDonald Corps headquarter buildings at Oak Brook, IL; Mountain Bell with an ISDN GTE GTD5, NT DMS100 and NEC for the Phonix 1987 ISS; Northwest Pacific Bell with an ISDN operator Northern Telecom ISDN interface; Southern Bell with a Northern Telecom ISDN 23B+D interface in Atlanta and #7 Signalling System; Pacific Bell's attempt to use a copper wire transmission technique to

transmit 2 voice and 5 data channels one at 9.6 Kb/s and four at 1.2 Kb/s with later changes to achieve a new sub rate ISDN interface; and Northwestern Bell's ISDN interface with NEC's systems.

- Strategic alliances have been made between Holland's Phillips and Siemens to turn out 1 and 4 MBIT memory chips.
- Rockwell purchased 3M's local area network subsidiary Interaction Systems and Allen Bradly to move it into the top twenty-five of the Data Communications 50 to compete with Siemens in factory automation.
- Siemens formed a joint marketing venture with Telecom Plus International to distribute PBXs and has a data packet switching supplier DATABIT.
- Bell South has chosen single mode fiber (4 Gb/s) to use in all applicants over 12,000 feet from office. It installed approximately 60,000 KM in 1984 and 70,000 KM in 1985 for the public network; including a 20,000 unit Florida subdivision with fiber optic cable providing: home security, remote utility monitoring and other services, as well as a joint venture with Siecor to form Fiberlan where Siecor, itself, is a joint venture with Corning Glass and Siemens A.G. It also pursued subrate standards such as 32K and 19.2K all within the 64K envelope as a national alternative to 2B + D. Pulselink their packet switched service will interface with the Public Data Networks with the intention to keep business on the public network.
- NWB filed to allow a digital transmission path between customers premises without going through the local exchange central office- Digicom.
- AT&T entered joint agreement with EDS on several major 20-30 million dollars networking projects.
- Pacific Telesis's Pacific Telesis International's Spanish subsidiary Pacific Telesis Iberica S.A. signed a 41 million dollar contract with Spain's National Telephone Co. (Compania Telefonica Nacional de Espana) to design, construct, supply and operate a telecommunications laboratory in Madrid using Bellcore assistance.
- The game becomes more and more international—where Northern Telecom obtained $250 million contract with NTT for 2 million lines of DMS-10. The FCC entered the AT&T—Siemens clash in France.

MARKET STRATEGIES

- Telephone Market had 200 companies providing sets for a 1984 1.25 billion dollar market. Customers wanted quality reliable sets; market reduced suppliers to 80 companies with AT&T having 20% of market.
- Key systems for small business sales peaked in 1984 at 4.7 million units and $2.8 billion. As sales dropped in 1985, average prices dropped from $300 to $225 per unit.
- PBX market of 3.5 billion (1985) has had 30% reduction in overall price.
- Micro stations, costing 7,000 to 15,000 are widely being used as low cost satellite terminals with 2-6' dish antennas in 4/6 gigahertz and 14/12 GHz frequency range. They were used by Federal Express's—ZAPMAIL service

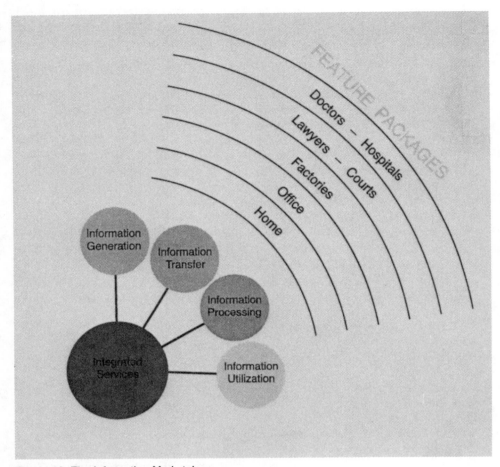

Fig. 14-10. The Information Marketplace.

for typical transmission of 56,000-128,000 bits per sec.

- Mobile telephone—205,000 (1985) phones in use. Costs have dropped from $2,500 to $700 per unit to $23/month rental to be more economically attractive to a wider range of small businesses.
- The U.S. Government requested bids for a $4.5 billion private telecommunication network using packet and circuit switched data transports, the largest such private network in the world.
- Data Communications Paul Strausse's survey analysis depicts a massive data industry with 86 billion in U.S. sales and a growth rate of 15%; even though, due to intense restructuring, there were layoffs of 75,000 people.
- Video conference centers are being established by ISACOMM sharing network sites.
- Most video conference meeting centers currently operate at 768K bt/s, while AT&T uses a full T1 rate at 1,544 Mb/s. Under this arrangement hosts (owners of the video conference sites) pay less for usage such as $350/hr

while non hosts pay an additional $200/hr for use (rental) of the site.

- AT&T's Software Defined Network (SDN) is to enable all locations of a corporation to tie together (even remote) by using conventional loops dedicated to SDN Traffic with Telco passing call information over a dedicated trunk to AT&T-SDN Supporting Central Office using No. 1AESS to No. 4ESS generic 4 feature package called CCSA code compatible, where CCSA Common Control Signalling Arrangement is the ageing private line network. It will later be supported in Feature Group D, which is not yet widely deployed. For this dedicated access AT&T's customer's pay the Telco 9¢ a minute.

- Teleconferencing, Telemarketing, Telebanking, Teleshopping are coming more into focus, especially with Telebanking achieving initial user acceptance.

- *World Market*—424 million access lines connected to the world's public telephone network; providing 210 billion/year revenue at $400-700 per line; with outside U.S. growth rate as 13% compared to 3% U.S.; capital expenditure for a new subscriber (customer) averages 3,500; $500 billion equipment market between 1986-1990 with China spending $650 million + per year. As new networks in Asia, Brazil, Venezuela, Mexico grow, North America's share will drop from 50% (1970) to 38% (1995) and Europe to 24%. Asia will grow to 32% by 1995, with Latin America Telecommunications market approaching $43 billion/year by 1990. World wide public and private purchases will increase at 8% a year through 1990. Data computers purchases will grow at 12-15% a year. Only one supplier Ericsson is in the number one position in two of the six regions (Latin America and Oceania); ITT was in the number one position in Europe and number two in Asia, Latin America and Oceania; while Siemens leads in Africa, is second in Europe and third in Latin America; with France's Alcatel-Thomson number two in Africa and number three in Europe. Digital switching programs are well underway in U.S., Canada, France, Italy, United Kingdom, Netherlands, Sweden, Korea, Taiwan, Malaysia, South America, Algeria, Morocco, Mexico and Australia; with a digital toll network in Japan; cellular mobile radio systems in U.S., Nordic countries, Japan, United Kingdom, Spain etc,; and more joint ventures between European and North American suppliers, such as: GTE/Siemens, AT&T/Phillips, and more mergers between suppliers within individual countries in United Kingdom, Italy, West Germany and the United States, such as the CGE and ITT merger.

- Jockeying for position for orders in 16% of French switching market was: AT&T and AT&T/Phillips with Compagne Generale d'Electricite (CGE) for No. 5ESS production in French market for CGCT Compagne Generale De Construction Telephonique, in return to help CGE's U.S. subsidiary CIT-Alcatel market E10 digital switch to BOCs, as well as talk between L.M. Ericsson and CGCT and DGT's Director General des Telecommunication's evaluation of ITT's System 12, which led to the ITT buyout.

- AT&T offers Megacom and Megacom 800 (different from 800 service and WATS (Wide Area Telecommunication Service)) because Megacom rates are based on destination and duration rather than geographic area called bands. Access to Megacom is via high capacity direct access private line for large users, as part of "migration strategy" to directly tie to AT&T, with SDN, which customers like Control Data will use and other large customers, such as the 25, who currently use EPSCS (Enhanced Private Switched Communication Service). SDN will thus enable heavy private line users, with multiple locations to design software defined private networks, based on AT&T's in place switched network.

ARCHITECTURE STRATEGIES

- AT&T's Information Systems Network (ISN), a packet switched baseband local area network can work in tandem with the company System 75 or 85 digital PBX and be used as a 19.2Kb/s per second local area network, with the System 85 expandable to handle 35,000 lines.
- Bellcore and other IEEE and ANSI steering organizations continue to attempt to ensure the network is compatible with open standard interfaces to ensure open architecture can be achieved in a reasonable and competitive

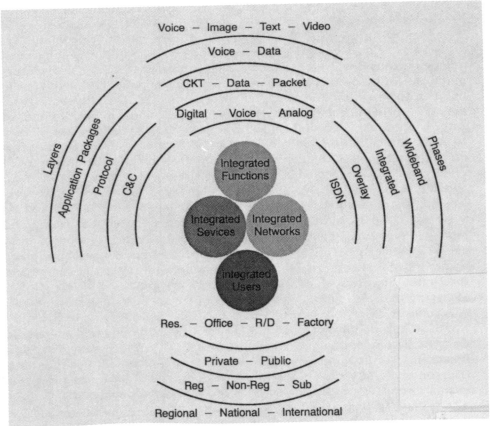

Fig. 14-11. Integrated Services — Integrated Networks.

marketplace without degrading the quality of the network, based on OSI model and CCITT recommendations.

- CCITT V.22 bis (second) will be the worldwide standard for 2.4Kb/s dial up modems with fall back to 1.2Kbts; defining physical and logical handshaking.

- Dept Of Navy Office Automation and Communication System's (DONOACS) aim is to curtail the proliferation of independent and incompatible computer-assisted administration schemes by providing a standard centrally controlled, decentrally operated, office automation network that enables different vendor's machines to transmit a file to one another. There are some 200 different word processing packages making this impossible, so they have defined a new word processing standard with the Bureau of Standards called Document Interchange Format (DIF) in which office automation vendors can use software translators, integrated with their word processor and operating systems, that translates their code to DIF Standard, based on an extended ASCII code set.

- Operational safeguard and network security measures such as encryption, authentication, terminal sequence numbers, passwords and log codes, physical versus logical terminal check, acknowledgment of single messages or groups of messages, system sequence numbers, event records, call back, and audit trails will be used to prevent, determine or diminish threats such as read messages on a circuit, insertion of a false message at a terminal, modification of real messages at a terminal, modification of real messages on a circuit, or attachment of a false terminal to a node.

- Movement of data in which eight consecutive zeros can affect the F bit in framing and in the secondary channel and control bits C/S would destroy network timing. It must be adequately addressed by new product offerings for integrated voice/data digital facilities using "clear channels" with standard interfaces to resolve European and American differences.

- NETWORK BRIDGES—IBM's Distributed Office Support System (DISOSS), which stores and retrieves documents in a central library and distributes them throughout networks, has been accepted by AT&T to link non IBM equipment with the DIOSS distributed office support system environment. AT&T will supply software to its 3B minicomputers to exchange revisable form documents with IBM. The WANG office equipment Professional Office Systems (PROFS) a similar package for a different set of IBM machines, WANG's Mailway and Boeings (BCS) document transfer services will interface to DISOSS, as well as General Electric's Information Service's document translation and distribution network and portions of MCI's electronic mail network link (Mailbag). The session and application level software will be based on logical unit (LU) 6.2 (IBM's peer to peer communications protocol). Digital Equipment Corp. DISOSS Document Exchange Facility resides on a DECNET/SNA Gateway, letting Users on a DECNET Network engage DISOSS features on a machine that belongs to a neighboring SNA network. Similarly, Burroughs, Data Generals (ECLIPSE MV family of processors) Hewlett-Packard and Datapoint are working on DISOSS bridges. Soft-switch sells directly to Users and Original Equipment Manufacturers (OEM) and will supply Wang the document format conversion software. It lets Wang, Xerox, NBI and Multimate exchange documents with DISOSS, PROFS and each other.

- AT&T's 3B2 and 3B5 computers on a 3BNET can link through a communications processor to an IBM main frame SNA 3270 software. The 3B allows synchronous terminals to emulate standard 3278 terminals to the IBM host's front end processors.

- UNIX based machines are adapted to handle both BSC and SNA protocols without alternating the standard operating system.

- FCC has difficulty assigning 200 Data Network Identification codes or DNICs to 2000 network operators, using X.121. The U.S. has asked CCITT for the numbering sequence from 3100 to 3169 and 3170 to 3299 to give it 200 DNICs, but this still does not resolve their needs with several National alternatives yet to be pursued.

- Ethernet has three versions. Ethernet specification version 1, Sept. 1980, Ethernet specification version 2, Nov. 1982 and IEEE 802.3 carrier—sense multiple access with collision detection (CSMA/CD) specification revision, Dec. 1982, the original version 1 was developed by Xerox, Digital Equipment Co. (DEC) and Intel. The main differences among the three versions lie in the connection from the data terminal equipment (DTE) controlled to the media access unit (MAU) transceiver interface. The Xerox designed data communications scheme has so far adhered to a baseband technique, capable of only 10 Mbit/sec. Developments to share the cable with facsimile, voice and video have led to a set of data transmission techniques proposed by DEC for a broadband Ethernet compatible with the baseband standard called Broadband Medium Attachment Unit and Broadband Medium Specifications. DEC's Broadband Ethernet Channel bandwidth of 18 MHz—also expressed as three 6 MHz TV channels—consists of 14 MHz for data transmission and 4 MHz for collision enforcement. The bandwidth supports the very high transmission speed of 10 Mbit/s for high speed computer to computer traffic.

- In baseband Ethernet networks, the maximum separation is 2800 meters (1.7 miles) between communication nodes. In DEC's Broadband Ethernet, implementation, the maximum node separation is 3800 meters (2.4 miles). The full length of which can be tapped by various terminal devices. The three tier IEEE 802.3 local network reference model is functionally identical to the data link and physical levels of the ISO-OSI model. IEEE has divided the data link layer into two functions: Logical level control and its underlaying medium-access control. IEEE standards are being established on three approaches to medium access control; CSMA/CD, token bus and token ring.

- SS No. 7 with the power to flexible interconnect clear (voice and data). 64Kb/s channels is the essence of the Integrated Services Digital Network, whose features of User access to full 64Kb/s channels with no bits stolen for signalling or syncronization, rapid establishment or modification of the destination, characteristics of the connection, and transmission of user data without disturbance through the existing connection—require the Common Channel Signalling System. On ISDN facilities, it is performed by the D channel. On the backbone network between telephone company exchanges, SS No. 7 will take on the common channel signalling task.

- To enable long strings of zeros for random data to be sent on digital facilities and not lose frame synchronization and not lose transmission capacity so that 64K becomes 56K, and to enable number new services such as 800 service, credit card checks, billing and rating information to be exchanged between offices, a separate out of band signalling channel is used.

- CCITT has developed two common channel signalling systems recommendations SS No. 6 and SS No. 7. No 6 was designed to work with low data rate 2.4K analog modems to carry 20 information +8 check bit messages. The No. 6 protocol is not layered and is a monolithic structure. SS No. 7 a signalling system for digital (pulse-code-modulation) trunks was to handle higher data rates and lower error rates (1 in 10^9 rather than 10^5) and use layered bit oriented protocols in conformance with ISO's seven layer OSI (X.200) reference model. Though SS No. 7 would be difficult to redesign after the OSI model was finished to take more advantage of the lower levels, it will accommodate most needs for the future ISDN networks. Though No. 7 is layered, the layers are not identical with the OSI model. The physical layer, data link layer and network layer of the OSI are related to its signalling data link level 1, link control function level 2, and common transfer function level 3 to provide the message transfer parts, network service parts and signalling connection control part. To provide full OSI addressing capability the message transfer part is supplemented by a signalling connection control part (SCCP). The transport, session, presentation and application layers are cross related to level 4—the user and application parts.

- The application in North America is to connect signalling transport points (STPs), which become the cross grid of signalling systems, that route, off the network, the destination status and network route availability information, before establishing the complete network connection. It will also be used by BOC's to handle INWATS, 800, and credit card validation services.

- The Link Layer protocol to be used on the D channels is LAP D, similar to LAP B (the balanced HDLC version used on X.25 connections) except two octet address fields are used for statistically multiplexing the various services provided on the D channel. The signalling formats to be used above LAP-D, and when LAP-D should be replaced with the message transfer part of SS No. 7 (thus becoming the E channel) enable the E channel to be used for PBX accesses. Using the SS No. 7 on PBX links would make a PBX capable of providing information concerning users behind the PBX (called or calling party's availability, capability and identity) and passing them through the network. CCIS6 (a common channel system based on SS No. 6) and AT&T's Embedded CCIS6 (ECIS6) and Telcom Canada's CCIS6 (TCIS6) provide vehicles for several internetworking, that provide SS No. 7's input and provide a model for moving ahead, as SS No. 7 becomes the key for ISDN by new networks of STP centers with local STPs to provide CLASS features and other "Feature Switch" programmable features, above the network, if so desired, or to INFO Switches within the network, closer to the User, as suggested in earlier analysis.

- A 1986 MAP demonstration based on 802.4 token Bus technology was an attempt for a complete standard for the factory using the OSI seven layer model, where MAP 2.1 version is specified for layers 1, 2, 4, 5 and parts of 3 and 7. The demo showed that AT&T, Digital Equipment, Gould, IBM, Hewlett-Packard, Motorola and Intel devices could communicate to each other on a network conforming to the MAP specification, Boeings Computer Service's Technical Office Protocol (TOP) and X.25.

- Virtual Private Networks for large firms, such as; Federal Express, the Bank of America and American Health Services, etc. are on the rise, as well as large networks, such as the Federal Telecommunications System. The FTS will have new switches and transmission at a cost of 1.3 billion. In 1984 it had 52 switching centers, 15,000 long distance trunks, and 35,000 access lines.

- They will be developed using ETN Electric Tandem Networks facilities for long haul carriers and local firms using Centrex or privately owned PBXs to tie users together to access the network; by using SDN the Software Definition Network of AT&T; or by Digital Termination Service (DTS) a point to point local distribution of voice and data over a special microwave frequency set aside by the FCC.

NETWORK STRATEGIES

- Scientists at Bell Laboratories pumped 4 gigabits—62,500 voice telephone calls or about as much information as contained in a 30 volume encyclope-

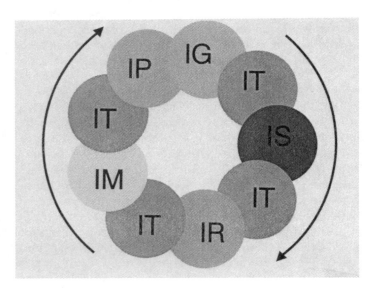

Fig. 14-12. C&C — ISDN Information Integration.

dia through a single optical fiber strand in a single second.

- AT&T estimated that at the end of 1985 its capacity of 1.03 billion circuit miles was 690 million miles less that that of its combined long distance competitors.
- A BOC may construct a user's private long distance network that bypasses AT&T. Though the breakup decrees forbids BOCs from providing interexchange routing it does not prohibit [BOC] from providing switching service to customers as end-users for originating and terminating traffic among dedicated interexchange circuits as part of a Centrex or PBX offering per H. H. Greene deregulation judgment.
- BOCs are putting fiber cables in the ground having 99 fibers but are only normally using 2 to 3 fibers initially.
- AT&T and MCI announce virtual networks that support bandwidth on demand, rather than leasing lines to solve network management problems.
- France's transport network froze, during peak hours for three days caused by a fault in customer node software by a surge of calls that overloaded host computers dispensing videotex services. The load of unanswered calls created unprecedented demands on transport nodes. The faulty software declared the node not coherent and propagated the error forcing the nodes to shut down. The crisis caused an acceleration of new traffic handling improvements as total number of ports are expected to double from 31,000 to 60,000 by 1990. In 1986 videotex was 20% of network traffic and 40% of the calls. It was expected to increase from 8,700 erlangs (MAX) to 40,000 by 1990.
- A RACE (Research and Development of Advanced Communications) Network in Europe is supported by France's Campagni des Machines Bull, Britain's GEC and STC, West Germany's Siemens and Italy's Olivette. They are joined by public carriers and government officials for the procurement of a billion dollar multipurpose wideband network.
- AT&T filed for its own Accunet 56 Kb/s interLATA Switched Digital Service based on CSDC, since BOCs could not offer the service past their local access and transport areas (LATAs) and because AT&T no longer had access to customers local loops. CSDC (Circuit Switched Digital Service) was used only to serve local service. Users will dial up a new 700 56X-XXXXX where the last five digits are unique to the destination switched 56Kb/s user.
- AT&T's network offering called Software Defined Network Service (SDNS) gives large customers control over their long distance networks and usage flexibility as a virtual private line network. Bandwidth is dynamically controlled by AT&T though the user is able to reallocate it. It can be used for many multiple sites or as backup for high volume point to point private data lines. SDNS is an enhancement to other AT&T switched private line network services. It currently offers customers—Common Control Switching Arrangement (CCSA) and Enhanced Private Switched Communications Service (EPSCS). Per Data Communications, AT&T indicates users would see a 20-30% decrease over private lines. SDNS will be accessible to users in 600 of AT&T's class 4 central offices locations, and where EPSCS was based.

In the past user reconfiguration has been restricted by the limited number of central office sites that support EPSCS.

- PULSE LINK was the underlying packet net for Knight-Ridders Viewtran videotex for the Miami area. Bell South was to use it to provide async to X25 to X75 protocol conversion services in Orlando, Columbia and Atlanta.

- Pacific Bell will permit users to access its packet network by one of four methods: Dial up access into ports on the packet switch (Northern Telcom SL-10); dedicated access via a Dataphone digital service (DDS); or 3002 analog voice line; and data over voice access into the switch. Rates are for 300-9,600 b/s from terminal and 9.6 to 56Kb/s between switch and computers of information providers who will build Bus and Res services. They have developed a new product to operate on voice lines and provide several data channels.

- Existing satellites will need to be "hardened" against EMP Billion Volt Pulses to protect from an accident such as the disintegration of a nuclear powered space vehicle.

- Since antenna size is inversely proportional to frequency, CB and 4-6 GHz requires a large antenna necessary for high speed trunking via T1, Microwave, and Fiber for digital multiplexing of numerous terrestrial 9.6K circuits. Alternately, Ku band (12/14 GHz) allows placement near data processing or PBX location but suffers from high degree of atmospheric attention. Due to C band saturation with terrestrial microwave, the trend is to Ku band with increased rf power.

- DOS-SC AT&T's Digital Data System with secondary channels or DDS 2 to let users run end to end circuit diagnostics has an alternative BOC offering based upon proposal by Bellcore. It is called Diginet, Megalink, Synchronet and Quickway by the different BOCs.

- GM will use a 18 mile lightwave network to link 14,000 phones and 23 switches into a single digital network.

- A 700 access to three new AT&T's offerings will provide: a 1,000 service that is designed for voice contact; a 2,000 service for data conferencing of multiple remote data devices; and a 3,000 service for simultaneous voice and data conversations using separate circuits.

- France is using special coaxial cables to transmit 560 Mb/s to carry approximately 8,000 digital channels. It is called SPCT 560 to provide digital connections between Paris provincial centers, using the basic design from CIT ALCATEL and SAT (Socie'te' Anonymede Te'le'communications) for the French Directorate General for Telecommunications (DGT) with the new Satellite broadband transmission capacity and 140 Mb/s microwave links. 70% of the network will then be digital by 1990.

- Proteon has a highspeed successor to its 10 Mbit/s token passing ring local network. ProNet 80 using a star configuration connects to 240 Digital Equipment Corp's Unibus or Multibus processors at a 120 Mbit/s signal rate, which translates into a throughput of 80 Mb/s.

- Security Pacific Company became Data Transport's first user Data Transport, a value-added packet network by MCI is the nearest market equivalent to AT&T's NET 1000 (which subsequently was terminated) or its regulated Accunet Packet Switched Service. MCI uses Northern Telcom's protocol assembler/disassembler (PAD) equipment, which can also be owned by the User.

- BOCs formulate Packet Switching Service, as they await FCC final decisions on strings tied to: location of switch in basic Telco, separate accounting procedures and clarification on ASYNC ASCII to X25 conversion rulings.
- Clear channel 64Kb/s that support data will not be available nationwide until the end of the century. Data will be provided by "restricted 64Kb/s" or 56Kb/s in America till then.
- AT&T's LAN based on 802.3 is called ST or LAN uses Unix System "Streams" and support Micro soft corp's MS-DOS 3.1 and MS-Net and 3Com's 3 + series software a series of seven applications packages to run on IBM Token Ring Ethernet and Starlan. The Unix "Streams" provide protocol and media interface so software developers can interface to Unix Kernel bypassing the hardware architecture on which Unix runs.
- Technology Insurance is becoming expensive, Lost in Space in 1984-5: BS-2—Japan, Westor VI Palapa B-2, Intelsat V F-9, Anik D-2 Arabsat 1A, Leasat 3, Leasat 4, Eutelsat ECS-3, SPACENET III at an insured value of $630 million.
- 1994 modems may cost $10 and be the size of a bug, as modems become components, with ISDN and the continuing "devolution" of modern technology into chips. Projected sales for 1990 are expected to dip and then double to 2 billion dollars for personal computer models supplied by Hayes ($80 M 1985), U.S. Robotics ($16.6M), Novation ($16M), Ventel ($15M) Rkon ($14M), UDS ($8M), Anchor Automation ($7M), Racal Vadic ($2.3M), and data terminals modems: AT&T ($202M), Codex Motorola ($148M), Racal-Milgo ($136M), Paradyne ($135M), Racal-Vadic ($100M), General Data Comm ($70M), UDS ($57.5), IBM ($46.5M).
- Key systems market (1985) looked like: AT&T (26%), TIE (20%), ITT (17%), Executone (3%), Toshiba (3%), Iwatsu (4%), NEC (5%), others 22% of a 2 billion dollar market, as proliferation of key system makers compete.
- COLAN—or Central Office based LAN may be called a high speed digital link in which voice and data is multiplexed together to a Centrex/Data Switch splitter and then handled respectively by the separate switches with data muxed at the 19.2Kbs rate using AT&T Data Kit Switching and special purpose DUVs made by General Data communication—DATAX 2000 voice data/voice multiplex with rates of 300 bits to 19.2 kilobits per sec. over twisted pair (unloaded).

PRODUCT STRATEGIES

- Expanded/enhanced Centrex will challenge PBXs with extended features once CI III + and the Huber strategy enable storage and forwarding of digitized voice, message services and database operations.
- If all of 1930 degree resentments are removed, IBM may be allowed to sell

- Information Generation
  - Information Transfer
    - Information Storage
      - Information Transfer
        - Information Retrieval
          - Information Transfer
            - Information Manipulation
              - Information Transfer
                - Information Presentation

Fig. 14-13. Information Flow.

software as part of hardware transactions to stop plug compatible SNA looks likes—AT&T's IBM PC compatible systems.
- European Computer Manufacturers Association ECMA has chosen IBM'S peer to peer Computer Linking Interface (Logical Unit 6.2), as a basis for the transaction processing protocol for the open systems interconnection (OSI) model, but this decision was challenged.
- IBM's token ring supports IEEE 802.5 Standard and General Motors Manufacturing Automation Protocol MAP. IBM's local area network software NET-BIOS has become a defacto standard for LAN software. IBM also has a 2 Mbits LAN (PC Network), as another microprocessor LAN.
- New top of the line processors by Cray (Cray II), IBM (3090) Burroughs and Data General are competing with new Japan family for speed and quality.
- AT&T's ACCUNET T45, a 44.73 Mbit/s long distance service, provides the equivalent of 5 to 8 T1 lines depending on distance with a short haul version called METROBUS.
- Japan makes 98% of world's facsimile machines. By 1990 there will be 2 million facsimile machines in Japan alone, using a Group 3 standard with a technique that can zip off a single page letter in less than a minute. A very fast borderline Group 3/4 facsimile gear like the NEC model (once used by Federal Express in its terminated ZAPMAIL service) can send a page in 3 seconds at 56 Kb/s. The more advanced Group 4 facsimile standard will send packets of data and connect directly to computer lines. It is being defined under the auspices of CCITT and should be an ISDN standard by 1990.
- IBM made arrangements to resell Stratus Computer's fault tolerant processor and Bytex's Matrix switches.
- PBXs are integrating local area network packet transport capabilities and

integrated voice/data terminal interfaces to their systems as well as the ability to tie two PBXs together; as seen in the AT&T System 75 and System 85 interface to their Information Systems Network (ISN) (8.65 Mb/s); the SL-1 and its Merideon (a high speed 40 megabits transport Bus using one or more T1/DS-1 channels to the SL/1 circuit switch), and Rolm's CBX-11 and IBM's Token Ring (16 Mb/s), as well as interfaces to the IBM PC 3270 terminal located between S and T at NT1 interface with Nodal switches between T and U at the U interface.

- Protocol conversion system such as IBM Series 1, Protocol computers, GTE Telenet, Dynatech, Amdahl, Ark, Datastream, and Dynapac have extensive competition in ASCII to IBM protocol conversion systems and dropping prices; but there will be new opportunity in ASYNC to X25 conversations.

- Users don't care about ISDN for their PBXs, it is more a central office feature. They are more interested in what PBX office systems can do for their data terminals to network them together and move files of information.

- CRAY 2 super computer was unveiled in 1986 as a 1 billion instruction per second, 246 billion word memory and 4.1 nanosec clockcycle. IBM may follow with a vector processor able to process many similar operations using general purpose processing as front end systems, similar to ILIAC IV objective in 1966.

- Illinois Bell issued a RFP for ISDN terminal equipment; a CRT type terminal with two integrated phone jacks to connect to their ISDN loops, as well as a data-voice multiplex RFP.

- STC PLC a UK electronics firm has demonstrated chip technology for ISDN interface that T1D1.3 group of ANSI considered, as an American ISDN standard interface. The group ruled out the ping-pong method, as they look at echo canceling techniques using an adaptive equalizer and a dipulse code. STC promoted a 3B2T code which supports 144 Kb/s with a transmission frequency of 108Kb/s. With 600 million subscriber lines world wide, it is a game of high stakes for chip manufacturers.

- Dial up 56Kb/s service is a dial up version of 56Kb/s DDS called Public-Switched Digital Service (PSDS) for CSDS (Circuit Switched Digital Capability), once supported by central offices. Systems in San Francisco and Chicago will connect $3,000 to $5,000 CPE equipment with 12¢ to 10¢ per minute usage cost, enabling 56k DDS customers to save money on dial up, if usage is under 2 1/2 hours per day. However, the advantage is for applications where ubiquitous use is desired to interface to multiple destinations, using such terminals as 56K picturephone.

- IBM's file translator rate on its 4 Mbits data rate token ring, using 512 byte packet files between any two processes attached to the local network, may be less then 200Kb/s for disk to disk. By conducting searches and retrievals simultaneously with network transmission, this could speed up to 1 Mbit/s with best possible at 2.2 Mb/s transmission rates, using 10 MIPS processor on memory to memory transfer.

- The dial up 56Kb/s teleco-accunet service works out to be around $.90-1.00 a minute. It does enable concentration of users by a PBX to the local switch to reduce costs to around .80 to .90/minute and share $50/month local line/PBX trunk access costs, making it more attractive to the local area networks to be switched by the public network and removed from DDS, as clusters of small offices. However, it must still compete against point to point DDS, which has a $1,000 average access cost and $3,000 for 1,000 mile distance cost. Hence, under $4,000-5,000 per month the user may still benefit from dial up switched access to multipoint locations. However, it is only for customers who can truly benefit from a higher speed (over a 2.4, 4.8, 9.6) digital data packet network. Video (56K) applications, that obviously generate higher usage, having terminals costing $50,-75,000 must still pay substantial costs for switched usage over point to point. Similar 1.5 Mbit/s higher resolution switched versus point to point considerations will still play a major role in attracting customers depending on price, as well as market packages for specific user groups. Here, price appears to be the deciding factor especially as FCC tariffs a carrier common line usage costs of 4¢/minute. This further drives large customers to bypass rather than remain on the switched network. Here, price must be viewed in terms of attracting *small, medium, and large* customers to use electronic public networks rather than use manual methods, separate private networks, or point to point networks.

- Display terminal customer controllers and modem manufacturers in Data Communications 1985 service indicated that they were becoming quite sophisticated in their terminal selection. Of the 2000 users interviewed, 1400 would recommend their terminal to another user with 200 undecided. The list of terminal manufacturers and available terminals has become quite impressive, as the terminals begin to internetwork in the 90s.
- High cost of high technology—ITT pulled plug on System 12 development after spending $165 million to bring Class 5 system switches and STP (Signal Transfer Point) systems to U.S. market having had orders from United Telephone of Florida, Century Telephone of Wisconsin and Bell South to field trial initial systems, as well as with Southern Bell and Pacific Bell for STPs. The move was to shift ITT focus to be overseas market. ITT's European companies had orders for about 10.75 million System 12 lines and 600,000 trunks or what ITT called 12 million "equivalent" lines. Many of those orders also included local manufacturing licenses, including a huge production deal in China. ITT's fourth-quarter $15 million loss came on sales of $6 billion. Net income for 1984's fourth quarter was $175 million on sales of $5.1 billion. The fourth quarter loss the result of the $160 million, or $1.13 per share, charge. ITT had said that without the charge, fourth quarter income would have totaled $145 million. For the year, ITT's net income fell 34 percent to $294 million or $1.89 per share, versus $448 million, or $2.97 per share, in 1984. Revenue in 1985 climbed 11 percent to $20 billion from previous year's restated $18 million. Finally, in mid 1986 ITT approached CGE France to sell them ITT's Telecommunication firms for approximately one and one half billion dollars, with 30% stock in joint venture.

- The Matrix switch fits into a network at a central site, such as a data processing center. Users channels connect to the Matrix switch. It does not switch channels to each other, but does enable the network manager to access and monitor otherwise dedicated computers to establish or deactivate any connection or reconfigure any portion of the network and enable rapid rerouting as a network controller.
- Technology advances, as a 32 bit transputer—a building block computer on a chip operating at 10 MIPS with OCCAM language—considered to be one of the fastest computers on a chip. It can be used in arrays, as a computing surface with hundreds linked together for video and data future broadband networks.
- Northern Telcom's PBX family Merideon, in which the smallest model comes with three commonly used operating systems (MS/DOS, CP/M and UNIX Level V), all work under Northern's proprietary operating system called XMS (Extended Management System). The larger models of the line currently have XMS, Xenix and UNIX and in time will have MS/DOS and CP/M. The Merideon based local network is provided on a double bus scheme of 40 Mbit/s as a "transport" for information flow and a 100 Mbit/s transport for administration and control.
- A central processor polls terminals for voice or data packets. The data network operates over two standard twisted pair wiring within a 4,000 foot diameter with up to several thousand terminals at 2.56 Mb/s. The Merideon line includes an X.25 gateway, a gateway to IBM's Systems Network Architecture (SNA), a gateway to Microsoft's MSNET local network (similar to IBM's PC network) and to the computer to PBX interface CPI, developed by Northern for DEC. Merideon features: windowing, voice and text, ICONs resembling Macintosh, Wang like word processing software, built in spreadsheets and a mouse.
- Per Mr. Phillips, a system protocol specialist, protocol converters can be located at numerous locations such as:

  - An asynchronous software driver resident in a host or front end processor.
  - A protocol converter can take the place of an SNA/SDLC 3278 controller between the synchronous host and asynchronous terminals.
  - Converter may connect to a single ASCII device.
  - A combination of protocol hardware and software may reside within a terminal.

- Protocol converters will play an ever increasing role to achieve: device independence, multiple protocols and hosts, additional security, programmable terminal support, modifiable character sets, printer passthrough, floating printer support, micro computer support, local networking that allows a multipoint, multiprotocol product which can be interconnected through a token passing network protocol and a distribution network, that uses a central unit communicating with small remote units by a private protocol. Packages such as DISOSS and Architectures such as APPC (Advanced Program to Program Communication) will allow protocol converters to support various manufacturers' word processing and office automation packages. Finally the connection of clusters of terminals such as IBM's personal computer 3270 over X.25 network. Integrated security such as proprietary error detection and recovery protocols on the asynchronous side, integrated secure dial-back hardware and built in Data Encryption Standards will be areas for future protocol converters.

- Telemanagement—call accounting, tracking moves, trouble log, bill reconciliation is becoming a major requirement for PBXs.

INFORMATION SERVICE STRATEGIES

Two powerful economic driving forces are changing manufacturing:

- First, to automate manufacturing by using computer controlled machines and robots, and to automate the flow of control of information in the factory from design to inventory to orders. This enables common lines to handle either a few special purpose systems, a limited production runs of various products, large three shift production runs, or separate lines for prototypes. This would enable a plant to have the flexibility of short production runs and allow different products from the same assembly line, as well as link islands of the factory together per product.
- Second, to automate the office behind the factory. Those who handle information rose from 45% (1960) to 56% (1983). One analyst's view of the office is: "that executives consist of 1% of the labor force and are 1% of the cost; designers are 19% of the labor force and 17% of the costs; operators are 8% of the force and 8% of the costs, and managers, security and operating staff are 66% of the force and 75% of the costs. Hence the information need for designers, managers, operation and staffs should address 90% of the costs and enable a 'Network of Conversations' to drastically improve the 'Content of the Conversations' from a business production perspective."
- Example: GM purchased Electronic Data Systems (EDS) and Hughes aircraft including Hughes Communications for 8 billion, where one of EDS's first tasks, at about 2 billion per year, was to automate and network GM's information based activities from management and accounting through inventory control, car design and control of manufacturing into a united global system using a 400 million dollar telecommunications network for GM's 250,000 telephones and thousands of computers to trim a 200 million annual phone bill and save in 10 years 360 million dollars in long distance charges.
- Result: The value of a machine in integrated facilities rises by the number of machines it can communicate unimpeded.
- Open Standards versus Open Architecture where Terminal A will be able to communicate with Terminal B may end up with two standards:
  — *OSI* will be the basis for manufacturing protocols MAP and Boeing's de-

sign automation protocol TOP as well as DCNA and ISA.

— *SNA* (IBMs) will be the alternative protocol as LANs and WANs are developed over the years, using various types of Nodal point systems to interface with the terminals and the network.

- Intelligent Terminal using powerful chip processors and megabit memory chips will continue to compete and challenge the common usage Intelligent Network Services.
- GSA (U.S. General Service Administration) requires a $450 million/year integrated network that must be capable of handling 1.5 Mb/s data services and full motion video and voice.
- Repair, Maintenance, Training and Credit and Leasing are offering 25% more revenue to computer firms. Though many firms are attempting to capitalize on training, some firms such as IBM and Computer Apple are working with firms to offer low cost training to encourage customer acceptance and understanding to promote usage and further sales.
- Britain's emphasis on futuristic research to prepare for the next phase of ISDN to make the best use of simultaneous voice, data and video is in two projects, Adminal and Unison, where both use star 2.048 megabit networks from British Telecom PTC.
- Adminal collaborators' British Telecom Marconi Research Center of Britain's General Electric Co., PLC and two university computer laboratories' task is to develop network management architectures, distributed computer techniques, and protocols for multimedia calls.
- Unison project is a collaboration of two vendors Logical VTS LTD, Acorn Computers LTD and three academic computer labs to link local networks and develop multimedia services, such as: file transfer and preparation of documents, using Cambridge Rings invented by Andrew Hopper called FASTRING, resembling IBM Token passing local network, using speed chip sets forming 8 bit interfaces to link rings together to a central ring, which can be made into a fast switch. The development of the switch will form a natural interface between the 8 Mb/s wideband Fastring networks and 2 Mb/s lines being installed by British Telcom.
- New publicly accessible database were growing, as new businesses at the rate of three per day in 1985. Databases, despite problems with videotex (easy to use data communicators) for the home, were growing as numerous specialized databases were developed such as: "electronic clipping service," which searched for information under key word headings. 1985 revenues were around 2 billion, up from 1984 revenues of 1.6 billion. During the initial formation period:

  — Dun and Bradstreet spent 101 million to buy Data Service and then 1.2 billion to purchase Nielsen, a market research line.
  — Gulf and Western spent $700 million to purchase Prentz-Hall.
  — News American spent $350 million for acquisition of Ziff-Davis' business publication.
  — McGraw-Hill's 55 million stock quotation distributor.

- Dow Jones and Oklahoma Publishing Co.'s $459 million purchase of 52% of Telerate, an electronic financial database about mortgage backed securities.
- Older firms, such as Reuters, now obtain 85% revenues from electric databases.
- France's anticipated Minitel's payback of 100 dollar terminal give away, will be three to four years from phone directories and database services revenues.
- Doctors pay $10 to check patient for previous malpractice suits, using "Physicians Alert."
- Easynet will provide user access to other networks such as Dialog, Mead, Newsnet and can also be a library.
- Dec and Honeywell have office videotex.
- IBM has Trintex and International Market Network—an international videotex network, a videotex research center and a videotex development group.

- Videotex is becoming a universal term meaning access to information. It is not necessarily limited to using ASCII.
- France has considerable success with "Chat" and computer games offerings, as people talk to each other via terminals.
- Though 88 million firms have TV sets, the real market for viewtron was the unused TV, that was not competing with television programs and was not a terminal costing $600.00.
- Trintex, a videotex venture with IBM, CBS and Sears Roebuck may cost $100 million for promotional expenses alone. It is planned to be a national full graphics capability videotex service, providing information, entertainment, advertising and shopping.
- AT&T, Time Inc, Bank America Corp. and Chemical Bank have formed Covideo.
- Britain's Prestal Videotex service began a financial service that grew to 2 million accesses in the first four months.
- For database transactions $.10 of every user's dollar goes to packet networks; who some estimate obtain 20-30% of their $300 million (1984) from electronic database publishers.
- ILL Bell offers remote access directory assistance service called "Directory Express" as test case for BOC's ability to provide database services. If allowed, terminals could be given away, similar to French situation so other firms may provide news, weather, home banking and shopping services and pay the BOC for access. The result is videotex!!
- National Security Decision Directive (NSDD) 145 suggest concern for a new category of information as sensitive but unclassified government or government or government derived information, whose loss could harm national security; such data, a defense official, during a congressional hearing, said could include: banking transactions, medical records and social security files—"Big Brother?"

- Instant Information versus Printed Information grew from 25% in 1975 to 75% (1988).

ISDN STRATEGIES

- ISO proposed a 14 digit standard worldwide zip code for public data networks, an 8 digit standard for Telex, a 12 digit format for public telephone networks, and a 15 digit format for future ISDN networks.
- Europe and America have had different ISDN network interface approaches over issues of time division multiplex or echo cancellation as basic interface, which effect chip manufactures strategies.
- X400 services data messaging protocol rides on top of recommended X25 network protocols in which P1 (the envelope) message transfer protocol and P2 the message content multimedia body enables flexibility to handle existing feature sets of electronic mail vendors and the RTS (reliable transfer services) serve. It enables a series of intermediary communications commands that act as a buffer between the presentation layer and the session layer.
- X32 a public dial up X25 standard for the public network will enable 1.2, 2.4 and 4.8 Kb/s (synchronous and full duplex) rates and various methods to identify users to the network. It can also be used across multiple users of a Telenet version. It may represent the future of packet switching.
- BITNET that links 68 universities in the U.S. and Canada through 188 nodes will be the catalyst for a European Academic and Research Network (EARN), financed by IBM, it will meet CCITT X.25, X.28 and X.21 protocols to link 300 university notes in 10 European Countries and Israel.
- AT&T has 9 offerings, which should be addressed, as to the role they will play in their overall Universal Information Network— ISDN transition per DATA COMMUNICATIONS:

  - CSDC (Circuit Switched Digital Capability) being sold to the operating companies by AT&T network systems. Converts analog local loop to 56-kbit/s digital channel. Uses time-compression multiplexing. First example of high-speed digital upgrade of local analog plant. 5E4 (Software module under development for the 5ESS). Along with hardware modules, will put primary-and basic-rate ISDN Interfaces on the 5ESS. Will ultimately process ISDN calls and recover from anomalies.

  - RSMs (Remote switching modules) distributed pieces of a 5ESS linked to a central 5ESS as extensions of internal circuitry. As ISDN Unfolds on 5ESS, same features on RSM. 36 installed in central offices as of March 1985.

  - DCP (Digital Communications Protocol) links PBX with terminal or telephone. Two 64-kbit/s information channels. Main difference from ISDN basic-rate interface; signalling channel is 8, not 16, kbit/s.

— DS1 (Digital Signalling Level 1) links PBXs and increasingly, PBXs to central offices. 23 64-kbit/s information channels (currently limited by bit-robbing). Signalling channel more rudimentary than that of ISDN Primary-rate interface, since DS1 is based on existing T1 technology.

— DCS (Distributed Communications System) data link between AT&T PBXs. Has subset of ISDN features. Unifies multilocation private networks. Could let user on one PBX see name of person calling from a telephone on another PBX.

— SDNS (Software-Defined Network Service) lets users manage and reconfigure a network's bandwidth on a channel-by-channel basis. AT&T views it as part of ISDN. Analysts views it as precursor that will be incorporated.

— DACS (Digital Access and Cross-Connect System) digital central-office hardware. Allows 64-kbit/s channels, currently as part of T1-capacity services, to be reconfigured from a terminal. Needed to reconfigure a flexible ISDN-type backbone network. Part of ISDN's supporting structure, not a user offering. May be replaced over time.

— CCR (Customer-Controlled Reconfigurability) lets customers run their DACS. Changes can be made in real time or according to a preplanned map. Follows ISDN principle of users managing their network resources. Uses control signals different from, but evolvable to, ISDN standards.

- ISDN standards for basic rate 144 Kb/s or 2B(64K) channels and 1D (16K) channel) and primary rate (American (1.544 Mb/s or 23B + 1 64K D channels) and European (2.048 b/s or 30B + 2-64K D channels)) were vigorously pursued by The Exchange Carriers Standards Association (ECSA) and by TIDI on accredited standards activity under the American National Standards Institute (ANSI). Line interfaces needed to be stabilized by the end of 1986 before chip manufacturers could design VLSI chips for use in new systems. The physical interface level for primary rate uses T1 two pair wiring and transmission techniques, and an echo cancellation (European, Japanese preference) or time compression multiplexing (American preferred). The D channel protocol facilitates control and signalling between customer site and the ISDN network. The Link Level protocol is referred to as LAP-D or link access procedure for the D channel is a permutation of LAP-B link protocol of X.25.
- Five million lines of Plessey's System X for British Telecom in 1987 at about $1.5 billion begins Britain's move into the information era, enabling reployment of electromechanical "data noisy" offices to provide single ISDN lines to support 64K and 8K channels. Systems X suppliers are Plessey and PLC.

Ericsson will supply about 800,000 lines of AXE10, while a North American supplier faces $50 million for re-engineering a major switch to this European market and are not as competitive.

- ISO has developed a universal addressing scheme to accommodate virtually every form of switched voice and data communications known, so future generations would have a common format for addressing and network routing of everything from Telex messages to local networks to packet data to long distance international telephone voice calls. It has called it the Draft Information Standard (DIS) or officially the Network Layor Addressing Plan DIS8348/DAD2 as an addendum to the larger ISO Network Services Definition, issued by ISO's TC97/SC6 committee. It will accommodate CCITT X.121 addressing for public data network (14 decimal digits); CCITT F.69—the Telex numbering plan (8 digits); CCITT E.167—the number plan for public switched telephone networks (12 digits); CCITT E.164—the futuristic ISDN numbering plan (15 digits); ISO DCC—for geographic defined addressing using 4 digit Data Country Code; ISO 6523 ICD binary or digital data device addressing using a 4 digit International Code Designator prefix, that identifies specific organization's International Networks, such as NATO, and the ISO-OSI binary data device addressing including 48-50 bit local network addresses, network service access point (NSAP) and so on.

- It uses a 20-octet field, if the address is binary encoded, or 40 character field, if composed of decimal characters. It will be the cornerstone for what the ISO open systems architecture is to achieve with regard to integrated voice and data. As an example, the first two decibel digits may indicate that an ISO DCC specified address follows and that it is binary encoded, the next four octets indicate the countries network, then 4 octets identify destination organization, two more octets specify the specific organization network or local network, and the last seven octets are the actual device address.

- IEEE'S 802.4 has defined a token passing standard for a media access control protocol (MAC) for central access to broadcast medium as well as 802.3 and 802.5 LAN Standards. They have become the U.S. Standards which the world computer industry must address, as well as new PBX's and CCITT working groups.

- X9.17 is a new security standard for American Banking Association, that will enhance X9.9, the Financial Institution Message Authentication Standard (FIMAS), to make it more widely accepted by the banking industry, as a process by which messages, that financial institutes receive from each other, can be verified. It was defined by ANSI working group X9E9, as a complementary standard called Financial Institution Key Management Standard X9.17.

GOVERNMENTAL STRATEGIES

- FCC rulings for data packet network were that basic Telcos must use separate Accounting Techniques and must charge themselves the circuit rate rather than book rate for digital links between packet switch and PADS.

- The services arenas of competitive offerings and charges for usage and access have become an on going saga as we see:

  - Ability to have interLATA provided by Telco tied to intraLATA competition.
  - Ability to have STS (Shared Tenant Service) question the very existence of the LATA Telco monopoly.
  - The access charges of $2 to $1.00 for the needy, to large user discounts to eliminate bypass, as well as interexchange revenue pool sharing's algorithms changed to discourage bypasses in more competitive regions— are areas to be resolved.
  - The local switch usage costs and trunk access usage costs to interexchange carriers needs to be further defined to discourage bypass and encourage local network usage.
  - To provide open architecture, to remove bottleneck, to enable open competition on information services, to provide non- regulated offerings of basic and enhanced services by basic Telco and its subsidiaries, to use separate cost accounting all need clearer definition over the 80s, during the ISDN formation period.
- The 1987 Huber analysis, adapted by Justice in their recommendation to Judge Greene, indicated allowing full competition by BOCs in all arenas other than interexchange (until "local monopoly" issues are resolved). This enabled BOC full data transport and information processing as well as manufacturing.

STRATEGY OF THE STRATEGIES

- The telecommunications industry's status in the late 80s was summed up by this users' observation: "Much is being said nowadays about the sales slump in the data processing hardware industry. Until now, sales representatives were mainly 'order takers.' Due to their clients' increased sophistication, however, the situation has changed drastically. What we found in our contacts with the vendors was that salespeople did not know intimately the products they were trying to sell, let alone those of their competitors. When we asked sales representatives questions about the data communications specifications of their products, we mostly received an absurd and wrong answer or a request to hold the question until they could bring in a data communications expert. If industry wants to increase its slow sales, it needs to upgrade the technical quality of its sales teams."
- There is growing acceptance that the transition of the telecommunications industry is far from complete in that the overall structure will be an evolving one for many years where technology, consumer needs, changing major/minor players, and new political and regulatory philosophies will occur, as regulators grapple with access charge, competition, bypass, equal access, and universal service questions, as well as Federal preemption over

State decisions on turf issues.

- Management has moved from *time and motion* (people as machines), to *human relations* (people with human needs, goals, desires), to *computer science* (efficiency via models), to *systems management* (work as part of an overall system), to *limited participatory management* (everyone working together with limited individual power), to *situations management* (different management styles depending on the situation), to *financial management* (bottom line for Wall Street as short term profit as the driving force of major decisions), to *management by conflict* (top division leaders fight it out), to *management by consensus* (Japan's solution to obtain group members' agreement participation and commitment). The 80s then showed a mixture of financial management and participation management with some system management in terms of computer science efficiently models—setting the stage for the new "P" manager planner.
- Planning—The 80s became a new battleground between central and decentral organization control, as some firms reduced central staff to give units more responsibility to plan there own destinies. However, as the units were required to be more market driven, they found their customers required integrated solutions, using products from other units. This produced a dilemma which was further expanded by the high cost of high technology. The need for the long range look of several years to incorporate future products offerings with existing or near term products into an integrated network offering became the essential key to success, requiring a new level of planning at the unit and at the centralized holding company to take advantage of the complete resources of the firm. This also required merges and/or joint partnerships between suppliers and suppliers, between suppliers and providers, and between providers and providers, within the communication industry, within the computer industry, and across both industries.

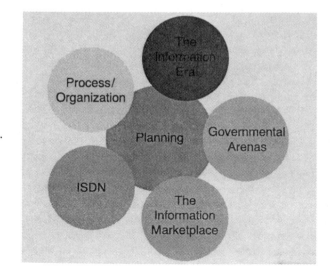

Fig. 14-14. Planning the Information Game.

Seven: A Final Look at Playing the Game

This book has attempted to show the issues and questions that must be addressed as working relationships, using planning and technology transfer processes, are established within recognized forums, such as ECSA—T1. An excellent example of the complexity of the game and the need for these relationships is the standards arena. Suppliers can no longer provide a formidable array of products for the providers without achieving agreements before development across fellow suppliers with the new and traditional providers. In the past, AT&T had dominated standards, some say with a competitive edge. As a result of divestiture many (some say too many) suppliers and providers are now heavily involved in identifying standards for user terminals to access the network, such as the early Basic Access User-Network S/T CCITT Recommendations. In the late 80s, the game became more intense as it shifted to address and resolve the many remaining standards, such as the primary rate U interface.

To understand the game is to understand the complexity of the play. Hence we will close this book of Telecommunications Management Planning with a detailed analysis of the ever-changing standards arena, as it is being actually played by the now seasoned and experienced players. Let us review how new standards are being identified, addressed and resolved. These agreements will form the basis for the ISDN Networks of the 90s, in preparation for the wideband (broadband) ISDN networks of the 21st century.

In Chapter 9, we saw the vision of the future presented by President Hudson of Northern Telecon. Now let us review the implementation considerations presented by BNR and Northern Telecon under the direction of Mr. Eckhart, Mr. Chattoe, and Mr. Yuen, as expressed eloquently in Telesis 1986 by Fung, Luetchford, and Scales:

"Successful deployment of ISDN will depend on the network's capability to maintain customer service continuity during the changeover to ISDN, while also offering new ISDN standard services. Some standards are not sufficiently mature for product and network development to proceed. The resolution of these standards issues is under active consideration in CCITT and in U.S. standards bodies, such as the Exchange Carrier Standards Association (ECSA) T1D1 subcommittee under the American National Standards Institute (ANSI).

"Key standards issues that must be resolved during this phase relate to the U-interface, access signalling protocols, data rate adaptation, and interworking between ISDN and existing numbering plans and networks.

"U-interface: The U-interface refers to the two-wire loop transmission system that conveys information between the four-wire, user-to-network interface (S/T—reference point) and the local exchange.

"When the first set of ISDN standards was ratified in 1984, the CCITT deliberately left the U-interface unspecified, and defined only a standard user-to-network, four-wire interface at the S/T reference point. By leaving the U-interface unspecified, the CCITT hoped to encourage the development of loop transmission systems that would be developed independently from terminal equipment connected at the S/T reference point. Regulatory considerations in the U.S., however, have resulted in the initiation of discussions in the T1D1 subcommittee of ECSA to develop a standard loop transmission interface at the U-reference point. At the ISDN '85 Symposium in Sandestin, Florida, the real merit of a U-interface standard emerged; namely, the availability of mass-market silicon devices for the digital loop.

"Access Signalling Protocols: There are a number of detailed issues with respect to access signalling that must be resolved before the initial implementation phase of ISDN. Current ISDN signalling protocols, defined in CCITT Recommendation Q.931, as well as Recommendation I.451 cover only basic call control. Extensions to basic call control, however, are required to cover access to such network features and supplementary services as hold, three-way calling, use of authorization codes, ring-again, and Key systems. These services, and others are currently being defined in CCITT and ECSA T1D1.

"In initial ISDN implementation, access to these network features can be accomplished using stimulus signalling, which provides a master-slave relationship between the network and the user. Stimulus signalling is based on the concept that the terminal reports feature key activation to the network; the network interprets the meaning of the specific feature activation and returns prompts to the user in the form of indicator-lamp states and audible tones. Use of stimulus signalling in the early trial period will guarantee that users, while migrating to ISDN, will maintain access to existing stimulus-oriented network features.

"Rate adaptation: Market success also requires a simple, low-cost, and readily available approach to rate adaptation, in order to ensure that existing data terminal equipment can be connected to the ISDN. The function of rate adaptation, performed in the terminal adapter, is to convert existing data rates (for example, 2400 bits per second) into 64-kilobit-per-second (kbit/s) B-channels. Because ISDN terminal equipment will ultimately use the full 64-kbit/s B-channel for data, rate adaptation—while initially essential in order to make use of existing terminals and technologies—is expected to be only an interim requirement.

"Two rate adaptation techniques are currently specified in CCITT: circuit mode and packet mode.

"Circuit mode, defined in CCITT Recommendation I.463, specifies rate adaptation of low bit-rate synchronous data into an 8-kbit/s subrate channel CCITT Recommendation. I.460 then specifies how the subrate channels are multiplexed into a 64-kbit/s channel. The packet-mode rate adaptation technique, defined in CCITT Recommendation I.462 (X.31), specifies that high level data link control (HDLC) flags (a specific 8-bit code) be repeatedly inserted into the channel bit stream, in order to increase the bit rate from the low bit-rate data input to the 64-kbit/s B-channel. HDLC is a protocol standard developed by the International Standards Organization (ISO).

"However, the circuit-switched data applications identified in the 1986-1987 field trials indicated that there is a major requirement to support existing asynchronous terminals; there are currently no CCITT ISDN Recommendations specifying rate adaptation for asynchronous terminals.

"BNR and Northern Telecom have recommended use of the Northern Telecom T-link rate adaptation technique. The major advantage of this technique is that it will support inter-working between ISDN circuit-switched data services and existing circuit-switched data services.

"BNR and Northern Telecom have also proposed enhancements to the I.463 Recommendation to provide for the longer term support of asynchronous terminals and interworking between ISDN components and existing network components. These enhancements are under active consideration in CCITT, ANSI-T1D1, and the European Computer Manufacturers Association (ECMA).

"Substantial agreement regarding the necessary additions to the standard has already been achieved in all three forums.

"ISDN numbering plan: Another important standards issue that must be addressed in the initial implementation phase of ISDN concerns numbering plans.

"Terminals connected to ISDN interfaces will be addressed using the ISDN numbering plan, defined in CCITT Recommendation I.331 (E.164). The ISDN numbering plan is based on the telephony numbering plan (Recommendation E.163) but provides additionally for network identification (network destination code). The ISDN numbering plan allows for up to 15 digits for the main address, compared to the telephony numbering plan that allows for only 12. Initial ISDN implementations in North America will continue to use the existing 10 digit North American numbering plan for both voice and data terminals. This is a valid subset of the ISDN numbering plan and will provide an optimal solution until ISDN becomes widely deployed.

"Current data network numbering plans (such as those defined in CCITT Recommendation X.121) are substantially different from the ISDN numbering plan. However, the ability of data terminals connected to the ISDN to communicate fully with data terminals connected to existing networks is a clear customer requirement. Consequently, specific arrangements must be agreed to for interworking between terminals addressed by different numbering plans.

"Substantial agreement is emerging for a long-term solution. This solution will provide a numbering and addressing plan indicator (NAPI) to indicate to the network the numbering plan of the destination terminal. For the short term, however, it is not practical to make the necessary changes to include NAPI in existing packet data networks or data terminal equipment connected to them. It is impractical simply because of the large number of these systems that exist.

"Thus, in order to meet early ISDN implementation needs, CCITT is evaluating a number of short-term solutions, based on using specific digits (known as escape codes) to indicate the numbering plan of the destination terminal. The approach adopted in initial ISDN implementations, in 1986-1987, is to use a unique data network identification code to "escape" into the ISDN numbering plan.

"Interworking: between numbering plans, equally important for the implementation and evolution of ISDN is the physical and protocol interworking between networks to meet existing service needs.

"During early implementation stages, many ISDNs will exist as islands. For market success, however, it is essential that these ISDN islands fully interwork with existing networks.

"Interworking between ISDN and existing packet data networks is currently specified in CCITT Recommendation I.462 (X.31). Substantial work is in progress in CCITT to provide more detailed interworking arrangements, including the necessary network requirements in the new I.500 Series of CCITT Recommendations.

"Initially, interworking of packet data connections between ISDNs, either connected directly or via existing packet data networks, will use an enhancement of existing CCITT Recommendation X.75, the packet gateway protocol between different packet networks.

"Required enhancements to X.75 include destination and transit network identification for routing requirements and for services, such as closed user group and call transfer, and requirements to allow for numbering plan interworking.

"To accommodate the increasing functionality required between ISDNs and packet data networks, vital to the business success of ISDN, a new network interworking interface has been proposed in CCITT. Examples of increasing functionality include indentification of data rate, bearer capability, negotiation of B- or D-channels on incoming calls, and data service requirements. It is expected that this new interface specification will be based on the ISDN primary rate interface, using the ISDN Q.931 out-of-band signalling protocol requirements.

"Interworking between ISDN and existing public-switched telephone networks (PSTN) is also, under leadership from BNR, being actively considered in CCITT. Typical examples of issues under debate include application of in-band tones and announcements versus the use of out-of-band D-channel signals, echo control arrangements in interworking situations, and the handling of voiceband modem traffic between PSTNs and ISDN.

"During the multi-node implementation stage of ISDN implementation, multiple ISDN nodes will be interconnected using common channel Signaling System No. 7 (SS7) in combination with digital transmission technology. SS7 has been adopted as the ISDN standard for out-of-band, digital signalling between network nodes. SS7, digital transmission technology, and standard signalling protocols will permit the network to offer features and services, including Centrex offerings, on a networkwide basis.

"Standards for network services, however, are currently in an immature state. The players have taken active roles in CCITT and T1D1 to consolidate the definitions of service features and signalling protocols to ensure consistency between access and network service standards.

"To assist in the development of the appropriate standards, standards-setting bodies are breaking service features down into elementary functions, or call-processing primitives. These elementary functions, called supplementary functional components (SFCs), can be used within different features, and they can be invoked using functional signalling. (Functional signalling is based on a peer-to-peer exchange of information between an intelligent terminal and the network.) Acceptance of SFCs is expected to expedite standardization in CCITT and T1D1 because SFCs would eliminate the need to agree on complex, bundled feature definitions.

"During this multinode implementation period, networking will be extended to PBXs via the ISDN primary rate interface (23B + D). This type of networking will permit service features on PBXs to interact with service features that are available in the public network. The interaction will provide users with a more universal access to wider range of services, and will improve the revenue potential of network providers.

"Initial features will include calling line identification and networkwide ring-again, whereby a subscriber may request the network to complete a connection to a busy line once the line becomes idle. Other features, more appropriate to virtual private networks, include city-wide Centrex features, such as uniform dialing plans. These dialing plans will provide multilocation four-digit dialing and automatic route selection features.

"During this implementation large businesses that operate in multiple locations will be served by a mix of PBX and Centrex exchanges. It will be crucial, therefore, during the network feature design process to ensure uniform operation not only between Centrex-to-Centrex nodes, but also between Centrex-to-PBX nodes and PBX-to-PBX nodes. An objective is that the user's perception of features will be the same, whether the user is served by a PBX or a Centrex node.

"The implication of this from a standards point of view is that the access signalling protocols must be designed to support both user invocation of a feature (that is, from a terminal) and networking of that feature (that is, between the PBX and the network) in a consistent manner.

"The ISDN D-channel functional signalling protocol (CCITT Recommendation Q.931) in conjunction with the link layer protocol (CCITT Recommendation Q.921) will support the intelligent peer-to-peer communication required for feature networking.

"The same message-based functional signalling may also be implemented in intelligent workstations. This implementation will offer users a powerful signalling capability to access new network features and services, also to communicate across the network via user-to-user signalling. User-to-user signalling is an ISDN capability whereby messages may be exchanged via out-of-band signalling, on an end-to-end basis.

"Standard network interfaces would also include provision of call progress information to indicate interworking with non-ISDN portions of the network. Thus, an ISDN user internetworking with a non-ISDN part of the network will be informed that services such as user-to-user signalling will not be supported, and that further call progress information will be received as in-band tones and announcements rather than as out-of-band functional messages.

"The interaction of network services with OA&M features must also be considered during this phase. Existing protocols currently under consideration in standards bodies are the Transaction Capabilities Application Part (TCAP) of SS7 as well as Northern Telecom's Network Operations Protocol (NOP). TCAP and NOP are based on CCITT Recommendations X.409/X.410.

"Provided that improved consistency between TCAP and X.409 and X.410 can be achieved, TCAP will be used for accessing network databases and potentially, for supporting new inquiry transaction services (such as videotext and credit card validation).

"NOP will be used to support ISDN operations and maintenance, including the potential of new features such as on-line customer network management.

"Evolution beyond 1990. Here the single-node and multinode phases of ISDN introduction will lay the foundation for the evolution of ISDN. By 1990, basic standards to support access technology, signalling for basic call control, and commonly used network features are expected to be stable and implemented in a range of network products.

"Beyond 1990, ISDN capabilities will be further exploited for additional services, including new packet data services and broadband applications. Additional revenue opportunities will become available, and cost savings through increased network flexibility and integrated OA&M functions will be achieved. New standards will be necessary during this stage to provide for the integration of basic and supplementary service control procedures.

"Additionally, broadband ISDN will require a new range of standards, including broadband service descriptions and broadband interfaces, both between the user and the network. Broadband ISDN will also provide for additional interconnection capability between existing local area networks (LANs) and emerging voice and data LANs.

"With the emergence of a wide range of network services for narrowband and broadband ISDN, and the need for integrated network operations systems, substantial focus on network protocol reference models, such as an extension to the ISDN reference models, such as in CCITT Recommendation 1.320, will be required.

"A network vision only a few years ago, ISDN is rapidly becoming a reality, as it moves from concept to implementation. Although substantial progress has been made in the area of standards, much remains to be done. BNR, Northern Telecom, and Bell Canada are unequivocally committed to implementing ISDN standards and will continue to assume a leadership role in the CCITT and ANSI standards organizations. Comprehensive access and network standards are key to the commercial success of ISDN. We remain dedicated to the pursuit of practical standards that can be implemented to provide end-user benefits and cost reductions in the network."

These, fortunately for our children and our children's children, are the goals and objectives of most of the players of The Information Game.

R.K. Heldman

711

Technical Terms and Acronyms

A wise man once said, "Terminology is 75% of any endeavor." The computer and communication industries have developed their own particular acronyms and terms, which are presented here for reference:

ABS—Alternate Billing Service
ACB—Automatic Call Back
ACBC—Automatic Callback Calling
ACD—Automatic Call Distribution
ACE—Automatic Calling Equipment
ACF—Advanced Communications Function
ACK—Automatic Message Acknowledgement
ACM—Association for Computing Machinery
A/D—Analog-to-Digital conversion
ADCCP—Advanced Data Communications Control Procedure
ADM—Add Drop Multiplexer
ADP—Automatic Data Processing
ADPCM—Adaptive Differential Pulse Code Modulation
ADTS—Automated Digital Terminal System
AEO—Analog End Office
AEPL—Acoustic Echo Path Loss
AFIPS—American Federation of Information Processing Societies
ALU—Arithmetic Logic Unit
AMA—Automatic Message Accounting

AM—Amplitude Modulation
ANI—Automatic Number Identification
ANSI—American National Standards Institute
APL—A Programming Language
ARQ—Automatic Message Repeat Request
ARPA—Advanced Research Project Agency
ASCII—American National Standard Code for Information Interchange
ASR—Automatic Send/Receive
AT—Access Tandem
ATM—Automated Teller Machine
ATPS—Access Tandem Packet Switch
ATTIS—AT&T Information Systems
AVD—Alternate Voice/Data

B8RZ—Bipolar violation every 8th pulse to Zero
B8ZS—Bipolar with 8 Zero Substitution
BANCS—Bell Administrative Network Communications System
BASIC—Beginner's All-purpose Symbolic Instruction Code
BCC—Block Check Character
BCD—Binary-Coded Decimal
BCG—B-Channel Gateway
BER—Bit Error Rate
BERT—Bit Error Rate Test
Bisync—Binary Synchronous Communication
BITS—Building Integrated Timing Supply
BIU—Bus Interface Unit
BLER—Block Error Rate
BOC—Bell Operating Company
B/S—Bits/sec.
BTAM—Basic Telecommunications Access Method
BVA—Billing Validation Application
Byte—8 Bit Segments

CABS—Carrier Access Billing System
CAD—Computer-Aided Design
CADV—Combined Alternate Data
CAI—Computer-Aided Instruction
CAM—Computer-Aided Manufacturing
CAMIS—Construction Activities Management Information Sys.
CAROT—Centralized Automatic Reporting On Trunks
CATV—Community Antenna Television
CBEMA—Computer Business Equip Manufacturers Association
CBX—Computerized Branch Exchange
CC—Common Control
CC—Country Code
CCC—CSDC Control Center
CCC—Clear Channel Capability

CCIA—Computer and Communications Industry Association
CCIS—Common Channel Interoffice Signaling
CCITT—International Telegraph and Telephone Consultative Committee
CCRS—Centrex Customer Rearrangement System
CCS—Hundred Call Seconds
CCS—Common Channel Signaling
CDAC—CSDC Design and Analysis
CEPT—Conference of European Postal and Telecommunications Administrations
C/F—Call Forwarding
CGA—Carrier Group Alarm
CI II—Computer Inquiry II
CI III—Computer Inquiry III
CICS—Customer Information Control System
CIIS—Customer Input and Inquiry System
CIMAP—Circuit Installation and Maintenance Assistance Package
CLASS—Customized Local Area Signaling Services
CMOS—Complementary Metal Oxide Semiconductor
CMS-1—Circuit Maintenance System-1
CMS-3—Circuit Maintenance System-3
CO—Central Office
COBOL—Common Business Oriented Language
COE—Central Office Equipment
COER—Central Office Equipment Reports
COF—Central Office Facility
COSMOS—Computer System for Mainframe Operations
COT—Central Office Terminal
CPC—Circuit Provisioning Center
CPE—Customer Premises Equipment
CP/M—Control Program for Microcomputers
CPMS—Cable Pressure Monitoring System
CPU—Central Processing Unit
CR—Carriage Return
CRC—Cyclic Redundancy Check
CRN—Customer Reconfigurable Network
CRSAB—Centralized Repair Service Attendant Bureau
CRT—Cathode-Ray Tube
CS—Circuit Switch
CSA—Carries Serving Area
CSDC—Circuit Switched Digital Capability
CSMA/CD—Carrier-Sense Multiple Access/Collision Detection
CSU—Channel Service Unit
CTS—Clear To Send
CTX—Centrex
CVSD—Continuous Variable-Slope Delta Modulation
C/W—Call Waiting

D—D Channel
D/A—Digital to Analog
DACS—Digital Access and Cross-connect System
DAS—Digital Assignment System
DASD—Direct-Access Storage Device
DBAS—DataBase Administration System
dB—Decibel
DBMS—DataBase Management System
DCC—Data Country Code
DCE—Data Circuit-Terminating Equipment
DCO—Digital Central Office
DCP—D-Channel Processor
DCPR—Detailed Continuing Property Record
DCS—Digital Cross-Connect System
DCT—Digital Carrier Trunk
DDCMP—Digital Data Communications Message Protocol
DDD—Direct Distance Dialing
DDP—Distributed Data Processing
DDS—Digital Data System
DEMUX—Demultiplexer
DEO—Digital End Office
DES—Data Encryption Standard
DFB—Distributed Feedback Laser
DFT—Digital Facility Terminal
DICT—Direct Inter-LATA Connecting Trunk
DID—Direct Inward Dialing
DIF—Digital Interface Frame
DIG—Digital
DIP—Dual In-line Pin
DLC—Digital Loop Carrier
DMA—Direct Memory Access
DMS-100—An NTI Central Office Switch
DNA—Digital Network Architecture
DNA—Dynamic Network Architecture
DNIC—Data Network Identification Code
DOD—Department Of Defence
DOS—Disk Operating System
DOTS—Digital Office Timing Supply
DPBX—Digital Private Branch Exchange
DPC—Destination Point Code
DR—Draft Recommendation
DS-0—Digital Signal level 0 (64 Kb/s)
DS-1—Digital Signal level 1 (1.544 Mb/s)
DS-1C—Digital Signal level 1C
DS-2—Digital Signal level 2
DS-3—Digital Signal level 3

DSA—Digital Serving Area
DSAC—Dialing Services Administration Center
DSC—Digital Service Center
DSI—Data Subscriber Interface
DSL—Digital Subscribers Line
DSN—Digital Service Node
DSU—Data Service Unit
DSX-0—DS-0 Cross Connect Frame
DSX-1—Digital Signal Cross-connect level 1
DTE—Data Terminal Equipment
DTMF—Dual Tone Multi-Frequency
DVO—Data Voice Office
DX—Destination Exchange

E-O—Electro-Optic
E1-TIRKS—Equipment Component System
EADAS/NM—Engineering and Administrative Data Acquisition System/Network Management
EBCDIC—Extended Binary Coded Decimal Interchange Code
EC—Equipment Controller
ECL—Emitter Coupled Logic
ECSA—Exchange Carrier Standards Association
EDP—Electronic Data Processing
EFB—Error Free Block
EFds—Error Free decisecond
EFRAP—Exchange Feeder Route Analysis Program
EFT—Electronic Funds Transfer
EHF—Extremely High Frequency
EIA—Electronic Industries Association
EM—Electromechanical
EMI—Electromagnetic Interference
EOA—End Of Address
EOB—End Of Block
EOM—End Of Message
EOT—End Of Transmission
EPROM—Erasable Programmable Read-Only Memory
EPS—Engineering and Planning System
EQTV—Extended Quality Television
ERL—Echo Return Loss
ES—Errored Second
ESF—Extended Super Frame Format
ESFDL—Extended Super Frame Data Link
ESS—Electronic Switching System
ET—Exchange Termination
ETB—End of Transmitted Block
ETN—Electronic Tandem Network

ETS—Electronic Tandem Switch
ETX—End Of Text

FACS—Facility Assignment and Control System
FAR—First Application Region
FCC—Federal Communications Commission
FDM—Frequency-Division Multiplexing
FEC—Forward Error Correction
FED—Far End Data
FEP—Front-End Processor
FEPS—Facility and Equipment Planning System
FEV—Far End Voice
FIPS—Federal Information Processing Standard
FM—Frequency Modulation
FMAC—Facility Maintenance and Administration Center
FN/SI—Feature Node/Service Interface
FNSI—FN Signaling Interface
FOA—First Office Application
FORTRAN—Formula Translation Language
FSD—Feature Specification Document
FSK—Frequency-Shift Keying
FX—Foreign Exchange

G—Giga—Prefix meaning one billion
GaAs—Gallium Arsenide (crystalline material)
Gb/s—Giga (Billion) bits per second
GDS/SSDAC—Generic Dispatch System/Special
GEN NTWK—Generation Network
GOC-TIRKS—0 Generic Order Control Component System
GOPL—"Good Old" Private Line
GOS—Grade of Service
GOSCAL—Grade of Service Calculator Program
GRIN-ROD—Gradient Index Rod

HALS—Hindered Amine Light Stabilizers
HASP—Houston Automatic Spooling Program
HCDS—High Capacity Digital Service
HCFE—High Capacity Front End
HDLC—High level Data Link Control
HDTV—High Definition Television
Hz—Hertz
HRX—Hypothetical Reference

IAM—Initial Address Message
IBT—Illinois Bell Telephone
IC—Inter-LATA Carrier
ICA—International Communications Association
ICC—Installation Control Center
IDCMA—Independent Data Communications Manufacturers Assoc.
IDLC—Integrated Digital Loop Carrier
IDN—Integrated Digital Network
IEC—Interexchange Carrier
IEEE—Institute of Electrical and Electronics Engineers
I/F—Interface
IF—Intermediate Frequency
IF—Interworking Functions
IFIPS—International Federation of Information Processing Soc.
IMS/VS—Information Management System/Virtual Storage
INA—Integrated Network Access
INE—Intelligent Network Elements
I/O—Input/Output
IO—Integrated Optics
IP—Intelligent Peripheral
IPL—Initial Program Load
IPM—Interruptions Per Minute
IPS—Integrated Provisioning System
IRC—International Record Carrier
ISC—International Switching Center
ISDN—Integrated Services Digital Network
ISO—International Organization for Standardization
ISSN—Integrated Special Services Network
ISUP—ISDN User Part
ITCAP—Integrated TOC-Based Costing Analysis Program
ITS—Integrated Test System
ITU—International Telecommunications Union
ITW—Integrated Test Workstation
IU—Interface Unit
IVDT—Integrated Voice/Data Terminal

JCL—Job Control Language
JES—Job Entry Subsystem
JMOS—Job Management Operations System

k—kilo = 1,000
Kb/s—Kilo (thousand) bits per second
KSR—Keyboard Send/Receive

LAC—Loop Assignment Center
LADT—Local Area Data Transport

LAN—Local Area Network
LAP—Link Access Procedure
LAPB—Link Access Protocol Balanced
LAPD—Link Access Protocol Delta channel
LATA—Local Access and Transport Area
LBRV—Low Bit Rate Voice
LD—Laser Diode
LDM—Limited-Distance Modem
LED—Light Emitting Diode
LEIS—Loop Engineering Information Systems
LFAC—Loop Facility Assignment and Control System
LIDB—Line Information Database
LIU—Line Interface Unit
LMOS/FE—Loop Maintenance Operations System/Front End
LMOS—Loop Maintenance and Operations System
LPC—Linear Predictive Coding
LPS—Local Packet Switch
LRC—Longitudinal Redundancy Check
LSD & F—Local Switching Demand and Forecast
LSI—Large-Scale Integration
LSSGR—Local Access Transport Area Switching System Generic Requirements
LSSGR—LATA Switching System Generic Requirements
LT—LATA Tandem
LTCT—LATA Toll Connect Trunk
LU6.2—IBM Data Communications Protocol

m—Milli
M—Mega
MAC—Media Access Control
MACS—Major Apparatus and Cable System
MAN—Metropolitan Area Network
MAS—Memory Administration System
MATMS—Material Management System
MBE—Molecular Beam Epitaxy
Mb/s—Mega (Million) bits per second
MCVF—Multi-Channel Voice Frequency
MESFET—Metal-Semiconductor Field Effect Transistor
MF—MultiFrequency
MFJ—Modified Final Judgement
MFT—Metallic Facility Terminal
MICR—Magnetic Ink Character Recognition
MIPS—Million Instructions Per Second
MLT—Mechanized Loop Testing System
MM—Micrometers
MMS—Memory Management System
MOS—Metal-Oxide Semiconductor

MOS—Mean Opinion Score
MOSFET—Metal-Oxide Semiconductor Field Effect Transistor
MPG—Microwave Pulse Generator
MTA—Message Transfer Agent
MTBF—Mean Time Between Failure
MTP—Message Transfer Part
MTS—Message Transfer System
MTS—Message Telephone Service
MTTR—Mean Time To Repair
Mux/DEMUX—Multiplexer/Demultiplexer
MVS—Multiple Virtual Storage

NAK—Negative Acknowledgment
NANP—North American Numbering Plan
NAPLPS—North American Presentation-Level Protocol Syntax
NARUC—National Association of Regulatory Utility Commis.
NBEC—Non-Bell Exchange Carrier
NBS/ICST—National Bureau of Standards/Institute for Computer Sciences and Technology
NC—Network Controller
NCC—Network Control Center
NCTA—National Cable Television Association
NCTE—Network Channel-Terminating Equipment
NDC—National Destination Code
NE—Network Element
NI—Network Interface
NIC—Near Instantaneous Companding
NM—Nanometer
NMA—Network Maintenance and Analysis
NOC—Network Operations Center
NPA—Numbering Plan Area
NPMS—Network Performance Management System
NPS—Network Planning System
NPS Dist—Network Planning System—Distribution
NPS IOF—Network Planning System—Interoffice Facilities
NPS TRAF—Network Planning System—Traffic
NPS WC—Network Planning System—Wire Center
NRZ—Non-Return to Zero
NRZI—Non-Return to Zero Inverted
NSA—Network Services Architecture
N(S)N—National (Significant) Number
NSTS—Network Services Test System
NT—Network Termination
NT1—Network Termination type 1 (Layer 1)
NT2—Network Termination type 2 (Layer 1-3)
NTE—Network Terminal Equipment

720

NTIA—National Telecommunications and Information Admin.
NTN—Network Terminal Number
NTP—Network Termination Point
NTSC signal—National Television Sys. Committee-Specified sig.

OC-3—Optical Carrier-Signal Level 3
OC-M—Optical Carrier-Level
OCR—Optical Character Recognition
OCU—Office Channel Unit
O-E—Opto-Electric
OEIC—Opto-Electronic Integrated Circuit
OEM—Original Equipment Manufacturer
OMAP—Operations, Maintenance and Administration Application Part
OPC—Origination Point Code
OPS—Operations Process System
OS—Operation System
OSI—Open Systems Interconnection
OSN—Operations System Network
OSP—Outside Plant
OSS—Operations Support System
OSS—Operator Services System
OSSP—Operations System Strategic Plan
OTC—Operating Telephone Companies

P(A)BX—Private (Automatic) Branch Exchange
PAD—Packet Assembler/Disassembler
PAM—Pulse Amplitude Modulation
P/AR—Peak to Average Ratio
PAX—Private Automatic Exchange
PBX—Private Branch Exchange
PC—Personal Computer
PC—Primary Center
PCM—Pulse Code Modulation
PCMAC—Personal Computer—Macintosh
PCNE—Processor Controlled Network Element
PCO—Plant Control Office
PDM—Pulse Duration Modulation
PDN—Public Data Network
PICS—Plug-in Inventory Control System
PIN—Positive Intrinsic Negative
PL/1—Programming Language One
PMU—Performance Monitoring Unit
POP—Point of Presence
POT—Point of Termination
POTS—"Plain Old" Telephone Service
PPSN—Public Packet Switched Network

PPSS—Public Packet Switched Services
PS—Packet Switch
PSAP—Public Safety Answering Point
PSDC—Public Switched Digital Capability
PSDS—Public Switched Digital Service
PSN—Packet Switched Network
PROM—Programmable Read-Only Memory
PSTN—Public Switched Telephone Network
PTT—Postal Telegraph and Telephone Public Network
PUC—Public Utility Commission
PVC—Private Virtual Circuit
PVN—Private Virtual Network
PWM—Pulse Width Modulation

Q and R—Quality and Reliability
QA/QS—Quality Assurance/Quality Surveillance
QAM—Quadrature Amplitude Modulation
QSAM—Quadrature Sideband Amplitude Modulation

R/T—Receiver/Transmitter
RCMAC—Recent Change Memory Administration Center
rf—Radio Frequency
RFD—Request For Development
RFI—Request For Information
RFP—Request For Proposal
RIT—Rate of Information Transfer
RJE—Remote Job Entry
RL—Return Loss
RMAS—Remote Memory Administration System
RMS—Root Mean Square
RO—Receive Only
ROLR—Receiving Objective Loudness Rating
ROM—Read-Only Memory
RPG—Report Program Generator
RPOA—Recognized Private Operating Agency
RSA—Repair Service and Answering
RSB—Repair Service Bureau
RSU—Remote Switching Unit
RT—Remote Terminal
RTS—Request To Send
RTTU—Remote Trunk Test Unit
RTU—Remote Terminal Unit
RTU—Right-To-Use
RX—Remote Exchange
RXO—Remote Exchange Office

SAPI—Service Access Point Identifier
SARTS—Switched Access Remote
SC—Secondary Channel
SC—Secondary Center
SCC—Switching Control Center
SCCP—Signalling Connection Control Part
SCCS—Switching Control Center System
SCP—Service Control Point
SCS—Scheduling and Coordination System
SDLC—Synchronous Data Link Control
SEAS—Signalling Engineering and Administration System
SES—Severely Errored Second
SES—Service Evaluation System
SHF—Super-High Frequency
SIT—Special Information Tones
SITA—Societe International de Telecommunication Aeronautique
SLC—Subscriber Loop Carrier
SLCCOT—SLC Central Office Terminal
SLCRT—SLC Remote Terminal
SLIC—Subscriber Line-Interface Card
SLS—Signalling Link Selection
SMF—Single-Mode Fiber
SMS—Service Management System
SN—Subscriber Number
SNA—Systems Network Architecture
SNR—Signal To Noise Ratio
SO—Service Order
SOAC—Service Order Application/Control
SOE—Standard Operating Environment
SOH—Start of heading
SONET—Synchronous Optical Network
SOP—Service Order Processor
SOS—Short Outage System
SP—Signal Processor
SP—Signaling Point
SPCS—Stored Program Control System
SPOOL—Simultaneous Peripheral Operation On Line
SQL—Structured Query Language
SRL—Singing Return Loss
SS7—Signaling System No. 7
SSC—Special Services Center
SSCP—System Services Control Point
SSDAC—Special Services Dispatch Administration Center
SSFS—Special Services Forecasting System
SSP—Service Switching Point
STP—Signal Transfer Point

STS-1—Synchronous Transport Signal Level 1
STS—Shared Tenant Services
STX—Start Of Text
SVC—Service
SWIFT—Society for Worldwide Interband Financial Tele.
SXS—Step-By-Step
SYNTRAN—Synchronous Transmission

T1—A U.S. Standards Committee
T1C1—T1 Standards Subcommittee on Carrier-to-CPE Interfaces
T1D1—T1 Standards Subcommittee on ISDN
T1M1—T1 Standards Subcommittee on Operations, Administration, and Maintenance
T1M1.4—A Working Group of T1M1 Standards Subcommittee
TA—Technical Advisory
TAN—Technician Access Network
TASC—Telecommunications Alarm Surveillance and Control
TASI—Time Assignment Speech Interpolation
TAU—Test Access Unit
Tb/s—Terabits per second (10 to the 12th bits/second)
TCAM—Telecommunications Access Method
TCAP—Transaction Capability Application Part
TCAS—T-Carrier Administration System
TDAS—Traffic Data Administration System
TDM—Time Division Multiplexing
TDMA—Time-Division Multiple Access
T1—1.544 Mbits/s Digital Carrier Facility (DS-1 Format)
T1C—3.152 Mbits/s Digital Carrier Facility (DS-1C Format)
T2—6.312 Mbits/s Digital Carrier Facility (DS-2 Format)
Telco—Telephone central office
TIP—Terminal Interface Processor
TIRKS—Trunks Integrated Records Keeping System
TL1—Transaction Language 1
TNDS/TK—Total Network Data System/Trunks
TNDS—Total Network Data System
TR—Technical Reference
TRBLS—Troubles
TRIF—Technical Requirements Industry Forum
TSC—Test System Controller
TSPS—Traffic Service Position System
TTL—Transistor-to-Transistor Logic

UART—Universal Asynchronous Receiver/Transmitter
UHF—Ultra High Frequency
USART—Universal Synchronous/Asynchronous Receiver Trans.

USITA — United States Independent Telephone Association
USRT — Universal Synchronous Receiver/Transmitter

VAN — Value-Added Network
VFN — Vendor Feature Node
VHF — Very High Frequency
VLF — Very Low Frequency
VLSI — Very Large Scale Integration
VM — Virtual Memory
VTAM — Virtual Telecommunications Access Method

WATS — Wide Area Telephone Service
WDM — Wavelength Division Multiplexing
WFA — Work and Force Administration

XB — Crossbar (X-Bar) Switching System
XC — Cross Connect
XFE — Cross Front End

Index

Edited by Carl D. Aron